Rick Steves'

CROATIA
& SLOVENIA
2007

Rick Steves & Cameron Hewitt

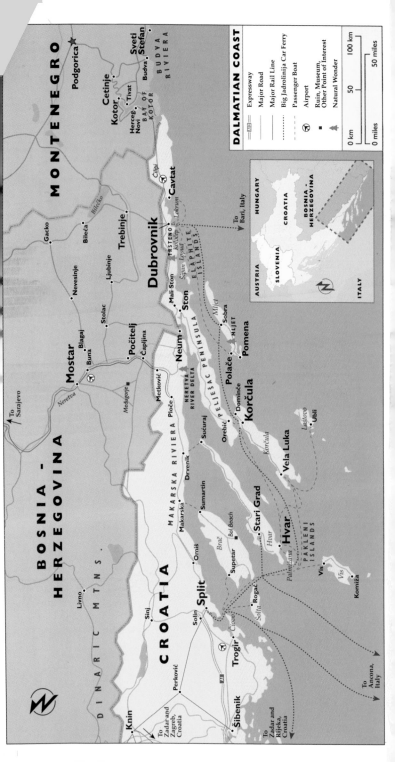

DALMATIAN COAST

- ━━━ Expressway
- ─── Major Road
- ─── Major Rail Line
- ⋯⋯⋯ Big Jadrolinija Car Ferry
- ─ ─ Passenger Boat
- ✈ Airport
- ■ Ruin, Museum, Other Point of Interest
- ◀ Natural Wonder

| 0 km | 50 | 100 km |
| 0 miles | 50 miles | |

MONTENEGRO

Podgorica

Sveti Stefan

Cetinje

Budva

BUDVA RIVIERA

Kotor

Tivat

BAY OF KOTOR

Herceg Novi

Cavtat

Trebinje

Bileća

Gacko

Ljubinje

Nevesinje

Lokrum

Dubrovnik

Šipan

Koločep

ELAPHITE ISLANDS

TRSTENO

Mali Ston

Ston

Stolac

Blagaj

Buna

Mostar

Počitelj

Čapljina

Neum

Metković

PELJEŠAC PENINSULA

Sobra

Mljet

MLJET

Pomena

Polače

BOSNIA - HERZEGOVINA

To Sarajevo

Neretva

Medugorje

Ploče

NERETVA RIVER DELTA

MAKARSKA RIVIERA

Sućuraj

Orebić

Dominče

Korčula

Korčula

Lastovo

Ubli

Vela Luka

Drvenik

Makarska

Sumartin

Brač

Bol Beach

Supetar

Omiš

Stari Grad

Hvar

Hvar

Hvar

PAKLENI ISLANDS

Palmižana

Vis

Vis

Komiža

Livno

DINARIC MTNS.

Sinj

Solin

Split

Čiovo

Solta

Rogač

Trogir

Perković

CROATIA

Knin

Šibenik

To Zadar and Zagreb, Croatia

To Zadar and Rijeka, Croatia

To Ancona, Italy

To Bari, Italy

AUSTRIA

SLOVENIA

HUNGARY

CROATIA

BOSNIA - HERZEGOVINA

ITALY

Rick Steves'

CROATIA
& SLOVENIA
2007

AVALON
TRAVEL

CONTENTS

Top Destinations in Croatia and Slovenia

INTRODUCTION

Set sail on the shimmering Adriatic, to a remote island whose name you can't pronounce, but whose wonders you'll never forget. Corkscrew your way up impossibly twisty mountain roads to panoramic vistas of cut-glass peaks. Lie on a beach in the hot summer sun, listening to the lapping waves as a Venetian-style bell tower overhead clangs out the hour. Ponder the fading scars of a recent war, and admire how skillfully the locals have revitalized their once-troubled region. Dine on a seafood feast and sip a glass of local wine as you watch the sunset dip into the watery horizon...feeling smug for discovering this place before all your friends did. Unfamiliar as they might seem, Slovenia and Croatia are what you've been looking for: stay-a-while seashore, soaring alpine peaks, epic history, delectable food and wine, and some of the friendliest people in Europe.

Here in the land where the Adriatic meets the Alps, there are countless ways to have fun. Begin your adventure by flipping through this book, which covers Croatia and Slovenia's best big-city, small-town, and back-to-nature destinations. You'll get all the information and suggestions necessary to wring the maximum value out of your limited time and money. If you're planning a trip of three weeks or less, this book is all you need.

Not long ago, Croatia and Slovenia—two of Europe's youngest nations—belonged to the union called Yugoslavia. Just over a decade and a half later, they're proudly independent and racing toward the future. Carefree Croatia, with a long and varied coastline, beckons vacationers with its dramatically scenic terrain, romantic old towns, sunshine-bathed pebbly beaches, and irrepressible seafaring spirit. Perky Slovenia surprises travelers with its tidy quaintness, breathtaking mountainscapes, colorful towns, and gregarious natives. And for good measure, I've also included detours into two other parts of the former Yugoslavia, each one offering a striking contrast to Croatia or Slovenia: the craggy coast of Montenegro, and the diverse and challenging town of Mostar, in Bosnia-Herzegovina.

Experiencing Europe's culture, people, and natural wonders economically and hassle-free has been my goal for three decades of traveling, tour guiding, and writing. With this book, I pass on to you all of the lessons I've learned, updated for 2007.

Rick Steves' Croatia & Slovenia covers the predictable biggies and adds a healthy dose of "Back Door" intimacy. Along with strolling the walls around Dubrovnik's peerless Old Town, you'll poke your way into a hidden little tavern clinging like a barnacle over the sea. I've been selective, including only the top destinations and sights. For example, Croatia has over a thousand islands. But why not focus on the very best? That's Korčula, Hvar, Rab, and Mljet.

The best is, of course, only my opinion. But after spending half my adult life researching Europe, I've developed a sixth sense for what travelers enjoy. Just thinking about the places featured in this book makes me want to polka.

This Information Is Accurate and Up-to-Date

This book is updated every year. Most publishers of guidebooks that cover a region from top to bottom can afford an update only every two or three years (and even then, it's often by e-mail or phone). Since this book is selective, it's possible to update it in person each summer. The prices and hours of sights listed in this book are accurate as of mid-2006—but I'm sure you'll understand that guidebooks begin to yellow even before they're printed. Still, if you're traveling with the current edition of this book, you're using the most up-to-date information available in print (for the latest, see www.ricksteves.com/update). Also at our Web site, you'll find a valuable list of reports and experiences—good and bad—from fellow travelers who have used my guidebooks (www.ricksteves .com/feedback).

Use this year's edition. People who try to save a few bucks by traveling with an old book learn the seriousness of their mistake... in Europe. Your trip costs about $10 per waking hour. Your time is valuable. This guidebook saves lots of time.

About This Book

Rick Steves' Croatia & Slovenia is a personal tour guide in your pocket. Better yet, it's actually two tour guides in your pocket: The co-author of this book is Cameron Hewitt, who edits guidebooks and leads Eastern Europe tours for my travel company, Rick Steves' Europe Through the Back Door. Inspired by his Slavic roots and by the enduring charm of the Croatian and Slovenian people,

Cameron has spent the last six years closely tracking the exciting changes in this part of the world. Together, Cameron and I keep this book up-to-date and accurate. For simplicity, we've shed our respective egos for this book and have become "I."

This book is organized by destination. Each destination is covered as a mini-vacation on its own, filled with exciting sights and convenient, affordable places to stay and eat. In each chapter, you'll find the following:

Planning Your Time contains a suggested schedule, with thoughts on how to best use your limited time.

Orientation includes tourist information, city transportation, and an easy-to-read map designed to make the text clear and your arrival smooth.

Sights are rated:

▲▲▲—Worth getting up early and skipping breakfast for;
▲▲—Worth getting up early for;
▲—Worth seeing if it's convenient;
No rating—Worth knowing about.

Sleeping and **Eating** feature descriptions and contact information for my favorite accommodations and restaurants.

Transportation Connections explains how to reach nearby destinations by train, bus, or boat.

There are **Country Introductions** for both Croatia and Slovenia, which give you an overview of each country's culture, customs, money, history, current events, cuisine, language, and other useful practicalities.

The **Understanding Yugoslavia** chapter sorts out the various countries and conflicts, giving you a good picture of why Yugoslavia was formed, and why it broke up.

The **appendix** is a traveler's tool kit, with telephone tips, a climate chart, a list of festivals and national holidays, tips on metric conversion, and a list of US embassies.

Browse through this book, choose your favorite destinations, and link them up. Then have a great trip! Traveling like a temporary local, you'll get the most out of every mile, minute, and dollar. As you travel the route I know and love, I'm happy you'll be meeting some of my favorite Europeans.

PLANNING

Trip Costs

The economies in both Croatia and Slovenia are thriving. Things aren't exactly cheap there—but they're still more affordable than countries to the west, such as Italy or Austria. If you're careful to avoid inflated tourist-trap prices (by following my tips on where to stay and where to eat), a trip to this region is a great value.

Top 10 Small Coastal Towns

1. Rovinj (Croatia)
2. Kotor (Montenegro)
3. Korčula (Croatia)
4. Hvar (Croatia)
5. Piran (Slovenia)

6. Rab (Croatia)
7. Sveti Stefan (Montenegro)
8. Trogir (Croatia)
9. Perast (Montenegro)
10. Poreč (Croatia)

Five components make up your trip cost: airfare, surface transportation, room and board, sightseeing and entertainment, and shopping and miscellany.

Airfare: Don't try to sort through the mess. Get and use a good travel agent. A basic round-trip flight from the US to Ljubljana or Dubrovnik should cost $800 to $1,200 (even cheaper in winter), depending on where you fly from and when. Always consider saving time and money in Europe by flying "open jaw" (into one city and out of another). The additional cost of flying into Ljubljana and out of Dubrovnik is often cheaper than the added expense (and wasted time) of an overland return trip to Ljubljana.

Surface Transportation: For the two-week whirlwind trip described on page 6, allow $150 per person for public transportation (train, bus, and boat tickets). Train travelers will probably save money by simply buying tickets along the way, rather than purchasing a railpass (see "Transportation," page 18). A basic car rental costs about $250 per person per week (based on two people splitting the cost of the car, tolls, gas, and insurance). Long-term car rental is cheapest when arranged in advance from the US, but exorbitant fees for dropping off in a different country can make long-term car rental prohibitively expensive if you're going to both Croatia and Slovenia (see "Car Rental," page 23).

Room and Board: You can thrive in Croatia and Slovenia on an average of $90 a day per person for room and board. A $90-a-day budget per person allows $15 for lunch, $20 for dinner, and $55 for lodging (based on two people splitting the cost of a $110 double room that includes breakfast). That's doable. Students and tightwads do it on $40 a day ($20 per hostel bed, $20 for meals).

Sightseeing and Entertainment: Sightseeing is cheap here. Major sights generally cost $3 to $6. Figure $10 to $25 for splurge experiences (e.g., watching the *Moreška* sword dance in Korčula, or seeing Slovenia's Lipizzaner stallions). You can hire your own private guide for four hours for about $100–150—a good value when divided among two or more people. An overall average of $20 a day works for most. Don't skimp here. After all, this category is the driving force behind your trip—you came to sightsee, enjoy, and experience Croatia and Slovenia. Fortunately for you, the region's best attractions—the sea, mountains, and sunshine—are free.

Shopping and Miscellany: Figure $1 per postcard, coffee, beer, and ice-cream cone. Shopping can vary in cost from nearly nothing to a small fortune. Good budget travelers find that this category has little to do with assembling a trip full of lifelong and wonderful memories.

When to Go

Tourist traffic in this part of Europe (especially the coastal towns) is extremely seasonal. The peak season hits suddenly and floods the towns like a tidal wave, only to recede a couple months later—leaving empty streets and dazed locals. In general, the tourist season runs roughly from May through September, reaching a peak in early August. June and September are my favorite months to travel in Croatia and Slovenia—I enjoy the smaller crowds, milder weather, and ability to grab a room almost whenever and wherever I like.

Peak Season: July and especially August are top season, when just about everything is likely to be open very long hours daily (occasionally closed for a midday siesta). It's also the busiest time of year. Visiting Croatia in July or August is like spending spring break in Florida—fun, but miserably crowded. Hotels charge top dollar, and you'll miss out on the "undiscovered" quality that pervades the rest of the year.

Shoulder Season: Early May through June and September through mid-October are shoulder season. Within this time span, late June and early September are nearly, but not quite, as crowded as peak season, but the rush subsides substantially in May and October.

Off-Season: Mid-October through early May are dead as a doornail. Many small coastal towns close down entirely, with only one hotel and one restaurant remaining open during the lean winter months, and most of the town's residents moving to the interior to hibernate. Anything that's open keeps very limited hours (weekday mornings only). The weather can be cool and dreary, and night will draw the shades on your sightseeing before dinnertime. You may find the climate chart in the appendix helpful.

Seasonal Changes: Because of this region's extreme seasonality, specifics such as opening times and prices are especially flexible. It's not unusual for a hotel to charge six different rates for the same room, depending on the time of year. Every year, I hike around these towns trying to pin down hours for TIs, travel agencies, and museums. And every year, they change. If you're here anytime outside of mid-summer, don't rely on my hours—call a

Croatia and Slovenia:
Best Two-Week Trip by Car

Day	Plan	Sleep in
1	Arrive Ljubljana's Brnik airport and take a taxi to Lake Bled	Lake Bled
2	Relax at Lake Bled	Lake Bled
3	Pick up car, drive through Julian Alps, end in Ljubljana	Ljubljana
4	Ljubljana	Ljubljana
5	Drive through the Karst and Piran to Rovinj*	Rovinj
6	Tour Istria	Rovinj
7	Drive to Plitvice Lakes via Istria's hill towns	Plitvice
8	Hike the lakes, then drive to Split and drop car	Split
9	Split	Split
10	To Hvar or Korčula	Hvar/Korčula
11	Relax on Hvar or Korčula	Hvar/Korčula
12	To Dubrovnik	Dubrovnik
13	Dubrovnik	Dubrovnik
14	Rent a car to day-trip to Montenegro's Bay of Kotor or to Mostar	Dubrovnik

* To save the substantial extra cost of picking up your car in one country and then dropping it off in another (see page 24), consider this plan: Drop your Slovenian car when you get to Ljubljana, enjoy the city for two nights without a car, then take the train directly to Rijeka (2.5 hours), pick up a different car, and drive to Rovinj (1.5 hours); or, to pack more sightseeing into your day, take the train from Ljubljana to Zagreb (2.5 hours), spend a few hours visiting Zagreb, then pick up a car and drive to Istria (about 3 hours). Note that public-transportation connections to Rovinj are difficult, so going via Rijeka or Zagreb is smoother.

By Public Transportation
This itinerary can be done entirely by public transportation, with a few modifications. Skip the Julian Alps, and take the bus from Lake Bled to Ljubljana. Skip Istria; instead, take the train from Ljubljana to Zagreb, see that city, then take a bus to Plitvice. The

bus connects Plitvice to Split, and from there, you'll continue down the Dalmatian Coast by boat or bus.

Even if you're using public transportation, seriously consider periodically renting a car for the day to be able to see the Julian Alps, Istria, or Montenegro's Bay of Kotor.

day or two ahead to double-check that the place you need (like a room-booking agency) will actually be open when you arrive.

Sightseeing Priorities

Depending on the length of your trip, here are my recommended priorities. Assuming you're traveling by public transportation, I've taken geographical proximity into account.

3 days:	Dubrovnik
5 days, add:	Choose between Korčula or Hvar
7 days, add:	Split and more island time
9 days, add:	Lake Bled and the Julian Alps
10 days, add:	Plitvice Lakes
12 days, add:	Ljubljana, Montenegro's Bay of Kotor
14 days, add:	Istria
16 days, add:	Mostar, the Karst
18 days, add:	Logarska Dolina, Zagreb
21 days, add:	Ptuj, Opatija, and more islands and coastal villages (Piran, Rab, Mljet)

The map on page 7 and the two-week itinerary on page 6 include all of the stops in the first 14 days.

As you plan your trip, don't underestimate the long distances. People tell me, "I've got four days, and I want to see Lake Bled and Dubrovnik"—not realizing they'll spend a least a full day connecting those two sights. If you only have a few days, consider focusing either on the Dalmatian Coast in the south, or on Slovenia and Istria in the north. For more details, see "Getting to the Dalmatian Coast" on page 152.

For some pointers on crafting a fun and varied Croatian itinerary, see "Where Should I Go?" on page 48.

Travel Smart

Your trip to Europe is like a complex play—easier to follow and really appreciate on a second viewing. While no one does the same trip twice to gain that advantage, reading this book's chapters on your intended destinations before your trip accomplishes much the same thing. As a practical matter (to avoid redundancy), many cultural or historical details are explained for one sight and not repeated for another—even if they would increase your understanding and appreciation of that second sight.

As you read through this book, note days of festivals, market days, and when sights are closed. When setting up your itinerary, anticipate problem days. Hotels are most crowded on Fridays and Saturdays, especially in resort towns. Saturdays in Europe are virtually weekdays with earlier closing hours. Sundays have the same pros and cons as they do for travelers in the US: Sightseeing attractions are generally open, shops, banks, and markets are closed, and city traffic is light. Rowdy evenings are rare on Sundays.

Be sure to mix intense and relaxed periods in your itinerary. Plan ahead for banking, laundry, picnics, post-office chores, and Internet stops. Every trip (and every traveler) needs at least a few slack days. Pace yourself. Assume you will return.

Reread this book as you travel and visit local tourist information offices. Upon arrival in a new town, lay the groundwork for a smooth departure—write down the schedule for the train or bus you'll take when you depart. Buy a phone card and use it for reservations and reconfirmations. Enjoy the hospitality of the Croatians and Slovenes. Slow down and ask questions. Most locals are eager to point you in their idea of the right direction. Wear your money belt, familiarize yourself with the local currency, and learn a simple formula to quickly estimate rough prices in dollars. Keep a notepad in your pocket for organizing your thoughts. Those who expect to travel smart, do.

RESOURCES

Tourist Offices

In the US

Each country's national tourist office is a wealth of information. Before your trip, get the free general information packet, and request any specifics you may want (such as regional and city maps and festival schedules).

Croatian National Tourist Office: Ask for their free brochures and maps. In the US, call 800-829-4416 or visit http://us.croatia.hr (cntony@earthlink.net).

Slovenian Tourist Office: They have a *Welcome to Slovenia* brochure, map, and information on various regions, hiking, biking, winter travel, and tourist farms. From the US, call Slovenian tel. 011-386-1-560-8823 or visit www.slovenia.info (info@slovenia.info).

In Europe

The local tourist information office is your best first stop in any new city. In this book, I'll refer to a tourist information office as a **TI** (though locally, you may see them marked TZ, for *turistička zajednica*). Throughout Croatia and Slovenia, you'll find TIs are usually well-organized and always have an English-speaking staff. Try to arrive, or at least telephone, before it closes. Have a list of questions ready, and pick up maps, brochures, and other information. Most local tourist offices in Croatia and Slovenia are run by the government, which means their information isn't colored by a drive for profit. This also means they're not allowed to make money by running a room-booking service—though they can almost always give you a list of local hotels and private rooms, and if they're not too busy, can call around for you to check on availability. Every town has at least one travel agency with a room-booking service. Even if there's no "fee," you'll pay more for the room than if you book direct, using the listings in this book.

Rick Steves' Guidebooks, Public Television Show, and Radio Show

With the help of my staff, I produce materials to help you plan your trip and travel smoothly.

Guidebooks: This book is one of a series of 30+ books on European travel that includes country guidebooks, city and regional guidebooks, and my budget-travel skills handbook, *Rick Steves' Europe Through the Back Door.* All are annually updated. My phrase books—for Italian, French, German, Spanish, and Portuguese—are practical and budget-oriented. My other books include *Europe 101* (a crash course on art and history), *European Christmas* (on traditional and modern-day celebrations), and *Postcards from Europe* (a fun memoir of my travels over 25 years). For a complete list of my books, see the inside of the last page of this book.

Public Television and Radio Shows: My television series, *Rick Steves' Europe,* covers European destinations. My weekly public radio show, *Travel with Rick Steves,* features interviews with travel experts from around the world. All the TV scripts and radio shows are at www.ricksteves.com. Listen to the shows at any time—or download them onto your MP3 player to take along on your trip.

Other Guidebooks

Especially if you'll be traveling beyond my recommended destinations, you may want some supplemental information. When you consider the improvements they'll make in your $3,000 vacation, $30 for extra maps and books is money well spent. Especially for several people traveling by car, the weight and expense are negligible. One budget tip can save the price of an extra guidebook.

The Rough Guides, which individually cover Croatia and Slovenia, are packed with historical and cultural insight. The Lonely Planet guides (with separate Croatia and Slovenia books, and a handy Western Balkans book that includes these two countries and more) are similar, but are designed more for travelers than for intellectuals. If choosing between these two titles, I buy the one that was published most recently. Students, backpackers, and nightlife-seekers should consider the Let's Go guides (by Harvard students, has the best hostel listings, updated annually). Dorling Kindersley publishes snazzy Eyewitness Guides covering Croatia and Dubrovnik and the Dalmatian Coast. While pretty to look at, these books weigh a ton and are skimpy on actual content. Since none of the above titles is updated annually, check the publication date before you buy.

The British entertainment publication *Time Out* sells a well-researched annual magazine with up-to-date coverage on Croatia, including the latest on hotels, restaurants, and nightlife (look for it at newsstands in Croatia, www.timeout.com).

If your travels take you to nearby countries, consider *Rick Steves' Best of Eastern Europe 2007,* which covers parts of Croatia and Slovenia, plus Hungary, Poland, the Czech Republic, and Slovakia. Like the book you're holding now, this title is updated annually in person.

More Recommended Reading and Movies

For information on Croatia and Slovenia past and present, consider these books and films:

Books: Lonnie Johnson's *Central Europe: Enemies, Neighbors, Friends* is the best history overview of Croatia, Slovenia, and their neighboring countries. Rebecca West's classic, bricklike *Black Lamb and Grey Falcon* is the definitive travelogue of the Yugoslav lands (written during a journey between the two World Wars). For a more recent take, Croatian journalist Slavenka Drakulić has written a trio of insightful essay collections from a woman's perspective: *Café Europa: Life After Communism; The Balkan Express;* and *How We Survived Communism and Even Laughed.*

Films: To grasp the wars that shook this region a decade and a half ago, there's no better film than the Slovene-produced *No Man's Land,* which won the 2002 Oscar for Best Foreign Film. The BBC produced a remarkable (but difficult-to-find) six-hour documentary series called *The Death of Yugoslavia,* featuring actual interviews with all of the key players. Croatian films worth watching include *Border Post* (2006); *How the War Started on My Island* (1996); *Underground* (1995); *Tito and Me* (1992); and *When Father Was Away on Business* (1985).

Maps

The black-and-white maps in this book, drawn by Dave Hoerlein, are concise and simple. Dave, who is well-traveled in Croatia and Slovenia, designed the maps to help you locate recommended places and get to the local TIs, where you can pick up a more in-depth map (usually free) of the city or region. Better maps are sold at newsstands and bookstores—take a look before you buy to be sure the map has the level of detail you want.

Drivers will want to pick up a good, detailed map in Europe. My favorite maps of the region are by the Slovenian cartographer

Kod & Kam (they have a store in Ljubljana—see page 329—but you can find these maps everywhere). Their 1:500,000-scale Croatia map (*Hrvaška* in Slovene, *Hrvatska* in Croatian) covers everything in this book (including Slovenia, Bosnia-Herzegovina, and most of Montenegro) with all the detail you'll need. For just Slovenia, pick up the good 1:300,000 *Autokarta Slovenija* map, sold at tourist shops everywhere (the black version, without the cardboard cover, is just as good and costs less—generally cheaper at TIs than at bookstores or travel agencies). If you'll be hiking, especially in the Slovenian Alps, you'll find no shortage of excellent, very detailed maps locally.

Since new expressways are constantly being built in these countries, an up-to-date map is essential—it can mean the difference between choosing an old, slow road or saving an hour by finding the brand-new highway.

PRACTICALITIES

Red Tape: Currently, Americans and Canadians need only a passport, but no visa or shots, to travel in Croatia and Slovenia. Make sure your passport is good for at least 90 days after your ticketed date of return to the US. It's also a good idea to pack a photocopy of your passport in your luggage in case the original is lost or stolen.

Borders: Even though Croatia and Slovenia used to be part of the same country, you will have to stop and show your passport when you cross a border. Whether by car or by train, border crossings are generally a non-event—flash your passport, maybe wait a few minutes, and move on.

Time: Croatia and Slovenia are six/nine hours ahead of the East/West Coasts of the US. In Europe—and throughout this book—you'll be using the 24-hour clock. After 12:00 noon, keep going—13:00, 14:00, and so on. For anything over 12, subtract 12 and add p.m. (14:00 is 2:00 p.m.)

Metric: Get used to metric. A liter is about a quart, four to a gallon. A kilometer is six-tenths of a mile. I figure kilometers to miles by cutting them in half and adding back 10 percent of the original (120 km: 60 + 12 = 72 miles, 300 km: 150 + 30 = 180 miles). For more on metric conversions, see the appendix.

Watt's Up? If you're bringing electrical gear, you'll need a two-prong adapter plug (sold cheap at travel stores in the US) and a converter (to convert the voltage from European to US). Travel appliances often have convenient built-in converters that "autosense" the proper voltage. On others, you may have to turn a voltage switch, marked 120V (US) and 240V (Europe).

Beaches: Croatia is known for its glimmering beaches.

However, most are pebbly or rocky rather than sandy. In addition to your swimsuit, you may want to pack (or buy in Europe) a pair of water shoes for wading.

News: For international news, Americans keep in touch with the *International Herald Tribune* (published almost daily throughout Europe). Every Tuesday, the European editions of *Time* and *Newsweek* hit the stands with articles of particular interest to European travelers. Sports addicts can get their fix from *USA Today*. News in English will be sold only where there's enough demand: in big cities and tourist centers. Good Web sites include www.europeantimes.com and http://news.bbc.co.uk.

Discounts: While discounts for sightseeing and transportation are not listed in this book, youths (under 18) and students (only with International Student Identity Cards) sometimes get discounts—but only by asking.

MONEY

Banking

Bring plastic (ATM, credit, or debit cards) along with a few hundred dollars in hard cash as an emergency backup. Traveler's checks are a waste of time (waiting at banks) and a waste of money (paying to purchase and then cash checks).

The best and easiest way to get local cash is to use the omnipresent bank machines (always open, low fees, and quick processing). The universal word for "cash machine" in Croatia and Slovenia is *Bankomat*. To withdraw cash, you'll need a card that can withdraw money from your bank account, plus a PIN code (note that European keypads show only numbers, no letters). Before you go, verify with your bank that your card will work, and inquire about "international transaction" fees (which can be up to $5 plus 5 percent per transaction). Alert your bank that you'll be making withdrawals in Europe; otherwise, the bank may not approve transactions if they perceive unusual spending patterns. Bring two cards in case one gets demagnetized or eaten by a temperamental machine. Since certain fees are charged per exchange, and most ATM screens top out at a certain amount, try to minimize "per visit" fees by pushing the "other amount" button and asking for a higher amount (though this is not always possible, especially in Croatia).

Bank machines often dispense high-denomination bills, which can be difficult to break (especially at odd hours). My strategy: Request an odd amount of money from the ATM (such as 450 kn instead of 500 kn); or, if that doesn't work, go as soon as possible to a bank or a large store (such as a supermarket) to break the big bills.

Visa and MasterCard are more commonly accepted than

Exchange Rates

Croatia and Slovenia use different currencies.

Croatia

Croatia still uses its traditional currency, the kuna (abbreviated kn locally, HRK internationally):

6 Croatian kunas (kn) = about $1

A kuna is broken into 100 smaller units, called lipas. There are coins of 1, 2, 5, 10, 20, and 50 lipas, and 1, 2, and 5 kunas. To convert Croatian kunas into dollars, divide by six (e.g., 5 kn = about $0.85; 70 kn = about $11; 200 kn = about $33).

Even though Croatia doesn't officially use the euro, many businesses (especially hotels) quote prices in euros for the convenience of their international guests. For maximum accuracy, I generally list the prices they gave me—so you'll notice that in the Croatia part of this book, some prices are in euros while others are in kunas.

Slovenia

Slovenia adopted the euro currency in January of 2007:

1 euro (€) = about $1.20

Like dollars, one euro (€) is broken down into 100 cents. You'll find coins ranging from one cent to two euros, and bills from five euros to 500 euros. To convert prices in euros to dollars, add 20 percent: €20 is about $24, €45 is about $55, and so on.

So, that 50-kn bottle of Croatian wine is about $8, the €20 Slovenian feast is about $24, and the 300-kn taxi ride through Zagreb is...uh-oh.

American Express. Just like at home, credit or debit cards work easily at larger hotels, restaurants, and shops, but smaller businesses prefer payment in local currency.

Because Croatia and Slovenia have different currencies, you may wind up with leftover cash from the previous country. Coins can't be exchanged once you leave the country, so try to spend them before you cross the border. But bills are easy to convert to the "new" country's currency. Regular banks have the best rates for changing currency (or traveler's checks). Post offices and train stations usually change money if you can't get to a bank.

You should use a money belt (a pouch with a strap that you buckle like a belt and wear under your clothes). Thieves target tourists. A money belt provides peace of mind, allowing you to

Damage Control for Lost or Stolen Cards

If you lose your credit, debit, or ATM card, you can stop people from using your card by reporting the loss immediately to the respective global customer-assistance centers. If you promptly report your card lost or stolen, you typically won't be held responsible for any unauthorized transactions on your account, although many banks charge a liability fee. Call these 24-hour US numbers collect: Visa (tel. 410/581-9994), MasterCard (tel. 636/722-7111), and American Express (tel. 336/393-1111).

At a minimum, have the following information ready: the name of the financial institution that issued you the card, along with the type of card (classic, platinum). Ideally, plan ahead: Pack photocopies of the backs of your cards (with the collect-call numbers), and write down your card numbers on a separate piece of paper that doesn't have your name on it. Providing the following information will allow for a quicker cancellation of your missing card: full card number, whether you are the primary or secondary cardholder, the cardholder's name exactly as printed on the card, billing address, home phone number, circumstances of the loss or theft, and identification verification (such as your birthdate, your mother's maiden name, or your Social Security number—memorize this, don't carry a copy). If you are the secondary cardholder, you'll also need to provide the primary cardholder's identification verification details. You can generally receive a temporary card within two or three business days in Europe.

carry lots of cash safely. Don't be petty about taking out money. Withdraw a week's worth of cash, stuff it in your money belt, and travel!

Tips on Tipping

A decade ago, tipping was unheard of in Croatia and Slovenia. But then came the tourists. Today, some waiters and taxi drivers are beginning to expect Yankee-sized tips when they spot an American. Tipping the appropriate amount—without feeling stingy, but also avoiding contributing to the overtipping epidemic—is nerve-wracking to conscientious visitors. Relax! Many locals still don't tip at all, so any tip is appreciated. As in the US, the proper amount depends on your resources, tipping philosophy, and the circumstances, but the following guidelines should help you out.

Restaurants: Tipping is an issue only at restaurants that have table service. If you order your food at a counter, don't tip. At restaurants that have a waitstaff, round up the bill 5–10 percent after a

---

Begin Your Trip at www.ricksteves.com

At our travel Web site, you'll find a wealth of **free information** on destinations covered in this book, including fresh monthly news and helpful tips from thousands of fellow travelers.

Our online Travel Store offers travel bags and accessories specially designed by Rick Steves to help you travel smarter and lighter. These include Rick's popular carry-on bags (wheeled and rucksack versions), money belts, totes, toiletries kits, adapters, other accessories, and a wide selection of guidebooks, planning maps, and DVDs.

Choosing the right railpass for your trip—amidst hundreds of options—can drive you nutty. We'll help you choose the best pass for your needs, plus give you a bunch of free extras.

Travel agents will tell you about mainstream tours of Europe, but they won't tell you about **Rick Steves' tours.** Rick Steves' Europe Through the Back Door travel company offers more than two dozen itineraries and 400+ departures reaching the best destinations in this book...and beyond. You'll enjoy great guides, a fun bunch of travel partners (with small groups of generally around 25), and plenty of room to spread out in a big, comfy bus. You'll find European adventures to fit every vacation length. To get our Tour Catalog and a free *Rick Steves Tour Experience* DVD (filmed on location during an actual tour), visit www.ricksteves.com.

---

good meal. My rule of thumb is to estimate about 10 percent, then round down slightly to reach a convenient total (for a 70-kn meal, I pay 75 kn—a tip of 5 kn, or about 7 percent). A 15 percent tip is overly generous, verging on extravagant. At some tourist-oriented restaurants, a 10 or 15 percent "service charge" may be added to your bill, in which case an additional tip is not necessary. If you're not sure whether your bill includes the tip, just ask.

Taxis: To tip the cabbie, round up about five percent (for a 71-kn fare, pay 75 kn). If the cabbie hauls your bags and zips you to the airport to help you catch your flight, you might want to toss in a little more. But if you feel like you're being driven in circles or otherwise ripped off, skip the tip.

Hotels: I don't tip at hotels, but if you do, give the porter the local equivalent of $0.50 for carrying bags, and, at the end of your stay, leave a dollar's worth of local cash for the maid if the room was kept clean.

Special Services: Tour guides at public sites sometimes hold out their hands for tips after they give their spiels. If I've already paid for the tour, I don't tip extra. In general, if someone in the service industry does a super job for you, a small tip (the equivalent of a dollar) is appropriate...but not required.

When in doubt, ask: If you're not sure whether (or how much) to tip for a service, ask your hotelier or the TI; they'll fill you in on how it's done on their turf.

VAT Refunds for Shoppers

Wrapped into the purchase price of your souvenirs is a Value Added Tax (VAT) of 18.5 percent in Croatia and 20 percent in Slovenia. If you spend a minimum amount (501 kn in Croatia, €63 in Slovenia) at a store that participates in the VAT refund scheme, you're entitled to get most of that tax back. Personally, I've never felt that VAT refunds are worth the hassle, but if you do, here's the scoop.

Ideally, the merchant will subtract the tax when you make your purchase (this is more likely to occur if the store ships the goods to your home). Otherwise, you'll need to do all this:

• **Get the paperwork.** Show the merchant your passport, and he or she will fill out the necessary refund document, called a "cheque."

• **Get your stamp at the border or airport.** Process your cheque(s) at your last stop in the country with the customs agent who deals with VAT refunds. It's best to keep your purchases in your carry-on for viewing, but if they're too large or dangerous (such as knives) to carry on, have them inspected before you check your bag. To qualify, your purchased goods should be unused. If you show up at customs wearing your Slovenian shoes, officials might look the other way—or deny you a refund.

• **Collect your refund.** You'll need to return your stamped documents to the retailer or its representative. Many merchants work with a service that has offices at major airports, ports, and border crossings, such as Global Refund (www.globalrefund.com) or Premier Tax Free (www.premiertaxfree.com). These services, which extract a 4 percent fee, usually can refund your money immediately in your currency of choice or credit your card (within two billing cycles). If you have to deal directly with the retailer, mail the store your stamped documents and then wait. It could take months.

Customs Regulations

You can take home $800 in souvenirs per person duty-free. The next $1,000 is taxed at a flat 3 percent. After that, you pay the individual item's duty rate. You can also bring in duty-free a liter of alcohol (slightly more than a standard-sized bottle of wine), a carton of cigarettes, and up to 100 cigars. As for food, anything in cans or sealed jars is acceptable. Don't bring back meat (even if it's dried and cured), cheeses, and fresh fruits and veggies. To check customs rules and duty rates, visit www.customs.gov.

TRANSPORTATION

If you're debating between public transportation and car rental, consider these factors: Trains, buses, and boats are best for single travelers; those who'll be spending more time in big cities or on islands; and those who don't want to drive in Europe. While a car gives you more freedom—enabling you to search for hotels more easily and carrying your bags for you—trains, buses, and boats zip you effortlessly from town to town, usually dropping you in the center, near the tourist office. Cars are great in the countryside, but a worthless headache in places like Ljubljana and Dubrovnik. If you're lacing the big cities together, the last thing you want is a car.

In some parts of Croatia and Slovenia, a car is helpful, if not essential: Istria (especially the hill towns), Rab, the Julian Alps, Logarska Dolina, the Karst, and Montenegro's Bay of Kotor. In other areas, a car is unnecessary: Ljubljana and most of the Dalmatian Coast (Dubrovnik, Split, Hvar, and Korčula). For most trips, the best plan is a combination: Use public transportation in some areas, then strategically rent a car for a day or two in a region that merits it. (I've noted which areas are best by car, and offered route and arrival instructions, throughout this book.)

Public Transportation

When checking timetables *(vozni red)*, arrivals are *prihodi* and departures are *odhodi; svaki dan* means "daily," but some buses don't go on Sundays *(nedjeljom)* or holidays *(praznikom)*.

Trains

Trains are ideal for certain routes in Croatia and Slovenia (such as between Ljubljana and Zagreb), and for connecting to other countries. But their usefulness is limited, and you'll find buses, boats, and flights better for most trips (all explained below).

For train timetables, the first place to check is Germany's excellent all-Europe timetable at http://bahn.hafas.de/bin/query .exe/en. You can also check www.slo-zeleznice.si for Slovenia, and www.hznet.hr for Croatia. Buy tickets at the train station (or on board, if the station is unmanned)—you rarely need a reservation.

Railpasses: While railpasses can be a good deal in some parts Europe, they usually aren't as useful in Croatia or Slovenia. Point-to-point tickets are affordable, and often the better option. If your travels are taking you beyond Croatia and Slovenia, consider a Eurail Selectpass, which covers unlimited travel for up to 15 travel

Public Transportation in Croatia and Slovenia

days (within a two-month period) in three, four, or five adjacent countries (Croatia and Slovenia are considered a single "country"). A separate combo-pass covers Hungary, Slovenia, and Croatia, and another pass covers Austria, Slovenia, and Croatia. Again, none of these passes is likely to save you much money, but if a pass matches your itinerary, give it a look and crunch the numbers. For all of the options, visit our Railpass Guide online at www.ricksteves .com/rail.

Buses

Buses often take you where trains don't. For example, train tracks run only as far south as Split; for destinations on the Dalmatian Coast farther south, you'll rely on buses (or boats). Even on some routes that are served by trains, buses are a better option. For example, Ljubljana and Lake Bled are connected by both train and bus—but the bus station is right in the town center of Bled, while the train station is a few miles away.

Confusingly, a single bus route can be operated by a variety of different companies, making it difficult to find comprehensive schedules. Some big cities have handy Web sites listing all connections (such as www.ap-ljubljana.si for Ljubljana, and www.akz .hr for Zagreb), but for smaller towns, the TI is your best source of information. Prices vary among companies, even for identical journeys. For popular routes during peak season, you'll want to buy your ticket in advance to ensure getting a seat (ask the local TI how far ahead to get to the bus station).

If you're headed south along the coast, sitting on the right side comes with substantially better scenery (sit on the left for northbound buses).

Boats

All along the Croatian Coast, slow car ferries and speedy catamarans inexpensively shuttle tourists between major coastal cities and quiet island towns. Boats run often in summer (June–early Sept), but frequency drops sharply off-season.

Croatians use the word **"ferry"** *(trajekt)* to describe a boat that takes cars (though walk-on passengers are also welcome). These move slowly but can run in virtually any weather. Watching the ferry crew scurrying around to load and unload cars and trucks onto their boat—especially if it's a small one—is a ▲▲▲ Croatian experience.

Increasingly, popular tourist destinations in Croatia are connected by much faster **catamarans,** which carry only passengers. These are efficient, but they have to slow down (or sometimes can't run at all) in bad weather.

Most of Croatia's boats are run by the state-run company called Jadrolinija (yah-droh-LEE-nee-yah), which operates a variety of vessels. Most notable are the four big Jadrolinija car ferries: *Marko Polo* and *Liburnija* go all the way down the coast from Rijeka to Dubrovnik, and cross to Bari, Italy; *Dubrovnik* and *Ivan Zajc* cross between Ancona and Split, and (in peak season, July–mid-Sept) also connect Split with Stari Grad (Hvar Island) and Korčula town. But Jadrolinija also runs smaller car ferries along the coast, as well as some faster catamarans.

Buy your ticket before boarding the boat. Each town has a Jadrolinija ticket office, which I've listed throughout this book; if the office isn't at the dock itself, there's always a small ticket kiosk that opens at the dock before each departure. The main Jadrolinija office is in Rijeka (tel. 051/666-111, fax 051/213-116, www .jadrolinija.hr). For non-Jadrolinija boats, such as the *Krilo* catamaran (described below), you may have to buy the tickets at a travel agency.

Boat rides are cheap for deck passengers: figure less than $40 per person on the big Jadrolinija car ferry from Rijeka in the north all the way to Dubrovnik in the south; shorter journeys—which you're more likely to take—are even more affordable. A car pays about $100 from Rijeka to Dubrovnik (progressively less for shorter trips). You're allowed to get off at any port en route, then get on a later boat on the same route—but you have to get your ticket validated before you leave the boat.

Advance reservations are not necessary for walk-on passengers on car ferries; you can almost always find a seat on the deck or in the on-board café. The lower-capacity catamarans can fill up, so it's wise to show up 30–60 minutes before departure time (get advice from the local TI).

Drivers cannot reserve in advance on most routes. This means you'll want to arrive at the dock up to a few hours early, especially in peak season. Again, since this flexes with the season, the local TI is your best resource for advice on how early to leave for the boat. Notice that on some islands, the car ferry port is a long drive from the main tourist town (for example, Vela Luka on Korčula Island is a 1-hour drive from Korčula town; Stari Grad on Hvar Island is a 20-minute drive from Hvar town).

You can buy food and drinks onboard most boats. It's not too expensive, but it's not top quality, either. Bring your own snacks or a picnic instead.

Because Jadrolinija has a virtual monopoly on coastal ferries, their routes don't always cater to customer demand. But a few new, private companies are beginning to compete with Jadrolinija. Most notably, a catamaran called *Krilo* is running an extremely handy service between Split, Hvar town, and Korčula town every day in summer.

Rumor has it that other, similar boats may be up and running soon—inquire locally.

The boat schedule information in this book changes every year, without fail. As my information is based on the 2006 schedules, it's essential to confirm before you make your plans. Jadrolinija's Web site (www.jadrolinija.hr) is useful, but they don't post future schedules very far in advance. Again, local TIs are the single best source of information for how their town is connected to the rest of the coast.

Cheap Flights

Each country has its own national air carrier: Croatia's is **Croatia Airlines** (www.croatiaairlines.com), while Slovenia has **Adria Airways** (www.adria-airways.com). Both airlines offer flights connecting their big cities to destinations within Croatia and Slovenia, and to most major European capitals. And both carriers sell a handful of seats on certain flights at deeply discounted promotional rates. For example, a Croatia Airlines "FlyPromo" ticket from Zagreb to Split or Dubrovnik can be as inexpensive as €30—cheaper and much faster than taking the bus. These cheap seats sell fast, so try to book several weeks ahead.

To connect to other parts of Europe, check with the low-cost airlines. Carriers that fly to cities in Croatia or Slovenia include **easyJet** (www.easyjet.com), **Ryanair** (www.ryanair.com), **SkyEurope** (www.skyeurope.com), and **Wizz Air** (www.wizzair .com). Prices are cheap—for example, SkyEurope flies between Budapest and Dubrovnik for less than $50 (but only in summer). However, there are some trade-offs for these cheap flights: minimal customer service, non-refundable tickets, and strict restrictions on the amount of baggage you're allowed to check without paying extra. In general, you'll be nickel-and-dimed every step of the way (e.g., no free drinks). Also note that you'll sometimes fly out of less convenient, secondary airports. Finally, be warned that many no-frills airlines save money by scheduling flights on the same plane extremely close together—so they can pack more flights into one day. But this means that a delay early in the day can trickle down and cause major delays later.

Europe by Air offers a Flight Pass, charging $99 per leg (plus taxes and airport fees) for flights within Europe. They partner with various well-established airlines, providing good coverage for low prices (most useful for Croatia Airlines flights to and from the Dalmatian Coast; tickets can be purchased only in US, www .europebyair.com, US tel. 888-321-4737).

Driving

Car Rental

It's cheaper to arrange long-term European car rentals in the US than in Europe. For short rentals of a day or two, I usually have no problem finding an affordable car on the spot (I've listed car-rental companies in this book)—but if your itinerary is set, it doesn't hurt to book ahead. All of the big American companies have offices throughout Croatia and Slovenia. Comparison-shop on the Web to find the best deal, or ask your travel agent.

Allow about $750 per person (based on two people sharing the car) to rent a small economy car for three weeks with unlimited mileage, including gas, parking, and insurance. I normally rent a small, inexpensive model like a Ford Fiesta or Škoda Fabia. You'll pay extra for collision damage waiver (CDW) insurance (described next). Be warned that dropping a car off in a different country—say, picking up in Ljubljana and dropping in Dubrovnik—can be prohibitively expensive (depends on distance, but the extra fee averages a few hundred dollars, and can exceed $1,000—see the sidebar for ways around this). Again, I prefer to connect long distances by train or bus, then rent cars for a day or two where they're most useful.

As a rule, always tell your car-rental company up front exactly which countries you'll be entering. Some companies levy extra insurance fees for trips taken with certain types of cars (such as BMWs, Mercedes, and convertibles) in certain countries. More importantly, as you cross borders you may need to show the proper paperwork, such as proof of insurance (often called a "green card"). Double-check with your rental agent that you have all the documentation you need before you drive off.

For driving in Croatia and Slovenia, it's wise to get an International Driving Permit ahead of time at your local AAA office ($10 plus two passport-type photos, www.aaa.com).

Insurance: For peace of mind, I spring for the Collision Damage Waiver insurance (CDW, about $15–25 per day), which limits my financial responsibility in case of an accident. Unfortunately, CDW now has a high deductible hovering at about $1,000–1,500. When you pick up your car, many car-rental companies will try to sell you "super CDW" at an additional cost of $7–15 per day to lower the deductible to zero. Consider the following alternatives.

Some credit cards offer zero-deductible collision coverage (similar to CDW) for no charge to their customers. Quiz your credit-card company on the worst-case scenario. You have to choose either the coverage offered by your car-rental company or by your credit-card company. This means that if you go with the credit-card coverage, you'll have to decline the CDW offered by

The Rental-Car Conundrum

Virtually everyone planning a trip by car to this region runs into the same problem: International drop-off fees for rental cars are astronomical. Generally there's no extra charge for picking up and dropping off a car in different towns within the same country, but you'll pay through the nose (often hundreds of dollars) to drop off across the border. This is especially frustrating when connecting some car-friendly parts of southern Slovenia (such as the Karst or Piran) with similar areas in northern Croatia (such as Istria or Plitvice Lakes National Park).

But by thinking creatively, you can avoid this huge and unnecessary expense. Let's say you want to pick up a car in Ljubljana, drive through Slovenia's Karst to Istria, then continue to Split and drop your car. Here are two possible alternatives: First, you could do a circuit around the sights of southern Slovenia, then head back up to Ljubljana (fast and easy, thanks to the short distances and speedy expressways), drop your Slovenian car there, and train into a northern Croatian city (such as Zagreb or Rijeka) to pick up a second car for your Croatian driving. Or you could take the train from Ljubljana into northern Croatia, pick up your rental car, then loop back up into Slovenia with the Croatian car before continuing south through Croatia.

the car-rental company. In this situation, some car-rental companies put a hold on your credit card for the amount of the full deductible (which can equal the value of the car). This is bad news if your credit limit is low—particularly if you plan on using that card for other purchases during your trip.

Another alternative is buying CDW insurance from Travel Guard ($9/day plus a one-time $3 service fee covers you up to $35,000, $250 deductible, US tel. 800-826-4919, www.travelguard .com). It's valid throughout Europe, but some car-rental companies refuse to honor it (mainly in Italy and Ireland). Oddly, residents of Washington State are not allowed to buy this coverage.

In summary, buying CDW from the car-rental company— along with the supplemental insurance to buy down the deductible, if you choose—is the easiest but priciest option. Using the coverage that comes with your credit card is cheaper, but can involve more hassle. If you're taking a short trip, an easy solution is to buy Travel Guard's very affordable CDW. For longer trips, consider leasing.

Leasing: If you'll be renting for three weeks or more, look into leasing (either through your travel agent or by going online to check the major companies' Web sites). Leasing allows you to

Driving: Distance and Time

avoid insurance costs and taxes, but you may have to pick up and drop off the car in Germany or Austria.

Driving Tips

Drivers should be prepared for twisty seaside and mountain roads, wonderful views, and plenty of tempting stopovers. As you approach any town, follow the *Centar* signs (usually also signed with a bull's-eye symbol). Get parking advice from your hotel, or look for the blue-and-white *P* signs.

Croatia and Slovenia are crisscrossed by an impressive network of expressways (*autocesta* in Croatian, *avtocesta* in Slovene). I don't call them "freeways" because they're not—you'll generally pay about €0.05 per kilometer (so a 50-kilometer trip is about €2.50, or $3). You'll take a toll-ticket when you enter the expressway, then submit it when you get off (but don't lose your ticket, or you'll pay the maximum).

Construction on these superhighways is ongoing, so it's not unusual to discover that a not-yet-finished expressway ends, requiring a transfer to an older, slower road. For example, the wonderfully speedy A-1 expressway goes only as far south as Split; from there southward along the Dalmatian Coast (including Dubrovnik), you'll follow the winding coastal road. (Likewise, you'll sometimes discover that a much faster road has been built between major destinations since your two-year-old map was published.) Secondary roads are usually in good repair, but they can be very twisty—especially along the coast or through the mountains. If you get way off the beaten track, you still might find gravel. Locals poetically describe these as "white roads." (Get it? No asphalt.)

A good map is essential (see page 11). While most roads are numbered, Croatians and Slovenes seem to ignore these numbers, which rarely appear on signs. Instead, navigate by town name—directional signs pointing to nearby towns and cities are at every major intersection.

If you'll be driving along the Dalmatian Coast, notice that between Split and Dubrovnik, you'll actually pass through Bosnia-Herzegovina for a few miles (the town of Neum; the borders are a breezy formality, but you may need to show your passport).

Keep a close eye out for bikers. You'll see scads of them on mountain roads, struggling to earn a thrilling downhill run.

Parking: Parking is a costly headache in big cities. You'll pay about $10–15 a day to park safely. Rental-car theft can be a problem in cities. Ask at your hotel for advice.

Laws and Regulations: Learn the universal road signs (see sidebar). Seat belts are required, and two beers under those belts are enough to land you in jail. (In Croatia, it's illegal to have any alcohol at all in your system if you're driving.)

More and more European countries—including Slovenia—require you to have your headlights on any time you're driving, even in broad daylight. Many cars are rigged to have lights go on and off automatically when you start and stop the engine. Be sure to ask about this regulation, and how your car's lights work, when you pick up your rental car.

Europe's Best Linguists

Why do Croatians and Slovenes speak English so well?

Residents of big, powerful Western European countries, such as Germany or Italy, might think that foreigners should learn their language. But Croatians and Slovenes are as practical as Germans and Italians are stubborn. They realize that it's unreasonable to expect an American to learn Croatian (5 million speakers worldwide) or Slovene (2 million). When only a few million people on the planet speak your language, it's essential to find a common language with the rest of the world—so they learn English early and well.

In Croatia, all schoolchildren start learning English in the third grade. (I've had surprisingly eloquent conversations with Croatian grade-schoolers.) And, since American television programs here are subtitled rather than dubbed, people get plenty of practice hearing American English (with a non-stop simultaneous translation). This means Croatians and Slovenes speak not textbook English, but *real* English—and can be more proficient in slang than some Americans.

Many times, I've heard a Norwegian and a Croatian conversing in English—a reminder that as Americans, we're lucky to speak the world's new lingua franca.

COMMUNICATING

Hurdling the Language Barrier

The language barrier in Croatia and Slovenia is actually smaller than in places like France, Italy, or Spain. You'll find that most people in the tourist industry—and virtually all young people—speak excellent English.

Of course, not *everyone* speaks English. You'll run into the most substantial language barriers in situations when you need to deal with a lesser-educated clerk or service person (train stations and post office counters, maids, museum guards, bakers, and so on). Be reasonable in your expectations. Croatian museum ticket-sellers are every bit as friendly and multilingual as they are in the US.

It helps to know a few words of the local language. Croatian and Slovene are closely related, but not identical. Still, they're similar enough that the same basic words work in both. For example, "hello" is *dobar dan* in Croatian, but *dober dan* in Slovene. I've listed the essential phrases in each country introduction, and more at the end of this book (beginning on page 457).

Pronouncing Croatian and Slovenian Place Names

Remember that *j* is pronounced as "y," and *c* is pronounced "ts." For the special characters, *č* is "ch," *š* is "sh," *ž* is "zh," and *đ* is similar to "j."

Name	Pronounced
Bohinj	BOH-heen
Brijuni (Islands)	bree-YOO-nee
Brtonigla	bur-toh-NEEG-lah
Dubrovnik	doo-BROHV-nik
Grožnjan	grohzh-NYAHN
Herzegovina	hert-seh-GOH-vee-nah
Hum	hoom
Hvar	hvahr
Istria	EE-stree-ah
Jadrolinija (Ferry Company)	yah-droh-LEE-nee-yah
Korčula	KOHR-choo-lah
Lipica (Lipizzaner Stud Farm)	LEE-peet-suh
Ljubljana	lyoob-lyee-AH-nah
Međugorje	MEDGE-oo-gor-yeh
Motovun	moh-toh-VOON

Croatian and Slovene have a few letters that are pronounced differently than in English, and they add a few diacritics—little markings below and above some letters. Here are a few rules of thumb for sounding out unfamiliar words:

J / j sounds like "y" as in "yellow"

C / c sounds like "ts" as in "cats"

Č / č and Ć / ć sound like "ch" as in "chicken"

Š / š sounds like "sh" as in "shrimp"

Ž / ž sounds like "zh" as in "leisure"

Đ / đ (only in Croatian) is like the "dj" sound in "jeans"

Croatian and Slovene are notorious for their seemingly unpronounceable consonant combinations. Most difficult are hv (as in *hvala*, "thank you") and nj (as in Bohinj, a lake in Slovenia). Foreigners are notorious for over-pronouncing these combinations. In the combination hv, the h is nearly silent; if you struggle with it, simply leave off the h (for *hvala*, just say "VAH-lah"; saying "huh-VAH-lah" sounds silly). When you see nj, the j is mostly silent,

Mljet (National Park)	muhl-YET
Opatija	oh-PAH-tee-yah
Otočac	OH-toh-chawts
Plitvice (National Park)	PLEET-veet-seh
Piran	pee-RAHN
Polače	POH-lah-cheh
Pomena	POH-meh-nah
Poreč	poh-RETCH
Postojna (Caves)	poh-STOY-nah
Predjama (Castle)	prehd-YAH-mah
Ptuj	puh-TOOey
Rab	rob
Radovljica	rah-DOH-vleet-suh
Rijeka	ree-YAY-kah
Rovinj	roh-VEEN
Škocjan (Caves)	SHKOHTS-yahn
Senj	sehn
Soča (River Valley)	SOH-chah
Vršič (Pass)	vur-SHEECH
Zagreb	ZAH-grehb

with a slight "y" sound that can be omitted: for Bohinj, just say BOH-heen. Listen to locals and imitate.

A few key words are helpful for navigation: *trg* (square), *ulica* (road), *cesta* (avenue), *autocesta* (expressway), *most* (bridge), *otok* (island), *trajekt* (ferry), and *Jadran* (Adriatic).

Throughout Croatia and Slovenia, German can be a useful second language (especially in Croatia, which is popular among German-speaking tourists). And a few words of Italian can also come in handy, especially in bicultural Istria.

Learn the key phrases and travel with a phrase book. Consider Lonely Planet's good *Eastern Europe Phrasebook*, which includes both Croatian and Slovene, or their in-depth, stand-alone *Croatian Phrasebook*.

Don't be afraid to interact with locals. The people of Croatia and Slovenia love visitors, and a friendly greeting in their language is an easy icebreaker. Give it your best shot. The locals will appreciate your efforts.

Telephones

Smart travelers learn the phone system and use it daily to reserve or reconfirm rooms, get tourist information, reserve restaurants, confirm tour times, or phone home.

Types of Phones

You'll encounter various kinds of phones in your European travels.

Pay phones—in booths, free-standing, or fixed to a wall—line the streets of Europe. Most are no longer coin-operated; you have to buy an insertable phone card, or use an international phone card (both options described under "Paying for Calls").

Hotel room phones are fairly cheap for local calls, but pricey for international calls, unless you use an international phone card.

American mobile phones work in Europe if they're GSM-enabled, tri-band (or quad-band), and on a calling plan that includes international calls. T-Mobile and Cingular have the best deals. For example, with a T-Mobile phone, you can roam all over Europe using your home number, and pay about $1 per minute for making or receiving calls. This option is the most convenient—and can be the most expensive.

Some travelers buy a **European mobile phone** in Europe (but if you're on a strict budget, skip mobile phones and use phone cards instead). The cheapest new phones cost around $75, plus $20–50 for the necessary "SIM card" to make it work (includes some prepaid calling time). A cheapie phone is often "locked" to work affordably only in the country where you buy it, but can also roam (for high rates) in other countries. For around $25 more, you can buy an "unlocked" phone that allows you to use different SIM cards in different countries—which saves money if you'll be making lots of calls. If you're interested, stop by any European shop that sells mobile phones; you'll see prominent store window displays. You aren't required to (and shouldn't) buy a monthly contract—buy prepaid calling time instead. As you use it up, buy additional minutes at newsstands or mobile-phone shops.

Paying for Calls

You can spend a fortune making phone calls in Europe...but why would you? Here's the skinny on different ways to pay, including the best deals.

European phone cards come in two types: official phone cards that you insert into a pay phone, and international phone cards that can be used from virtually any phone.

• **Insertable phone cards** can be purchased at post offices, newsstands, and tobacco shops. Simply take the phone off the hook, insert the prepaid card, wait for a dial tone, and dial away. The price of the call (local or international) is automatically deducted while you talk. These cards only work in the country where you buy them (so your Slovenian phone card is worthless in Croatia). Insertable phone cards are a good deal for calling within Europe, but it's cheaper to make your overseas calls with an international phone card.

• **International phone cards** allow you to call home cheap (generally around 25–50 cents per minute). Unlike the official phone cards, an international phone card is *not* inserted into the phone. Instead, you dial the toll-free number listed on the card, reaching an automated operator. When prompted, you dial in a scratch-to-reveal code number, also written on the card. Then dial your number. Since these cards are not insertable, you can use them from any phone—including the one in your hotel room (if your phone is set on "pulse," switch it to "tone"). These cards are not quite as cheap as similar cards in Western Europe, but they're catching on here fast—so rates are sure to drop as more choices become available. Look for fliers advertising long-distance rates, or ask about the cards at Internet cafés, newsstands, souvenir shops, and youth hostels. There are many different brands. Simply request an international telephone card, tell the vendor where you'll be making most calls ("to America"), and he'll select the brand with the best deal. Make sure the access number you dial is toll-free, not a local number (or else you'll be paying for a local call *and* deducting time from your calling card). These cards usually work only in the country where you buy them, but some brands work internationally. Buy a lower denomination in case the card is a dud.

Dialing direct from your hotel room without using an international phone card is usually quite expensive for international calls, but it's convenient. Always ask first how much you'll be charged. Keep in mind that you have to pay for local and occasionally even toll-free calls.

Receiving calls in your hotel room is often the cheapest way to keep in touch with the folks back home—especially if your family has an inexpensive way to call you (either a good deal on their long-distance plan, or a prepaid calling card with good rates to Europe). Give them a list of your hotels' phone numbers before you go. As you travel, send your family an e-mail or make a quick pay-phone call to set up a time for them to call you, and then wait for the ring.

Metered phones are available in phone offices and sometimes in bigger post offices. You can talk all you want, then pay the bill when you leave—but be sure you know the rates before you have a lengthy conversation.

Coin-operated phones, while rare, still exist in some areas. If making a call, have a bunch of coins handy—they go fast.

VoIP (Voice over Internet Protocol), which is an option only for those traveling with a laptop computer, allows VoIP users to talk with each other for free via their computers over a fast Internet connection. Look into Skype (www.skype.com) and Google Talk (www.google.com/talk).

US calling cards (such as the ones offered by AT&T, MCI, and Sprint) are the worst option. You'll nearly always save a lot of money by paying for your call in any of the other ways described previously.

How to Dial

Calling from the US to Europe, or vice versa, is simple—once you break the code. The European calling chart on page 450 will walk you through it. Remember that European time is six/nine hours ahead of the East/West Coasts of the US.

Dialing Domestic Calls: Croatia and Slovenia, like much of the US, use an area-code dialing system. If you're dialing within an area code, you just dial the local number to be connected; but if you're calling outside your area code, you have to dial both the area code (which starts with a 0) and the local number. For example, Dubrovnik's area code is 020, and the number of one of my recommended Dubrovnik hotels is 453-834. To call the hotel within Dubrovnik, just dial 453-834. To call it from Split, dial 020/453-834.

Making International Calls: When making an international call to Croatia or Slovenia, first dial the international access code of the country you're in (011 from the US or Canada, 00 if you're calling from Europe), then the country code for the place you're calling (385 for Croatia, 386 for Slovenia), then the area code (*without* its initial 0) and the local number. For example, to call the Dubrovnik hotel from the US, dial 011, 385 (Croatia's country code), 20 (Dubrovnik's area code without the initial zero), and 453-834.

To call my office in Edmonds, Washington, from Europe, I dial 00 (Europe's international access code), 1 (US's country code), 425 (Edmonds' area code), and 771-8303.

If you see a phone number that begins with +, you have to replace the + with the international access code (again, that's 011 from the US or Canada, 00 from Europe). For a listing of country codes, see the appendix.

E-mail and Mail

E-mail: These days, almost every hotel has an e-mail address and Web site (included in this book). In fact, most hoteliers prefer to receive your booking online rather than by fax or phone. Some family-run pensions can become overwhelmed by the volume of e-mail they receive, so be patient if you don't get an immediate response.

Many hotels have an Internet terminal in the lobby for guests (which I've noted in this book)—sometimes free, sometimes for a fee. I've also listed some Internet cafés, but your hotelier or TI can steer you to the nearest Internet access point.

If you're traveling with a laptop, you'll find that wireless Internet access, or Wi-Fi (sometimes called "WLAN" in Europe), is gradually being installed in hotels and progressive B&Bs. Some charge by the minute, while others are free. On a typical trip with my laptop, I can get online at about half of my hotels.

Mail: You can get stamps at the neighborhood post office, at newsstands inside fancy hotels, and at some mini-marts and card shops. While you can arrange for mail delivery to your hotel (allow 10 days for a letter to arrive), phoning and e-mailing are so easy that I've dispensed with mail stops altogether.

SLEEPING

The accommodations situation in Croatia and Slovenia is quirky and complicated. There are two basic choices: either a big hotel or what locals call "private accommodations"—a rented apartment *(apartman)* or a room in a private home *(soba*, pronounced SOH-bah; plural *sobe*, SOH-bay). I've explained the ins and outs of each in this section.

Whether I'm evaluating a hotel or a private room, I look for the same qualities: it must be friendly, comfortable, professional-feeling, centrally located, English-speaking, and family-run. Obviously, a place meeting every criterion is rare, and all of my recommendations fall short of perfection—sometimes miserably. But I've listed the best values for each price category, given the above criteria. My favorites are small, family-run hotels (which are rare), and friendly local people who rent "hotelesque" private rooms without a reception desk (which are thankfully abundant).

In Croatia, most hotels are outrageously expensive, but private accommodations are an excellent value. My recommendations range from $15 bunks to $300-plus splurges, but most cluster around the same price range. For a well-located standard double room in peak season on the Croatian Coast, plan on spending $125–200 in a big resort hotel; $60–110 in a small hotel or a "hotelesque" private room or apartment (with your own bathroom, TV, and other amenities); or $45–65 for a more basic private room with a shared bathroom.

Slovenia has a wider range of affordable small hotels (about $90–120 in Ljubljana, and $70–90 in small towns and the countryside), which make private accommodations a lesser value there.

Remember that some accommodations quote their rates in euros, while others use kunas. For maximum accuracy, I generally

Sleep Code

I've divided the rooms into three categories, based on the price for a standard double room with bath:

$$$ **Higher Priced**
$$ **Moderately Priced**
$ **Lower Priced**

To save space while giving specific information, I've described my recommended hotels with a standard code. Prices listed are per room, not per person. When a range of prices is listed for a room, the price fluctuates with room size or season. Hotels usually accept credit cards and include a buffet breakfast (unless otherwise noted); private accommodations rarely do either. Virtually all of my recommended accommodations are run by people who speak English; if they don't, I mention it in the listing.

S = Single room (the price for one person in a double is often slightly more).
D = Double or twin.
T = Triple (often a double bed with a single bed moved in).
Q = Quad (an extra child's bed is usually cheaper).
b = Private bathroom with toilet and shower or tub.

According to this code, a couple staying at a "Db-480 kn, cash only" place in Dubrovnik would pay a total of 480 Croatian kunas (about $80) for a double room with a private bathroom. Credit cards are not accepted, but you can assume they speak English.

list the prices they gave me.

At either type of accommodation, rates vary wildly by season, with August being the most expensive. Also at both types, short stays (of less than three nights) are discouraged, especially in peak season. Expect to pay 20–50 percent extra if you're staying just one or two nights, and don't be surprised if some places have a one-week minimum in summer.

Three or four people can save money by requesting one big room. Traveling alone can be expensive: A single room is often only 20 percent cheaper than a double.

Discos and nightclubs are proliferating in the old town centers of many cities in this book—including Dubrovnik, Split, and Ljubljana. I've noted the specific hotels that suffer the worst noise. If you're a light sleeper, make a point of requesting a quiet room. Non-smoking rooms are rare—so be very specific and assertive if you need a room that's strictly non-smoking.

If there seems to be no hot water, try flipping the switch with a picture of a water tank, usually next to the light switch. In many *sobe,* the hot-water tank is tiny—about big enough for one American-length shower. So two people traveling together may want to practice the "Navy shower" method (water, soap up, rinse)...or the second one may be in for a chilly surprise. The incredibly high water pressure in Croatian showers only makes the hot water go that much faster (turn the faucet on only partway to help stretch the precious hot water).

For environmental reasons, towels are often replaced in hotels only when you leave them on the floor. In private accommodations and some cheap hotels, they aren't replaced at all, so hang them up to dry and reuse. The cord that dangles over the tub or shower in big resort hotels is not a clothesline—you pull it if you've fallen and can't get up.

Before accepting a room, confirm your understanding of the complete price (including, for example, extra fees for short stays). Pay your bill the evening before you leave to avoid the time-wasting crowd at the reception desk in the morning, especially if you need to rush off to catch your train. The only tip my recommended accommodations would like is a friendly, easygoing guest. And, as always, I appreciate feedback on your experiences.

Private Accommodations (*Sobe* and Apartments)

Private accommodations offer travelers a characteristic and money-saving alternative for a fraction of the price of a hotel. Again, you have two options: a *soba* (room) or *apartman* (apartment).

Often run by empty-nesters, private accommodations are similar to British bed-and-breakfasts...minus the breakfast (ask your host about the best nearby breakfast spot). Generally the more you pay, the more privacy and amenities (private bathroom, TV, air-conditioning, kitchenette) you get. The simplest *sobe* allow you to experience Croatia on the cheap, at nearly youth-hostel prices, while giving you a great opportunity to connect with a local family. The fanciest *sobe* are downright swanky, allowing for near-hotel anonymity. Apartments are bigger and cost more than *sobe,* but they're still far cheaper than hotels.

Registered *sobe* have been rated by the government using a system that assigns stars based on amenities. Three stars means that you'll have your own bathroom, two stars means that the bathroom's down the hall, and one star is rock-bottom basic. If you don't like the idea of sharing a toilet with strangers, look for three stars and you'll do fine. (Apartments always have private bathrooms, plus some modest kitchen facilities.) Many, but not all, three-star *sobe* also have TV and air-conditioning (but usually no telephone). The prices for private accommodations generally fluctuate with the seasons, and remember that stays of fewer than three nights almost always come with a 20–30 percent surcharge.

You can reserve most *sobe* in advance (usually by e-mail). This represents a major financial risk for your host, who loses money if you don't show up. For this reason, some hosts may ask you to send cash or a check as a deposit. *Sobe* hucksters who accost you on the street can be very aggressive about luring travelers away from their reserved rooms. But if you've booked a room at a particular place, you owe it to them to show up.

If you like to travel spontaneously, you'll have no problem finding *sobe* as you go. Locals hawking rooms meet each arriving boat, bus, and train. Many of these *sobe* have not been classified by the government, but they can sometimes turn out to be a good deal. The person generally shows photos of her place, you haggle for a price, then she escorts you to your new home. Be sure you understand exactly where it's located (i.e., within easy walking distance of the attractions) before you accept—ask to see the location on a map, and find out how long it takes to walk into town.

You can also keep an eye out for rooms as you walk or drive through town—you'll see blue *sobe* and *apartman* signs everywhere. It's actually fun to visit a few homes and make a deal. While it takes nerve to just show up without a room, this is standard operating procedure for backpackers.

As a last resort, you can enlist the help of a travel agency to find you a room—but you'll pay 10–30 percent extra (various agencies are listed in this book; to search from home, try www.dubrovnikapartmentsource  .com for Dubrovnik, or www.adriatica.net for all of Croatia).

I'm accustomed to staying in hotels. But on my last trip to Dubrovnik, I found all of the hotels booked up. With some trepidation, I stayed in a *soba*...and I'll never go back to a Croatian resort hotel again. I've made it my mission to convince you to sleep in *sobe*, too.

Hotels

Even under communism, Yugoslavs were savvy businesspeople. To maximize beach-tourism occupancy in the 1960s and 1970s, they razed quaint Old World buildings to make way for new, big resort hotels. Most of these coastal hotels housed refugees from inland Croatia during the war, and many have been only lightly renovated since.

Today, many of these hotels still have the same old communist-era dark-wood furnishings, moldy-college-dorm ambience, "beach" access (often on a concrete pad), a travel-agency desk selling tours in the lobby, and a seaview apéritif bar. These hotels are just fine with the busloads of European tourists who head south for a week-long summer holiday. But Americans are appalled at how much you have to spend for such low quality.

For years, these hulking communist-era hotels sat around Croatia's prettiest towns, begging for a thorough renovation. The good news: It's finally happening. The bad news: Instead of sprucing the hotels up to acceptable standards for a moderate price range, most are being turned into four- or five-star luxury hotels. While the renovated hotels are gorgeous, they're also exorbitant. Those in the Croatian tourist industry believe this will do great things for tourism, but it prices people like you and me out of the big-hotel market.

Fortunately, *sobe* and apartments are stepping up to fill the mid-budget accommodations void. Another promising development is that a handful of new, smaller, family-run hotels are opening up around Croatia. These are usually much more reasonably priced than the big resorts—and friendlier, to boot. I've listed my favorites.

Hostels

For $15 to $20 a night, travelers of any age can stay at a youth hostel. While official hostels admit nonmembers for an extra fee, it's best to join the club and buy a youth hostel card before you go (call Hostelling International at US tel. 202/783-6161 or order online at www.hiayh.org). To increase your options, consider the many independent hostels that don't require a membership card (www.hostels.com).

Throughout Croatia, hostels are a relatively new concept. Usually official hostels are poorly located, in bad repair, and particularly institutional, while independent hostels are loosely run and grungier than the European norm. If you need a cheap bed and don't gravitate to either of these extremes, private accommodations are always a good option. Slovenia's hostels are much better. In fact, one of Europe's most innovative hostels is in Ljubljana: Celica, a renovated former prison (see page 348).

At any hostel, cheap meals are sometimes available, and kitchen facilities are usually provided for do-it-yourselfers. Expect crowds in the summer, snoring, and lots of youth groups giggling and making rude noises while you try to sleep. Hosteling is ideal for those traveling single: prices are per bed, not per room, and you'll have an instant circle of friends. More and more hostels are getting their business acts together, taking credit card reservations over the phone and leaving sign-in forms on the door for each available room. If you're serious about traveling cheaply, get a card, carry your own sheets, and cook in the members' kitchens.

Making Reservations

It's possible to travel at any time of year without reservations (especially if you arrive early in the day). But given the erratic accommodations values and the quality of the gems I've found for this book, I'd highly recommend that you book rooms ahead as soon as your itinerary is set—or at least call ahead for rooms a day or two in advance as you travel. Even if a hotel clerk or *sobe* host says they're fully booked, you can try calling between 9:00 and 10:00 on the day you plan to arrive. That's when they know who'll be checking out and just which rooms will be available. I've taken great pains to list telephone numbers with long-distance instructions (see "Telephones," earlier in this chapter and in the appendix). Use the telephone and the convenient phone cards. Most hotels listed are accustomed to English-only speakers. Most hotel receptionists or *sobe* hosts will trust you and hold a room until 16:00 (4:00 p.m.) without a deposit, though some will ask for a credit-card number. Honor (or cancel by phone) your reservations. Long distance is cheap and easy from public phone booths. Again, don't let these people down—I promised you'd call and cancel if for some reason you won't show up.

If you know exactly which dates you need and really want a particular place, reserve a room well in advance before you leave home. To reserve from home, e-mail, call, or fax the hotel or *sobe*. Phone and fax costs are reasonable, e-mail is a steal, and simple English is usually fine. To fax, use the form in the appendix (or find it online at www.ricksteves.com/reservation). A two-night stay in August would be "2 nights, 16/8/07 to 18/8/07." (Europeans write the date in this order—day/month/year—and accommodations jargon counts your stay from your day of arrival through your day of departure.)

If you e-mail or fax a reservation request and receive a response with rates stating that rooms are available, this is not a confirmation. You must confirm that the rates are fine and that indeed you want the room for the agreed-upon dates. (Don't just assume you can extend upon arrival; take the time to consider in advance how long you'll stay.) The hotel or *sobe* host will often request one night's deposit. A credit-card number and expiration date will usually work. Be sure to fax your card number (rather than e-mail it) to keep it private, safer, and out of cyberspace. If you use your credit card for the deposit, you can pay with your card or cash when you arrive; if you don't show up, you'll be billed for one night. Ask about the cancellation policy when you reserve; sometimes you may have to cancel as much as two weeks ahead to

Balkan Flavors

All of the countries of the Balkan Peninsula—basically from Slovenia to Greece—have several foods in common. The Ottomans from today's Turkey, who controlled much of this territory for centuries, imported some goodies that remained standard fare here long after they left town. Whether you're in Slovenia, Croatia, Bosnia-Herzegovina, Montenegro, Serbia, or Albania, here are some local tastes worth seeking out.

A popular fast food you'll see everywhere is **burek** (BOO-rehk)—phyllo dough filled with meat, cheese, spinach, or apples. The more familiar **baklava** is phyllo dough layered with honey and nuts.

Grilled meats are a staple of Balkan cuisine. You'll most often see **ražnjići** (RAZH-nyee-chee—small pieces of steak on a skewer, like a shish kebab) and **ćevapčići** (cheh-VAHP-chee-chee—minced meat formed into a sausage-link shape, then grilled). Sometimes you'll come across **pljeskavica** (plehs-kah-VEET-suh—similar to *ćevapčići,* except the meat is in the form of a hamburger-like patty).

While Balkan cuisine favors meat, a nice veggie comple-ment is **đuveđ** (JOO-vedge)—a spicy mix of stewed vegeta-bles, flavored with tomatoes and peppers.

And you just can't eat any of this stuff without the ever-present condiment **ajvar** (EYE-var). Made from red bell pepper and eggplant, *ajvar* is like ketchup with a kick. Many Americans pack a jar of this distinctive, flavorful sauce to remember the flavors of the Balkans when they get back home.

avoid paying a stiff penalty. Reconfirm your reservations several days in advance for safety.

EATING

Croatia and Slovenia offer good food for reasonable prices—espe-cially if you venture off the main tourist trail. This is affordable sightseeing for your palate.

The food of this region is surprisingly diverse. Choosing between strudel and baklava on the same menu, you're constantly reminded that this is a land where East meets West. I've listed the specific specialties in each country introduction, but throughout Croatia and Slovenia you'll sink your teeth into lots of delicious Italian-style food (pizzas and pastas), as well as succulent seafood and fine local wines. You'll also find some pan-Balkan elements that distinguish the cuisine throughout the former Yugoslavia (see sidebar).

At fish restaurants, seafood is often priced by weight—either by kilogram or by hectogram (100 grams, or one-tenth of a kilogram). A one-kilogram portion feeds two hungry people or three light eaters. When I list price ranges for main dishes at restaurants, I don't include the super-top-end seafood splurges (such as lobster).

When restaurant-hunting, choose a spot filled with locals, not the place with the big neon signs boasting, "We Speak English and Accept Credit Cards." Venturing even a block or two off the main drag leads to local, higher-quality food for less than half the price of the tourist-oriented places. Most restaurants tack a menu onto their door for browsers and have an English menu inside. Only a rude waiter will rush you. Good service is relaxed (slow to an American).

When you're in the mood for something halfway between a restaurant and a picnic meal, look for take-out food stands, bakeries (with sandwiches and small pizzas to go), delis with stools or a table, department-store cafeterias, salad bars, or simple little eateries for fast and easy sit-down restaurant food.

TRAVELING AS A TEMPORARY LOCAL

We travel all the way to Europe to enjoy differences—to become temporary locals. You'll experience frustrations. Certain truths that we find "God-given" or "self-evident"—like cold beer, ice in drinks, bottomless cups of coffee, hot showers, cigarette smoke being irritating, and bigger being better—are suddenly not so true. One of the benefits of travel is the eye-opening realization that there are logical, civil, and even better alternatives. A willingness to go local ensures that you'll enjoy a full dose of local hospitality.

Fortunately for you, hospitality is a local forte. The friendliness of Croatians and Slovenes has always shone through during difficult times—and now that they're enjoying an unprecedented prosperity, they're even more excited to show off their beautiful homeland.

If there is a negative aspect to the European image of Americans, we can appear loud, aggressive, impolite, rich, and a bit naive. While Europeans look bemusedly at some of our Yankee excesses—and worriedly at others—they nearly always afford us individual travelers all the warmth we deserve.

While updating my guidebooks, I hear over and over again that my readers are considerate and fun to have as guests. Thank

How Was Your Trip?

Were your travels fun, smooth, and meaningful? If you'd like to share your tips, concerns, and discoveries, please fill out the survey at www.ricksteves.com/feedback or e-mail me at rick @ricksteves.com. I personally read and value your feedback. Thanks in advance—it helps a lot.

you for traveling as temporary locals who are sensitive to the culture. It's fun to follow you in my travels.

Judging from all the positive comments I receive from travelers who have used this book, it's safe to assume you'll enjoy a great, affordable vacation—with the finesse of an experienced, independent traveler.

Thanks, and happy travels!

BACK DOOR TRAVEL PHILOSOPHY
From *Rick Steves' Europe Through the Back Door*

Travel is intensified living—maximum thrills per minute and one of the last great sources of legal adventure. Travel is freedom. It's recess, and we need it.

Experiencing the real Europe requires catching it by surprise, going casual..."Through the Back Door."

Affording travel is a matter of priorities. (Make do with the old car.) You can travel—simply, safely, and comfortably—anywhere in Europe for $100 a day plus transportation costs. In many ways, spending more money only builds a thicker wall between you and what you came to see. Europe is a cultural carnival, and, time after time, you'll find that its best acts are free and the best seats are the cheap ones.

A tight budget forces you to travel close to the ground, meeting and communicating with the people, not relying on service with a purchased smile. Never sacrifice sleep, nutrition, safety, or cleanliness in the name of budget. Simply enjoy the local-style alternatives to expensive hotels and restaurants.

Extroverts have more fun. If your trip is low on magic moments, kick yourself and make things happen. If you don't enjoy a place, maybe you don't know enough about it. Seek the truth. Recognize tourist traps. Give a culture the benefit of your open mind. See things as different but not better or worse. Any culture has much to share.

Of course, travel, like the world, is a series of hills and valleys. Be fanatically positive and militantly optimistic. If something's not to your liking, change your liking. Travel is addictive. It can make you a happier American as well as a citizen of the world. Our Earth is home to six and a half billion equally important people. It's humbling to travel and find that people don't envy Americans. Europeans like us, but, with all due respect, they wouldn't trade passports.

Globe-trotting destroys ethnocentricity. It helps you understand and appreciate different cultures. Regrettably, there are forces in our society that want you dumbed down for their convenience. Don't let it happen. Thoughtful travel engages you with the world—more important than ever these days. Travel changes people. It broadens perspectives and teaches new ways to measure quality of life. Rather than fear the diversity on this planet, travelers celebrate it. Many travelers toss aside their hometown blinders. Their prized souvenirs are the strands of different cultures they decide to knit into their own character. The world is a cultural yarn shop, and Back Door travelers are weaving the ultimate tapestry. Join in!

CROATIA

CROATIA

(Hrvatska)

Sunny beaches, succulent seafood, and a taste of *la dolce vita*...in Eastern Europe?

Croatia is known for two very different reasons: as a top fun-in-the-sun tourist destination, and as the site, just more than a decade ago, of one of the most violent European wars in generations. Thankfully, the bloodshed is in the past. While a trip to Croatia offers curious travelers the opportunity to understand a ripped-from-the-headlines piece of recent history, most visitors focus instead on its substantial natural wonders: mountains, waterfalls, caves, sun, sand, and sea.

With thousands of miles of seafront and more than a thousand islands, Croatia's coastline is Eastern Europe's Riviera. Holiday-makers love its pebbly beaches, predictably balmy summer weather, and melt-in-your-mouth seafood. Croatia is also historic—from ruined Roman arenas and Byzantine mosaics to Venetian bell towers and Hapsburg villas, past rulers have left their mark.

Croatia feels more Mediterranean than Eastern European. Historically, Croatia has more in common with Venice and Rome than Vienna or Budapest. Especially on the coast, it's sometimes difficult to distinguish this lively, chaotic place from Italy. If you've become accustomed to the Germanic efficiency of Slovenia, Croatia's relaxed and unpredictable style can come as a shock. Be prepared to fall victim to the "Croatian Shrug"—a simple gesture meaning, "Don't know, don't care." But most visitors happily put up with Croatia's minor frustrations to take advantage of its postcard beauty and laid-back rhythm. After all, you're on vacation.

If you want to blow through a lot of money here, you can. Croatian hotels, especially on the coast, are a terrible value, and there are plenty of touristy restaurants happy to overcharge you. But if you know where to look, there are also wonderful budget alternatives—foremost among them *sobe* (rooms in private homes). *Sobe* are a comfortable compromise: new-feeling, fresh, hotelesque doubles with a private bathroom and TV, for half the cost of a moldy room in a crumbling resort hotel just down the beach (for details, see page 35). If you sleep in *sobe* and eat at non-touristy restaurants (which I've also recommended), your money will go farther than you might expect.

Europeans are reverent sun-worshippers, and on sunny days, virtually every square inch of coastal Croatia is occupied by a sun-bather on a beach towel. Nude beaches are a big deal, especially for vacationing Germans and Austrians. If you want to work on an all-around tan, seek out one of the beaches marked *FKK* (from the German *Freikörper Kultur,* or "free body culture"). First-timers get comfortable in a hurry, finding they're not the only pink novices on the rocks. But don't get too excited—these beaches are most beloved by people you'd rather see with their clothes on.

Every Croatian coastal town has two parts: The time-warp old town, and the obnoxious resort sprawl. Main drags are clogged with gift shops selling shell sculptures and tasteless T-shirts. While European visitors enjoy this tacky-trinket tourism, Americans visiting Europe are generally more interested in Old World charm. Fortunately, it's generally easy to ignore this scene and instead poke your way into twisty old medieval lanes, draped with drying laundry and populated by gossiping housewives and soccer-playing kids.

Croatian popular music, the mariachi music of Europe, is the ever-present soundtrack of a Dalmatian vacation. Oliver Drago-jević—singing soulful Mediterranean ballads with his gravelly, passionate voice—is the Croatian Tom Jones. Known simply as "Oliver," this immensely popular crooner gets airplay across Europe, and has spawned many imitators. More traditional is the hauntingly beautiful *klapa* music—men's voices harmonizing a cappella, like barbershop with a soothing Adriatic flavor.

Croatia may be Europe's second most ardently Catholic coun-try (after Poland). During the Yugoslav era, religion was down-played and many people gave up the habit of attending Mass (or mosque) regularly. But as the wars raged in the early 1990s, many Croatians rediscovered their religion. In Croatia's churches today, you may be surprised by how many people you see worshipping.

In the Yugoslav era, Croatia was flooded with tourists—both European and American—who fell in love with its dramatic beauty and fun-loving ambience. In its heyday, Croatia hosted about 10 million visitors a year, who provided the country with about a third of its income. But then, for several years after the war, Croatia floundered. Just five years ago, the streets of Dubrovnik were empty, lined with souvenir shops manned by desperate-looking vendors. But in the last year or two, locals are breathing a sigh of relief as the number of visitors returns to pre-war highs. With astonishing speed, Croatia is becoming one of Europe's top desti-nations.

Today's Croatia is crawling with a Babel of international guests, speaking German, French, Italian, every accent of English...and a smattering of Croatian. And yet, despite the tourists, this place remains distinctly and stubbornly Croatian. You'd have to search pretty hard to find a McDonald's.

Helpful Hints

Stow Your Euros: Tourists are notorious for confusing euro bills with Croatian kuna bills (both modeled after the old German *Deutschmark*, and therefore similar). Make a point of deep-storing all euros while outside the euro zone, or you'll be paying about seven times more than you should to enjoy Croatia.

Telephones: Croatia's phone system uses area codes. To make a long-distance call within the country, start with the area code. To call Croatia from another country, first dial the international access code (00 if calling from Europe, 011 from US or Canada), 385 (Croatia's country code), the area code (without the initial zero), and the local number. To call out of Croatia, dial 00, the country code of the country you're calling (see chart in appendix), the area code if applicable (may need to drop initial zero), and the local number.

Croatia's pay phones work on insertable phone cards (buy at newsstands or kiosks). Cheap, prepaid international calling cards are appearing here with decent rates (about 1 kn/min). But beware: Some cards work only with a local Split or Zagreb number—a toll call from a pay phone (no toll-free access number).

Free Tourist Help by Phone: The "Croatian Angels" service gives free information over a toll-free line in English (tel. 062/999-999, mid-June–Sept daily 8:00–24:00).

Addresses: Addresses listed with a street name and followed by "b.b." have no street number.

Slick Pavement: Old towns, with their well-polished pavement stones and many slick stairs, can be quite treacherous, especially after a rainstorm. Tread with care.

Siesta: Croatians eat their big meal at lunch, then take a traditional Mediterranean siesta. This means that many stores, museums, and churches close in the mid-afternoon. It can make for frustrating sightseeing...but you're on vacation. If you can't beat 'em...join 'em.

Anatomy of the Croatian Coast

Croatia's 3,600 miles of coastline is divided into three regions (north to south): Istria, the wedge-shaped peninsula just south of Slovenia; the Kvarner Gulf, with the big, industrial port city of Rijeka and lots of islands; and the romantic Dalmatian Coast, with Croatia's most famous towns. Here's an anatomy lesson of the Croatian coast, from north to south.

Croatia

Istria

The Istrian Peninsula—the most Italian-feeling part of Croatia—is notable for its diversity. The coast here is green and sloping, rather than rocky and jagged. Of Istria's many resort towns, the best are **Rovinj** (giddily atmospheric peninsular Old Town) and **Poreč** (high-capacity beach resort with Byzantine-mosaics-packed church). **Pula** is a big, industrial city with impressive Roman ruins, including one of the best-preserved amphitheaters anywhere. Istria has an equally enjoyable interior, with charming hill towns (including **Motovun, Grožnjan,** and **Hum**), truffle-packed forests, and dozens of small vineyards. Because of the richness and earthiness of its attractions, Istria's tourist board is trying to cultivate its image as a new Tuscany.

Just north of Istria is the Slovenian coastal town of **Piran.**

The Kvarner Gulf

The long stretch of coast between Istria and Dalmatia—the Kvarner Gulf—is anchored by the big, unappealing port city and transportation hub of **Rijeka** at the north. Next door to Rijeka, the old Hapsburg resort of **Opatija** offers a refreshingly genteel contrast to the creaky old towns elsewhere. Stretching south is a

Where Should I Go?

The perfect Croatian vacation is like a carefully refined recipe—a dash of this, a pinch of that, a slow simmer...and before long, you've got a delicious feast. Overwhelmed with options, people often ask me how to prioritize their time. The "Anatomy of the Croatian Coast" overview should help you get your bearings. But when you're ready for the next step, here's my tried-and-true recipe:

Begin with the biggies. Dubrovnik is a must, period. If you like big cities, Split is endlessly entertaining. Plitvice Lakes National Park, while difficult to reach, rarely disappoints.

Fold in one or two of seafront villages. Croatian coastal towns are all variations on the same theme: A warm stone Old Town with a Venetian bell tower, a tidy boat-speckled harbor, ample seafood restaurants, a few hulking communist-era resort hotels on the edge of town, and *sobe* and *apartman* signs by every other doorbell. Of course, each town has its own personality and claims to fame: Rovinj feels particularly Venetian, Rab has four bell towers, Korčula has a fjord-like backdrop and a fish-skeleton street plan, Hvar has a particularly lazy ambience and great nightlife, and Trogir has a yacht- and stroll-friendly seaside promenade. About a dozen other towns, not covered in this book, are more of the same. Beach bums, sightseers, yachters, historians, partiers—everyone you'll talk to has their own favorite town. Don't trust this advice blindly. Try out a few and choose your own top town.

Add some spice. This is my secret ingredient. After you've been to one or two of the coastal resorts, you could head for another one...or you could use that time for something completely different. Some of these options are easy and convenient—the Roman ruins of Pula, the hilltop hamlets of the Istrian interior, the imported-Austrian-resort feel of Opatija. But my favorites involve crossing borders and broadening horizons. Montenegro's Bay of Kotor, while enjoying some of the same seaside thrills as Croatia, is a different country entirely—and feels like it. And Mostar, Bosnia-Herzegovina—with vibrant Muslim culture, striking Turkish architecture, thought-provoking war damage, and an inspiring Old Bridge—feels a world away. A year from now, you'll barely remember the difference between all those little seaside towns you toured. But you'll never forget the mosques of Mostar.

rugged, desolate, sparsely populated coastline. But just offshore are several welcoming island getaways: **Rab** (my favorite, with a skinny Old Town peninsula), **Pag, Krk, Lošinj,** and **Cres.**

Dalmatian Coast

As you continue south and pass **Zadar** (a mid-sized city with a mildly interesting Old Town), you reach Croatia's main attraction: the Dalmatian Coast. South of Zadar is **Šibenik,** a resort town with some nice old churches, and **Trogir,** a little village on an island. Across the bay from Trogir is bustling **Split**—the capital of the coast, boasting a vibrant seaside promenade and a lived-in warren of twisting lanes sprouting out of a massive Roman palace. Split is the main transport hub for the Dalmatian Coast (lots of boat, bus, train, and plane connections), but it's also a worthwhile destination in its own right.

Dalmatian Islands: Off the coast between Split and Dubrovnik are a half-dozen inviting islands, each with its share of resort towns. These include **Brač, Vis,** and my favorites: **Hvar** and **Korčula.**

Pelješac Peninsula: Across the channel from Korčula Island is the town of **Orebić,** which is at the tip of the **Pelješac Peninsula.** This rugged, mountainous peninsula is famous for its wine (*plavac* grapes—see page 57). At the base of the peninsula is **Ston,** a humble little town with too-big fortifications climbing the hill behind it.

Bosnia-Herzegovina: Just north of where the Pelješac Peninsula joins the mainland, the main coastal road passes through a little segment of Bosnia-Herzegovina, including the town of **Neum.** About 90 minutes inland is the unofficial capital of Herzegovina, **Mostar**—famous for its still-thriving Muslim culture (tensely sharing the town with Catholic Croats) and its rebuilt Turkish-style Old Bridge.

Dubrovnik and Nearby: Dubrovnik is the final stop on the Dalmatian Coast, and easily the single best destination in Croatia. With a giant, walled Old Town and an epic history, Dubrovnik is like Venice without the canals. Just north of Dubrovnik are the **Elaphite Islands**—an archipelago including **Lopud** (the most developed island), **Koločep,** and **Šipan.** These islands are popular with tourists, but relatively rustic. Beyond Dubrovnik, near the airport and the Montenegrin border, is **Cavtat.**

The Montenegrin Coast: Just south of Dubrovnik, in Montenegro, is the **Bay of Kotor,** with gnarled fjord-like inlets. You'll pass through little towns (including the remarkably fortified town of **Kotor**) as you travel along the twisty road.

Croatia Almanac

Official Name: Republika Hrvatska, or just Hrvatska for short.

Snapshot History: After losing its independence to Hungary in A.D. 1102, Croatia watched as most of its coastline became Venetian and its interior was conquered by Ottomans. Croatia was "rescued" by the Hapsburgs, but after World War I it became part of Yugoslavia—a decision most Croats regretted until they finally gained independence in 1991 through a bitter war with their Serbian neighbors.

Population: Of the country's 4.5 million people (similar to Louisiana), 90 percent are ethnic Croats (Catholic) and 4 percent are Serbs (Orthodox). (The Serb population was more than double that before the ethnic cleansing of the 1991–1995 war.) About 1 percent of Croatians are Bosniak (Muslim). "Croatians" are citizens of Croatia; "Croats" are a distinct ethnic group made up of Catholic South Slavs. So Orthodox Serbs living in Croatia can be Croatians, but they can't be Croats (since they're not Catholic).

Latitude and Longitude: 45°N and 15°E (similar latitude to Venice, Italy; Ottawa, Canada; or Portland, Oregon).

Area: 22,000 square miles, similar to West Virginia.

Geography: This boomerang-shaped country has two terrains: Stretching north to south is the long, hilly Mediterranean coastline (3,600 miles of beach, including more than 1,100 offshore islands), which is warm and dry. Rising up from the sea are the rugged Dinaric Mountains (which also cover virtually all of neighboring Bosnia-Herzegovina). To the northeast, beginning at about Zagreb, Croatia's flat, inland "panhandle" (called Slavonia) has hot summers and cold winters.

Biggest Cities: The capital, Zagreb (in the northern interior), has 780,000; Split (along the southern Dalmatian Coast) has 189,000; and Rijeka (on the northern coast) has 150,000.

Economy: Much of the country's wealth ($56 billion GDP, $12,400 GDP per capita) comes from tourism, banking, and trade with Italy. The country is still recovering from the turmoil of the 1990s: Unemployment is a stiff 14 percent, corruption is deeply rooted, and Croatia is still a European Union outsider.

Croatian History

For nearly a millennium, bits and pieces of what we today call "Croatia" were batted back and forth between foreign powers: Hungarians, Venetians, Ottomans, Hapsburgs, and—of course— Yugoslavs. Only in 1991 did Croatia (violently) regain its independence.

Currency: 1 kuna (kn, or HRK) = about 17 cents, and 6 kunas = about $1. *Kuna* is Croatian for "marten" (a fox-like animal), recalling the long-ago era when fur pelts were used as currency.

Government: The country's prime minister (currently Ivo Sanader, head of the majority party in parliament) is conservative, while the directly elected (but more figurehead) president, Stipe Mesić, is left-of-center. The single-house assembly (Sabor) of 152 legislators is elected by popular vote.

Flag: The flag has three horizontal bands (red on top, white, and blue) with a traditional red-and-white checkerboard shield in the center.

The Average Croatian: The average Croatian will live to age 74 and have 1.4 children. One in four uses the Internet. The average Croatian absolutely adores the soccer team Dinamo Zagreb and absolutely despises Hajduk Split...or vice versa.

Notable Croatians: A pair of big-league historical figures were born in Croatia: Roman Emperor Diocletian (A.D. 245–313) and explorer Marco Polo (1254?–1324). More recently, many Americans whose name ends in "-ich" have Croatian roots, including actor John Malkovich and Ohio politicians Dennis Kucinich and John Kasich, not to mention baseball legend Roger Marich...I mean, Maris. More Croatian athletes abound: NBA fans might recognize Toni Kukoč or Gordan Giricek, and at the 2002 and 2006 Winter Olympic Games, the women's downhill skiing events were dominated by Janica Kostelić. Actor Goran Višnjić (from TV's *ER*) was born and raised in Croatia, and served in the army as a paratrooper. You've likely never heard of the beloved Croatian sculptor Ivan Meštrović, but you'll see his expressive works all over the country. Inventor Nikola Tesla (1856–1943) would be world-famous today if America had opted for his alternating current (AC) instead of Thomas Edison's direct current (DC). And a band of well-dressed 17th-century Croatian soldiers stationed in France gave the Western world a new fashion accessory—the *cravate*, or necktie (for the full story, see page 165).

Early History

Croatia's first inhabitants were the Illyrians (ancestors of today's Albanians). Romans began to settle the Dalmatian Coast as early as 229 B.C., and in the fourth century A.D., Emperor Diocletian built his retirement palace in the coastal town of Split. The Slavic Croats—ancestors of today's Croatians—arrived in the seventh century, and in A.D. 925, the Dalmatian duke Tomislav united most of present-day Croatia.

Loss of Independence

By the early 12th century, the Croatian kings had died out, and neighboring powers (Hungary, Venice, and Byzantium) threatened the Croats. For the sake of self-preservation, Croatia entered into an alliance with the Hungarians in 1102—and for the next 900 years, Croatia was ruled by foreign states. The Hungarians gradually took more and more power from the Croats, exerting control over the majority of inland Croatia. Meanwhile, the Venetian Republic conquered most of the coast and peppered the Croatian Adriatic with bell towers and statues of St. Mark. Through it all, the tiny Republic of Dubrovnik flourished—paying off whomever necessary to maintain its independence, and becoming one of Europe's most important shipbuilding and maritime powers.

The Ottomans conquered most of inland Croatia in the 15th century, and challenged the Venetians—unsuccessfully—for control of the coastline. In the 17th century, the Ottomans were forced out and the Hapsburgs arrived, taking over inland Croatia. After Venice and Dubrovnik fell to Napoleon, the coast went to the Hapsburgs—beginning a long tradition of Austrians basking on Croatian beaches.

The Yugoslav Era, World War II, and the Ustaše

When the Austro-Hungarian Empire broke up at the end of World War I, Croats banded together with the Serbs, Bosnians, and Slovenes in the union that would become Yugoslavia. But virtually as soon as Yugoslavia was formed, many Croats already had regrets. The Croats worried that the Serbs would steer Yugoslavia to their own purposes. So when the Nazis invaded and installed a puppet government—called the Ustaše—many Croats supported them, believing that fascism could provide them with greater independence from Serbia. Ustaše concentration camps were used to murder not only Jews and Roma (Gypsies), but also Serbs. Hot-tempered debate rages even today about how many Serbs died at the hands of the Ustaše—estimates vary wildly, from 25,000 to over a million, but most legitimate historians put the number in the hundreds of thousands.

Cardinal Alojzije Stepinac was one Croat who made the mistake of backing the Ustaše. By most accounts, Stepinac was a mild-mannered, extremely devout man who didn't agree with the extremism of the Ustaše...but also did little to fight it. When Tito came to power, he arrested, tried, and imprisoned Stepinac, who died under house arrest in 1960. In the years since, Stepinac has become a martyr for Catholics and Croat nationalists. But even though he's the single most revered figure of Croatian Catholicism, Stepinac remains highly controversial and unpopular among Serbs.

At the end of World War II, the Ustaše were forced out by

After the War

Some Americans shy away from Croatia, clinging to decade-old memories of wartime images on the nightly news. But those who venture here are, without exception, amazed by how peaceful and stable today's Croatia feels. Croatia's primary tourist region—the coast—was barely touched by the war (except Dubrovnik, which has been painstakingly restored). The interior is sprinkled with destroyed homes and churches—some standing gutted, skeletons of their original structures—but these villages are gradually being refurbished.

The only actual danger is that much of the Croatian interior was once full of landmines. Most of these mines have been removed, and fields that may be dangerous are usually clearly marked. As a precaution, stay on roads and paths, and don't go wandering through overgrown fields and deserted villages.

The biggest impact from the war has been on the people. Throughout the country, but especially in the war-torn interior, sadness and resentment hang heavy in the air. Though the country is repairing itself admirably, the Croatians' souls will take the longest to heal. They're still cheerful and welcoming—but a little less enthusiastically than before.

For more on Croatia during and after the war, see the Understanding Yugoslavia chapter, page 436.

Tito's Partisan army, and Croatia once again became part of a united Yugoslavia. The union would hold together for more than 40 years, until it broke apart under Serbian President Slobodan Milošević and Croatian President Franjo Tuđman.

For all the details on Yugoslavia and its breakup, see the Understanding Yugoslavia chapter, page 436.

Independence Regained

Croatia's declaration of independence from Yugoslavia in 1991 was met with fear and anger on the part of its Serb residents. Even before independence, the first volleys of a bloody war had been fired. The war had two phases: First, in 1991, Croatian Serbs declared independence from the new nation of Croatia, forming their own state and forcing out or murdering any Croats in "their" territory (with the thinly disguised support of Slobodan Milošević). Then a tense cease-fire fell over the region until 1995, when the second phase of the war ignited: Croatia pushed back through the Serb-dominated territory, reclaiming it for Croatia and forcing out or murdering Serbs living there. For details on this bloody war, see the Understanding Yugoslavia chapter.

Franjo Tuđman
(1922-1999)

Independent Croatia's first president was the controversial Franjo Tuđman (FRAHN-yoh TOOJ-mahn). Tuđman began his career fighting for Tito on the left, but later had a dramatic ideological swing to the far right. His anti-communist, highly nationalistic HDZ party was the driving force for Croatian statehood, making him the young nation's first hero. But even as he fought for independence from Yugoslavia, his own ruling style grew more and more authoritarian. Just a few years after his death, Tuđman remains a polemical figure.

Before entering politics, Tuđman was a historian. He revered the Ustaše, Croatia's Nazi-affiliated government during World War II, that murdered hundreds of thousands of Serbs and Jews in concentration camps. (Because the Ustaše governed the first independent Croatian state since the 12th century, Tuđman figured that these quasi-Nazis were the original Croatian "freedom fighters.") When Croatia voted for independence and Tuđman was elected president in 1990, he immediately reintroduced many Ustaše symbols, including the red-checkerboard flag and the currency (the kuna)—both still fixtures of Croatian life today. These acts raised eyebrows worldwide, and raised alarms in Croatia's Serb communities.

Tuđman espoused many of the same single-minded attitudes about ethnic divisions as the ruthless Serbian leader Slobodan Milošević. In fact, Tuđman and Milošević had secret, Hitler-and-Stalin-esque negotiations for divvying up Bosnia-Herzegovina. When Tuđman's successor moved into the president's office, he

Imagine becoming an independent nation after nine centuries of foreign domination. The Croatians seized their hard-earned freedom with a nationalist fervor that bordered on fascism. This was a heady and absurd time, which today's Croatians recall with disbelief, sadness...and maybe a tinge of nostalgia.

In the Croatia of the early 1990s, even the most bizarre notions seemed possible. Croatia's first post-Yugoslav president, the extreme nationalist Franjo Tuđman, proposed implausible directives for the new nation—such as privatizing all of the nation's resources and handing them over to 200 super-elite families (which, thankfully for everyone else, never happened). The government began calling the language "Croatian" rather than "Serbo-Croatian," creating new words from specifically Croat roots (see "Croatian Language," on page 59). The Croats even briefly considered replacing the Roman alphabet with the ninth-century Glagolitic script to invoke Croat culture and further differentiate Croatian from Serbia's Cyrillic discovered a top-secret hotline to Milošević's desk. And even today, Croatian newspapers routinely turn up decade-old photos of clandestine summits between the two leaders in Vienna.

To ensure that he stayed in power, Tuđman played fast and loose with his new nation's laws. He was notorious for changing the constitution as it suited him. By the late 1990s, when his popularity was slipping, Tuđman extended Croatian citizenship to anyone in the world who had Croatian heritage—a ploy aimed at getting votes from Croats living in Bosnia-Herzegovina, who were sure to line up with him on the far right.

Through it all, Tuđman kept a tight grip on the media, making it illegal to report anything that would disturb the public—even if true. When Croatians turned on their TV sets and saw the flag flapping in the breeze to the strains of the national anthem, they knew something was up...and switched to CNN to get the real story. In this oppressive environment, many bright, young Croatians fled the country, causing a "brain drain" that hampered the post-war recovery.

Tuđman died of cancer at the end of 1999. While history will probably judge him harshly, the opinion in today's Croatia is qualified. Most agree that Tuđman was an important and even admirable figure in the struggle for Croatian statehood, but he ultimately went too far and got too greedy. Tuđman's political party is still active, frequently naming streets, squares, and bridges for this "hero" of Croatian nationalism. But if he were alive, Tuđman would be standing trial in The Hague.

alphabet. Fortunately for tourists, this plan didn't take off.

After Tuđman's death in 1999, Croatia began the new millennium with a more truly democratic leader, Stipe Mesić. The popular Mesić, who was once aligned with Tuđman, had split off and formed his own political party when Tuđman's politics grew too extreme. Tuđman spent years tampering with the constitution to give himself more and more power, but when Mesić took over, he reversed those changes and handed more authority back to the parliament.

Croatia Today

In 2003, Croatia applied for membership in the European Union. It's officially an EU candidate country, but several roadblocks stand in its way. Most notably, some officers who fought in the recent war are still wanted to stand trial before the International Criminal Tribunal for the Former Yugoslavia (ICTY) in The Hague, Netherlands. Many Croatians feel that the soldiers branded

GENERAL
ANTE GOTOVINA

as "war criminals" by The Hague are actually heroes of their war of independence. The highest-profile figure so far is Ante Gotovina, a lieutenant general accused of atrocities against Serb civilians. Arrested in Spain in December of 2005, Gotovina is currently standing trial in The Hague. As a sign of support, photos of him have appeared in towns throughout Croatia. Gotovina's name means "cash." Many Croatians are grousing, "To get into the EU, we have to pay cash *(gotovina)*!"

Some Croatians are skeptical about joining the EU for other reasons. One Croatian said to me, "We were just badly divorced. We're not ready to be married again." For the other countries that recently joined the EU, a concern with EU membership was that the new members' citizens would flood to the West. Some Croatians are worried about the opposite: Westerners buying up Adriatic beachfront property.

Despite the controversy, pro-EU President Stipe Mesić's re-election in 2005 is a clear signal that most Croatians are optimistic about becoming a part of a united Europe. Mesić has repeatedly voiced his dedication to tracking down those wanted by The Hague, and is viewed both by most Croatians and by international observers as precisely the kind of moderate, modern, European-minded leader a fledgling country such as Croatia needs to lead it into the 21st century.

Croatian Food

Like its people, the food in Croatia's different regions has been shaped by various influences—predominantly Italian, Turkish, and Hungarian. No single cuisine is distinctly Croatian.

Balkan flavors are everywhere—especially in the inland part of the country (such as near the Plitvice Lakes), where Ottoman influences were strongest (see "Balkan Flavors" on page 39). To the north (Zagreb) and east (Slavonia), the food has more of a Hungarian flavor—heavy on meat, and served with cabbage, noodles, or potatoes.

On the Dalmatian Coast, seafood is a specialty, and the Italian influence is obvious. Dalmatians say that a fish should swim three times: first in the sea, then in olive oil, and finally in wine—when you eat it. You can get all kinds of seafood along the coast: fish, scampi, mussels, calamari, you name it. Remember that prices for seafood dishes are listed either by the kilogram (1,000 grams) or by the 100-gram unit (figure about a half-kilo, or 500 grams—that's about one pound—for a large portion). Consider *riblja juha*—fish soup.

If you're not a seafood eater, there's plenty of pizza and pasta to choose from. Another Dalmatian specialty is *pašticada*—braised beef in a wine-and-herb sauce, usually served with gnocchi (not unlike beef Stroganoff). Dalmatia is also known for its mutton. Since the lambs graze on salty seaside herbs, the meat—often served on a spit—has a distinctive flavor.

There are many good local varieties of cheese made with sheep's or goat's milk. Pag, an island in the Kvarner Gulf, produces a famous, very salty, fairly dry sheep's-milk cheese *(paški sir)*, which is also said to be flavored by the herbs the sheep eat.

Throughout Croatia, salad is served with the main dish unless you request that it be brought beforehand. For dessert, you'll find lots of good, homemade ice cream *(sladoled)*. Dalmatia's typical dessert is flan (crème caramel), which they call *rozata*.

As in most Slavic countries, *voda* is water, *kava* gets you coffee, *pivo* is beer, and *vino* gets you wine. Mineral water is *mineralna voda*. Jamnica is the main Croatian brand of bottled water, but you'll also see Bistra and Studenac. The most popular Croatian beers are Ožujsko and Karlovačko, but Slovene-produced Laško is also common. Along the coast, locals find it refreshing to drink wine mixed with mineral water. When toasting with some new Croatian friends, raise your glass with a hearty *"Živjeli!"* (ZHEE-vyeh-lee).

The quality of Croatia's wine declined under the communists, as much of the industry was state-run and focused on mass production. Now that the communists are gone, vintner families are returning to their roots—literally—and bringing quality back to Croatian wine. The north of the country primarily produces whites *(bijelo vino)*, usually dry *(suho)* but sometimes semi-dry *(polusuho)* or sweet *(slatko)*. The sunny mountains north of Zagreb are covered with vineyards producing whites. From Slavonia (Croatia's inland panhandle), you'll find *graševina*—crisp, dry, and acidic (like Welsh Riesling); Krauthaker and Enjingi are well-respected brands. The Istrian Peninsula corks up some good whites, including *malvazija*, a very popular, light, mid-range wine (Muscat is also popular). Each Adriatic island produces its own wine. For example, on Korčula, look for *pošip* and *grk;* on Vis, it's *vugava*.

As you move south, into the Dalmatian Coast, the wines turn red—which Croatians actually call "black wine" *(crno vino)*. The most common grape here is called *plavac* (more specifically *plavac mali*, or "little blue")—a distant cousin of Californian Zinfandel

Key Croatian Phrases

English	Croatian	Pronounced
Hello. (formal)	*Dobar dan.*	DOH-bahr dahn
Ciao. (both "Hi" and "Bye"—informal)	*Bog.*	bohg
Do you speak English?	*Govorite li engleski?*	GOH-voh-ree-teh lee EHN-glehs-kee
yes / no	*da / ne*	dah / neh
Please. / You're welcome.	*Molim.*	MOH-leem
Can I help you?	*Izvolite?*	EEZ-voh-lee-teh
Thank you.	*Hvala.*	HVAH-lah
I'm sorry. / Excuse me.	*Oprostite.*	oh-PROH-stee-teh
Good.	*Dobro.*	DOH-broh
Goodbye.	*Do viđenija.*	doh veed-JAY-neeah
one / two	*jedan / dva*	YEH-dahn / dvah
three / four	*tri / četiri*	tree / CHEH-teh-ree
five / six	*pet / šest*	peht / shehst
seven / eight	*sedam / osam*	SEH-dahm / OH-sahm
nine / ten	*devet / deset*	DEH-veht / DEH-seht
hundred	*sto*	stoh
thousand	*tisuća*	TEE-soo-chah
How much?	*Koliko?*	KOH-lee-koh
local currency	*kuna*	KOO-nah
Where is...?	*Gdje je...?*	guh-DYEH yeh
...the toilet	*...vece*	VEHT-seh
men	*muški*	MOOSH-kee
women	*ženski*	ZHEHN-skee
water / coffee	*voda / kava*	VOH-dah / KAH-vah
beer / wine	*pivo / vino*	PEE-voh / VEE-noh
Cheers!	*Živjeli!*	ZHEE-vyeh-lee
the bill	*račun*	RAH-choon

For more Croatian phrases, see page 457.

grapes. Generally speaking, the best coastal reds are produced on the long Pelješac Peninsula, across from Korčula. On the Pelješac Peninsula are specific regions with especially good reputations: Dingač is known as having the best possible climate for growing *plavac* grapes (Grgić, a brand produced by a Croatian-American vintner, is tops); wines from Postup are also good. Aside from the Pelješac Peninsula, the island of Hvar produces good wines (also using *plavac* grapes).

To request a menu, say, *"Meni, molim"* (MEH-nee, MOH-leem; "Menu, please"). To get the attention of your waiter, say *"Konobar"* (KOH-noh-bahr; "Waiter"). When he brings your food, he'll likely say, *"Dobar tek!"* ("Enjoy your meal!"). When you're ready for the bill, ask for the *račun* (RAH-choon).

Croatian Language

Croatian was once known as "Serbo-Croatian," the official language of Yugoslavia. Most Yugoslav republics—including Croatia, Serbia, and Bosnia-Herzegovina—spoke this same language (though Slovene is quite different). And while each of these countries has tried to distance its language from that of its neighbors since the war, the languages spoken in all of these places are still very similar. The biggest difference is in the writing: Croatians and Bosnians use our Roman alphabet, while Serbs use Cyrillic letters.

In recent years, Croatia has attempted to artificially make its vocabulary different from Serbian. A decade ago, you'd catch a plane at the *Aerodrom*. Today, you'll catch that same flight at the *Zračna Luka*—a new coinage that combines the old Croatian words for "air" and "port." These new words, once created, are artificially injected into the lexicon. Croatians watching their favorite TV show will suddenly hear a character use a word they've never heard before...and think, "Oh, we have another new word."

Remember, *c* is pronounced "ts" (as in "bats"). The letter *j* is pronounced as "y." The letters *č* and *ć* are slightly different, but they both sound more or less like "ch"; *š* sounds like "sh" and *ž* sounds like "zh" (as in "leisure"). One Croatian letter that you won't see in other languages is *đ*, which sounds like the "dj" sound in "jeans." In fact, this letter is often replaced with "dj" in English.

When attempting to pronounce an unfamiliar word, the accent is usually on the first syllable (and never on the last). Confusingly, Croatian pronunciation—even of the same word—can vary in different parts of the country. This is because modern Croatian has three distinct dialects, called Kajkavian, Shtokavian, and Chakavian—based on how you say "what?" (*kaj?*, *što?*, and *ča?*, respectively). That's a lot of variety for a language with only five million speakers.

ZAGREB

While Zagreb doesn't have the urban bustle of Split or the stay-awhile charm of Ljubljana, the Croatian capital offers historic neighborhoods, worthwhile museums, a thriving café culture, and an illuminating contrast to the beaches. As a tourist destination, Zagreb pales in comparison to the sparkling coastal towns. But you can't get a complete picture of modern Croatia without a visit here—away from the touristy resorts, in the lively and livable city that is home to one out of every six Croatians (pop. 780,000).

Zagreb began as two walled medieval towns, Gradec and Kaptol, separated by a river. As Croatia fell under the control of various foreign powers—Budapest, Vienna, Berlin, and Belgrade—the two hill towns that would become Zagreb gradually took on more religious and civic importance. Kaptol became a bishopric in 1094, and it's still home to Croatia's most important church. In the 16th century, the Ban (Croatia's governor) and the Sabor (parliament) called Gradec home. The two towns officially merged in 1850, and soon after, the railroad connecting Budapest with the Adriatic port city of Rijeka was built through the city. Zagreb prospered.

After centuries of being the de facto religious, cultural, and political center of Croatia, Zagreb officially became a European capital when the country declared its independence in 1991. In the ensuing war with Serbia, Zagreb was hardly damaged—Serbian bombs hit only a few strategic targets (the bloodiest fighting was to the east and south of here).

Today, just over a decade later, Zagreb has long since repaired the minimal damage, and the capital feels safe, modern, and accessible.

CITY HISTORY
MUSEUM
UPPER
MEŠTROVIĆ ATELIER
ST. MARK'S
BAN'S PALACE
**MUSEUM OF
NAIVE ART**
GRADEC
FUNICULAR
TOWN
SABOR
KAPTOL
STONE
GATE
MARKET
**RIBNJAK
PARK**
CATHEDRAL
VLASKA
ILICA
PANSKA
**ARTS +
CRAFTS
MUSEUM**
OCTAGON
GALLERY
BOGO
MESN
FRANKO
TESLINA
JURISCEVA
POST
RACKOGA
MASARYKOVA
LOWER
HEBRANGOVA
TOWN
BOSKOVICEVA
GAJEVA
ZERJAVICEVA
**MIMARA
MUSEUM**
MIHANOVICEVA
**P
A
R
K**
HATZOVA
KNEZA
PETRN
PALMO
DRASKO
**BOTANICAL
GARDENS**
POST
BRANIMIROVA
**TRAIN
STATION**
TO
BUS
STATION
DCH

¼ MILE
400 METERS
RADICEVA
TKALCICEVA
KAPTOL
DEMETROVA
RIBNJAK

1 Hotel Dubrovnik
2 Hotel Astoria
3 Hotel Jadran
4 Hotel Central
5 Hostel Fulir
6 Tkalčićeva St.
  Eateries
7 Nokturno Rest.
8 Sandwich Bar Pingvin
9 Mimice Restaurant
10 Vinodol Restaurant
11 Restaurant Jägerhorn
12 Millennium Ice Cream

★ = JELAČIĆ
  SQUARE

13 Marko Polo
   Travel Agency
14 Plitvice Lakes
   Office

Planning Your Time

Most visitors just pass through Zagreb, but the city is worth a look. Check your bag at the station and zip into the center for a quick visit—or consider spending the night.

You can get a decent sense of Zagreb in just a few hours. With whatever time you have, make a beeline for Jelačić Square to visit the TI and get oriented. Take the funicular up to Gradec, visit the excellent Museum of Naive Art, and stroll St. Mark's Square. Then wander down through the Stone Gate to the lively Tkalčićeva

scene (good for a drink or meal), through the market (closes at
14:00), and on to Kaptol and the cathedral.

With more time, visit some of Zagreb's museums, wander the
series of parks called the "Green Horseshoe," or head to the enjoyable nearby town of Samobor (see the end of this chapter).

If you're moving on from Zagreb to Plitvice Lakes National
Park (see next chapter), be warned that there are generally no
buses between 17:30 and 22:00 (or sometimes later). Confirm your
bus departure carefully to ensure that you don't get stranded in
Zagreb.

ORIENTATION

(area code: 01)
Zagreb, just 30 minutes from the Slovenian border, stretches from
the foothills of Medvednica ("Bear Mountain") to the Sava River.
In the middle of the sprawl, you'll find the modern **Lower Town**
(Donji Grad, centered on **Jelačić Square**) and the historic **Upper
Town** (Gornji Grad, comprising the original hill towns of **Gradec**
and **Kaptol**). To the south is a U-shaped belt of parks, squares, and
museums that make up the "Green Horseshoe." The east side of
the U is a series of three parks, with the train station at the bottom
(south) and Jelačić Square at the top (north).

Zagrebians have devised a brilliant scheme for confusing
tourists: Street names can be depicted several different ways. For
example, the street that is signed as ulica Kralja Držislava ("King
Držislav Street") is often called by locals simply Držislavova
("Držislav's"). So if you're looking for a street, don't search for an
exact match—be willing to settle for something that just has a lot
of the same letters.

Tourist Information

Zagreb has two TIs. The bigger, better one is at **Jelačić Square**
(Mon–Fri 8:30–20:00, Sat 9:00–17:00, Sun 10:00–14:00, sometimes longer hours in summer, Trg bana Jelačića 11, tel. 01/481-
4052, www.zagreb-touristinfo.hr); the other is just a few blocks
south, between Jelačić Square and the train station along the west
side of **Zrinjevac Park** (Mon–Fri 9:00–17:00, closed Sat–Sun, Trg
Nikole Šubića Zrinskoga 14, tel. 01/492-1645). Zagreb's TIs offer
piles of free, well-produced tourist brochures that desperately
try to convince visitors to do more than just pass through. Pick
up the one-page city map (with handy transit map and regional
map on back), the *Zagreb Info A–Z* booklet (including accommodations and restaurant listings), the monthly events guide,
the great *City Walks* brochure (with a couple of mildly diverting
self-guided walking tours), the museum guide, the booklet about

Zagreb Essentials

English	Croatian	Pronounced
Jelačić Square	Trg bana Jelačića	turg BAH-nah YEH-lah-chee-chah
Gradec (original civic hill town)	Gradec	GRAH-dehts
Kaptol (original religious hill town)	Kaptol	KAHP-tohl
Café street between Gradec and Kaptol	Tkalčićeva (or "Tkalči" for short)	tuh-KAHL-chee-chay-vah (tuh-KAHL-chee)
Main Train Station	Glavni Kolodvor	GLAHV-nee KOH-loh-dvor
Bus Station	Autobusni Kolodvor	OW-toh-boos-nee KOH-loh-dvor

the surrounding region, and more.

The **Zagreb Card** gives you free transportation and discounts on Zagreb sights for 72 hours (90 kn, sold at TI). This usually doesn't make sense for folks who are day-tripping here, but it can be a good deal if you're taking the city tour (next) and doing some sightseeing.

To get oriented, consider the fun daily **city tours** (2-hour walking tour: 95 kn, usually Mon–Thu; 3-hr bus-plus-walking tour: 150 kn, usually Fri–Sun; 25 percent discount on either tour with Zagreb Card). For the weekday walking tour, just show up at the TI; for the weekend bus-plus-walk, call the TI by 14:00 the day before to confirm the schedule, reserve a space, and request an English guide. The same company runs theme tours and excursions into the surrounding countryside (about 2/month, tel. 01/481-4052, www.event.hr).

Arrival in Zagreb

By Train: Zagreb's Main Train Station (Glavni Kolodvor) is conveniently located a few blocks south of Jelačić Square on the Green Horseshoe. The straightforward arrivals hall has a train information desk, ticket windows, ATMs, WCs, and newsstands. The left-luggage office is at the left end of the station, with your back to the tracks (look for low-profile *garderoba* sign, open daily 24 hours). To reach the city center, go straight out the front door. You'll run into a taxi stand, and then the tracks for tram #6 (buy 6.50-kn ticket from kiosk, then hop on: direction Črnomerec zips you to Jelačić Square; direction Sopot takes you to the bus station—the third stop, just after you turn right and go under the big overpass). If you walk straight ahead through the long, lush park, you'll wind up at the bottom of Jelačić Square in 10 minutes.

By Bus: The user-friendly bus station (Autobusni Kolodvor) is a few long blocks southeast of the Main Train Station. The station has all the essentials—ATMs, post office, mini-grocery store, left-luggage counter...everything from a smut store to a chapel. Upstairs, you'll find ticket windows and access to the buses (follow signs to *perone;* wave ticket in front of turnstile to open gate). Tram #6 (in direction Črnomerec) takes you to the Main Train Station, then on to Jelačić Square.

By Plane: Zagreb's airport is 10 miles south of the center (tel. 01/626-5222, www.zagreb-airport.hr). The Croatia Air bus connects the airport to Zagreb's bus station (30 kn, every 30 min, 25-min trip). Figure around 200 kn for a taxi from the airport to the center.

Getting Around Zagreb

The main mode of public transportation is the **tram,** operated by ZET (Zagreb Electrical Transport, www.zet.hr). A single ticket (good for 90 min in one direction, including transfers) costs 8 kn if you buy it from the driver (6.50 kn at kiosk, ask for *ZET karta*—zeht KAR-tah). A day ticket *(dnevna karta)* costs 18 kn. The most useful tram for tourists is #6, connecting Jelačić Square with the train and bus stations.

Taxis start at 19 kn, then run 7 kn per kilometer (20 percent more Sun and at night, 3 kn extra for each piece of baggage; beware of corrupt cabbies—ask for an estimate up front, or call Radio Taxi, tel. 01/970 or 01/661-0200).

Helpful Hints

Important Days: Virtually all Zagreb museums are closed on Sunday afternoon and all day Monday. On Sunday morning, the city is thriving—but by afternoon, it's extremely quiet.

Ferry Tickets: If you're heading for the Dalmatian Coast, note that there isn't a Jadrolinija ferry office in the center. But you can reserve and buy tickets at the **Marko Polo** travel agency (Mon–Fri 9:00–17:00, Sat 9:00–13:00, closed Sun, Masarykova 24, tel. 01/481-5216).

Plitvice Lakes Office: If you're going to Plitvice Lakes National Park, you can get a preview and ask any questions at their helpful information office in Zagreb (Mon–Fri 8:00–16:00, closed Sat–Sun, a block in front of Main Train Station at Trg Kralja Tomislava 19, tel. 01/461-3586).

SELF-GUIDED WALK

Zagreb's Upper Town

The following one-way circular orientation walk, worth ▲▲, begins at Jelačić Square. The entire route takes about an hour at a leisurely pace (not counting museum stops).

Jelačić Square (Trg bana Jelačića): The "Times Square" of Zagreb bustles with life. It's lined with cafés, shops, trams,

 Baroque buildings, and the TI. When Zagreb consisted of the two hill towns of Gradec and Kaptol, this Donji Grad ("lower town") held the townspeople's farm fields. Today, it features a prominent equestrian statue of national hero **Josip Jelačić** (YOH-seep YEH-lah-cheech, 1801–1859), a 19th-century governor who extended citizens' rights and did much to unite the Croats within the Hapsburg Empire. In Jelačić's time, the Hungarians were exerting extensive control over Croatia, even trying to make Hungarian the official language. Meanwhile, Budapesters revolted against Hapsburg rule in 1848. Jelačić, ever mindful of the need to protect Croatian cultural autonomy, knew that he'd have a better shot at getting his way from Austria than from Hungary. Jelačić chose the lesser of two evils, and fought alongside the Hapsburgs to put down the Hungarian uprising. In the Yugoslav era, Jelačić was considered dangerously nationalistic, and this statue was taken down. But when Croatia broke away in 1991, Croatian patriotism was in the air, and Jelačić returned. Though Jelačić originally faced his Hungarian foes to the north, today he's staring down the Serbs to the south.

Get oriented. If you face Jelačić's statue, a long block to your left is a funicular that takes you up to one of Zagreb's original villages, Gradec. To the right, look for the TI. If you leave the square ahead and to the right, you'll reach the other original village, Kaptol, and the cathedral (you can't miss its huge, pointy, Neo-Gothic spires—visible from virtually everywhere in Zagreb). If you leave the square ahead and to the left, you'll come to the market (Dolac) and the lively café street, Tkalčićeva.

For now, we'll head up to Gradec. Go a long block down the busy Ilica. On the way, consider ducking inside the big shopping gallery on the left (at #5; look for the tie shop from the chain called Croata—for the story, see page 165). Then continue up Ilica and turn right on Tomićeva, where you'll see a small **funicular** (ZET Uspinjača) crawling up the hill. Dating from the late 19th century, this funicular is looked upon fondly by Zagrebians—both as a bit of nostalgia and as a way to avoid some steps. You can walk up if you want, but the ride is more fun and takes only 55 seconds (3 kn, validate ticket in orange machine before you board, leaves every 10 min daily 6:30–21:00).

Gradec: From the top of the funicular, you'll enjoy a fine panorama over Zagreb. The tall tower you face as you exit is one of Gradec's original watchtowers, the **Burglars' Tower** (Kula Lotršćak). After the Tatars ransacked Central Europe in the early 13th century, King Béla IV decreed that towns be fortified—so Gradec built a wall and guard towers (just like Kraków and Budapest did). Look for the little cannon in the top-floor window. Every day at noon, this cannon fires a shot, supposedly to commemorate a 15th-century victory over the besieging Ottomans. Zagrebians hold on to other traditions, too—the lamps on this hill are still gas-powered, lit by a city employee every evening.

Head up the street next to the tower. Little remains of medieval Gradec. When the Ottomans overran Europe, they never managed to take Zagreb—but the threat was enough to scare the nobility into the countryside. When the Ottomans left, the nobles came back, and replaced the medieval buildings here with Baroque mansions. At the first square, to the right, you'll see the Jesuit **Church of St. Catherine.** It's not much to look at from the outside, but the interior is intricately decorated. The same applies to several mansions on Gradec. This simple-outside, ornate-inside style is known as "Zagreb Baroque."

As you continue up the street, on the left you'll see the **Croatian Museum of Naive Art**—Zagreb's best museum, and well worth a visit (see listing under "Sights"). In the next block, on the left, look for the monument to Nikola Tesla (1856–1943), a prominent Croatian scientist who championed alternating current as an alternative to Thomas Edison's direct current.

At the end of the block, you'll come to the low-key **St. Mark's Square** (Markov trg), centered on the **Church of St. Mark.** The original church here was from the 12th century, but only a few fragments remain. The present church's colorful tile roof, from 1880, depicts two coats of arms.
On the left, the red-and-white checkerboard symbolizes north-central Croatia, the three lions' heads stand for the Dalmatian Coast, and the marten (*kuna*, like the money) running between the two rivers (Sava and Drava) represent Slavonia—Croatia's northern, inland panhandle. On the right is

the seal of Zagreb: a walled city with wide-open doors (strong, but still welcoming to visitors...like you). The interior is a bit stark, livened up by a few sculptures by Ivan Meštrović, whose former home is about a block straight ahead (go down the street behind the church on the left-hand side, and you'll see the museum on the right; see listing under "Sights").

As you face the church, to the right is the **Sabor,** or parliament. From the 12th century, Croatian noblemen would gather here to make important decisions regarding their territories. This gradually evolved into today's modern parliament. (If you walk along the front of the Sabor and continue straight ahead 2 blocks, you'll run into the Zagreb City Museum, described under "Sights".)

Across the square from the Sabor (to your left as you face the church) is the **Ban's Palace** (Banski Dvori), today the offices for the president and prime minister. This was one of the few buildings in central Zagreb destroyed in the recent war. In October of 1991, the Serbs shelled it from afar, knowing that Croatian President Franjo Tuđman was inside...but Tuđman survived.

Walk from Gradec to Kaptol: For an interesting stroll from St. Mark's Square to the cathedral, head down the street (Kamenita ulica) to the right of the parliament building. Near the end of the street, you'll see the oldest **pharmacy** in town—recently restored and gleaming (c. 1355, on the right, marked *gradska ljekarna*).

Just beyond, you'll reach Gradec's oldest surviving gate, the **Stone Gate** (Kamenita Vrata). Inside is an evocative chapel. The focal point is a painting of Mary that miraculously survived a major fire in 1731. When this medieval gate was reconstructed in the Baroque style, they decided to turn it into a makeshift chapel. The candles (purchased in the little shop and lit in the big metal box) represent Zagrebians' prayers, and the stone plaques on the wall give thanks *(Hvala)* for prayers that were answered. You may notice people doing the sign of the cross as they walk through here, and often a crowd of worshippers gather, staring intently at the painting. Mary was made the official patron saint of Zagreb in 1990.

As you leave the Stone Gate and come to Radićeva, turn right. Take the next left, onto the street called **Krvavi Most**—"Blood Bridge." At the end of Krvavi Most, you'll come to **Tkalčićeva.** This lively café-and-restaurant street used to be a river—the natural boundary between Gradec and Kaptol. The two towns did not always get along, and sometimes fought against each other. Blood was spilled, and the bridge that once stood here between them became known as Blood Bridge. By the late 19th century, the towns had united, and the river began to stink—so they covered it over with this street.

As you cross Tkalčićeva, you enter the old town of Kaptol. You'll come to the **market** *(dolac),* packed with colorful stalls selling produce of all kinds (Mon–Sat 7:00–14:00, Sun 7:00–13:00). At the back-left corner is the fragrant fish market *(ribarnica)*, and under your feet is an indoor part of the market *(tržnica)*, where farmers sell farm-fresh eggs and dairy products (same hours as outdoor market, entrance down below in the direction of Jelačić Square).

Your walk is over. On the other side of the market, visit the cathedral (see description in "Sights").

SIGHTS

Museums in Gradec

▲▲**Croatian Museum of Naive Art (Hrvatski Muzej Naivne Umjetnosti)**—This remarkable spot is one of the most enjoyable little museums in Croatia. It features expressionistic paintings by untrained peasant artists of the mid-20th century. These stirring images—fantasy worlds rich with detail—are well worth a look. The exhibit kicks off with works by the movement's star, Ivan Generalić, then moves on to his followers. Mijo Kovačić's paintings are particularly striking, with hauntingly detailed layers of twisted tree branches (10 kn, pick up the English explanations as you enter, Tue–Fri 10:00–18:00, Sat–Sun 10:00–13:00, closed Mon, ulica Sv. Čirila i Metoda 3, tel. 01/485-1911, www.hmnu.org).

▲**Ivan Meštrović Atelier**—Ivan Meštrović, the only Croatian artist worth remembering, lived in this house from 1922 until 1942 (before he fled to the US during World War II). The house has been converted into a delightful gallery of the artist's works, displayed in two parts: residence and studio. Split's Meštrović Gallery is the definitive museum of the 20th-century Croatian sculptor, but if you're not going there, Zagreb's gallery is a convenient place to gain an appreciation for the prolific, thoughtful artist (20 kn, 20-kn English catalog, Tue–Fri 10:00–18:00, Sat–Sun 10:00–14:00, closed Mon, behind St. Mark's Square at Mletačka 8, tel. 01/485-1123). For more on Meštrović, see page 165.

Zagreb City Museum (Muzej Grada Zagreba)—This collection, with a modern, engaging exhibit that sprawls over two floors of an old convent, traces the history of the city through town models, paintings, furniture, clothing, and other artifacts. After buying your ticket, head through the door and turn left, then work your way up through the ages. But save your time and energy for the most interesting section: the early days of independence from Yugoslavia (including an exhibit on damage sustained during the warfare) and a hall of illuminating propaganda posters (20 kn, English descriptions, Tue–Fri 10:00–18:00, Sat–Sun 10:00–13:00, closed Mon, at north end of Gradec at Opatička 20, tel. 01/485-1361, www.mdc.hr/mgz).

Cathedral (Katedrala)

By definition, Croats are Catholics. Before the recent war, relatively few people practiced their faith. But as the Croats fought with their Orthodox and Muslim neighbors, Catholicism took on a greater importance. Today, more and more Croats are attending Mass. This is Croatia's single most important church, worth ▲.

In 1094, when a diocese was established at Kaptol, this church quickly became a major center of high-ranking church officials. In the mid-13th century, the original cathedral was destroyed by invading Tatars, who actually used it as a stable. It was rebuilt, only to be destroyed again by an earthquake in 1880. The current version—undergoing yet another renovation for the last several years—is Neo-Gothic. Surrounding the church are walls with pointy-topped towers (part of a larger archbishop's palace) that were built for protection against the Ottomans. The full name is the Cathedral of the Assumption of the Blessed Virgin Mary and the Saintly Kings Stephen and Ladislav (whew!)—but most locals just call it "the cathedral."

Step inside (free, Mon–Sat 10:00–17:00, Sun 13:00–17:00). Look closely at the silver relief on the first **altar:** a scene of the Holy Family doing chores around the house (Mary sewing, Joseph and Jesus building a fence...and angels helping out).

In the front-left corner, find the tombstone of **Alojzije Stepinac.** He was the Archbishop of Zagreb in World War II, when he shortsightedly supported the Nazis—thinking, like many Croatians, that this was the ticket to greater independence from Serbia. When Tito came to power, he put Stepinac on trial and sent him to jail for five years. But Stepinac never lost his faith, and remains to many the most important inspirational figure of Croatian Catholicism.

As you leave the church, look to the back of the left apse. This strange script is the **Glagolitic alphabet** *(glagoljca),* invented by Byzantine missionaries Cyril and Methodius in the ninth century to translate the Bible into Slavic languages. Though these missionaries worked mostly in Moravia (today's eastern Czech Republic), their alphabet caught on only here, in Croatia. (Glagolitic was later adapted in Bulgaria to become the Cyrillic alphabet—still used in Serbia, Russia, and other parts east.) In 1991, when Croatia became its own country and nationalism surged, the country flirted with the idea of making this the official alphabet.

The Green Horseshoe

With extra time, stroll around the Green Horseshoe (the U-shaped belt of parks and museums in the city center). The museums here aren't nearly as interesting as those on Gradec, but may be worth a peek on a rainy day.

Mimara Museum (Muzej Mimara)—This grand, empty-feeling building displays the eclectic collection of a wealthy Dalmatian, ranging from ancient artifacts to paintings by European masters. While the names are major—Rubens, Rembrandt, Velázquez, Renoir, Manet—the paintings themselves are minors. Still, art buffs may find something to get excited about (20 kn, 90-kn English guidebook, otherwise virtually no English, Tue–Sat 10:00–17:00, Thu until 19:00, Sun 10:00–14:00, closed Mon, Rooseveltov trg 5, tel. 01/482-8100).

Arts and Crafts Museum (Muzej za Umjetnost i Obrt)—This decorative arts collection of furniture, ceramics, and clothes is well-displayed. From the entry, go upstairs, then work your way clockwise and up to the top floor—passing through each artistic style, from Gothic to the present. It's mostly furniture, with a few paintings and other items thrown in (20 kn, some rooms have laminated English descriptions to borrow, otherwise very limited English, Tue–Sat 10:00–19:00, Sun 10:00–14:00, closed Mon, Trg Maršala Tita 10, tel. 01/488-2111, www.muo.hr).

Botanical Garden (Botanički Vrt)—For a back-to-nature change of pace from the urban cityscape, wander through this relaxing garden, run by the University of Zagreb (free, Mon–Tue 9:00–14:30, Wed–Sun 9:00–18:00, Wed–Sun until 19:00 in summer, at southwest corner of the Green 'Shoe).

SLEEPING

Hotels in central Zagreb are very expensive—you won't get much for your money. I prefer sleeping in Ljubljana or at Plitvice Lakes National Park, both of which offer better values. But if you must stay in Zagreb, these are the best deals right in the main tourist zone.

$$$ **Hotel Dubrovnik** has an ideal location (at the bottom of Jelačić Square) and 268 business-class rooms (small Sb-780 kn, bigger Sb-880–950 kn, Db with 1 big bed-1,050 kn, twin Db-1,200 kn, suite-1,400–1,600 kn, extra bed-250 kn, rooms overlooking the square don't cost extra—try to request one, often cheaper on weekends, prices soft, non-smoking floors, elevator, Gajeva 1, tel. 01/486-3555, fax 01/486-3506, www.hotel-dubrovnik.hr, reservations@hotel-dubrovnik.hr).

Sleep Code

(€1 = about $1.20, 6 kn = about $1, country code: 385, area code: 01)
S = Single, **D** = Double/Twin, **T** = Triple, **Q** = Quad, **b** = bathroom. English is spoken at each place. Unless otherwise noted, credit cards are accepted, breakfast is included, and the modest tourist tax (7 kn per person, per night) is not.

To help you sort easily through these listings, I've divided the rooms into three categories based on the price for a standard double room with bath:

$$$ **Higher Priced**—Most rooms 800 kn or more.
$$ **Moderately Priced**—Most rooms between 500–800 kn.
$ **Lower Priced**—Most rooms 500 kn or less.

$$$ **Hotel Astoria,** a Best Western, was recently renovated from top to bottom. Now it offers 102 smallish but plush rooms and a high-class lobby. It's on a grimy street near the train station, so I wouldn't splurge here unless I were in town on a weekend, when rates drop by a third (Sb-850–970 kn, Db-1,100 kn; Fri–Sun: Sb-570 kn, Db-735 kn; prices can also be soft on some weekdays, fancier suites also available, elevator, Petrinjska 71, tel. 01/480-8900, fax 01/480-8908, www.bestwestern.com, info@hotelastoria.hr).

$$ **Hotel Jadran** has 49 decent rooms near the cathedral, a few blocks east of Jelačić Square (Sb-510 kn, Db-717 kn, Tb-894 kn, some street noise—request quiet room, elevator, Vlaška 50, tel. 01/455-3777, fax 01/461-2151, www.hup-zagreb.hr, jadran @hup-zagreb.hr).

$$ **Hotel Central**'s 76 overly perfumed rooms are comfortable and modern, and the price is right. This place seems to get a little better every year, and the location—right across from the Main Train Station—is convenient for rail travelers (Sb-550–600 kn, Db with one big bed-720 kn, twin Db-780 kn, bigger Db-830 kn, extra bed-160 kn, elevator, Branimirova 3, tel. 01/484-1122, fax 01/484-1304, www.hotel-central.hr, info@hotel-central.hr).

$ **Hostel Fulir,** named for a legendary Zagrebian bon vivant, is energetically run by Davor and Leo, a pair of can-do Croats who lived in Ohio. It's new, colorful, and friendly, with a big 10-bunk dorm and a smaller four-bed room sharing two bathrooms. Just a few steps from Jelačić Square, this hostel puts you in the heart of Zagreb (€19.50 per bunk, includes sheets, no breakfast, free lockers, Internet access, upstairs at the end of the courtyard at Radićeva 3a, tel. 01/483-0882, mobile 098-193-0552, www.fulir-hostel.com).

EATING

For the perfect place to sip a lazy cup of coffee, look no further than Jelačić Square—Zagreb's heart and soul. To venture a little farther, try these places.

On Tkalčićeva: This is Zagreb's main café street, "restaurant row," and urban promenade rolled into one. It's a parade of fashionable locals, and *the* place to see and be seen. Wander here and choose your favorite spot (starts a block behind Jelačić Square, next to the market). For good pizza and pasta, wander a few feet up Skalinska (near the Jelačić Square end of the street) to find **Nokturno,** with a lively interior and fun outdoor seating (18–30-kn pizzas, pastas, and salads, 25–45-kn meat and fish dishes, daily 9:00–1:00 in the morning, Skalinska 4, tel. 01/481-3394).

At the Market (Dolac): Zagreb's lively market offers plenty of options (Mon–Sat 7:00–14:00, Sun 7:00–13:00). Buy a fresh picnic direct from the producers. Or, for something already prepared, duck into one of the many cheap restaurants and cafés on the streets around the market. The middle level of the market, facing Jelačić Square, is home to a line of places with cheap food and indoor or outdoor seating.

Sandwich Bar Pingvin is a favorite for quick, cheap, tasty sandwiches. The photo menu—featuring sandwiches with chicken, turkey, steak, fish, even salmon—makes ordering easy. They'll wrap it all in a piece of grilled bread and top it with your choice of veggies and sauces (16–24 kn, open long hours daily, Teslina 7).

Mimice, a local institution and an old-habits-die-hard favorite of the older generation, serves up simple fish dishes (20–30 kn, order starches and sauces separately). Choose what you want from the limited menu, pay, and take your receipt to the next counter to claim your food. Then eat it standing or sitting on high stools (closed Sun, Jurišićeva 21). As Zagreb is a Catholic town, you'll have to wait in line if you're here on a Friday.

Vinodol is your white-tablecloth classy dinner spot, with a peaceful covered terrace and a smartly appointed dining room under an impressive vaulted ceiling (55–90-kn main dishes, daily 10:00–24:00, Teslina 10, tel. 01/481-1427).

Restaurant Jägerhorn shares a delightful garden courtyard with a serene waterfall. The menu includes game (60–90 kn) and simpler grilled dishes (45–90 kn; daily 10:00–22:30, at the end of a courtyard a block from Jelačić Square at Ilica 14, tel. 01/483-3877). They also rent 13 small, musty, overpriced rooms.

Ice Cream!: Zagreb's favorite *sladoled* (Italian gelato-style ice cream) is at **Millennium,** just a block from Jelačić Square. With giant mounds of the widest variety of flavors I've seen in Croatia, this is the city's best dessert stop (Mon–Sat 8:00–23:00, Sun 9:00–23:00, Bogovićeva 7, tel. 01/481-0850).

TRANSPORTATION CONNECTIONS

From Zagreb by Train to: Rijeka (3/day, 4 hrs), **Split** (3/day, 5.5 hrs, plus 1 direct night train, 8 hrs), **Ljubljana** (8/day, 2.5 hrs), **Vienna** (2/day, 6.5 hrs), **Budapest** (2/day, 5 or 7 hrs), **Lake Bled** (via Lesce-Bled, 5/day, 3.5 hrs).

By Bus to: Samobor (about 3/hr, 30 min), **Plitvice Lakes National Park** (about hourly until 17:30, 2–2.5 hrs; then none until about 22:00), **Rijeka** (hourly, 3.5 hrs), **Rovinj** (8/day, 5–8 hrs), **Pula** (almost hourly, 3.75–6 hrs), **Split** (about 2/hr, 5–9 hrs), **Dubrovnik** (2 in the early morning, sometimes 1–2 midday, then 4–6 overnight, 11–12.5 hrs), **Korčula** (1/night, 13.5 hrs).

Bus schedules can be sporadic (e.g., several departures clustered around the same time, then nothing for hours)—confirm carefully locally (at the TI; schedules also online at www.akz.hr). Popular buses, such as the afternoon express to Split, can fill up quickly in peak season. Unfortunately, it's impossible to buy bus tickets anywhere in the center, so to guarantee a seat, you'd have to get to the station early (locals suggest even two hours in advance). Better yet, call the central number for the bus station to check schedules and reserve the bus you want: tel. 060-313-333 (from abroad, dial +385-1-611-2789). If you can't get an English speaker on the line, and the TI isn't too busy, they might be able to call for you.

Near Zagreb: Samobor

This charming little town, tucked between Zagreb and the Slovenian border, is where city dwellers head to unwind, get away from the clattering trams, and gorge themselves on sausages and cream cakes. Cuddled by hiker-friendly hills, bisected by a picturesque stream, favored by artists and poets, and proud of its tidy square, Samobor is made to order for a break from the big city.

ORIENTATION

Samobor (with 15,000 people, plus 20,000 more in the surrounding area) has a pleasantly compact tourist zone. Virtually anything you'd want to see or do is within sight of its centerpiece, King Tomislav Square (Trg kralja Tomislava). A stream called Gradna cuts through the middle of town.

Tourist Information

The eager TI is dead center on the main square (Mon–Fri 8:00–19:00, Sat 9:00–19:00, Sun 10:00–19:00, Trg kralja Tomislava 5, tel. 01/336-0044, www.samobor.hr). Pick up the free, handy map-guide, and get suggestions for restaurants and hikes.

Getting There

By public transportation, you'll have to arrive by **bus** via Zagreb (about 3/hr, 20 kn, 30-min trip). Once at Samobor's bus station, go to the end of the station that has all of the kiosks. From there, walk five minutes (past the covered produce market) toward the big, yellow steeple that marks the main square.

By **car,** Samobor is just off the main Zagreb-Ljubljana expressway. Exit following signs for Samobor, then follow the bull's-eyes to the *Centar*. Once at the main square, drive over the little covered bridge to reach the parking lot (5 kn/hr, put ticket on dashboard).

SIGHTS

Samobor is more about ambience than about sightseeing. Stroll the main square, sit at a café, gaze at the surrounding hills, and contemplate a hike. For extra credit, you can drop into the town's sleepy Samobor Museum (5 kn, Tue–Fri 8:00–15:00, Sat–Sun 9:00–13:00, closed Mon, across the covered bridge from the main square at Livadićeva 7, tel. 01/336-1014).

SLEEPING

(6 kuna = about $1, country code: 385, area code: 01)
Both of central Samobor's hotels are more welcoming and a much better deal than anything in downtown Zagreb. Rail or bus travelers might find it too much of a hassle to sleep in Samobor, but drivers may prefer to avoid urban traffic by sleeping here, then day-tripping by bus (30 min) into Zagreb.

$ Hotel Livadić, named for a Croatian patriot and Samobor native, has 23 rooms with elegant, old-fashioned decor over a classy café right on the main square (Sb-360–410 kn, Db-465 kn, bigger Db-530 kn, Tb-531 kn, 6 percent cheaper if you pay cash, Trg kralja Tomislava 1, tel. 01/336-5850, fax 01/336-5851, www .hotel-livadic.hr).

$ Hotel Lavica, more businesslike and less personal, rents 33 slightly worn rooms next to a pleasant park just across the covered bridge from the main square (Sb-232 kn, Db-314 kn, Tb-396 kn, Livadićeva 5, tel. 01/336-8000, fax 01/336-6611, www.lavica-hotel .hr, info@lavica-hotel.hr).

EATING

Samobor is highly regarded among Zagrebians for its cuisine, and the TI loves to recommend specific restaurants. First, an apéritif: Samobor's own Bermet is a sweet red wine made with fruits and grasses from the Samobor hills. As it's an acquired taste, start with just a sip. The local sausage, *češnjovke,* is traditionally eaten with the town's own mustard, *Samoborska Muštarda* (sold in little ceramic pots). Round out your meal with a piece of cream cake, or *kremšnita* (curiously similar to Lake Bled's specialty).

PLITVICE LAKES NATIONAL PARK

(Nacionalni Park Plitvička Jezera)

Plitvice (PLEET-veet-seh) is one of Europe's most spectacular natural wonders. Imagine Niagara Falls diced and sprinkled over a heavily forested Grand Canyon. There's nothing like this lush valley of 16 terraced lakes, laced together by waterfalls and miles of pleasant plank walks. Countless cascades and water that's both strangely clear and full of vibrant colors make this park a misty natural wonderland. Years ago, after eight or nine visits, I thought I really knew Europe. Then I discovered Plitvice, and realized you can never exhaust Europe's surprises.

Planning Your Time

Plitvice deserves at least a few good hours. Since it takes some time to get here (two hours by car or bus from Zagreb), the most sensible plan is to spend the night in one of the park's hotels (no character, but comfortable and convenient) or a nearby private home (cheaper, but practical only if you're driving). If you're coming from the north (e.g., Ljubljana), head to Zagreb in the morning, spend a few hours seeing the Croatian capital, then take the bus (no buses 17:30–22:00) or drive to Plitvice in the late afternoon to spend the night at the park. Get up early and hit the trails (ideally by 8:30 or 9:00); by early afternoon, you'll be ready to move on (perhaps by bus to the coast, or back to Zagreb). Two nights and a full day at Plitvice is probably overkill for all but the most avid hikers.

Getting to Plitvice

Plitvice Lakes National Park, a few miles from the Bosnian border, is two hours by car south of Zagreb on National Road #1 (a.k.a. D-1).

By **car** from Zagreb, you'll take the expressway south for about an hour, exiting at Karlovac (marked for *1* and *Plitvice*). From here, D-1 takes you directly south about another hour to the park. For information about driving onward from Plitvice, see "Route Tips for Drivers" at the end of this chapter.

Buses leave from Zagreb's main bus station in the direction of Plitvice. Various bus companies handle the route; just go to the ticket window and ask for the next departure (about 70 kn, trip takes 2–2.5 hours). Buses run from Zagreb about hourly until 17:30, and then there are generally no departures until 22:00 (or sometimes later). With the opening of the new freeway connecting Zagreb and Split, some buses now bypass the park altogether, so confirm that your bus will actually stop at Plitvice. (The driver may be willing to take you to your specific hotel, or, worst-case scenario, he'll drop you at the official Plitvice bus stop, which is a 10-min walk beyond the hotels.) Confirm the schedule online (www.akz.hr) or at the Plitvice office in Zagreb (Mon–Fri 8:00–16:00, closed Sat–Sun, Trg Kralja Tomislava 19, tel. 01/461-3586).

By car or bus, you'll see some thought-provoking terrain between Zagreb and Plitvice. As you leave Karlovac, you'll pass through the village of **Turanj,** part of the war zone just a decade ago. The destroyed, derelict houses belonged to Serbs who have not come back to reclaim and repair them. Farther along, about 25 miles before Plitvice, you'll pass through the striking village of **Slunj,** picturesquely perched on travertine formations (like Plitvice's) and surrounded by sparkling streams and waterfalls. If you're in a car, this is worth a photo stop. This town, too, looks very different than it did before the war—when it was 30 percent Serb. As in countless other villages in the Croatian interior, the Orthodox church has been destroyed...and locals still seethe when they describe how occupying Serbs "defiled" the town's delicate beauty.

ORIENTATION

(area code: 053)
Plitvice's 16 lakes are divided into the Upper Lakes (Gornja Jezera) and the Lower Lakes (Donja Jezera). The park officially has two entrances *(ulaz),* each with ticket windows and snack and gift shops. Entrance 1 is at the bottom of the Lower Lakes, across the busy D-1 road from the park's best restaurant, Lička Kuća (see "Eating," page 85). Entrance 2 is about 1.5 miles south, at the

cluster of Plitvice's three hotels (Jezero, Plitvice, and Bellevue; see "Sleeping," page 83). There is no town at Plitvice. The nearest village, Mukinje, is a residential community mostly for park workers (boring for tourists, but has some good private room options).

Cost and Hours: The price to enter the park during peak season (April–Oct) is a hefty 110 kn (70 kn Nov–March, ticket good for entire stay, including park entry, boat, shuttle bus, and parking). Park hours vary (generally from 7:00 in summer, 8:00 in spring and fall, and 9:00 in winter; closes at dusk). Night owls should note that the park never "closes"; these hours are for the ticket booths and the boat and shuttle bus system. You can just stroll right into the park at any time, provided that you aren't using the boat or bus. For fewer tour-group crowds, visit early or late in the day.

Tourist Information

A handy map of the trails is on the back of your ticket, and big maps are posted all over the park. The big 20-kn map is a good investment; the various English-language guidebooks are generally poorly translated and not very helpful (both sold at entrances, hotels, and shops throughout the park). The park has a good Web site: www.np-plitvicka-jezera.hr.

Getting Around Plitvice

Of course, Plitvice is designed for hikers. But the park has a few ways (included in entry cost) to help you connect the best parts.

By Shuttle Bus: Buses connect the hotels at Entrance 2 (stop ST2, below Hotel Jezero) with the top of the Upper Lakes (stop ST4) and roughly the bottom of the Lower Lakes (stop ST1, a 10-min walk from Entrance 1). Between Entrance 2 and the top of the Upper Lakes is an intermediate stop (ST3, at Galovac lake)—designed for tour groups, available to anyone, and offering a convenient way to skip the less interesting top half of the Upper Lakes. Buses start running early and continue until late afternoon (frequency depends on demand—generally 3–4/hr; buses run from March until the first snow—often Dec). Note that the park refers to its buses as "trains," which confuses some visitors. Also note that no local buses take you along the major road (D-1) that connects the entrances. The only way to get between them without a car is by shuttle bus (inside the park) or by foot (about a 40-min walk).

By Boat: Low-impact electric boats ply the waters of the biggest lake, Kozjak, with three stops: below Hotel Jezero (stop P1), the bottom of the Upper Lakes (P2), and at the far end of Kozjak, at the top of the Lower Lakes (P3). From Hotel Jezero to the Upper Lakes is a quick five-minute ride; the boat goes back and forth continuously. From the Upper Lakes to the Lower

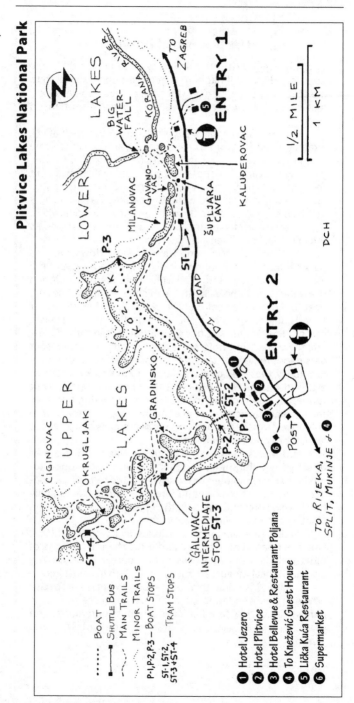

Plitvice Lakes National Park

BOAT
SHUTTLE BUS
MAIN TRAILS
MINOR TRAILS

P-1, P-2, P-3 – BOAT STOPS

ST-1, ST-2,
ST-3 & ST-4 – TRAM STOPS

1 Hotel Jezero
2 Hotel Plitvice
3 Hotel Bellevue & Restaurant Poljana
4 To Kneževič Guest House
5 Lička Kuća Restaurant
6 Supermarket

1/2 MILE
1 KM

LOWER LAKES
UPPER LAKES
BIG WATERFALL
KORANA RIVER
TO ZAGREB
ENTRY 1
KALUĐEROVAC
ŠUPLJARA CAVE
GAVANOVAC
MILANOVAC
 KOZJAK
GRADINSKO
GALOVAC
OKRUGLJAK
CIGINOVAC
OLD ROAD
ENTRY 2
POST
TO RIJEKA, SPLIT, MUKINJE & 4
"GALOVAC" INTERMEDIATE STOP ST-3
P-3
ST-1
ST-2
P-1
P-2
ST-4
DCH

The Science of Plitvice

Virtually every visitor to Plitvice eventually asks the same question: How did it happen? A geologist once explained to me that Plitvice is a "perfect storm" of unique geological, climatic, and biological features you'll rarely find elsewhere on earth.

Plitvice's magic ingredient is calcium carbonate ($CaCO_3$), a mineral deposit from the limestone. Calcium is the same thing that makes "hard water" hard. If you have hard water, you may get calcium deposits on your cold-water faucet. But these deposits build up only at the faucet, not inside the pipes. That's because when hard water is motionless (as it usually is in the pipes), it holds on to the calcium. But at the point where the water is subjected to pressure and movement—as it pours out of the faucet—it releases the calcium.

Plitvice works the same way. As water flows over the park's limestone formations, it dissolves the rock, and the water becomes supersaturated with calcium carbonate. When the water is still, it holds on to the mineral—which causes the beautiful deep-blue color of the pools. But when the water speeds up and spills over the edge of the lakes, it releases carbon dioxide gas. Without the support of the carbon dioxide, the water can't hold on to the calcium carbonate, so it gets deposited on the lake bed and at the edges of the lakes. Eventually, these deposits build up to form a rock called travertine (the same composition as the original limestone, but formed in a different way). The travertine coating becomes thicker, and barriers—and eventually dams and new waterfalls—are formed. The ongoing process means that Plitvice's landscape is always changing.

And why is the water so clear? For one thing, it comes directly from high-mountain runoff, giving it little opportunity to become polluted or muddy. Also, the calcium carbonate in the water both gives it more color and makes it highly basic, which prevents the growth of plant life (such as certain algae) that could cloud the water.

Wildlife found in the park includes deer, wolves, wildcats, lynx, wild boar, voles, otters, and more than 160 species of birds (including eagles, herons, owls, grouse, and storks). The lakes (and local menus) are full of trout. Perhaps most importantly, Plitvice is home to about 50 brown bears—a species now extremely endangered in Europe. You'll see bears, the park's mascot, plastered all over the tourist literature (and in the form of a scary representative in the lobby of Hotel Jezero).

Lakes takes closer to 20 minutes, and the boat goes about twice per hour—often at the top and bottom of every hour. (With up to 10,000 people a day visiting the park, you might have to wait for a seat on this boat.) Unless the lake freezes (about every five years), the boat also runs in the off-season—though frequency drops to hourly, and it stops running earlier.

SIGHTS AND ACTIVITIES

Plitvice is a refreshing playground of 16 terraced lakes, separated by natural travertine dams and connected by countless waterfalls.

Over time, the water has simulta-neously carved out, and, with the help of mineral deposits, built up this fluid landscape.

Plitvice became Croatia's first national park in 1949. On Easter Sunday in 1991, the first shots of Croatia's war with Yugoslavia were fired right here—in fact, the war's first casualty was a park policeman, Josip Jović. The Serbs occupied Plitvice until 1995, and most of the Croatians you'll meet here were evacuated and lived near the coastline as refugees. Today, the war is a fading memory, and the park is again a popular tourist destination, with 750,000 visitors each year (relatively few from the US).

Hiking the Lakes

Plitvice's system of trails and boardwalks makes it possible for visi-tors to get immersed in the park's beauty. (In some places, the path leads literally right up the middle of a waterfall.) The official park map and signage recommend a variety of hikes, but there's no need to adhere strictly to these suggestions; invest in the big 20-kn map and create your own route.

I like hiking uphill from the Lower Lakes to the Upper Lakes, which offers slightly better head-on views of the best scenery. (Even though this route has a gradual uphill slope, remember that if you go the other way—downhill—there's a steep climb back up at the end.) I've described a one-way hiking route (going uphill), divided between Upper and Lower. Walking briskly and with a few photo stops, figure on an hour for the Lower Lakes, an hour for the Upper Lakes, and a half-hour to connect them by boat. It's essential to get an early start (9:00 or even 8:30) to get in front of the hordes of international tour groups that descend on the trails each morning.

Start at the...

Lower Lakes (Donja Jezera)—The lower half of Plitvice's lakes are accessible from Entrance 1. If you start here, the route marked *G2* (intended for groups, but doable for anyone) leads you along the boardwalks to Kozjak, the big lake that connects the Lower and the Upper Lakes (see below).

From the entrance, you'll descend down a steep path with lots of switchbacks, as well as thrilling views over the canyon of the Lower Lakes. As you reach the lakes and begin to follow the boardwalks, you'll have great up-close views of the travertine formations that make up Plitvice's many waterfalls. See any trout? If you're tempted to throw in a line, don't. Fishing is strictly forbidden. (Besides, they're happy.)

Near the beginning of the Lower Lakes trails, an optional 10-minute detour (to the right) takes you down to the **Big Waterfall** (Veliki Slap). It's the biggest of Plitvice's waterfalls, where the Plitvica River plunges 250 feet over a cliff into the valley below. Depending on recent rainfall, the force of the Big Waterfall varies from a light mist to a thundering deluge.

After seeing the Big Waterfall, continue on the boardwalks. On the left, a smaller trail branches off towards **Šupljara Cave.** You can actually climb through this slippery cave all the way up to the trail overlooking the Lower Lakes (though it's not recommended). This unassuming cavern is a surprisingly big draw. In the 1960s, several German and Italian "Spaghetti Westerns" were filmed at Plitvice and in other parts of Croatia (which, to European eyes, has terrain similar to the American West). The most famous, *Der Schatz im Silbersee (The Treasure in Silver Lake),* was filmed here at Plitvice, and the treasure was hidden in this cave. The movie—complete with *Deutsch*-speaking "Native Americans"—is still a favorite in Germany, and popular theme tours bring German tourists to movie locations here in Croatia. (If you drive the roads near Plitvice, keep an eye out for strange, Native American–sounding names such as Winnetou—fictional characters from these beloved stories of the Old West, by the German writer Karl May.)

After Šupljara Cave, you'll stick to the east side of the lakes, then cross over one more time to the west, where you'll cut though a comparatively dull forest. You'll emerge at a pit-stop-perfect clearing with WCs, picnic tables, a souvenir shop, and a self-service restaurant. Here you can catch the shuttle boat across Lake Kozjak to the bottom of the Upper Lakes (see "Getting Around Plitvice," earlier in this chapter). While you're waiting for the next boat (usually every 30 min), visit the friendly old ladies in the kiosks selling wheels of cheese and a variety of strudel (10 kn per piece).

Lake Kozjak (Jezero Kozjak)—The park's biggest lake, Kozjak, connects the Lower and Upper Lakes. The 20-minute boat ride between Plitvice's two halves offers a great chance for a breather. You can hike between the lakes along the west side of Kozjak, but the scenery's not nearly as good as in the rest of the park.

Upper Lakes (Gornja Jezera)—Focus on the lower half of the Upper Lakes, where nearly all the exotic beauty is. From the boat dock, signs for *C* and *G2* direct you up to Gradinsko Lake through the most striking scenery in the whole park. Enjoy the stroll, take your time, and be thankful if you have an extra-large memory card for your digital camera.

After Gradinsko Lake, when you reach the top of Galovac Lake, you'll have three options:

1. Make your hike a loop by continuing around the lake (following *H* and *G1* signs back to the P2 boat dock), then take the boat back over to the hotels (P1 stop).

2. Hike a few steps up to the ST3 bus stop to catch the shuttle bus back to the hotels (more efficient, but doesn't give you a second look at the lakes).

3. Continue hiking up to the top of the Upper Lakes; you'll get away from the crowds and feel like you've covered the park thoroughly. From here on up, the scenery is less stunning, and the waterfalls are fewer and farther between. At the top, you'll finish at shuttle bus stop ST4 (with food stalls and a WC), where the bus zips you back to the hotels.

Nice work!

SLEEPING

At the Park

The most convenient way to sleep at Plitvice is to stay at the park's lodges. Book any of these hotels through the same office (reservation tel. 053/751-015, fax 053/751-013, www.np-plitvicka-jezera .hr, info@np-plitvicka-jezera.hr; reception numbers for each hotel listed next). Because of high volume in peak season, the hotels often don't return e-mails; it's better to call or fax for a reservation—they speak English.

$$$ Hotel Jezero is big and modern, with all the comfort—and charm—of a Holiday Inn. It's well-located right at the park entrance, and offers 200 rooms that feel newish, but generally have at least one thing that's broken. Rooms facing the park have big glass doors and balconies (July–Aug: Sb-€83, Db-€118; May–June and Sept–Oct: Sb-€76, Db-€108; Nov–April: Sb-€61, Db-€86, elevator, reception tel. 053/751-500).

Sleep Code

(€1 = about $1.20, country code: 385, area code: 053)
English is spoken, credit cards are accepted, and breakfast is included at each place. The tourist tax (€1 per person, per day) is not included in these prices.

To help you sort easily through these listings, I've divided the rooms into three categories based on the price for a standard double room with bath in peak season:

$$$ Higher Priced—Most rooms €100 or more.
  $$ Moderately Priced—Most rooms between €50–100.
    $ Lower Priced—Most rooms €50 or less.

$$ Hotel Plitvice, a better value than Jezero, offers 50 rooms and mod, wide-open public spaces on two floors with no elevators. For rooms, choose from economy (fine, older-feeling; July–Aug: Sb-€72, Db-€96; May–June and Sept–Oct: Sb-€65, Db-€82; Nov–April: Sb-€50, Db-€70), standard (just a teeny bit bigger; July–Aug: Sb-€77, Db-€106; May–June and Sept–Oct: Sb-€70, Db-€96; Nov–April: Sb-€55, Db-€74), or superior (bigger still, with a sitting area; July–Aug: Sb-€82, Db-€116; May–June and Sept–Oct: Sb-€75, Db-€106; Nov–April: Sb-€60, Db-€84, reception tel. 053/751-100).

$$ Hotel Bellevue is simple and bare-bones (no TVs or elevator). It has an older feel to it, but the price is right and the 80 rooms are perfectly acceptable (July–Aug: Sb-€55, Db-€74; May–June and Sept–Oct: Sb-€50, Db-€68; Nov–April: Sb-€40, Db-€54, reception tel. 053/751-700).

Near the Park

While the park's lodges are the easiest choice for non-drivers, those with a car should consider these cheaper alternatives.

$ Knežević Guest House, with 11 bright, modern rooms, is a new family-run hotel a five-minute drive south of the park in the nondescript workers' town of Mukinje. The street is modern and dull, but the yard is peaceful, with an inviting hammock (Db-€35, breakfast-€5, family rooms; driving south from the park, take first right turn into Mukinje and you'll see #57; tel. 053/774-081, mobile 098-168-7576, www.knezevic.hr, guest_house@vodatel.net, daughter Kristina speaks English).

$ *Sobe*: Drivers looking for character and preferring to spend €40, rather than €80, should simply find a room in a private home, advertised with *sobe* signs for miles on either side of the park. For details, see page 35.

EATING

The park runs all of the restaurants at Plitvice. These places are handy, and the food is tasty and affordable. If you're staying at the hotels, you have the option of paying for half-board with your room (lunch or dinner, €12 each). This option is designed for the restaurants inside hotels Jezero and Plitvice, but you can also use the voucher at other park eateries (you'll pay the difference if the bill is more). The half-board option is worth doing if you're here for dinner, but don't lock yourself in for lunch—you'll want more flexibility as you explore Plitvice (excellent picnic spots and decent food stands abound inside the park).

Hotel Jezero and **Hotel Plitvice** both have big restaurants with good food and friendly, professional service (half-board for dinner, described above, is a good deal; or order à la carte: fish and meat dishes 60–100 kn; both open daily until 23:00).

Lička Kuća, across the pedestrian overpass from Entrance 1, has a wonderfully dark and smoky atmosphere around a huge open-air wood-fired grill (grilled trout-50 kn, more elaborate dishes up to 100 kn, daily 11:00–24:00, tel. 053/751-024).

Restaurant Poljana, behind Hotel Bellevue, has the same boring, park-lodge atmosphere in both of its sections: cheap, self-

service cafeteria (25–40 kn) and sit-down restaurant with open wood-fired grill (same choices and prices as the better-atmosphere Lička Kuća, above; both parts open daily but closed in winter, tel. 053/751-092).

For **picnic** fixings, there's a small supermarket at Entrance 2, and another one with a larger selection across road D-1 (use the pedestrian overpass). The boat docks come with a few eating options. At the P3 boat dock, locals sell homemade goodies, and at the P1 boat dock, you can buy grilled meat and drinks.

TRANSPORTATION CONNECTIONS

To reach the park, see "Getting to Plitvice," earlier in this chapter. Moving on from Plitvice is trickier. Buses pass by the park in each direction—northbound (to **Zagreb**, 2–2.5 hrs) and southbound (to coastal destinations such as **Split**, 4–6 hrs, and **Dubrovnik**, 9–10 hrs).

There is no bus station—just a low-profile *Plitvice Centar* bus stop shelter. To reach it from the park, go out to the main road from either Hotel Jezero or Hotel Plitvice, then turn right; the bus stops are just after the pedestrian overpass. The one on the hotel side of the road is for buses headed for the coast; the stop on the opposite side is for Zagreb. But here's the catch: Many buses that pass through Plitvice don't stop (either because they're full, or because they don't have anyone to drop off there). You can stand at the bus stop and try to flag one down, but it's safer to get help from the park's hotel staff. They can help you figure out which bus suits your schedule, then they'll call ahead to be sure the bus stops for you. If you don't want to make the 10-minute walk out to the bus stop, someone at the hotel can usually drive you out for a modest fee.

Route Tips for Drivers

Plitvice's biggest disadvantage is that it's an hour away from the handy A-1 expressway that connects northern Croatia to the Dalmatian Coast. You have two ways to access this expressway from Plitvice:

At Karlovac: From Plitvice, drive about one hour north on D-1 to the town of Karlovac, where you can take A-1 north to **Zagreb** or south to the **Dalmatian Coast** (first reaching **Zadar,** then **Split**). Once you're on A-1 southbound, you can also access A-6, which leads west to **Rijeka, Opatija,** and **Istria.**

At Otočac: From Plitvice, go south on D-1, then go west on road #52 to the town of Otočac (about 1.5 hours through the mountains from Plitvice to Otočac). After Otočac, you can get on A-1 (north to **Zagreb,** south to the **Dalmatian Coast**); or continue west and twist down the mountain road to the seaside town of Senj, on the main coastal road of the **Kvarner Gulf.** From Senj, it's about an hour north along the coast to **Rijeka,** then **Opatija;** or an hour south to Jablanac, where you can catch the ferry to **Rab Island.**

During the recent war, the front line between the Croats and Serbs ran just east of **Otočac** (OH-toh-chawts), and bullet holes still mar the town's facades. But today Otočac is putting itself back together, and it's a fine place to drop into a café for a coffee, or pick up some produce at the outdoor market. The Catholic church in the center of town, destroyed in the war but now rebuilt, has a memorial out back with its damaged church bells. Just up the main street, beyond the big, grassy park, is the Orthodox church. Otočac used to be about one-third Serbian, but the Serbs were forced out during the war, and this church fell into disrepair. But, as Otočac and Croatia show signs of healing, about two dozen Serbs have returned to town and re-opened their church—if the door's open, take a look inside (for more on the Serbian Orthodox Church, see page 234).

ISTRIA

Rovinj • Pula • The Brijuni Islands • Poreč • Hill Towns

Idyllic Istria (EE-stree-ah; "Istra" in Croatian), at Croatia's northwest corner, reveals itself to you gradually and seductively. Pungent truffles, Roman ruins, striking hill towns, quaint coastal villages, carefully cultivated food and wine, and breezy Italian culture all compete for your attention...and you're always the winner. The wedge-shaped Istrian Peninsula, while not as famous as its southern rival (the much-hyped Dalmatian Coast), is giving Dalmatia a run for its money.

The Istrian coast, with gentle green slopes instead of the sheer limestone cliffs found along the rest of the Croatian shoreline, is more serene than sensational. It's lined with pretty, interchangeably tacky resort towns, such as the tourist mecca Poreč (worthwhile only for its Byzantine mosaic-packed basilica). But one seafront village reaches the ranks of greatness: romantically creaky Rovinj, my favorite little town on the Adriatic. Down at the tip of Istria is big, industrial Pula, offering a bustling urban contrast to the rest of the time-passed coastline, plus some impressive Roman ruins (including an amphitheater so remarkably intact, you'll marvel that you haven't heard of it before). Just offshore are the Brijuni Islands—once the stomping grounds of Maršal Tito, whose ghost still haunts a national park peppered with unexpected attractions.

But Croatia is more than the sea, and diverse Istria offers some of the country's most appealing reasons to head inland. In the Istrian interior, you'll find vintners painstakingly reviving a delicate winemaking tradition, farmers pressing that last drop of oil out of their olives, trained dogs sniffing out truffles in primeval forests, and a smattering of fortified medieval hill towns—including the tiny, rugged artists' colony of Grožnjan, and the popular

Istria Overview

village of Motovun, with sweeping views over the surrounding terrain.

Planning Your Time

Istria offers an exciting variety of attractions compared to the relatively uniform, if beautiful, string of island towns farther south. While some travelers wouldn't trade a sunny island day for anything, I prefer to sacrifice a little time on the Dalmatian Coast for the diversity that comes with a day or two exploring Istria's hill towns and other unique sights.

Istria at a Glance

▲▲▲**Rovinj** Extremely romantic, Venetian-style coastal town with an atmospheric Old Town and salty harbor.

▲▲**Pula** Big, industrial port town packed with Roman ruins, including one of the world's best-preserved amphitheaters.

▲▲**Motovun** Touristy but enjoyable hill town with a fun rampart walk offering sweeping views over inland Istria.

▲▲**Grožnjan** Sleepy artists' colony hill town in the interior.

▲**Brijuni Islands** Tito's former summer residence, now a national park with a Tito museum, mini-safari, and other offbeat sights.

Hum Miniscule, touristy town deep in the interior.

Poreč Big coastal resort squeezed full of European holidaymakers, plus a church with some of the most intact Byzantine mosaics in Croatia.

Istria's main logistical advantage is that it's easy to reach and to explore. Just a quick hop from Venice or Slovenia, compact little Istria is made-to-order for a quick, efficient visit.

With a car and two weeks to spend in Croatia and Slovenia, Istria deserves two days, divided between its two big attractions: the coastal town of Rovinj and the hill towns of the interior. Ideally, make your home base for two nights in one area, and daytrip to the other. (For a suggested hill town driving itinerary, see page 119.) To wring the most out of limited Istrian time, the city of Pula and its Roman amphitheater are well worth a few hours. The fun but time-consuming Brijuni Islands merit a detour only if you've got at least three days.

Getting Around Istria

Istria is a cinch for **drivers,** who find distances short and roads and attractions well-marked (though summer traffic can be miserable, especially on weekends). While Istria has no four-lane expressways, it is neatly connected by a speedy two-lane highway nicknamed the *ipsilon* (the Croatian word for the letter Y, which is what the highway is shaped like). One branch of the "Y" (A-9) runs roughly parallel to the coast from Slovenia to Pula, about six miles inland; the other branch (A-8) cuts diagonally northeast to the Učka Tunnel (leading to Rijeka). You'll periodically come to toll booths, where you'll pay a modest fee for using the *ipsilon*. Following road signs here is easy (navigate by town names), but if you'll be driving a lot, pick up a good map to more easily navigate the back roads. My favorite is the Kod & Kam 1:100,000 *Istra* map (available in local bookstores and some TIs).

If you're relying on **public transportation,** Istria is less desirable: The towns easiest to reach (Poreč and Pula) are the least interesting. While it may be possible to patch together some of the better sights (such as Rovinj and the hill towns) by bus, it's probably not worth the hassle. Even if you're doing the rest of your trip by public transportation, consider renting a car for a day or two in Istria.

Driving from Istria to Rijeka (and the Rest of Croatia): Istria meets the rest of Croatia at the big port city of Rijeka (see the Kvarner Gulf chapter). There are two ways to get to Rijeka: The faster alternative is to take the *ipsilon* road via Pazin to the Učka Tunnel (28-kn toll), which emerges just above Rijeka and Opatija (for Rijeka, you'll follow the road more or less straight on; for Opatija, you'll twist down to the right, backtracking slightly to the seashore below you). Or you can take the slower but more scenic **coastal road** from Pula via Labin. After going inland for about 25 miles, this road jogs to the east coast of Istria, which it hugs all the way into Opatija, then Rijeka. From Rijeka, you can easily hook into Croatia's expressway network (for example, take A-6 east to A-1, which zips you north to Zagreb or south to the Dalmatian Coast).

By Boat to Venice: Venezia Lines connects Venice with Rovinj, Poreč, and Pula, as well as Piran (in Slovenia) and other Adriatic destinations (such as Ravenna and Ramini in Italy, and Opatija in Croatia). The company also allows you to sail between some of these same towns (for example, a handy Rovinj–Piran boat runs on some days when there's no buses on that route). While designed for day-trippers from Istria to Venice, this service can also be used one-way. For details, see www.venezialines.com.

Rovinj

Rising dramatically from the Adriatic as though being pulled up to heaven by its grand bell tower, Rovinj (roh-VEEN, Rovingo in Italian) is a welcoming Old World oasis in a sea of tourist kitsch. Among the villages of Croatia's coast, there's something particularly romantic about Rovinj. Some locals credit the especially strong Venetian influence here—it's the most Italian town in Croatia's most Italian region. Rovinj's streets are delightfully

Istrian Food and Wine

Though much of Croatia is arid and barren, Istria's fertile soil produces a cornucopia of delicious ingredients. Istrian cuisine is hearty, humble countryside grub. Like the Istrian people, it's a mix of various cultural influences—Italian-style elements, farmer fare, and seafood. Pastas such as gnocchi and fusilli are popular, as is *pršut*, the air-cured ham that's Istria's answer to prosciutto (see sidebar on page 319). Food here is distinctly Mediterranean, with lots of olives and wine. You'll often find game on the menu.

Istria is also a major wine-growing region, producing about 80 percent whites. Istrian vintners are particularly

proud of their *malvazija* (mahl-VAH-zee-yah; sometimes spelled Malvasia in English)—a light white wine that can be either sweet *(slatko)* or dry *(suho)*. *Malvazija* wines are produced throughout Europe, but Istria's *malvazija* is indigenous. The red *teran* is also popular, as is Merlot. *Teran*, a heavy wine from *refošk* grapes, is sometimes blended with Merlot to soften its flavor. *Teran* pairs well with *pršut*. Because many Istrian vintners are relatively recent to the job—having gotten into the craft when the industry was privatized at the end of communism—the focus is on quality, not quantity...so few Croatian wines are exported.

twisty, its ancient houses are characteristically crumbling, and its harbor—lively with real-life fishermen—is as salty as they come. Like a little Venice on a hill, Rovinj is the stage set for your Croatian seaside dreams.

Rovinj was wealthy and well-fortified in the Middle Ages. It boomed in the 16th and 17th centuries, when it was flooded with refugees fleeing both the Ottoman invasions and the plague. But by the late 18th century, Rovinj was a forgotten Venetian outpost. After Napoleon seized the region, then was defeated, Rovinj became part of Austria. While the Venetians had neglected Istria, the Austrians invested in it—bringing the railroad, gas lights, and a huge Ronhill tobacco factory (recently replaced by

an enormous, state-of-the-art facility farther inland). The Austrians chose Pula and Trieste to be the empire's major ports—cursing those cities with pollution and sprawl, while allowing Rovinj to linger in its trapped-in-the-past quaintness.

Before long, Austrians discovered Istria as a handy escape for a beach holiday. Tourism came to Rovinj in the late 1890s, when a powerful Austrian baron bought one of the remote, barren islands offshore and brought it back to life with gardens and a grand villa. Before long, another baron bought another island...and a tourist boom was underway. In more recent times, Rovinj has become a top destination for nudists. The resort of Valalta, just to the north, is a popular spot for those seeking "southern exposure"... as a very revealing brochure at the TI explains (www.valalta.hr). Whether you want to find PNBs (pudgy nude bodies), or avoid them, remember that the German phrase *FKK* (*Freikörper Kultur,* or "free body culture") is international shorthand for nudism.

Rovinj is the most atmospheric of all of Croatia's small coastal towns. Unfortunately, it's also one of the most over-promoted—as you approach, you pass endless billboards touting hotels, restaurants, and tour companies. But if you survive this tacky gauntlet, the commercialism melts away as soon as you set foot in Rovinj's Old Town.

Planning Your Time

Rovinj is hardly packed with diversions. You can get the gist of the town in a one-hour wander. The rest of your time is for enjoying the ambience. When you're ready to overcome your inertia, there's no shortage of day trips (all outlined in this chapter). Be aware that much of Rovinj closes down from November through Easter.

ORIENTATION

(area code: 052)

Rovinj, once an island, is now a peninsula. The Old Town is divided in two parts: a particularly charismatic chunk on the oval-shaped peninsula, and the rest (with similarly time-worn buildings) on the mainland. Where the mainland meets the Old Town is a broad, bustling public space called Tito Square (Trg Maršala Tita). The Old Town peninsula—traffic-free except for the occasional moped—is topped by the massive bell tower of the Church of St. Euphemia. At the very tip of the peninsula is a small park.

Tourist Information

Rovinj's helpful TI, facing the harbor, has several handy, free materials including a town map and an info booklet (summer daily 8:00–22:00; off-season Mon–Fri 8:00–15:00, Sat 8:00–13:00,

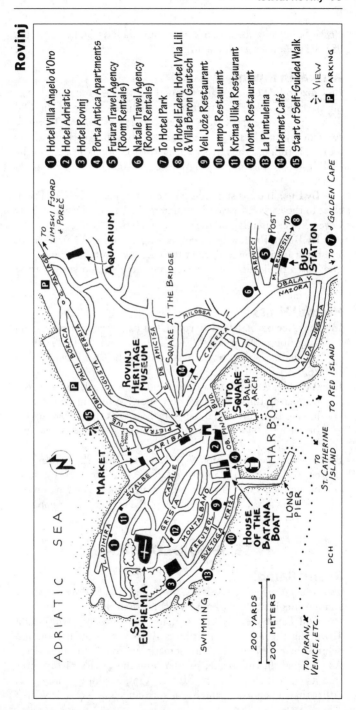

Rovinj

1. Hotel Villa Angelo d'Oro
2. Hotel Adriatic
3. Hotel Rovinj
4. Porta Antica Apartments
5. Futura Travel Agency (Room Rentals)
6. Natale Travel Agency (Room Rentals)
7. To Hotel Park
8. To Hotel Eden, Hotel Vila Lili & Villa Baron Gautsch
9. Veli Jože Restaurant
10. Lampo Restaurant
11. Krčma Ulika Restaurant
12. Monte Restaurant
13. La Puntuleina
14. Internet Café
15. Start of Self-Guided Walk

↑ VIEW

P PARKING

closed Sun; along the embankment at Obala Pina Budičina 12, tel. 052/811-566, www.tzgrovinj.hr).

Arrival in Rovinj

By Car: Follow *Centar* signs through the little roundabout to the big parking lot on the waterfront immediately north of the Old Town, just up the shore from the classic view of Rovinj. There are two side-by-side lots, so if the one closer to town—used mostly by locals—is full, use the farther one (5 kn/hr). Hotels away from the Old Town are individually signposted as you approach the town center.

By Bus: The bus station is on the south side of the Old Town, close to the harbor. Leave the station to the left, then walk on busy Carera street directly into the center of town.

By Boat: The few boats connecting Rovinj to Venice, Piran, and other Istrian towns dock at the long pier protruding from the Old Town peninsula. Simply walk up the pier, and you're in the heart of town.

Helpful Hints

Internet Access: **A-Mar Internet Club** has several terminals and long hours (Mon–Fri 8:00–22:00, Sat–Sun 8:00–23:00, on the main drag in the mainland part of the Old Town, Carera 26, tel. 052/841-211).

Local Guide: **Renato Orbanić** is a laid-back musician who enjoys wandering through town with visitors. While light on heavy-hitting facts, his casual tour somehow suits this easygoing little town (€60 for a 2-hour tour, mobile 091-521-6206, rorbanic @inet.hr).

Best Views: The postcard view of Rovinj is from the parking lot embankment at the north end of the Old Town (at the start of the "Self-Guided Walk"). For a different perspective on the Old Town, head for the far side of the harbor on the opposite (south) end of town.

SELF-GUIDED WALK

Rovinj Ramble

This orientation walk, worth ▲▲, introduces you to Rovinj in about an hour. Begin at the parking lot just north of the Old Town.

Old Town View: There are many fine views of Rovinj's Old Town, but this is the most striking. Boats bob in the harbor, and behind them Venetian-looking homes seem to rise from the deep. As you soak in this scene, ponder how the town's history created its current shape: In the Middle Ages, Rovinj was an island, rather than a peninsula, and it was surrounded by a double wall—

a protective inner wall and an outer seawall. Because it was so well-defended against pirates and other marauders (not to mention the plague), it was extremely desirable real estate. And yet, it was easy to reach from the mainland, allowing it to thrive as a trading town. With more than 10,000 residents at its peak, Rovinj became immensely crowded, explaining today's pleasantly claustrophobic Old Town.

Over the centuries—as demand for living space trumped security concerns—the town walls were converted into houses, with windows grafted on to their imposing frame. Gaps in the wall, with steps that seem to end at the water, are where fishermen would pull in to unload their catch directly into the warehouse on the bottom level of the houses. (Later you can explore some of these lanes from inside the town.) Today, if you live in one of these houses, the Adriatic is your backyard.

• *In the little park near the sea, notice the big, blocky...*

Communist-Era Monument: Dating from the time of Tito, this celebrates the Partisan army's victory over fascism in World War II, and also memorializes the victims of that war. With typical Yugoslav grace and subtlety, this jarring block shatters the otherwise harmonious time-warp vibe of Rovinj. Fortunately, it's the only modern structure anywhere near the Old Town.

• *Now continue toward town, stopping to explore the covered...*

Market: The front part of the market, near the water, is for souvenirs. But natives delve deeper in, where everything is local and mostly homemade: produce, wine, olive oil, and *rakija* (the powerful firewater popular throughout the Balkans). The hall labeled *Ribarnica/Pescheria* at the back of the market is where you'll find fresh, practically wriggling fish. This is where locals gather ingredients for their favorite dish, *brodet*—a stew of various kinds of seafood mixed with olive oil and wine...all of Istria's best bits rolled into one dish. It's simmered and generally served with polenta (unfortunately, it's rare in restaurants).

• *Continue up the broad street, named for **Giuseppe Garibaldi**—one of the major players in late-19th-century Italian unification. Imagine: Even though you're in Croatia, Italian patriots are celebrated in this*

Italo-Croatia

Apart from its tangible attractions, one of Istria's hallmarks is its biculturalism: It's an engaging hybrid of Croatia and Italy. Like most of the Croatian Coast, Istria has variously been controlled by Illyrians, Romans, Byzantines, Slavs, Venetians, and Austrians. After the Hapsburgs lost World War I, most of today's Croatia joined Yugoslavia—but Istria became part of Italy. During this time, the Croatian vernacular was suppressed, while the Italian language and culture flourished. This extra chapter of Italian rule left Istrians with an identity crisis. After World War II, Istria joined Yugoslavia, and Croatian culture and language returned. But many people here found it difficult to abandon their ties to Italy.

Today, Croatians are proud of Istria...and so are Italians. Istria pops up on Italian weather reports. Not long ago, Italy's then-Prime Minister Silvio Berlusconi declared that he still considered Istria part of Italy—and he wanted it back.

People who live here don't worry about the distinction. Locals insist that they're not Croatians and not Italians—they're Istrians. They don't mind straddling two cultures. Both languages are official (and often taught side-by-side in schools), street signs are bilingual, and most Istrians dabble in each tongue—often seeming to foreign ears as though they're mixing the two at once. I used to think that Dalmatia was the most relaxed, most "Italian-feeling" part of Croatia... until I got to know Istria better.

As a result of their tangled history, Istrians have learned how to be mellow and take things as they come. They're gregarious, open-minded, and sometimes seem to thrive on chaos. A twentysomething local told me, "My ancestors lived in Venice. My great-grandfather lived in Austria. My grandfather lived in Italy. My father lived in Yugoslavia. I live in Croatia. My son will live in the European Union. And we've all lived in the same town."

very Italian-feeling town (see the "Italo-Croatia" sidebar, above). After one long block, you'll come to the wide cross-street called...

Square at the Bridge (Trg na Mostu): This marks the site of the medieval bridge that once connected the fortified island of Rovinj to the mainland. Back then, the island was populated mostly by Italians, while the mainland was the territory of Slavic farmers. But as Rovinj's strategic importance waned, and its trading status rose, the need for easy access became more important than the canal's protective purpose—so in 1763, it was filled in. The two populations integrated, creating the bicultural mix that survives today.

• *Across from Trg na Mostu, notice the* **Rovinj Heritage Museum,** *described under "Sights and Activities," later in this section. Now proceed to the little fountain in the middle of the square (near Hotel Adriatic)...*

Tito Square (Trg Maršala Tita): This wide-open square at the entrance to the Old Town is the crossroads of Rovinj. The **fountain,** with a little boy playing a spiny fish like a bagpipe, is one of the square's newest features—it dates only from the Yugoslav period.

From here, you're a few steps from Rovinj's crowded **harbor,** with fishing vessels and excursion boats that shuttle tourists out to the offshore islands. Of Rovinj's own little archipelago, the two most popular islands for a visit are St. Catherine (Sveta Katarina) and Red Island (Crveni Otok). Each has a hotel and its own share of beaches.

If you were to walk down the **embankment** between the harbor and the Old Town (past Hotel Adriatic), you'd find the TI and a delightful "restaurant row" with several tempting places for a drink or a meal. Many fishermen pull their boats into this harbor, then simply walk their catch across the street to a waiting restaurateur.

Face the Old Town entrance gate, called the **Balbi Arch.** The winged lion on top is a reminder this was Venetian territory for centuries.

• *Head through the gate into the Old Town, and begin walking up...*

Grisia Street: Just inside the gate, on the left, is the old Town Hall. Notice another Venetian lion, as well as other historic crests embedded in the wall.

The main "street" (actually a tight lane) leading through the middle of the island from the Balbi Arch is choked with tourists during the midday rush and lined with art galleries. This inspiring town has attracted many artists, some of whom display their works along this colorful stretch.

As you explore, remember that, as crowded as it is today, little Rovinj was even more packed-to-the-gills in the Middle Ages. Keep an eye out for arches that span narrow lanes—the only way a walled city could grow. Many of these additions created hidden little courtyards, nooks, and crannies that make it easy to get away from the crowds and claim a corner of the town for yourself. Another sign of Rovinj's overcrowding are the distinctive chimneys poking up above the rooftops. These chimneys, added long after the buildings were first constructed, made it possible to heat previously underutilized rooms…and squeeze in even more people.

• *At the top of town is the can't-miss-it…*

Church of St. Euphemia (Sv. Eufemija): Rovinj's landmark Baroque church, worth ▲, dates from 1754 (free, generally open daily 10:00–18:30, maybe later for Mass, often closed off-season). It's watched over by an enormous 190-foot-tall **campanile,** a replica of the famous bell tower on St. Mark's Square in Venice. The tower is topped by a copper weathervane depicting St. Euphemia, the church's namesake (explained next). Local fishermen look to this saintly weathervane for direction: When Euphemia is looking out to sea, it means the stiff, fresh Bora wind is blowing, bringing dry air from the interior—and good weather for fishing. But if she's facing the land, the humid Jugo wind will soon bring bad weather from the sea. (For more on Croatian winds and weather, see the sidebar on page 136.)

The church is named for **St. Euphemia,** the virtuous daughter of a prosperous early-fourth-century family in Chalcedon (near today's Istanbul). Euphemia used her family's considerable wealth to help the poor. Unfortunately, her pious philanthropy happened to coincide with anti-Christian purges by the Roman Emperor Diocletian. When she was 15 years old, Euphemia was arrested for refusing to worship the local pagan idol. She was brutally tortured, her bones broken on a wheel (notice the wheel next to her on top of the weathervane). Finally she was thrown to the lions as a public spectacle. But, the story goes, the lions miraculously refused to attack or maul her—only nipping her gently on one arm. The Romans murdered Euphemia anyway, and her remains were later rescued by Christians. In the year 800, a gigantic marble sarcophagus containing St. Euphemia's relics somehow found its way into the Adriatic and floated all the way up to Istria, where Rovinj fishermen found it bobbing in the sea. They towed it back to town, where a crowd gathered. The townspeople realized what it was, and wanted to take it up to the Church of St. George (where we are now). But nobody could move it…until a young boy with two young calves showed up. He said he'd had a dream of St. Euphemia—and, sure enough, he succeeded in dragging her relics to where they still lie. While St. George remains the town's official co-patron saint, most people here are all about Euphemia.

Before you go **inside,** notice the relief of St. Euphemia holding the church just outside the entrance. The vast, somewhat gloomy interior boasts some fine altars of Carrara marble (a favorite medium of Michelangelo's). Services here are celebrated using a combination of Croatian and Italian, suiting the town's mixed population. Don't miss the chapel containing the relics of St. Euphemia (at the front-right corner, as you face the altar). That famous sarcophagus—whose front panel, behind the glass, is opened with much fanfare every September 16, St. Euphemia's feast day—is flanked by frescoes depicting her most memorable moment (protected by angels, as a bored-looking lion tenderly nibbles at her right bicep), and her arrival here in Rovinj (with burly fishermen looking astonished as the young boy succeeds in moving the giant sarcophagus). Note the depiction of Rovinj fortified by a double crenellated wall—looking more like a castle than like the creaky fishing village of today.

• *Your tour is finished. Before heading back down into town, you can visit the park out at the tip of the peninsula, just below this church.*

SIGHTS AND ACTIVITIES

House of the Batana Boat (Kuća o Batani)—Rovinj has a long, noble shipbuilding tradition, and this tiny but interesting museum gives you the whole story on the town's distinctive *batana* boats. These flat-bottomed vessels are favored by local fishermen for their ability to reach rocky areas close to shore that are rich with certain shellfish. Using high-tech exhibits, the museum explains how the boats are built and introduces you to some of the salty old sailors who use them (find the placemat with wine stains, and put the glass in different circles to hear various seamen talk in the Rovinj dialect). Upstairs is a wall of photos of *batana* boats still in active use, and a video screen showing *betinada* music—local music with harmonizing voices, mandolin, guitar, and bass. There's no posted English information, so pick up the comprehensive English flyer as you enter (10 kn; June–Sept daily 10:00–15:00 & 17:00–22:00; Oct–Dec and March–May Tue–Sun 10:00–13:00 & 15:00–17:00, closed Mon; closed Jan–Feb; Obala P. Budicin 2, tel. 052/805-266).

Rovinj Heritage Museum (Zavičajni Muzej Grada Rovinja)—This ho-hum museum combines art old (obscure classic painters) and new (obscure contemporary painters from Rovinj) in an old mansion. Rounding out the collection are some model ships and a small archaeological exhibit (15 kn; summer Tue–Sun 9:00–12:00 & 19:00–22:00, closed Mon, may open midday in peak season; winter Tue–Sat 9:00–13:00, closed Sun–Mon; Trg Maršala Tita 11, tel. 052/816-720, www.muzej-rovinj.com).

Aquarium (Akvarij)—This century-old collection of local sea life is one of Europe's oldest aquariums (12 kn, daily in summer 9:00–21:00, progressively shorter hours off-season, a 10-min walk up the coast from the parking lots at Obala G. Paliage 5, tel. 052/804-712).

Swimming—The most central spot to swim or sunbathe is on the rocks along the embankment on the south side of the Old Town peninsula (just under Hotel Rovinj). For bigger beaches, head for the offshore islands, or go to the wooded Golden Cape (Zlatni Rat) south of the harbor (past the big, waterfront Hotel Park). This cape is lined with walking paths and beaches, and shaded by a wide variety of trees and plants.

SLEEPING

In Rovinj's Old Town

All of these accommodations are on the Old Town peninsula, rather than the mainland section of the Old Town. While Rovinj has no hostel, *sobe* are a good budget option.

$$$ Hotel Villa Angelo d'Oro is your top Old Town splurge. The location—on a peaceful street just a few steps off the water—is ideal, and the public spaces (including a serene garden bar and sauna/whirlpool area) are rich and inviting. The 23 rooms don't quite live up to the fuss, but if you want your money to talk your way into the Old Town, this is the place (mid-July–Aug: Sb-905 kn, Db-1,600 kn; May–mid-July and Sept: Sb-776 kn, Db-1,346 kn; cheaper Oct–Dec and March–April, closed Jan–Feb, pricier suites also available, no elevator, dinner in their restaurant-205 kn per person, Vladimira Švalbe 38–42, tel. 052/840-502, fax 052/840-111, www.angelodoro.hr, hotel.angelo@vip.hr).

Sleep Code

(€1 = about $1.20, 6 kn = about $1, country code: 385, area code: 052)

S = Single, **D** = Double/Twin, **T** = Triple, **Q** = Quad, **b** = bathroom. The modest tourist tax (7 kn or €1 per person, per night, lower off-season) is not included in these rates. Hotels accept credit cards and include breakfast in their rates, while most *sobe* accept only cash and don't offer breakfast. Everyone listed here speaks at least enough English to make a reservation (or knows someone nearby who can translate).

To help you sort easily through these listings, I've divided the rooms into three categories based on the price for a standard double room with bath in peak season:

$$$ Higher Priced—Most rooms 700 kn (€97) or more.
$$ Moderately Priced—Most rooms between 400–700 kn (€55–97).
$ Lower Priced—Most rooms 400 kn (€55) or less.

$$$ Hotel Adriatic, a lightly renovated holdover from the communist days, features 27 rooms overlooking the main square, where the Old Town peninsula meets the mainland. The quality of the drab, worn rooms doesn't justify the high prices...but the location does. Of the big chain of Maistra hotels, this is the only one in the Old Town (slippery rates depend on demand, mid-June–early Sept: Sb-410–492 kn, non-view Db-670–834 kn, twin Db with view-746–908 kn; shoulder season: Sb-305–365 kn, non-view Db-462–582 kn, view twin Db-536–656; 20 percent more for 1- or 2-night stays, all Sb are non-view, closed mid-Oct–March, Trg Maršala Tita, tel. 052/815-088, fax 052/813-573, www.maistra.hr, adriatic@maistra.hr).

$$$ Hotel Rovinj enjoys an incredible location at the tip of the Old Town peninsula, and—unlike most Rovinj hotels—it's not owned by a big company. The bad news is that they're in the midst of an extensive renovation, and may be closed in 2007. When they re-open, prices will probably skyrocket (old rates were Db-€70–104 in peak season, less off-season, likely higher in 2007, closed Nov–Easter, Sv. Križa 59, tel. 052/811-288, fax 052/840-757, hotel-rovinj@pu.t-com.hr).

$$ Porta Antica is an agency renting five beautifully decorated apartments over an Old Town restaurant facing the harbor. While you may not get a warm welcome, the location and price are excellent (small apartment with no view-540 kn mid-July–mid-Sept, 360 kn June–mid-July, 288 kn off-season; bigger sea-view apartment-720 kn/504 kn/396 kn; deluxe view apartment with terrace-864 kn/612 kn/468 kn). The same agency rents other rooms in town, including two in the Old Town and others in the outlying areas—if you rent one of these, establish clearly where it is (prices are for 2 people—86 kn more per extra person, no breakfast, cash only, 3-night minimum June–Sept, 2-night minimum Oct–May, open year-round, next door to TI, mobile 099-680-1101, www .portaantica.com, portaantica@yahoo.it).

$ *Sobe:* Several agencies rent private rooms in the Old Town for great prices (figure Db-€20–40, depending on season, location, and size). The catch: In peak season, you'll pay double for a one-night stay, and 20–50 percent extra for a two- or three-night stay (this surcharge is sometimes waived off-season). Just about everyone in town has a line on rooms. These two agencies are English-friendly and handy to the bus station: **Futura Travel** (across from bus station at Benussi 2, tel. 052/817-281, fax 052/817-282, www .futura-travel.hr) and **Natale** (Carducci 4, tel. & fax 052/813-365, www.rovinj.com).

On the Mainland

To escape the high prices of Rovinj's Old Town, consider the resort neighborhood just south of the harbor. While the big hotels themselves are an option, I prefer cheaper alternatives in the same area. The big hotels are signposted as you approach town (follow signs for *hoteli,* then your specific hotel). Once you're on the road to Hotels Eden and Park, the other two are easy to reach: Villa Baron Gautsch is actually on the road to Hotel Park (on the right, brown *pansion* sign just before Hotel Park itself); Hotel Vila Lili is a little farther on the main road toward Eden (to the left just after turnoff for Hotel Park, look for *Vila Lili* sign). All of these options are about a 15-minute uphill walk from the Old Town.

$$$ Masitra Hotels: The local hotel conglomerate, Maistra, has several hotels in the lush parklands just south of the Old Town (www.maistra.hr). Most Americans—looking for proximity to the Old Town rather than plush rooms, a big lounge, and hotel-based activities—will prefer to save money and stay at one of my other listings. **Hotel Park** has 202 thoroughly renovated but boring rooms in a colorized communist-era hull, and a seaside swimming pool with great views over the Old Town. From here, you can walk along the scenic harborfront promenade into town (July–Aug: Sb-€75–90, Db-€130–160; shoulder season: Sb-€60–70, Db-€100–120; even cheaper off-season, closed Jan–Feb, tel. 052/811-077, fax 052/816-977, park@maistra.hr). **Hotel Eden** offers 330 upscale, imaginatively updated rooms with oodles of contemporary style behind a brooding communist facade. This flagship hotel is the fanciest one in the Maistra chain, but it's a bit farther from the Old Town—frustrating without a car (July–Aug: Sb-€100–115, Db-€175–200; shoulder season: Sb-€75–85, Db-€125–140; even cheaper off-season, closed Dec–March, tel. 052/800-400, fax 052/811-349, eden@maistra.hr). Both hotels have air-conditioning, elevators, and free parking (20 percent more for 1–2 nights, prices include dinner at hotel—skip this half-board option to save about €3 per person). The Maistra chain also has several other properties (including the Old Town's Hotel Adriatic, described previously, and other more distant, cheaper options).

$$$ Hotel Vila Lili is a charming, family-run hotel over a restaurant on a quiet lane in a modern part of town. Its 16 pleasant rooms have slightly tacky resort decor, but they're comfortable and reasonably close to the Old Town (July–Aug: Sb-445 kn, Db-780 kn; shoulder season: Sb-445 kn, Db-620–700 kn; pricier suites also available, cheaper off-season, no extra charge for 1-night stays, elevator, parking-30 kn/day, Mohorovičića 16, tel. 052/840-940, fax 052/840-944, www.hotel-vilalili.hr, vila-lili@pu.t-com.hr).

$$ Villa Baron Gautsch is a pension with 17 simple but comfortable rooms (Aug: Db-444 kn; July and Sept: Db-368 kn;

shoulder season: Db-266–296 kn; 20 percent more for less than 3 nights, 40 kn extra for balcony, closed Nov–mid-April, cash only, no elevator, Ronjgova 7, tel. 052/814-042, fax 052/840-537, www .baron-gautsch.com).

EATING

Interchangeable restaurants cluster where Rovinj's Old Town meets the mainland, and all around the harbor. Choose the place with

the view or menu you like best—or delve a bit farther into the heart of the peninsula to one of my other recommendations. Be warned that most of these eateries—like much of Rovinj—close for the winter (roughly November to Easter).

Along Rovinj's "Restaurant Row": The easiest dining option is to stroll the Old Town embankment overlooking the harbor (Obala Pina Budičina), which changes its name to Svetoga Križa and cuts behind the buildings after a few blocks. While these restaurants are all about the same, a few are notable. **Veli Jože** is a reliable pleaser that's in all the guidebooks (Sv. Križa 1), while **Lampo** has scenic seating right on the water (Sv. Križa 22).

Krčma Ulika, a truly classy hole-in-the-wall run by Inja Tucman, has a mellow, cozy interior strewn with art. The simple menu, featuring gourmet Mediterranean food, changes based on what's fresh. The food is prepared right in a corner of the tight six-table dining room (12-kn cover, 50–80-kn main dishes, Wed–Mon 18:30–2:00 in the morning, Fri–Sun also 13:00–15:00, closed Tue except in peak season, closed off-season, Vladimira Švalbe 34, tel. 052/818-089).

Monte Restaurant is your upscale, white-tablecloth splurge. With tables strewn around a covered terrace just under the town bell tower, this atmospheric place features international cuisine with a French Mediterranean flair (100–140-kn main dishes, daily 12:00–15:00 & 19:00–23:00, reserve ahead in peak season, Montalbano 75, tel. 052/830-203, Đekić family).

La Puntuleina is a fancy spot near the tip of the Old Town peninsula with one of the most scenic seafront settings in town. This restaurant, cocktail bar, and wine bar features pricey Mediterranean cuisine served in the contemporary dining room or outside on tables literally scattered along the rocks overlooking a swimming hole. Some visitors—overwhelmed by Rovinj's romanticism, not to mention the wine—have been known to leap from their cocktail table directly into the sea (60–100-kn pastas, 100–160-kn main dishes, Thu–Tue 12:00–15:00 & 18:00–22:00, closed Wed except in peak season, on the Old Town embankment past the harbor at Sv. Križa 38, tel. 052/813-186). If the food is priced too steeply for your budget, consider dropping by for a drink.

TRANSPORTATION CONNECTIONS

From Rovinj by Bus to: Pula (about hourly, 45 min), **Poreč** (6–8/day, 1 hr), **Rijeka** (6/day, 3.5 hrs), **Zagreb** (8/day, 5–8 hrs), **Split** (1/day, 11 hrs), **Dubrovnik** (nightly, 15 hrs), **Piran** (1/day July–Aug, otherwise transfer in Poreč and Portorož), **Ljubljana** (1/day in season, 5.5 hrs), **Venice** (1/day early in the morning, 8 hrs). Bus information: tel. 052/811-453.

Route Tips for Drivers

Just north of Rovinj, on the coastal road to Poreč, you'll drive briefly along the **Limski Fjord** (Limski Zaljev), a seven-mile-long inlet. Supposedly the famed pirate Captain Morgan was so enchanted by this canal that he retired here, founding the nearby namesake town of Mrgani. Local tour companies sell boat excursions into the fjord, which is used to raise much of the shellfish that's slurped down at local restaurants. It's mildly thrilling if you've never been to Norway, but not worth going out of your way to see. Along the fjordside road, you'll pass kiosks selling grappa (firewater, a.k.a. *rakija*), honey, and other homemade concoctions.

Pula

Pula (Pola in Italian) isn't quaint. Istria's biggest city is an industrial port town with traffic, smog, and sprawl...but it has the soul of a Roman poet. Between the shipyards, you'll discover some of the top Roman ruins in Croatia, including its stately amphitheater—a fully intact mini-Colosseum that marks the entry to a seedy Old Town with ancient temples, arches, and columns.

Strategically situated at the southern tip of the Istrian Peninsula, Pula has long been a center of industry, trade, and military might. In 177 B.C., the city became an important outpost of the Roman Empire. It was destroyed during the wars following Julius Caesar's death, and rebuilt by Emperor Augustus. Many of Pula's

most important Roman features—including its amphitheater—
date from this time (early first century A.D.). But as Rome fell, so
did Pula's fortunes. The town changed hands repeatedly, caught
in the crossfire of wars between greater powers—Byzantines,
Venetians, and Hapsburgs. After being devastated by Venice's
enemy Genoa in the 14th century, Pula gathered dust as a ghost
town...still militarily strategic, but otherwise abandoned.

In the mid-19th century, Italian unification forced the
Austrian Hapsburgs—whose navy had been based in Venice—to
look for a new home for their fleet. In 1856, they chose Pula, and
over the next 60 years, the population grew thirtyfold. (Despite
the many Roman and Venetian artifacts littering the Old Town,
most of modern Pula is essentially Austrian.) By the dawn of the
20th century, Pula's harbor bristled with Austro-Hungarian warships, and it had become the crucial link in a formidable line of
imperial defense that stretched from here to Montenegro. As one
of the most important port cities of the Austro-Hungarian Empire,
Pula attracted naval officers, royalty...and a young Irishman named
James Joyce on the verge of revolutionizing the literary world.

Today's Pula, while no longer quite so important, remains
a vibrant port town and the de facto capital of Istria. It offers
an enjoyably urban antidote to the rest of this stuck-in-the-past
peninsula.

Planning Your Time

Pula's sights, while top-notch, are quickly exhausted. Two or three
hours should do it: Visit the amphitheater, stroll the circular Old
Town, and maybe see a museum or two. As it's less than an hour
from Rovinj, there's no reason to spend the night.

ORIENTATION

(area code: 052)
Although it's a big city, the tourist's Pula is compact: the amphitheater and, beside it, the ring-shaped Old Town circling the base
of an old hilltop fortress. The Old Town's main square, the Forum,
dates back to Roman times.

Tourist Information

Pula's well-organized TI overlooks the Old Town's main square,
the Forum. It offers a free map and information on the town and
all of Istria (May–Oct daily 9:00–22:00, maybe until 24:00 in peak
season; Nov–April Mon–Sat 9:00–19:00, Sun 10:00–16:00; Forum
3, tel. 052/219-197, www.pulainfo.hr).

To **rent a car** in Pula, **Avis** (Riva 14, tel. 052/224-350) is
most central. **Europcar** (mobile 091-430-3040) and **Hertz** (tel.

052/210-868) are at the airport (3.5 miles northeast of the center; figure an 80-kn taxi trip).

Arrival in Pula

By Car: Pula is about a 45-minute drive south of Rovinj. Approaching town, follow *Centar* signs, then *Amfiteatar.* The easiest parking is right next to the can't-miss-it amphitheater (4 kn/hr).

By Bus: The bus station is just up the street and around the corner from the amphitheater. Exit the station to the left and walk up the busy street (ulica 43 Istarske Divizije) about 10 minutes, bearing left to the amphitheater.

By Train: The train station is a 10-minute walk from the amphitheater, near the waterfront (in the opposite direction from the Old Town). Walk with the coast on your right until you see the amphitheater.

SELF-GUIDED WALK

Welcome to Pula

This walk is divided between Pula's two most interesting attractions: The Roman amphitheater, and the circular Old Town. About an hour for each is plenty. More time can be spent sipping coffee *al fresco* or dipping into museums.

• *Begin at Pula's landmark...*

Amphitheater (Amfiteatar)

Of the dozens of amphitheaters left around Europe and North Africa by Roman engineers, Pula's is the sixth-largest (435 feet long and 345 feet wide), and one of the best-preserved any-where (20 kn, daily in summer 8:00–21:00, shorter hours off-season, 30-kn audioguide).

Go inside and explore the interior, climbing up the seats as you like. An "amphi-theater" is literally a "double theater"— imagine two theaters, without the back wall behind the stage, stuck together to maximize seating. Pula's amphitheater was built over several decades (first century A.D.) under the reign of three of Rome's top-tier emperors: Augustus, Claudius, and Vespasian. It was completed around 80 A.D., about the same time as the Colosseum in Rome. It remained in active use until the beginning of the fifth century, when gladiator battles were outlawed.

Notice that the amphitheater is built into the gentle incline of a hill. This economical plan, unusual for Roman amphitheaters, saved on the amount of stone needed, and provided a natural foundation for some of the seats (notice how the upper seats incorporate the slope). It may seem like the architects were cutting corners, but they had to raise the ground level at the lower end of the amphitheater to give it a level foundation. The four rectangular towers anchoring the amphitheater's facade are also unique. These once held wooden staircases for loading and unloading the amphitheater more quickly. At the top of each tower was a water reservoir, used for powering fountains that sprayed scents over the crowd to mask the stench of blood.

And there was plenty of blood. Imagine this scene in the days of the gladiators. More than 20,000 cheering fans from all social classes filled the seats. The Romans made these spectacles cheap—distracting commoners with a steady diet of mindless entertainment prevented discontent and rebellion. (Hmm...*American Idol,* anyone?) Canvas awnings rigged around the top of the amphitheater shaded many seats. The fans surrounded the "slaying field," which was covered with sand to absorb blood spilled by man and beast, making it easier to clean up after the fight. This sand *(harena)* gave the amphitheater its nickname...arena.

The amphitheater's "entertainers" were gladiators. Some gladiators were criminals, but most were prisoners of war from lands conquered by Rome, who dressed and used weapons according to their country of origin. A colorful parade kicked off the spectacle, followed by simulated fights with fake weapons. Then the real battles began. Often the fights represented stories from mythology or Greek or Roman history. Most ended in death for the loser. Sometimes gladiators fought exotic animals—gathered at great expense from far corners of the empire.

After the fall of Rome, builders looking for ready-cut stone picked apart structures like this one. Sometimes the scavengers were seeking the iron hooks that were used to connect the stone—in these oh so "Dark Ages," the method for smelting iron from ore was lost. Most of this amphitheater's interior structures—such as steps and seats—are now in the foundations and walls of Pula's buildings...not to mention palaces in Venice, across the Adriatic. In fact, in the late 16th century, the Venetians planned to take this entire amphitheater apart, stone by stone, and reassemble it on the island of Lido on the Venetian lagoon. A heroic Venetian senator—still much revered in Pula—convinced them to leave it where it is. Despite these and other threats, the amphitheater's exterior has been left gloriously intact. Today the amphitheater is still used to stage spectacles—from Pavarotti to Marilyn Manson—with seating for about 5,000 fans.

Amphorae

In museums, hotels, and restaurants all along the Croatian coast, you'll see amphorae. An amphora is a jug that was used to transport goods when the ancient Greeks ruled the seas, through about the seventh century B.C. These tall and skinny ceramic jugs—many of them lost in ancient shipwrecks—litter the Adriatic coastline.

Amphorae were used to transport oil, wine, and fish on long sea journeys. They're tapered at the bottom because they were stuck into sand (or placed on a stand) to keep them upright in transit. They also have a narrow neck at the top, often with two large handles. In fact, the name comes from the Greek *amphi pherein*, "to carry from both sides." The taller, skinnier amphorae were generally used for wine, while the fat, short ones were for olive oil. Because amphorae differ according to their purpose and nationality, archaeologists find them to be a particularly useful clue for dating shipwrecks and determining the country of origin of lost ships.

Before leaving, don't miss the museum exhibit (in the "subterranean hall," down the chute marked #17). This takes you down to the lower level of the amphitheater, where gladiators and animals were kept between fights. When the fight began, gladiators would charge up a chute and burst into the arena, like football players being introduced at the Super Bowl. As you go down the passage, you'll walk on a grate over an even lower tunnel. Pula is honeycombed with tunnels like these, originally used for defense. Inside, the exhibit—strangely dedicated to "viniculture and olive-oil production in Istria in the period of antiquity" instead of, you know, gladiators—shows off three huge presses for making olive oil, as well as a collection of amphorae (see sidebar).

• *From the amphitheater, it's a few minutes' walk to Pula's Old Town, where more Roman sights await.*

Old Town (Stari Grad)

• *Exit the amphitheater to the left and walk up the busy road (Amfiteatarska ulica) along the small wall, bearing right at the fork. When you reach the big park on your right, look for the little, car-sized...*

Town Model: Use this handy model of Pula to get oriented. Next to the amphitheater, the little water cannon spouting into the air marks where you're standing. The big star-shaped fortress on the hill is Fort Kaštel, designed by a French architect but dating from the Venetian era (1630). Read the Roman town plan into this model: At the center (on the hill) was the *castrum*, or military base. At the base of the hill (the far side from the amphitheater) was the forum, or town square. During Pula's Roman glory days, the hillsides around the *castrum* were blanketed with the villas of rich merchants. The Old Town, which clusters around the base of the fortress-topped hill, still features many fragments of the Roman period, as well as Pula's later occupiers. We'll take a counterclockwise stroll through this ancient zone.

• *Continue along the street, again bearing right (on Kandlerova ulica) at the fork. Notice the Roman ruins on your right. Just about any time someone wants to put up a new building, they find ruins like these. Work screeches to a halt while the valuable remains are excavated.*

After about three blocks, on your right-hand side, you'll see Pula's...

Cathedral (Katedrala): This church combines elements of the two big Italian influences on Pula: Roman and Venetian.

Dating from the fifth century, the Romanesque core of the church (notice the skinny, slit-like windows) marks the site of an early-Christian seafront settlement in Pula. The Venetian Baroque facade and bell tower are much more recent (early 18th century). Typical of the Venetian style, notice how far away the austere bell tower is from the body of the church. The bell tower's foundation is made of stones that were scavenged from the amphitheater.

• *Keep walking through the main pedestrian zone, past all the tacky souvenir shops. After a few more blocks, you emerge into the...*

Forum: Every Roman town had a forum, or main square. All these centuries later, Pula's Forum still serves the same function, and has kept the old Roman name. When replacing some of the old paving stones a couple of years back, workers discovered (to everyone's astonishment...or not) more Roman ruins. This delayed construction, as the ruins needed to be excavated, studied, and (likely) covered with glass. The square may still be torn up for your visit, but get as close as you can to the center of the square and take a look around.

Two important buildings front the north end of the square, where you entered. The smaller building (on the left, with the columns) is the first-century A.D. Roman **Temple of Augustus** (Augustov Hram). Built during the reign of, and dedicated to,

Augustus Caesar, this temple took a direct hit from an Allied bomb in World War II, but was rebuilt after the war. It's the only one remaining of three such temples that once lined this side of the square. As Rome fell, its long-subjugated subjects in Pula had little respect for the former empire's symbols, and many temples didn't survive. Others were put to new use: Part of an adjacent temple (likely dedicated to Diana) was incorporated into the bigger building on the right, Pula's medieval **Town Hall** (Gradska Palača). (You can still see Roman fragments embedded in the back of this building.) The Town Hall encapsulates many centuries of Pula architecture: Romanesque core, Gothic reliefs, Renaissance porch, Baroque windows...and a few Roman bits and pieces.

• *Consider dropping by the TI on this square before continuing our circular stroll down the main drag, Sergijevaca. After one block, detour a block to the right to the next two sights, which are situated in a strangely undeveloped field. At the near end of the field, hiding near the entryway of an apartment block, find the...*

Roman Floor Mosaic (Rimski Mozaik): Uncovered by locals who were cleaning up from World War II bombs, this third-century floor was carefully excavated and cleaned up for display right where it was laid nearly two millennia ago. (Notice that the Roman floor level was about six feet below today's.) The centerpiece of the mosaic depicts the punishment of Dirce. According to the ancient Greek legend, King Lykos of Thebes was bewitched by Dirce and abandoned his pregnant queen. The queen gave birth to twin boys (depicted in this mosaic), who grew up to kill their deadbeat dad and tie Dirce to the horns of a bull to be bashed against a mountain. This same story is famously depicted in the twisty *Toro Farnese* sculpture partly carved by Michelangelo (on display in Naples' Archaeological Museum).

• *Now continue to the little chapel at the far end of the field.*

Basilica of St. Mary Formosa (Kapela Marije Formoze): We've seen plenty of Roman and Venetian bric-a-brac, but this chapel survives from the time of another Istrian occupier: Byzantium. For about 170 years after Rome fell (the sixth and seventh centuries A.D.), this region came under the control of the Byzantine Empire, and was ruled from Ravenna (across the Adriatic, south of Venice). Much of this field was once occupied by a vast, richly decorated basilica. This lonely chapel is all that's left, but it still gives a feel for the architecture of that era—including the Greek cross floor plan (with four equal arms) and heavy brick vaulting.

• *Back on the main drag (Sergijevaca), continue a few more blocks through Pula's most colorful and most touristy neighborhood, until you arrive at the...*

Arch of Sergius (Slavoluk Sergijevaca): This Roman trium-
phal arch, built under the Emperor Titus, honors Lucius Sergius
Lepidus, who fought on the side of
Augustus in the civil wars that swept
the empire after Julius Caesar's
assassination. Statues of Lucius and
two of his relatives once stood on
the three blocks at the top of the
arch. (Squint to see the *Sergivs* name
on each block.)

• *Before going under the arch, look
to your left to see a famous Irishman
appreciating the view from the terrace
of...*

Café Uliks: In October of 1904,
a young writer named James Joyce moved from Dublin to Pula

with his girlfriend, Nora Barnacle. By day,
he taught English to Austro-Hungarian
naval officers at the Berlitz language school
(in the building marked by the plaque). By
night, he imagined strolling through his
hometown as he penned short stories that
would eventually become the collection
Dubliners. But James and Nora quickly
grew bored with little Pula, and moved to
Trieste in March of 1905. Even so, Pula
remains proud of its literary connections.

• *Now pass through the arch, into a square
next to remains of the...*

Town Wall: In the pavement, you see the footprint of what
was formerly a much more elaborate entrance gate. To your left are
remains of the city wall, with an inviting path up top. If you're not
short on time, consider a detour to a lively nearby square: Continue
straight ahead from the arch for two bustling blocks (up in-love-
with-life Flanatička ulica, brimming with shops and cafés), and
you'll reach **National Square** (Nardoni Trg)—home to the 19th-
century market hall.

• *Back at the town wall, with the arch at your back, take a left and
walk under the leafy canopy next to the wall. Keep an eye out (mostly on
your left, along the wall) for more Roman remains. Among these are the
Twin Gates (Porta Gemina), marking the entrance to a garden that's
home to the **Archaeological Museum of Istria** (listed under "Sights").
With more time, you can also consider a trip to the hilltop fortress, **Fort
Kaštel**. Otherwise, we've completed our circular tour—the amphitheater is just around the corner.*

SIGHTS

Archaeological Museum of Istria (Arheološki Muzej Istre)—If Pula's many ruins intrigue you, here's the place to expand your knowledge. This museum, over a century old, shows off some of what you've seen in the streets, plus lots more—stone monuments, classical statues, ancient pottery...you name it (12 kn; summer Mon–Sat 9:00–12:00, Sun 10:00–15:00; winter Mon–Fri 9:00–15:00, closed Sat–Sun; Carrarina 3, tel. 052/218-603, www.mdc.hr/pula).

On the hill behind the museum is its highlight, the remains of a **Roman Theater** (Rimsko Kazalište). Part of the stage is still intact, along with the semicircle of stone seats (some of which are still engraved with the names of the wealthy theatergoers who once sat there). This was the smaller of the two theaters in Roman Pula; the second was south of the center (and is no longer intact today).

Fort Kaštel—For a bird's-eye view over the town, head up to its centerpiece fortress. This deserted-feeling place, hosting the Historical Museum of Istria, is worth visiting only for the chance to wander the ramparts. While neither the museum nor the fortress is worth the hike up here, it's a good way to kill some extra time in Pula, and sample the views over the town and amphitheater (various trails lead up from the streets below).

TRANSPORTATION CONNECTIONS

By Bus from Pula to: Rovinj (about hourly, 45 min), **Poreč** (12/day, 1 hr), **Opatija** (almost hourly, 2 hrs), **Rijeka** (almost hourly, 2.5 hrs), **Zagreb** (almost hourly, 3.75–6 hrs), **Dubrovnik** (nightly, 14 hrs), **Piran** (1/day July–Aug only, 3.5 hrs), **Portorož** near Piran (2/day July–Aug, 1/day off-season, 3.5 hrs), **Venice** (1/day, 5 hrs). Note that bus connections are more frequent on weekdays (fewer departures Sat–Sun).

By Train to: Zagreb (3/day, 6 hrs, transfer in Rijeka; in summer also 1 night train with very early arrival in Zagreb, 8 hrs), **Ljubljana** (1/day, 6 hrs, transfer in Rijeka; plus 1 more Mon–Fri, 5.5 hrs).

The Brijuni Islands

The Brijuni Islands (bree-YOO-nee, Brioni in Italian)—an archipelago of 14 islands just offshore from the southern tip of the Istrian Peninsula—were a favorite haunt of Maršal Tito, the leader of communist Yugoslavia. The main island, called Great Brijuni (Veli Brijun), was where Tito liked to show off the natural wonders of his beloved Yugoslavia to visiting dignitaries and world leaders.

Brijuni: Center of the Non-Aligned World

Many visitors to the former Yugoslavia mistakenly assume this country was part of the Soviet Bloc. It most decidedly wasn't. While the rest of "Eastern Europe" was liberated by the Soviets at the end of World War II, Yugoslavia's own, homegrown Partisan army forced the Nazis out themselves. This allowed the country—and its new leader, the war hero Maršal Tito—a certain degree of self-determination following the war. While the new Yugoslavia was socialist, it was not Soviet socialism. After formally breaking ties with Moscow in 1948, Tito steered his country toward a "Third Way" between the strict and stifling communism of the East, and the capitalist free-for-all of the West. (For more on Tito's system, see the Understanding Yugoslavia chapter on page 436.)

Many other countries also didn't quite fit into the easy East-versus-West dichotomy embraced by the US, USSR, and Europe. On July 19, 1956, the Brijuni Declaration—signed by Tito, Jawaharlal Nehru of India, and Abdel Nasser of Egypt—created the Non-Aligned Movement (NAM). Members recognized each other's sovereignty and respected each leader's right to handle domestic issues however he or she saw fit.

As Tito's international prominence grew, the list of visitors to his Brijuni Islands hideaway began to read like a Who's Who of post-WWII world leaders. In addition to Nehru and Nasser, Tito hosted Haile Selassie (Ethiopia), Yasser Arafat (Palestinian States), Fidel Castro (Cuba), Indira Gandhi (India), Muammar al-Gaddafi (Libya), Queen Elizabeth II (Great Britain), Willy Brandt (West Germany), Leonid Brezhnev (USSR)...not to mention Elizabeth Taylor (US) and Sophia Loren (Italy).

In principle, the NAM was envisioned to compete with NATO and the Warsaw Pact. But as the world's politics have changed, many NAM members are now closely allied with other, more powerful nations. And when Yugoslavia broke up, the countries that emerged preferred to join NATO and the EU.

So whatever happened to the rest of the NAM? It's still going strong, encompassing virtually all of Africa, the Middle East, and Southeast Asia. While the EU and the US wrestle for bragging rights as the world's new superpower, the NAM represents 55 percent of the world's population. In 2006, Fidel Castro hosted the most recent NAM summit in Havana.

Today the island is a national park that combines serene natural beauty with quirky Yugoslav sights—offering a strange but enjoyable time capsule of the Tito years.

As you'll see from the remains of previous occupants (Romans, Byzantines, Venetians, Austrians—even dinosaurs), Tito wasn't the first to fall in love with Brijuni. Its first tourist boom came at the turn of the 20th century, when Austrian entrepreneur Paul Kupelwieser developed Brijuni into a world-class health resort. Between the World Wars, it hosted many notables, from Douglas Fairbanks and John Rockefeller to Richard Strauss and Hirohito. But when Tito took power, he claimed the islands for himself, making Brijuni his summer residence from 1949 until 1979. During this time, the island hosted a steady stream of VIP visitors from the East, West, and the non-aligned world (see sidebar on previous page). Just three years after Tito's death, in October of 1983, Brijuni opened to the public as a national park.

Getting There: You can only get to Great Brijuni Island on one of the national park's boats. These depart from the town of Fažana, five miles north of Pula and 20 miles south of Rovinj. From Rovinj, drive southeast to Bale, where you'll get on the *ipsilon* highway and continue south. In Vodnjan, watch for the easy-to-miss turnoff (on the right) marked for Fažana and Brijuni. Once in Fažana, follow brown *Brijuni* signs and park along the water (confirm with park ticket office that your parking spot is OK).

Cost and Information: The price varies depending on the time of year: July–Aug-180 kn, June and Sept-170 kn, April–May and Oct-140 kn, Nov–March-100 kn; includes entry to the park, the boat to the island, and a guide (see "English Tour," below). Tel. 052/525-882, www.brijuni.hr, izleti@brijuni.hr.

Hours: From April through October, the first boat departure is at 6:40 and the last trip is at 21:45 (last return from Brijuni at 23:00). The number of departures to the island varies with the time of year: July–Aug about hourly, 14/day; May–June and Sept 12/day; April and Oct 10/day. Sporadic boats run in the off-season (roughly Nov–Easter), but they're intended for people who live on the island.

English Tour: You're required to go to the island with a four-hour guided tour, much of which is spent on a little tourist train. The only English-language tour usually departs Fažana daily at 11:30. It's important to call ahead to confirm the schedule and reserve a space on the tour (call at least a day before, or three days ahead in peak season, tel. 052/525-882).

If you can't make it on the English tour, you're welcome to join any tour you like (Croatian, German, Italian, etc.). While it's possible to slip away from your group and explore the island on your own, park officials discourage it. (But, since hotel guests on the island can move about freely, it's generally no problem.) Staying with the tour for most of the trip is wise in any event, as there's lots of ground to cover in a limited amount of time. It's possible to rent bikes at the hotel where the boat puts in. You're technically required to take the same boat back with the rest of your tour, but this isn't closely monitored.

Visiting the Island: Great Brijuni Island can be visited only with a tour. After a 15-minute crossing from the mainland town of Fažana, visitors arrive at the island's main harbor, a hub of activity and the site of its two hotels (Neptun-Istra Hotel and Karmen Hotel, Sb-€95–105, Db-€164–178 in peak season, www.brijuni.hr). Outside of this area, the island is largely undeveloped, with just a few tourist facilities and houses of people who live here. There are virtually no cars—most people get around by bike, golf cart, or the little tourist train you'll board to begin your tour. As you spin around the island, you'll enjoy views over its endlessly twisty coast, with cove after tranquil cove. Your guide will impart both dry facts and eye-rolling legends while you putter past several intriguing sights, periodically giving you a chance to get off the train and explore a few of them up close.

The tour's highlight is the **"Tito on Brijuni"** exhibit. Dating from 1984—four years after his death, and before the end of Yugoslavia—this exhibit celebrates the cult of personality surrounding the head of this now-deceased nation. The museum (with English descriptions) features countless photos of Tito in every Brijuni context imaginable—strolling, sunbathing, skeet shooting, schmoozing with world leaders and movie stars, inspecting military officers, playing with camels given to him by Muammar al-Gaddafi, and so on. Smaller side-exhibits include a taxidermy collection of exotic animals given to Tito by foreign leaders from around the world, and photos of Paul Kupelwieser, the Austrian magnate who put Brijuni on the tourist map.

This reverent approach to Tito may lead you to ask: Do people still like Tito? The short answer is...yes. While his strongman tactics in the early days of his presidency could be downright ruthless, the eventual balance he struck between communism and capitalism, and between the competing interests of his ethnically diverse nation, led to this region's most stable and prosperous era. More than a quarter-century after his death, and a decade after the recent wars, many former Yugoslavs increasingly respect and appreciate Tito's efforts to make a go of it. Pictures of Tito still hang in the living rooms of many Croatians' homes.

Another high point of the island tour is the **safari,** featuring a diverse menagerie of animals brought here for Tito as gifts by visiting heads of state. Because many of the non-aligned nations are in Africa, Asia, or other non-European regions, some of these beasts are particularly exotic. Aside from the Istrian ox and Istria's trademark goat, you'll see llamas, camels, Somali sheep, Shetland ponies, chamois, and more. Your train may stop for a visit with Sony and Lanka, a pair of Indian elephants given to Tito by Indira Gandhi, the former prime minister of India. There once were camels, cheetahs, ostriches, monkeys, bears, and bobcats as well, but most of these have gone to the great non-aligned safari in the sky, and their bodies are now preserved at the "Tito on Brijuni" exhibit (described previously).

Other attractions you may see on Brijuni: an ancient, gnarled olive tree supposedly dating from the fourth century; the remains of a first-century Roman *villa rustica*, or country estate; the ruined street plan of a Byzantine fort; a 15th-century Gothic church with an exhibit on frescoes and Glagolitic (early Croatian) script; a Venetian summer house that hosts an archaeology museum; an Austro-Hungarian naval fort (Brijuni was strategically important back when Pula was Austria's main naval base); and footprints left by a dinosaur who vacationed here 120 million years before Tito.

Birders can look for some of the 250 avian species that live on the island in the summer. Gardeners may spot some exotic, non-native plant species (more gifts, to go along with all those animals), such as Australian eucalyptus. And Republicans can drool over the golf course, a reminder that Brijuni is attempting to cultivate a ritzy image. In fact, the fashion company that shares the islands' Italian name (Brioni)—a favorite suit-maker of Donald Trump and James Bond—is developing a super-exclusive polo tournament here. Your tour's lengthy stop at the bar/gift shop is yet another indication that, while some remember Tito fondly, good ol' capitalism is here to stay.

Poreč

When you tell Europeans you're going to Istria, they say, "Ah, you must go to Poreč!" Poreč (poh-RETCH, Parenzo in Italian), the tourist capital of the Istrian coast, is the kind of resort where locals brag about how many hotel beds it has, rather than how many museums, churches, or gelato stands are packed into its Old Town. They're also proud to have more than their share of "blue-flag beaches" (which they call *lagunas*)—meaning that the water is crystal-clear for swimming. Finally, Poreč has won several "Croatia's cleanest city" contests. None of this makes for very compelling sightseeing, but...there you go.

Despite the town's appeal to Europeans, most American visitors find Poreč too big to be charming, but too small to be exciting. Its only real sight is the basilica, with its exquisite mosaics. Beyond that, it's mostly interesting as a case study on how Germans like to vacation: Set up camp for a week at a distant resort hotel, bake in the sun, and occasionally trek into the Old Town for dinner. Think of it as the Croatian Acapulco.

Planning Your Time

For the typical speedy American visitor, spending time in Rovinj, Piran, Pula, or the Istrian interior is more satisfying. If you're still curious, see Poreč en route or as a day trip: Zip in, stroll the Old Town, ogle the mosaics in the basilica, then move on. Despite its many hotels, Poreč lacks soul—I prefer sleeping elsewhere.

ORIENTATION

(area code: 052)

Like so many Croatian coastal towns, the Old Town of Poreč is on a peninsula. Surrounding it are miles of hotels-and-concrete sprawl. Traffic into the city funnels into Zagrebačka street, which passes the TI and ends at the spacious square named Trg Slobode. From there, Decumanis street marches right through the middle of the Old Town.

Tourist Information

Visit the TI to pick up the information booklet, sightseeing guide, and city map (July–Aug daily 8:00–21:00, progressively shorter hours off-season until winter Mon–Sat 8:00–16:00, closed Sun, a few steps from Trg Slobode at Zagrebačka 9, tel. 052/451-293).

Arrival in Poreč

The bus station and big parking lot straddle the base of the Old Town.

Drivers follow *Centar* and *Parking* signs to reach the big lot nearest the Old Town (take ticket as you enter and bring it with you; when leaving Poreč, pay at the kiosk before returning to your car, then wave paid ticket at exit to open gate). From the lot, walk uphill past the parking kiosk and the market until you reach big Zagrebačka boulevard, with the grass median. Turn right and continue up Zagrebačka, passing the TI (on your right) en route to Trg Slobode and the Old Town.

The **bus** station is at the other end of the Old Town. Exit the station to the right and go through the little park to the seafront and Old Town. Just up the hill is Trg Slobode and the nearby TI.

SIGHTS

▲Euphrasian Basilica (Eufrazijeva Bazilika)—This sixth-century church is a gold mine for fans of Byzantine mosaics. The otherwise dull interior is domi-nated by the mosaics in the apse surrounding the main altar. The top row depicts Jesus surrounded by the 12 apostles, the medal-lions around the arch celebrate 12 female martyrs, and front and cen-ter are Mary and Jesus surrounded by angels and martyrs—including Bishop Euphrasius, holding his

namesake basilica in his arms (second from left). These date from the 170-year period after the fall of Rome (roughly 530–700 A.D.), when Istria was part of the Byzantine Empire and was ruled from Ravenna (near Venice, across the Adriatic). The more recent (13th-century) canopy over the altar was inspired by the one in St. Mark's Basilica in Venice. Don't miss another set of mosaics in the floor just inside the door (free entry, open long hours daily, no shorts, a block off the Old Town's main drag on—where else?—Eufrazijava street).

For more mosaics, drop into the attached **museum,** with sev-eral mosaic fragments scattered around two floors (10 kn, daily 10:00–17:00). Or climb the **bell tower** to get a bird's-eye view of Poreč for 10 kn.

TRANSPORTATION CONNECTIONS

From Poreč by Bus to: Rovinj (6–8/day, 1 hr), **Pula** (12/day, 1 hr), **Piran** (3/day July–Aug only), **Portorož** near Piran (3/day July–Aug, 1/day off-season).

Hill Towns of the Istrian Interior

Most tourists in Croatia focus on the coast. But after a while, all those seafront villages begin to feel the same. To break up the monotony, head for the hinterland. Some of the best bits of the Croatian interior lie just a short drive inland from Rovinj. Dotted with picturesque hill towns, speckled with wineries and olive-oil farms, embedded with precious truffles, and grooved by meander-ing rural roads, the Istrian interior is worth a visit. Tucked below, between, and on top of the many hills are characteristic stone-walled villages, designed to stay cool in summer and warm in winter. The local tourist board is carefully manicuring this region's image as *the* hot new spot to find hill towns, backcountry drives, and a relaxed and relaxing lifestyle. It's working. These days, some travelers even mention Istria in the same breath as Tuscany or Provence...but maybe that's just the *malvazija* wine and truffle oil talking.

Poking around and exploring on your own is a good option here. But for a more efficiently organized visit, I've covered the

basics below. Start with the two top-notch hill towns: the tiny, rugged, relatively un-trampled artists' colony of Grožnjan; and the popular Motovun, with sweeping views. A third hill town, tiny but touristy Hum, is a fine way to round out your day with a longer drive.

As you explore, you'll see frequent signs for wineries, olive-oil producers, and truffle shops. (But remember that it's illegal to drive in Croatia if you've had any alcohol at all—bring a designated driver, or simply buy some wine to have back at your hotel.) There's an itinerary for every interest, and the Istrian tourist board publishes a stack of well-produced brochures on every topic you can imagine (available at local TIs). One recent trend in Istria is the emergence of *agroturizam*s. Like Italian *agritrismos* or Slovenian tourist farms, these are working farms that try to involve tourists in a meaningful way—sometimes just for a meal or overnight stay, but occasionally actually participating in the daily workings of the farm. For more information, pick up the free brochure (available locally), or visit www.istra.hr.

Getting Around the Istrian Interior

By Public Transportation: While it's possible to see some parts of inland Istria by public transportation, connections are frustrating. The large hill town of Pazin is the region's transit hub, with buses to Rovinj, Pula, Poreč, and Motovun—but not Grožnjan, Hum, or Brtonigla.

By Car: The region is ideal by car. For a full day of hill town-hopping in the Istrian interior, follow my suggested clockwise route. Though I've described the trip starting from Rovinj, you can begin wherever you like.

From Rovinj, take the fast *ipsilon* highway north to Buje (between the *ipsilon* and Buje, consider stopping for a meal in **Brtonigla**). From Buje, continue through Krasica and watch for the turn-off to take the twisty back road to **Grožnjan.** After Grožnjan, wind down to the mercifully flat and straight road (#44) that follows the Mirna River Valley eastward, to Motovun (well-signed off the main road). Consider dropping by the Zigante truffle shop in **Livade** before leaving the main road and winding around back of Motovun's hill to find the corkscrew road up. After seeing **Motovun,** you can head back to your home base along the main valley road. Or, with more time, continue farther east to **Hum** (follow the main valley road east to Buzet, then to Roč, then look for the turn-off on the right to Hum, along the **Glagolitic Lane**). From Hum, you're very close to the northeast branch of the *ipsilon* highway (A-8), which leads right back to Rovinj (via Pazin). (Note that Hum is also just a few miles from the Učka Tunnel to Rijeka, if you're continuing to the east.)

While you'll traverse some slow and windy roads, this entire trip is quick—you could do the entire circle (including Hum) without stops in less than three hours.

This route is just a rough framework. Venture off it. Run down leads from locals. Follow intriguing signs to wine-tastings, restaurants, and *agroturizam*s. Sniff out some truffles in the Motovun Forest. You will see lots of other tourists, but this area isn't Tuscany...yet. There may just be some gems in the Istrian interior waiting for you to discover.

Brtonigla

Brtonigla (bur-toh-NEEG-lah, Verteneglio in Italian, literally "black soil") is a tiny wine village surrounded by vineyards. It's a bit closer to the sea than the other hill towns in this chapter, and sits above gentle slopes rather than a dramatic hilltop. But this deserted-feeling little burg is a welcome antidote to the tourist crowds on the coast, and it's home to a luxurious hotel/restaurant and a well-regarded local eatery. Still, if you're not eating or sleeping here, give it a pass.

Getting There: Brtonigla is well-marked off the main *ipsilon* highway (coming north from Rovinj, but still south of Buje). Once in town, you'll find just a handful of haphazard streets.

SLEEPING AND EATING

In Brtonigla
$$$ San Rocco Hotel and Restaurant is a family-run hotel suitable for a serious splurge. A few years ago this was the abandoned shell of a traditional Istrian house; now, after an extensive renovation partly subsidized by the local government, it's a cushy and

elegant hotel with traditional beams-and-stone decor and all the modern amenities. With 12 rooms, an outdoor pool, a sauna, and distant views of the Adriatic, it's a welcoming retreat. "Premier" rooms come with views or Jacuzzi tubs, but the simpler "classic" rooms are plenty comfortable (April–Sept: "classic" Db-€133, "premier" Db-€149; Oct–March: "classic" Db-€123, "premier" Db-€133; Sb-35 percent less, no extra charge for 1-night stays, air-con, elevator, Srednja ulica 2, tel. 052/725-000, fax 052/725-026, www .san-rocco.hr, info@san-rocco.hr, Fernetich family). Its **restaurant**—open to guests and non-guests alike—features traditional Istrian cuisine in a dressy setting (100-kn mains, 200-kn truffle splurges, 300–500-kn fixed-price meals, daily 13:00–24:00).

Konoba Astarea, a restaurant down the street and around the corner, is a local favorite for traditional, take-your-time Istrian cuisine with a focus on fish and lamb. Anton Kernjus and his staff don't print an English menu, but they'll explain your options. Choose between the warmly cluttered, borderline-kitschy dining room huddled around an open fire, or the terrace with faraway sea views. It's smart to reserve ahead (60–100-kn meals, daily 11:00–23:00, tel. 052/774-384).

Grožnjan

Grožnjan (grohzh-NYAHN, Grisignana in Italian) is your trapped-in-a-time-warp Istrian hill town. Its setting, artfully balanced on the tip of a vine-and-olive-tree-covered promontory, is pleasing, if not thrilling. The time-passed character of its sleepy lanes invites you to get lost and leave your itinerary on your dashboard. Not long ago, Grožnjan was virtually forgotten. But now several artists have taken up residence here, keeping it Old World but with a spiffed-up, bohemian ambience.

Grožnjan has virtually no "sights," but it's a delightful place to go for a stroll. The town church's bell tower is its only landmark. To get the lay of the land, take a 10-minute town wander: Facing the church facade, go left (past the wine-and-truffle bar) and loop

clockwise through town, past the shaded square with Café Pintur, then the Italian Cultural Center and Caffè Bar Arta. Don't worry about addresses or finding a particular place; whether you want to or not, you'll find yourself walking in circles, and quickly see what there is to see. Instead, let your pulse slow and enjoy being a castaway on this isolated, tranquil hilltop. If gallery-browsing is your idea of fun, this is the place.

Tourist Information: The humble TI is in the center of town (generally open Sat–Sun 10:00–12:00 & 17:00–19:00, closed Mon–Fri, maybe longer in peak season, less off-season, Gorjan 3, tel. 052/776-131, www.groznjan-grisignana.hr and www.tz -groznjan.hr).

Arrival in Grožnjan: All roads lead to the convenient parking lot, a few steps from the traffic-free village.

SLEEPING AND EATING

In Grožnjan

$ Café Pintur, a nondescript restaurant on a cozy Grožnjan square just downhill from the church, rents four small but comfy top-floor rooms. The Černeka family doesn't speak much English, but that's part of the charm (Sb-200 kn, Db-300 kn, about 20 kn less for more than 2 nights; includes breakfast Sept–May, or 25 kn extra June–Aug; cash only, no elevator, Mate Gorjana 9, mobile 098-586-188, tel. & fax 052/776-397, ivan.cerneka@pu.t-com.hr).

Café Pintur's restaurant, open long hours daily in summer, serves up basic pasta and grilled meats. The only other restaurant in town, **Bastia,** is a bit bigger, with a similar menu and hours (across the square, and sharing a leafy terrace with Pintur). For a scenic drink, try **Caffè Bar Arta,** clinging to the cliff near the Italian Cultural Center (closed Mon, Trg Karner 3).

Enoteka Zigante, a branch of the Istrian truffle empire (see page 126), has a small wine-and-truffle bar offering a more genteel nibbling experience (wine-tastings and light dishes such as cheese and *pršut,* Mon–Thu 10:00–20:00, Fri–Sun 10:00–21:00, until 22:00 in peak season, ulica Gorjan 5, tel. 052/721-998).

Since Grožnjan has such limited dining options, consider venturing to a countryside *agroturizam* for dinner. Or head to the restaurants in Brtonigla or Motovun.

Motovun

Dramatically situated high above vineyards and a truffle-filled forest, Motovun (moh-toh-VOON, Montona in Italian) is the best-known and most-touristed of the Istrian hill towns. And for good reason: Its hilltop Old Town is particularly evocative, with a colorful old church and a rampart walk with spine-tingling vistas across the entire region. It's hard to believe that race-car driver Mario Andretti was born in such a tranquil little traffic-free hamlet. Today Motovun's quiet lanes are shared by locals, tourists, and artists—who, as in Grožnjan, began settling here a generation ago, when it was nearly deserted.

ORIENTATION

(area code: 052)

Motovun is the steepest hill town listed in this chapter. Most every-thing of interest to tourists is huddled around its tippy-top. The one

and only gate into town deposits you at the main square, with the church on your left and Hotel Kaštel on the right. From there, you're just about two blocks in every direction from a sheer drop-off. This hilltop zone is circled by an old rampart that today offers Motovun's most scenic stroll.

Tourist Information

Motovun doesn't have an official TI, but the gang at Hotel Kaštel dispenses tourist information. During the day, you can drop into their travel agency on the main square, called Istria Magica (Mon–Sat 7:00–16:00, closed Sun, to the right as you face Hotel Kaštel, at Trg Andrea Antico 8, tel. 052/681-750); at other times, ask at the hotel reception desk (listed under "Sleeping" later in this section).

Arrival in Motovun

Motovun's striking hilltop setting comes with a catch: Visitors usually have to hike up part of the way. A steep, twisty road con-nects the base of the hill with the Old Town up top. If it's not too crowded, drive as far up this road as possible until you're directed to park in the lot partway up (near the lower church, a steep 15-min uphill walk to the main square, 5 kn/hr). In busier peak times, this lot might be full, so you may have to wait a few minutes for a car to leave; or you can park in the big lot at the foot of the hill and walk all the way up (during very busy times, such as the Film Festival, a shuttle bus may be taking visitors up the hill). If you're staying at Hotel Kaštel, you should be allowed to drive up much closer to town—ask when you reserve.

SELF-GUIDED WALK

Welcome to Motovun

The following commentary will bring some meaning to your Motovun hilltop stroll.

As you pass below the town's wall, you'll go through the first of two **defensive gateways.** Inside this passage, notice the various insignias from Motovun's history lining the walls—look for the Venetian lion, the Latin family tombstone, and the seal of Motovun (with five towers being watched over by an angel). The area above the gate was a storehouse for weapons in the 15th century, when Motovun first flourished.

Emerging from the gateway, you're greeted by sweeping views of the valley below on your right-hand side. Just up and to the left, you'll find the second defensive gateway, which leads to the heart of the **Old Town.**

To your left as you come through the main gate is the yellow town church, **St. Stephen's.** While unassuming from the out-

side, this austere house of worship has an impressive pedigree: It was designed by the famous Venetian architect Andrea Palladio (1508–1580), who greatly influenced the Neoclassical architecture of Washington, DC. The interior is a little gloomy but refreshingly lived-in—used more by locals than by tourists. On the left, notice a painting of the heart of Jesus, its eyes following you around the church (free, paltry 1-kn English pamphlet, generally open daily 10:00–18:00 and during frequent services).

As you stand on the square in front of the church, imagine Motovun during its annual **film festival,** when it's filled with 20,000 movie-lovers from throughout the region and around the world—often including a minor celebrity or two. This square fills to capacity, and films are projected on a giant screen at the far end (generally late July or early Aug, www.motovunfilmfestival.com).

At the other end of the square is a leafy little piazza dominated by the big **Hotel Kaštel**—the main industry in town. In addition to its rooms and restaurant, Hotel Kaštel serves as the town TI and base of operations during the annual film festival, and even offers

truffle-finding excursions for tourists in the fall (about €100/person).

From Hotel Kaštel, follow the signs to the **ram- parts.** Take the 10-minute stroll around the Old Town on these fortifications. As you breathe in the stunning panorama, notice that well-defended Motovun has been fortified three times—two layers of wall up top, and a third down below.

SLEEPING

In Motovun

$$ Hotel Kaštel, the only big-hotel-in-a-small-town option in the Istrian interior, is a pleasant family-run place dominating Motovun's hilltop. The 30 rooms (most of which have views) are colorful and comfortable, and the location couldn't be better in this little burg. This is where bigwigs in town for the local film festival call home—ask the staff about recent star-sightings (July–Aug: Sb-€49, Db-€82, Tb-€76; June and Sept: Sb-€45, Db-€76, Tb-€69; May and Oct: Sb-€43, Db-€69, Tb-€64; pricier apartments available, cheaper off-season, 20 percent more for 1- or 2-night stays, no elevator, Trg Andrea Antico 7, tel. 052/681-607, fax 052/681-652, www.hotel-kastel-motovun.hr, info@hotel-kastel-motovun.hr).

$$ Pension Miro, just below and across from the gate to the main square, is a low-key, simply furnished, no-frills guest house renting 10 rooms (six have private bathrooms, while four top-floor rooms share one bathroom). As the guest house is operated by a local travel agency, it has no real reception—so you're on your own (when you reserve, clearly communicate your arrival time). There's no breakfast, but you're free to use the kitchen and the view terrace (D with shared bathroom-400 kn for 1 night, 370 kn for 2 nights, 300 kn for 3 or more nights; Db-430 kn for 1 night, 400 kn for 2 nights, 340 kn for 3 or more nights; singles pay about 250 kn, cash only, Kanal 10, tel. 052/681-970, fax 052/616-409, mobile 091-587-2847, www.montonatours.com, info@montonatours.com). Since this agency also rents other rooms and apartments throughout the region, be very clear on the location before you book.

$ At Bella Vista, on the steep road leading up to town, the Kotiga family rents two apartments with cute decor and balconies that offer sweeping views across the countryside (Db-€40, cash only, on the way up to the main gate at Kanal 27, tel. & fax 052/681-724, mobile 098-219-607, www.apartmani-motovun.com).

EATING

In Motovun

Any of these three restaurants, in the center of Motovun, are fine for a straightforward meal: **Barbakan Konoba** (on the left just before the main gate into the Old Town, Wed–Sun 12:30–15:30 & 18:30–23:30, closed Mon–Tue); **Taverna** (actually inside the main gate itself, on the right; Thu–Tue 12:00–21:00, closed Wed); or the restaurant at **Hotel Kaštel** (on the main square—also listed under

Truffle Mania

A mysterious fungus with a pungent, unmistakable flavor has been all the rage in Istria for the last decade or so. Called *tartufi* in both Croatian and Italian, these precious tubers have been gathered here since Roman times, and were favored by the region's Venetian and Austrian rulers. More recently, local peasants ate them as a substitute for meat (often mixed with polenta) during the lean days after World War II.

In 1999, Istrian Giancarlo Zigante discovered a nearly three-pound white truffle. In addition to making Giancarlo Zigante a very wealthy man (see "Zigante Tartufi" listing, below), this giant truffle legitimized Istria on the world truffle scene. Today, Istria is giving France's Provence and Italy's Piedmont a run for their money in truffle production. Most of Istria's truffles are concentrated in the Motovun Forest, the damp, oak-tree-filled terrain surrounding Motovun, Livade, and Buzet.

A truffle is a tuber that grows entirely underground, usually at a depth of eight inches near the roots of oak trees. Since no part of the plant grows aboveground, they're particularly difficult to find...and, therefore, valuable. Traditionally, Istrian truffle-gatherers use specially trained dogs to find truffles. This is most productive at night, when the darkness forces the dog to rely more on its sense of smell rather than sight. Once a truffle is located, the gatherer digs it up with a specially designed tool that looks like a wooden handgun with a long, narrow shovel at the end. There are two general types of truffles: white (more

"Sleeping," above; daily 7:00–10:00 & 13:00–15:00 & 19:00–21:00). For a truffle feast, head across the valley to **Zigante** in Livade (described next).

Near Motovun, in Livade: Zigante Tartufi

The little crossroads village of Livade, sitting in the valley facing the back of Motovun's hill, is home to the first and last name in Istrian truffles. In 1999, Giancarlo Zigante unearthed the biggest white truffle the world had ever seen—2.9 pounds, as verified by *The Guinness Book of World Records*. This single hunk of fungus—now revered as if a religious relic—kicked off a truffle craze that continues in Istria today (see sidebar, above). If you're a truffle connoisseur, or just curious, make a pilgrimage to this truffle mecca.

Zigante's large facility here is divided into two parts:

The **Zigante Tartufi shop** offers a big room with shelves upon shelves of both fresh and packaged truffle products (plus local wines, olive oils, brandies, and more). There's also a little tasting

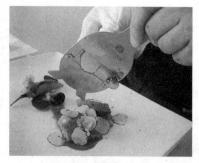

valuable and with a milder flavor—*Tubermagnatum,* known as the "Queen of the Truffles") and black. Each type of truffle has a "season"—a specific time of year when its scent is released, making it easier to find. Once dug up, they look pretty unassuming—like a tough, dirty pinecone.

Truffles can be eaten in a variety of ways. Thanks to their powerful and distinctive kick, they're often used sparingly for flavor—grated like parmesan cheese, or truffle oil sprinkled over a dish. But you'll also find them in cheese, salami, olive oil, pâté, and even ice cream. Some people find that the pungent, musty aftertaste follows them around all day...and all night, when its supposed aphrodisiac qualities kick in.

What drives people to pay so royally for a fragrant little hunk of fungus is, I'll admit, beyond me. But then, I never understood the appeal of Beanie Babies, either. If you're a truffle nut, you'll find yourself in heaven here; if not, you may appreciate the chance to sample a little taste of truffle. While you do that, ponder how one giant tuber changed the economy of an entire region.

table where you can sample the earthy goods, and a brain-sized replica of that famously massive chunk of white truffle. A small jar of preserved truffles will run you 50–130 kn, depending on the size, type of truffle, and preparation. You can even pick up a recipe sheet telling you what to do with the precious stuff once you get it home (daily 9:00–21:00, Livade 7, tel. 052/664-030, www.zigantetartufi.com).

The adjacent **Restaurant Zigante,** one of Istria's fanciest (and most expensive), dishes up all manner of truffle specialties. The decor—inside or out on the terrace—is white-tablecloth classy, the service is deliberate but friendly, and the truffles, as if on a cooking game show, are prepared in a dizzying variety of ways. If you want the full dose of this local delicacy from a place that knows its truffles, this is a worthwhile splurge (150–300-kn main dishes, 350–450-kn fixed-price meals, daily 12:00–23:00, Livade 7, tel. 052/664-302).

Hum

According to its marketing plan, Hum (pronounced "hoom," Colmo in Italian) is the "smallest town in the world." While there are, no doubt, hamlets even tinier than its population of 16 people, as of a few decades ago—when first it laid claim to this honor—Hum had a town hall, church, school, post office, and all the other trappings of a "town"...so it wins the title on a technicality. Smart gimmick.

Unfortunately, these days Hum is also, per capita, the most touristy town in the world—crammed with visitors who come to stroll through its streets, drop some kunas in its single souvenir shop, or dine at its lone restaurant (Humska Konoba, lunch and dinner, open daily mid-May–mid-Oct, closed Mon mid-March–mid-May and mid-Oct–mid-Nov, Sat–Sun only mid-Nov–mid-March, tel. 052/660-005).

But despite its quirks and its one-trick commercialism, Hum is genuinely engaging. At the far corner of Istria—just up the road from Mount Učka, which forms the natural boundary with the neighboring Kvarner Gulf—Hum feels remote, rugged, and (if you don't run into any tour buses) forgotten by modern times.

You'll enter Hum through its main gate, formed by part of its 11th-century castle. Once inside the characteristic Old Town, you'll find cobbled lanes connecting the stone houses and 19th-century town church (with five altars). It's more rustic-feeling than the other villages in this chapter, with rougher paving stones, more overgrowth, and an even more pronounced yesteryear quality. And yet, you'll still spot several *sobe* signs and a souvenir shop. Popular mementos—sold at the restaurant and the shop—are little ceramic tiles with your initials using the Glagolitic alphabet (see below).

Getting There: Coming from Motovun on the road following the Mirna River, you'll pass through Buzet, following signs for Lupoglav and Rijeka. The turn-off for Hum (and the Glagolitic Lane) is on the right. When you're finished in Hum, you're not far from the A-8 highway back to the south (the coast), or onward to the east (Rijeka via the Učka Tunnel).

Near Hum: The Glagolitic Lane

The road leading south to Hum from the Mirna Valley is the **Glagolitic Lane** (Aleja Glagoljaša), commemorating a ninth-century alphabet once used for written Croatian. While the alphabet hasn't been widely used for centuries, Croatians recognize it as an integral and unique part of their cultural heritage. And in the area around Hum, they've clung to the dinosaur alphabet even more than in other parts of the country—claiming it was commonly used here into the 20th century. Today, the alphabet is even taught in some schools, and children have poetry contests and spelling bees in Glagolitic. Along the Glagolitic Lane to Hum, you'll see various monuments to this alphabet, including giant Glagolitic characters standing in a field, as well as a sort of "Rosetta Stone" on top of a hill (on the left, just before Hum) comparing the Glagolitic, Cyrillic, and (our) Roman alphabet.

THE KVARNER GULF

Opatija • Rijeka • Rab

The long stretch of Croatian coast from Istria to Dalmatia—between the cities of Rijeka and Zadar—offers twisty seaside roads, functional port towns and fishing villages, some of the country's most rugged scenery, and no real knockout sights. Croatia offers more bang for your buck to the north (Istria) and the south (Dalmatia)—but if you're connecting these zones, the Kvarner Gulf offers several suitable stopovers.

Kvarner's best mainland town is its northern gateway: the former Hapsburg resort of Opatija. Shot through with the faded elegance of an upper-crust history, Opatija is, if nothing else, a welcome change of pace from the salty Venetian-flavored towns along the rest of the Croatian coast. Nearby, the big industrial port city of Rijeka is best avoided, unless you're changing buses or boats there.

South of Opatija and Rijeka, the Kvarner coastline is stark and desolate—any traces of settlement long since blown away by the battering Bora wind (see sidebar on page 136). But offshore, sheltered from the elements, are several inviting island getaways. Each of the main islands—Krk, Cres, Lošinj, Rab, and Pag—has its own character and appeal. But the best Kvarner village is Rab town, on the island of the same name. Rab's pretty, peninsular Old Town, bristling with Venetian-style bell towers, overlooks a shimmering harbor and beaches full of happy swimmers and sunbathers.

Planning Your Time

The Kvarner Gulf is "passing-through" territory. While destinations in this chapter have their fans, first-timers seeing Croatia in a hurry should give the region a miss. But if you have plenty of time

The Kvarner Gulf

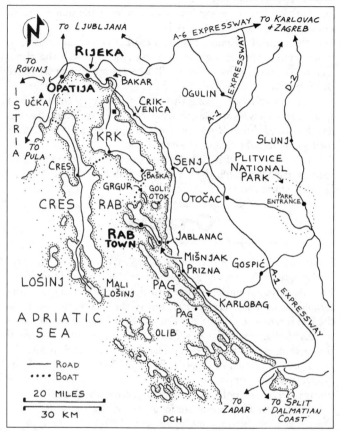

and your own wheels, and you're driving through anyway, Opatija and Rab are worthy overnight stops.

Driving Between Northern Croatia and Dalmatia

If you're driving between northern Croatia (Zagreb, Plitvice, Istria, or Opatija) and the Dalmatian Coast (Zadar, from where the expressway zips to Split), you have two options: Use the fast inland A-1 expressway, or follow the slow Kvarner Gulf coastal road all the way down.

The **A-1 expressway** option is boring but faster and far more efficient, especially from Zagreb or Plitvice. If you're coming from Zagreb, just take A-1 directly to Split; from Plitvice, drive south, then west to Otočac to pick up the expressway. From Istria or Opatija, you have two options for accessing A-1 that take about the same amount of time: Head east (inland) from Rijeka on A-6 to join A-1; or, more interesting, drive the Kvarner coastal road as far south as Senj, then cut inland and up over the mountains to Otočac, where you can get on A-1.

The two-lane **Kvarner coastal road** is twisty and slow, but more scenic. Speedy sightseers won't find it worth the time. Compared to the expressway, you'll lose at least an hour if you're coming from Istria or Opatija, and much more if you're starting in Zagreb or Plitvice. Along this road, you'll enjoy good but not spectacular views—similar to what you'll see in Dalmatia, but less developed. From Rijeka, just follow signs for Split and Zadar (being careful not to get on the expressway).

If you want to visit **Rab,** be sure to take the Kvarner coastal road; at Jablanac, catch the car ferry to Rab (see "Route Tips for Drivers" at the end of this chapter).

Opatija

Opatija (oh-PAH-tee-yah) is not your typical Croatian beach town. In the late-19th-century golden age of the Austro-Hungarian Empire, this unassuming village near the port of Rijeka was transformed into the Eastern Riviera, one of the swankiest resorts on the Mediterranean. While the French, British, and German aristocracy sunbathed on France's Côte d'Azur, the wealthy elite from the eastern half of Europe—the Hapsburg Empire, Scandinavia, and Russia—partied in Opatija. Baroque, Neoclassical, and Art Nouveau villas popped up along its coastline as it became the sunny playground for barons, dukes, and other aristocrats.

While the Hapsburgs are long gone, Opatija retains the trappings of its genteel past. Most of Croatia evokes the time-passed Mediterranean, but Opatija whispers "belle époque." It may be the classiest resort town in Croatia, with more taste and less fixation on postcards and seashells. Most people don't come to Croatia for this chic scene. But if rustic seaside villages are wearing on you, Opatija is a pleasant return to high-class civilization.

Thanks to its sheltered location nestled under high mountain peaks, Opatija is protected from the Bora wind, enjoying instead a light, refreshing breeze from Učka Mountain. This gives Opatija a particularly mild and enjoyable climate—the perfect match for its refined ambience.

ORIENTATION

(area code: 051)
Opatija is basically a one-street town: Obala Maršala Tita, lined on both sides by stately hotels, follows the seafront. The town's focal point is Gortana Square (Trg V. Gortana). You can walk from one end of the tourist zone to the other in about 20 minutes.

Tourist Information
Opatija's helpful TI is right on the main drag. Pick up the map, information booklet, and list of hotels (July–Aug Mon–Sat 8:00–22:00, Sun 12:00–22:00, progressively shorter hours off-season, closed Sun in winter, Obala Maršala Tita 101, tel. 051/271-310, www.opatija-tourism.hr).

SIGHTS

Begin on Opatija's centerpiece, **Gortana Square** (Trg V. Gortana), with sweeping sea views, a marbled Croatian "Walk of Fame" (with one or two names you might recognize), and a seawater swimming pool. From here, Opatija lines up along its main drag, **Obala Maršala Tita,** still fronted by ornate villas that would seem more at home in Vienna than they do in Croatia. Austrians and other tourists stroll here hand-in-hand, taking in the views, dipping into high-class boutiques, and snapping photos of the fancy facades as they go. Joining them, you, too, may soon find yourself thinking of this place as the "Monte Carlo of Croatia."

A few steps toward the sea, stretching in either direction along the waterfront, is a scenic promenade called the **Lungomare.** This

is another wonderful spot for strolling, and offers striking views across the bay to Rijeka (which looks much better from afar).

As for sightseeing...well, Opatija is not that kind of place. If you like, you can drop into the *opatija* (abbey) that gave the town its name, the **Abbey of St. Jacob** (Opatija Sv. Jakov, right along the Lungomare below the TI). Nearby, an outdoor theater shows movies or concerts nightly in peak season (near the ferry landing; weather permitting, check with TI for schedule). You'll also stumble upon many manicured parks.

SLEEPING

Opatija is chock-a-block full of swanky resort hotels. While prices are high, you get a lot of luxury for your money (unlike hotels in most small coastal villages). Sleeping in Opatija is definitely preferable to overnighting in Rijeka.

$$$ *Big and Fancy:* These two chain hotels are my favorites of the many opulent Opatija hotels. They've got the most striking Hapsburg facades in town, and both have luxurious rooms (air-con, elevator, and all the amenities). Each can also refer you to other, similar chain properties (price range depends on season—top price is for Aug): **Hotel Bristol** (78 rooms, part of Vienna International chain, Sb-€70–100, Db-€100–145, Obala Maršala Tita 108, tel. 051/706-300, fax 051/706-301, www.hotel-bristol.hr, info@hotel -bristol.hr) and **Hotel Agava** (76 rooms, part of Ugo chain, Sb-€77–100, Db-€112–146, Obala Maršala Tita 89, tel. 051/278-100, fax 051/278-021, www.ugohoteli.hr, info@ugohoteli.hr).

$$$ *Smaller and Family-Run:* These two small hotels, run by the Brko family, are well-located a few steps from the lively Gortana Square (to the right as you face the water): **Hotel Galeb,** with 20 comfortable rooms and three stars, has more character than most Opatija hotels (July–Aug: Sb-€85, Db-€110; €15 less in June and Sept, €25 less Oct–May; €20 more for sea view, 10 percent less if you pay cash, pricier suites also available, elevator, Obala Maršala Tita 160, tel. 051/271-177, tel. & fax 051/271-349, www .hotel-galeb.hr, hotel-galeb@ri.t-com.hr). **Hotel Savoy,** across the street, comes with four stars, 32 rooms, a swimming pool, more class, and higher prices (about 20 percent more expensive than

---

Sleep Code

(€1 = about $1.20, country code: 385, area code: 051)
S = Single, **D** = Double/Twin, **T** = Triple, **Q** = Quad, **b** = bathroom. The modest tourist tax (€1 per person, per night, lower off-season) is not included in these rates. Hotels generally accept credit cards and include breakfast in their rates, while most *sobe* accept only cash and don't offer breakfast. Everyone listed here speaks English.

To help you sort easily through these listings, I've divided the rooms into three categories based on the price for a standard double room with bath in peak season:

  $$$ Higher Priced—Most rooms €100 or more.
  $$ Moderately Priced—Most rooms between €60–100.
  $ Lower Priced—Most rooms €60 or less.

Galeb, elevator, Obala Maršala Tita 129, tel. 051/710-500, fax 051/272-680, www.hotel-savoy.hr, info@hotel-savoy.hr).

TRANSPORTATION CONNECTIONS

Opatija is connected to the nearby transportation hub of **Rijeka** twice each hour by bus (30-min trip).

Rijeka

The industrial city of Rijeka (ree-YAY-kah; it translates as "River") became Croatia's biggest port under Austro-Hungarian rule. It's dainty little Opatija's bigger, burlier brother. Like Opatija, much of Rijeka's architecture is reminiscent of the glory days of the Hapsburgs. But unlike Opatija, most of Rijeka's buildings haven't been renovated in the last century or so, giving it a seedy, gritty, past-its-prime feel. Avoid Rijeka if you can. However, since it's a major transportation hub, there's a good chance you'll pass through. Here are the basics.

The bus station, train station, and ferry terminal are within a few blocks of each other in a bustling waterfront business zone. The sector is crossed by two one-way streets (going in opposite directions): Ivana Zajca (or the "Riva," along the waterfront, runs west to east) and Adamićeva (which changes its name a few times as it cuts east to west through town).

A block above these two streets is the **Korzo,** an almost-charming pedestrianized zone packed with shops, restaurants,

 and the **TI** (at the widest part of the Korzo, near the well-signed McDonald's; mid-June–mid-Sept Mon–Sat 8:00–20:00, Sun 9:00–14:00; mid-Sept–mid-June Mon–Fri 8:00–20:00, Sat 8:00–14:00, closed Sun; Korzo 33, tel. 051/335-882, www.tz-rijeka.hr).

The **train station** is a few blocks west of the Korzo. On arrival, exit the station to the right and walk 10 minutes to the water. You'll first come to the bus station, then the ferry terminal. The Korzo is just above them.

The **bus station** is basically a big parking lot in the middle of the chaos, near the west end of the Korzo. You'll see the big boats along the waterfront as you exit your bus. To get to the train station, face the water and turn right, following the busy street about 10 minutes.

The Bora
Or, How to Predict Croatian Coastal Weather

When asked what tomorrow's weather will bring, a salty Croatian boat captain looks to the mountains and feels the stiff wind on his face. "Sun," he says. "The Bora brings good weather."

Like any people whose fate is tied to the sea, coastal Croatians can extrapolate a breeze or a front of clouds into a full-blown weather report. While this is a precise art cultivated over a lifetime, even the casual tourist can learn a few tried-and-tested clues from the natives.

Croatian coastal weather is shaped by a mighty wind called the Bora (named for the Greek Boreas, the North Wind; sometimes called "Bura" in Croatian, or "Burja" in Slovene). Much like the infamous mistral wind that's an unavoidable fact of life in France's Provence, the Bora has an indelible impact on this region's weather, vegetation, architecture, and tourism.

The Dinaric Mountains, which rise sharply up from the sea all along the Croatian Coast, act as a barrier for cold, cloudy weather. As the air on the coastal side of the mountains heats up, the air behind the snowcapped peaks stays cool. Something's gotta give to equalize this temperature and pressure differential. A white fringe of clouds builds up along the ridge of the mountains, as the cool air moves toward the warm air—a sure sign that the Bora is about to blow. When all that pent-up air finally escapes, the Bora comes screaming down the slopes to the sea.

The Bora occurs anywhere that mountains create two different climates in nearby terrains, including Slovenia's Karst. But the Bora's power is at its peak along the Kvarner Gulf—especially where a gap in the mountains provides a natural funnel toward the sea (such as at Senj and at Karlobag). It's strongest in the winter, when the temperature differential between the interior and the coast is most pronounced. Farther south, such as in Dalmatia, the inland remains warmer and the Bora is milder.

The Bora is not constant—it's strongest at midday, and made up of intermittent, fierce gusts than can reach 150 miles per hour. Young children have been known to "fly" through the air

The **ferry terminal** is at the east end of the waterfront. The Jadrolinija ticket office is in the building with the big *Jadrolinija* sign (at Riva 16, second building east of bus station, ticket office at far right end of building as you face it).

Some of Rijeka's **car-rental** offices are conveniently located right downtown, on the main harborfront street called Ivana Zajca, or the "Riva": **Avis** is at #8 (Mon–Sat 8:00–20:00, Sun 8:00–12:00, tel. 051/311-135) and **Hertz** is at #6 (Mon–Fri 8:00–12:00 & 17:00–20:00, Sat 8:00–13:00, closed Sun, tel. 051/311-098). **Europcar** is for short distances because of the Bora. The Kvarner coastal road is closed several times each year to trucks, buses, and other high-profile vehicles, for fear they'll be blown over. And occasionally Kvarner Gulf ferries (such as the Jablanac–Mišnjak connection to Rab Island) must wait patiently for the Bora to die down. After a day or two of a stiff winter Bora, everything is coated with a thin layer of salt, like ash after a volcano.

The good news: As the Bora rushes toward the coast, it sweeps bad-weather clouds away with it—leaving in its wake clear, cooler air and sunshine.

In summer, the much milder version of this wind—which usually bathes the coast in a refreshing breeze each evening, when the interior cools faster than the sea—is called a Maestral. Sporadic mini-Bora gusts at night are known as Burin.

The Bora's unpopular cousin is the wind called Jugo (YOO-goh, meaning "south"—as in "Yugo-slavia"). The Jugo originates as a moist air mass gathering over the Adriatic, which creates a low-pressure vortex. Finally it blows northward toward Croatia, bringing with it hot, humid, and stormy weather. Because humid conditions foster disease, an ancient superstition considers the Jugo wind evil, and the refreshing Bora wind good. Notice that the Bora and the Jugo are the yin and yang of Croatian winds, blowing in opposite directions and with opposite effects.

When all else fails, you can always fall back on the reliable old saying, which also exists in Croatian: "Red sky at night, sailor's delight." If light from the sunset is able to leak through the bottom of a bank of clouds on the western horizon, it's a sign that clearer weather lies just beyond...and should arrive by morning.

Of course, these adages are highly generalized. Croatia's coast is made up of a series of microclimates. Each island has its own very specific weather conditions, which is why one island may grow olives, the next one lavender, the next red wine grapes, and the next white wine grapes. If you really want to know what sort of weather is on the way, ask a local.

much less handy, at the airport on the nearby island of Krk (mobile 091-4303-038).

TRANSPORTATION CONNECTIONS

From Rijeka by Boat to: Rab (1/day, 1.5-hr catamaran in summer, 2-hr car ferry in winter), the **Dalmatian Coast** (slow Jadrolinija car ferry, 4/week in summer, 2/week in winter, all depart in the evening and go overnight to Split, then onward down the coast;

figure 11 hrs to **Split,** 18 hrs to **Korčula,** 21 hrs to **Dubrovnik**).

From Rijeka by Train to: Zagreb (3/day, 4 hrs), **Ljubljana** (2–3/day direct, 2.5 hrs), **Budapest** (1/day, 10 hrs, transfer in Zagreb; plus direct but long night train, 14 hrs).

From Rijeka by Bus to: Opatija (2/hr, 30 min), **Senj** (hourly, 1.5 hrs), **Rab town** (2/day, 3.5 hrs), **Pula** (almost hourly, 2.5 hrs), **Rovinj** (6/day, 3.5 hrs), **Zagreb** (hourly, 3.5 hrs), **Split** (nearly hourly, 8.5 hrs), **Dubrovnik** (2/day, 12 hrs), **Ljubljana** (2/day, 2.5 hrs).

Rab

Rab (pronounced "Rob," like the man's name) is the most appealing Croatian island north of the Dalmatian Coast. Though it's one of the greenest islands in the northern Adriatic, its northern half (including where the ferry from the mainland docks) is an eerily dry, rocky moonscape—the result of saltwater blown ashore by harsh Bora winds (see sidebar). But on the seaward side of the island, you'll find lush vegetation, as well as the island's main town, also called Rab. Rab's Old Town peninsula is nestled along a sleepy harbor. Along the spine of the Old Town are four different Venetian-style campaniles (bell towers)—Rab's claim to touristic fame. A relaxing seafront promenade runs behind the Old Town.

Rab was independent and strong in the 14th century, but soon after became a backwater outpost of Venice. In the 19th

century, when Rab was part of the Hapsburg Empire, Austrians found its beaches a fine place to catch some rays (their descendants still do). In fact, Rab Island kicked off the nude-beach boom that's still going strong in Croatia: In 1936, England's King Edward VIII came to Rab on holiday with his soon-to-be wife, Wallis Simpson. Edward wanted to work on an all-over tan, so he went through the proper channels to have one of Rab's beaches designated for nudists. Inspired by the English monarch's example, other visitors to Rab followed suit (er, dropped suit)... and a phenomenon was born. Keep your eyes peeled for the letters *FKK (Freikörper Kultur,* German for "free body culture"), which is pan-European code for nudism.

Rab Town

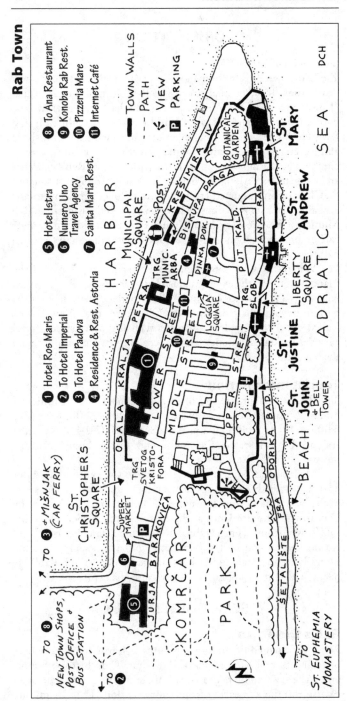

1 Hotel Ros Maris
2 To Hotel Imperial
3 To Hotel Padova
4 Residence & Rest. Astoria

5 Hotel Istra
6 Numero Uno Travel Agency
7 Santa Maria Rest.

8 To Ana Restaurant
9 Konoba Rab Rest.
10 Pizzeria Mare
11 Internet Café

TOWN WALLS
PATH
VIEW
P PARKING

ORIENTATION

(area code: 051)

The Old Town of Rab is on a long, tapering peninsula alongside a tidy harbor. Three parallel streets run the length of the peninsula: **"Lower Street"** (Donja ulica, just off the harbor, a narrow lane with a few cafés and discos); **"Middle Street"** (Srednja ulica, a few steps higher, the bustling main drag lined with souvenir shops and ice-cream stands); and **"Upper Street"** (Gornja ulica, a steep climb up at the top of the peninsula, with most of Rab's churches and campaniles). Along the harbor are Rab's two biggest squares: St. Christopher's Square (Trg Svetog Kristofora), with a makeshift art gallery and steps leading up into the park; and businesslike Rab Municipal Square (Trg Municipium Arba), a huddle of *al fresco* café umbrellas surrounded by the TI, the post office, and the town hall.

Where the Old Town peninsula attaches to the rest of the island, you'll find the extensive, lush **Komrčar Park,** which is filled with trees and crisscrossed with walking paths. A few steps off the harbor, beyond the park from the Old Town, is a **"New Town"** (called Palit) with modern amenities such as grocery stores, travel agencies, bakeries, an open-air produce market, a post office, and the bus station.

Tourist Information

The **TI,** with a smattering of local brochures, is on Municipal Square (generally open daily June–Sept 8:00–22:00, Oct–May 8:00–14:00, Trg Municipium Arba 8, tel. 051/771-111, www.tzg -rab.hr). In peak season, there's a second, smaller branch near the bus station in the New Town.

Most of Rab's travel agencies—where you can find a *soba* or apartment, rent bikes and scooters, and sign up for excursions—are in the New Town. More convenient is the only travel agency in the Old Town, **Numero Uno,** at the corner of the harbor where the Old Town peninsula meets the mainland (open long hours daily in season, shorter hours off-season, between the big supermarket and Hotel Istra on Šetalište Markantuna de Dominisa, tel. 051/724-688, www.numero-uno.hr and www.dmmedia.com).

SELF-GUIDED WALK

Rab's Old Town

Don't get bogged down figuring out which campanile is which, or trying to make too much of Rab's humdrum history. Simply enjoy the lazy ambience. Instead of sightseeing, use Rab as an excuse to take a vacation from your vacation. This 30-minute walk will give you the lay of the land.

Begin at the big **St. Christopher's Square** (Trg Svetog Kristofora). Peruse the starving artists' work and admire the sculp-

ture fountain. These star-crossed lovers, from the island's two big feuding families, are the protagonists of Rab's favorite legend. Kalifront (the bronze guy with the goatee) was desperately in love with a peasant girl named Draga (in the fountain). But since Draga had taken a vow of celibacy to the Roman goddess Diana, she couldn't give in to Kalifront's advances. Draga begged Diana for help, and Diana turned her to stone to prevent any hanky-panky. Tears from the petrified Draga became the spring of a fountain of youth. Diana punished the randy Kalifront by turning him into a half-man-half-tree, fed by the spring of his unrequited lover—and sentenced to watch her eternally from afar.

Look across the harbor to the ridge that runs along the spine of the island. Notice the little **stone walls** climbing up the hill. These walls, called *gromače*—which you'll see throughout the region—traditionally served three purposes: to mark property boundaries, to prevent erosion, and to provide a convenient place for farmers to get rid of big rocks unearthed while tilling.

Continue into town on **Middle Street** (Srednja ulica, near the

base of the big staircase). You'll pass restaurants, galleries, tacky souvenir shops (with T-shirts so obscene you can only admire their creativity), and the town's Internet café (look for @ sign on left; Mon–Sat 10:00–14:00 & 18:00–24:00, Sun 18:00–24:00). Along the way, stop to drool over a few of the ice-cream *(sladoled)* stands—many run by Kosovo Albanians who live on Rab. When you emerge into the little piazza with the pillared loggia, detour through the tunnel on the left.

Municipal Square (Trg Municipium Arba), the second of Rab's two harborfront squares, is home to several outdoor cafés, the recommended Astoria restaurant, and the TI (at the far corner, near the waterfront). At the top-right corner of the square (with the harbor at your back), find the family-run **Natura Rab** shop, selling all-organic, all-local products from Rab, including various types of olive oil, honey, lavender, and *rakija*—the local firewater,

The Dark History of Rab

For some more serious, somber sightseeing—and a severe contrast to otherwise lighthearted Rab—you can pay your respects at the remains of a **concentration camp** operated by Mussolini's occupying forces during World War II. Tens of thousands of Jews and political prisoners (many of them Slovenes) were interned here; thousands of them died. It's odd to think this facility was Italian, rather than German—making this, for many, a surprising footnote in WWII history. The site is now a graveyard memorial (on the road to Lopar, about 3 miles northwest of Rab town).

Offshore from Rab Island (to the north) are two smaller islands with a troubled history. After Yugoslav President-for-Life Tito split from Moscow in 1948 to pursue his own brand of communism, he arrested Yugoslavs who remained loyal to the Soviet Union. Many of them ended up on the "gulag island" of **Goli Otok** ("Barren Island"). In a strange parallel to the US's McCarthyism, the late 1940s and early 1950s were an era of great anti-Soviet paranoia in communist Yugoslavia. This period—called *Informbiro*, after the Soviet secret police—is the subject of the Oscar-nominated Croatian film *When Father Was Away on Business*. Near Goli Otok, **Grgur Island** hosted a women's prison in the early Yugoslav era. Prisoners were forced to carve Tito's name and a giant star of communism into the hillside (still faintly visible). It's difficult to visit these islands, but you may see them as you drive around Rab Island and along the mainland.

like Italian grappa (July–Aug daily 9:30–13:00 & 19:00–23:00, shorter hours off-season, www.natura-rab.hr). Just to the right of Natura Rab is the old Rector's Palace (marked with a distinctively carved balcony), the former residence of the Venetian governor.

With your back to the harbor, go to the top-left corner of the square, with the post office (notice the wall of old-fashioned wooden mailboxes inside). Walk down the street the P.O. is on (Biskupa Draga) until you emerge into a sweet little **botanical garden.** This peaceful oasis is watched over by a statue of St. Marin—the Rab-born stonecutter who went to Italy and founded San Marino, which remains an independent nation today. (If you continue out the far end of the garden, you'll reach the tip of the Old Town peninsula.)

Take the ramp up from the garden, and find your way to the start of **Upper Street** (Gornja ulica), marked by a big church and a piazza with palm trees. As you stroll along this street with the sea on your left, you'll pass several little monasteries and churches, four of which boast Rab's trademark bell towers (in order: Saints Mary, Andrew, Justine, and John the Evangelist). If a church is open, poke inside (or look through the grate to see the interior); some of them have modest museums attached. You can climb the first **bell tower** (St. Mary, 5 kn, closed for a long midday siesta), but it's better to climb the fourth tower, by the ruins of the seventh-century Church of St. John (Sveti Ivan), because it's free and always open.

Halfway along Upper Street, you'll reach **Liberty Square** (Trg Slobode), marked by a single, huge Holm oak. Stairs behind the tree lead down to the embankment that runs behind the peninsula—a fine place for swimming or strolling (see "Activities").

Beyond the fourth bell tower, Upper Street runs into a small staircase. Go up the stairs and into the garden courtyard, where more stairs on the right lead up to the top of a rampart with a fine view over Rab's rooftops. Continuing past the courtyard leads you into the park—a nicely shaded place to relax.

ACTIVITIES

Swimming—As with most beaches in Croatia, Rab's are largely pebbly or rocky. The best swimming area is along the back (non-harbor) side of the Old Town

peninsula and park (accessed from Liberty Square/Trg Slobode on Upper Street—see above). This concrete sidewalk, running along the waterfront, has a few low-key cafés and several sets of steps into the sea that make things easy for swimmers. (To stretch your legs, continue along this embankment for about 30 minutes to the Franciscan Monastery of St. Euphemia—not worth going out of your way for, but a suitable excuse for a waterfront stroll.)

Reaching the island's sandy beaches (away from the Old Town) take a little more effort. Sahara Beach, the best beach, is clothing-optional (some people wear swimsuits, but most are nude). It's at the north end of the island, past the town of Lopar (easiest to take the bus to the town of San Marino, then water taxi or walk to Sahara—get details at Rab TI).

Shopping—Trinkets don't get much tackier than the ones on Rab. But with a little searching, you can find some worthwhile souvenirs (try the Natura Rab shop on the Municipal Square—described in the "Self-Guided Walk"). Look for local honey, grape brandy, and lavender. The next island over, Pag, produces a tasty cheese called *paški sir*—with an herby/salty flavor that is said to come from the sea-air-blown vegetation the sheep graze on.

Other Activities—To get out and see the island, you can rent a bike or scooter, or join an excursion by bus or boat (all are available at hotel reception desks and at travel agencies—see "Tourist Information," earlier in this chapter). Boat captains along the harborfront offer cruises to various secluded coves on Rab and nearby islands. With a bike, you can ride the trails in Kalifront and Frkanj (get a good map when you rent your bike).

SLEEPING

(€1 = about $1.20, country code: 385, area code: 051)
I've listed the top-season prices (August). Each hotel charges progressively less off-season.

$$$ **Hotel Ros Maris** is your best big-hotel splurge. Perfectly located on the harborfront in the middle of the Old Town peninsula, it was renovated with plush, modern class in 2005. The 146 pampering rooms share a swimming pool and several sunbathing areas. As it's surrounded by discos, it can be a little noisy at night—but the air-conditioning and solid windows keep things sleepable (Sb-€155, Db-€215, air-con, elevator, Obala P. Krešimira 4, tel. 051/778-899, fax 051/724-206, www.rosmaris.com, reservations@rosmaris.com).

$$$ *Imperial Rab Hotels:* Rab's other big hotels are run by this single company, which offers lightly renovated communist "comfort" at too-high prices. The best-located option is the **Hotel Imperial,** with 134 rooms in the park just beyond the end of the harbor (Sb-€60, Db-€100, €4 more for sea view). **Hotel Padova** looms across the harbor from the Old Town (a 20-minute walk away; Db-€130–190 depending on view and amenities). Both hotels have elevators and air-conditioning, and can be booked through the same office: tel. 051/724-184, www.imperial.hr, sale @imperial.hr.

$$ **Residence Astoria** rents eight new, comfortable apartments over the restaurant of the same name, in a restored Venetian palazzo right in the center of town. As it overlooks the bustling Municipal Square, it can be noisy at night—especially since there's no air-conditioning (€60–110 depending on size and amenities, one-week minimum July–Aug, 1- or 2-night stays possible but unlikely in peak season, closed mid-Oct–April, Trg Municipium Arba 7, tel. 051/774-844, www.astoria-rab.com, astoria@email .t-com.hr).

$$ **Hotel Istra,** at the corner of the harbor where the Old Town peninsula meets the mainland, is an old communist-style hotel, now run by the Renić family. Its 100 rooms are dingy and

not air-conditioned, but the location and lack of other affordable options makes it worth considering (Sb-€50, Db-€90, €4 more for a balcony, elevator, Šetalište Markantuna de Dominisa b.b., tel. 051/724-134, fax 051/724-050, www.hotel-istra.hr, hotel-istra @hi.t-com.hr).

$ Sobe *and Apartments:* As elsewhere in Croatia, the best budget option is to stay in a room in a private home *(soba)* or rent an apartment. Every travel agency in Rab has a line on rooms; Numero Uno is well-located and well-established (see "Tourist Information," earlier in this chapter).

EATING

Rab has a cuisine scene typical for a Croatian resort town—a dozen pizzerias, a half-dozen seafood joints, and some splurges—but a few eateries stand above the rest. All of these recommendations (except Ana) are in the Old Town. As with everything in Rab, opening times flex with the season (long hours daily in summer with a mid-afternoon break, shorter hours or closed entirely off-season).

Astoria is a good choice for a splurge, with high-quality food, including lots of delectable seafood options. Sit inside, or out on the terrace, overlooking the Municipal Square (40–75-kn pastas, 70–130-kn main dishes, open daily for lunch and dinner, closed 15:00–18:00, on Trg Municipium Arba 7, tel. 051/774-844).

Santa Maria specializes in grilled meat, but you'll also find fish on the menu. With the most impressive interior in town—including nautical decor reminiscent of its namesake ship, and a giant old-fashioned skylight that pulls in a refreshing breeze—it's an enjoyable place for a meal (daily 10:00–14:00 & 17:00–23:00; just beyond the end of Middle Street, continue straight up the narrow alley after the piazza with the loggia, on the right at Dinke Dokule 6, tel. 051/724-196).

Ana Restaurant serves up pastas, seafood, and Balkan-style grilled meats in a residential-feeling area just beyond the New Town commercial center. My only listing outside the Old Town, it lacks the charm—and crowds—of the Old Town eateries, but the food is delicious (35–45-kn pizzas and pastas, 60–90-kn main dishes, pricier seafood splurges, daily 11:00–15:00 & 18:00–24:00; go up the New Town's main drag, then turn right just after the open-air produce stalls and look for signs, Palit 80, tel. 051/724-376).

Konoba Rab, run by the father-and-son Vidas family, has good seafood and an over-the-Croatian-village-rooftops interior (daily 10:00-14:00 & 17:00-23:00; about halfway down Middle Street, look for sign leading up the stairway to Upper Street, Kneza Branimira 3, tel. 051/725-666).

Pizza: There's no shortage of pizza and pasta eateries in Rab's Old Town. I enjoy **Pizzeria Mare,** serving up pizza with a soft and tasty crust (35–45-kn pizzas and pastas, daily 9:00–22:00, entrances from both Middle and Lower Streets, Srednja ulica 8).

TRANSPORTATION CONNECTIONS

By Public Transportation

Getting to Rab can be frustrating by public transportation. It's easy to reach by boat from Rijeka, but it's slow and complicated to continue southward (such as to the Dalmatian Coast). This makes it difficult to visit Rab efficiently between northern destinations (like Slovenia or Istria) and the Dalmatian Coast. It's generally much faster to skip Rab and connect north and south by plane, train, or bus—see "Getting to the Dalmatian Coast," page 152.

Without a car, the easiest way to reach Rab in summer is by **fast catamaran** from Rijeka (1/day in each direction; generally leaves from Rab's harborfront at 6:45 Mon–Sat, at 9:45 Sun; return boat leaves Rijeka in the afternoon; 1.5-hour trip; generally runs June–Sept only). In the winter, the Rab–Rijeka route is operated by a slower car ferry (1/day, 2 hrs). Rab Island is also connected by other ferries and by taxi boats to nearby islands (such as Krk to the north), and a regular car ferry keeps it linked to the mainland (see "Route Tips for Divers," next).

Buses connect Rab to the mainland using the Mišnjak–Jablanac ferry. Buses to the north are easy and straightforward: **Rijeka** (2/day, 3.5 hrs), **Senj** (partway up the coast to Rijeka—see below; 3/day, 2 hrs), and **Zagreb** (2/day direct in summer, 5.5 hrs; off-season you'll usually transfer in Senj). Destinations to the south (such as Zadar, at the start of the Dalmatian Coast) are more complex and very slow, since you'll be following the windy coastal road all the way down to Zadar (connections speed up from Zadar to Split). To get on a southbound bus from Rab, you'll have to take one of the northbound buses (just described) across to the mainland, then transfer to a southbound bus. After the ferry docks at Jablanac, the bus climbs up to a roadside bus stop called Magistrala, where you can transfer (often requires a long wait for the next bus); or continue another 45 minutes north to **Senj** to transfer. Carefully confirm the transfer schedule at the station before you set out. Rab's bus station is in the New Town (bus info: tel. 051/724-189).

Route Tips for Drivers

Rab is a relatively straightforward stopover if you have a **car.** Driving along the Kvarner coastal road between Rijeka and Zadar, you'll pass above Jablanac (follow signs off the main road down a twisty one-way road to this coastal port town). In summer, the Rapska Plovidba car ferry makes the 20-minute crossing continuously between Jablanac and Mišnjak, a lonely dock at the very barren end of Rab Island (a 15-minute drive along the length of the island from Rab town). In the busiest times (weekends in July–Aug), you may have to wait up to a few hours to drive your car on. Off-season, the ferry still crosses at least eight times per day.

You'll be struck by how desolate the coast feels as you drive along the Kvarner coastal road. Between Jablanac (with the Rab ferry) and Rijeka, the most appealing spot for a break is **Senj** (pronounced "sehn"—the j is mostly silent, but has a slight *y* sound). Senj has a little harbor and a modest square with a jumble of outdoor cafés. The town is watched over by the boxy fortress of a band of pirates called the Uskoks. These were Croat and Bosniak refugees forced out of their homes in the interior when the Ottomans invaded in the 16th century. After resettling here in Senj, they became pirates and began terrorizing the Adriatic coastline. While they claimed to target only Ottoman ships, they also harassed anyone who traded with the Ottomans—including Venice. Finally the Austrians—bowed by political pressure from the Venetians—put down the Uskoks. Today Senj is the best jolt of civilization along this road, with busloads of tour groups constantly dropping off here for a coffee-and-WC break. This means that the natives of Senj—perhaps harkening back to their pirate ancestors—are adept at overcharging and shortchanging visitors. Check your bill carefully against the posted menu prices.

Senj is also the easiest point where the Kvarner coastal road connects to the speedy A-1 expressway that runs parallel to the coast inland. From Senj, a well-traveled road cuts away from the coast and soon begins twisting up the coastal mountain range. After about an hour, you'll arrive at the war-scarred town of Otočac, where you can access A-1. (For more on Otočac, see page 86.)

SPLIT

Dubrovnik is the darling of the Dalmatian Coast, but Split (pronounced as it's spelled) is Croatia's "second city" (after Zagreb), bustling with 189,000 people. If you've been hopping along the coast, landing in urban Split feels like a return to civilization. While most Dalmatian coastal towns seem made for tourists, Split is real and vibrant—a shipbuilding city with ugly sprawl surrounding an atmospheric Old Town, which teems with Croatians living life to the fullest.

Though today's Split throbs to a modern, young beat, its history goes way back—all the way to the Roman Empire. Along with all the trappings of a modern city, Split has some of the best Roman ruins this side of Italy. In the fourth century A.D., the Roman Emperor Diocletian (245–313) wanted to retire in his native Dalmatia, so he built a huge palace here. Eventually, the palace was abandoned. Then locals, fleeing seventh-century Slavic invaders, moved in and made themselves at home, and a medieval town sprouted from the rubble of the old palace. In the 15th century, the Venetians took over the Dalmatian Coast, adding on to the city and building several small palaces. But even as Split grew, the nucleus remained the ruins of Diocletian's Palace. To this day, 2,000 people live or work inside the former palace walls. A maze of narrow alleys is home to fashionable boutiques and galleries, wonderfully atmospheric cafés, and Roman artifacts around every corner.

Planning Your Time

Split is southern Croatia's transit point—a hub for bus, boat, train, and flight connections to other destinations in the country and abroad. This means that many visitors to Dalmatia only change

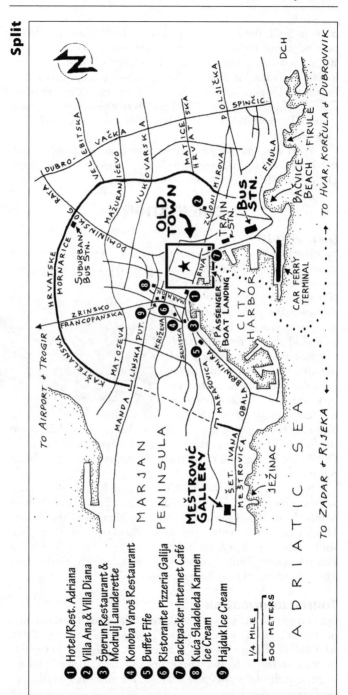

Split

1 Hotel/Rest. Adriana
2 Villa Ana & Villa Diana
3 Šperun Restaurant & Modrulj Launderette
4 Konoba Varoš Restaurant
5 Buffet Fife
6 Ristorante Pizzeria Galija
7 Backpacker Internet Café
8 Kuća Sladoleda Karmen Ice Cream
9 Hajduk Ice Cream

boats in Split. But the city is the perfect real-life contrast to the lazy, prettified Dalmatian beach resorts—it deserves a full day. Begin by strolling the remains of Diocletian's Palace, then have lunch or a coffee break along the Riva promenade. After lunch, browse the shops or visit a couple of Split's museums (the Meštrović Gallery, which is a long walk or short bus ride from the Old Town, is tops). Promenading along the Riva with the natives is *the* evening activity.

With a second day (or en route to or from northern destinations), you could spend some time in nearby Trogir—an enjoyable Dalmatian village (see the end of this chapter).

ORIENTATION

(area code: 021)

Split sprawls, but almost everything of interest to travelers is around the City Harbor (Gradska Luka). At the top of this harbor is the Old Town (Stari Grad). Between the Old Town and the sea is the Riva, a waterfront pedestrian promenade lined with cafés and shaded by palm trees. The main ferry terminal (Trajektni Terminal) juts out into the harbor from the east side. Along the harborfront embankment between the ferry terminal and the Old  Town are the long-distance bus station (Autobusni Kolodvor) and the forlorn little train station (Željeznička Stanica). West of the Old Town, poking into the Adriatic, is the lush and hilly Marjan peninsula.

Split's domino-shaped Old Town is made up of two square sections. The east half was once Diocletian's Palace, and the west half is the medieval town that sprang up next door. The shell of Diocletian's ruined palace provides a checkerboard street plan, with a gate at each end. At the center of the former palace is the Peristyle square (Peristil), where you'll find the TI, cathedral, and highest concentration of Roman ruins.

Tourist Information

Split's disinterested TI is on the Peristyle square, in the very center of Diocletian's Palace (Mon–Fri 8:00–20:00, Sat–Sun 8:00–13:00, tel. 021/345-606, www.visitsplit.com). Pick up the free town map, monthly events guide, and other materials. The TI also sells books, maps, and the Splitcard (museum discount card—not worth considering for most visits).

Split Essentials

English	Croatian	Pronounced
Old Town	Stari Grad	STAH-ree grahd
City Harbor	Gradska Luka	GRAHD-skah LOO-kah
Harborfront Promenade	Riva	REE-vah
Peristyle (old Roman square)	Peristil	PEH-ree-steel
Soccer Team	Hajduk	HIGH-dook
Local Sculptor	Ivan Meštrović	EE-vahn MESH-troh-veech
Adriatic Sea	Jadran	YAH-drahn

Arrival in Split

For all the details on getting to the Dalmatian Coast, see page 152.

By Boat, Bus, or Train: Passenger boats (like the speedy *Krilo* catamaran to Hvar and Korčula) put in at the Obala Lazareta embankment right in front of the Old Town. Bigger **car ferries** use the main terminal (Trajektni Terminal) at the far end of the harbor. If you arrive at this ferry terminal, wade through the *sobe* hawkers to the main terminal building, where you'll find ATMs, WCs, a grocery store, and offices for all of the main ferry companies, including Jadrolinija (open long hours daily).

Split's **car ferry** terminal, **bus station** (Autobusni Kolodvor), and **train station** (Željeznička Stanica) all share a busy and very practical strip of land called Obala Kneza Domagoja, on the east side of the City Harbor. From any of them, you can see the Old Town and Riva; just walk around the harbor toward the big bell tower (about a 10-min walk). Along the way, you'll pass travel agencies, baggage-check offices, locals trying to rent rooms, a post office, and Internet cafés. Arriving or leaving from this central location, you never need to deal with the concrete, exhaust-stained sprawl of outer Split.

By Plane: Split's airport (Zračna Luka Split-Kaštela) is across the big bay (Kaštelanski Zaljev), 15 miles northwest of the center, near the town of Trogir. A bus leaves Split 90 minutes before each Croatia Airlines flight (and some other companies' flights) from the small Air Terminal near the southeast corner of Diocletian's Palace, and meets each arriving flight at the airport (30 kn, 40 min). Figure on paying a hefty 300 kn for a taxi to the center.

Getting to the Dalmatian Coast

Three recent developments help make the long trip down to Dalmatia nearly painless: an expressway, a high-speed train line, and budget flights.

By Car or Bus: Thanks to Croatia's new A-1 super-expressway, the road trip from Zagreb to Split—which used to take seven hours—now takes less than five. Travelers who used to opt for an all-day journey or a bleary-eyed night bus now leave Zagreb after an early dinner, and arrive in Split before bedtime. In the coming years, the expressway will be extended south to Dubrovnik, making that trip even quicker. For the latest, see www.hac.hr. For more details on the two different driving routes from northern Croatia to Dalmatia, see page 131.

By Train: Croatian Railways' new "tilting train" line connects Zagreb to Split three times a day. Because the trains can tilt slightly, and the tracks are banked, the new line is able to shave significant time off the trip—making it from the capital to the Dalmatian Coast in just five and a half hours.

By Plane: Several low-cost airlines connect Dalmatia to northern Croatia and the rest of Europe. Even the national carrier, Croatia Airlines, often has surprisingly cheap tickets between Zagreb and Dubrovnik or Split. For more details, see page 22.

By Boat: Overnight boats sail in each direction between Rijeka (on the northern Croatian coast—4 hours by train from Zagreb and 2.5 hours by train from Ljubljana) and Split. While it's still much slower than the first three options, this can be a romantic way for nautical types to get to Dalmatia.

Airport info: tel. 021/203-506, www.split-airport.hr.

By Car: Drivers are treated to the ugly side of Split as they approach (don't worry—it gets better). Coming into town, begin by following *Centar* signs. The road forks while you're still outside of downtown: One way is simply marked *Centar* (west end of Old Town), while the other directs you to the bus and train stations and the ferry terminal (east end of Old Town). Ask your hotel which is more convenient (many hotels are individually sign-posted at the fork). If you follow the signs for the ferry terminal, you'll pop out right at the southeast corner of Diocletian's Palace (by the Green Market). For handy (but expensive) parking, continue straight when the road swings left to the ferry terminal, and you'll drive right into a parking lot just outside the palace walls (10 kn/hr).

Driving around the city center can be tricky—Split is split by its Old Town, which is welded to the harbor by the pedestrian-only Riva promenade. This means drivers needing to get 300 yards from one side of the Old Town to the other must drive about 15 minutes entirely around the center, which can be miserably clogged with traffic. A semicircular ring road makes this better than it might be. To get to the west end, you'll go through a tunnel under the Marjan peninsula. To reach the car-ferry terminal (east side), follow *Trajektni* signs (look for the tiny ferry icon).

Helpful Hints

Internet Access: Internet cafés are plentiful in the Old Town; look for signs, especially around the Peristyle square. Closer to the stations and ferry terminal is **Backpacker C@fé,** run by Australian Steve Potter. This place has Internet access, coffee and drinks with outdoor eating, and used guidebooks and paperbacks for sale (daily July–Aug 6:00–24:00, shoulder season 8:00–21:00, even shorter hours off-season, near the beginning of Obala Kneza Domagoja, tel. 021/338-548). Modrulj Launderette (below) also has Internet access.

Post Office: A modern little post office is next to the bus station (Mon–Sat 7:00–21:00, closed Sun, on Obala Kneza Domagoja).

Laundry: Modrulj Launderette, a rare coin-operated launderette, is well-run by an Australian couple, Shane and Julie (50 kn/load self-service, 75 kn/load full-service, air-con, Internet access, left-luggage service; April–Oct daily 8:00–20:00; Nov–March Mon–Sat 9:00–17:00, closed Sun; Šperun 1, tel. 021/315-888). It's conveniently located just off the harbor at the west end of the Old Town, near the recommended Šperun and Konoba Varoš restaurants—handy if multitasking is your style.

Travel Agency: Turistički Biro, between the two halves of the Old Town on the Riva, books *sobe* and hotels, sells guidebooks and maps, and sells tickets for excursions (mid-June–Sept Mon–Fri 8:00–21:00, Sat 8:00–20:00, open Sun 8:00–13:00 mid-July–Aug only; Oct–mid-June Mon–Fri 8:00–20:00, Sat 8:00–13:00, closed Sun; Riva 12, tel. & fax 021/347-100, turist-biro-split@st.t-com.hr).

Baggage Check: The train and bus stations both have safe and efficient baggage-check services *(garderoba)*. If one is very crowded, the other may be empty—check both before waiting in a long line. At the opposite (west) end of the Old Town, Modrulj Launderette also has a left-luggage service (see above).

Wine Shop: At **Vinoteka Bouquet,** at the west end of the Riva (near the restaurants and launderette on Šperun street),

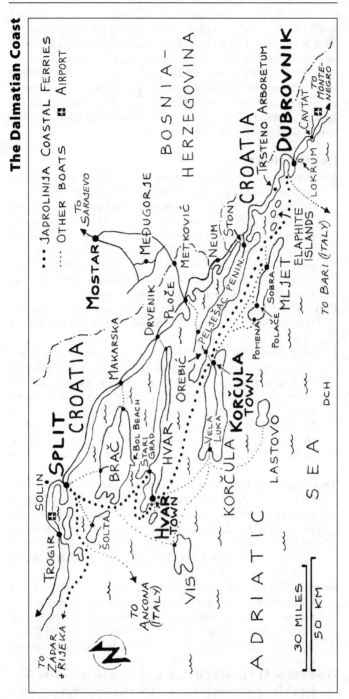

The Dalmatian Coast at a Glance

Trying to decide how to divvy up your Dalmatian days? Here are my favorite spots, listed in order of priority, and with a suggestion of how long to spend at each one on a fast-paced trip.

▲▲▲**Dubrovnik** Croatia's single best attraction is a giant, walled Old Town filled with engaging museums, delicious seafood restaurants, and happy tourists. If you visit one place in Croatia, make it Dubrovnik. Allow two days or more.

▲▲▲**Split** The perfect big-city antidote to the small-town quaintness on the rest of the Dalmatian Coast, Split's center-piece is an Old Town built on the goose-pimpling remains of a Roman palace. Long considered merely the "transfer point" of Dalmatia, bustling Split is worth exploring in its own right. Allow a full day.

▲▲**Korčula** This "mini-Dubrovnik" island village features a scenic, walled Old Town peninsula with a looming fjord-like backdrop. Proudly historic Korčula has more than its share of offbeat museums, plus beaches in abundance. Allow a full day or more.

▲▲**Hvar** A mellow, low-impact island town with a shimmering harbor, hilltop fortress, and lively nightlife, Hvar is increasingly popular with fun-seekers. Hvar is less immediately striking but more seductively relaxing than Korčula. Allow a full day or more.

▲**Mljet National Park** If you like your islands without civilization, head for this carefully preserved getaway, great for hiking, biking, and swimming. Allow a day (most convenient as a side-trip from Dubrovnik).

Trogir This sleepy little village, across the bay from Split, is best known as a convenient spot to moor your yacht. Less thrilling than the bigger, better Hvar and Korčula, Torgir's biggest advantage is its easy proximity to Split. Allow a half-day.

For more on day trips from Dubrovnik, see page 248.

knowledgeable Denis can help you pick out a bottle of Croatian wine to suit your tastes (Mon–Fri 8:30–12:30 & 17:00–20:30, Sat 9:00–13:30, closed Sun, Obala Hrvatskog Narodnog Preporoda 3, tel. 021/348-031). For a wine primer before you visit, see page 57.

Getting Around Split

Most of what you'll want to see is within walking distance, but some sights (such as the Meštrović Gallery) are more easily reached by bus or taxi.

By Bus: Local buses, run by Promet, cost 9 kn per ride (or 8 kn if you buy ticket from a kiosk; ask for a *putna karta;* zone 1 is fine for any ride within Split, but you need the 19-kn zone 4 ticket for the ride to Trogir). Validate your ticket as you board the bus. Suburban buses to towns near Split (such as Salona or Trogir) generally use the Suburban Bus Station (Prigradski Autobusni Kolodvor), a 15-minute walk due north of the Old Town on Domovinskog rata. Bus information: www.promet-split.hr.

By Taxi: Taxis start at 18 kn, then cost around 8 kn per kilometer. Figure 50–60 kn for most rides within the city (for example, from the ferry terminal to most hotels)—but if going from one end of the Old Town to the other, it can be faster to walk. To call for a taxi, try Radio Taxi (tel. 021/970).

TOURS

Of Split

The only regularly scheduled **walking tours** of Split are run by Lifejacket Adventures, based at Modrulj Launderette (90 kn, April–Nov nearly nightly at 20:00—call ahead to confirm; tours depart from in front of launderette, last about 2 hours, and include a drink at the end; mobile 098-931-6400).

To hire your own **private guide,** contact the guide association, with an office on the Old Town's Peristyle square (330 kn for 2 people on a 2-hour tour, about 50 kn per person after that; June–Aug Mon–Fri 9:00–13:00 & 15:00–19:00, Sat 9:00–14:00, closed Sun; May and Sept Mon–Fri 9:00–17:00, Sat 9:00–15:00, closed Sun; even shorter hours Oct–April; tel. 021/360-058, tel. & fax 021/346-267, mobile 098-361-936).

From Split

Lifejacket Adventures, run by Australian couple Shane and Julie, works hard to come up with culturally meaningful excursions that connect travelers to the Croatia they came to see. You can choose among various full-day and multi-day trips to nearby islands. To get out on the open sea, consider their day trip to Brač Island on an authentic, old-fashioned *falkuša* fishing boat (730 kn, departs daily in summer at 8:30, includes a visit to the 16th-century Blaca Monastery and a traditional lunch with wine before returning to Split at 20:30). Once a week, the *falkuša* takes romantics out on a sunset tour, including traditional snacks and a swim on Čiovo Island (150 kn, 15 kn for drinks). They also arrange custom excursions, with a focus on kayaking, hiking, wine, history, archaeological sites, and rock climbing. Reserve ahead for any of these trips (call mobile 098-931-6400 or stop by Split's launderette, which Shane and Julie also run—see "Helpful Hints"; www .lifejacketadventures.com).

Elite Travel and **Atlas Travel** offer a variety of excursions from Split (mostly full-day, about €45–65). Itineraries include a tour of Split and Trogir, whitewater rafting on the nearby Cetina River, the island of Brač, the island of Hvar, Brač and Hvar together, the island of Korčula, Dubrovnik, and Plitvice Lakes National Park. This can be a quick, convenient way to get to places that are time-consuming to reach by public transportation. Get information and tickets at any travel agency, such as the Turistički Biro on the Riva (see "Tourist Information").

SELF-GUIDED WALK

Diocletian's Palace (Dioklecijanova Palača)

Split's only ▲▲▲ sight is the remains of Roman Emperor Diocletian's enormous retirement palace, sitting on the harbor in the heart of the city. Since the ruins themselves are now integrated into the city's street plan, exploring them is free (though you'll pay to enter a few parts—such as the cellars and the cathedral/mausoleum). Because fragments of the palace are poorly marked, and there are not yet any good guidebooks or audioguides for tracking down the remains, Split is a good place to take a walking tour or hire a local guide (see "Tours"). This self-guided tour explains the basics. To begin the tour, stand in front of the palace (at the east end of the Riva, at the corner with the map of Split and palace illustration) to get oriented.

Background: Diocletian grew up just inland from Split, in the town of Salona (Solin in Croatian)—which was then the capital of Dalmatia. He worked his way up the Roman hierarchy and became emperor (A.D. 284–305). Despite all of his achievements, Diocletian is best remembered for two questionable legacies: dividing the huge empire among four emperors (which helped administer it more efficiently, but began a splintering effect that arguably led to the empire's decline); and torturing and executing Christians, including thousands right here on the Dalmatian Coast.

As Diocletian grew older, he decided to return to his homeland for retirement. (Since he was in poor health, the medicinal sulfur spring here was another plus.) His massive palace took only 11 years to build—and this fast pace required a big push (more than 2,000 slaves died during construction). Huge sections of his palace still exist, modified by medieval and modern developers alike. To get a sense of the original palace, check out the big illustration posted across from the palace entry.

Palace Facade: The "front" of today's Split—facing the harbor—was actually the back door of Diocletian's Palace. There was no embankment in front of the palace back then, so the water came right up to this door—sort of an emergency exit by boat.

Visually trace the outline of the gigantic palace, which was more than 600 feet long on each side. On the corner to the right stands a big, rectangular guard tower (one of the original 16). To the left, the tower is gone and the corner is harder to pick out (look for the beginning of the newer-looking buildings). Erase in your mind the ramshackle two-story buildings added 200 years ago, which obscure the grandness of the palace wall.

Halfway up the facade, notice the row of 42 arched window frames (mostly filled in today). Diocletian and his family lived in the seaside half of the palace. Imagine him strolling back and forth along this fine arcade, enjoying the views of his Adriatic homeland. The inland, non-view half of the palace was home to 700 servants, bodyguards, and soldiers.

• *Now go through the door in the middle of the palace (known as the "Brass Gate"; under the* Substructure of Diocletian's Palace *banner). Just inside the door is the entrance to...*

Diocletian's Cellars (Podromi): Since the palace was built on land that sloped down to the sea, these chambers were built to level out the main floor (like a modern "daylight basement"). The cellars weren't used for storage; they were filled with water from three different sources: a freshwater spring, a sulfur spring, and the sea. Later, medieval residents used them as a dump. Rediscovered only in the last century, the cellars enabled archaeologists to derive the floor plan of some of the palace's long-gone sections. Today, these underground chambers are used for art exhibits and a little strip of souvenir stands. But before you go shopping,
explore the cellars at this end (15 kn, skimpy 10-kn guidebook; hours sporadic, but generally opens daily at 9:00 and closes June–Aug at 21:00, Sept at 20:00, May and Oct at 18:00, April at

Diocletian's Palace

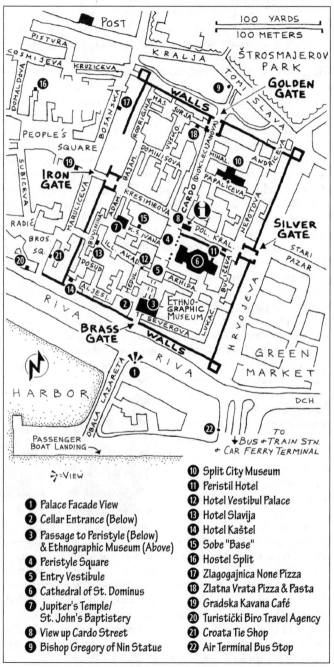

➤ =VIEW

1. Palace Facade View
2. Cellar Entrance (Below)
3. Passage to Peristyle (Below) & Ethnographic Museum (Above)
4. Peristyle Square
5. Entry Vestibule
6. Cathedral of St. Dominus
7. Jupiter's Temple/ St. John's Baptistery
8. View up Cardo Street
9. Bishop Gregory of Nin Statue
10. Split City Museum
11. Peristil Hotel
12. Hotel Vestibul Palace
13. Hotel Slavija
14. Hotel Kaštel
15. Sobe "Base"
16. Hostel Split
17. Zlagogajnica None Pizza
18. Zlatna Vrata Pizza & Pasta
19. Gradska Kavana Café
20. Turistički Biro Travel Agency
21. Croata Tie Shop
22. Air Terminal Bus Stop

17:00; Nov–March Mon–Sat 9:00–14:00, closed Sun).

Wander through the labyrinthine area beyond the ticket desk (on the left, or west, side of the palace). When those first villagers took refuge in the abandoned palace from the rampaging Slavs in 641, the elite lived upstairs, grabbing what was once the emperor's wing. They carved the rough holes you see in the ceiling to dump their garbage and sewage. Over the generations, the basement (where you're standing) filled up with waste and solidified, ultimately becoming a once-stinky, then-precious bonanza for 20th-century archaeologists. Today, the huge, vaulted main hall is used for everything from flower and book shows to fashion catwalks. As you poke around, notice the unexcavated wings—a compost pile of ancient lifestyles, awaiting the tiny shovels and toothbrushes of future archaeologists. The headless black granite sphinx is one of 13 that Diocletian brought home from Egypt. The two beams on display once supported floorboards overhead (see the holes on either side of the vaults).

You can also explore the cellars on the east side (same ticket). Among other things, you'll see a semicircular marble table used by the Romans, who—as shown in Hollywood movies—ate lying down (three would lounge and feast, while servants dished things up from the straight side).

• *When you're finished, head back to the main gallery, where you can shop your way down the passage and up the stairs into the...*

Peristyle (Peristil): This square was the centerpiece of Diocletian's Palace. As you walk up the stairs, the entry vestibule into the residence is above your head, Diocletian's mausoleum (today's Cathedral of St. Dominus) is to your right, and the street to Jupiter's Temple is on your left. The little chapel straight ahead houses the TI, and beyond that is the narrow street to the former main entrance to the palace, the Golden Gate.

Go to the middle of the square and take it all in. The red granite pillars—which you'll see all over Diocletian's Palace—are from Egypt, where Diocletian spent many of his pre-retirement years. Imagine the pillars defining fine arcades—now obscured by medieval houses. (As the Peristyle is undergoing a lengthy restoration, you may notice some of the ruins are lighter-colored than others.) The black sphinx is the only one of Diocletian's collection of 13 that's still (mostly) intact. Here or elsewhere in the Old Town, you're likely to run into a roving band of CD-selling *klapa* singers, performing traditional a cappella harmonies.

• *Climb the stairs (above where you came in) into the domed, open-ceilinged...*

Entry Vestibule: Impressed? That's the idea. This was the grand entry to Diocletian's living quarters, meant to wow visitors. Emperors were believed to be gods. Diocletian called himself "Jovius"—the son of Jupiter, the most powerful of all gods. Four times a year (at the change of the seasons), Diocletian would stand here and overlook the Peristyle. His subjects would lie on the ground in worship, praising his name. Notice the four big niches at floor level, which once held statues of the four tetrarchs who ruled the unwieldy empire after Diocletian retired. The empty hole in the ceiling was once capped by a dome (long since collapsed), and the ceiling itself was covered with frescoes and mosaics. Wander out back to the harbor side through medieval buildings (some with seventh-century foundations), which evoke the way local villagers came in and took over the once-spacious and elegant palace. Back in this area, you'll find the beautifully restored new home of the **Ethnographic Museum** (described under "Sights and Activities" later in this chapter).

• *Now go back into the Peristyle square and turn right, climbing the steps to the...*

Cathedral of St. Dominus (Katedrala Sv. Duje): The original octagonal structure was Diocletian's elaborate mausoleum, built in the fourth century. But after the fall of Rome, it was converted into the town's cathedral. Construction on the bell tower began in the 13th century and took 300 years to complete. Before you go inside, notice the sarcophagi ringing the cathedral. In the late Middle Ages, this was prime post-mortem real estate, since being buried closer to a cathedral improved your chances of getting to heaven.

Step inside the oldest building used as a cathedral anywhere in Christendom (5 kn, get the 10-kn combo-ticket that includes Jupiter's Temple—see below, daily 7:00–19:00, may be closed for midday siesta, Kraj Sv. Duje 5, tel. 021/344-121). Imagine the place in pre-Christian times, with Diocletian's tomb in the center. The only surviving decor from those days are the granite columns and the relief circling the base of the dome (about 50 feet up)—a ring of carvings heralding the greatness of the emperor. The small, multicolored marble pillars around the top of the pulpit (near the entry) were scavenged from Diocletian's sarcophagus. These pillars are all that survive of Diocletian's remains.

Diocletian brutally persecuted his Christian subjects, sometimes in the crypt of this very building. To kick off his retirement upon his arrival on the Dalmatian Coast, he had Bishop Dominus of Salona killed, along with several thousand Christians. When Diocletian died, there were riots of happiness. In the seventh century, his mausoleum became a cathedral dedicated to the martyred bishop. The extension behind the altar was added in the ninth century, and the doors are 12th-century walnut originals. The sarcophagus of St. Dominus (to the right of the altar, with early-Christian carvings) was once the cathedral's high altar. To the left of today's main altar is the altar of St. Anastasius—lying on a millstone, which is tied to his neck. On Diocletian's orders, this Christian martyr was drowned in the Adriatic. Posthumous poetic justice: Now Christian saints are entombed in Diocletian's mausoleum...and Diocletian is nowhere to be found.

For another 5 kn, you can climb steep steps to the top of the **bell tower.** You'll be rewarded with sweeping views of Split, but it's not for claustrophobes or those scared of heights. The building's **crypt** was also recently opened to the public (5 kn, yet another separate ticket).

Jupiter's Temple/St. John's Baptistery: Remember that Diocletian believed himself to be Jovius (that's Jupiter, Jr.). On exiting the mausoleum of Jovius, worshippers would look straight ahead to the temple of Jupiter. (Back then, of course, all of these medieval buildings weren't cluttering up the view.) Make your way through the narrow alley, past another headless, pawless sphinx, to explore the small temple (using the 10-kn combo-ticket you bought at the cathedral, same hours as cathedral; if it's locked, go ask the guy at the cathedral to let you in).

The temple has long since been converted into a baptistery—with a big 12th-century baptismal font and a statue of St. John by the great Croatian sculptor Ivan Meštrović (EE-vahn MESH-troh-veech, see page 165). The half-barrel vaulted ceiling is considered the best preserved of its kind anywhere. Every face and each patterned box is different.

• *Back at the Peristyle square, stand in front of the TI with your back to the entry vestibule (and harbor). The little street just beyond the TI (going left to right) connects the east and west gates. If you've had enough Roman history, head right (east) to go through the "Silver Gate" and find Split's busy, open-air Green Market. Or, head to the left (west), which takes you to the "Iron Gate" and People's Square (see below), and, beyond that, the fresh-and-smelly fish market. But if you want to see one last bit of Roman history, continue straight ahead up the...*

Cardo: This street—which translates as "Hot Street"—was the most important in Diocletian's Palace, connecting the main entry with the heart of the complex. As you walk, you'll pass a bank with modern computer gear all around its exposed Roman ruins (first building on the right, look through window), a Venetian merchant's palace (a reminder that Split was dominated by Venice from the 15th century on—step into his courtyard, first gate on left), an alley to the **City Museum** (on the right—see "Sights and Activities"), and a fan shop for Hajduk Split, the city's extremely popular soccer team (on left, with *Umbro* sign).

• *Before long, you'll pass through the...*

Golden Gate (Zlatna Vrata): This great gate was the main entry of Diocletian's Palace. Its name came from the golden statues of Diocletian and other Roman VIPs that once adorned it. Standing inside the gate itself, you can appreciate the double-door design that kept the palace safe. Also notice how this ancient building is now being used in very different ways from its original purpose. Up above on the outer wall, you can see the bricked-in windows that contain part of a Dominican convent. At the top of the inner wall, notice somebody's garden terrace.

Go outside the gate, where you'll get a much clearer feel for the way the palace looked before so many other buildings were grafted on. Straight ahead from here is Salona (Solin), which was a major city of 60,000 (and Diocletian's hometown) before there was a Split. The big statue by Ivan Meštrović is **Bishop Gregory of Nin,** a 10th-century Croatian priest who tried to convince the Vatican to allow sermons during Mass to be said in Croatian, rather than Latin. People rub his toe for good luck (though only non-material wishes are given serious consideration).

• *Your tour is finished. Now enjoy the rest of Split.*

SIGHTS AND ACTIVITIES

In or near the Old Town
▲▲Strolling the Riva (Obala Hrvatskog Narodnog Preporoda)—The official name for this seaside pedestrian drag is the "Croatian National Revival Embankment," but locals just call it "Riva" (Italian for "harbor"). This is the town's promenade, an integral part of Mediterranean culture. After dinner, Split residents collect their families and friends for a stroll on the Riva. It offers some of the best people-watching in Croatia; make it a point to be here for an hour or two after dinner. At the west end of the Riva, the people-parade of Croatian culture turns right and heads away from the water, up Marmontova. The stinky smell that sometimes accompanies the stroll isn't a sewer. It's sulfur—a reminder that the town's medicinal sulfur spas have attracted people here since the days of Diocletian.

▲People's Square (Narodni Trg)—The lively square at the center of the Old Town is called by locals simply *Pjaca,* pronounced the same as the Italian *piazza*. Stand in the center and enjoy the bustle. Look around for a quick lesson in Dalmatian history. When Diocletian lived in his palace, a Roman village popped up here, just outside the wall. Face the former wall of Diocletian's Palace (behind and to the right of the 24-hour clock tower). This was the western gate, or so-called "Iron Gate." By the 14th century, a medieval town had developed, making this the main square of Split. The city's grand old café, Gradska Kavana, has been the Old Town's venerable meeting point for generations (drinks and cakes but no meals, daily 7:00–24:00). Across the square, the white building jutting out into the square was once the City Hall, and now houses temporary exhibitions. The loggia is all that remains of the original Gothic building. Directly to your left as you face the loggia is the Nakić House, built in the early-20th-century Viennese Secession style—a reminder that Dalmatia was part of the Hapsburg Empire, ruled by Vienna, from Napoleon's downfall through World War I. The lane on the right side of this building leads to Split's fish market (Ribarnica).

Ethnographic Museum (Etnografski Muzej)—This museum uses temporary exhibits to show off the culture, costumes, and customs of Dalmatia. The collection was recently transplanted to this gorgeously renovated early-medieval palace, hiding on the upper level of the Old Town behind Diocletian's entry vestibule. Check out the artsy "golden fleece" entry door. On the ground floor, you'll find the remains of a seventh-century church. The upstairs exhibit often includes a look at traditional folk dress (10 kn, some English explanations; June–mid-Sept Mon–Fri 9:00–21:00, Sat 9:00–13:00, closed Sun; mid-Sept–May Mon–Fri 9:00–14:00, Sat 9:00–13:00, closed Sun; Severova 7, tel. 021/344-164).

Split City Museum (Muzej Grada Splita)—This museum traces how the city grew over the centuries. It's a bit dull, but it can help you appreciate a little better the layers of history you're seeing in the streets. The ground floor displays Roman fragments (including coins from the days of Diocletian) and temporary exhibits. The upstairs focuses on the Middle Ages (find the terrace displaying carved stone monuments), and the top floor goes from the 16th century to the present (10 kn, some English descriptions, 75-kn guidebook is overkill; May–Sept Tue–Fri 9:00–21:00, Sat–Sun 9:00–16:00, closed Mon; Oct–April Tue–Fri 9:00–16:00, Sat–Sun 10:00–13:00, closed Mon; Papalićeva 1, tel. 021/344-917, www .mgst.net).

The 15th-century Papalić Palace, which houses the City Museum, is a sight all its own. At the end of the palace, near Cardo street, look up to see several typical Venetian-style Gothic-Renaissance windows. The stone posts sticking out of the wall next to them were used to hang curtains.

Radić Brothers Square (Trg Braće Radića)—A Venetian cita-del watches over this square, just off the Riva between the two halves of the Old Town. After Split became part of the Venetian Republic, there was a serious danger of attack by the Ottomans, so octagonal towers like this were built all along the coast. But this imposing tower had a second purpose: to encourage citizens of Split to forget about any plans of rebellion. In the middle of the square is a studious sculpture by Ivan Meštrović of the poet Marko Marulić, who is considered the father of the Croatian language. Marulić was the first to write literature in the Croatian vernacular, which before then had generally been considered a backward peas-ants' tongue.

On the downhill (harbor) side of the square is **Croata,** a neck-tie boutique that loves to explain how Croatian soldiers who fought with the French in the Thirty Years' War (1618–1648) had a distinc-tive way of tying their scarves. The French found it stylish, adopted it, and called it *à la Croate*—or eventually, *cravate*—thus creating the modern tie that many people wear to work every day throughout the world. Croata's selection includes ties with traditional Croatian motifs, such as the checkerboard pattern from the flag or writing in the ninth-century Glagolitic alphabet. Though pricey, these ties are good souvenirs (cheaper ties-149 kn, top-quality ties-399 kn, Mon–Fri 8:00–20:00, Sat 8:00–14:00, closed Sun).

Green Market—This lively open-air market bustles at the east end of Diocletian's Palace. Locals shop for produce and clothes here, and there are plenty of tourist souvenirs as well. Browse the wide selection of T-shirts, and ignore the creepy black-market tobacco salesmen who mutter at you: *"Cigaretta?"*

Split's Outskirts
▲▲Meštrović Gallery (Galerija Meštrović)—Split's best art museum is dedicated to the sculptor Ivan Meštrović (1883–1962), the most important and most famous of all Croatian artists. Many

of Meštrović's finest works are housed in this palace, designed by the sculp-tor himself. If you have time, it's worth the 20-minute walk or short bus or taxi ride from the Old Town.

Meštrović grew up in a family of poor, nomadic farm workers just inland from Split. At an early age, his drawings and wooden carvings showed promise, and a rich family took him in and made sure he was properly trained. He eventually went off to school in Vienna, where he fell in with the Secession movement and found fame and fortune. Later in life—like Diocletian before him—Meštrović returned to Split and built a huge seaside mansion (today's Meštrović Gallery). During World War II, Meštrović moved abroad to escape the Nazi puppet government and lectured at Notre Dame (in Indiana, not France) and Syracuse (in New York, not Italy).

You'll see Meštrović's works all over Split and throughout Croatia. Most are cast bronze, depicting biblical, mythological, political, and everyday themes. Whether whimsical or emotional, Meštrović's expressive, elongated faces—often with a strong-profile nose—connect with the viewer. In this collection, don't miss *Job*, howling with an agony verging on insanity—carved by the artist in exile, as his country was turned upside-down by World War II. A moving contrast is the quietly poignant *Roman Pietà*, with mournful faces at painful angles pondering the dead body of Christ (20 kn, in summer Tue–Sat 9:00–21:00, Sun 12:00–21:00, closed Mon, shorter hours off-season—call to confirm it's open before making the trip, Šetalište Ivana Meštrovića 46, tel. 021/340-800, www .mdc.hr/mestrovic).

If you enjoy the gallery, continue walking five more minutes down Šetalište Ivana Meštrovića to **Kaštelet Chapel** ("Chapel of the Holy Cross"), a 16th-century fortified palace Meštrović bought to display his wooden carvings of Jesus' life. The centerpiece is a powerful wooden crucifix (included in ticket for gallery, but open shorter hours: in summer Tue–Sat 9:30–16:00, Sun 12:00–17:00, closed Mon; even shorter hours off-season).

Marjan Peninsula—This long, hilly peninsula extends west from the center of Split. This is where Split goes to relax, with out-of-the-way beaches and lots of hiking trails (great views and a zoo on top).

Hit the Beach—Since it's more of a big city than a resort, Split's beaches aren't as scenic (and the water not as clear) as small towns elsewhere along the coast. The beach that's most popular—and crowded—is Bačvice, in a sandy cove just east of the main ferry terminal. You'll find less crowded beaches just to the east of Bačvice. Locals like to hike around Marjan, the peninsular city park (see above), ringed with several sunbathing beaches.

NIGHTLIFE

The Riva—Every night in Split, the sea of Croatian humanity laps at the walls of Diocletian's Palace along the town's pedestrian promenade. Choose a bench and watch life go by, or enjoy a drink at one of the many outdoor cafés.

Old Town Pubs—Wander the labyrinthine lanes of the Old Town to find the pub of your choice. Several cluster along Majstora Jurja

Sleep Code

(€1 = about $1.20, 6 kn = about $1, country code: 385, area code: 021)
S = Single, **D** = Double/Twin, **T** = Triple, **Q** = Quad, **b** = bathroom. The modest tourist tax (7 kn or €1 per person, per night, lower off-season) is not included in these rates. Hotels generally accept credit cards and include breakfast in their rates, while most *sobe* accept only cash and don't offer breakfast. All my recommended accommodations speak English.

To help you sort easily through these listings, I've divided the rooms into three categories based on the price for a standard double room with bath in peak season:

$$$ **Higher Priced**—Most rooms 800 kn (€110) or more.
  $$ **Moderately Priced**—Most rooms between 500–800 kn (€70–110).
    $ **Lower Priced**—Most rooms 500 kn (€70) or less.

(just inside Golden Gate and—facing outside—to the left about a block) and near Radić Brothers Square (Trg Braće Radića; from the square's statue of Marulić, enter the Old Town and bear right, following the beat).

Bačvice Beach—This family-friendly beach by day becomes a throbbing party zone for young locals late at night. Since all Old Town bars have to close by 1:00 in the morning, night owls hike on over to the Bačvice crescent of clubs. The three-floor club complex is a cacophony of music, with the beat of each club melting into the next—all with breezy terraces overlooking the harbor.

SLEEPING

Several new hotels have cropped up in Split over the last few years, but there still aren't enough beds in peak season—so hoteliers are shameless about gouging their customers.

Many of my recommended hotels are conveniently located in the Old Town. Unfortunately, this is also a happening nightlife zone, so you're likely to encounter some noise (especially on weekends). Bring earplugs and request a quiet room, if one is available. Old Town bars are required to close by 1:00 in the morning, so at least things will quiet down before the birds start chirping. To locate these accommodations, see the maps on pages 149 and 159.

$$$ **Peristil Hotel** is my favorite Old Town splurge, with 12 classy rooms over a restaurant just steps from the couldn't-be-more-central square of the same name. Well-run by the Caktaš

family, it's homey and convenient, if a bit pricey (July–Aug: Sb-850 kn, Db-1,000 kn; May–June and Sept–Oct: Sb-750 kn, Db-900 kn; Nov–April: Sb-650 kn, Db-800 kn; air-con, stairs with no elevator, just behind TI and inside Silver Gate at Poljana Kraljice Jelene 5, tel. 021/329-070, fax 021/329-088, www.hotelperistil .com, hotel.peristil@email.t-com.hr).

$$$ Hotel Vestibul Palace is the swankiest splurge in Split. Tucked in a corner just behind the entry vestibule on the upper level of Diocletian's Palace, this plush new place offers seven rooms with maximum comfort and style for maximum prices (July–Sept: Sb-980–1,150 kn, Db-1,650 kn; Oct–June: Sb-820–960 kn, Db-1,400 kn; prices depend on size and amenities of room, pricier suites also available, air-con, Iza Vestibula 4, tel. 021/329-329, fax 021/329-333, www.vestibulpalace.com, info@vestibulpalace.com).

$$$ Hotel Adriana has 15 nice, new-feeling rooms perched right above the people-packed Riva. Choose between harborview front rooms or quieter back rooms. Unfortunately, the place suffers from absentee management and iffy service, and the rooms are an afterthought to the busy restaurant (Sb-650 kn, Db-850 kn, 100 kn less off-season, pricier apartments also available, air-con, elevator, Riva 8, tel. 021/340-000, fax 021/340-008, www.hotel-adriana.hr, info@hotel-adriana.hr).

$$ Villa Ana may just be the best small hotel on the Dalmatian Coast, with five modern, comfortable rooms in a smart little house a five-minute walk from the Old Town. This delightful, free-standing stone home is well-run by Danijel Bilobrk and his family. Though it's in a boring urban neighborhood, it's pristine and welcoming inside (Sb-600 kn, Db-750 kn, Tb-850 kn, roughly 150 kn less Nov–March, air-con, reception open 7:00–24:00, may be closed Dec–Feb, street parking or a tight little parking spot, 2 long blocks east of Old Town up busy Kralja Zvonimira, follow the driveway-like lane opposite Koteks skyscraper to Vrh Lučac 16, tel. 021/482-715, fax 021/482-721, www.villaana-split.hr, info @villaana-split.hr).

$$ Villa Diana, a new place right next door to Villa Ana (see above), has six similar but smaller rooms over a lively cocktail bar. It's a lesser value than the Ana, but still plenty nice and comfortable (April–Oct: Sb-610 kn, Db-750 kn; Nov–March: Sb-550 kn, Db-690 kn; pricier apartments also available, air-con, Kuzmanića 3, follow walking directions for Villa Ana, tel. & fax 021/482-451, www.villadiana.hr, info@villadiana.hr).

$$ Hotel Slavija shares a tiny square with some very popular late-night discos and cafés, so it can be noisy—especially on weekends (new windows attempt, with only some success, to keep out the throbbing dance beat; try requesting a quieter back room). Each of its 25 starkly modern rooms is a little different, some with balconies for no extra charge. Ongoing improvements are planned, so rates may increase in the near future (Sb-550 kn, Db-790 kn, Tb-900, suites, huge family rooms, air-con, a block from Radić Brothers Square at Buvinina 2—look for the low-profile sign at the top of a white staircase, tel. 021/323-840, fax 021/323-868, www .hotelslavija.com, info@hotelslavija.com).

$ Hotel Kaštel, run by the quirky Čaleta family, has seven rooms and five apartments at the end of a forgotten alley just inside the wall of Diocletian's Palace. The rooms (some with views overlooking the Riva) are basic but newish, making this a decent budget choice. It's in a slightly quieter area than some Old Town hotels, and most of the rooms have double-paned windows, but a little noise can sneak in (complicated pricing structure, figure Db-€60–65 July–Aug, €50–55 June and Sept, cheaper off-season, 10 percent less for Sb, Mihovilova širina 5, mobile 091-120-0348, www.kastelsplit.com, info@kastelsplit.com).

$ Sobe "Base" has three of the nicest rooms in the Old Town, each with most of the big hotel amenities (including Internet terminals). You can't be more central: All of the rooms—over an artsy gallery—overlook the front steps of the cute little Jupiter's Temple (Sb/Db-450 kn, no extra charge for 1- or 2-night stays, cash only, air-con, Kraj Svetog Ivana 3, tel. 021/317-375, mobile 098-361-387, www.base-rooms.com, mail@base-rooms.com). Because a bustling nightlife zone is just around the corner, expect some nighttime noise (even though the double-paned windows do their darnedest to provide silence).

$ Other *Sobe:* Though there are very few *sobe* inside Split's Old Town, there are plenty within a 10-minute walk. As in any coastal town, you can simply show up at the boat dock or bus station, be met by locals trying to persuade you into their rooms, and check out the best offer (about 250 kn for a double). Or you can try the **Turistički Biro,** a booking agency. You can generally make a reservation in advance, then drop by their office, pay, pick up your welcome packet, and head off to your awaiting landlady. Or you can just drop in—they can always find you something (mid-July–mid-Aug: S-240 kn, Sb-280 kn, D-350 kn, Db-400 kn; June–mid-July and mid-Aug–Sept: S-190 kn, Sb-220 kn, D-300 kn, Db-340 kn; Oct–May: S-170 kn, Sb-190 kn, D-250 kn, Db-290 kn; plus 7 kn per person, per night for tourist tax, no breakfast, 30 percent less for stays of 4 nights or more; office open mid-June–Sept Mon–Fri 8:00–21:00, Sat 8:00–20:00, open Sun 8:00–13:00 mid-July–mid-Sept only, otherwise closed Sun; Oct–mid-June Mon–Fri 8:00–20:00, Sat 8:00–13:00, closed Sun; Riva 12, tel. & fax 021/347-100, turist-biro-split@st.t-com.hr).

$ Hostel Split is a brand-new place just off of Narodni Trg in the very heart of town. Run by a pair of Aussie women with the simple slogan "booze & snooze," it's Split's most central hostel option (€17 per person in 6–8-bed rooms, €3 cheaper off-season, 8 Narodni Trg, tel. 021/342-787, www.splithostel.com, info @splithostel.com).

EATING

Split's Old Town has oodles of atmosphere, but if you venture just a couple of blocks west of the Old Town, you'll discover my three favorite places (Šperun, Konoba Varoš, and Buffet Fife). To locate most of these eateries, see the map on page 149; for None and Zlatna Vrata, see the map on page 159.

Šperun Restaurant has a classy, cozy Old World ambience and a passion for good Dalmatian food. Zdravko Banović and his son Damir serve a mix of Croatian and "eclectic Mediterranean," specializing in seafood. A "buffet" table in the lower dining room shows you what you're getting, so you can select your ideal meal (not self-service—order from the waiter). This place distinguishes itself by offering a warm welcome and high-quality food for reasonable prices (35–50-kn pastas, 40–80-kn meat and seafood, air-con interior, a few sidewalk tables, reservations wise June–Aug, daily 9:00–23:00, Šperun 3, tel. 021/346-999).

Konoba Varoš, though pricier than Šperun and a bit impersonal, is beloved by natives and tourists alike for its great food. Serious, vest-wearing waiters serve a wide range of Croatian cooking (including pastas, seafood, and meat dishes) under droopy fishnets. Their 60-kn carpaccio starter—thinly sliced strips of raw meat or fish sprinkled with lemon and olive oil and served with lettuce and cheese—will get you in an Adriatic-seaside mood (55–95-kn main dishes, lots of groups, reservations smart—busiest 20:00–22:00, daily 9:00–24:00, Ban Mladenova 7, tel. 021/396-138).

Buffet Fife is your cheap, dream-come-true fish joint, where a colorful local crowd shares rough wood tables, and the waitstaff seem brusque until you crack them up. Zvonko (the charming-as-a-cartoon waiter) ignores the menu, declaring, *"Ja sum meni!"* (*"I am the menu!"*) to the chuckles of his regulars. You can eat in the tiny, mostly locals bar in the main building; out front, on the tourist-laden terrace; or across the alley, in their little annex (35–45-kn main dishes, 10-kn sides, daily 7:00–24:00, walk 200 yards along the waterfront west of Old Town to Trumbičeva obala 11, poorly marked—look for salty locals standing out front, tel. 021/345-223).

Fast and Cheap: **Zlagogajnica None** ("Grandma's") is a stand-up or take-away pizza joint handy for a quick bite in the Old Town. In addition to pizzas, sandwiches, and bruschettas with various toppings, they serve up a pair of traditional pizza-like specialties (with crust on bottom and top, like a filled pizza): *viška pogača,* with tomatoes, onion, and anchovy; and *soparnik,* with a thin layer of spinach, onion, and olive oil (8–18 kn, Sun–Fri 7:00–23:00, closed Sat except in summer, just outside Diocletian's Palace on the skinny street that runs along the wall at Bosanska 4, tel. 021/347-252).

Pizzerias: **Zlatna Vrata** ("Golden Gate"), right in the Old Town, offers wood-fired pizzas and pasta dishes. The food and interior are nothing special, but there's wonderful outdoor seating in a tingle-worthy Gothic courtyard with pointy arches and lots of pillars (30–50 kn, Mon–Sat 7:00–24:00, closed Sun except maybe in summer, just inside the Golden Gate and—as you face outside—up the skinny alley to the left, on Majstora Jurja, tel. 021/345-015). **Ristorante Pizzeria Galija,** at the west end of the Old Town, has a local following and good wood-fired pizza, pasta, and salads (25–50-kn pizzas and pasta dishes, air-con, Mon–Sat 9:00–24:00, Sun 12:00–24:00, just a block off of the pedestrian drag Marmontova at Tončićeva 12, tel. 021/347-932).

On the Riva: **Restaurant Adriana** is your only choice for dining (not just drinks and desserts) on the harborfront promenade. It's packed with tourists, so you'll get crank-'em-out food and service for top prices. But with entertaining people-watching, it's not a bad place for a slow meal or scenic drink (55–90-kn main dishes, 45–50-kn pizzas, daily 7:00–24:00, Riva 8, tel. 021/340-000).

Gelato: Split has several spots for delicious Italian gelato-style ice cream *(sladoled).* Locals swarm to a pair of ice-cream parlors near Trg Gaje Bulata (the modern shopping square—with a McDonald's, big Prima mall, and modern-looking church—at the end of the Marmontova pedestrian drag just beyond the northwest corner of the Old Town): **Kuća Sladoleda Karmen** (daily 8:00–24:00, hides behind the building in the middle of the square, facing the modern church on Kačićeva) and **Hajduk** (daily 8:00–24:00, a block west from the top of Marmontova and around the corner from Galija pizzeria at Matošićeva 4). To my taste buds, these two spots are much better than the other options in town.

TRANSPORTATION CONNECTIONS

Split Boat Connections

As the transport hub for the Dalmatian Coast, Split has good boat connections to most anywhere you want to go. Big car ferries use the main ferry terminal at the end of the harbor, while passenger boats (including fast catamarans) depart from the handy Obala Lazareta embankment just in front of the Old Town. Be warned that the following boat information, based on the 2006 schedules,

Sailing Between Croatia and Italy

Many travelers are tempted to splice a little bit of Croatia into their Italian itinerary, or vice versa. But zipping across the Adriatic isn't as effortless as it seems. Most sea crossings involve an overnight on the boat, and the Italian towns best connected to Croatia—Ancona, Pescara, and Bari—are far from Italy's top sights. Plan thoughtfully. For example, if you're in northern Italy and want to sample Croatia, it's much easier to dip into Slovenia and Istria than it is to get all the way down to Croatia's Dalmatian Coast.

If you decide to set sail, you have several options, run by various companies. Split is the primary hub, but you can also go from other cities (usually Dubrovnik or Zadar; some international ferries also call at the small Dalmatian islands). Almost all boats go to Ancona, Italy, which is about two-thirds of the way up the Italian coast (on the calf of Italy's "boot"). Others go to Pescara, about 100 miles south of Ancona; and to Bari, near the southern tip of Italy (the heel). Most trips are overnight and last 8–10 hours, but there are faster daytime catamarans.

Slow Night Boats: Figure about €40 per person for one-way deck passage (about 10–20 percent more in peak season, roughly July–Aug; sometimes even more on weekends). On-board accommodation costs extra (about €10 per person for a couchette in a 4-berth compartment, €45 per person in 2-bed compartment with private shower and WC). Three different companies operate night boats to Italy:

Jadrolinija goes from Split to Ancona, from Split to Pescara, from Zadar to Ancona, and from Dubrovnik to Bari (tel. 051/211-444, www.jadrolinija.hr).

Blue Line sails from Split to Ancona, stopping en route at either Stari Grad (on Hvar Island) or Vis Island (can book at Split Tours travel agency in Split, tel. 021/352-533, www.bli-ferry.com).

is highly subject to change—always confirm before you make your plans. Split's Jadrolinija boat ticket office is in the main ferry terminal (see "Arrival in Split," page 151), with several smaller branch offices between there and the Old Town (tel. 021/338-333).

Big Jadrolinija Car Ferries: These hulking boats generally leave Split early in the morning (at 6:30 or 7:00) and head south, stopping at **Stari Grad** on Hvar Island (20-min bus ride from Hvar town; 5/week July–mid-Sept, 2/week mid-Sept–June, 1.75 hrs; the catamarans described next are faster and take you right to Hvar town), **Korčula town** (5/week July–mid-Sept, 3/week June, 2/week mid-Sept–May, 3.5–6 hrs), and **Dubrovnik** (2/week year-round, 8.25–9.25 hrs, more with transfer in Korčula). You can also sleep

Azzurraline goes between Bari and Dubrovnik, and between Bari and Kotor, Montenegro (Croatian tel. 020/313-178, Italian tel. 080-592-8400, www.azzurraline.com).

Most nights in summer, at least one of these companies is running a night boat. Other companies serving these routes come and go each year—ask the Split TI or poke around Split's main terminal building to discover the latest.

Fast Daytime Boats: There are some speedier crossings available. But because these boats are faster and smaller, they're also weather-dependent—so they don't run off-season. **Aliscafi SNAV** connects Split and Ancona in just 4.5 hours (€65 one-way, or €85 in peak season—late July–early Sept). They also zip from Split to Stari Grad (on Hvar Island), then on to the Italian town of Pescara (4.75 hours total, €70 one-way, or €90 in peak season; all boats sail daily mid-June–mid-Sept, Croatian tel. 021/322-252, Italian tel. 081-428-5555, www.snav.it). **La Riviera Lines** sometimes runs a similar fast boat between Termoli, Italy, and Korčula or Hvar (Italian tel. 0875-82248, www.lariveralines.com).

Trains Within Italy: From **Ancona,** you can catch a train to Venice (almost hourly, 4.25–5.25 hrs, most transfer in Bologna), Florence (almost hourly, 3–4.25 hrs, most transfer in Bologna), or Rome (8/day direct, 3–4.5 hrs). From **Pescara,** trains head to Rome (6/day direct, 3.75–4.25 hrs) and Florence (almost hourly, 4.5–5.25 hrs, transfer in Bologna). From **Bari,** you can hop a train to Naples (6/day, 3.75–6 hrs, most transfer in Caserta), Rome (3/day direct, 4.75 hrs), or Florence (8/day, 6.75–8.5 hrs, transfer in Rome or Bologna).

Northern Italy/Croatia: Venice is connected by boat to several seaside towns in northern Croatia and Slovenia. For details, see page 90.

Note that in Italian, Split is called Spalato (which is also the sound you hear if seasickness gets the best of you).

on the boat as it heads north to **Rijeka** (2/week, 11 hrs overnight).

Other Boats to Hvar Island: Ideally, catch a boat heading to Hvar town, the most interesting part of the island. Speedy **Jadrolinija catamarans** run from Split to Hvar town twice a day June through September (departing Split at 11:30 and 15:00, 50 min to Hvar town, occasionally stops at Milna on Brač Island). A different company runs the similar *Krilo* catamaran directly from Split to Hvar town (June–Sept: departs Split daily at 17:00; Oct–May: departs Split 4/week at 16:00; 1.25 hrs to Hvar town). Six days a week in the summer, a much **slower car ferry** putters from Split to Hvar town (late June–early Sept only, departs Split at 10:00, arrives Hvar at 12:00; even though this is a car ferry, only foot passengers can get on and off at Hvar). Finally, if you're desperate, you can also reach Hvar Island on the **frequent slow car ferries** from Split to the town of Stari Grad, across the island from Hvar town (at least 3/day, more in summer; from Stari Grad, it's an easy 20-minute bus trip into Hvar town).

Other Boats to Korčula Island: Many of the same boats that go to Hvar town (described previously) continue on to Korčula Island. The most convenient is the *Krilo* **catamaran,** which takes you right to Korčula town (June–Sept: departs Split daily at 17:00; Oct–May: departs Split 4/week at 16:00, 2.75 hrs to Korčula). The other boats leave you at Vela Luka, at the far end of Korčula Island from Korčula town (buses meet arriving boats to take passengers on the one-hour trip into Korčula town). The 15:00 **Jadrolinija catamaran** goes from Split to Hvar town, then to Vela Luka (June–Sept, 1.75 hrs to Vela Luka, occasionally stops at Mlina on Brač Island). Slower **car ferries** also go from Split to Vela Luka (2/day late June–early Sept, 1/day late Sept–early June, 2.75 hrs).

Sailing to Italy: See the sidebar on page 172.

Split Overland Connections

By Bus to: Zagreb (at least hourly, 5–8 hrs, depending on route, about 140 kn), **Dubrovnik** (almost hourly, less off-season, 5 hrs, about 100 kn), **Korčula** (1 night bus leaves 24:45 and arrives 6:00, 90–125 kn), **Trogir** (at least hourly, 30 min, about 20 kn), **Zadar** (at least hourly, 3 hrs, about 70 kn), **Rijeka** (nearly hourly, 8.5 hrs). Zagreb-bound buses sometimes also stop at **Plitvice** (confirm with driver and ask him to stop; about 8/day, 4–6 hrs, 70–80 kn). Each of these routes is served by multiple companies, which charge slightly different rates, so the prices listed here are rough estimates. Reservations for buses are generally not necessary, but always ask about the fastest option—which can save hours of bus time. Bus info: www.ak-split.hr, tel. 021/338-483 or toll tel. 060-327-777.

By Train to: Zagreb (3/day, 5.5 hrs, plus 1 direct night train, 8 hrs). Train info: tel. 021/338-525 or toll tel. 060-333-444.

Near Split: Trogir

Just 12 miles northwest of Split is Trogir, a tiny, medieval-architecture-packed town surrounded by water. This made-for-tourists village lacks the real-world heart and soul of Split, and it's more or less identical to a dozen other Croatian coastal resort towns (Korčula and Hvar are bigger and better—see pages 195 and 177). But even though it's nothing to jump ship for, Trogir is an easy day trip for those looking to get away from urban Split.

Trogir is a small island, wedged between the mainland and

the much bigger Čiovo island. Busy
bridges connect it to the rest of the
world at the east end, and a big soccer field squeezed between imposing
watchtowers anchors the west end. In
the middle is a tight medieval street
plan of twisty marbled-stone lanes.

Getting There: You have two
options for reaching Trogir from
Split, both roughly the same price
(15–20 kn). The faster, easier option
is to take a bus from Split's **main bus
station,** next to the City Harbor.
Any bus going north (for example, to Šibenik, Zadar, or even
Rijeka) will usually stop at Trogir (2/hr, about 30 min, simply go
to ticket window and ask for next bus to Trogir). Note that in the
busiest summer months, some long-distance buses may not want
to take you (preferring to give your seat instead to someone paying
for a longer trip). The other option is to take **local bus #37,** which
leaves from Split's inconveniently located Suburban Bus Station
(Prigradski Autobusni Kolodvor, a 15-min walk north of Old
Town on Domovinskog rata). Because this bus makes several stops
along the way, it can take 45–60 min, depending on traffic (leaves
every 20 min)—avoid it if you can. You'll need a ticket for zone 4
(19 kn, buy at ticket window or on bus).

Arrival in Trogir: Both buses drop you off at the mainland
market, just across the canal from the island. Cross the bridge
into town and wander straight ahead for two blocks (bearing left);
you'll run into the main square.

Tourist Information: At the main square, named for Pope
John Paul II (Trg Ivana Pavla II), you'll find the TI (June–Sept
daily 8:00–21:00, off-season closed afternoons and Sat–Sun, tel.
021/885-628, www.dalmacija.net/trogir.htm).

Sights: On the main square is the town's centerpiece, the
Cathedral of St. Lawrence (Katedrala Sv. Lovre). Built in the
13th through 17th centuries, the cathedral drips with history. The
bell tower alone took 200 years to build, leaving it a textbook lesson in Dalmatian architecture styles: straightforward Gothic at
the bottom, Venetian Gothic in the middle, and Renaissance at
the top. The cathedral's front entryway—the ornately decorated,
recently restored Radovan's Portal—is worth a gander. Inside, it's
dark, very old-feeling, and packed with altars. The treasury (5 kn)
features some beautiful 15th-century carved-wood cabinets filled
with ecclesiastical art and gear.

The town's other sights—both dull—are the **Town Museum**
(Muzej Grada), a few blocks north (toward the mainland) from

the main square, and the **Monastery of St. Nikola** (Samostan Sv. Nikole), a few blocks south (toward Čiovo island).

But Trogir isn't for museum-going; it's for aimless strolling. And the best place for that is along the wide, beautifully manicured **harborfront promenade** along the southern edge of town (Obala bana Berislavića). Lined with expensive restaurants, and clogged with giddy, ice-cream-licking tourists, this promenade is the highlight of a visit to Trogir. Often the enormous yachts of the rich and famous put in here, giving wanderers something to yak about. At the far end of the promenade, the **Kamerlengo Fortress** has a lookout tower with fine views over the town and region (10 kn).

Sleeping in Trogir: I see no reason to sleep in this little burg. But if you do, consider **$$ Hotel Concordia,** with 14 fine rooms at the end of the embankment (view Sb-350 kn, non-view Db-500 kn, small Db with view-550 kn, big Db with view-600 kn, 50 kn cheaper in winter, air-con, Obala bana Berislavića 22, tel. 021/885-400, fax 021/885-401, concordia-hotel@st.t-com.hr).

HVAR

Hvar is a rising star in the tourism world. Each year, another magazine or TV show includes it on a list of "world's top 10 most beautiful islands," and a young, international, jet-set crowd speaks of it as the next big thing. Hvar's hip cachet, and its easy proximity to Split, has quickly turned this tidy little fishing village into one of the top destinations on the Dalmatian Coast.

The island's main town, also called Hvar, lacks the fortified mini-Dubrovnik feel of rival Korčula—Hvar's straightforward Old Town melts into the harbor rather than dominating it. But as you get to know it, Hvar reveals itself to be a fun-loving, easygoing place to be on vacation. The rhythm of life here is soothing and natural, and a stroll through Hvar's back alleys is as rewarding as any village in Croatia. Hvar's quirky museums, while far from time-consuming, are enjoyable. The formidable fortress hovering above town provides restless beach bums with a good excuse for a hike, and rewards hikers with stunning views. And if you're seeking nightlife, many Croatians describe happening Hvar as a "party town" after hours.

History? Sure, Hvar's got that, too. Its tongue-twisting name comes from the ancient Greek settlement here: Pharos. Greeks from the island of Paros migrated here in the fourth century B.C., attracted by the fertile farmland. Since then, it's been occupied by Slavs, Venetians, Hapsburgs, and—today—tourists, all of whom have left their mark.

But the town is just the beginning. Hvar Island—which insists it's both the sunniest and greenest in Dalmatia—has plenty to offer visitors here long enough to do some exploring. Known for its fragrant fields of lavender and its red and white wines (which love the island's perfect combination of wind and sunshine), Hvar Island's gentle climate is appreciated by tourists and farmers alike. Every corner and cove of Hvar has something to offer, but for speedy tourists, the most obvious and easiest side-trip from Hvar town is the Pakleni Islands, a small archipelago just offshore.

Planning Your Time

For most, one Dalmatian island is enough—choose either Hvar or Korčula, and give it at least two nights and a full day. (To help you choose, see "The Dalmatian Coast at a Glance" on page 155.)

With a full day on Hvar, do your sightseeing in the morning, before the weather gets too hot and while the church sights are open (the cathedral and both monasteries close for lunch at 12:00). Then use the rest of the day to relax, swim at the beaches, explore the Old Town, hike up to the fortress, or take a trip out to Palmižana on the Pakleni Islands (this excursion works well in the late afternoon—take a dip while it's still hot, then hike over to Vlaka for your dinner reservation at Dionis).

Be warned that July and especially August are peak-of-the-peak season. When you ask locals about crowds in August, they roll their eyes and groan. It can be downright impossible to find a room, and the "undiscovered" back lanes and "hidden" offshore islands are jam-packed with tourists. In August, consider giving Hvar a miss. Conversely, the town is completely dead off-season (roughly mid-Oct–mid-May)—many hotels, restaurants, and even museums shut their doors for winter hibernation. The best times to visit Hvar are mid-May through the end of June, and September through mid-October.

ORIENTATION

(area code: 021)
First off, "Hvar" is pronounced like it's spelled, but the H is nearly silent. If you struggle with it, just say "var" (but don't say "huh-var," which just sounds silly to locals).

Hvar town (with about 4,000 residents) clusters around its harbor. The harbor's eastern embankment (to the right, with your back to the water) is where the big boats put in, and home to the Jadrolinija boat ticket office, most travel agencies, and the post office. Branching off to the east from the end of the harbor is Hvar's long, wide main

Hvar

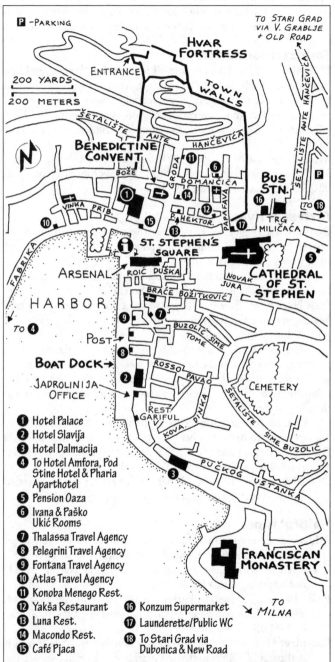

P –PARKING

TO STARI GRAD
VIA V. GRABLJE
& OLD ROAD

HVAR
FORTRESS

ENTRANCE

TOWN
WALLS

200 YARDS
200 METERS

ŠETALIŠTE

ANTE HANČEVIĆA

N

BENEDICTINE
CONVENT

ANTE HANČEVIĆA

BOŽE

GRODA

⓫

⑥

DOMANČIĆA

BUS
STN.

P

① ➡

⑭ +

⑫

PAPAFAVA

⑯

TO ⑱

VINKA PRIB.

⑮

P. HEKTOR.

⑰

TRG
MILIČAĆA

⑩

⓭

FABRIKA

ℹ

ST. STEPHEN'S
SQUARE

⑤

ARSENAL

ROIĆ DUŠKA

NOVAK
JURA

CATHEDRAL
OF ST.
STEPHEN

HARBOR

BRAĆE BOŽITKOVIĆ

TO ④

⑨

⑦

BUZOLIĆ ŠIME

TOME

CEMETERY

POST

⑧

BOAT DOCK→

②

ROSSOL
PAVAO

JADROLINIJA
OFFICE

REST.
GARIFUL

KOVA DINKA

ŠETALIŠTE ŠIME BUZOLIĆ

③

PUČKOG USTANKA

① Hotel Palace
② Hotel Slavija
③ Hotel Dalmacija
④ To Hotel Amfora, Pod
   Stine Hotel & Pharia
   Aparthotel
⑤ Pension Oaza
⑥ Ivana & Paško
   Ukić Rooms
⑦ Thalassa Travel Agency
⑧ Pelegrini Travel Agency
⑨ Fontana Travel Agency
⑩ Atlas Travel Agency
⓫ Konoba Menego Rest.
⑫ Yakša Restaurant
⓭ Luna Rest.
⑭ Macondo Rest.
⑮ Café Pjaca

⑯ Konzum Supermarket
⑰ Launderette/Public WC
⑱ To Stari Grad via
   Dubonica & New Road

FRANCISCAN
MONASTERY

TO
MILNA

square, St. Stephen's Square (Trg Svetog Stjepana). The Old Town scampers up the hills in either direction from St. Stephen's Square. Overlooking the town and harbor is a mighty hilltop fortress.

Tourist Information

Hvar's informative, no-nonsense TI is in the big Arsenal building right on the main square, a few steps from the harbor. Pick up the helpful free map and mini-guidebook; ask about this month's events calendar; and confirm details for your day trips and ferry connections (flexible hours, but generally mid-June–Aug daily 8:00–14:00 & 15:30–22:00; May–mid-June and Sept–Oct Mon–Sat 8:00–14:00 & 16:00–20:00, Sun 8:00–12:00; Nov–April Mon–Sat 8:00–14:00, closed Sun; Trg Svetog Stjepana, tel. 021/741-059, www.tzhvar.hr).

Arrival in Hvar

By Boat: Passenger boats to **Hvar town** arrive on the harbor's eastern embankment. Simply exit and walk to the left—you'll run right into St. Stephen's Square.

Car ferries to Hvar Island (including the big Jadrolinija coastal ferries) arrive just outside the town of **Stari Grad,** across the island from Hvar town. Buses are timed to meet arriving boats and take passengers over the island's picturesque spine to Hvar town (20 min, 10 kn).

By Bus: Hvar's bus station is just beyond the far end of St. Stephen's Square from the harbor. As you get off your bus, you can see the main tower of the cathedral—marking the town center, a two-minute walk away. The island's few **taxis** generally hang out at the bus station.

By Car: All car ferries come to the town of Stari Grad. There are two ways to drive to Hvar town: The speedy, newer road via Dubovica to the south; or the slower, windy road (through prettier, less-traveled terrain) via Brusje to the north. In Hvar, you can park by the bus station. Be warned that the car ferries can be crowded in summer—waiting two hours or more is not unusual.

Helpful Hints

Addresses: Everyone in Hvar ignores numbers, and even street names (you'll constantly see *b.b.*, meaning "without number"). Navigate with maps (a good one is available free at the TI) and by asking locals for directions.

Post Office: It's along the harbor's main (eastern) embankment, inside a little fenced courtyard (Mon–Fri 7:00–20:00, Sat 7:00–14:00, closed Sun).

Laundry: Hvar has a rare self-service launderette. You'll find it at the public toilets under the market on the main square (no

joke—look for big, blue *toillet* sign; 50-kn wash, 40-kn dry;
June–Oct daily 7:00–21:00; Nov–May Mon–Sat 7:00–12:00
& 16:00–18:00, closed Sun; to the left as you face the cathedral at Trg Svetog Stjepana 1).

Boat Tickets: You can get tickets for most connections at the
Jadrolinija office (open long hours daily in summer but closed
13:00–15:00 and Sun after 13:00, along the embankment
where the big boats put in, tel. 021/741-132). To buy tickets
for the *Krilo* catamaran to Split or Korčula, you'll have to go
to the **Pelegrini** travel agency at the opposite end of Hotel
Slavija (tel. 021/742-743, pelegrini@inet.hr).

Summer Fun: You name it, Hvar has it. Various agencies in towns
rent cars, scooters, bikes, motorboats, and more—just look for
signs or ask at the TI.

SIGHTS

▲▲St. Stephen's Square (Trg Svetog Stjepana)—Hvar's main
square, which is supposedly Dalmatia's biggest, is a relaxed and

relaxing people zone surrounded
by inviting cafés filled with deliri-
ously sun-baked tourists. For a
quick tour, begin by the harbor and
face the cathedral.

To your right is the **Arsenal**
building (housing the TI)—a
reminder of Hvar's nautical importance through history, thanks to its
ideal location on the sailing route
between Venice and the Mediterranean. During the town's seafaring heyday, ships were repaired and supplied in this huge building
that still dominates the town.

Many of Hvar's buildings date from the 16th and 17th centuries, when it was an important outpost of the Venetian Republic.
Facing the cathedral, notice that the Old Town spreads out in two
directions. During the Venetian period, the population was seg-
regated along this axis. To the left lived the well-to-do patricians,
protected within the city wall (looking up the hill to the fortress,
you can see the crenellated walls reaching down to embrace this
neighborhood). To the right, outside the wall, dwelled the humble
plebeians—who worked hard and paid high taxes, but had no say
in government. In the 16th century, these two populations came
to blows, scuffling sporadically over the course of a century. The
Venetians finally decided enough was enough, and sent a modera-
tor to restore peace...and this medieval Dr. Phil pulled it off. As
a symbol of the reconciliation, part of the Arsenal building was

converted into a **communal theater.** Built in 1612, this was the first municipal theater in Europe. It still serves this purpose, but may be closed for restoration in 2007.

Across the square from the Arsenal, the building with the arches and tower is the **Loggia,** all that remains of a 15th-century palace for the rector (who ruled the island as a representative of Venice). This was the town's court of justice, and important decisions were announced from the stepped pillar in front (with the flagpole). This pillar also served as the town pillory, for publicly humiliating prisoners. During Hapsburg control in the early 20th century, most of the palace was torn down to build the town's first resort hotel; today, that building—appropriately called the Palace Hotel—still stands just behind the Loggia.

Walk toward the cathedral, stopping at the first big gap on the left. You can see the top of a never-finished **Venetian palace,** with its distinctive Venetian-style windows. A descendant of the former owner recently bought back this palace, with plans to restore it. But workers began to uncover layer after layer of Hvar's history: blocks of stone from the Greek island of Paros, Illyrian coins, and Roman mosaics. The renovation is planned to continue, and may include a small museum to display artifacts found during construction. If you were to head two blocks up this street, you'd run into the yellow Benedictine Convent and its loveable lace museum; if you continued beyond the convent, you'd reach the trailhead for the fortress up above. But before leaving the square, visit the cathedral (convent, fortress, and cathedral described later in this section).

Then poke around Hvar's **back streets.** As you wander, especially on the left (north) side of the square, look up to find more characteristic Venetian windows. You'll also spot stone tabs jutting out from house facades. The ones with holes were used to hang color-coded curtains: White for a birth, black for a death. Also notice the gleaming white limestone everywhere, which is quarried locally. An often-repeated (but false) legend that the US White House was built of this same stone is temptingly plausible.

Cathedral of St. Stephen (Sv. Stjepan)—Hvar's centerpiece is its Renaissance-era cathedral, with a distinctive three-humped gable (representing the Holy Trinity) and open-work steeple. The interior comes with a few tales from Hvar's storied past (free, daily 8:00–12:00 & 16:30–20:00).

The **bronze entrance doors,** completed by a popular Croatian sculptor in 1990, combine religious themes with important elements of life on Hvar. On the left door, top to bottom, you'll see the Creation; Madonna and Baby Jesus surrounded by the circle of stars (representing the European Union—reflecting Croatians' desire to be considered part of Europe); vineyards (both literal and as a symbol of heaven); and a procession of penitence, a fixture

of life among religious locals. On the right door, you'll see a dove (representing peace and the Holy Spirit); fishermen (an actual part of Hvar life, but also representing the Church's "fishers of men" evangelical philosophy); and a boat, sailing into the future.

Inside, work your way counterclockwise around the church. At the right-front chapel, the tabernacle behind the yellow cloth (under the big crucifix) holds an important piece of Hvar history: a crucifix that supposedly shed tears of blood on the eve of a major 1510 uprising of the plebeians against the patricians. (This spooked the rebels enough to postpone the uprising a few months.) Behind the main altar, you'll see wooden choir stalls rescued from an earlier Gothic church destroyed during an Ottoman attack in 1571. Notice the two pulpits: the right one, with St. Paul and his sword, is for reading or singing the Epistles; the left one, with the eagle (representing St. John), is used for reading the Gospels. The left-front chapel features the tomb of St. Prosperus, Hvar's "co-patron saint," who shares the credit with the more famous St. Stephen. People pray to Prosperus for good health. On his feast day, May 10, the lid is opened and you can actually see his preserved body. The figures flanking the tomb represent faith and strength.

▲▲**Benedictine Convent (Samostan Benediktinki) and Lace Museum**—Hvar's most appealing sight is this nun-run attraction, inside a convent where 13 Benedictine sisters spend their lives (they never go outside). When they're not praying, the sisters make lace using fibers from the *agava* (a cactus-like plant with broad, flat, tapered, spiny leaves—see the sample next to the desk as you enter). First, they tease the delicate threads out of the plant, then wash, bleach, and dry them. Finally, they weave the threads into intricate lace designs. The painstaking procedure is made even more challenging by Hvar's unpredictable weather: The humid southerly Jugo wind causes tangles, while the dry northern Bora wind makes the fibers stiff and difficult to work with.

You'll see samples of the nuns' work, both new and old—some yellowed specimens date from the late 19th century (the oldest ones are in the back room). The sisters are particularly happy to make lace for bishops and cardinals. And when the *other* Benedict—the XIV—became pope in 2005, they created a lace papal emblem for him as a gift.

Rounding out the museum are ecclesiastical gear, some bishops' vestments (with the Baby Jesus below them wearing an *agava*-lace shirt), ancient kitchenware discovered in this house, a stone sink and baptismal font, an actual well, and some amphora jugs. Out in front of the building is a statue of St. Benedict, the patron saint of Europe, reading his daily routine in a book: *ora et labora* ("pray and work"). You'll notice the museum is also called the Hanibal Lucić Museum, for a prominent Renaissance poet whose daughter-in-law donated this property to the church (10 kn, skimpy 20-kn multilingual booklet, June–Aug Mon–Sat 10:00–12:00 & 17:00–19:00, closed Sun; it's technically closed Sept–May, but you can ring the bell to the right of the main door to get in during these same hours—use the door in the yellow building; tel. 021/741-052).

▲**Franciscan Monastery (Franjevački Samostan)**—This interesting sight—with an offbeat museum, Hvar's most famous painting, an ancient tree, and a pair of monks—is worth the 10-minute stroll from the Old Town (15 kn; May–Oct Mon–Sat 10:00–12:00 & 17:00–19:00, closed Sun; Nov–April it's technically closed, but the TI can call to see if they'll let you in during these hours).

Starting in the 15th century, this monastery was a hospice for sailors who encountered illness on treacherous sea journeys. As you enter, notice that the cloister's floor is slanted inward to capture rainwater. Pipes took this pure water out to the waterfront, where passing ships could use it to replenish their supplies.

The focal point of the monastery is its impressive painting of the **Last Supper** (c. 1640). According to legend, a passing ship had a passenger who was severely ill with scurvy, so they left him on a small offshore island, where monks took pity on him. He asked for the biggest canvas they could find, and painted this. (This may be more than a myth—historians recently found a letter inviting the presumed artist to Hvar.) The U-shaped table in the painting provides the framework for some bold experimentation with perspective. Facing Jesus, front and center, is Judas, identified by several clues. In his left hand (hard to see) is a bag of coins, and his right hand is dipping bread into wine (after Jesus had predicted that the one who did this would betray him). The yellow of his garment symbolizes betrayal, and the red indicates that the betrayal led to the spilling of blood. Under the table by Judas is a cat, representing lust. On the lower left, we see a beggar (accompanied by a dog, symbolizing fidelity)—likely a self-portrait by the artist, grateful to the monks who nursed him back to health.

The museum has a few more rooms, including an exhibit of currency from the fourth century B.C. (Greek coins with an image of Zeus) until today (see the rapid evolution of Croatia's currency since its independence); a collection of amphora jugs; and paintings by Venetian artists and modern Croatian artists.

The final attraction, out in the relaxing garden (beyond the museum), is an enormous cypress tree whose gnarled branches are held up by big supports. Scientists believe this ancient tree—probably around 250 years old—was struck by lighting, which caused the branches to spread out and become flatter than usual.

On the way over to the monastery, take a look inside **Restaurant Gariful** (at the end of the embankment, by the green lighthouse, lots of outdoor seating). You know the fish is fresh, because it's swimming around inside the floor (50–110-kn main dishes, daily 12:00–24:00, tel. 021/742-999).

▲Hvar Fortress (Fortica Hvar)—Visiting this mighty castle above the Old Town is a good excuse for a sturdy 20-minute hike to

break up your lazy Hvar day. This huge fortification was built over several generations, beginning in the 13th century. In the 14th century, Spanish engineers did their part to bulk up the fortress (giving it the nickname "Španjola"). In 1571, the townspeople fled here for sanctuary during an attack by the

Ottomans (on their way to the famous Battle of Lepanto), but just a few years later, the fortress was devastated when lightning hit a gunpowder store. In the 19th century, the occupying Austrians put their own touches on the castle. Today it's used as a catering facility and tourist attraction (10 kn, daily in summer 8:00–24:00, shoulder season 8:30–21:00, much shorter hours—and often closed—off-season).

From the Old Town, hike up the steep street called Groda to the road passing above town. Once on that road, look for the

nearby gate with the picture of a castle for another steep hike up a switchback trail (stay on the main path—side-paths that seem like shortcuts are actually dead-ends). Once inside the fort, there's very little in the way of posted descriptions, but the views over town

are terrific. You can also climb down into the prison, sip a drink at the café/bar, and visit the one-room "Marine Archaeological Museum" (hiding inside the blocky central part of the fortress; look for *amphorae* sign). This display features booty found at three different Dalmatian shipwrecks, including a collection of amphora jugs (for more on these jugs, see the sidebar on page 108). According to the exhibit, one out of every 50 voyages in antiquity ended in a shipwreck. (And you thought flying was dangerous.)

The complex on the higher hill nearby was built by Napoleon (which is also its nickname among locals). In the 1970s, it was converted into an astronomic and seismographic observatory.

ACTIVITIES

Swimming—With typically Dalmatian crystal-clear water, Hvar is a great swimming town. Also typically Dalmatian, virtually all of the swimming areas are rocky or pebbly. As you walk along the coastline in either direction from town, you'll spot concrete pads and ladders trying to seduce you into the cool blue (these are generally open to the public, but you may have the option of renting a beach chair). The town's main beach, Pokonji Dol, is about a 20-minute walk east of town—simply follow the coast. Just offshore is a small, barren island of the same name topped with a lonely little lighthouse. If you continue eastward along the coast, you'll hit another popular beach, at Milna (2.5 miles from Hvar town).

Many people—especially the clothing-optional crowd—prefer to take a water taxi across the bay to the Pakleni Islands (described below). The island of Jerolim and the bay of Stipanska (or is it *Strip*anska?) on the island of Marinkovac are particularly good places to spot (or sport?) some bare skin. The beach at Palmižana is another popular swim destination because it's partly "sandy" (translation: smaller pebbles).

Hike from Velo Grablje—For a vigorous hike on Hvar Island, consider taking the one daily bus that uses the scenic old road to Stari Grad, and get off at the village of Velo Grablje (about 7 miles east of Hvar town). This modest settlement, once famous for its lavender oil production, is now a near-ghost town on a rugged plateau with far-off views of the sea. From Velo Grablje, you can hike back down into Hvar (via M. Grablje, then Milna and its nice beach), with views along the way. The TI can give you details (bus generally departs Hvar town at 11:50—confirm at TI or bus station).

Excursions—Joining a day-trip excursion is a handy way to reach nearby destinations (generally available June–Oct, 200–400 kn per person). The most popular options are trips around Hvar Island and the nearby Pakleni Islands, Vis Island, Brač Island and the beach at Bol, Korčula, Mljet National Park, Dubrovnik, river rafting, and more. The two big Croatian companies have

offices in Hvar: **Atlas** (at the top of the harbor) and **Elite** (at Pelegrini travel agency, along the embankment). Aside from these big operators, salespeople hawk various boat excursions along the embankment.

Near Hvar: The Pakleni Islands (Pakleni Otoci)

These islands, just offshore from Hvar town, are a popular and easy back-to-nature day-trip destination. The name means the "Devil's Islands" in Croatian, but in the local dialect, *pakleni* refers to the resin used to seal the hulls of ships. As noted above, some of the smaller islands (Jerolim and Marinkovac) are known for their nude beaches, and little else. But for a bit more civilization, set your sights on the biggest island, known as **"Palmižana"** for its main settlement (the island is officially named Svetog Klement, but nobody calls it that). The only real "town" on this island is Palmižana (pahl-mee-ZHAH-nah; sounds like "parmesan-a")— which is basically a modest marina and a handful of cafés huddled around a beach. From there, you can hike through the woods and scramble your way to some postcard-perfect hidden coves.

Getting There: Excursion boats ferry tourists out to the islands every summer morning from the harbor in front of the Hvar TI—just look for signs to the specific island, beach, or cove that you want. It costs about 50 kn round-trip per person; most boats take people over between 9:00 and 11:00, then go back to fetch them home around 16:00 or 17:00 (about 30 min each way to Palmižana). This works well, provided you want to spend the entire day stranded on a tropical island.

An efficient sightseer might prefer just a few hours of island time—enough for a quick dip, a hike, and maybe a meal. For this purpose, you can pay double for a faster, private **water taxi** to zip you there in just 15 minutes, and then pick you up whenever you like. I had a good experience with one of these speedy taxis, helmed by English-speaking Luka. I called him 15 minutes before I wanted to head over, and again 15 minutes before I came back—door-to-door service to any island you like (100 kn round-trip per person, 2-person minimum—so a single rider pays double, mobile 098-959-5094). Luka's blue boat is inflatable and designed for speed (rather than comfort), so the ride may be a bit rough.

Planning Your Time: If you're relatively fit and have a few hours to spare, try this plan: Ride with Luka to Palmižana, hit the Vinogradišće beach, hike across the island to the settlement of Vlaka, have lunch or dinner at Konoba Dionis, call Luka, and ride with him from Vlaka back to Hvar.

Beach at Vinogradišće Cove: The most popular spot for swimming on the island is the beach at Vinogradišće. To get here

Near Hvar

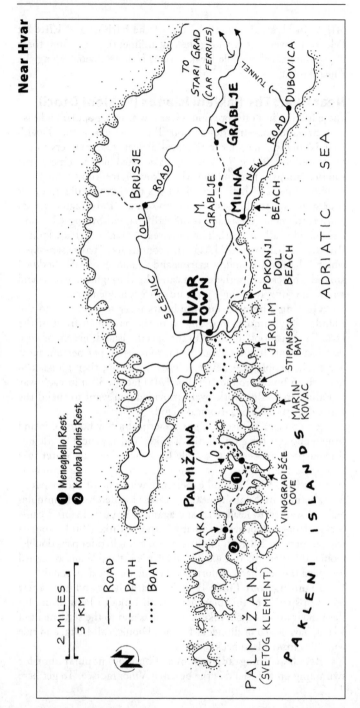

① Meneghello Rest.
② Konoba Dionis Rest.

N

2 MILES
3 KM

—— ROAD
‑ ‑ ‑ PATH
· · · · BOAT

TO
STARI GRAD
(CAR FERRIES)

V. GRABLJE

DUBOVICA

TUNNEL

BRUSJE

OLD ROAD

M. GRABLJE

MILNA

NEW ROAD

BEACH

POKONJI DOL BEACH

SCENIC

HVAR TOWN

ADRIATIC SEA

JEROLIM

STIPANSKA BAY

MARIN‑KOVAC

PALMIŽANA

VINOGRADIŠĆE COVE

VLAKA

PALMIŽANA (SVETOG KLEMENT)

PAKLENI ISLANDS

from the Palmižana marina, hike up the trail (to the left, past the little cantina). When the road forks, take the middle fork and follow the restaurant signs (they're all at the beach). While it's not as "undiscovered" as you might hope, Vinogradišće is certainly a picturesque spot, with a small patch of semi-sand surrounded by rocks and concrete pads for catching some rays. A smattering of sailboats on the horizon rounds out the idyllic Croatian scene.

Hike to Vlaka: For a hardy 45-minute (2-mile) hike on a rough trail with some pleasant views—and a restaurant reward at the end (Konoba Dionis, described below)—trek across the top of the island to the little settlement of Vlaka (wear good shoes and bring water). From Palmižana, first follow signs to Meneghello. After you pass Meneghello Restaurant and some of its bungalows (described below), there's a fork in the path—go right (following the faint red marking on the wall to Vlaka). You'll climb up to the crest of the island, on a very narrow and rocky trail. A few side paths fork down to various bays, but stay on the main trail along the top of the island (generally marked with red-painted rocks). You'll periodically break through the trees for views over secluded coves and nearby islands. Finally, the path leads down along yet another pretty cove before sending you back over the top of the island to Vlaka and Konoba Dionis.

Eating at Palmižana: Several lazy cafés surround the Vinogradišće beach at Palmižana. A bit higher on the hill is **Meneghello,** run by a family of the same name that's been in Palmižana for over a century. They serve mostly seafood on a colorful, funky terrace (90–100-kn combo plates, fishy splurges for a bit more, open long hours daily April–Oct, reservations smart for dinner, follow signs from the Palmižana marina, tel. 021/717-270). Meneghello's restaurant is the centerpiece of a complex of rentable, color-coded bungalows that bunny-hop through an overgrown botanical garden down to the beach (www.palmizana.hr).

Eating at Vlaka: The culinary highlight of the island is at the other end, in Vlaka. **Konoba Dionis** is a charming stone hut with just six tables on a covered terrace, overlooking vineyards, an olive grove, and the distant sea. The electricity comes from a generator, and the water comes from the sky (except during droughts, when it's brought over from the mainland)—so the cuisine is straightforward, traditional Dalmatian dishes, and the focus is on relaxation. Their "aubergine pie" is a tasty eggplant lasagna (70–120-kn main dishes, mid-May–mid-Oct daily 12:00–24:00, closed off-season, mobile 098-167-1016 or 091-765-6044). Tourists often make the long journey over to Dionis, only to find it's already full—reservations (especially for lunch) are a must.

SHOPPING

You'll see little souvenir kiosks everywhere on Hvar. The big item here is lavender, produced on the island for the last century or so. In addition to making things smell nice, some locals swear by its medicinal properties: Massage some lavender oil on your temples to cure a headache, or rub it on your chest for asthma. You'll see it sold in bottles or sachets—a fragrant souvenir (that helps keep your luggage smelling nice, too).

SLEEPING

As with other small coastal towns, Hvar suffers from a lack of accommodations options. The big hotels are pricey, but, as usual, *sobe* are your salvation (see page 35). And, if you don't mind a bit of a walk from the Old Town, there are some fine little private hotels on the outskirts. It can be hard to find a room in July and especially August (when all accommodations boost their rates); book as far ahead as possible for these times. Any time of year, your biggest hurdle is that nearly all of the small (cheaper) places charge 30 percent more for stays less than three nights—try to negotiate your way out of this if it's not peak season.

In the Old Town

$$$ *Sunčani Hvar Hotels:* Most of the big hotels in town are operated by the same company, Sunčani Hvar. These hotels are currently undergoing a long-term, multi-phase renovation to bring them all up to four-star (read: expensive) status, so in the coming years, they'll take turns being partly or entirely closed. Those that are fully renovated and have already re-opened—such as the Amfora—boast super-modern rooms with strikingly contemporary decor. Prices vary dramatically depending on season, view, size, how recently the rooms were renovated, and the direction the wind is blowing. The cheapest, un-renovated doubles (such as at the faded old Hotel Palace) start around €150 in peak season... and go up from there. The most notable locations include **Hotel Palace,** a few steps off the main square, at the end of the harbor; **Hotel Slavija,** along the embankment where the big boats dock; **Hotel Dalmacija,** around the corner from Slavija, just east of the Old Town; and **Hotel Amfora,** on the other side of the harbor, a 10-minute walk west of the Old Town. If you've got deep pockets and are tempted by good locations and big-hotel amenities, you can book any of the Sunčani Hvar hotels through the same office: tel. 021/750-750, fax 021/750-751, www.suncanihvar.hr, reservations @suncanihvar.com. But I'd save some kunas and enjoy more local color by sleeping in one of the following options instead.

Sleep Code

(€1 = about $1.20, 6 kn = about $1, country code: 385, area code: 021)
S = Single, **D** = Double/Twin, **T** = Triple, **Q** = Quad, **b** = bathroom. The modest tourist tax (7 kn or €1 per person, per night, lower off-season) is not included in these rates. Hotels generally accept credit cards and include breakfast, while most *sobe* accept only cash and don't offer breakfast. Everyone listed here speaks at least enough English to make a reservation (or knows someone nearby who can translate).

To help you sort easily through these listings, I've divided the rooms into three categories based on the price for a standard double room with bath in peak season:

$$$ **Higher Priced**—Most rooms 700 kn (€97) or more.
$$ **Moderately Priced**—Most rooms between 400–700 kn (€55–97).
$ **Lower Priced**—Most rooms 400 kn (€55) or less.

$$ Pension Oaza is a charming little oasis behind the bus station, a few steps off the main square. Virginia (who's French) and Mateo (a salty Croatian) run their own little "country farm" in the town center, with a vegetable garden, goats, donkeys, and a pair of oafish dogs. They rent five cozy little rooms with older furnishings, an apartment, and a private villa in the corner of the ranch. If you take the half-board option (€15 per person more than the rates listed here), you'll dine on traditional Croatian cuisine prepared with the pension's own produce (July–Aug: Db-€70, villa-€100, apartment-€200; June and Sept: Db-€50, villa-€80, apartment-€160; Oct–May: Db-€40, villa-€60, apartment-€120; 30 percent more for 1- or 2-night stays, cash only, includes breakfast, Hanibala Lucića 4, tel. & fax 021/741-201, mateo.novak-bilweis@st.t-com.hr). Follow the little steep-walled lane at the end of the bus station parking lot, and you'll spot the sign on your right.

$ Ivana and Paško Ukić offer the best *sobe* I've found in Hvar, with two new-feeling apartments and one room sharing a quiet square with a little church a few steep blocks above the main square (Db-280–360 kn July–Aug, 240 kn June, 200 kn May and Sept–Oct, 180 kn Nov–April, apartments about 40 kn more, no breakfast, 1- or 2-night stays are possible if they're not too busy, cash only, air-con, tel. 021/741-810, Ivana speaks just enough English to make a reservation, or call fluent daughter Lidija at mobile 098-917-0652). From the cathedral, walk three blocks up toward the fortress, then look for the little church to your left.

$ *More* **Sobe** *and Apartments:* Stepping off the boat or bus, you'll be approached by hordes of people hoping to recruit you into their rooms. As you wander the streets, you'll see *sobe* and *apartman* signs everywhere. If you arrive without a reservation, the TI can point you in the right direction. For more options, consider going through an agency. Figure anywhere from €25 to €65, and likely more, for a double in peak season (30 percent more for 1- or 2-night stays). Most of Hvar's *sobe* and apartments have private bathrooms. Four different agencies in Hvar can book rooms (all are open sporadic hours, based on season; the first three are right along the embankment where the big boats dock, while the last is across the harbor): **Thalassa** (tel. 021/742-908, thalassa@st.t-com.hr), **Pelegrini** (tel. 021/742-743, pelegrini@inet.hr), **Fontana** (tel. 021/742-133, www.happyhvar.com, info@happyhvar.com), and **Atlas** (tel. 021/741-911, atlas-hvar@st.t-com.hr).

In the Residential Area West of the Old Town

These two hotels are in a quiet, nondescript residential neighborhood just beyond the big Hotel Amfora west of the Old Town.

$$$ **Pod Stine Hotel** ("Under Stones") feels like the sunny hideout of a reclusive writer. At the edge of town overlooking a mini-arboretum and a beautiful cove, this place features smart contemporary decor and 45 upscale-feeling rooms. If you don't mind the 20-minute walk into town, it's a more intimate and enjoyable splurge than the big hotels (mid-July–Aug: non-view Sb-885–1,180 kn, seaview Sb-1,425–1,805 kn, non-view Db-930–1,240 kn, seaview Db-1,500–1,900 kn; 10–15 percent cheaper May–mid-July and Sept, 40–50 percent cheaper April and Oct, closed Nov–March, higher prices are for rooms with balcony, no extra charge for 1- or 2-night stays, air-con, elevator, free parking, Podstine b.b., tel. 021/740-400, fax 021/740-499, www.podstine.com, hotel@podstine.com).

$$ **Pharia Aparthotel** has 10 new-feeling, straightforward rooms and 11 apartments in two buildings. The neighborhood is dull and the rooms are nothing special, but they're well-priced for the proximity to the Old Town—about a 15-minute walk (July–Aug: Sb-444 kn, non-view Db-696 kn, seaview Db-800 kn; progressively cheaper off-season, closed mid-Oct–April, more for suites and apartments, 30 percent more for 1- or 2-night stays, air-con, Majerovica b.b., tel. 021/778-080, fax 021/778-081, www.orvas-hotels.com, info@orvas-hotels.com).

EATING

Hvar is packed with similar places serving up plates of grilled fish and meat, with pasta and pizza rounding out the predictable options. But the following, more interesting spots are a break from the same old seaside fare.

Konoba Menego, run by the Kovačević family, offers the chance to try cuisine from Dalmatia and throughout Croatia. The user-friendly menu lists the town or region of origin for each specialty. Portions are small, so think of it as Croatian tapas: Two people can order three or four dishes to share, and sample a variety of regional flavors. Dine in the cozy enclosed terrace or in the atmospheric dining room, with air-dried ham *(pršut)* hanging from the rafters (40–70-kn portions, bigger 90–130-kn combination plates, daily 11:30–14:30 & 17:00–24:00, on the steep lane called Groda leading up to the fortress, reservations smart, tel. 021/742-036).

Yakša is a dressy new splurge that oozes style, serving updated Dalmatian cuisine with international flair. They pride themselves on using only the freshest of ingredients, and brag that all their produce (and olive oil) is grown right here on Hvar. The dining room is in the heart of a gorgeously restored 16th-century palazzo with columns and arches between the tables. Or sit outside on the covered sidewalk or in their enclosed patio (100–120-kn main dishes, just off the cathedral end of the main square at Hektorovićeva b.b.—look for the arches in the illuminated dining room, reservations smart, tel. 021/717-202).

Hvar's "Restaurant Row": The streets just above the main square (to the left, as you face the cathedral) are full of restaurants slinging similar Dalmatian and Mediterranean fare. Outdoor tables make it easy to window-shop and find your favorite. In this zone, two places are particularly well-regarded: **Luna** (colorful, lively decor and a delightful rooftop terrace, Mediterranean cuisine, 60–120-kn main dishes, daily 12:00–14:30 & 18:00–23:00, tel. 021/741-400) and **Macondo** (fun, tight sidewalk seating or nondescript dining room, 70–100-kn meat and fish main dishes, open long hours daily except closed Sun lunch, tel. 021/742-850).

Breakfast: If you're sleeping in a *soba*, you're on your own for breakfast. Small **bakeries** are scattered around town. For something more substantial, drop into **Café Pjaca** on the main square across from the TI ("Ferry Express" continental breakfast-30 kn, "Theater Breakfast" with eggs and meat-40 kn, daily 7:00–23:00, cool modern decor). Finally, most of the **big hotels** charge nonguests a reasonable 50 kn to gorge themselves at their breakfast buffets.

Picnic Supplies: There's a big, handy **Konzum** supermarket near the bus station (Mon–Sat 7:00–21:00, Sun 8:00–13:00).

TRANSPORTATION CONNECTIONS

Hvar Boat Connections

Big car ferries use the port at Stari Grad, across the island from Hvar town (a 20-min bus ride; local buses are scheduled to connect Hvar town with these boats). Smaller passenger-only catamarans leave from the harbor in the heart of Hvar town. For non-drivers going to either Split or Korčula, the catamarans are much better, since their departure point is more convenient and they make the trip faster. As always, confirm your plans in advance—boat schedules are subject to change (the following information is based on 2006 schedules).

Big Jadrolinija Car Ferries from Stari Grad: These big boats head north, to **Split** (4/week July–mid-Sept, 2/week mid-Sept–June, 1.75 hrs); and south, to **Korčula town** (4/week July–mid-Sept, 2/week mid-Sept–June, 3.5 hrs) and **Dubrovnik** (2/week year-round, 6.5 hrs). Jadrolinija also runs frequent additional car ferries from Stari Grad to **Split** (at least 3/day, more in summer).

Boats from Hvar Town to Split and Korčula Island: The handy *Krilo* **catamaran** heads for Split in the morning, and for Korčula town in the afternoon (daily June–Sept, 4/week Oct–May, 1.25 hrs to Split, 1.75 hrs to Korčula; in Hvar, buy tickets at Pelegrini travel agency). A **Jadrolinija catamaran** connects Hvar town twice daily to Split and once daily to Vela Luka (at the far end of Korčula Island, a 1-hr bus ride to Korčula town; boat ride takes 1 hr to Split, 45 min to Vela Luka). And late June though early September, Jadrolinija's **slower car ferry** also goes to Split and Vela Luka (Split: 6/week, 2 hrs; Vela Luka: daily, 1.5 hrs; even though this is a car ferry, only foot passengers can get on and off in Hvar town).

Hvar Overland Connections

Hvar's **buses** only connect you to other parts of the island. For farther-flung destinations (such as Dubrovnik or Zagreb), you'll take a boat to Split, then connect by bus from there. About six buses a day cross the island between Hvar town and Stari Grad, and there's always a bus coordinated to meet the big ferries at Stari Grad (in which case you want Stari Grad's "Trajekt" stop rather than its Old Town stop).

KORČULA

While not yet matching the fame of Dubrovnik or Split, the little island town of Korčula (KOHR-choo-lah) offers one of the most pleasant stopovers on the Dalmatian Coast. Conveniently located midway between Dubrovnik and Split, Korčula boasts an atmospheric Old Town, some surprisingly engaging museums, and a dramatic, fjord-like mountain backdrop.

Korčula was founded by ancient Greeks. It became part of the Roman Empire, and was eventually a key southern outpost of the Venetian Republic. Four centuries of Venetian rule left Korčula with a quirky Gothic-Renaissance mix and a strong siesta tradition. Korčulans take great pride in the fact that Marco Polo was born here in 1254—the explorer remains the town's poster boy. Korčula is also known for its traditional *Moreška* sword dance.

You'll discover that there are two Korčulas: the tacky seaside resort and the historic Old Town. Savvy visitors ignore the tourist sprawl and focus on Korčula's medieval quarter, a mini-Dubrovnik poking out into the sea on a picture-perfect peninsula. Tiny lanes branch off the humble main drag like ribs on a fishbone. This street plan is designed to catch both the breeze and the shade. All in all, this laid-back island village is an ideal place to take a vacation from your busy vacation.

Planning Your Time

Korčula offers little to do besides taking it easy. Wander the medieval Old Town, explore the handful of tiny museums, kick back at a café or restaurant, or bask on the beach. If you're here on a Thursday, be sure to catch the performance of the *Moreška* dance (also Mon July–Aug). One day is more than enough for Korčula—

but because of sometimes-sparse ferry schedules, you may end up stranded here for longer. With the extra time, consider a one-day package excursion to Mljet Island and its national park.

ORIENTATION

(area code: 020)
The long, skinny island of Korčula runs alongside the even longer, skinnier Pelješac Peninsula (famous for its wine—see page 59). The main town and best destination on the island—just across a narrow strait from Pelješac—is also called Korčula.

Korčula is centered on its compact **Old Town** (Stari Grad) peninsula, which is connected to the mainland at a big staircase leading to the Great Land Gate. In the area in front of this staircase, you'll find ATMs, travel agencies, the Jadrolinija ferry office, several Internet cafés, the Konzum supermarket, a colorful outdoor produce market, and other handy tourist services.

Stretching to the south and east of the Old Town is **"Shell Bay,"** surrounded by a strip of tacky tourist shops and resort hotels. This seamier side of Korčula—best avoided—caters mostly to Europeans here to worship the sun for a week or two.

To the west of Old Town is the serene waterfront street **Put Sv. Nikola,** where you'll find several *sobe* (including Rezi Depolo's—see "Sleeping," page 203), great views back on the Old Town, and more locals than tourists.

Tourist Information

Korčula's we-try-harder TI, run by Stanka Kraljević, is next to Hotel Korčula on the west side of the Old Town waterfront (mid-June–Sept Mon–Sat 8:00–15:00 & 16:00–22:00, Sun 9:00–14:00; Oct–mid-June Mon–Sat 8:00–15:00, closed Sun, may be open Sun in shoulder season; tel. 020/715-701, www.korcula.net). Pick up the free cartoon map (marked with "rambling paths") and *Korčula* magazine (with maps, pictures, hotel information, and other town information).

Arrival in Korčula

For all the details on getting to the Dalmatian Coast, see page 152.

By Boat: The big Jadrolinija ferries can arrive on either side of the Old Town peninsula, depending on the wind. (The Orebić

Korčula

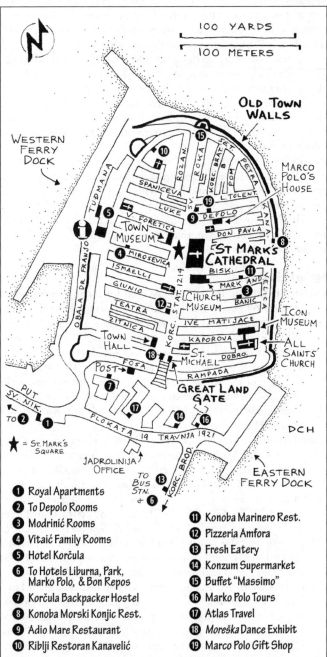

100 YARDS

100 METERS

N

OLD TOWN WALLS

WESTERN FERRY DOCK

MARCO POLO'S HOUSE

ST MARK'S CATHEDRAL

MARKO POLO'S HOUSE

ICON MUSEUM

ALL SAINTS' CHURCH

EASTERN FERRY DOCK

GREAT LAND GATE

★ = ST. MARK'S SQUARE

JADROLINIJA OFFICE

TO BUS STN.

DCH

1 Royal Apartments
2 To Depolo Rooms
3 Modrinić Rooms
4 Vitaić Family Rooms
5 Hotel Korčula
6 To Hotels Liburna, Park, Marko Polo, & Bon Repos
7 Korčula Backpacker Hostel
8 Konoba Morski Konjic Rest.
9 Adio Mare Restaurant
10 Riblji Restoran Kanavelić

11 Konoba Marinero Rest.
12 Pizzeria Amfora
13 Fresh Eatery
14 Konzum Supermarket
15 Buffet "Massimo"
16 Marko Polo Tours
17 Atlas Travel
18 *Moreška* Dance Exhibit
19 Marco Polo Gift Shop

passenger ferry and the fast catamarans generally dock at the west side of town.) From either side of the peninsula, it's just a two-minute walk to where it meets the mainland and all of the services described in "Orientation," earlier in this chapter.

A few boats (car ferries from Orebić and Drvenik) use the Dominče dock two peninsulas east of Korčula (near Hotel Bon Repos). Regular buses connect this dock with Korčula.

Some boats from Split and Hvar town arrive at Vela Luka, at the far end of Korčula Island. Each boat arriving at Vela Luka is met by a bus waiting to bring arriving travelers to Korčula town (about 1 hour).

By Bus: The bus station is at the southeast corner of Korčula's Shell Bay. If you leave the station with the bay on your right, you'll reach the Old Town. If you leave with the bay on your left, you'll get to hotels Liburna, Park, and Marko Polo.

By Car: See "Route Tips for Drivers" at the end of this chapter. Once in Korčula town, there's plenty of free parking at the bus station along the marina.

Helpful Hints

Jadrolinija Office: This office, essential for sorting through and confirming boat schedules, is located where the Old Town meets the mainland (peak season Mon–Fri 8:00–20:00, Sat 8:00–13:00 & 18:00–22:00, Sun 6:00–13:30, much shorter hours off-season—depends on boat schedules, tel. 020/715-410, www.jadrolinija.hr). But note that they don't sell tickets for the convenient *Krilo* catamaran to Hvar town and Split (buy *Krilo* tickets at Marko Polo Tours—see next). For a run-down of the confusing boat options to and from Korčula, see the end of this chapter.

Travel Agencies: Korčula has two major travel agencies. At either one, you can book an excursion, browse shelves of books and souvenirs, and get information about car rental and other activities: **Marko Polo Tours** (also sells tickets for *Krilo* catamaran; located just outside the Old Town gate at Biline 5, tel. 020/715-400, fax 020/715-800) and **Atlas Travel** (Trg 19 Travnja, tel. 020/711-231, fax 020/715-580). Both agencies are open similar hours (long hours daily in summer, closed for mid-afternoon break in shoulder season, open Mon–Sat mornings and closed Sun in winter).

Festivals: Korčula has a couple of fun annual festivals. The Marco Polo Festival is in late June and early July, with lots of exhibitions, concerts, dances, and a parade with a costumed Marco Polo returning to his native Korčula after his long visit to China. For 10 days at the beginning of September, Korčula remembers the great 1298 naval battle that took place just offshore, when the Genoese captured Marco Polo. The festivities culminate in a 14-ship reenactment, complete with smoke and sound effects.

SIGHTS

Korčula's few sights cluster within a few yards of each other in the Old Town. I've listed them roughly in order from the Great Land Gate (the Old Town's main entry) to the tip of the Old Town peninsula. All museums are officially "closed" November through April, but most will usually open by request (ask the TI to call for you...or just try knocking on the door).

▲▲*Moreška* **Dance**—Lazy Korčula snaps to life when locals perform a medieval folk dance called the *Moreška* (moh-REHSH-kah). The plot helps Korčulans remember their hard-fought past: A bad king takes the good king's bride, the dancing forces of good and evil battle, and there's always a happy ending (80 kn, June–mid-Oct every Thu at 21:00, July–Aug also Mon at 21:00, in Gradska Vijećnica outdoor theater next to Great Land Gate, or in a nearby congress center if bad weather; buy tickets from travel agency, at your hotel, or at the door).

▲**Great Land Gate (Veliki Revelin)**—A noble staircase leads up to the main entrance to the Old Town. Like all of the town's towers,

it's adorned with the Venetian winged lion and the coats of arms of the doge of Venice (left) and the rector of Korčula (right; the offset coat of arms below was the rector who later renovated the gate). You can climb the tower to visit a small exhibit on the *Moreška* dance and enjoy panoramic town views (10 kn, generally May–Oct daily 9:30–21:30, may be closed for midday break in shoulder season, likely closed Nov–April, English descriptions).

Just inside the gate is **Franjo Tuđman Square,** renamed in 2001 for the controversial first president of an independent Croatia (see page 54). During the war, Tuđman was considered a hero. In later years, it was revealed that he had held secret negotiations with the Serbian leader Slobodan Milošević. As the key figure of a recent-but-bygone era that combined both joy and terror, Tuđman remains controversial in today's Croatia. But members of his party are still in power and hold local offices throughout the country, and sometimes adorn a square or street with his name.

On the left inside the gate is the 16th-century **Town Hall and Rector's Palace.** The seal of Korčula (over the center arch) symbolizes the town's importance as the southernmost bastion of the Venetian Republic: St. Mark standing below three defensive towers. The little church on the other side of the square is dedicated to **St. Michael** (Crkva Sv. Mihovila). Throughout Croatia, you'll often find churches to St. Michael just inside the town gates, as he is believed to offer saintly protection from enemies. Notice that a passageway connects the church to the building across the street—home to the Brotherhood of St. Michael, one of Korčula's many religious fraternal organizations (see "Icon Museum," page 202).

• *Now begin walking up the...*

Street of the Korčulan Statute of 1214 (Ulica Korčulanskog Statuta 1214)

—This street is Korčula's backbone—in more ways than one (remember that the street plan is designed as a fish skeleton). While most medieval towns slowly evolved with twisty, mazelike lanes, Korčula was carefully planned. The streets to the west (left) of this one are straight, to allow the refreshing northwesterly Maestral winds into town. To the east (right), they're curved (notice you can't see the sea) to keep out the bad-vibe southeasterly Jugo winds.

The street's complicated name honors a 1214 statute—the oldest known written law in Central Europe—with regulations about everyday life and instructions on maintaining the walls, protecting nature, keeping animals, building a house, and so on. As you head up the street, look up to notice some interesting decorations on the houses' upper floors.

• *If you continue up the street, you'll reach St. Mark's Square (Trg Sv. Marka). From here, you're a few steps from the next four sights.*

▲St. Mark's Cathedral (Katedrala Sv. Marka)

—Korčula became a bishopric in the 14th century. In the 19th century—36 bishops later—the Hapsburgs decided to centralize ecclesiastical power in their empire, and removed Korčula's bishop. The town still has this beautiful "cathedral"—but no bishop. On the ornately decorated tympanum above the main door, you'll see another Venetian statue of St. Mark (flanked by Adam and Eve). Inside, above the main altar, is an original Tintoretto painting (recently restored in Zagreb). As you leave, notice the weapons on the back wall, used in some of the pivotal battles that have taken place near strategically situated Korčula (free, May–Oct daily 9:00–14:00 & 17:00–19:00, may be open all day long in peak season, closed during church services, generally closed Nov–April but may be open Mon–Fri 9:00–12:00 after Easter).

▲**Church Museum (Opatska Riznica)**—This small museum has an unusual and fascinating collection. Try to find the following items: a ceremonial necklace from Mother Teresa (who came from Macedonia, not far from here—she gave this necklace to a friend from Korčula), some old 12th-century hymnals, two tiny drawings by Leonardo da Vinci, a coin collection (including a 2,400-year-old Greek coin minted here in Korčula), some Croatian modern paintings, and two framed reliquaries with dozens of miniscule relics (15 kn, May–Oct Mon–Sat 9:00–19:00, closed Sun except sometimes in the morning, may be open later in peak season and have shorter hours in shoulder season, generally closed Nov–April but may be open Mon–Fri 9:00–12:00 after Easter).

▲**Town Museum (Gradski Muzej)**—Housed in an old mansion, this museum does a fine job of bringing together Korčula's eclectic claims to fame. It's arranged like a traditional Dalmatian home: shop on the ground floor, living quarters in the middle floors, kitchen on top. Notice that some of the walls near the entry have holes in them. Archaeologists are continually doing actual "digs" into these walls to learn how medieval houses here were built.

On the ground floor is a lapidarium, featuring fragments of Korčula's stone past (see the first-century Roman jugs). Upstairs is a display on Korčula's long-standing shipbuilding industry, including models of two modern steel ships built here (the town still builds ship parts today). There's also a furnished living room and, in the attic, a kitchen. This was a smart place for the kitchen—if it caught fire, it was less likely to destroy the whole building. Notice the little WC in the corner. A network of pipes took kitchen and other waste through town and out to sea (10 kn, limited posted English information—pick up the free English guide brochure at entry; mid-June–Aug Mon–Sat 9:30–21:00, closed Sun; Sept–mid-June Mon–Fri 8:00–15:00—if it's locked, try knocking, closed Sat–Sun).

Marco Polo's House (Kuća Marka Pola)—Korčula's favorite son is the great 13th-century explorer Marco Polo. Though Polo sailed under the auspices of the Venetian Republic, and technically was a Venetian (since the Republic controlled this region), Korčulans proudly claim him as their own. Marco Polo was the first Westerner to sail to China, bringing back amazing stories and exotic goods (like silk) that Europeans had never seen before. After his trip, Marco Polo fought in an important naval battle against the Genoese near Korčula. He was captured, taken to Genoa, and imprisoned. He told his story to a cellmate, who wrote it down, published it, and made the explorer a world-class and much-in-demand celebrity. To this day, kids in swimming pools around the world try to find him with their eyes closed.

Today, Korčula is the proud home to "Marco Polo's House"—

actually a more recent building on the site of what may or may not have been his family's property. The house is in poor repair, but most of the property has been purchased by the city to open to visitors. Currently you can just climb the tower and wander the gardens, but in the coming years the town hopes to turn the complex into a world-class museum about the explorer (10 kn, likely open May–Oct only; just north of cathedral on—where else?—ulica Depolo).

Across the street from the house's entrance, you'll find a clever **Marco Polo gift shop** selling various relatively classy items relating to the explorer—herbs, brandies, honey, and so on. Each one comes with a little tag telling a tale of M.P.—for example, how he invented the word "million" (because no existing word was superlative enough for his discoveries). There's even a life-size Marco Polo and Kublai Khan you can pose with (daily in summer 9:00–21:00, shorter hours off-season, closed in winter, ulica Depolo 1A).

▲**Icon Museum (Zbirka Ikona)**—Korčula is known for its many brotherhoods—centuries-old fraternal organizations that have sprung up around churches. The Brotherhood of All Saints has been meeting every Sunday after Mass since the 14th century, and they run a small but interesting museum of icons. These golden religious images were brought back from Greece in the 17th century by Korčulans who had been fighting the Ottomans on a Venetian warship (10 kn, hours depend on demand, but generally May–Oct daily 10:00–13:00 & 17:00–20:00, may be open all day long in peak season, closed Nov–April—but try ringing the bell, on Kaprova ulica at the Old Town's southeast tip).

Brotherhoods' meeting halls are often connected to their church by a second-story walkway. Use this one to step in to the Venetian-style **All Saints' Church** (Crkva Svih Svetih). Under the loft in the back of the church, notice the models of boats and tools—donated by Korčula's shipbuilders. Look closely at the painting to the right of the altar. See the guys in the white robes kneeling under Jesus? That's the Brotherhood, who commissioned this painting.

▲**Old Town Walls**—For several centuries, Korčula held a crucial strategic position: This was one of the most important southern outposts of the Venetian Republic (the Republic of Dubrovnik started at the Pelješac Peninsula, just across the channel). The original town walls around Korčula date from at least the 13th century, but the fortifications were extended (and new towers built) over several centuries to defend against various foes of Venice—mostly Ottomans and pirates.

The most recent tower dates from the 16th century, when the Ottomans attacked Korčula. The rector and other VIPs fled to the mainland, but a brave priest remained on the island and came up with a plan. All of the women of Korčula dressed up as men, and then everybody in town peeked over the wall—making the Ottomans think they were up against a huge army. The priest prayed for help, and the strong northerly Bora wind blew. Not wanting to take their chances with the many defenders and the weather, the Ottomans sailed away, and Korčula was saved.

By the late 19th century, Korčula was an unimportant Hapsburg beach town, and the walls had no strategic value. The town decided to quarry the top half of its old walls to build new homes (and to improve air circulation inside the city). While today's walls are half as high as they used to be, the town has restored many of the towers, giving Korčula its fortified feel. Each one has a winged lion—a symbol of Venice—and the seal of the rector of Korčula when the tower was built.

ACTIVITIES

Swimming—The water around Korčula is clean and popular for swimming. You'll find pebbly beaches strewn with holiday-goers all along Put Sv. Nikola, the street that runs west from the Old Town. Another popular swimming spot is at the very end of the Old Town peninsula.

Excursions—Various companies offer day-long excursions to nearby destinations (generally available June–Oct, each itinerary offered 2–3 times per week). The most popular options are Dubrovnik (420 kn) and the national park on Mljet Island (310 kn, includes park entry fee). Korčula's two big travel agencies—Marko Polo and Atlas—sell tickets for different companies. If one isn't running a tour to the destination you want, the other might be (both agencies are listed under "Helpful Hints" earlier in this chapter). Several new, more active tour companies have popped up recently, offering canoe trips, snorkeling, kayaking, and other "adventures"—look for flyers around town (Sokol is well-regarded, www.korcula-adventures.com).

SLEEPING

Korčula's accommodations options are extremely limited. There are five hotels in town—all decaying, overpriced, resort-style hotels, and all owned by the same company (which is, in turn, government-run). The lack of competition keeps quality low and prices ridiculously high—which makes *sobe* a particularly good alternative.

Sobe

My favorite *sobe* in Korčula offer similar comfort to the hotels at far lower prices—some of them with TVs and air-conditioning, to boot.

Sleep Code

(€1 = about $1.20, 6 kn = about $1, country code: 385, area code: 020)
S = Single, **D** = Double/Twin, **T** = Triple, **Q** = Quad, **b** = bathroom. The modest tourist tax (7 kn or €1 per person, per night, lower off-season) is not included in these rates. The hotels accept credit cards and include breakfast in their rates, while most *sobe* accept only cash and don't offer breakfast. Everyone listed here speaks at least enough English to make a reservation (or knows someone nearby who can translate).

To help you sort easily through these listings, I've divided the rooms into three categories based on the price for a standard double room with bath in peak season:

$$$ **Higher Priced**—Most rooms 700 kn (€97) or more.
$$ **Moderately Priced**—Most rooms between 400–700 kn (€55–97).
$ **Lower Priced**—Most rooms 400 kn (€55) or less.

$$ Royal Apartments are some of the most hotelesque (and most expensive) rooms in town. The five apartments are classy and new, making the place feel more like a small hotel with no real reception desk—arrange your arrival time carefully (July–Aug: small apartment-€80, big apartment-€90; June and Sept: small apartment-€70, big apartment-€80; closed Oct–May, no extra charge for 1- or 2-night stays, no breakfast, cash only, air-con, well-marked with green awning just west of Old Town at Trg Petra Šegedina 4, mobile 098-184-0444, royalapt@ica.net, Jelavić family).

$ Rezi and Andro Depolo, probably distant relatives of Marco, rent four comfy rooms on the bay west of the Old Town. Three of the rooms offer beautiful views to the Old Town, and the five-minute stroll into town is pleasant and scenic. English-speaking Rezi is very friendly and works to make her guests feel welcome (Db-200 kn, or 240 kn July–Aug, room with kitchen-40 kn more, 30 percent more for 1- or 2-night stays, continental breakfast-25 kn, big breakfast-35 kn, cash only, air-con, Put Sv. Nikola 43; walk along waterfront from Old Town with bay on your right, look for *sobe* sign at the yellow house set back from the street, just before the two monasteries; tel. 020/711-621, viladepolo@hotmail.com).

$ Lenni and Periša Modrinić, both of whom are outgoing and speak good English, rent three tight, modern, comfortable rooms and two apartments right in the heart of the Old Town (Db-€45, or €50 July–Aug; apartment-€55, or €60 July–Aug; €5 less off-season, 10 percent more for 1- or 2-night stay, no breakfast, cash only, air-con, near Konoba Marko Polo restaurant at Jakova Baničevića 13, tel. 020/711-400, www.ikorcula.net/lenni, perisa .modrinic@du.t-com.hr).

$ The **Vitaić family** is a father-and-sons operation renting three rooms in the Old Town (July–Aug: Db-400 kn; May–June and Sept–Oct: Db-250 kn; closed Nov–April, no extra charge for 1- or 2-night stays, no breakfast, cash only, Dinko Mirošević 8, tel. 020/715-312, mobile 098-932-7670, avitaic@net.hr).

$ Booking *Sobe* Through an Agency: While you can walk along Put Sv. Nikola and generally find a fine deal on a private room, you can also book one through one of Korčula's travel agencies for an additional 20 percent (figure Db-€35–50 in high season, €20–35 off-season, 30 percent more for 1- or 2-night stays). For information on the two main agencies—Marko Polo Tours and Atlas Travel—see "Helpful Hints," earlier in this chapter.

Hotels

All five of Korčula's hotels are owned by HTP Korčula. If you don't want to stay in a *soba*, these are the only game in town. You can reserve rooms at any of them through the main office (tel. 020/726-336, fax 020/711-746, www.korcula-hotels.com, marketing @htp-korcula.hr; at all hotels, credit cards are accepted, there is no air-con, and there are no non-smoking rooms). I've listed peak-season prices with breakfast only; rates are progressively lower the farther off-season you get. You can pay 10 percent more per person for half-board (dinner at the hotel). It's much cheaper to stay a week or longer. There's a long-term plan to renovate all of these hotels, but so far the Marko Polo is the only one that's seen any progress.

$$$ Hotel Korčula has by far the best location, right on the waterfront alongside the Old Town. It has a fine seaside terrace restaurant and friendly staff, even if the 20 rooms are outmoded and waaay overpriced. The rooms are on two floors: The more expensive "first-floor" rooms (actually on the third floor) have big windows and sea views; the cheaper "second-floor" rooms (actually on the fourth floor) have tiny windows and no views (July–Aug: Sb-720–900 kn, Db-960–1,200 kn; June and Sept: Sb-546–683 kn, Db-780–976 kn; cheaper Oct–May, reception tel. 020/711-078).

$$$ *Other Hotels:* Three more hotels cluster a 15-minute walk away, around the far side of Shell Bay. All are poorly maintained, overpriced (similar rates to Hotel Korčula), and relatively inconvenient to the Old Town, but they share a nice beach. **Hotel Marko Polo** has 94 crisp, newly renovated rooms and an elevator; they plan to renovate the lobby and pool area in 2007 (reception tel. 020/726-004). **Hotel Liburna,** with a clever split-level design that reflects the skyline of the Old Town, has 109 rooms, some of them accessible by elevator; half the rooms face the sea and cost an additional 10 percent (reception tel. 020/726-006). Dreary **Hotel Park** has 153 rooms (reception tel. 020/726-100). The fifth hotel, **Hotel Bon Repos**—another 15 minutes by foot from the Old Town—is, in every sense, the last resort.

Hostel

$ Korčula Backpacker, well-run by a South African–born Croat named Zlatko, is a youthful, fun-loving, easygoing place nicknamed the "Happy House." The 10-minute time limit on the shared bathrooms is strictly enforced (no locks on the doors). The ground-floor bar spills out into a nearby square, becoming a popular hangout on summer evenings (4- and 6-bed dorms, plus a 15-bed attic slumbermill dubbed the "fun club"; prices per bed: 120 kn mid-July–Aug, 100 kn mid-June–mid-July, 90 kn May–mid-June and Sept, closed Oct–April, no breakfast, cash only, Internet access, boat and bike rental, right where the Old Town meets the mainland on Trg Petra at Šegedina Hrvatske Bratske Zajednice 6, tel. 020/716-755, mobile 098-997-6353, www.korculabackpacker.com, bookings@korculabackpacker.com).

EATING

Korčula has plenty of interchangeable seafood restaurants. These are all good options, but (with the exception of Fresh) everything in town is pretty similar—make your decision based on atmosphere and what looks best to you.

Konoba Morski Konjic ("Moorish Seahorse") has tables spilling along the seawall, offering *al fresco* dining with salty views and jaded service. If you want romantic harborside dining, this is your best option (60–100-kn main dishes, daily 8:00–24:00).

Adio Mare, with fine seafood, may have the best decor in town: a cavernous stone dining room, or a tiny little upstairs nook (50–100-kn main dishes, daily 17:30–24:00, sometimes also 12:00–14:00 in peak season, near Marco Polo's House, tel. 020/711-253).

Riblji Restoran Kanavelić, near the far end of the Old Town peninsula, serves good seafood. Choose between the big outdoor terrace or the formal-feeling dining room (non-seafood dishes from 30 kn, 60–120 kn for seafood, daily 18:00–23:00, tel. 020/711-800).

Konoba Marinero has pleasantly nautical decor and a simple menu of Dalmatian specialties (50–100-kn main dishes, Easter–Oct daily 11:00–24:00, closed Nov–Easter, Marka Andrijića 13, tel. 020/711-170).

Pizzas and Pasta: **Pizzeria Amfora,** along the route of the people-parade up Korčula's main drag in the Old Town, features good, inexpensive, quick pizzas and pastas. Squeeze into the small dining room, or enjoy the sidewalk tables (35–50 kn, long hours daily, tel. 020/711-739).

Quick and Tasty: **Fresh,** an innovative new spot run by a Canadian-Croatian couple, offers 25-kn wraps and 20-kn smoothies. If you want a break from grilled seafood and pizza, this is the place (July–Aug daily 9:00–2:00 in the morning, until 19:00 in shoulder season, closed in winter, along Shell Bay behind the sunken-ship playground on the way to the bus station).

Picnics: Just outside the main gate, you'll find a lively produce market and a big, modern, air-conditioned Konzum supermarket (next to Marko Polo Tours). A short stroll from there, down Put Sv. Nikola, takes you to beach perches with the best Korčula views. Otherwise, there are plenty of picnic spots along the Old Town embankment.

A Scenic Drink: The best setting for drinks is at **Buffet "Massimo,"** a youthful-feeling cocktail bar in a city-wall tower at the very tip of the Old Town peninsula. You can have a drink on one of three levels: the downstairs bar, the main-floor lounge, or climb the ladder (at your own risk) to the tower-top terrace (terrace is only for cocktail-sippers—no beer or wine). If you're up top, notice the dumbwaiter for hauling up drinks (daily in summer 18:00–2:00 in the morning, shoulder season 17:30–1:00 in the morning, closed Nov–April, tel. 020/715-073).

TRANSPORTATION CONNECTIONS

Korčula is reasonably well-connected to the rest of the Dalmatian Coast by boat, but service becomes sparse in the off-season. If you're here during a lull in the sailing schedule, buses are your ticket out of town. No matter when you travel, it's smart to carefully study current boat schedules when planning your itinerary, as they are always subject to change (the following information is based on the 2006 schedules).

Korčula Boat Connections

Boats big and small depart from the embankment surrounding Korčula's Old Town peninsula. Which side of the peninsula a boat uses can depend on the weather—be flexible and inquire locally about where to meet your boat. Some boats leave from other parts of the island, most notably the town of Vela Luka (at the opposite tip of the island, a 1-hour bus ride from Korčula town—described below). Other boats, including the car ferry to Orebić (described under "Route Tips for Drivers" at the end of this chapter), leave from the Domince dock, about a five-minute drive east of Korčula town.

Big Jadrolinija Car Ferries: From Korčula town, these huge, handy vessels go north, to **Stari Grad** on Hvar Island (20-min bus ride from Hvar town; 4/week July–mid-Sept, 2/week mid-Sept–June, 3.5 hrs; the catamaran described next is faster and takes you right to Hvar town) and **Split** (5/week July–mid-Sept, 3/week June, 2/week mid-Sept–May, 3.5–6 hrs); or south, to **Sobra** on Mljet Island (1.25-hr bus ride from the national park, 3/week July–Sept, 2/week June, none Oct–May, 2 hrs; for details, see next) and **Dubrovnik** (5/week July–Sept, 4/week June, 2/week Oct–May, 3–4 hrs).

Speedy *Krilo* Catamaran from Korčula Town to Hvar Town and Split: A speedy catamaran called *Krilo* leaves Korčula town at 6:00 and zips to Hvar town and Split (daily June–Sept, 4/week Oct–May, 1.75 hrs to Hvar, 2.75 hrs to Split, some summer boats stop at Prigradica on Korčula Island—in which case these times are longer). In Korčula, tickets for the *Krilo* boat are sold at Marko Polo Tours—not the Jadrolinija office (35 kn one-way to Hvar, 55 kn to Split). Since it returns from Split and Hvar the same afternoon, this extremely handy catamaran allows you to effortlessly day-trip to either place (see "Transportation Connections" for each town).

From Vela Luka to Hvar Town and Split: There are additional boats to points north, but they usually require a very early bus from Korčula town (departing at 4:10) to the port at Vela Luka, an hour away at the other end of the island. A Jadrolinija **fast catamaran** goes daily from Vela Luka to both Hvar town and Split (Mon–Sat departs at 5:30, Sun at 8:00, 45 min to Hvar, 2 hrs to Split). A much slower **car ferry** also travels daily from Vela Luka to Split (departs Mon–Sat at 6:30, Sun at 14:45, 2.75 hrs, does not stop at Hvar town). From late June through early September, a second car ferry leaves Vela Luka for Split every afternoon, stopping at Hvar town en route (1.5 hours to Hvar town, 3.75 hrs to Split, does not stop at Hvar on Sat). Since reaching Vela Luka from Korčula town is a hassle, carefully confirm these boat schedules and understand all your options (at the Korčula TI or Jadrolinija office) before you get up early to make the trip.

To the National Park on Mljet Island: Public transportation connections between Korčula town and Mljet Island (see Near Dubrovnik chapter) are surprisingly poor. The big Jadrolinija car ferries go only to the town of Sobra, a long 1.25-hour bus ride from the national park (see connections above); worse yet, most of these ferries arrive in Sobra in the evening. If you want to day-trip to Mljet and return to Korčula, take an excursion instead (described on page 203). Looking at a map, it seems logical to do Mljet National Park en route from Korčula to Dubrovnik. In reality, it rarely works—it's better to go to Dubrovnik, then day-trip back out to Mljet using the speedy *Nona Ana* catamaran (see page 259). If you're determined to see Mljet on the way to Dubrovnik, one possibility is to go to the national park with an excursion, then leave the excursion and continue on to Dubrovnik using the catamaran—but this doesn't always work (see "The Excursion Loophole," next).

The Excursion Loophole: If you're desperate to reach a particular place from Korčula, and too impatient to wait for regularly scheduled service, consider paying for an excursion...then "forgetting" to return with the rest of your group (but tell your guide so they don't wait around for you). Sometimes you'll pay full-price, but occasionally you'll only be charged half. Be warned that this is far from a sure thing: Sometimes the agencies aren't willing to let you do it, and excursions can be sold out. And obviously it's much more expensive than a boat ticket (especially if they charge you full price). But, if you're in need, it's worth a try. Ask at Atlas and Marko Polo travel agencies, and try to look as pathetic as possible.

Korčula Bus Connections
All buses from Korčula town (except those to Vela Luka) first drive to Dominče, where they meet the car ferry to cross over to Orebić, on the Pelješac Peninsula. Don't be surprised if you have to get off the bus, walk onto the ferry, and meet a different bus across the channel. It takes close to two hours to drive the length of the Pelješac Peninsula and meet the main coastal road.

From Korčula Town by Bus to: Dubrovnik (peak season: 2/day, 3–4 hrs; off-season: Mon–Sat 1/day with an early departure, Sun 2/day), **Zagreb** (1/day, 9–13.5 hrs depending on route), **Split** (1/day, 5 hrs, same bus goes to Zagreb), **Vela Luka** (at far end of island, Mon–Fri 7/day, Sat 6/day, Sun 4/day, 1 hr, first bus at 4:10 gets you to the early-morning ferries—see above).

Route Tips for Drivers: Between Korčula and the Mainland
The island of Korčula is connected to the mainland by a small car ferry that runs between Dominče—about a mile east of Korčula town—and Orebić, across the channel on the Pelješac Peninsula (50 kn/car, 12 kn/passenger, 15-min crossing, departs Dominče at the top of most but not all hours—check carefully in Korčula, departs Orebić at :30 past most hours).

If you're driving via the mainland, you'll first cross on this car ferry to Orebić on the Pelješac Peninsula, which is known for its wines. The Pelješac Peninsula is extremely long and narrow, and the roads are very rough, so it can take longer than you'd expect to reach the main coastal road (figure 1.5–2 hours). Where the peninsula meets the mainland, you'll see the cute little "Great Wall of

Croatia" town of Ston.

If you're heading south to **Dubrovnik,** the coastal road zips you right there (about an hour from Ston). If you're heading north to **Split,** soon after joining the coastal road you'll actually pass through Bosnia-Herzegovina for a few miles (around the town of Neum—just flash your passport as you enter and exit the country).

Because of the ferry crossing and the long drive along the Pelješac Peninsula, driving from Split to Korčula is time-consuming and tiring. (Notice on the map that the whole time you're driving down the coast parallel to the Pelješac Peninsula, you're actually going in the opposite direction from Korčula—then you have to backtrack as you head up the peninsula itself.) Instead, I prefer to take the longer car ferry the whole way from Split to Vela Luka, at the far end of Korčula Island (described above; allow 1 hour for the drive from Korčula town to Vela Luka, about 315 kn per car). The scenic and relaxing 2.75-hour boat ride saves you more than that much driving time.

DUBROVNIK

Dubrovnik is a living fairy tale that shouldn't be missed. It feels like a small town today, but 500 years ago, Dubrovnik was a major maritime power, with the third biggest navy in the Mediterranean. Still jutting confidently into the sea and ringed by thick medieval walls, Dubrovnik deserves its nickname: the Pearl of the Adriatic. Within the ramparts, the traffic-free Old Town is a fun jumble of quiet, cobbled back lanes; tasty seafood restaurants; narrow, steep alleys; and kid-friendly squares. After all these centuries, the buildings still hint at old-time wealth, and the central promenade remains the place to see and be seen.

The city's charm is the sleepy result of its no-nonsense past. Busy merchants, the salt trade, and shipbuilding made Dubrovnik rich. But the city's most valued commodity was always its freedom—even today, you'll see the proud motto *Libertas* displayed all over town (see *"Libertas"* sidebar on page 213).

Dubrovnik flourished in the 15th and 16th centuries, but an earthquake destroyed nearly everything in 1667. Most of today's buildings in the Old Town are post-quake Baroque, although a few palaces, monasteries, and convents displaying a rich Gothic-Renaissance mix survive from Dubrovnik's earlier Golden Age.

Dubrovnik remained a big tourist draw through the Tito years, bringing in much-needed hard currency from Western visitors. Consequently, the city was never given the hard socialist patina of other Yugoslav cities (such as the nearby Montenegrin capital Podgorica, then known as "Titograd").

As Croatia violently separated from Yugoslavia in 1991, Dubrovnik became the only coastal city to be pulled into the fighting (see "The Siege of Dubrovnik" sidebar, page 224). Imagine having your youthful memories of good times spent romping in the surrounding hills replaced by visions of heavily armed soldiers shooting down on your hometown. The city was devastated, but Dubrovnik has been repaired with amazing speed. The only physical reminders of the war are lots of new, orange roof tiles. Locals, relieved the fighting is over but forever hardened, are often willing to talk about the experience with visitors—offering a rare opportunity to grasp the harsh realities of war from an eyewitness perspective.

While the war killed tourism in the 1990s, today the crowds are most decidedly back. In 2006, locals began to cautiously say, "I think it's finally about as many visitors as before the war." While Europeans and Australians have been flocking here for years, Americans have only just begun to re-discover Dubrovnik. If I had to pick just one place to visit in Croatia, this would be it. Go now, before it's as overrun as Venice...you're almost too late.

Planning Your Time

While Dubrovnik is low on impressive museums, it's one of those places that you never want to leave. The real attraction here is the city itself, and its relaxing, breezy ambience. While Dubrovnik could easily be "seen" in a day, a second or third day to unwind makes the long trip here more worthwhile.

To hit all the key sights in a single day, start at the Pile Gate, just outside the Old Town. Walk around the city's walls to get your bearings, then work your way down the main drag (following my "Welcome to Dubrovnik" self-guided walk). As you explore, drop in at any museums or churches that appeal to you. To squeeze the most into a single day (or with a second day), consider a boat excursion from the Old Port (Lokrum Island, just offshore, requires the least brainpower).

Dubrovnik also makes an excellent home base for day trips into the surrounding area, including a dizzying array of island getaways, plus a pair of particularly striking international destinations (Bosnia-Herzegovina's Mostar and Montenegro's Bay of Kotor). I enjoy staying three or four nights, for maximum side-tripping flexibility. For options, see the next chapter.

ORIENTATION

(area code: 020)

All of the sights worth seeing are in Dubrovnik's traffic-free, walled **Old Town** (Stari Grad) peninsula. The main pedestrian promenade through the middle of town is called the Stradun; from this artery, the Old Town climbs steeply uphill in both directions to the walls. The Old Town connects to the mainland through three gates (Pile Gate, to the west; Ploče Gate, to the east; and

Libertas

Libertas—liberty—has always been close to the heart of every Dubrovnik citizen. Dubrovnik was a proudly independent republic for centuries, even as most of Croatia became Venetian and Hungarian. Dubrovnik believed so strongly in *libertas* that it was the first foreign state in 1776 to officially recognize an upstart, experimental republic called the United States of America.

In the Middle Ages, the city-state of Dubrovnik (then called Ragusa) had to buy its independence from whomever was strongest—Byzantium, Venice, Hungary, the Ottomans—sometimes paying off more than one at a time. Dubrovnik's ships flew whichever flags were necessary to stay free, earning the nickname "Town of Seven Flags." As time went on, Europe's big-league nations were glad to have a second major seafaring power in the Adriatic to balance the Venetian threat. A free Dubrovnik was more valuable than a pillaged, plundered Dubrovnik.

In 1808, Napoleon conquered the Adriatic and abolished the Republic of Dubrovnik. After Napoleon was defeated, the fate of the continent was decided at the Congress of Vienna. But Dubrovnik's delegate was denied a seat at the table. The more powerful nations, no longer concerned about Venice and fed up after years of being sweet-talked by Dubrovnik, were afraid that the delegate would play old alliances off of each other to reestablish an independent Republic of Dubrovnik. Instead, the city became a part of the Hapsburg Empire, and entered a long period of decline.

Libertas still hasn't died in Dubrovnik. In the surreal days of the early 1990s, when Yugoslavia was reshuffling itself, a movement for the creation of a new Republic of Dubrovnik gained some momentum (led by a judge who, in earlier times, had convicted others for the same ideas). But today's locals are content to be part of an independent Republic of Croatia.

the smaller Buža Gate, at the top of Boškovićeva). The Old Port (Gradska Luka), with leisure boats to nearby destinations, is at the east end of town. While greater Dubrovnik has about 50,000 people, the local population within the Old Town is just 5,000 in the winter—and even less in summer, when many residents move out to rent their apartments to tourists.

The **Pile** (PEE-leh) neighborhood, a pincushion of tourist services, is just outside the western end of the Old Town (through Pile Gate). Right in front of the gate, you'll find a TI (with Internet access, see below), ATMs, a post office, a Croatia Airlines office, taxis, buses (fanning out to all the outlying neighborhoods), a cheap

Greater Dubrovnik

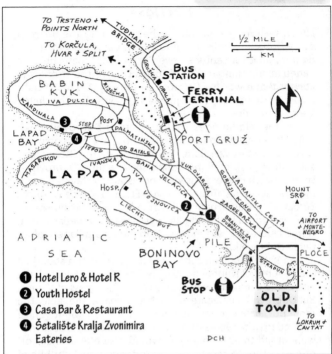

TO TRSTENO +
POINTS NORTH

TUĐMAN BRIDGE

TO KORČULA,
HVAR + SPLIT

½ MILE
1 KM

BUS STATION

FERRY TERMINAL

PORT GRUŽ

BABIN KUK

IVA DULCICA

KARDINALA

STJEČKA

GRUŠKA OBALA

STEP

POST

LAPAD BAY

PALMATINSKA

MASARYKOV

ISPOD

OD BATALE

IVANSKA

BANA

VUKOVARSKA

GORNJI KONO

JADRANSKA CESTA

L A P A D

IVA JELACICA

HOSP.

VOJNOVICA

ZAGREBAČKA

MOUNT SRĐ

TO AIRPORT + MONTE-NEGRO

LIECHT.

PUT

BRANITELJA DUBROVNIKA

A D R I A T I C
S E A

BONINOVO BAY

PILE

PLOČE

STRADUN

BUS STOP

OLD TOWN

TO LOKRUM + CAVTAT

❶ Hotel Lero & Hotel R
❷ Youth Hostel
❸ Casa Bar & Restaurant
❹ Šetalište Kralja Zvonimira
Eateries

DCH

Konzum grocery store, and the Atlas Travel Agency (which books private rooms—see "Helpful Hints," page 217). Just off this strip are some of Dubrovnik's best *sobe* (rooms in private homes—see "Sleeping," page 236). This is also the starting point for my self-guided "Welcome to Dubrovnik" walk (see page 220).

A mile or two away from the Old Town are beaches peppered with expensive resort hotels. My favorites are around **Boninovo Bay** (not too far from the Old Town—see page 241), but most cluster on the lush **Lapad Peninsula** to the west (buses run frequently from just outside Pile Gate and take about 15 min). Across the bay from Lapad Peninsula is **Port Gruž,** with the main bus station and ferry terminal.

In 2005, Dubrovnik re-named two of its busiest streets to commemorate the recent war. The road once called Dr. Ante Starčevića, which stretches from the Pile Gate toward Boninovo Bay and the Lapad Peninsula, became Branitelja Dubrovnika ("Street of the Dubrovnik Defenders"). The road once called Put Republike became Vukovarska (named for the northern Croatian city devastated by a Serb siege). I've used the current names in this chapter, but don't be confused by out-of-date maps and publications.

Dubrovnik Essentials

English	Croatian	Pronounced
Old Town	Stari Grad	STAH-ree grahd
Old Port	Stara Luka	STAH-rah LOO-kah
Pile Gate	Gradska Vrata Pile	GRAHD-skah VRAH-tah PEE-leh
Ploče Gate	Gradska Vrata Ploče	GRAHD-skah VRAH-tah PLOH-cheh
Main Promenade	Stradun	STRAH-doon
Adriatic Sea	Jadran	YAH-drahn

Tourist Information

Dubrovnik's TI has four branches (hours can fluctuate with demand, www.tzdubrovnik.hr): right on the main drag in the **Old Town,** a few blocks in from the Pile Gate (daily May–Oct 8:00–22:00, Nov–April 8:00–20:00, tel. 020/321-561); in the **Pile** neighborhood just outside the Old Town, 100 yards up the street from the Pile Gate (May–Oct daily 8:00–20:00; Nov–April Mon–Fri 9:00–16:00, Sat 9:00–13:00, closed Sun; Branitelja Dubrovnika 7, tel. 020/427-591; Internet access in the same office); across the street from the Jadrolinija ferry dock at **Port Gruž** (same hours as Pile TI, Gruška obala, tel. 020/417-983); and a little window at the **bus station** (open long hours daily).

All the TIs are government-run and legally can't sell you anything—but they can answer questions and give you a copy of the free monthly information booklet *Dubrovnik Riviera,* which contains helpful maps, hotel and restaurant listings, bus and ferry schedules, current museum prices and hours, and more. The TIs also give out a free monthly events brochure and a town map. If you need a room and the TI isn't busy, they might be willing to call around to find a place for you.

Arrival in Dubrovnik

For details on getting to the Dalmatian Coast, see page 152.

By Boat: The big boats arrive at Port Gruž, two miles north-west of the Old Town. On the road in front of the ferry terminal, you'll find a bus stop (#1, #1a, #1b, and #3 go to Old Town's Pile Gate; wait on the embankment side of the street) and a taxi stand (figure 70 kn to the Old Town and most accommodations). Across the street is the Jadrolinija office (with an ATM out front) and a TI. You can book a private room *(soba)* at Atlas Travel Agency (room-booking desk in boat terminal building) or at Gulliver Travel Agency (behind TI). You'll also be ambushed by locals wanting you to stay at their place (for more on the *sobe* option, see page 236).

By Bus: Dubrovnik's big, new bus station (Autobusni Kolodvor) is just beyond the ferry terminal along the Port Gruž embankment (about 2.5 miles northwest of the Old Town). It's pretty basic: pay toilets, baggage check (10 kn, daily 4:30–22:00), a little TI window, and a helpful bus information window. To reach the Old Town's Pile Gate, walk straight ahead through the bus stalls, then bear right at the main road to the city bus stop (#1, #1a, #1b, or #3 to Pile). A taxi to the Old Town and most accommodations runs about 75 kn.

By Plane: Dubrovnik's small airport (Zračna Luka) is in a place called Ćilipi, 13 miles south of the city. A Croatia Airlines bus meets most arriving flights at the airport (30 kn, 40 min). Figure around 250 kn for a taxi or hotel shuttle between the airport and the center (though some cabbies are charging as much as 300 kn). Airport info: tel. 020/773-333, www.airport-dubrovnik.hr.

To get *to* the airport, you can take the same Croatia Airlines bus, which leaves from Dubrovnik's bus station 90 minutes before most flights. If you're staying in or near the Old Town, you'll find it more convenient to catch the airport bus at a stop that's just above the Old Town: From the Old Town's main drag, hike up steep Boškovićeva street and go through the wall at the Buža Gate. Once outside, continue straight under the arch and up the stairs, then swing right at the fire station onto the busy Krešimira street; the bus stop is a few steps up the road, by the old cable-car station. The airport bus reaches this stop a few minutes after leaving the main bus station—wave it down or it might pass you by (confirm schedule at TI or bus station).

By Car: Coming from the north, you'll drive over the super-modern Tuđman Bridge (which locals call simply "the new bridge"). Immediately after crossing the bridge, you can either turn left to twist down to the bus station, ferry terminal (with some car-rental drop-off offices), and Lapad Peninsula; or you can continue straight, toward the Old Town. If you're headed for the Old Town, you'll pass above the Port Gruž area, then take the right turn-off marked *Dubrovnik* (with the little bull's-eye). You'll go through a tunnel, then turn left for *Centar*, and begin following the brown signs for *Grad* (Old Town); individual big hotels are also signed from here. You'll wind up just above the Old Town walls. Follow *Centar* and blue *P* signs to parking (there's a handy but expensive lot—nicknamed "the tennis court" by locals—just behind the wall); you can also go around the right side of the wall to the bustling Pile neighborhood (described under "Orientation"). Your *soba* host or hotel can suggest the easiest parking lot for where you're sleeping.

Helpful Hints

Dubrovnik Summer Festival: Dubrovnik is most crowded during its Summer Festival, a month and a half of theater and musical performances held annually from July 10 to August 25 (www.dubrovnik-festival.hr).

Other Musical Events: Recently Dubrovnik has been working hard to offer traditional music outside of festival time. From April through October, free open-air folk music shows take place each Saturday or Sunday around 11:00 in the area near St. Blaise's Church. For something a little more formal, spirited folk-music concerts are performed for tourists twice weekly in the Lazareti (old quarantine building) just outside the Old Town's Ploče Gate (80 kn, usually at 21:30). In the winter (Nov–Feb), there are two tourist-oriented musical events per week—folk, classical, and other types of music. For the latest on any of these events, ask the TI.

Travel Agency: You'll see travel agencies all over Dubrovnik. At any of them, you can buy seats on an excursion, rent a car, book a room, and pick up a pile of brochures. The biggest operation is **Atlas.** Their newest and most convenient office—which may be open in 2007—is in the big, can't-miss-it building just outside the Pile Gate; if that's not open yet, try their smaller branch just down the nearby alley at Sv. Đurđa 4 (June–Sept Mon–Sat 8:00–20:00, Sun 8:00–13:00; Oct–May Mon–Fri 8:00–19:00, Sat 8:00–15:00, closed Sun; tel. 020/442-574, fax 020/323-609, www.atlas-croatia.com, atlas.pile@atlas.hr). They also have an office at the ferry terminal building at Port Gruž.

Internet Access: You'll see Internet signs all over town. When staying in the Old Town, my favorite is the modern **Netcafé,** with speedy terminals right on Prijeko street, the "restaurant row" (daily 9:00–23:00, until 1:00 in the morning in summer, Prijeko 21, www.netcafe.hr). When sleeping in the Pile neighborhood, I use the **Dubrovnik Internet Centar** inside the Pile TI (5 kn/15 min; May–Oct daily 8:00–22:00, maybe later in peak season; Nov–April Mon–Sat 8:00–21:00, closed Sun; Branitelja Dubrovnika 7).

Car Rental: The big international chains such as **Avis** (tel. 020/773-811), **Europcar** (mobile 091-430-3031), and **Hertz** (tel. 020/425-000) have offices both at the airport and near the Port Gruž embankment where the big boats come in. In addition, the many travel agencies closer to the Old Town also have a line on rental cars. Figure €50–60 per day, including taxes, insurance, and unlimited mileage (at the bigger chains, there's usually no extra charge for drop-off elsewhere in Croatia). Be sure the agency knows if you're crossing a border (such as Montenegro or Bosnia-Herzegovina) to ensure you

Dubrovnik at a Glance

▲▲▲ **Stradun Stroll** Charming walk through Dubrovnik's vibrant Old Town, ideal for coffee, ice cream, and people-watching. **Hours:** Always open.

▲▲▲ **Town Walls** Scenic mile-long walk along top of 15th-century fortifications encircling the city. **Hours:** July–Aug daily 8:00–19:30, progressively shorter hours off-season until 10:00–15:00 in mid-Nov–mid-March.

▲**Franciscan Monastery Museum** Tranquil cloister, medieval pharmacy-turned-museum, and a century-old pharmacy still serving residents today. **Hours:** Daily 9:00–18:00, until 17:00 or maybe even earlier off-season.

▲**Cathedral** Eighteenth-century Roman Baroque cathedral and treasury filled with unusual relics such as a swatch of Jesus' swaddling clothes. **Hours:** Mon–Sat 9:00–20:00, Sun 11:00–17:30.

▲**Dominican Monastery Museum** Another relaxing cloister with precious paintings, altarpieces, and manuscripts. **Hours:** Daily May–Sept 9:00–18:00, off-season until 17:00.

▲**Institute for the Restoration of Dubrovnik** Photos and videos of the recent war and an exhibit on restoration work. **Hours:** June–Sept Mon–Fri 9:00–13:00, closed Sat–Sun; rotating exhibits Oct–May.

▲**Serbian Orthodox Church and Icon Museum** Active church serving Dubrovnik's Serbian Orthodox community, and museum with traditional religious icons. **Hours:** Church—daily 8:00–13:00 & 17:00–19:00, short services daily at 8:30 and 19:00, longer liturgy

have the proper paperwork.

Best Views: Walking the Old Town walls at sunset is a treat—film disappears fast. The Fort of St. Lawrence, perched above the Pile neighborhood cove, has great views over the Old Town. A stroll east of the city walls offers nice views back on the Old Town (best light early in the day).

Better yet, if you have a car, head south of the city in the morning for gorgeously lit Old Town views over your right shoulder; various turn-offs along this road are ideal photo stops. The best one, known locally as the "panorama point," is where the road leading up and out of Dubrovnik meets the

Sun at 9:00; museum—May–Oct Mon–Sat 9:00–14:00, closed Sun; Nov–April Mon–Fri 9:00–14:00, closed Sat–Sun.

▲Rupe Granary and Ethnographic Museum Good folk museum with tools, jewelry, clothing, and painted eggs above immense underground grain stores. **Hours:** June–Oct daily 9:00–18:00; Nov–May Mon–Sat 9:00–14:00, closed Sun.

Rector's Palace Antique furniture, guns, coins, and old prison cells in the former home of Venetian rectors who ruled Dubrovnik in the Middle Ages. **Hours:** May–Oct daily 9:00–18:00; Nov–April Mon–Sat 9:00–14:00, closed Sun.

Maritime Museum Contracts, maps, paintings, and models from Dubrovnik's days as a maritime power and shipbuilding center. **Hours:** Vary with demand, usually June–Aug daily 9:00–18:00, Sept–Oct Mon–Sat 9:00–17:00, Nov–May Mon–Sat 9:00–14:00, generally closed Sun off-season.

Aquarium Tanks of local sea life housed in huge, shady old fort. **Hours:** Daily July–Aug 9:00–21:00, progressively shorter hours off-season until 9:00–13:00 Nov–March.

Synagogue Museum Europe's second-oldest synagogue and Croatia's only Jewish museum, with 13th-century Torahs and Holocaust-era artifacts. **Hours:** May–Oct daily 10:00–20:00; Nov–April Mon–Fri 10:00–15:00, closed Sat–Sun.

War Photo Limited Thought-provoking photographic look at contemporary warfare. **Hours:** June–Sept daily 9:00–21:00; May and Oct Tue–Sat 10:00–16:00, Sun 10:00–14:00, closed Mon; closed Nov–April.

main road that passes above the town (look for the pull-out on the right, with tour buses). Even if you're heading north, in good weather it's worth a quick detour south for this view.

Getting Around Dubrovnik

If you're staying in or near the Old Town, everything is easily walkable. But those sleeping on Boninovo Bay or the Lapad Peninsula will want to get comfortable with the buses—they work great, and the system is easy.

By Bus: Libertas runs Dubrovnik's public buses. Tickets, which are good for an hour, are cheaper if you buy them in advance from a kiosk or your hotel (8 kn, ask for *autobusna karta*, ow-toh-BOOS-nah KAR-tah) than if you buy them from the bus driver (10 kn). When you enter the bus, validate your ticket in the machine. All buses stop near the Old Town, just in front of the Pile Gate (buy tickets at the newsstand right by the stop). From here, they fan out to just about anywhere you'd want to go (hotels on Boninovo Bay, Lapad Peninsula, and the ferry terminal and long-distance bus station). You'll find bus schedules and a map in the TI booklet.

By Taxi: Taxis start at 25 kn, then cost 8 kn per kilometer. The handiest taxi stand for the Old Town is just outside the Pile Gate. The biggest operation is Radio Taxi (tel. 020/970).

TOURS

Two new companies—Dubrovnik Walks and Dubrovnik Walking Tours—offer similar one-hour **walking tours** of the Old Town daily at 10:00 (100 kn, daily, look for fliers at TI). But these tours are pricey and brief, touching lightly on the same basic information explained in this chapter. For an in-depth look at the city, consider hiring your own local guide: **Štefica Ćurić** really knows her stuff and can give you an insider's look at the city (480 kn/2 hrs, mobile 091-345-0133, dugacarapa@yahoo.com). The TI can also help you find a local guide (same price as Štefica). Finally, two big companies (Atlas and Elite) offer expensive **bus-plus-walking tours** of Dubrovnik (about 200 kn, 2 hours).

To get out of town, you can rent a car (see "Helpful Hints"), or consider hiring your own **driver.** Friendly Pepo Klaić, who speaks great English, can drive you just about anywhere near Dubrovnik, including Mostar, Montenegro, or Korčula (€250 for the full day, tel. 020/436-194, mobile 098-427-301, pepoklaic@yahoo.com). Note that Pepo is a driver, not a tour guide. It's cheaper to rent a car and do it yourself, but if you'd rather have someone else do the driving, this is a handy option.

For information on guided excursions from Dubrovnik to nearby destinations, see the next chapter.

SELF-GUIDED WALK

Welcome to Dubrovnik: Strolling the Stradun

Running through the heart of Dubrovnik's Old Town is the Stradun promenade—packed with people and lined with sights. This walk, worth ▲▲▲, offers an ideal introduction to Dubrovnik's charms. It takes about a half-hour, not counting sightseeing stops.

• *Begin at the busy square in front of the west entrance to the Old Town, the Pile (PEE-leh) Gate.*

Pile Neighborhood: This bustling area is the nerve center of Dubrovnik's tourist industry—it's where the real world meets the fantasy of Dubrovnik (for all the details, see "Orientation," page 212). Across from the big Atlas Travel Agency building is a leafy café terrace. Wander over to the edge of the terrace and take in the imposing walls of the Pearl of the Adriatic. The huge, fortified peninsula just outside the city walls is the **Fort of St. Lawrence** (Tvrđava Lovrijenac), Dubrovnik's oldest fortress and one of the top venues for the Dubrovnik Summer Festival. Shakespearean plays are often performed here, occasionally starring Goran Višnjić, the Croatian actor who has become an American star on the TV show *ER*. You can climb this fortress for great views over the Old Town (covered by same ticket as Old Town walls).

• *Now go through the...*

Pile Gate (Gradska Vrata Pile): Just before you enter the gate, notice the image above the entrance of **St. Blaise** (Sveti Vlaho in Croatian) cradling Dubrovnik in his arm. You'll see a lot more of Blaise during your time here—we'll find out why later on this walk.

Inside the outer wall of the Pile Gate and to the left, a white sign shows where each bomb dropped on the Old Town in the recent war.

Passing the rest of the way through the gate, you'll find a lively little square surrounded by landmarks. To the left, a steep stairway leads up to the imposing **Minčeta Tower.** This is a good starting point for Dubrovnik's best activity, walking around the top of the wall (see "Sights" later in this chapter).

Next to the stairway is the small **Church of St. Savior** (Crkva Svetog Spasa). Appreciative locals built this votive church to thank God after Dubrovnik made it through a 1520 earthquake. When the massive 1667 quake destroyed the city, this church was one of the only buildings left intact. And during the recent war, the church survived another close call when a shell exploded on the ground right in front of it (you can still see pockmarks from the shrapnel).

The big, round structure in the middle of the square is **Onofrio's Big Fountain** (Velika Onofrijea Fontana). In the Middle Ages, Dubrovnik had a complicated aqueduct system that brought water from the mountains seven miles away. The water ended up here, at the town's biggest fountain, before continuing through the city. This plentiful supply of water, large reserves of salt (a key source of Dubrovnik's wealth), and a massive granary (now the Rupe Museum, described on page 235) made little, independent Dubrovnik very siege-resistant.

The big building on the left just beyond the small Church of St. Savior is the **Franciscan Monastery Museum.** This building, with a delightful cloister and one of Europe's oldest pharmacies, is worth touring (described on page 228).

• *When you're finished taking in the sights on this square, continue along...*

The Stradun: Dubrovnik's main promenade—officially called Placa, but better known as the Stradun—is alive with locals and

tourists alike. This is the heartbeat of the city: an Old World shopping mall by day and sprawling cocktail party after dark, when everybody seems to be doing the traditional evening stroll—flirting, ice-cream-licking, flaunting, and gawking. A coffee and some of Europe's best people-watching in a prime Stradun café is one of travel's great $3 bargains.

When Dubrovnik was just getting its start in the seventh century, this street was a canal. Romans fleeing from the invading Slavs lived on the island of Ragusa, and the Slavs settled on the shore. In the 11th century, the canal separating Ragusa from the mainland was filled in, the towns merged, and a unique Slavic-Roman culture and language blossomed. While originally much more higgledy-piggledy, this street was rebuilt in the current, more straightforward style after the 1667 earthquake.

During your time in Dubrovnik, you'll periodically hear the rat-a-tat-tat of a drum echoing through the streets from the Stradun. This means it's time to head for this main drag to get a glimpse of the colorfully costumed "town guards" parading through town (and a cavalcade of tourists running alongside them, trying to snap a clear picture). You may also see some of these characters standing guard outside the town gates. It's all part of the local tourist board's recent efforts to make their town even more atmospheric.

• *At the end of the Stradun is a lane leading to the Ploče Gate. Just before this lane is the lively Luža Square. Its centerpiece is...*

Orlando's Column (Orlandov Stup): Columns like this were typical of towns in northern Germany. Dubrovnik erected the column in 1417, soon after it had shifted allegiances from the oppressive Venetians to the Hungarians. By putting a northern European symbol in the middle of its most prominent square, Dubrovnik decisively distanced itself from Venice. Anytime a decision was made by the Republic, the town crier came to Orlando's Column and announced the news. The step he stood on indicated the importance of his message—the higher up, the more important the news. It was also used as the pillory, where people were publicly punished. The thin line on the top step in front of Orlando is exactly as long as the statue's forearm. This mark was Dubrovnik's standard measurement—not for a foot, but for an "elbow."

• *Now stand in front of Orlando's Column and orient yourself with a...*

Luža Square Spin-Tour: Orlando is looking toward the **Sponza Palace** (Sponza-Povijesni Arhiv). This building, from 1522, is the finest surviving example of Dubrovnik's Golden Age in the 15th to 16th centuries. It's a combination of Renaissance (ground-floor arches) and Venetian Gothic (upstairs windows). Houses up and down the main promenade used to look like this, but after the 1667 earthquake, they were replaced with boring uniformity. This used to be the customs office *(dogana)*, but now it's an exhaustive archive of the city's history, with temporary art exhibits and a war memorial. The poignant **Memorial Room of Dubrovnik Defenders** (on the left as you enter) has photos of dozens of people from Dubrovnik who were killed fighting the Serbs in 1991. A TV screen and images near the ceiling show the devastation of the city. Though the English descriptions are (perhaps unavoidably) slanted to the Croat perspective, it's compelling to look in the eyes of the brave young men who didn't start this war...but were willing to finish it (free, daily 10:00–15:00, often later).

To the right of Sponza Palace is the town's **Bell Tower** (Gradski Zvonik). The original dated from 1444, but it was rebuilt when it started to lean in the 1920s. The big clock may be an octopus—but only one of its hands tells time. Below that, the circle shows the phase of the moon (the greener, the fuller the moon). At the bottom, the old-fashioned digital readout tells the hour (in Roman numerals) and the minutes (in five-minute increments). At the top of each hour (and again three minutes later), the time is clanged out on the bell up top by two bronze bell ringers, Maro and Baro. (If this all seems like a copy of the very similar clock on St. Mark's Square in Venice, locals are quick to point out that this clock predates that one by several decades.) The clock still has to be wound every two days. Notice the little black hole between the moon phase and the "digital" readout: The clock-winder opens this window to get some light. During the recent war, the clock-winder's house was destroyed—with the keys inside. For days, the clock bell didn't run. But then, miraculously, the keys were discovered lying in the street. The excited Dubrovnik citizens came together in this square and cheered as the clock was wound and the bell chimed, signaling to the soldiers surrounding the city that

The Siege of Dubrovnik

In June of 1991, Croatia declared independence from Yugoslavia. Within weeks, the nations were at war (for more on the war, see the Understanding Yugoslavia chapter, page 436). Though warfare raged in the Croatian interior, nobody expected that the bloodshed would reach Dubrovnik.

At 6:00 in the morning on October 1, 1991, Dubrovnik residents were stunned to see Yugoslav warships on the horizon. Then the explosions began. The ships shelled the hillsides above Dubrovnik to disable a strategic communications tower (which you can see today) and clear the way for land troops, who quickly surrounded the city. Within a month, the Serb-dominated Yugoslav National Army began bombing the Pearl of the Adriatic. At first, the attacks were focused on strategic military positions on the outskirts of town. But then, shockingly, they aimed their guns at the Old Town. Defenseless townspeople took shelter in their cellars, and sometimes even huddled together in the city wall's 15th-century forts. For the first time in centuries, Dubrovnik's city walls were used to protect its people from an invading army.

Dubrovnik resisted the siege better than anyone expected. The Serbs were hoping that residents would flee the town, allowing the Yugoslav National Army to move in. But the people of Dubrovnik stayed. Dubrovnik's defenders held the fort atop Mount Srđ (just above the Old Town), while the Serbs controlled nearby mountaintops. All supplies had to be carried up to the fort by foot or by donkey. Dubrovnik wasn't prepared for war, so they had to improvise their defense. Many brave young locals lost their lives when they slung old hunting rifles over their shoulders and, under the cover of darkness, climbed the hills above Dubrovnik to meet the Serbs face-to-face.

After eight months of bombing, Dubrovnik was liberated by the Croatian army, which attacked Serb positions from the north. By the end of the war, 100 civilians were dead, as well as more than 200 Dubrovnik citizens who lost their lives actively

they hadn't won yet.

The big building to the right of the Bell Tower is the **City Hall** (Vijećnica). Next to it is **Onofrio's Little Fountain** (Mala Onofrijea Fontana), the little brother of the one at the other end of the Stradun. Beyond that is the **Gradska Kavana,** or "Town Café." This hangout—historically Dubrovnik's favorite spot for gossiping and people-watching—was recently renovated, with seating all the way through the wall to the Old Port. Just down the street from the Town Café is the Rector's Palace, and then the cathedral (for more on each, see "Sights").

Behind Orlando is **St. Blaise's Church** (Crkva Sv. Vlaha), fighting for their hometown (much revered today as "Dubrovnik Defenders"). More than two-thirds of Dubrovnik's buildings had been damaged, and more than 30,000 people had to flee their homes—but the failed siege was finally over.

Why was Dubrovnik—so far from the rest of the fighting—dragged into the conflict? The Serbs wanted to catch the city and surrounding region off-guard, gaining a toehold on the southern Dalmatian Coast so they could push north to Split. They also hoped to ignite pro-Serb passions in the nearby Serb-dominated areas of Bosnia-Herzegovina and Montenegro. But perhaps most of all, Yugoslavia wanted to hit Croatia where it hurt—its proudest, most historic, and most beautiful city, the tourist capital of a nation dependent on tourism. (It seems their plan backfired. Locals now say, "When Serbia attacked Dubrovnik, they lost the war"—because images of the historic city under siege swayed international public opinion *against* the Serbs.)

The war initially devastated the tourist industry. Now, to the casual observer, Dubrovnik seems virtually back to normal. Aside from a few pockmarks and bright, new roof tiles, there are scant reminders of what happened here just over a decade ago. But even though the city itself has been repaired, the people of Dubrovnik are forever changed. Imagine living in an idyllic paradise, a place that attracted and awed visitors from around the world...and then watching it gradually blown to bits. It's understandable that Dubrovnik citizens are a little less in love with life than they once were.

Dubrovnik has no real museum about its recent war, but two small sights can help you piece together the story: the Memorial Room of Dubrovnik Defenders in the Sponza Palace on Luža Square (page 223); and, a few blocks away across the Stradun, the Institute for the Restoration of Dubrovnik (page 233). Another sight, War Photo Limited, expands its scope to war photography from around the world (page 232).

dedicated to the patron saint of Dubrovnik. You'll see statues and paintings of St. Blaise all over town, always holding a model of the city in his left hand. According to legend, a millennium ago St. Blaise came to a local priest in a dream and warned him that the up-and-coming Venetians would soon attack the city. The priest alerted the authorities, who prepared for war. Of course, the prediction came true. St. Blaise has been a Dubrovnik symbol—and locals have resented Venice—ever since.

• *Your tour is finished. From here, you've got plenty of sightseeing options (all described under "Sights"). As you face the Bell Tower, you can go up the street to the right to reach the Rector's Palace and cathedral; you can walk through the gate straight ahead to reach the Old Port; or you can head through the gate and jog left to find the Dominican Monastery Museum. Even more sights—including an old synagogue, an Orthodox church, two different exhibits of war photography, and the medieval granary—are in the steep streets between the Stradun and the walls.*

SIGHTS

All of Dubrovnik's sights are inside the Old Town's walls. Note that three of Dubrovnik's sights are covered by a single 50-kn "collective ticket": the Rector's Palace, Maritime Museum, and Rupe Ethnographic Museum (plus an uninteresting 16th-century Croatian writer's house). If you'll be visiting at least two of these museums, this ticket will save you money (available at any participating sight).

Town Walls (Gradske Zidine)

Dubrovnik's single best attraction—easily worth ▲▲▲—is strolling the scenic mile around the city walls. As you meander along

this lofty perch—with a sea of orange roofs on one side, and the actual sea on the other—you'll get your bearings and snap pictures like mad of the ever-changing views. Bring extra film and your map, which you can use to pick out landmarks and get the lay of the land.

There have been walls here almost as long as there's been a Dubrovnik. The fortifications were beefed up in the 15th century, when the Ottoman navy became a threat. Around the perimeter are several substantial forts, which protected residents both during the Republic of Dubrovnik's Golden Age and during the recent war.

Walking the walls also offers the best illustration of the damage Dubrovnik sustained during the recent war. It's easy to see that more than 70 percent of Dubrovnik's roofs were replaced after the bombings (notice the new, bright-orange tiles—and how some buildings salvaged the old tiles, but have 20th-century ones underneath).

You can enter the walls at three points: just inside the Pile Gate, near the Dominican Monastery north of the Ploče Gate, and by the Maritime Museum south of the Old Port. The highest point is the empty Minčeta Tower, above the Pile Gate at the west end of town. The tower rewards those who climb it with a fine view. If you climb here first from the Pile Gate and then proceed

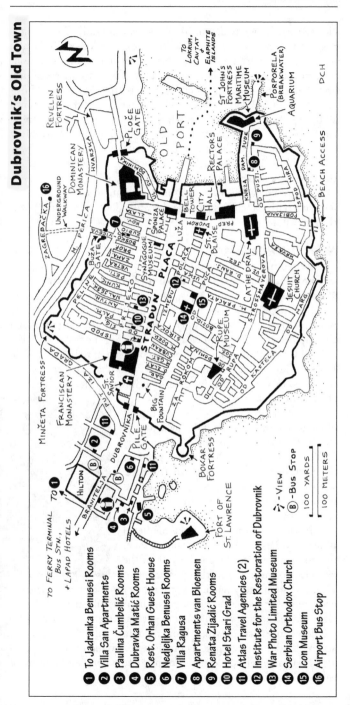

Dubrovnik's Old Town

1 To Jadranka Benussi Rooms
2 Villa San Apartments
3 Paulina Čumbelić Rooms
4 Dubravka Matić Rooms
5 Rest. Orhan Guest House
6 Nedjeljka Benussi Rooms
7 Villa Ragusa
8 Apartments van Bloemen
9 Renata Zijadić Rooms
10 Hotel Stari Grad
11 Atlas Travel Agencies (2)
12 Institute for the Restoration of Dubrovnik
13 War Photo Limited Museum
14 Serbian Orthodox Church
15 Icon Museum
16 Airport Bus Stop

clockwise, it's mostly downhill all the way around. (Posted signs suggest you go counterclockwise, so if it's crowded, you may find it's easier to go with the flow of other wall-walkers.) Speed demons with no cameras can walk the walls in less than an hour; strollers and shutterbugs should plan on longer (50 kn to enter walls, July–Aug daily 8:00–19:30, progressively shorter hours off-season until 10:00–15:00 in mid-Nov–mid-March). Note that posted opening times indicate when the walls close, *not* the last entry—ascend at least an hour before this time if you want to make it all the way around. Your ticket also includes the Fort of St. Lawrence outside the Pile Gate (described in self-guided walk, above).

You can rent a 40-kn audioguide, separate from the admission fee, for a narrated circular tour of the walls (look for salesmen near the entry points).

Near the Pile Gate

This museum is just inside the Pile Gate.

▲**Franciscan Monastery Museum (Franjevački Samostan-Muzej)**—In the Middle Ages, Dubrovnik's monasteries flourished. While all you'll see here are a fine cloister and a one-room museum in the old pharmacy, it's a delightful space. Enter through the gap between the small church and the big monastery (20 kn, daily 9:00–18:00, until 17:00 or maybe even earlier off-season, Placa 2). Just inside the door, a century-old pharmacy still serves residents. (You'll see the monastery's original medieval pharmacy at the far end of the cloister.)

Explore the peaceful, sun-dappled **cloister.** Examine the capitals at the tops of the 60 Romanesque-Gothic double pillars. Each one is different. Notice that some of the portals inside the courtyard are made with a lighter-colored stone—these had to be repaired after being damaged in the recent war.

In the far corner stands the medieval **pharmacy.** Part of the Franciscans' mission was to contribute to the good health of the citizens, so they opened this pharmacy in 1317. The monastery has had a pharmacy in continual operation ever since. On display are jars, pots, and other medieval pharmacists' tools. The sick would come to get their medicine at the little window (on left side), which limited contact with the pharmacist and reduced the risk of passing on disease. Around the room, you'll also find some relics, old manuscripts, and a detailed painting of early 17th-century Dubrovnik.

Near Luža Square

These sights are at the far end of the Stradun (nearest the Old Port). As you stand on Luža Square facing the Bell Tower, the Rector's Palace and Cathedral are up the street called Pred Dvorom to the right, and the Dominican Monastery Museum is through the gate by the Bell Tower and to the left.

Rector's Palace (Knežev Dvor)—In the Middle Ages, the Republic of Dubrovnik was ruled by a rector (similar to a Venetian doge), who was elected by the nobility. To prevent any one person from becoming too powerful, the rector's term was limited to one month. Most rectors were in their 50s—near the end of the average lifespan, and less likely to shake things up. During his term, a rector lived upstairs in this palace. Because it's been plundered twice, this empty-feeling museum isn't as interesting as most other European palaces—but it does offer a glimpse of Dubrovnik in its glory days (35 kn, covered by 50-kn "collective ticket"; May–Oct daily 9:00–18:00; Nov–April Mon–Sat 9:00–14:00, closed Sun; some posted English information, skip the 30-kn audioguide, 6-kn English booklet is helpful, Pred Dvorom 3).

The exterior is decorated in the Gothic-Renaissance mix (with particularly finely carved capitals) that was so common in Dubrovnik before the 1667 earthquake. The courtyard is a venue for the Summer Festival, hosting music groups ranging from the local symphony to the Vienna Boys' Choir.

In the courtyard is the only secular statue created during the centuries-long Republic. Dubrovnik republicans, mindful of the dangers of hero-worship, didn't believe that any one citizen should be singled out. They made only one exception—for Miho Pracat (a.k.a. Michaeli Prazatto), a rich citizen who donated vast sums to charity and willed a fleet of ships to the city. But notice that Pracat's statue is displayed in here, behind closed doors, not out in public. The ground floor has some other exhibits, including some old prison cells. Supposedly these were placed within earshot of the rector's quarters, so the Big Guy could hear the moans of the prisoners...and stay honest.

On the mezzanine level (stairs on right as you enter), you'll find an impressive collection of antique pharmacy jars, a decent display of furniture, a wimpy gun exhibit, and a ho-hum coin collection. On the upper floor (stairs on left as you enter, across from mezzanine stairs) are old apartments that serve as a painting gallery. The only vaguely authentic room is the red room in the corner, decorated more or less as it was in 1500, when it was the rector's office. Mihajlo Hamzić's exquisite *Baptism of Christ* painting, inspired by Italian painter Andrea Mantegna, is an early Renaissance work from the "Dubrovnik School" (see "Dominican Monastery Museum").

▲**Cathedral (Katedrala)**—Dubrovnik's original 12th-century cathedral was funded largely by the English king Richard the Lionhearted. On his way back from the Third Crusade, Richard was shipwrecked nearby. He promised God that if he survived, he'd build a church on the spot where he landed—which happened to be on Lokrum Island, just offshore. At Dubrovnik's request, Richard agreed to build his token of thanks inside the city instead. It was the finest Romanesque church on the Adriatic... before it was destroyed by the 1667 earthquake. This version is 18th-century Roman Baroque. Inside, you'll find a painting from the school of Titian *(Assumption of the Virgin)*, a stark contemporary altar, and a quirky treasury *(riznica)* packed with 138 relics (church entry free, treasury entry-10 kn, both open Mon–Sat 9:00–20:00, Sun 11:00–17:30).

Examining the **treasury** collection, notice that there are three locks on the treasury door—the stuff in here was so valuable, three different VIPs (the rector, the bishop, and a local aristocrat) had to agree before it could be opened. On the table near the door are several of St. Blaise's body parts (pieces of his arm, skull, and leg—all encased in silver). In the middle of the wall directly opposite the door, look for the crucifix with a piece of the "true cross." On a dig in Jerusalem, St. Helen (Emperor Constantine's mother) discovered what she believed to be the cross that Jesus was crucified on. It was brought to Constantinople, and the Byzantine czars doled out pieces of it to Balkan kings. Note the folding three-paneled altar painting (underneath the cross). Dubrovnik ambassadors packed this on road trips (such as their annual trip to pay off the Ottomans) so they could worship wherever they traveled. On the right side of the room, the silver casket supposedly holds the actual swaddling clothes of the Baby Jesus (or, as some locals call it somewhat less reverently, "Jesus' nappy"). Dubrovnik bishops secretly passed these clothes down from generation to generation...until a nun got wind of it, and told the whole town. Pieces of the cloth were cut off to miraculously heal the sick, especially new mothers recovering from a difficult birth. No matter how often it was cut, the cloth always went back to its original form. Then someone tried to use it on the wife of a Bosnian king. Since she was Muslim, it couldn't help her, and it never worked again. Whether or not it's true, this legend hints at the prickly relationships between faiths (not to mention male chauvinism) here in the Balkans.

▲**Dominican Monastery Museum (Dominikanski Samostan-Muzej)**—You'll find many of Dubrovnik's art treasures—paintings, altarpieces, and manuscripts—gathered around the peaceful Dominican Monastery cloister inside the Ploče Gate (15 kn, art buffs enjoy the 60-kn English book, daily May–Sept 9:00–18:00, off-season until 17:00).

One room contains paintings from the **"Dubrovnik School,"** the Republic's circa-1500 answer to the art boom in Florence and Venice. While the 1667 earthquake destroyed most of these paintings, about a dozen survive, and five of those are in this room. Don't miss the triptych by Nikola Božidarović, with St. Blaise holding a detailed model of 16th-century Dubrovnik (left panel)—the most famous depiction of Dubrovnik's favorite saint.

The striking **church** is decorated with modern stained glass, a fine 13th-century pulpit that survived the earthquake (reminding visitors of the intellectual approach to scripture that characterized the Dominicans), and a precious 14th-century Paolo Veneziano crucifix hanging above the high altar. The most memorable piece of art in the church is the *Miracle of St. Dominic,* showing the founder of the order bringing a child back to life (over the altar to the right, as you enter). It was painted in the Realist style (late 19th century) by Vlaho Bukovac.

Near the Old Port (Stara Luka)

The picturesque Old Port, carefully nestled behind St. John's Fort, faces away from what was Dubrovnik's biggest threat, the

Venetians. The long seaside building across the bay on the left is the Lazareti, once the medieval quarantine house. In those days, all visitors were locked in here for 40 days before entering town. A bench-lined harborside walk leads around the fort to a breakwater, providing a peaceful perch. At the port, you can haggle with captains selling excursions (described in the next chapter).

Maritime Museum (Pomorski Muzej)—By the 15th century, when Venice's nautical dominance was on the wane, Dubrovnik emerged as a maritime power and the Mediterranean's leading shipbuilding center. The Dubrovnik-built "argosy" boat (from "Ragusa," an early name for the city) was the Cadillac of ships, frequently mentioned by Shakespeare. This small museum traces the history of Dubrovnik's most important industry with contracts, maps, paintings, and models—all well-described in English. Don't miss the poorly marked upstairs section, with the best exhibits. Boaters will find the museum particularly interesting (35 kn, covered by 50-kn "collective ticket," 5-kn English booklet, hours depend on demand, usually June–Aug daily 9:00–18:00, Sept–Oct Mon–Sat 9:00–17:00, Nov–May Mon–Sat 9:00–14:00, generally closed Sun off-season, upstairs in St. John's Fort, at far—or south—end of Old Port, tel. 020/323-904).

Aquarium (Akvarij)—Dubrovnik's aquarium, housed in the cavernous St. John's Fort, is an old-school place, with 27 tanks on one floor. A visit here allows you a close look at the local marine life, and provides a cool refuge from the midday heat (30 kn, kids-10 kn, English descriptions, daily July–Aug 9:00–21:00, progressively shorter hours off-season until 9:00–13:00 Nov–March, ground floor of St. John's Fort, enter from Old Port).

Between the Stradun and the Mainland

These two museums are a few steps off the main promenade toward the mainland.

Synagogue Museum (Sinagoga-Muzej)—When Jews were forced out of Spain in 1492, a steady stream of them passed through here en route to today's Turkey. Finding Dubrovnik to be a flourishing and relatively tolerant city, many stayed. Žudioska ulica ("Jewish Street"), just inside Ploče Gate, became the ghetto in 1546. It was walled at one end, and had a gate (which would be locked at night) at the other end. Today, the same street is home to the second-oldest synagogue in Europe (after Prague's), which contains Croatia's only Jewish museum. The top floor houses the synagogue itself. Notice the lattice windows that separated the women from the men (according to Orthodox Jewish tradition). Below that, a small museum with good English descriptions gives meaning to the various Torahs (including a 13th-century one from Spain) and other items—such as the written orders *(naredba)* that Jews in Nazi-era Yugoslavia had to identify their shops as Jewish-owned and wear armbands. (The Ustaše—the Nazi puppet government in Croatia— interned and executed not only Jews and Roma/Gypsies, but also Serbs and other people they considered undesirable; see page 52.) Of Croatia's 25,000 Jews, only 3,000 survived the Holocaust. Today Croatia has about 2,000 Jews, including 12 Jewish families who call Dubrovnik home. A rabbi visits this synagogue a few times each year from Zagreb (10 kn, 10-kn English booklet; May–Oct daily 10:00–20:00; Nov–April Mon–Fri 10:00–15:00, closed Sat–Sun; Žudioska ulica 5, tel. 020/321-028).

War Photo Limited—If the tragic story of wartime Dubrovnik has you in a pensive mood, drop by this gallery with images of warfare from around the world. The brainchild of photojournalist Wade Goddard, this thought-provoking museum attempts to show the ugly reality of war through raw, often disturbing photographs taken in the field. Well-displayed on two floors, the exhibit changes every two months or so. Note that the focus is not on Dubrovnik, but on war anywhere and everywhere (25 kn; June–Sept daily 9:00–21:00; May and Oct Tue–Sat 10:00–16:00, Sun 10:00–14:00, closed Mon; closed Nov–April; Antuninska 6, tel. 020/322-166, www.warphotoltd.com).

Between the Stradun and the Sea

▲**Institute for the Restoration of Dubrovnik (Zavod za Obnovu Dubrovnika)**—This small photo gallery is the closest thing Dubrovnik has to a museum about its recent war. The front two rooms display images of bombed-out Dubrovnik, each one juxtaposed with an image of the same building after being restored. The back room offers rotating exhibits about efforts to restore Dubrovnik to its pre-siege glory. The photos are too few, but still illuminating. The highlight of the exhibit is a video showing a series of breathless news reports from a British journalist stationed here during the siege. As you watch shells devastating this glorious city, and look in the eyes of its desperate citizens at their darkest hour, you might just begin to grasp what went on here not so long ago (free; June–Sept Mon–Fri 9:00–13:00, closed Sat–Sun; Oct–May the same space is used for rotating exhibits on other topics; Zuzorić 6, tel. 020/324-060).

▲**Serbian Orthodox Church and Icon Museum (Srpska Pravoslavna Crkva i Muzej Ikona)**—Round out your look at Dubrovnik's faiths (Catholic, Jewish, and Orthodox) with a visit to this house of worship—one of the most convenient places in Croatia to learn about Eastern Orthodox Christianity. Remember that people from the former Yugoslavia who follow the Orthodox faith are, by definition, ethnic Serbs. With all the (perhaps understandably) hard feelings about the recent war, this church serves as an important reminder that all Serbs aren't bloodthirsty killers.

Dubrovnik never had a very large Serb population (an Orthodox church wasn't even allowed inside the town walls until the mid-19th century). During the recent war, most Serbs fled, created new lives for themselves elsewhere, and see little reason to return. But some old-timers remain, and Dubrovnik's dwindling, aging Orthodox population is still served by this church. The candles stuck in the sand and water (to prevent fire outbreaks) represent prayers: The ones at floor level are for the deceased, while the ones higher up are for the living. The gentleman selling candles encourages you to buy and light one, regardless of your faith, so long as you do so with the proper intentions and reverence (free entry, good 20-kn English book explains the church and the museum, daily 8:00–13:00 & 17:00–19:00, short services daily at 8:30 and 19:00, longer liturgy Sundays at 9:00, Od Puča 8). For a

The Serbian Orthodox Church

Because the emphasis of this book is on the Catholic areas of the former Yugoslavia, it's easy to overlook the rich diversity of faiths in this region. Dubrovnik's Serbian Orthodox Church, as well as several Orthodox churches in Kotor, Montenegro (see page 303), offer an invaluable opportunity to learn about a faith that's often ignored by visitors.

As you explore an Orthodox church, notice that there are no pews. Worshippers stand through the service, as a sign of respect (though some older parishioners sit on the seats along the walls). Women stand on the left side, men on the right (equal distance from the altar—to represent that all are equal before God). The Orthodox Church uses essentially the same Bible as Catholics, but it's written in the Cyrillic alphabet, which you'll see displayed around any Orthodox church. Following Old Testament Judeo-Christian tradition, the Bible is kept on the altar behind the iconostasis, the big screen in the middle of the room covered with curtains and icons (golden paintings of saints), which separates the material world from the spiritual one. At certain times during the service, the curtains are pulled back so the congregation can see the Holy Book.

Unlike many Catholic church decorations, Orthodox icons are not intended to be lifelike. Packed with intricate symbolism, and cast against a shimmering golden background, they're meant to remind viewers of the metaphysical nature of Jesus and the saints rather than their physical form, which is considered irrelevant. You'll almost never see a statue, which is thought to overemphasize the physical world...and, to Orthodox people, feels a little too close to the "Thou shalt not worship graven images" thing. Orthodox services generally involve chanting (a dialogue that goes back and forth between the priest and the congregation), and the church is filled with the evocative aroma of incense.

The incense, chanting, icons, and standing up are all intended to heighten the experience of worship. While many Catholic and Protestant services tend to be more of a theoretical and rote consideration of religious issues (come on—don't tell me you've never dozed through the sermon), Orthodox services are about creating a religious experience. Each of these elements does its part to help the worshipper transcend the physical world and enter into communion with the spiritual one.

primer on the Orthodox faith, see the sidebar.

A few doors down, hiding above an art gallery, you'll find the **Icon Museum** (10 kn; May–Oct Mon–Sat 9:00–14:00, closed Sun; Nov–April Mon–Fri 9:00–14:00, closed Sat–Sun). This small collection features 78 different icons (paintings of saints, generally on a golden background—a common feature of Orthodox churches) from the 15th through the 19th centuries, all identified in English. In the library—crammed with old shelves holding some 12,000 books—look for the astonishingly detailed calendar, with portraits of hundreds of saints.

▲Rupe Granary and Ethnographic Museum (Etnografski Muzej Rupe)—This huge, 16th-century building was Dubrovnik's biggest granary. *Rupe* means "holes"—and it's worth the price of entry just to peer down into these cavernous underground grain stores, designed to maintain the perfect temperature to preserve the seeds (63 degrees Fahrenheit). When the grain had to be dried, it was moved upstairs—which today houses a surprisingly well-presented Ethnographic Museum, with tools, jewelry, clothing, instruments, painted eggs, and other folk artifacts from Dubrovnik's colorful history (35 kn, covered by 50-kn "collective ticket," borrow English-language info sheet, well-stocked gift store; June–Oct daily 9:00–18:00; Nov–May Mon–Sat 9:00–14:00, closed Sun). This museum hides several blocks uphill from the main promenade toward the sea (climb up Široka, which becomes Od Domina on the way to the museum).

ACTIVITIES

Swimming—If the weather's good and you've had enough of museums, spend a sunny afternoon at the beach. There are no sandy beaches on the mainland near Dubrovnik, but there are lots of suitable pebbly options, plus several concrete perches. Ask your host or hotelier where the nearest beach is. The most convenient public beaches are Banje (just outside Ploče Gate, east of Old Town) and the beach in the middle of Lapad Bay (near Hotel Kompas). There's also a delightful rocky beach clinging onto the outside of the Old Town's wall (with a smaller branch of Cold Drinks "Buža," described on page 236): Climb the steep steps behind the cathedral, and look for the door in the wall with the *No Toples No Nudist* sign. Locals prefer to swim on Lokrum Island (where Toples and Nudist are most certainly permitted), because there are fewer tourists there.

NIGHTLIFE

Dubrovnik's Old Town is one big, romantic parade of relaxed and happy people out strolling. The main drag is brightly lit and packed with shops, cafés, and bars, all open late. This is a fun scene. And if you walk away from the crowds, out on the port, or even up on the city walls, you'll be alone with the magic of the Pearl of the Adriatic. Everything feels—and is—very safe after dark.

Bars—Cold Drinks "Buža," clinging scenically to Dubrovnik's outer wall, is a fine place for a drink day or night (see listing on page 245). **Hard Jazz Caffè Troubadour** is cool, owned by a former member of the Dubrovnik Troubadours—Croatia's answer to the Beatles (or, perhaps more accurately, the Turtles). On balmy evenings, 50 comfy wicker chairs with tiny tables are set up theater-style in the dreamy courtyard facing the musicians. Step inside to see old 1970s photos of the band (30–40-kn drinks, daily 9:00–24:00, live jazz nightly from about 22:00 or whenever the boss shows up, often live piano at other times, next to cathedral at Bunićeva Poljana 2, tel. 020/323-476). **Hemingway's Cocktail Bar,** a few steps from the cathedral on Pred Dvorom, is an outdoor lounge with big overstuffed chairs at a fine vantage point for people-watching (50-kn cocktails, daily 9:00–2:00 in the morning, shorter hours off-season).

SLEEPING

You basically have two options in Dubrovnik: a centrally located room in a private home *(soba);* or a big resort hotel on a distant beach, a bus ride away from the Old Town. Since Dubrovnik hotels are generally a poor value, I highly recommend giving the *sobe* a careful look. For locations, see the map on page 227.

Be warned that the Old Town is home to many popular discos. My listings are quieter than the norm, but if you're finding a place on your own, you may discover you have a late-night soundtrack—particularly if you're staying near the Stradun.

No matter where you stay, prices are much higher mid-June through mid-September. Reserve ahead in these peak times, especially during the Summer Festival (July 10–Aug 25 every year).

Sobe (Private Rooms): A Dubrovnik Specialty

In Dubrovnik, you'll almost always do better with a *soba* than with a hotel. All of my favorite *sobe* are run by friendly English-speaking Croatians, and are inside or within easy walking distance of the Old Town. There's a range of places, from simple and cheap rooms where you'll share a bathroom, to downright fancy places with private facilities and satellite TV, where you can be as anonymous

---

Sleep Code

(€1 = about $1.20, 6 kn = about $1, country code: 385, area code: 020)
S = Single, **D** = Double/Twin, **T** = Triple, **Q** = Quad, **b** = bathroom. The modest tourist tax (7 kn or €1 per person, per night, lower off-season) is not included in these rates. Hotels generally accept credit cards and include breakfast in their rates, while most *sobe* accept only cash and don't offer breakfast. All Dubrovnik hotels provide free guest parking. Everyone listed here speaks English.

To help you sort easily through these listings, I've divided the rooms into three categories based on the price for a standard double room with bath in peak season:

$$$ **Higher Priced**—Most rooms 700 kn (€97) or more.
  $$ **Moderately Priced**—Most rooms between 400–700 kn (€55–97).
   $ **Lower Priced**—Most rooms 400 kn (€55) or less.

---

as you like. Most *sobe* don't include breakfast, so I've listed some suggestions on page 245.

You'll find the highest concentration of good *sobe* just outside the Old Town's Pile Gate. This Pile (PEE-leh) neighborhood offers all the conveniences of the modern world (grocery store, bus stop, post office, travel agency, etc.), just steps from Dubrovnik's magical Old Town.

Before you choose, carefully read the information on page 35. It's easy and smart to book one of these places direct, but you can also go through an agency (for an additional charge) or make a deal with a *sobe* hustler on arrival. While the town is pretty tight in July and August, you can generally find a €40 double (with a bathroom down the hall) if you're nervy enough to just show up.

In the Pile Neighborhood, Behind the Bus Stop

These two places feel plenty private, and each room gets its own bathroom. They're uphill (away from the water) from the Pile Gate's bus stop.

$$ Jadranka and Milan Benussi, a middle-aged professional couple, rent four rooms in a quiet, traffic-free neighborhood. Their stony-chic home, complete with a leafy terrace, is a steep 10-minute hike above the Old Town. Jadranka speaks good English, enjoys visiting with her guests, and gives her place modern Croatian class (July–Aug: small Db-410 kn, big Db-480 kn, small apartment-660 kn, big apartment with balcony-740 kn; June and Sept: small Db-370 kn, big Db-410 kn, small apartment-590 kn, big apartment-660 kn; Oct–May: small Db-330 kn, big Db-370 kn, small apartment-520 kn, big apartment-590 kn; 20 percent more for 1- or 2-night stays, no breakfast, cash only, all rooms have air-con and kitchenettes, Miha Klaića 10, tel. 020/429-339, mobile 098-928-1300, www.dubrovnik-online.com/apartments_benussi, mbenussi@inet.hr). To find the Benussis, go to the big Hilton hotel just outside the Pile Gate (across from the TI). Walk up the little stepped lane called Marijana Blažića at the upper-left corner of the Hilton driveway. When that lane dead-ends, go left up Baltazara Bogišića (more steps) until you see a little church on the left. The Benussis' house is just before this church.

$$ Villa San, run by the Ahmić family, offers four nice apartments overlooking the bus stop directly in front of the Pile Gate (July–Sept: Db-€60; May–June: Db-€50; Oct–April: Db-€40; singles discouraged, no extra charge for short stays, no breakfast, cash only, above the bank behind the bus stop—go around left side to find entrance at Tiha 2, tel. 020/411-884, mobile 098-178-5620, www.villa-san.com, info@villa-san.com).

In the Pile Neighborhood, near the Cove by Restaurant Orhan

These places cluster around a quiet, no-name cove a five-minute walk from the Old Town. This waterfront neighborhood's landmark—and best breakfast spot (50 kn for omelet or continental breakfast, served daily 8:00–11:00)—is Restaurant Orhan, which also rents rooms of its own. Dubravka Matić, whose *sobe* are listed here, will do your laundry even if you're not staying with her (70 kn/load). To reach this cove, leave the Pile Gate TI to the right (on ulica u Pilama), then go down the first flight of stairs on your right; wind down the lanes to the little bay and the lane called Od Tabakarije.

$ Paulina Čumbelić is a kind, gentle woman renting four old-fashioned rooms in her homey, clean, and peaceful house (July–Aug: S-200 kn, D-300 kn, T-450 kn; other times: S-170 kn, D-260 kn, T-350 kn; 20 percent more for 1- or 2-night stays, no breakfast, cash only, closed in winter, Od Tabakarije 2, tel. 020/421-327, mobile 091-530-7985).

$ Dubravka Matić is a charming young mom renting out three classy, tidy, and simple rooms in her cozy home. You'll truly feel you're sharing her house, but thanks to friendly Dubravka, that's not a problem (July–Aug: S-200 kn, D-300 kn; other times: S-170 kn, D-260 kn; includes tax, 20 percent more for 1- or 2-night stays, no breakfast, cash only, she'll do your laundry for 70 kn/load, Frana Antice 2, tel. 020/311-904, mobile 098-938-8281, m_dubby@yahoo.com).

$ Restaurant Orhan Guest House allows hotel anonymity at *sobe* prices. Its 11 simple rooms—in a couple of different buildings around the corner from the restaurant—are air-conditioned, well-located, and quiet, with modern bathrooms. As the rooms are an afterthought to the restaurant, don't expect a warm welcome (Sb or Db-400 kn, 100 kn more for 1-night stays, breakfast-50 kn, cash only, Od Tabakarije 1, tel. & fax 020/414-183).

$ Nedjeljka Benussi, Jadranka Benussi's sister-in-law (see above), rents three modern, new-feeling rooms sharing two bathrooms and a pretty view (July–Aug: D-400 kn, T-550 kn; Sept–June: D-300 kn, T-450 kn; 20 percent more for 1-night stays, no breakfast, cash only, slightly closer to the Old Town than the others and near the small Atlas Travel Agency office at Sv. Đurđa 4, tel. 020/423-062, mobile 098-175-699).

In the Old Town, Above the Stradun Promenade

$$ Villa Ragusa offers the nicest rooms for the price in the Old Town. Pero and Valerija Carević have renovated a 600-year-old house at the top of town (a steep walk up from the Stradun) that was damaged during the war. The five comfortable, modern rooms come with atmospheric old wooden beams, antique furniture, and thoughtful touches. There are three doubles with bathrooms (including a top-floor room with breathtaking Old Town views for no extra charge—request when you reserve), and two singles that share a bathroom. The Carevićs live off-site, a few miles outside of town, so be sure to let them know when you'll arrive. Since they don't live in the house, it's more private and hotelesque than other *sobe*—you're basically on your own after you check in (July–Aug: S-€40, Db-€80; May–June and Sept–Oct: S-€30, Db-€60; Nov–April: S-€25, Db-€50; 30 percent more for 1- or 2-night stays, €8 breakfast can be eaten here or at nearby Stradun café, cash only, air-con, lots of stairs with no elevator, Žudioska ulica 15, tel. 020/453-834, mobile 098-765-634, http://villaragusa.netfirms.com, villa.ragusa@du.t-com.hr). Pero offers his guests airport transfers for €20.

In the Old Town, near St. John's Fort

These two places are near St. John's Fort, at the end of the Old Port. To find them from the cathedral, walk toward the big fort tower along the inside of the wall (follow signs for *akvarij*).

$$$ Apartments van Bloemen, well-run by a Brit named Marc and his Croatian wife Silva, offers four apartments just inside the big fort. The prices are too high, and it's in all the guidebooks, but the apartments are big, well-equipped, and homey-feeling, each with its own bathroom and kitchen (June–Sept-€120, April–May and Oct–Nov-€90, less Dec–March, smaller apartment-30 percent less, 20 percent more for 1- or 2-night stays, no breakfast, cash only, near the aquarium at Bandureva 1, tel. 020/323-433, www.karmendu.com, apartments@karmendu.tk).

$ Renata Zijadić, a mom who speaks good English, offers four well-located rooms with slanting floors, funky colors, and over-the-top antique furniture. A single and a double (both with great views) share one bathroom; another double features an ornate old cabinet and its own bathroom; and the top-floor apartment comes with low ceilings and fine vistas (July–Aug: S-220 kn, D-300 kn, Db-360 kn, apartment-600 kn, 20 percent more for 1- or 2-night stays; Sept–June: S-180 kn, D-260 kn, Db-300 kn, apartment-400 kn; no breakfast, cash only, follow signs for wall access and walk up the steps marked *ulica Stajeva* going over the street to find Stajeva 1; tel. 020/323-623, renatadubrovnik@yahoo.com).

Sobe-Booking Web Sites and Agencies

Several Web sites put you in touch with Dubrovnik's *sobe* and apartments. For example, www.dubrovnikapartmentsource.com, run by an American couple, offers a range of carefully selected, well-described accommodations. You can browse a variety of options, then reserve your choice and pay a non-refundable deposit by credit card. Another, bigger operation—with a wider selection but less personal attention—is www.adriatica.net. Of course, you'll save yourself and your host money if you book direct, but these sites are convenient.

If you arrive without a reservation and the TI isn't too busy, they might be able to call around and find you a *soba* for no charge. Otherwise, just about any travel agency in town can help you, on the spot or in advance...for a fee. **Atlas** is the biggest operation (figure Db-€48 in July–Aug, €34 in shoulder season; for more on Atlas, see page 217).

Hotels

If you must stay in a hotel, you have only a few good options. There are just two hotels inside the Old Town walls—and one of them charges $500 a night (Pucić Palace, www.thepucicpalace.com). Any big, resort-style hotel within walking distance of the Old Town will run you at least €150. These inflated prices drive most visitors to the Lapad Peninsula, a 15-minute bus ride west of the Old Town. But values on Lapad aren't much better, so I prefer the closer neighborhood near Boninovo Bay.

In general, Dubrovnik hotels are stuck in one of two ruts: refusing to renovate, and wringing the maximum income out of pathetic old rooms; or aggressively renovating so they can earn that extra star and begin charging double.

In the mass-tourism tradition, most European visitors choose to take the half-board option at their hotel (i.e., dinner in the hotel restaurant). This can be convenient and a good value, but I'd rather not be tied down to eating at my hotel—the Old Town is full of well-priced little eateries worth going out of your way for (see "Eating").

In the Old Town

$$$ Hotel Stari Grad knows it's the only real hotel option in the Old Town—and charges accordingly. Still, it's worth considering: eight modern yet nicely old-fashioned rooms a half-block off the Old Town's main drag. While gloomy, overpriced old hotels sit on desolate beaches two miles away, this smartly appointed place offers true class and an excellent location...for those smart enough to book ahead. The rooftop breakfast terrace (summer only) enjoys a spectacular view over orange tiles (July–Sept: Sb-980 kn, Db-1,400 kn; April–June and Oct: Sb-805 kn, Db-1,150 kn; Nov–March: Sb-595 kn, Db-850 kn; plus silly "insurance" charge of 7 kn per person per night, 10 percent more for 1- or 2-night stays, air-con, lots of stairs with no elevator, Od Sigurate 4, tel. 020/322-244, fax 020/321-256, www.hotelstarigrad.com, info @hotelstarigrad.com).

Near Boninovo Bay

If you want a big hotel, Boninovo Bay is your best bet. Above this bay are Dubrovnik's only three-star hotels within walking distance of the Old Town (not to mention the city's only youth hostel). These places offer slightly better prices and closer proximity to the Old Town than the farther-out Lapad Bay resorts. Boninovo Bay is an uphill 20-minute walk or five-minute bus ride from the Old Town (straight up Branitelja Dubrovnika). Once you're comfortable with the buses, the location is great (from Pile Gate, take #1a, #3, #4, #5, #6, #8, or #9; you'll see the bay on your left as you climb the hill, then get off at the stop after the traffic light). To reach the hotels from the Boninovo bus stop, go up Pera Cingrije (the busy road running along the top of the cliff overlooking the sea). There's a super little 24-hour bakery, Pekarnica Klas, on the right (across the street from the cliff-hanging Hotel Bellevue).

$$$ Hotel R, with just 10 rooms, feels friendlier and less greedy than all the big resort hotels (July–mid-Sept: Sb-€75, Db-€117; June and late Sept: Sb-€62, Db-€96; May and Oct: Sb-€50, Db-€74; April: Sb-€43, Db-€66; closed Nov–March, 20 percent more for 1- or 2-night stays, 10 percent more for balcony, half-board-€10, just beyond the big Hotel Lero at Iva Vojnovića 32, tel. 020/333-200, fax 020/333-208, www.hotel-r.hr, helpdesk @hotel-r.hr).

$$$ Hotel Lero, 250 yards up the street from the bus stop, has 160 modern and fresh rooms. It might be closed for renovation sometime in 2007 (or re-opened...and more expensive)—call ahead. Choose between sea views with some road noise, or quieter back rooms (early July–late Sept: Sb-€110, Db-€140; May–early July and late Sept–mid-Oct: Sb-€85, Db-€106; even less in winter; in busy times, you may be quoted more than these rates—try asking for a better deal; air-con, elevator, Internet access, €5 each for lunch or dinner, Iva Vojnovića 14, tel. 020/341-333, fax 020/332-123, www.hotel-lero.hr, hotel-lero@du.t-com.hr).

$ Dubrovnik's fine **Youth Hostel** is a quiet, modern, and well-run by proud manager Laura. It's quite institutional, with fresh, woody dorms (82 beds in 19 rooms; bed in 4- to 6-bed dorm: 115 kn July–Aug, 100 kn June and Sept, 90 kn May and Oct, 80 kn Nov–April; 10 kn more for non-members, includes sheets and breakfast, 5 kn less without breakfast, open daily 7:00–2:00 in the morning, up the steps at ulica bana Jelačića 15–17, tel. 020/423-241, fax 020/412-592, www.hfhs.hr, dubrovnik@hfhs.hr). From the Boninovo bus stop, go down Pera Čingrije toward Hotel Bellevue, but take the first right uphill onto ulica bana Jelačića and look for signs up to the hostel on your left. Several houses nearby rent rooms to those who prefer a double...and pick off hostelers as they approach.

EATING

In the Old Town

While the Old Town is packed with busy restaurants, my first two recommendations distinguish themselves by providing quality as if there were no easy tourist buck. This makes them very popular with natives and in-the-know visitors—expect lines throughout normal dining hours (no reservations possible). Anywhere you eat, breezy outdoor seating is a no-brainer, and scrawny, adorable kittens beg for table scraps.

Konoba Kamenice, a no-frills fish restaurant, is the locals' unanimous choice for Dubrovnik's best eatery. This place offers inexpensive, fresh, and delicious seafood dishes on a charming market square, as central as can be in the Old Town. Some of the waitstaff are notorious for their playfully brusque service—but loyal patrons put up with it to enjoy the huge, splittable plates. Arrive early, or you'll have to wait (most main dishes 30–55 kn, daily 7:00–24:00, until 22:00 off-season, Gundulićeva poljana 8, tel. 020/323-682, no reservations).

Lokanda Peskarija, facing the Old Port, is popular for its fine seafood and pretty harborside setting—close to all the tourism, yet still peaceful. Servings are hearty and come in a pot, "home-style."

Dubrovnik's Old Town Restaurants

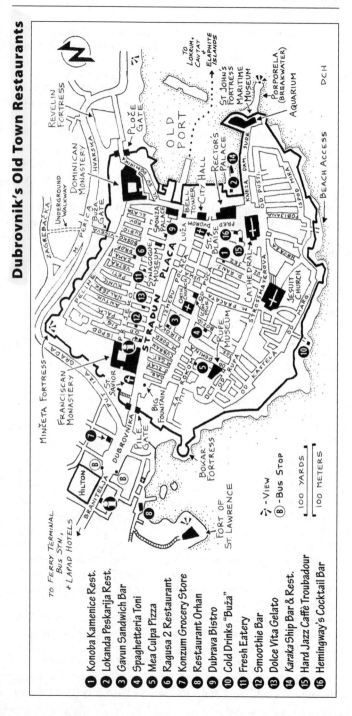

1. Konoba Kamenice Rest.
2. Lokanda Peskarija Rest.
3. Gavun Sandwich Bar
4. Spaghetteria Toni
5. Mea Culpa Pizza
6. Ragusa 2 Restaurant
7. Konzum Grocery Store
8. Restaurant Orhan
9. Dubrava Bistro
10. Cold Drinks "Buža"
11. Fresh Eatery
12. Smoothie Bar
13. Dolce Vita Gelato
14. Karaka Ship Bar & Rest.
15. Hard Jazz Caffè Troubadour
16. Hemingway's Cocktail Bar

The 45-kn seafood risotto easily feeds two, and sharing is no problem. The menu's tiny—with only seafood options, and not much in the way of vegetables—but the value is appreciated (most main dishes 30–60 kn, daily 12:00–24:00, very limited indoor seating fills up fast, lots of wonderful outdoor tables, tel. 020/324-750, no reservations). This is a good place to try the typical Dubrovnik dessert, *rozata* (crème caramel).

Sandwiches: **Gavun Sandwich Bar** is a handy spot to grab a good meal on the go. If you'd like a taste of the sea, your options include marinated sardines and anchovies. Ask for a 50-kn combination appetizer plate with some homemade cornbread to enjoy at a streetside table, or have them wrap it up in a 20–30-kn sandwich to go (also pizza and omelets, daily 9:00–23:00, until 21:00 in winter, may close in bad weather since there's no indoor seating, 50 yards off main drag at Široka 3—the widest side street, midway up the Stradun).

Pasta: **Spaghetteria Toni** is a cozy seven-table place popular with natives and tourists for its reliably good pasta and reasonable prices (also has ample outdoor seating, 30–50-kn pastas, daily in summer 11:00–23:00, midday break and closed Sun in winter, closed Jan, Nikole Božidarevića 14, tel. 020/323-134).

Pizza: **Mea Culpa** is popular for its cheap and tasty pizzas and salad bar; take-out is also available (huge, splittable 35–50-kn pizzas, daily 8:00–24:00, until 23:00 in winter, just off the main drag at Za Rokom 3, tel. 020/323-430).

The Old Town's "Restaurant Row": **Prijeko street,** a block toward the mainland from the Stradun promenade, is lined with outdoor, tourist-oriented eateries—each one with a huckster out front trying to lure in diners. (Many of them aggressively try to snare passersby down on the Stradun, as well.) This is hardly a local scene, but a stroll along here is fun, the atmosphere is lively, the sales pitches are entertainingly desperate, and the food is generally acceptable (if overpriced). If any place along here has an edge, it's **Ragusa 2,** which is open year-round and has the longest tradition (the Rudenjak family has been in the restaurant business since 1929). With white tablecloths and fancy presentation, it's a classy place to splurge (most main dishes 50–110 kn, daily 8:00–24:00, corner of Prijeko and Zamanjina at Zamanjina 12, tel. 020/321-661). By the way, Ragusa 1—also run by the Rudenjak family—is in New York City.

Picnic in the Old Town: Pick up picnic grub at Konzum (the cheapest grocery store in town, just outside Pile Gate), at the open-air produce market (each morning near the cathedral), or at the Gavun Sandwich Bar (see above). Good picnic spots include the shady benches overlooking the Old Port, the Porporela breakwater (beyond the Old Port and fort—comes with a swimming area, sunny no-shade benches, and views of Lokrum Island), and the green, welcoming park in what was the moat just under the Pile Gate entry to the Old Town.

Breakfast: If you're sleeping in a *soba*, you'll likely be on your own for breakfast. Fortunately, you have plenty of cafés and pastry shops to choose from, and your host probably has a favorite she can recommend. In the Pile neighborhood, I like **Restaurant Orhan,** which also rents rooms (50 kn for omelet or continental breakfast, served daily 8:00–11:00, right on the cove; see listing in "Sleeping" section). In the Old Town, **Dubrava Bistro** has fine outdoor seating at the most colorful end of the Stradun (30–40-kn egg dishes, daily from 8:00, Placa 6, tel. 020/321-229).

Drinks with a View: **Cold Drinks "Buža"** offers, without a doubt, the most scenic spot for a drink. Perched on a cliff above

the sea, clinging like a barnacle to the outside of the city walls, this is a peaceful, shaded getaway from the bustle of the Old Town...the perfect place to watch cruise ships sail into the horizon. *Buža* means "hole in the wall"—and that's exactly what you'll have to go through to reach this place. Filled with mellow tourists and bartenders pouring wine from tiny screw-top bottles into plastic cups, it comes with castaway views and Frank Sinatra ambience. This is supposedly where Bill Gates hangs out when he visits Dubrovnik (16–30-kn drinks, small munchies, summer daily 9:00–into the wee hours, closed mid-Nov–Jan, find doorway in city wall marked *Cold Drinks* up the stairs and behind Jesuit St. Ignatius' Church). It can be tough to get a table in peak season, but you might be able to reserve by calling owner Danko on his mobile phone (091-589-4936).

Wraps and Smoothies: For a break from the grilled fish and pizza, sink your teeth into an American-style wrap. **Fresh,** a lively, popular hangout with a young backpacker following, features tasty 25-kn wraps, 20-kn smoothies, and patented "beer towers" for a powerful buzz (take-away available, daily 9:00–1:00 in the morning, Vetranićeva 4). Fresh's "smoothies," while tasty, are basically party drinks. For a serious smoothie operation—where they custom-make your smoothie using fresh fruit—head a few blocks down the Stradun to **Smoothie Bar** (15–22-kn smoothies, also a low-key bar with 30-kn mixed drinks such as margaritas and mojitos, June–Oct daily 10:00–24:00, shorter hours off-season, closed Dec–Feb, Palmotićeva 5, mobile 098-186-7440).

Ice Cream: Dubrovnik has lots of great gelato, but locals swear by the stuff at **Dolce Vita** (daily 9:00–24:00, a half-block off the Stradun at Nalješkovićeva 1A, tel. 020/321-666).

Avast ye Hearties: By day, a recent replica of the 14th-century *Karaka* ship takes tourists on excursions. But by night, the same ship docks at the Old Port and welcomes aboard landlubbers who want drinks with a nautical atmosphere (10 kn to walk around the boat, or pay 10–30 kn for a drink and go on board for free, food also served, sit out on the deck or inside, May–Oct nightly 20:00–24:00 in good weather, look for the old-fashioned ship in the Old Port).

On Lapad Bay

If you want a break from the Old Town, consider venturing to Lapad Bay. Many visitors to Dubrovnik actually sleep here, in overpriced resort hotels. While the accommodations are a bad value, the ambience is pleasant and Lapad is worth an evening stroll (easy bus ride or a 60-kn taxi trip from the Old Town).

The **Šetalište Kralja Zvonimira** is an amazingly laid-back pedestrian lane where bars have hammocks, Internet terminals are scattered through a forested park, and a folksy Croatian family ambience holds its own against the better-funded force of international tourism. Stroll from near Hotel Zagreb to the bay, where you'll find my favorite splurge restaurant (described next) and schmaltzy music nightly on the harborside terrace of Hotel Kompas. From Hotel Kompas, a romantic walk—softly lit at night—leads along the bay through the woods, with plenty of private little stone coves for lingering.

Casa Bar and Restaurant provides the best harborside, candlelit, romantic dining in the area, with a straightforward, user-friendly menu offering traditional cooking with fresh ingredients. Tables overlook Lapad Bay, and English-speaking owner Gonzales enjoys exploring the menu with his diners (80 kn per fish plate, open long hours daily, on the bay just beyond Hotel Kompas' restaurant, Pučića 1, tel. 020/438-710).

TRANSPORTATION CONNECTIONS

From Dubrovnik by Big Jadrolinija Car Ferry: The big boats leave Dubrovnik in the morning and go to **Korčula** (5/week July–Sept, 4/week June, 2/week Oct–May, 3–4 hrs), **Stari Grad** on Hvar Island (2/week year-round, 6.5 hrs), **Split** (2/week June and Sept, 3/week July–Aug, 8.25–9.25 hrs), and **Rijeka** (2/week year-round, 21 hrs including overnight from Split to Rijeka). Boat schedules are subject to change—confirm your plans at a local TI, or see www.jadrolinija.hr. For connections to Mljet National Park on the speedy *Nona Ana* catamaran, see page 259.

By Bus to: Split (almost hourly, less off-season, 5 hrs), **Korčula** (peak season: 2/day, 3–4 hrs; off-season: Mon–Sat 1/day, Sun 2/day), **Zagreb** (6/day, 10 hrs), **Mostar** in Bosnia-Herzegovina (2/day in summer, 1/day off-season, 4 hrs), **Kotor** in Montenegro (2/day, 2.5–3 hrs), **Pula** and **Rovinj** (nightly, 14 hrs to Pula, 15 hrs to Rovinj). For bus information, call 060-305-070 (a pricey toll line, but worth it).

By Plane: To quickly connect remote Dubrovnik with the rest of your trip, consider a cheap flight (see "Getting to the Dalmatian Coast," page 152.) For information on Dubrovnik's airport, see page 216.

NEAR DUBROVNIK

Excursions from Dubrovnik's Old Port •
Trsteno Arboretum • Mljet National Park

Stretching up and down the glimmering Dalmatian Coast from Dubrovnik are a variety of worthwhile getaways. Just offshore from the Old Town—and accessible via scenic boat trip from its historic port—are enticing islands and villages, where time stands still for lazy vacationers: the playground islet of Lokrum, the sights-studded archipelago of the Elaphite Islands, and the serene resort town of Cavtat. To the north is a lush and diverse arboretum called Trsteno, with a playful fountain, a 600-year-old aqueduct, a villa, a chapel...and, oh yeah, plants galore. A bit farther afield is the long, sparsely populated island called Mljet—a third of which is carefully protected as one of Croatia's most appealing national parks, where you can hike, bike, boat, and swim to your heart's content. And there's no better place to "come home to" than Dubrovnik—after a busy day exploring the coastline, strolling the Stradun to unwind is particularly sweet.

Planning Your Time

Give yourself a least a full day and two nights to experience Dubrovnik itself. But if you can spare the time, set up in Dubrovnik for several nights and use your extra days for some of these excursions. (This also gives you the luxury of keeping an eye on the weather reports, and saving the most weather-dependent activities for the sunniest days.)

I've listed these day trips in order of ease from Dubrovnik—the farther down the list, the more difficult to reach (with Montenegro and Bosnia-Herzegovina—the most time-consuming—covered in their own chapters). Choose the trips that sound best to you (see the sidebar on page 250), and ask locals and other travelers for their impressions...or for new leads.

Getting There

Lokrum, Cavtat, and the Elaphite Islands are easy to reach by **excursion boat** from Dubrovnik's Old Port; the rest are farther afield, best reached by **boat** (Mljet) or **car/bus** (Montenegro, Bosnia-Herzegovina, Trsteno). I've listed public transportation options for each, but consider renting a car for the day—or even splurging for your own private driver (see page 220).

Alternatively, the two big, competing travel agencies in Dubrovnik—Atlas and Elite—offer €40–60 **guided excursions** (by bus and/or boat) to nearby destinations. Popular itineraries include everything mentioned in this chapter, plus Korčula and others. Atlas and Elite are basically interchangeable, and you can buy tickets at most travel agencies and hotel lobbies (schedules and prices change frequently—look for fliers or inquire locally). If one company isn't running a tour to your preferred destination when you're in town, check with the other one (Atlas: tel. 020/442-574, www.atlas -croatia.com; Elite: tel. 020/358-200, www.elite.hr).

I recently went on Elite's day trip to Mostar (described in the Bosnia-Herzegovina chapter). The excursion efficiently packed several interesting destinations into a single day, but it was crowded (49 tourists on a 50-seat bus) and the guide alternated between English and French, with commentary that was uninspired at best ("The bridge is 300 meters long and 90 meters tall"). But these excursions can be a convenient way to tackle a complicated day trip if you don't want to hassle with taking public transportation or renting a car. And if you're an independent type, you can slip away from the group once you know the rendezvous time and place—although on far-flung trips, the time actually spent at your destination can be too short for much time on your own.

Excursions from Dubrovnik's Old Port

At Dubrovnik's salty Old Port, local captains set up tiny booths to hawk touristy boat trips. It's fun to chat with them, page through their sun-faded photo albums, and see if they can sell you on a short cruise (rough prices listed for each trip).

Lokrum Island

This island, just offshore from the Old Town, provides a handy escape from the city. Lokrum features a monastery-turned-Hapsburg-palace, a small botanical garden, an old military fort,

Dubrovnik Day Trips at a Glance

Here are your options, listed roughly in order of priority. The international excursions to Montenegro and Bosnia-Herzegovina—which are worth considering for overnight stops—are covered more thoroughly in the next two chapters.

▲▲▲**The Bay of Kotor** For rugged coastal scenery that arguably rivals anything in Croatia, head south of the border to newly independent Montenegro. The Bay of Kotor is a dramatic, fjord-like inlet crowned by the historic town of Kotor, with twisty Old World lanes, one of Europe's best town walls, and oodles of atmosphere. Allow a full day or more.

▲▲**Mostar** The side-trip with the highest degree of cultural hairiness—but potentially also the most rewarding—lies to the east, in Bosnia-Herzegovina. With its iconic Old Bridge, intriguing glimpse of European Muslim lifestyles, and still-vivid examples of war damage, Mostar is unforgettable. Not for everyone, this trip merits ▲▲▲ for adventurous travelers interested in Islam or in recent history. Allow a full day or more.

▲**Mljet National Park** While this largely undeveloped island is time-consuming to reach from Dubrovnik, Mljet offers an opportunity to romp on an island without all those tacky tourist towns. Serious nature-lovers eager to get away from civilization may find it a ▲▲▲ experience. Allow a full day.

▲**Trsteno Arboretum** Gardeners will enjoy this surprisingly engaging botanical garden just outside Dubrovnik, punctuated

hiking trails, a café, some rocky beaches, and a little lake called the "Dead Sea" (Mrtvo More) that's suitable for swimming. Since the 1970s, when Lokrum became the "Island of Love," it's been known for its nude sunbathing. If you'd like to (carefully) subject skin that's never seen the sun to those burning rays, follow the *FKK* signs from the boat dock for about five minutes to the slabs of waterfront rock, where naturalists feel right at home. Boats run regularly from Dubrovnik's Old Port (35 kn round-trip, 5 kn for a map, hourly in summer 9:00–17:00, July–Aug until 19:00, none Oct–March).

by a classical-style fountain and aqueduct. Allow a half-day.

Lokrum Island The most convenient excursion from Dubrovnik, this little island—just a short hop offshore from the Old Port—is a good chance to get away from (some of) the tourists. Allow a few hours.

Elaphite Islands This inviting archipelago offers a variety of island experiences without straying too far from Dubrovnik. With more time, Korčula (for a small town) or Mljet (for a back-to-nature experience) are better, but the "Elafiti" (as they're known) are more convenient. Allow a half-day to a full day.

Cavtat A charming resort/beach town en route to the Montenegrin border, Cavtat is more handy than must-see. Allow a few hours.

Međugorje Devout Catholics may want to consider a trip to this pilgrimage site in Bosnia-Herzegovina, with a holy hill visited daily by an apparition of the Virgin Mary. Allow a full day or more.

Budva Riviera Montenegro's best stretch of sandy beaches isn't worth a special trip, but it's a fun excuse for a drive if you've got extra time to kill. The highlight is the famous resort peninsula of Sveti Stefan. Allow a full day or more.

Elaphite Islands (Elafiti)

This archipelago, just north of Dubrovnik, is popular among day-trippers because you can hit three different islands in a single day. The main island, **Lopud,** has most of the attractions: a lively little town, boat and bike rental, and some rare sandy beaches. The other two islands—**Koločep** and **Šipan**—are less developed and (for some) a bit boring. Along the way, you'll discover fishing ports, shady forests, and forgotten escape mansions of old Dubrovnik aristocracy. The easiest way to cruise the Elafiti is to buy an excursion at Dubrovnik's Old Port, which includes a "fish picnic" cooked up by the captain as you cruise (about 250 kn with lunch, 180 kn without, prices often soft—feel free to bargain, several boats depart daily around 10:30, return around 18:00). You generally spend three hours on Lopud and about 45 minutes each on Koločep and

Šipan. For a more romantic route to the Elafiti, consider the old-time ship cruise (described at the end of this section). To get to the Elaphite Islands without a tour (on a cheap ferry), you'll sail from Dubrovnik's less convenient Port Gruž.

Cavtat

This sleepy little resort town—just 12 miles to the south, near the Montenegrin border—offers a milder alternative to bustling Dubrovnik (www.tzcavtat-konavle.hr). Best known as a handy spot to find a room when Dubrovnik's booked up, Cavtat's biggest appeal is that it's a fun excuse to take a cruise somewhere. Holiday-makers who can look past the concrete resort hotels enjoy Cavtat's small-town ambience, people-filled seafront promenade, and inviting beaches. Meanwhile, sightseers find a few diversions to keep them busy: a mausoleum with eclectic flair designed by Croatian sculptor Ivan Meštrović (see page 165); a monastery with some fine Renaissance paintings; the Baltazar Bogišić Collection, with a large library and other items once belonging to a wealthy lawyer; and a museum displaying early-modernist paintings by Cavtat-born portraitist Vlaho Bukovac. Boats to Cavtat leave regularly from Dubrovnik's Old Port (80 kn round-trip, about 45 min each way, hourly return boats from Cavtat).

Old-Time Ship Cruise

For a trip back in time, go for a cruise on one of the traditional vessels from Dubrovnik's Golden Age. The *Tirena* and the *Karaka*—a pair of old-fashioned sailing ships—have recently been restored, and routinely take to the sea for excursions. They do the basic Elaphite Islands cruise, as well as various theme trips (sunset cruise, Mozart cruise, and dinners with Richard the Lionheart or the Medicis). Nautical types who might enjoy these cruises can look for fliers around town.

Trsteno Arboretum

Take a stroll through the shaded, relaxing botanical garden in Trsteno, just up the coast from Dubrovnik. Non-gardeners may find it a bit dull, but Trsteno is a horticulturalist's heaven. Spread over 63 acres on a bluff overlooking the sea, this arboretum features hundreds of different Mediterranean, Asian, and American plants (each one labeled in six languages, including English). The whole complex is laced with easy footpaths and sprinkled with fun attractions—a column-studded Renaissance Garden, a desolate villa, a little chapel, an old mill and olive-oil press, and a sea-view

pavilion. As you wander, the world melts away and you're alone with the sounds of nature: wind, water, birds, and frogs. The garden's centerpiece is the whimsical 18th-century Neptune Fountain, featuring the god of the sea flanked by water-spouting nymphs and fishes, and holding court over a goldfish-stocked, lily-padded pond. Circling around behind the fountain, you'll discover that it's fed by an impressive 15th-century, 230-foot-long aqueduct (park entry-20 kn, daily May–Oct 7:00–19:00, Nov–April 8:00–15:00, tel. 020/751-019, www.hazu.hr/ENG/arboretum.html).

Getting There: Trsteno works best with a car, particularly if you're taking your time driving to Dubrovnik from the north (the main coastal road goes through the town of Trsteno, right past the well-marked arboretum). You can also take the bus from Dubrovnik (10–20 kn depending on company, buses run about hourly from bus station, 20–30 minutes; sometimes you'll go on a slow city bus, other times on a fast long-distance bus—any northbound bus can drop you in Trsteno, so ask at the bus station which bus is next). Coming back is trickier: Wait at the bus stop with the glass canopy by the park entrance and wave down any Dubrovnik-bound bus that passes (at least hourly).

Mljet National Park

Carefully protected against modern development, the island hideaway of Mljet National Park offers a unique back-to-nature escape. With ample opportunities for hiking, swimming, biking, and boating—and without a nightclub, tacky T-shirt, or concrete "beach" pad in sight—Mljet is a potential trip-capping highlight for active, outdoorsy types.

Though Mljet Island is one of Dalmatia's largest, it has fewer than 1,500 residents. Nearly three-quarters of the island is covered in forest, leaving it remarkably untamed. Aside from its beautiful national park, Mljet offers some of the most memorable tales of the Croatian coast—the poet Homer, his protagonist Ulysses, and the Apostle Paul all spent time here...or so the locals love to boast.

Most Croatians rave about Mljet. Take it with a grain of salt. The park, while enjoyable, is a bit overrated. One jaded local told me, "Mljet is basically Hvar or Korčula with no towns." But if that sounds like your kind of scene, make the trip.

Planning Your Time

Thanks to a handy catamaran connection, Mljet works perfectly as a full-day side-trip from Dubrovnik. But because of inconvenient boat schedules to other destinations, it's tricky to splice into a one-way itinerary (say, between Korčula and Dubrovnik). So if you want to visit Mljet, either do it as a day trip on your own from Dubrovnik, or buy a package day-trip excursion from Korčula, Hvar, or Split. For details, see "Transportation Connections" at the end of this chapter.

No matter how you arrive, one day is plenty for Mljet. I've suggested a day-trip plan under "Sights and Activities," on page 257.

Be warned that everything's very seasonal and weather-dependent, so visiting outside of peak season (June–Sept) may come with some frustration.

ORIENTATION

The island of Mljet (muhl-YET) is long (23 miles) and skinny (less than two miles). The western third of the island is the national park. You're likely to reach the island via one of three port towns: **Polače** (POH-lah-cheh) and **Pomena** (POH-meh-nah) are handy entry points into the national park, while **Sobra** (SOH-brah)—far to the east of the park—is much less convenient (a 1.25-hour bus trip across the island from the park). The *Nona Ana* catamaran from Dubrovnik puts in at Polače; most excursions use Pomena; and the car ferries (the big Jadrolinija Korčula–Dubrovnik car ferry, plus smaller ferries to the mainland) use Sobra.

Polače and Pomena flank the heart of the national park. The national park itself is centered on a pair of saltwater "lakes," called simply **Great Lake** (Veliko Jezero) and **Small Lake** (Malo Jezero). The two lakes meet at a cute little bridge, appropriately named **Small Bridge** (Mali Most), where you can rent kayaks and bikes, and catch a boat out to the little **island** in the Great Lake. A 15-minute walk around the Great Lake from the Small Bridge brings you to **Pristanište** (meaning, roughly, "transit hub"), where you can also catch a boat to the island or a shuttle bus to Polače. Also nearby is the cliff-climbing town of **Goveđari**, home to many of the people who work at the park, but not interesting to tourists.

Everything's well-signed, and there are enough landmarks that it's difficult to get really lost. Even so, I bought the 30-kn detailed park map (at the entry kiosk) and was glad I had it.

Tourist Information

The **TI** is in Polače, just across from where the Dubrovnik catamaran docks (mid-June–Aug daily 8:00–20:00; April–mid-June and

Mljet National Park

TO KORČULA
VIA EXCURSION BOAT

TO DUBROVNIK
VIA EXCURSION BOAT

TO DUBROVNIK
VIA NONA ANA
CATAMARAN

800 YARDS

800 METERS

N

TO SOBRA
(CAR FERRIES)

SMALL
BRIDGE

POLAČE

POMENA

GOVEĐARI

BABINE
KUĆE

PRISTA-
NIŠTE

MONTOKUC

SOLINE

SMALL
LAKE

GREAT
LAKE

VELIKI
MOST

—— PAVED ROAD

– – – PATH

•••• BOAT

ST. MARYS
CHURCH

ADRIATIC   SEA   DCH

Sept–Oct daily 8:00–13:00 & 17:00–20:00; Nov–March Mon–Fri
8:00–13:00, closed Sat–Sun; tel. 020/744-086). The TI is run by
a pair of friendly, can-do Mljet boosters named Ivan and Daniel.
Both also work at the island's lone hotel, the **Hotel Odisej** in
Pomena—which acts as a second tourist information point. The
hotel is a hub of services for visitors (for hotel guests and non-guests
alike): bike, scooter, car, and boat rentals; scuba diving and sailing lessons; walking tours around the island; cruises to some of the
island's caves; and even help finding private accommodations. For
more on the hotel, see "Sleeping and Eating," later in this chapter.

The general-information Web site for the island (including the
towns, Hotel Odisej, *sobe* and apartments, and more) is www.mljet
.hr; for information on the national park, visit www.np-mljet.hr.

Arrival in Mljet

At Polače: Arriving on the *Nona Ana* catamaran from Dubrovnik,
exit the boat to the right, walk a few steps, and look for the TI
on your left. A few minutes' walk up the coast (near the Roman
ruins) is a kiosk where you can buy your park entry ticket and catch
a minibus to the Pristanište transit hub at the Great Lake (runs

The Tales of Mljet

For a mostly undeveloped island, Mljet has had a surprisingly busy history. Home to Illyrians, Greeks, Romans, Slavs, Venetians, Hapsburgs, Yugoslavs, and now Croatians, the island has hosted some interesting visitors (or supposed visitors) that it loves to brag about.

Around the eighth century B.C., the Greek epic poet Homer possibly spent time here. He was so inspired by Mljet that he used it as the setting for one of the adventures of his hero Ulysses (a.k.a. Odysseus). This was the island where Ulysses fell in love with a beautiful nymph named Calypso, and shacked up with her in a cave for seven years. Today there's a much-vaunted "Ulysses' Cave" (Odisejeva Spilja) a 40-minute hike below the island's main town, Babino Polje (at the far end of the island—skip it unless you're a Ulysses groupie).

Flash forward nearly a millennium, when a real-life traveler found his way to Mljet. According to the Bible (Acts 28), the Apostle Paul was shipwrecked on an island called "Melita"—likely this one—for three months. While on the island, he was bitten by a deadly snake, which he threw into a fire. The natives were amazed that he wasn't affected by the poison, and he proceeded to cure their ailments. This event was long believed to have happened on the similarly named isle of Malta, in the Mediterranean Sea. But more recently, many historians believe Paul was on Mljet. The most convincing argument: Malta never had poisonous snakes. Incidentally, Mljet no longer does, either—the Austrians imported an army of Indian mongooses to rid the island of problematic serpents. Because of this historical footnote, people from Mljet are nicknamed "mongooses" by other Croatians.

The heroics continue with today's "mongooses." There have been over 100 fires on the island in the last 20 years (most caused by lightning, some by careless visitors), but only three have spread and caused significant destruction. That's because the people of Mljet—well aware of the fragility of the island that provides their income—are also a crack volunteer firefighting force, ready to spring into action and save their island at the first wisp of smoke.

hourly, scheduled to coincide with boat arrival). From Pristanište, you can take a boat out to the island in the Great Lake (about hourly), or walk around the lake toward the Small Bridge, Small Lake, and on to Pomena.

At Pomena: If you arrive at Pomena, you're most likely on a package excursion, in which case your park entry ticket is included and you'll probably stick with your guide for a while. But in case you're on your own, exit the boat to the left (passing Hotel Odisej) and buy your park entry ticket at the kiosk. A few steps up the road beyond the kiosk, you'll see a shortcut to the right that takes you up and down some steps on your way to the Small Lake; once at the lake, bear left and continue to the Small Bridge, where you can catch the boat to the island in the Great Lake or rent a bike or kayak.

Note that there's no official bus between Polače and Pomena, but Hotel Odisej operates a shuttle to coincide with the Dubrovnik catamaran. Several informal minibus-taxis can also take you for a fee.

At Sobra: If you come on a car ferry, you're in for a long haul over to Polače and Pomena—about a 1.25-hour bus trip on twisty roads. Avoid arriving via Sobra unless you're desperate.

SIGHTS AND ACTIVITIES

Mljet National Park

All of the following attractions are inside the park. The steep 90-kn entry fee includes the shuttle bus from Polače to the Great Lake and a boat ride to the lake's island. The park is open daily May–mid-Oct 7:00–19:00, shorter hours in shoulder season, closed Nov–Feb; park information tel. 020/744-041.

Day-Trip Plan: If you're doing the trip on your own from Dubrovnik, try this itinerary: From Polače, take the minibus to Pristanište, where you can catch the boat to the island in the Great Lake. Take the boat back to Mali Most (Small Bridge), where you can rent a bike for a ride around the Great Lake. If you're heating up, take a dip in the Small Lake at the beach near the Small Bridge. When you're ready for a bit of civilization, walk into Pomena and relax by the seaside, then take the hotel's shuttle bus or a minibus-taxi back to Polače to catch the catamaran back home to Dubrovnik. With more energy, skip Pomena and hike up to Montokuc (you can hike down to Polače on the other side).

The Lakes—The "Great Lake" and "Small Lake" are technically bays—fed by the sea and affected by ocean currents (as you'll clearly see if you're at the little channel by the Small Bridge at the right time of day). Scientists love these lakes, which contain various shellfish species unique to Mljet.

The Island—The main activity in the park is taking a boat out to the Great Lake's little island-in-an-island (boats depart about hourly from the Small Bridge and from Pristanište). The tiny island's main landmark is St. Mary's Church (Sv. Marija) and the attached monastery, left behind by Benedictine monks who lived on Mljet starting in the 12th century. While the monastery complex has been modified over the ages, fragments of the original

Romanesque structure still survive. You can hike the easy trail up to the top of the island, passing remains of fortifications and old chapels, and look for the island's only permanent residents: a handful of goats, donkeys, and chickens. You'll have about an hour on the island, but it only takes half that to see everything—then relax with an overpriced drink at the restaurant by the boat dock.

Biking—The Great Lake is surrounded by a paved, mostly level road that's good for an hour or two of pedaling (unfortunately, you can't go all the way around because the path is broken by the channel connecting the lakes to the sea). The path around the Small Lake is rough and rocky, making biking there more difficult. The handiest place to rent a bike for a quick ride around the Great Lake is right at the lake itself, by the Small Bridge (20 kn/1 hr, 80 kn/6 hrs, 100 kn/day). Other bike rental points are scattered around the island, including in both Polače and Pomena. But those towns are separated from the lakes—and from each other—by steep hills, making biking from either town to the lakes a headache for casual bikers.

Swimming—Options are everywhere, most temptingly at the Great Lake and Small Lake. In fact, even though it's fed by seawater, the Small Lake is always about seven degrees Fahrenheit warmer than the sea. The beach by the Small Bridge is particularly handy.

Boating—You can rent kayaks at the Small Bridge. Motorized boats—except for the occasional local resident's dinghy—aren't allowed on the island's lakes.

Hiking to Montokuc—The most rewarding hike takes you up to the national park's highest point, Montokuc. At 830 feet above sea level, this is a serious, steeply uphill hike—skip it unless you're in good shape, and be sure to bring water (allow at least one hour round-trip at a steady pace). The trail runs between Polače, at the north end of the island, and the village of Soline, beyond the far end of the Great Lake (past the old, broken bridge called Veliki Most). If you're doing this or any other hike, the 30-kn park map is essential (available at park entry kiosks and other merchants).

SLEEPING AND EATING

(€1 = about $1.20, country code: 385, area code: 020)

$$$ Hotel Odisej, the only hotel on the island, has more charm than most renovated communist hotels. Sitting right on the waterfront, with 157 rooms, it's a predictably comfortable home base (July–Aug: non-view Sb-€59–67, Sb with seaview and balcony-€93–103, non-view Db-€88–100, Db with seaview or balcony-€104–118, Db with seaview and balcony-€132–148; cheaper in shoulder season, no extra charge for 1- or 2-night stays, closed mid-Oct–mid-April, air-con, elevator, tel. 020/362-111, fax 020/744-042, www.hotelodisej.hr, info@hotelodisej.hr).

$–$$ Sobe *and Apartments:* Mljet has a wide range of private accommodations, with a few in each town or village. *Sobe* run about €15–20 per person in peak season, or €10–15 off-season; for apartments, figure €40–60 for two people in peak season, €25–40 off-season (20 percent more for 1- or 2-night stays). If you arrive without a room, the TI in Polače or Hotel Odisej in Pomena can help you find something. If you're looking in advance, check out the island Web site, www.mljet.hr. I'd choose a place in the population centers of Polače or Pomena (for their easy access to the park) or in the cute Great Lake–front village of Babine Kuće (near the Small Bridge). To really get away from it all, little end-of-the-road Soline (near the channel connecting the Great Lake to the sea) is rustic and remote, and has several options.

For **eating,** many good restaurants are scattered around the island. None are particularly worth seeking out—just eat when it fits your itinerary (or bring a picnic).

TRANSPORTATION CONNECTIONS

Between Mljet and Dubrovnik: The only easy public transportation connections are to Dubrovnik. The speedy **catamaran** called *Nona Ana* runs daily in each direction (in summer: Dubrovnik to Sobra, then on to Polače—departs Dubrovnik at 9:00, arrives Polače at 10:40, also stops at Elaphite Islands on Sat; returning, it departs Polače at 18:20, arrives Dubrovnik at 20:00; in winter, it still runs daily, but it leaves most days at 10:00 and returns at 16:00—and about half the time, it only goes as far as Sobra, not Polače). It's pricey (75 kn one-way, 150 kn round-trip) but very handy. In summer, this gives you a solid seven hours to enjoy Mljet's charms—just about right. The catamaran leaves from Dubrovnik's Port Gruž, but since it's not run by Jadrolinija, you buy tickets at the little Atlantagent kiosk next to the boat (across the street from the Jadrolinija office). The ticket window opens one hour before departure; in peak season (July–Aug), it's smart to show up around 8:00 to be sure you get on the boat. Information: www.alpex.hr or www.atlantagent.com/none_ana.html, tel. 020/419-044.

Between Mljet and Other Destinations: All other destinations (including Korčula, Hvar, and Split) are more conveniently connected to Mljet by **excursion** than by public transit. The approximately €40 price tag for an all-day excursion seems high, but remember that it includes the 90-kn (€12) admission fee and saves you the hassle of getting to the island on your own. Otherwise, you can reach Mljet only by the **car ferry** that stops at Sobra (2–3/week in peak season going between Dubrovnik and

Korčula, plus other connections from the mainland).

On paper, there's no good way to visit Mljet en route between destinations (say, on the way from Dubrovnik to Korčula). But it might work if you're creative. If the excursion boats aren't full—and they rarely are—you can buy a last-minute, one-way ticket for a fraction of the full price. So, for example, you can take the 9:00 catamaran from Dubrovnik to Mljet, enjoy the park, then continue on to Korčula in the evening on one of the day-trip boats. (It works vice-versa, too: Pay for a morning excursion from Korčula to Mljet, then continue to Dubrovnik on the public catamaran.) Call the staff at Hotel Odisej—who know which excursions are coming to town—the night before to see if they have any ideas. The downside: You can't arrange this in advance, and there's always a chance the boat will be full—and you'll be stranded on Mljet for the night.

BOSNIA-HERZEGOVINA

BOSNIA-HERZEGOVINA

Mostar and Međugorje

I know what you're thinking: War. Bloodshed. Destruction. The early 1990s weren't kind to Bosnia-Herzegovina. But apart from its tragic separation from Yugoslavia, the country has long been—and still remains—a remarkable place, with ruggedly beautiful terrain, a unique mix of cultures and faiths, kind and welcoming people who pride themselves on their hospitality, and some of the most captivating sightseeing in southeastern Europe. After all, little Bosnia-Herzegovina—with fewer than four million people—is still a country with three faiths, three languages, and two alphabets.

There are still parts of Bosnia-Herzegovina that I wouldn't feel comfortable visiting without a guide, but two destinations are safe, stable, and within easy reach of the Dalmatian Coast: the Turkish-flavored city of Mostar, and the Catholic pilgrimage site of Međugorje. These places are worth considering as a detour—both geographical and cultural—from the Croatian mainstream.

Mostar, still scarred by war, recently restored its famous 16th-century Old Bridge—one of Europe's most inspirational sights. Mostar also offers an illuminating and unique glimpse of a culture that's both devoutly Muslim and fully European. In the cobbled Old Town surrounding the bridge, you can poke into several mosques, tour old-fashioned Turkish-style houses, shop your way through a bazaar of souvenir stands, and hear the call to prayer echoing across the rooftops.

Međugorje, where six residents have reported seeing visions of the Virgin Mary, is of interest mostly to pilgrims. While other visitors scratch their heads and say, "Is that all there is?" many observant Catholics find something powerful here.

Nervous travelers may want to give Bosnia-Herzegovina a miss. While Mostar and Međugorje are generally considered safe for tourists, they can be unsettling, thanks to in-your-face war damage and an exotic mélange of cultures that goes against the European grain. Bosnia-Herzegovina presents a jarring but fascinating contrast to what you'll see in Croatia or Slovenia—and yet, somehow it still fits with those places, giving inquisitive visitors a more complete understanding of the former Yugoslavia.

Getting Around Bosnia-Herzegovina

The destinations I've covered in this chapter aren't as easy to reach as they should be from the Dalmatian Coast, but connections are workable.

By Package Tour: Taking an excursion from a Dalmatian resort town is the most efficient and accessible—but least rewarding—way to visit Mostar or Međugorje. These all-day tours are sold from Split, Hvar, Korčula, Dubrovnik, and other Croatian coastal destinations for about €50–60. The best tours max out their time in Mostar itself (it still won't be enough); avoid the tours that include a pointless boat trip on the Neretva River. Those that add on a quick visit to the worthwhile town of Počitelj are a better deal. Atlas and Elite are the biggest operators; ask for details at any travel agency in Dalmatia.

By Car: Coming with your own car gives you maximum flexibility, but you may find Mostar—which has poor signage—stressful to drive in. For specific route information, see "Route Tips for Drivers" on page 279. If you do plan to drive here, let your car-rental company know in advance to ensure you have the appropriate paperwork for crossing the border.

By Bus: Bus connections are sparse but possible (see page 278).

Mostar

Mostar represents the best and the worst of Yugoslavia. During the Tito years, it was an idyllic mingling of cultures—Catholic Croats, Orthodox Serbs, and Muslim Bosniaks living together in harmony, their differences spanned by an Old Bridge that epitomized an optimistic vision of a Yugoslavia where ethnicity didn't matter. And yet, as the country unraveled in the early 1990s, Mostar was gripped by a gory three-way war among those same peoples...and that famous bridge crumbled into the Neretva River.

More than any other destination in this book, Mostar rearranges your mental furniture. Most startling are the many vivid and thought-provoking signs of the war. The Old Town has been

Bosnia-Herzegovina Almanac

Official Name: Bosnia in Hercegovina (abbreviated "BiH"); the *in* means "and"—Bosnia *and* Herzegovina (the country's two regions—see "Geography," below). The tongue-twisting name "Herzegovina" (hert-seh-GOH-vee-nah) comes from the German word for "dukedom" (*Herzog* means "duke").

Snapshot History: Bosnia-Herzegovina's early history is similar to the rest of the region: Illyrians, Romans, and Slavs (oh, my!). The country's story parts ways with Croatia's in the late 15th century, when Turks from the Ottoman Empire began a 400-year domination of the country. Many of the Ottomans' subjects converted to Islam, and their descendants remain Muslims today. After the Hapsburgs forced out the Ottomans in 1878, Bosnia-Herzegovina became part of the Austro-Hungarian Empire, then Yugoslavia, until it declared independence in October of 1991. The bloody war that ensued came to an end in 1995. (For details, see the Understanding Yugoslavia chapter near the end of this book.)

Population: Because no census has been conducted since before the recent war, the population can only be estimated at about four million. (There were about 100,000 identified casualties of the war, but many estimates of total casualties are double that number.) Someone who lives in Bosnia-Herzegovina, regardless of ethnicity, is called a "Bosnian." A southern Slav who practices Islam is called a "Bosniak." Today, about half of all Bosnians are Bosniaks (Muslims), about a third are Orthodox Serbs, and about 15 percent are Catholic Croats. Traditionally, Bosniaks lived in the towns and cities, while Serbs and Croats farmed the countryside.

Political Divisions: As a part of the Dayton Peace Accords that ended the conflict here in 1995, the nation is divided into three separate regions: The Federation of Bosnia and Herzegovina (FBiH, shared by Bosniaks and Croats, very roughly in the western and central parts of the country), the Republika Srpska (RS, dominated by Serbs, generally to the north and east), and the Brčko District (BD, a tiny corner of the country, with a mix of the ethnicities). For the most part, each of the three native ethnic groups stay in "their" part of this divided country, but tourists can move freely between them.

Language: Technically, Bosnia-Herzegovina has three languages—Bosnian, Serbian, and Croatian. But all three are mutually intelligible dialects of what was recently considered a single language: Serbo-Croatian. Bosniaks and Croats use basically the same Roman alphabet we do, while Serbs generally use the

Cyrillic alphabet. You'll see both alphabets on currency and other official documents. Many people also speak English.

Area: 19,741 square miles (like Vermont and New Hampshire combined, or slightly larger than Slovakia).

Geography: Bosnia and Herzegovina are two distinct regions that share the same mountainous country. Bosnia constitutes the majority of the country (in the north, with a continental climate), while Herzegovina is the southern tip (about a fifth of the total area, with a hotter Mediterranean climate). Mostar is the biggest city and unofficial capital of Herzegovina—so saying you're in "Bosnia" while you're here is totally wrong.

Red Tape: To enter Bosnia-Herzegovina, Americans and Canadians need only a passport (no visa required). Make sure your passport is good for at least 90 days after your ticketed date of return to the US.

Economy: Bosnia-Herzegovina is struggling. Officially, there's a 45 percent unemployment rate, but in reality it's likely closer to 25 or 30 percent. The per capita GDP is $6,800.

Currency: The official currency is the Convertible Mark (Konvertibilna Marka, abbreviated KM locally, BAM internationally). The official exchange rate is $1 = about 1.50 KM. But merchants in these destinations are willing to take (and may actually prefer) euros or Croatian kunas, converting prices with a simple, universal formula:

2 KM = €1 = 8 kunas (= about $1.20)

For a visit of just a few hours, you won't need to get any local currency.

Telephones: Bosnia-Herzegovina's country code is 387. If calling from another country, first dial the international access code (00 in Europe, 011 in the US), then 387, then the area code (minus the initial zero), then the number.

Flag: The flag of Bosnia-Herzegovina, adopted after the recent war, is a blue field with a yellow triangle along the top edge. The three points of the triangle represent Bosnia-Herzegovina's three peoples (Bosniaks, Croats, Serbs), and the triangle also resembles the physical shape of the country. A row of white stars underscores the longest side of the triangle. These stars—and the yellow-and-blue color scheme—resemble the flag of the European Union (a nod to the EU's efforts to bring peace to the region).

mostly restored. But a few steps outside this tourist zone, burned-out husks of buildings, unmistakable starburst patterns in the pavement, and bullet holes everywhere are a constant reminder that the city is still recovering—physically and psychologically. In an age when we watch TV news coverage of conflicts abroad with the same detachment we give Hollywood blockbusters, Mostar provides an unpleasant but essential reminder of how real and how destructive war can be.

Western visitors may also be struck by the immediacy of the Muslim culture that permeates Mostar. Here at a crossroads of civilizations, minarets share the sky-line with church steeples. During the Ottomans' 400-year control of this region, many Slavic subjects converted to Islam (see sidebar on page 272). And, although the Ottomans retreated in the late 19th century, they left behind a rich architectural, cultural, and religious legacy that has forever  shaped Mostar. Five times each day, loudspeakers on minarets crackle to life, the call to prayer warbles through the streets, and Mostar's Muslim residents flock into the mosques. In many parts of the city, you'd swear you were in Turkey.

If these factors intrigue you, read on—Mostar has so much more to offer. Despite the scars of war, its setting is stunning: straddling the banks of the gorgeous Neretva River, with tributaries and waterfalls carving their way through the rocky landscape. The sightseeing—mosques, old Turkish-style houses, and that spine-tingling Old Bridge—is more engaging than much of what you'll find in Croatia or Slovenia. And it's cheap—hotels, food, and museums are less than half the prices you'll pay in Croatia.

If Mostar were a little more stable, if its service standards were a bit higher, and if it had frequent, effortless bus connections to the Dalmatian Coast, it would be one of the premier destinations in the former Yugoslavia. Over the next several years, all of those things may come to pass—and you'll have seen it before it really took off.

Planning Your Time

Because of its cultural hairiness, a detour into Bosnia-Herzegovina feels like a real departure from a Dalmatian vacation. But actually, Mostar is easier to reach from Dubrovnik or Split than many popular Dalmatian islands (it's just a three-hour drive or bus ride from either city).

Mostar

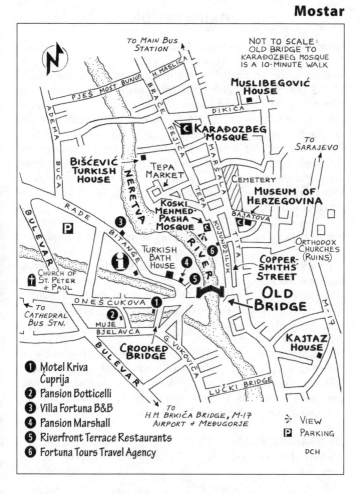

TO MAIN BUS STATION

NOT TO SCALE: OLD BRIDGE TO KARAĐOZBEG MOSQUE IS A 10-MINUTE WALK

N

H. MASLIĆA

BRAĆE

PJEŠ MOST BUNUR

FEJIĆA

DIKIĆA

MUSLIBEGOVIĆ HOUSE

KARAĐOZBEG MOSQUE

ADEMA

BUĆA

RADE

TO SARAJEVO

NERETVA

BIŠĆEVIĆ TURKISH HOUSE

TEPA MARKET

TARA

TEPA

CEMETERY

MUSEUM OF HERZEGOVINA

BAJATOVA

BULEVAR

P

BITANGE

KOSKI MEHMED-PASHA MOSQUE

RIVER

KUJUNDŽILUK

ORTHODOX CHURCHES (RUINS)

❸

❻

TURKISH BATH HOUSE

ℹ

TATA

COPPER-SMITHS STREET

CHURCH OF ST. PETER & PAUL

❹

❺

OLD BRIDGE

M-17

TO CATHEDRAL BUS STN.

ONESĆUKOVA

❶

MUJE BJELAVCA

❷

G. VUKOVIĆA

KAJTAZ HOUSE

CROOKED BRIDGE

BULEVAR

LUČKI BRIDGE

TO H.M. BRKIĆA BRIDGE, M-17 AIRPORT & MEĐUGORJE

❶ Motel Kriva Ćuprija
❷ Pansion Botticelli
❸ Villa Fortuna B&B
❹ Pansion Marshall
❺ Riverfront Terrace Restaurants
❻ Fortuna Tours Travel Agency

↗ VIEW
P PARKING

DCH

The vast majority of tourists in Mostar are day-trippers from the coast, which means the Old Town is packed midday, but empty in the morning and evening. You can get a good feel for Mostar in just a few hours, but a full day gives you time to linger and ponder.

You have three basic options: take a package tour from Dalmatia; rent a car for a one-day side-trip into Mostar; or (my favorite) spend the night here en route between Croatian destinations. To work a Mostar overnight into your itinerary, consider a round-trip plan that takes you south along the coast, then back north via Bosnia-Herzegovina (for example, Split-Hvar-Korčula-Dubrovnik-Mostar-back to Split).

ORIENTATION

(country code: 387; area code: 036)

Mostar—a mid-sized city with just over 100,000 people—is situated in a basin surrounded by mountains and split down the middle by the emerald-green Neretva River. Bosniaks live mostly on the east side of the river, and Croats on the west (though increasingly the populations are mixing again). Visitors move freely throughout the city, and most don't even notice the division. The cobbled, Turkish-feeling Old Town (called the "Stari Grad" or—borrowing a Turkish term—the "Stara Čaršija") surrounds the town's centerpiece, the Old Bridge. Timid tourists feel most comfortable in the Old Town sector, and that's where I've focused my sightseeing and hotel recommendations.

The skyline is pierced by the minarets of various mosques, but none is as big as the two major Catholic (Croat) symbols in town, both erected since the recent war: The giant white cross on the hilltop (placed where Croat forces shelled the Bosniak side of the river, including the Old Bridge); and the enormous (almost 100-foot-tall) bell tower of the Church of Sts. Peter and Paul. A monumental Orthodox Church once stood on the hillside across the river, but it was destroyed in the war when the Serbs were forced out, and never rebuilt.

A note about safety: Mostar is as safe as any city its size—but it doesn't always *feel* safe. You'll see bombed-out buildings everywhere, even in the core of the city. Some are marked with *Warning! Dangerous Ruin* signs, but for safety's sake, never wander into any building that appears damaged or deserted.

Arrival in Mostar

For arrival by **bus** or by **car,** see "Transportation Connections" on page 278.

Tourist Information

Pick up a free town map at the **TI** (summer daily 9:00–19:00, may be longer July–Aug, shorter hours in shoulder season, likely closed Dec–March, just a block from the Old Bridge on Rade Bitange street, tel. 036/580-275, www.bhtourism.ba).

More central and often more helpful is the **Fortuna Tours** travel agency, right in the heart of the Old Town (at the top of Coppersmiths' Street). In addition to selling all the tourist stuff, they can book you a local guide (about €50 for a 1.5-hour tour, reserve in advance)—an excellent investment in this challenging town (open long hours daily, Kujundžiluk 2, tel. 036/551-887, main office tel. 036/552-197, fax 036/551-888, www.fortuna.ba, fortuna_mostar@bih.net.ba).

If someone approaches you offering to be your guide, ask the price in advance (they often charge ridiculously high rates). If they seem cagey or overpriced, decline politely. The Fortuna Tours guides are better anyway.

Need Convertible Marks? The most convenient **ATM** in town is to the left of Fortuna Tours' door (but remember that kunas and euros are also accepted here).

SIGHTS

I've described these sights as they appear along a handy route through the Old Town. From the Ottoman era all the way through the end of World War II, Mostar had fewer than 15,000 residents—so this compact central zone was pretty much all there was until the city became industrialized and grew like crazy during the Tito years.

Be warned that opening times (and, well, just about everything else) are particularly sporadic in Mostar. Be flexible.

• *Begin at the western end of the...*

▲▲▲**Old Bridge (Stari Most)**—One of the most evocative sights in the former Yugoslavia, this iconic bridge confidently spanned the Neretva River for more than four centuries. Traditionally considered the point where East meets West, the Old Bridge is as symbolic as it is beautiful. Dramatically arched and flanked by two boxy towers, the bridge is striking...even without knowing its history.

Before the Old Bridge, the Neretva was spanned only by a rickety suspension bridge, guarded by *mostari* ("watchers of the bridge") who gave the city its name. Commissioned in 1557 by the Ottoman sultan Süleyman the Magnificent, and completed just nine years later, the Old Bridge was a technological marvel for its time..."the longest single-span stone arch on the planet." (In other words, it's the granddaddy of the Rialto Bridge in Venice.) Because of its graceful keystone design—and the fact that there are empty spaces inside the structure—it's much lighter than it seems. And yet, nearly four hundred years after it was built, the bridge was still strong enough to support the weight of Nazi tanks that rolled in to occupy Mostar. Over the centuries, it became the symbol for the town and region—a metaphor in stone for the way that the diverse faiths and cultures here were able to bridge the gaps that divided them.

In the early 1990s, this city of Bosniaks, Croats, and Serbs began to groan under the pressure of politicians' propaganda. In October of 1991, Bosnia-Herzegovina—following Croatia's and Slovenia's example, but without the blessing of its large Serb minority—declared independence from Yugoslavia. Soon after, the Serb-dominated Yugoslav National Army invaded. Mostar's Bosniaks and Croats joined forces to battle the Serbs, and succeeded in claiming the city as their own and forcing out the Serb residents.

But even as they defended their city from the final, distant bombardments of Serb forces, the Bosniaks and Croats began to squabble. Neighbors, friends, and even relatives took up arms against each other. The city became divided: The Croats controlled the west side of the river (under the big mountain), while the Bosniaks occupied the east side and a small strip on the west side. The Old Bridge frequently got caught in the crossfire. Old tires were slung over its sides, to absorb some of the impact from nearby artillery or shrapnel.

In November of 1993, Croats began shelling the bridge from the top of the mountain (where the cross is now). Several direct hits caused the venerable Old Bridge to lurch, then tumble in

pieces into the river. The decision to destroy the bridge was partly strategic—to cut off a Bosniak-controlled strip on the west bank from Bosniak forces on the east. (News footage from the time shows Bosniak soldiers scurrying back and forth over the bridge.) But there can be no doubt that, like the siege of Dubrovnik, the attack was also partly symbolic: the destruction of a bridge representing the city's Muslim legacy.

After the war, city leaders decided to rebuild the Old Bridge. Chunks of the original bridge were dredged up from the river. But the stone had been compromised by soaking in the water for so long, so it couldn't be used (you can still see these pieces of the old Old Bridge on the riverbank below). Staying true to their pledge to do it authentically, restorers quarried new stone (a limestone called *tenelija*) from the original quarry, and each stone was hand-carved. Then they assembled the stones with the same technology used by the Ottomans 450 years ago: Workers erected wooden scaffolding and fastened the stones together with iron hooks cast in lead. The project cost over $13 million, funded largely by international donors and overseen by UNESCO.

It took longer to rebuild the bridge in the 21st century than it did to build it in the 16th century. But on July 23, 2004, the new Old Bridge was inaugurated with much fanfare, and was immediately embraced by both the city and the world as a sign of reconciliation. Feel the shivers run down your spine as you walk over the Old Bridge today, and ponder its troubled yet inspirational past.

On a lighter note: One of Mostar's favorite traditions is for young men to jump from the bridge 75 feet down into the Neretva (which remains icy cold even in summer). Done both for the sake of tradition, and to impress girls, this custom was carried on even during the time the destroyed bridge was temporarily replaced by a wooden one. Now the tower on the west side of the bridge houses the office of the local "Divers Club," a loosely run organization that carries on this longstanding ritual. On hot summer days, you'll see divers making a ruckus and collecting donations at the top of the bridge. For the right price, one of them might take the plunge.

• *Continue over the Old Bridge and drop into the free photo exhibition on the right. Then turn left with the street and walk along...*

▲▲**Coppersmiths' Street (Kujundžiluk)**—This lively strip, with the flavor of a Turkish bazaar, offers some of the most colorful shopping this side of Istanbul. You'll see Mostar's characteristic bridge depicted in every possible way, along with blue-and-white "evil eyes" (believed in the Turkish culture to keep bad spirits at bay), old Yugoslav army kitsch, and hammered-copper decorations (continuing the long tradition that gave the street its name). Partway up, the homes with the colorfully painted facades double as galleries for local artists. The artists live and work upstairs, then sell their work right on this street. This is the most touristy street in Mostar (and maybe in all of Bosnia-Herzegovina), so don't expect any bargains. Still, it's fun.

• *Continue up to the Fortuna Tours office and its handy ATM (see "Tourist Information," earlier in this chapter). Then bear left up the cobbled street. About halfway along this street, on the left-hand side, look for the entrance to the...*

▲**Koski Mehmed-Pasha Mosque (Koski Mehmed-Paša Džamija)**—Mostar's Bosniak community includes several practicing Muslims. Step into this courtyard for a look at one of Mostar's many mosques (€1 to enter mosque, €2.50 includes mosque and minaret, open long hours daily). This mosque, dating from the early 17th century, is notable for its cliff-hanging riverside location, and because it's particularly accessible for tourists. The information here generally applies to the other mosques in Mostar, as well:

The fountain *(šadrvan)* in the courtyard allows worshippers to wash before entering the mosque, as directed by Islamic law. It's also refreshing in this hot climate, and the sound of running water helps worshippers concentrate.

The minaret—the slender needle jutting up next to the

The Muslims of Mostar

While recent Muslim immigrants are becoming a fixture in many European cities, Bosnia-Herzegovina is one place where Muslims have continuously been an integral part of the cultural tapestry for centuries.

During the 400 years that Mostar was part of the Ottoman Empire, the Muslim Turks (unlike some Catholic despots at the time) did not forcibly convert their subjects. However, it was advantageous for non-Turks to adopt Islam (for lower taxes and better business opportunities), so many Slavs living here became Muslims. In fact, within 150 years of the start of Ottoman rule, half of the population of Bosnia-Herzegovina was Muslim.

The Ottomans became increasingly intolerant of other faiths as time went on, and uprisings by Catholics and Orthodox eventually led to the end of Ottoman domination in the late 19th century. But even after the Ottomans left, many people in this region continued practicing Islam, as their families had been doing for centuries. These people constitute an ethnic group called "Bosniaks," and many of them are still practicing Muslims today (following the Sunni branch of the Muslim faith). Keep in mind that most Bosniaks are Slavs—of the same ethnic stock as Croats and Serbs—and look pretty much the same as their neighbors, although some Bosniaks have ancestors who married into Turkish families, and may have some Turkish features.

Due to the recent actions of a small but attention-grabbing faction of Muslim extremists, Islam is burdened with a bad reputation in the Western world. But judging Islam based on

dome—is the Islamic equivalent of the Christian bell tower. In the old days, the *muezzin* (prayer leader) would climb the tower five times a day and chant, "There is only one God, and Muhammad is his prophet." In modern times, loudspeakers are used instead. When Muslims hear this call to prayer, they come to a mosque to pray. (If they can't come at that particular moment, they're allowed to worship when and where they are able—so long as they do it five times each day.)

While it's usually expected to remove your shoes to enter a mosque, this one is accustomed to tourists, so they've put a special covering on the floor. Near the front of the mosque, you may see some of the small, overlapping rugs that are below this covering

Osama bin Laden and al-Qaeda is like judging Christianity based on Timothy McVeigh and the Ku Klux Klan. Visiting Mostar is a unique opportunity to get a taste of a fully Muslim society, made a bit less intimidating because it wears a more-familiar European face.

Here's an admittedly basic and simplistic outline (written by a non-Muslim) designed to help travelers from the Christian West understand a very rich but often misunderstood culture worthy of respect:

Muslims, like Christians and Jews, are monotheistic. They call their god Allah. The most important person in the Islamic faith is Muhammad, Allah's most important prophet, who lived in the sixth and seventh centuries A.D.

The "five pillars" of Islam are the same among Muslims in Bosnia-Herzegovina, Turkey, Iraq, Indonesia, the US, and everywhere else. Followers of Islam should:

1. Say and believe, "There is only one God, and Muhammad is his prophet."

2. Pray five times a day, facing Mecca. Modern Muslims explain that it's important for this ritual to include several elements: washing, exercising, stretching, and thinking of God.

3. Give to the poor (one-fortieth of your wealth, if you are not in debt).

4. Fast during daylight hours through the month of Ramadan. Fasting is a great social equalizer and helps everyone to feel the hunger of the poor.

5. Visit Mecca. This is interpreted by some Muslims as a command to travel. Muhammad said, "Don't tell me how educated you are, tell me how much you've traveled."

Good advice for anyone, no matter what—or if—you call a higher power.

(reserved for shoes-off worshippers).

Once inside, notice the traditional elements of the mosque. The niche *(mihrab)* across from the entry is oriented toward Mecca (the holy city in today's Saudi Arabia)—the direction all Muslims face to pray. The small stairway *(mimber)* that seems to go nowhere is symbolic of the growth of Islam—Muhammad had to stand higher and higher to talk to his growing following. This serves as a kind of pulpit, where the cleric gives a speech,

similar to a sermon or homily in Christian church services. No priest ever stands on the top stair, which is symbolically reserved for Muhammad.

The balcony just inside the door is traditionally where women worship. For the same reason I find it hard to concentrate on God at aerobics classes, Muslim men decided prayer would go better without the enjoyable but problematic distraction of bent-over women between them and Mecca. These days, women can also pray on the main floor with the men, but they still must avoid physical contact.

Muslims believe that capturing a living creature in a painting or a sculpture is inappropriate. (In fact, depictions of Allah and the prophet Muhammad are strictly forbidden—remember the newspaper cartoon controversy in Denmark?) Instead, mosques are filled with ornate patterns and Arabic calligraphy (of the name "Muhammad" and important sayings from the Quran).

The mosque's courtyard is shared by several merchants. When you're done haggling, head to the terrace behind the mosque for the best view in town of the Old Bridge.

• *Just after this mosque, the traffic-free cobbles of the Old Town end. Take a right and walk up one block to the big graveyard, filled with many soldiers killed in the recent war (notice how many headstones date from 1994 and 1995). Near this cemetery is another mosque. Go up the wide staircase next to that mosque to the...*

Museum of Herzegovina (Muzej Hercegovine)—This humble but worthwhile little museum collects fragments of this region's rich history, including several items from its Ottoman period. There's no English (in fact, there's barely any Bosnian), and without a tour guide the exhibits are difficult to appreciate—especially the small room commemorating the house's former owner, Dzemal Bijedić. But the museum is made worthwhile by a deeply moving, ▲▲ film that traces the history of the town through its Old Bridge: fun circa-1957 footage of the diving contests; harrowing scenes of the bridge being pummeled, and finally toppled, by artillery; and a stirring sequence showing the bridge's reconstruction and grand re-opening, with divers leaping off it once again (€0.50, ask about "film?" as you enter, Mon–Fri 9:00–14:00, Sat 10:00–12:00, closed Sun, Bajatova 4—walking up these stairs, it's the second door that's marked for the museum, under the overhanging balcony).

• *Backtrack to where you left the Old Town. Notice the **Tepa Market**, with locals hawking—and buying—produce, in the area just beyond the pedestrian zone. Now go straight ahead (with the produce market on your left) along the lively street called **Braće Fejića**. You're in the "new town," where locals sit out in front of boisterous cafés sipping Turkish (or "Bosnian") coffee while listening to the thumping beat of* *distinctly Eastern-sounding music. At the palm tree, detour a block to the left to reach...*

Bišćević Turkish House (Bišćevića Kuća)—This is your best city-center look at a traditional Turkish home (€1, generally open daily March–Oct 8:00–20:00, Nov–Feb 9:00–15:00, Bišćevića 13). Dating from 1635, this is typical of old houses in Mostar, which mix Oriental style with Mediterranean features. Notice that it's surrounded by a high wall—protection from the sun's rays, from thieves...and from prying eyes. You'll begin by stepping into the courtyard *(hajat)*, with stones set in geometrical forms in the floor (for example, the five-sided star, representing the five times a day Muslims pray). Notice the traditional fountain *(šadrvan)*, like

those at the entrance to a mosque. As you enter the covered, open area *(hama)*, notice the intricately carved tops of the wooden pillars. The big chests against the wall were used to bring the dowry when the homeowner took a new wife. Take your shoes off before you climb up the wooden staircase. Imagine how this stairway could be pulled up for extra protection in case of danger. The main gathering room *(divanhan)* in the back of the house—designed in a circle, so people could face each other, cross-legged, for a good conversation—has a dramatic view overlooking the Neretva.

If you're intrigued by this, consider dropping by Mostar's two other Turkish houses (both charge a modest entry fee). The **Kajtaz House** (Kajtazova Kuća), hiding up a very residential-feeling alley a few blocks from the Old Bridge, feels lived-in because it still is (in the opposite direction from most of the other sights, at Gaše Ilića 21). The grander, more ornamental **Muslibegović House** (Muslibegovića Kuća) is a bit more recent and modern-feeling, and therefore less homey and colorful (just two blocks uphill from the Karađozbeg Mosque).

• *Go back to the main café street and continue to the...*

▲Karađozbeg Mosque (Karađoz- begova Džamija)—The city's main mosque was completed in 1557, the same year work began on the Old Bridge. This mosque, which welcomes visitors, feels less touristy than the one back in the Old Town (€1 to enter, €2.50 includes mosque entry and minaret, daily May–Sept 9:00–19:30, Oct–April 10:00–15:00). Before entering the gate

into the complex, look for the picture showing the recent war damage sustained by this mosque, since repaired. You'll see that this mosque has most of the same elements as the one we saw earlier (read the description for the Koski Mehmed-Pasha Mosque, above). But here, most of the decorations are original—notice several gaps in the designs, giving you a sense of which parts of the mosque were damaged in the war.

• *If you're heading back over the Old Bridge, detour left after crossing it and follow the little valley to the...*

▲Crooked Bridge (Kriva Ćuprija)—This miniature Old Bridge was built nearly a decade before its more famous sibling, suppos-

edly to practice for the real deal. It spans the creek called Radobolja as it winds over waterfalls and several mills on its way to join the Neretva. Damaged—but not destroyed—during the war, the bridge was swept away several years later by floods. The bridge you see today is a recent reconstruction.

• *Just two blocks away from the river beyond the Crooked Bridge is the street called...*

Bulevar—This "Boulevard" was once the modern main drag of Mostar. But as fighting raged between the Croat and Bosniak

forces, this street became the front line—and virtually all of its buildings were destroyed. Then as now, the area to the east of here (toward the river) was controlled by Bosniaks, while the western part of town (toward the big mountain and the giant bell tower) was Croat territory.

SLEEPING

Mostar has a surprising concentration of new, friendly, accessible, and very affordable little hotels right in the city center. Each of these places is small, with English-speaking staff, and will provide a comfortable home base for your time here. None of these is a full-service hotel, so don't expect an all-night reception desk.

$$ Motel Kriva Ćuprija ("Crooked Bridge"), by the bridge of the same name, is clearly the best bet in town. Tucked between waterfalls in a picturesque valley a few steps from the Old Bridge, it's an appealing oasis with six rooms, three apartments, and a

Sleep Code

(€1 = about $1.20, country code: 387, area code: 036)
S = Single, **D** = Double/Twin, **T** = Triple, **Q** = Quad, **b** = bathroom.
To help you sort easily through these listings, I've divided the
rooms into two categories based on the price for a standard
double room with bath in peak season:

$$ Higher Priced—Most rooms €50 or more.
$ Lower Priced—Most rooms less than €50.

restaurant with atmospheric outdoor seating (Db-€55, apartment-
€60, includes breakfast, cash only, air-con, Kriva Ćuprija 2, tel.
036/550-953, mobile 061-135-286, www.motel-mostar.de, motel
-mostar@web.de, *se habla español*).

$ Pansion Botticelli, just up the valley from the Crooked
Bridge, has five colorful, artsy rooms (Sb-€30, Db-€40, prices can
be soft during slow times, breakfast-€5, cash only, Muje Bjelavca
6, mobile 063-319-057, botticelli@reklamiraj.com). You can also
book through Fortuna Tours (see next), where the owner works.

$ Villa Fortuna B&B, in a nondescript urban neighborhood
a few minutes' walk farther away from the Old Bridge, has five
tasteful, modern, air-conditioned rooms. The rooms are just above
the main office of Fortuna Tours, and you'll reserve through them
(Sb-€30, Db-€40, prices can be soft during slow times, break-
fast-€5, cash preferred, tel. 036/552-197, fax 036/551-888, fortuna
_mostar@bih.net.ba). Fortuna Tours can also put you in touch
with locals renting rooms and apartments.

$ Pansion Marshall has two apartments sharing a kitchen on
a tidy courtyard between the former Turkish bath and a popular
(and noisy) nightlife zone, also very close to the Old Bridge (Db-
€40, €30 in winter, extra bed-€15, breakfast-€3, cash only, air-con,
Rade Bitange 8, mobile 061-529-433, www.apartmanimarshall
.com, marshall@apartmanimarshall.com).

EATING

Most of Mostar's tourist-friendly restaurants are conveniently con-
centrated in the Old Town. If you walk anywhere that's cobbled,
you'll stumble onto dozens of tempting restaurants serving tradi-
tional food (grilled meats are especially popular—read "Balkan
Flavors," on page 39, before you dine).

Before choosing, find your way into the several levels of res-
taurants that clamber up the riverbank with perfect views of the
Old Bridge. To reach these, go over the bridge to the west side of

the river, and bear right on the cobbles until you get to the old Turkish bathhouse, or *hamam* (with the copper humps on the roof). To the right of the bathhouse is the entrance to a lively courtyard surrounded with cafés and restaurants. Continuing toward the river from the courtyard, stairs lead down to several of the riverfront terraces. While you'll have menus pushed in your face as you walk, don't hesitate—poke around to find your favorite bridge view before settling in for a drink or a meal.

TRANSPORTATION CONNECTIONS

From Mostar by Bus: Not surprisingly for a divided city, Mostar has two different bus terminals. The Main Bus Station is on the east (Bosniak/Muslim) side of the river, while the Cathedral Bus Station is a city bus stop near the cathedral on the west (Croat/Catholic) side of the river (across the street from the modern cathedral, near the intersection of Biskupa Čule and Biskupa Buconjća). A taxi between either station and the Old Town should cost less than 8 KM.

Confirm schedules—and which station your bus leaves from—carefully, as this information is particularly subject to change. Buses go to **Međugorje** (7/day, 50 min, actually a yellow public bus from Cathedral Bus Station, 3 KM), **Sarajevo** (11/day, 2.5 hrs, from Main Bus Station, 13.50 KM), **Zagreb** (1 night bus/day, 9.5 hrs, 67 KM), **Split** (5/day, 4 hrs, can be from either bus station—ask locally about your specific bus, 20 KM), **Dubrovnik** (2/day in summer, 1/day off-season, 4 hrs, from Main Bus Station, 18 KM—but note that all Dubrovnik buses leave early in the day, making an afternoon return from Mostar to Dubrovnik impossible). Service to **Korčula** is sporadic—sometimes once per week, sometimes none at all.

By Train: Mostar is on the train line that runs from **Ploče** (on the Croatian coast between Split and Dubrovnik) to **Sarajevo** and on to **Zagreb.** This train generally runs once daily, leaving Ploče at 6:40, stopping in Mostar at about 8:17, arriving Sarajevo at 10:34 and, after a long trip, Zagreb at 19:47 (going the other way, it's Zagreb-8:57, Sarajevo-18:18, Mostar-20:41, Ploče-22:05). Additional trains may also follow this route.

Route Tips for Drivers

The most convenient entry point into Bosnia-Herzegovina from the Dalmatian Coast is the town of **Metković,** about halfway between Dubrovnik and Split. (If you're driving there from Dubrovnik or Korčula, you'll actually cross into Bosnia-Herzegovina twice—including the short stretch of coastline that Bosnia-Herzegovina still controls, with the town of **Neum.**)

Near Metković, the main coastal road jogs away from the coast and around the striking **Neretva River Delta**—the extremely fertile "garden patch of Croatia," which produces a significant portion of Croatia's fruits and vegetables. The Neretva is the same river that flows under Mostar's Old Bridge upstream—but in Metković, it spreads out into 12 branches as it enters the Adriatic, flooding a vast plain and creating a bursting cornucopia in the middle of an otherwise rocky and arid region. Enjoying some of the most plentiful sunshine on the Croatian coast, as well as a steady supply of irrigation water, the Neretva Delta is as productive as it is beautiful.

After passing through Metković, you'll cross the border into **Bosnia-Herzegovina,** then continue straight on the main road (M-17) directly into Mostar. As you drive, you'll see destroyed buildings and occasional roadside memorials bearing the likenesses of fresh-faced soldiers who died in the recent war.

Along the way are a few interesting detours: In Čapljina, you can turn off toward **Međugorje** (described later in this chapter).

Soon after, a mountaintop castle tower on the right side of the road marks the medieval town of **Počitelj**—an artists' colony (both before and after the war) with a compelling mix of Christian and Muslim architecture, including a big mosque and a multi-domed bathhouse. It's well worth pulling over and strolling around this steep village.

With extra time, just before Mostar (in Buna), you can detour a few miles along the Buna River into **Blagaj**—the historical capital of the region until the arrival of the Ottomans. This is the site of a mountain called Hum, which is topped by the ruins of a hilltop castle that once belonged to Herzog ("Duke") Stjepan, who gave Herzegovina its name. Deep in Blagaj is an impressive cliff face with a scenic house marking the source of the Buna River. The building, called the Tekija, is actually a former monastery for Turkish dervishes (an order that emphasizes poverty and humility,

Enter the Dragon

Reconciliation works in strange and unexpected ways. In the early 2000s, idealistic young Mostarians formed the Urban Movement of Mostar, which searched for a way to connect the still-feuding Catholic and Muslim communities. As a symbol of their goals, they chose the deceased kung-fu movie star Bruce Lee, who is beloved by both Croats and Bosniaks for his characters' honorable struggle against injustice. A life-size bronze statue of Lee was unveiled with fanfare in November of 2005 in Veliki Park. Unfortunately, soon after, the statue was damaged. Whether or not the vandalism was ethnically motivated is unclear, but many locals hope the ideals embodied in the statue will continue to bring the city together.

and is famous for the way they whirl when in a worshipful trance); inside is a modest museum with the graves of two important dervishes. Today the area is surrounded by gift shops and a big restaurant with fine views over the river and cliff.

Approaching **Mostar** on M-17, you'll pass the airport, then turn left at your first opportunity to cross the river. After crossing the bridge, bear right onto Bulevar street, and continue on that main artery for several blocks (passing several destroyed buildings). At the street called Rade Bitange (just after the giant church bell tower), turn right to find the public parking lot—less than a 10-minute walk from the Old Bridge. Be warned that signage is poor; if you get lost, try asking for directions to "Stari Most" (STAH-ree most)—the Old Bridge.

Rugged-but-Scenic Route to Dubrovnik: Mostar's Croats will tell you that the only way to Dubrovnik is to follow the Neretva River straight out to the sea, then take the main coastal road south (as described above). But if you're adventurous and want to head way off the beaten track, you can also make the trip inland, through parts of Bosnia-Herzegovina that are under Serb control. Various back roads curve through desolate terrain—directed only by signs using the Cyrillic alphabet—to Trebinje, a Serb town with a picturesque church high on a hill overlooking a plateau. From there, it's a twisty but spectacular drive down to the coast—you'll pop out of the mountains just south of Dubrovnik. Since this takes longer than the main coastal route, it's best left to hardy travelers with plenty of time.

Međugorje

Međugorje is an unassuming little village that ranks with Lourdes, Fátima, and Santiago de Compostela as one of the most important pilgrimage sites in all of Christendom. To the cynical non-Catholic, it's just a strip of crassly commercial hotels, restaurants, and rosary shops leading up to a dull church, all tied together by a silly legend about a hilltop apparition. But as you look into the tear-filled eyes of the pilgrims who've journeyed here, it's clear that to some, there's so much more than what's on the surface.

For true believers, Međugorje represents a once-in-a-lifetime opportunity to tread on sacred soil: a place where, over the last 26 years, the Virgin Mary has appeared to six local people. Even though the Vatican has declined to recognize the apparitions, that doesn't stop hundreds of thousands of Catholics from coming here each year. More than 30 million pilgrims have visited Međugorje since the sightings began—summer and winter, war (which didn't touch Međugorje) and peace, rain and shine. People from Ireland, Italy, Germany, Spain, the US, and just about everywhere that has Catholics make the trek here.

Planning Your Time

Unless you're a pilgrim (or think you might be a pilgrim), skip Međugorje—it's an experience wasted on non-believers. (The only "attractions" are an unexceptional modern church, a couple of hilltop hikes, and pilgrim-spotting.)

If you do go, the easiest way is to take a day-trip excursion from the Dalmatian Coast (sold from Split, Dubrovnik, and Korčula). Otherwise, plan to spend the night, or sleep in Mostar two nights and day-trip into Međugorje. It's also possible to wake up in Dubrovnik, take an early bus to Međugorje, then take the afternoon bus (generally around 17:00) to Split. Be warned that there's no afternoon bus from Međugorje to Dubrovnik.

ORIENTATION

(country code: 387; area code: 036)
Međugorje (MEDGE-oo-gor-yeh, sometimes spelled "Medjugorje" in English) is basically a one-street town—most everything happens in the half-mile between its post office (where the bus stop is) and the main church, St. James (Crkva Sv. Jakova). On the hills

Međugorje Mary

What compels millions to flock to this little village in the middle of nowhere? The official story goes like this: On the evening of June 24, 1981, two young women were gathering their sheep on the hillside above Mostar. They came across a woman carrying a baby who told them to come near. Terrified, they fled, only to realize later that this might have been a vision of the Virgin Mary. They returned the next night with some friends, and saw the apparition again.

In the 26 years since, six different locals (including the two original seers) claim to have seen the vision, and some of them even say they see it regularly to this day. They also say that Mary has given them 10 secrets—predictions of future events that will portend Judgment Day. Written on a piece of parchment, these are kept safely at the home of one of the seers. They have said they will reveal each of these secrets, 10 days before the event occurs, to the local parish priest, who will then alert the world.

But official representatives of the Vatican are not among the believers. According to Catholic law, such visions must be "certified" by the local bishop—and the one around here doesn't buy it. One cause for suspicion is that the six seers, before witnessing the visions, were sometimes known to be troublemakers. (In fact, they later admitted that they went up the hill that fateful night not to chase wayward sheep, but to sneak a smoke.) One investigator even suggested that they invented the story as a prank, only to watch it snowball out of control once they told it to the local priest. The Vatican has showed strong signs of disbelief and disapproval. In their eyes, Catholics are allowed to *travel* to Međugorje, but not make a *pilgrimage* there—and shouldn't believe the story.

Whether or not the story is true is, to a certain extent, beside the point—that people *believe* it's true is why they come here.

behind the church are two trails leading to pilgrimage sites.

Vox Tours is one of many travel agencies along the main strip where you can find a room, rent a car, hire a local guide, buy ferry tickets for Croatia, and use the Internet (Mon–Fri 8:30–17:00, Sat 8:30–14:00, closed Sun, tel. 036/650-922, fax 036/650-771, vox -tours@tel.net.ba).

By the way, Međugorje is clearly a "Croat" sight. While this may seem odd (after all, you're in Bosnia-Herzegovina, not Croatia), remember that any Catholic from the former Yugoslavia is called a Croat. Virtually every local person you'll meet in Međugorje is, strictly speaking, a Bosnian Croat.

SIGHTS

The center of pilgrim activity is **St. James' Church** (Crkva Sv. Jakova), which was built before the apparitions. The exterior and interior are both pretty dull, but that doesn't stop the pilgrims from worshipping here at all times of day (inside and outside). Out in front of the church are posted maps that are useful for getting oriented, and a white statue of the Virgin Mary that attracts a lot of attention from pilgrims.

As you face the church, there are two trails leading up to the hills. Behind and to the left of the church is **Apparition Hill** (at Podbrdo), where the sightings occurred (a 1-mile hike, topped by a statue of Mary). Directly behind the church is the **Great Hill** (Križevac, or "Cross Mountain"), where a giant hilltop cross, which predates the visions, has become a secondary site of pilgrimage (1.5-mile hike). Pilgrims often do one or both of these hikes barefoot, as a sign of penitence.

Around back of the church is a makeshift amphitheater with benches, used for outdoor services. Beyond that is a path. You'll pass some Stations of the Cross, then (on the right) a giant statue of the **Resurrected Savior** (Uskrsli Spasitelj), also known as the "Weeping Knee." While the elongated, expressionistic sculpture—exemplifying Christ's suffering—is striking in itself, the eternal dampness of its right knee attracts the most attention from pilgrims. Miraculously (or not), it's always wet—go ahead and touch the spot that's been highly polished by worshippers and skeptics alike.

Believers and non-believers both appreciate the parade of kitsch that lines the **main street** leading up to the church. While rosaries are clearly the big item, you can get basically anything you want stamped with Catholic imagery (Mary is particularly popular, for obvious reasons).

SLEEPING

The main street has dozens of hotels and pensions catering to pilgrims.

$ Hotel Martin, well-run by Martin Ilić, is set back slightly from the main road. With 40 comfortable rooms, it's an easy choice (Db-€44, cash only, air-con, elevator, tel. 036/651-541, fax 036/651-505, www.martin.ba, martin.ilic@tel.net.ba). Don't confuse this with the Pansion Martin, much farther out of town.

$ Vox Tours can help find you a room (approximate prices: Db-€38, €49 for half-board, €66 for full board; for contact information, see "Orientation," on page 281).

EATING

The main street is lined with straightforward, crank-'em-out eateries catering to tour groups. For something a little more atmospheric and fun, head for **Gardens Restaurant** (near the post-office end of the main drag). This place—with a lively bar and wine cellar on the ground floor, a classy dining room upstairs, and the namesake garden terrace out back—serves tasty international cuisine. Somewhat youthful, but still respectable, it's a nice place to unwind at the end of a long pilgrimage (10–12-KM pastas, 15–20-KM main dishes, daily 8:00–24:00, tel. 036/650-499, www.medjugorje-gardens .com).

MONTENEGRO

MONTENEGRO

The Bay of Kotor and the Budva Riviera

If Dubrovnik is the grand finale of a Croatian vacation, then Montenegro is the encore. Europe's youngest nation awaits just south of the border, with dramatic scenery, a refreshing rough-around-the-edges appeal, and the excitement of a giddy new independence. If you're looking for the "next Croatia," look no further.

Montenegro is generally Orthodox, and shares a strong cultural affinity with Serbia. But while landlocked Serbia can feel businesslike, Montenegro boasts an easygoing seaside spice. With its laid-back Mediterranean orientation, sparkling coastline, and more than its share of Catholic churches (left behind by past Venetian and Austrian rulers), Montenegro also has a lot in common with Croatia.

And yet, crossing the border, you know you've left the sleek, prettified-for-tourists spit-and-polish of Croatia for a place that's grittier, raw, and a bit exotic. While the showpiece Dalmatian Coast avoided the drab, boxy dullness of the Yugoslav era, less affluent Montenegro wasn't so lucky. Between the dramatic cliffs and historic villages, you'll drive past grimy, broken-down apartment blocks and some truly unfortunate resort-hotel architecture. Montenegro is also a noticeably poorer country than its northern neighbor...with all that entails.

Still, nothing could mar the natural beauty of Montenegro's mountains, bays, and forests. For a look at the untamed Adriatic, a spin on the winding road around Montenegro's steep and secluded Bay of Kotor is a must. The area's main town, also called Kotor, has been protected from centuries of would-be invaders by its position at the deepest point of the fjord—and by its imposing town wall, which scrambles in a zigzag line up the mountain behind it. Wander the enjoyably seedy streets of Kotor, drop into some Orthodox churches, and sip a coffee at an *al fresco* café. With more time, beach bums will head for the Budva Riviera, and celebrity-seekers can day-

dream about past glories in the striking hotel-peninsula of Sveti Stefan.

Planning Your Time

Montenegro's Bay of Kotor is the single most satisfying day trip from Dubrovnik. I've organized the information in this chapter to help you do the trip yourself by car, or you can take a package excursion that follows basically the same route (see page 249 in the Near Dubrovnik chapter). With one day, I'd do this trip and linger a few hours in Kotor before heading back to Dubrovnik. With extra time, or if you tire of Kotor quickly, tack on a drive up over the mountains to Cetinje, or a jaunt to the Budva Riviera.

The Bay of Kotor

With dramatic cliffs rising out of the glimmering Adriatic, ancient towns packed with history and thrilling vistas, an undeveloped ruggedness unlike anything in Croatia, and a twisty road to tie it all together, the Bay of Kotor represents the best of Montenegro. To top it off, it's easy to reach by car from Dubrovnik.

Getting There

By Car: Driving is easily the best option, giving you maximum flexibility for sightseeing. I've narrated a handy self-guided driving tour, below. Consider renting a car (see page 217) or hiring a driver (page 220) from Dubrovnik to do the trip efficiently.

By Bus: Recently bus service between Dubrovnik and Montenegro—discontinued for years after the war—has resumed. However, the schedule is still in flux, so confirm schedules carefully (likely 2/day each way between Dubrovnik and Kotor town, 2.5–3 hrs).

By Excursion: Several Dubrovnik-based tour companies offer package excursions to Kotor. For details, see page 249 in the Near Dubrovnik chapter.

Montenegro Almanac

Official Name: After being part of "Yugoslavia," then "Serbia and Montenegro," the Republic of Montenegro (Republika Crna Gora) officially declared its independence on June 3, 2006. Montenegro—or Crna Gora in the native language—means "Black Mountain," from the days when sailors saw dark, thickly forested cliffs as they approached. Ironically, these trees no longer exist. (The name may also come from a specific mountain in the country's interior.)

Snapshot History: Long overshadowed by its Croatian and Serbian neighbors, Montenegro has gone quietly about its own business for centuries, well-insulated from the outside world's influence by its inhospitable terrain. Only in 2006 did the country finally achieve independence, in a landmark vote to secede from Serbia, its influential and sometimes overbearing "big brother."

Population: Montenegro is home to 630,000 people. Of these, the vast majority are Eastern Orthodox Christians (43 percent Montenegrins, 32 percent Serbs), with minority groups of Muslims (including Bosniaks and Albanians, about 15 percent total) and Catholics (1 percent).

Area: 5,415 square miles (slightly smaller than Connecticut).

Red Tape: Americans and Canadians need only a passport (no visa required) to enter Montenegro. Make sure your passport is good for at least 90 days after your ticketed date of return to the US.

Geography: Montenegro is characterized by a rugged, rocky terrain that rises straight up from the Adriatic and almost immediately becomes a steep mountain range. The country has 182 miles of coastline, about a third of which constitutes the Bay of Kotor. The only real city is the dreary capital in the interior, Podgorica (137,000 people). Each of Yugoslavia's six republics had

SELF-GUIDED DRIVING TOUR

The Bay of Kotor

The Bay of Kotor (Boka Kotorska, sometimes translated as "Boka Bay" in English) is Montenegro's most enjoyable and most convenient attraction for those based in Dubrovnik. This self-guided driving tour narrates the drive from the Croatian border to the town of Kotor, in the Bay of Kotor's deepest corner. The Montenegrin border is about 45 minutes south of Dubrovnik (simply follow the main coastal road south, past Cavtat and the airport). From the border, you can make it to Kotor in about an hour without stopping, but with all the diversions en route you should a town called Titograd...and Podgorica was Montenegro's.

Economy: As a fledgling new country, Montenegro has a sky-high unemployment rate (around 27 percent). The recent privatization of its economy (including its dominant industry, aluminum) and the aggressive development of its tourist trade (such as soliciting foreign investment to build new luxury hotels) should improve matters in the coming years. But for now, Montenegro's per capita GDP is just $3,800—a fraction of Croatia's or Slovenia's.

Currency: Though it's not a member of the European Union, Montenegro uses the euro as its official currency. €1 = about $1.20.

Alphabet: The official language is Serbian, but the local dialect is known informally as Montenegrin. While you'll occasionally see signs using the Cyrillic alphabet, most Montenegrins use the same Roman alphabet as Croatia and Slovenia. In the modern age of the Internet and a united Europe, Cyrillic is becoming something of a dinosaur here.

Telephones: Montenegro's country code is 382. When calling from another country, first dial the international access code (00 from Europe, 011 from the US), then 382, then the area code (minus the initial zero), then the number. Older sources may still list the country code as 381. This was once the code for Serbia and Montenegro, but it was phased out here in early 2007.

Flag: It's a red field surrounded by a gold fringe. In the middle is the national seal: a golden, two-headed eagle topped with a single crown, holding a scepter in one hand and a ball in the other. This symbolizes the balance between church and state. The eagle's body is covered by a shield depicting a lion with one paw raised (representing the resurrected Christ).

plan for much more time. Coming back, you can trim a good half-hour off the drive by crossing the fjord at its narrowest point, using the Lepetani–Kamenari ferry (described on page 297).

• *From the Croatian border, you'll approach the coast at the town called...*

Igalo

Driving through Igalo, keep an eye out (on the right) for a big concrete hotel called **Institut Dr. Simo Milošević** (no relation to Slobodan). This internationally regarded spa, especially popular among Scandinavians, offers treatment for arthritis and other nerve disorders. Capable of hosting more than 1,000 patients at once, this complex boasts that it's one of the world's premier treatment facilities for these conditions. Yugoslav President-for-Life Tito had a villa nearby, and took treatments here (www.igalospa.com).

• *A couple of miles beyond Igalo, you enter the biggest city you'll see today...*

Herceg Novi

The drab economic and industrial capital of the Bay of Kotor, Herceg Novi (with 25,000 people), is hardly the prettiest introduction to this otherwise striking landscape. Herceg Novi flourished during the Hapsburg boom of the late 19th century, when a railroad line connected it to Dubrovnik, Sarajevo, and Vienna. Back then, Austrians vacationed here—but more recent development has been decidedly less elegant than the Hapsburgs'. While there is a walled Old Town core to Herceg Novi, it's not worth stopping to see—Kotor town (at the end of this drive) is better by far.

As you drive through Herceg Novi, watch for **banana trees.** Locals pride themselves on their particularly mild climate, kept warm year-round thanks to the natural protection provided by the surrounding fjord. Supposedly, "it never drops below nine degrees Celsius (48 degrees Fahrenheit)." While these banana trees are just decorative (the fruit they produce is too small to eat), they're a local symbol. So is the mimosa flower, which blooms all winter long, and is the inspiration for the town's annual Mimosa Festival—held each February, when the rest of Europe (including most of Montenegro) is under a layer of snow.

Other than the banana trees and mimosas, Herceg Novi is basically a mess. Why so much ugliness compared to Croatia? For one thing, Tito viewed Croatia's Dalmatian Coast as a gold mine of hard Western currency—so he was inclined to keep it Old World–charming. And Croatia remained in the cultural and political orbit of Zagreb, which was motivated to take good care of its historic towns. But Belgrade, which exerted more influence on Montenegro, didn't offer it the same degree of TLC. And because Montenegro has traditionally been poorer than Croatia, its officials are more susceptible to bribery and corruption. ("Would a few thousand dinar convince you to ignore my new hotel's code violations?") To this day, locals aren't crazy about the Serbs who flock here in summer for as-cheap-as-possible beach holidays. Instead, Montenegrins are encouraging the construction of new, high-class resort hotels to lure high rollers from around the world (such as James Bond, who recently played poker in the fictional *Casino Royale* on the Montenegrin coast—actually filmed in the Czech Republic).

The Bay of Kotor

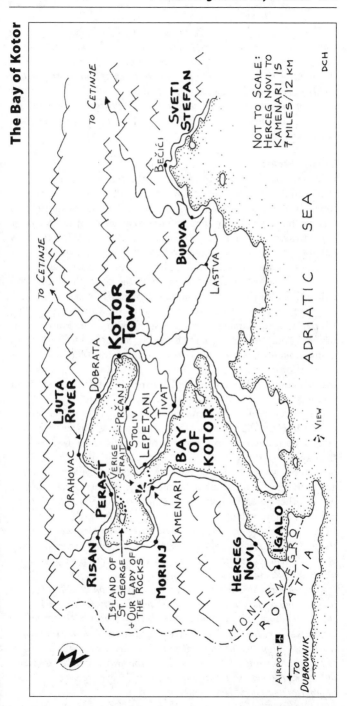

To Cetinje

Sveti Stefan

Bečići

Budva

Lastva

ADRIATIC SEA

Not to Scale:
Herceg Novi to
Kamenari is
7 miles/12 km

DCH

To Cetinje

Kotor Town

Ljuta River

Dobrata

Prčanj

Stoliv

Lepetani

Tivat

Verige Strait

Orahovac

Perast

Bay of Kotor

View

Risan

Island of
St. George
+ Our Lady of
the Rocks

Kamenari

Morinj

Herceg Novi

Igalo

Montenegro

Croatia

Airport

To Dubrovnik

• *As you go through Herceg Novi, follow signs for* Kotor. *Soon you'll emerge into a more rustic setting. This fjordside road is lined with fishing villages, some now developed as resorts (including a few with severe communist-era touches). After passing the town of* **Kamenari** *(with a handy ferry—described below—you could use to come home), watch for a convenient gravel pull-out on the right (likely packed with tour buses, by the small white lighthouse). Pull over to check out the narrowest point of the fjord, the...*

Verige Strait

This tight bottleneck is the secret to the Bay of Kotor's success: Any would-be invaders had to pass through here to reach the port towns inside. It's narrow enough to carefully monitor (not even a quarter-mile wide), but deep enough to allow even today's large ships through (more than 130 feet deep). Because this extremely narrow strait is relatively easy to defend, whoever controlled the inside of the fjord was allowed to thrive virtually unchecked.

Centuries before Christ, even before the flourishing of Roman culture, the Bay of Kotor was home to the Illyrians—the mysterious ancestors of today's Albanians. In the third century B.C., Illyrian Queen Teuta spanned this strait with an ingenious ship-wrecking mechanism to more effectively collect taxes. To this day, many sunken ships litter the bottom of this bay. (Teuta was a little too clever for her own good—her shrewdness and success attracted the attention of the on-the-rise Romans, who seized most of her holdings.)

In later times, the Venetians came up with an even more elaborate plan: Place cannons on either side of the strait, with a clear shot at any entering ships. Looking across the wide part of the bay, notice the town of Perast (by the two islands). Perast—our next stop—was also equipped with cannons that could easily reach across the bay. Thanks to this extensive defense network, Ottomans or any other potential invaders were unlikely to penetrate the bay, either by sea or by land.

• *Continue driving around the fjord. If you're ready for a meal, consider stopping in the town of* **Morinj** *for the fine food and gorgeous setting of the Konoba Ćatovića Mlini restaurant (described on page 306). Otherwise, continue around the bay.*

After going through Morinj and some other small villages, you'll pass through the larger resort town of **Risan.** *Back in Greek times, when the Bay of Kotor was known as "Sinus Rhizonicus," Risan was the leading town of the bay. Later, during the Illyrian Queen Teuta's brief three-year reign, Risan was her capital. Today the town is still home to the scant remains of Teuta's castle (on the hilltop just before town), but it's mostly notable for its giant communist eyesore hotel—named, appropriately enough, Hotel Teuta.*

The History of Kotor

With evidence of prehistoric settlements dating back to 2,500 B.C., the Bay of Kotor has been a prized location for millennia. Its unique bottleneck shape makes the Bay of Kotor the single best natural harbor between Greece and Venice.

One of the earliest known civilizations in Kotor (third century B.C.) was that of the Illyrians, whose Queen Teuta held court here until her lands were conquered by the Romans. Later, when the Roman Empire split (fourth century A.D.), Montenegro straddled the cultural fault line between West (Roman Catholic) and East (Orthodox). As Rome crumbled in the sixth and seventh centuries, the Slavs moved in. Initially rejecting Roman culture, many later converted to Christianity (some Orthodox, some Catholic).

By the 10th century, Montenegro's Slavs had organized into a sovereign state, affiliated with but partially independent from the Byzantine (Eastern Roman) Empire. Thanks to its protected location and a hinterland that was ideal for cattle breeding, medieval Kotor became a major city of the salt trade.

The Bay of Kotor further flourished in the 14th century, under the Serbian emperor Dušan the Mighty. Notorious for his aggressive law enforcement—chopping off the hand of a thief, lopping off the nose of a liar—Dušan made the Bay of Kotor a particularly safe place to do business. One of his strategies was making the nobility responsible for safe passage. If a visiting merchant was robbed, the nobleman who controlled that land would be ruthlessly punished. Soon 2,000-horse caravans could pass without a worry along this fjord. During storms, ships would routinely seek protection in this secluded bay.

But the Serbian Empire went into steep decline after Dušan. As the Ottomans threatened to invade in the 15th century, Kotor's traders turned to Venice for help. The Venetian Republic would control this bay for the next 450 years, and it was never taken by enemies. In fact, Montenegro managed to entirely evade Ottoman rule...unlike its neighbors Albania, Kosovo, Serbia, and Bosnia-Herzegovina.

In the late 19th century, when Venice fell to Napoleon, the Bay of Kotor came briefly under the control of France, then Austria. Feudal traditions fell by the wayside, industry arrived, and the area's old-fashioned economy went into a sharp decline. As trading wealth dried up, the Bay of Kotor entered a period of architectural stagnation. But thanks to this dark spell in Montenegrin history, today's visitors can enjoy some wonderfully preserved time-warp towns.

*Continue on to **Perast**. Approaching town, you can take the right fork (marked with brown sign) directly down into Perast; or you can first pass above town (left fork) for sweeping views over the bay, then backtrack down into the town center when the roads meet up again at the far end of town.*

Perast

This second-best town on the fjord (after Kotor) is considered the "Pearl of Venetian Baroque." It's well worth taking some time to wander and explore its buildings and enjoy its relaxed small-town feel (minus the bustle of bigger Kotor).

Remember that Perast, with its cannons aimed at the Verige Strait across the bay, was an essential link in the Bay of Kotor's fortifications. In exchange for this important duty, Venice rewarded Perast with privileged tax-free status. Perast became extremely wealthy. Ornate mansions proliferated during its heyday, the 17th and 18th centuries. But after Venice fell to Napoleon, and the Bay of Kotor's economy changed, Perast's singular defensive role disappeared. With no industry, no hinterland, and no natural resources, Perast stagnated—leaving it a virtual open-air museum of Venetian architecture.

Find your way to the tallest steeple in town, overlooking a long and narrow harborfront square. Perast is centered on its too-big (and incomplete) church, **St. Nicholas**—

dedicated to the patron saint of fishermen, of course. It was originally designed to extend out into the sea (the old church, still standing, was to be torn down). But Napoleon's troops came marching in before the builders got that far, so the plans were abandoned—and this massive part-church was simply grafted on to the existing, modest church instead.

Go inside (€1, generally open April–Nov daily 9:00–19:00, closed during Mass, closed Dec–March except by request—ask locals around the church if someone can let you in). Beyond the small sanctuary, you'll find a treasury with relics and icons. Past that is what was to be the main apse (altar area) of the unfinished massive church (notice it's at a right angle to the actual, in-use altar of the existing smaller church). The rough, unadorned brick walls are a reminder that they didn't get very far. Check out the model of the ambitious never-built church, and the priceless crucifix from the Tiepolo school. The Baroque main altar is by Bernini's student Francesco Cabianca, who lived in this area and was always trying to pay off his gambling debts.

If you have the time and energy, pay €1 to climb the **church tower** for the view.

Perast's only other "sight" is its **Town Museum,** skippable unless you've got time to kill (along the water near the start of town, in the ornate building with the arcade and balcony, €1, daily 9:00–18:00).

• *Before leaving Perast, take a close look at the two islands just offshore (and consider paying them a visit)...*

St. George (Sv. Đorđe) and Our Lady of the Rocks (Gospa od Škrpjela)

These twin islands—one natural, the other man-made—come with a fascinating, if hard-to-believe, story.

The **Island of St. George** (the smaller, rocky island with the trees), named for the protector of Christianity, was part of the for-

tification of the Bay of Kotor. This natural island had a small underwater reef nearby. According to legend, two fishermen noticed a strange light emanating from this reef in the early-morning fog. Rowing out to the island, they discovered an icon of Our Lady. From then on, local seamen returning home from a journey would drop a rock into the 65-foot-deep sea in this same place, gradually forming an entire island over the centuries.

Flash forward to today's **Our Lady of the Rocks** (the flat island with the dome-topped church)—created after more than 500 years of rocks were dumped here. In the 17th century, locals built a Baroque church on this holy site, and filled it with symbols of thanks for answered prayers: model ships made of silver from thankful sailors, 2,500 silver and gold votive plaques from other grateful worshippers, 68 canvases by a local painter, and a huge collection of wedding rings given by those who had nothing else to offer.

Boats to these islands leave from in front of St. Nicholas' Church in Perast—look for the guys with the T-shirts (often yellow) that say *Go to Island* (€2 per person each way).

• *When you're ready to move on, continue around the fjord. After the large town of Orahovac, you'll cross a bridge spanning the don't-blink-or-you'll-miss-it...*

Ljuta River

According to locals, this is the "shortest river in the world"—notice that the source (bubbling up from under the cliff) is just to the left of the bridge, and it meets the sea just to the right. Short as it is,

Europe's Newest Country

Montenegro, like Croatia and Slovenia, was one of the six republics that constituted the former Yugoslavia. When these republics began splitting away in the early 1990s, Montenegro—always allied closely with Serbia, and small enough to slip under the radar—decided to remain in the union. When the dust had settled, four of the six Yugoslav republics had seceded (Croatia, Slovenia, Bosnia-Herzegovina, and Macedonia), while only two remained united as "Yugoslavia": Serbia and Montenegro.

At first, Montenegrin Prime Minister Milo Đukanović was on friendly terms with Serbia's Slobodan Milošević. But in the late 1990s, as Milošević's stock plummeted, Montenegro began to inch away from its big brother Serbia. Serbia—eager to keep its access to the coast—made concessions that allowed Montenegro to gradually assert its independence. One benchmark came in 1996, when Montenegro adopted the German Mark as its official currency to avoid the inflating Yugoslav dinar.

By 2003, the country of Yugoslavia was no more, and the loose union was renamed "Serbia and Montenegro." Thus began a three-year "transition period" that allowed Montenegro to test the waters of real independence. During this time, "Serbia and Montenegro" were united only in defense—legislation, taxation, currency, and most governmental functions were separate. And it was agreed that after three years, Montenegro would be allowed to hold a referendum for full independence.

it's hardly a trickle—in fact, its name means "Angry River" for its fierce flow during heavy rains. The river actually courses underground for several miles before it gets here. Like the Karst area south of Ljubljana, this is a karstic landscape—limestone that's honeycombed with underground rivers, caves, and canyons. Many other waterfalls and streams feed the Bay of Kotor with snowmelt from the surrounding mountains. Because of this steady natural flushing, locals brag that the bay's water is particularly clear and clean. (Croatians—who claim that Montenegro dumps sewage into the sea—aren't convinced.)

Out in the bay near the river, watch for roped-off mussel farms. These are most successful at points where mountain water enters the bay.

• *Continuing along the fjord, as you pass through the town of Dobrota, look across the bay to the village of...*

Prčanj

This town is famous as the former home of many centuries' worth of wealthy sea captains. When the Bay of Kotor was part of the

That fateful vote took place on May 21, 2006. In general, ethnic Montenegrins tended to favor independence, while ethnic Serbs (who felt that Serbs and Montenegrins were basically the same anyway) wanted to stay united with Serbia. To secede, Montenegro needed 55 percent of the vote. By the slimmest of margins—half a percent, or just 2,300 votes—the pro-independence faction won. On June 3, 2006, Montenegro officially declared independence. (For good measure, two days later, Serbia declared independence as well.) Ironically, a few days after the countries separated, a united "Serbia and Montenegro" national soccer team took the field at the 2006 World Cup.

Today's Montenegrins are excited to have their own little country and enthusiastic about eventually joining the European Union, but must now face the daunting reality of going it alone without Serbian help. Serbia's greatest concern is that in losing Montenegro, it's also lost its lone outlet to the sea—both for shipping and for holiday-making. Serbia also worries that Montenegro's successful bid for independence might inspire a similar movement in Kosovo (which technically remains a province of Serbia).

But for many people in both countries, independence is an epilogue rather than a climax. Shortly after the referendum, I asked a Montenegrin when the countries would officially separate. He chuckled and said, "Three years ago."

Austrian Empire, Emperor Franz Josef came to Prčanj. Upon being greeted by some 50 uniformed ship captains, he marveled that such a collection of seafarers had been imported for his visit... not realizing that every one of them lived nearby.

• *Keep on driving. When you see the giant moat with the town wall, and the smaller wall twisting up the hill above, you'll know you've arrived in* **Kotor** *(described on the next page). After visiting Kotor (and the Budva Riviera, if you choose), it'll be time to head...*

Back to Croatia: Lepetani–Kamenari Ferry Shortcut

When you're ready to return to Dubrovnik, you can go back the way you came. Or, for a quicker route, consider the ferry that cuts across the narrow part of the fjord (between the towns of Lepetani and Kamenari). On the Kotor side of the bay, the boat departs from the town of Lepetani. From Kotor, you have two options: First, simply continue driving on the waterfront road clockwise around the bay (through Prčanj and Stoliv) until you land in Lepetani. Or, second, take the high-altitude road that twists up the valley just beyond Kotor (and offers some of the best views back on the town and the bay), and follow signs to Tivat. (Note that a faster route, via a new tunnel under this mountain, has long been under construction, and may open sometime in 2007.) The high-altitude route cuts the corner over the top of the peninsula, depositing you just up the road from the large town of Tivat. (If you're coming from Budva, simply follow signs into Tivat.) Once in Tivat, continue straight through on the main road to reach Lepetani, which is a few miles beyond the end of town. No matter how you approach, remember that "ferry" is *trajekt* (it's also signed for Herceg Novi—the big city across the bay). The boat goes continuously, and the crossing takes just four minutes (it takes longer to load and unload all the cars than it does to cross). A small car and its passengers pay €2.50 each way.

Alternatively, because the ferry goes both ways, you could take it in the morning to get to Kotor (or the Budva Riviera) first thing, then take your time working back around the bay the slow way home.

Kotor

Butted up against a steep cliff, cradled by a calm sea, naturally sheltered by its deep-in-the-fjord position, and watched over by an imposing network of fortifications, the town of Kotor is as impressive as it is well-protected. Though it's enjoyed a long and illustrious history, today's Kotor is a time-capsule retreat for travelers seeking a truly unspoiled Adriatic town.

There's been a settlement in this location at least since the time of Christ. The ancient town of Catarum—named for the Roman word for "contracted" or "strangled," as the sea is at this point in the gnarled fjord—was first mentioned in the first century A.D. Like the rest of the region, Kotor's next two millennia were layered with history as it came under control of a series of foreign powers: Illyrians, Romans, Serbs, Venetians, Napoleonic soldiers, Austrians, Tito's Yugoslavia...and now, finally, Montenegrins. Each group left its mark, and Kotor has its share of both Catholic and Orthodox churches, plus monuments and reminders of plenty of past colonizers and conquerors.

Through all those centuries, Kotor avoided destruction by warfare. But it was damaged by earthquakes—including the same 1667 quake that leveled Dubrovnik (known here as the "Great Shaking"), as well as a devastating 1979 earthquake that the city is still cleaning up from.

With an extremely inviting Old Town that seems custom-built for aimless strolling, Kotor is an idyllic place to while away a few hours. Though it's sometimes called a "little Dubrovnik,"

Kotor is low-key, less ambitious, and much smaller than its more famous neighbor. Yet visitors find that Kotor—with its own special spice that's exciting to sample—is a hard place to tear yourself away from.

ORIENTATION

Kotor (or Cattaro in Italian) has a compact Old Town shaped like a triangle. The two sides facing the bay are heavily fortified by a thick wall, and the third side huddles under the cliff face. A meandering defensive wall climbs the mountainside directly behind and above town.

The Old Town's maze-like street plan is confusing, but it's small and atmospheric enough that getting lost is fun rather than frustrating. Important buildings are labeled with red banners, which are tied into the town map and audioguide (both available at the TI).

Note that locals virtually ignore addresses, including the names of streets and squares. Most Old Town addresses are represented simply as "Stari Grad," then a number (useless if you're trying to navigate by streets). To make matters worse, a single square can have several names—so one map labels it Trg od Katedrale (Cathedral Square), while another calls it Pjaca Sv. Tripuna (Piazza of St. Tryphon). My advice: Don't fret about street or square names. Simply navigate with a map and by asking locals for directions. Thanks to the very manageable size of the Old Town, this is easier than it sounds.

Tourist Information

The **TI** is in a kiosk just outside the Old Town's main entrance gate (to the left as you face the gate; hours vary with demand—generally daily July–Aug 8:00–23:00, April–June and Sept–mid-Nov 8:00–21:00, mid-Nov–March 9:00–15:00, tel. 082/325-950, www.tokotor.com). Pick up the free map and browse the collection of guidebooks and souvenirs. You can also rent an audioguide that narrates a stroll through the Old Town (€1/hr).

When the TI is closed—or even when it's open—consider stopping by the **Forza Cattaro** travel agency and souvenir shop, just inside the gate to the left. They're a good source of information, and all manner of Montenegrin T-shirts and doodads (open long hours daily, tel. 082/304-069, www.forzakotor.com).

Arrival in Kotor

By Car: Approaching town, you'll first see Kotor's substantial wall overlooking a canal. You can park in one of two lots: immediately across from the main gate (to the right just after crossing the bridge by the wall); or in the lot across the canal (on the left just before the bridge by the wall—you'll be sent back here if the first lot is full). Either is a quick walk from the Old Town entrance.

By Bus: The bus station is about a half-mile south of the Old Town. Arriving here, simply exit to the right and walk straight up the road—you'll run into the embankment and town wall in 10 minutes.

SIGHTS

Kotor's Old Town

Because of its tangled alleys and irregular street plan, Kotor feels bigger than it is. But after 10 minutes of wandering, you'll discover you're going in circles and realize it's actually very compact. (In fact, aimless wandering is Kotor's single best activity.) How such a cute town manages to be so delightfully lazy and traffic-free, without being utterly overrun by tourists, I'll never know. But it can't last.

As you ramble, keep an eye out for these key attractions. I've listed them roughly in the order of a counterclockwise route through town, beginning outside the main entrance gate.

▲**Main Town Gate (Glavna Gradska Vrata)**—The bustling square fronting the bay and waterfront marina now welcomes tourists. But for centuries, its purpose was exactly the opposite. As the primary point of entry into this heavily fortified town, it was the last line of defense. Before the embankment was built, the water came directly to this door, and there was only room for one ship to tie up at a time (near where the cannons are today). If a ship got this far (through the gauntlet we saw back at the Verige Strait), it was carefully examined here again (and taxes were levied) before its passengers could disembark. This may seem paranoid, but realize that pirates could fly the flag of a friend to get through the strait, only to launch a surprise attack once here. By the way, pirates' primary booty wasn't silver or gold, but men—kidnapped for ransom, or, if ransom wasn't paid, as slaves to row on ships.

Check out the pinkish gate itself. The oldest parts of this gate date from 1555. It once featured a Venetian lion, then the double-headed eagle of the Austro-Hungarian Empire. But today, most of the symbolism touts Tito's communism (notice the stars). The big date (November 21, 1944) commemorates when this area was liberated from the Nazis by Tito's homegrown Partisan army. The Tito quote *(tuđe nećemo svoje nedamo)* means, roughly, "Don't take what's ours, and we won't take what's yours"—a typically provocative statement in these troubled Balkans.

• *Notice the TI in the kiosk just to the left of the gate. Passing through the gate, the Forza Cattaro travel agency (with more good tourist info)*

Kotor

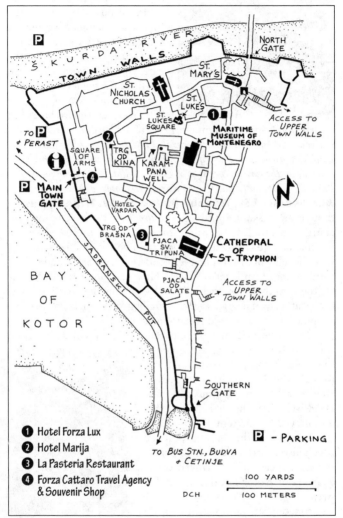

❶ Hotel Forza Lux
❷ Hotel Marija
❸ La Pasteria Restaurant
❹ Forza Cattaro Travel Agency
  & Souvenir Shop

🅿 – PARKING

TO BUS STN., BUDVA
& CETINJE

100 YARDS
100 METERS

DCH

is on the left. You'll emerge into the...

Square of Arms (Trg od Oržja)—Welcome to Kotor. This café-lined street is ringed with artifacts of the city's complex history. Do a quick spin-tour of the square. Looking to the left, you'll see a long building lined with cafés. This was once the palace of the rector, who ruled Kotor on behalf of Venice; later, it was the Kotor town hall. Beyond that, two buildings poke out into the square (on either side of the lane leading out of the square). The one on the right is the Venetian arsenal, the square's namesake. The one on the left

is the "French Theater," named for its purpose during the time this area was under Napoleon's control. Ninety degrees to the right, directly across from the gate you just came through, you'll see the town's Bell Tower, one of Kotor's symbols. In the little recessed square just right of that, you'll spot the communist-era Hotel Vardar.

• *If you need euros, there are several ATMs around this square. Then walk down the long part of the square directly ahead of where you entered, on the lane to the right of Hotel Vardar. You'll find yourself in Pjaca Sv. Tripuna (a.k.a. Trg od Katedrale), home to the...*

▲**Cathedral of St. Tryphon (Katedrala Sv. Tripuna)**—Even though most Kotorians are Orthodox, Kotor's most significant church is Catholic. According to legend, in A.D. 809, Venetian merchants were sailing up the coast from Nicea (in today's Turkey) with the relics of St. Tryphon—a third-century martyr, and today's patron saint of gardeners. A storm hit as they approached the Bay of Kotor, so they took shelter here. Every time they tried to leave, the weather worsened...so they finally got the message that St. Tryphon's remains should remain in Kotor.

The earliest, Romanesque parts of this church, dating from the mid-12th century, are made of limestone from the Croatian island of Korčula. But the church has been rebuilt after four different earthquakes—most extensively after the 1667 quake, when it achieved its current Renaissance-Baroque blend. This 1667 earthquake, which also contributed to Dubrovnik's current appearance, destroyed three-quarters of Kotor's buildings. A fire swept the city, and all of the dead bodies attracted rats (and with them, the plague)—a particularly dark chapter in Kotor's history. Why are the two towers different? There are plenty of legends, but the most likely is that restorers working after 1667 simply ran out of money before they finished the second one. Notice the Church of Our Lady of Health way up on the hill above this church (part of the town fortifications—described below).

Go inside the cathedral (€1, open daily in peak season 8:30–18:00, often closed off-season). The main part of the church is marginally interesting: tree-trunk columns, alternating between red and white; Byzantine-style paintings on the arches; and a fine

15th-century silver-and-gold altar covered by a delicate canopy. But the best part is the reliquary, upstairs. Find the stairs at the back-left corner of the church (as you face the altar) and walk up to the chapel. Behind the Baroque altar (by Bernini's student Francesco Cabianca, whose work we saw in Perast) and the screen, you'll see 48 different relics. In the center is St. Tryphon—his bones in a sarcophagus, and his head in the golden chalice to the right. Just to the right of the screen, examine the fascinating icon of the Madonna and Child from the 15th century. The painting exemplifies this town's position as a bridge between Western and Eastern Christianity: The faces, more lifelike, are Western-style (Catholic) Gothic; the stiff, elongated bodies are more Eastern (Orthodox) and Byzantine-style.

• *Exit the church. Notice the **La Pasteria** restaurant immediately across from the cathedral, with good Italian-style fare and scenic al fresco tables (see "Eating," later in this chapter). When you're ready to continue, face the cathedral facade and exit the square to your left (at the back-left corner of the square). In a block, you'll wind up on a little square that's home to the...*

Maritime Museum of Montenegro (Pomorski Muzej Crne Gore)—Like so many Adriatic towns, Kotor's livelihood is tied to the sea. This humble museum explores that important heritage. Ringing the top of the main room upstairs are 98 coats of arms representing aristocratic families who have lived here—a reminder of the richness of Kotor's history. There's also a display of rifles and swords (some with fun ornamental decorations), and some great model ships (€1.50, pick up the English brochure; summer Mon–Sat 8:00–18:00, Sun 8:00–12:00; winter Mon–Sat 8:00–14:00, Sun 8:00–12:00; on Trg Grgurina, tel. 082/325-646). The museum is housed in the Gregorina Palace, one of dozens of aristocratic mansions that dot the Old Town—yet another reminder of the historically high concentration of wealth and power in this little settlement.

• *Facing the museum, go around the left side. On the left, you'll pass the...*

Karampana—This well served as Kotor's only public faucet until the early 20th century. As such, it was also the top place in town for gossip, like the office water cooler. It's said that if your name is mentioned here, you know you've arrived.

• *Continue straight past the well into the next square...*

St. Luke's Square (Trg Svetog Luke)—Serbian Orthodox churches are scattered all over Kotor's Old Town, including two on this pretty square (also known as "Greek Square" and "St. Nicholas' Square"). Serbian Orthodox churches often have a squat design with narrow windows and portly domes. Little St. Luke's Church (Crkva Sv. Luka), in the middle of the square, dates from the 12th century. During the Venetian era, it did double duty as both an Orthodox and a Catholic church. The bigger and much newer St. Nicholas' Church (Crkva Sv. Nikola), at the far corner, was built in the early 20th century—but, because of its Neo-Byzantine design, has similarly spherical domes and slit-like windows.

Notice how the crosses on the steeples of St. Nicholas' Church differ from Western Christian churches. In addition to the arms

of the cross, Orthodox crosses often have a second, smaller crossbar near the top (representing the *I.N.R.I.* plaque that was displayed above Jesus' head). Sometimes Orthodox crosses also feature a third, angled crossbar at the bottom. Many believe that rather than being nailed directly to the cross, Jesus' feet were nailed to a crossbar like this one to prolong his suffering. The slanted angle represents Jesus' forgiveness of the thief crucified to his right (the side that's pointing up)...and suggests where the unrepentant thief on his left ended up.

Stepping into these (or any other Orthodox) churches, you'll immediately notice some key differences from Catholic churches: no pews (worshippers stand through the service as a sign of respect), tall and skinny candles (representing prayers), and a screen of icons, called an iconostasis, in the middle of the sanctuary to separate the material world from the holy world (where the Bible is kept). For more about Orthodox worship, see the sidebar on page 234.

• *If you go down the street to your left as you face St. Nicholas, you'll wind up back at the Square of Arms. But first try getting lost, then found again, in Kotor's delightful maze of streets. The town's final attraction is above your head.*

▲▲**Town Walls (Gradske Zidine)**—Kotor's fortifications begin as stout ramparts along the waterfront, then climb up the sheer cliff face behind town in a dizzying zigzag line. If there's a more elaborate city wall in Europe, I haven't seen it. A proud Kotorian bragged to me, "These fortifications cost more to build than any palace in Europe."

Imagine what it took to create this "Great Wall of Kotor": nearly three miles long, along an extremely inaccessible terrain. It was built in fits and starts over a millennium (9th–19th centuries, though most of it was during the Venetian occupation in the 17th and 18th centuries). Its thickness varies from six to 50 feet, and the tallest parts are 65 feet high. Sections higher on the hill—with thinner walls, before the age of gunpowder—are the oldest, while the thick walls along the water are most recent. It was all worth it: The fortified town survived many attacks, including a two-month Ottoman siege in 1657.

If you're in great shape, Kotor's best activity is scrambling along the walls and turrets above the Old Town. This involves climbing 1,500 steps (an eleva-  tion gain of more than 700 feet)—so don't overestimate your endurance or underesti- mate the heat. ("Am-I-*that*-out- of-shape?" tourists routinely find themselves winded and stranded high above town.) It's best to tackle the walls clock- wise. (Even if you're not doing the hike, you can visually trace this route.) Find the entrance at the back-left corner of town (near St. Mary's Church, through the alley with the two arches over it, including one with a Venetian lion). Pay the €1 entry fee and begin hiking up. Climb as high as the **Church of Our Lady of Health** (Crkva Gospe od Zdravlj). While some believe this church has miraculous healing powers, most everyone agrees it offers some of the best views down over Kotor. From this church, you can either cut back down toward the Old Town, or—if you're not exhausted yet—keep hiking up to the tippy-top **Fortress of St. John.** Built on the remains of fortifications from the Illyrians, this was the headquarters for the entire wall network below it. Then head back down, enjoying your reward: a downhill walk with head-on views of the Bay of Kotor.

Near Kotor: Cetinje

With extra time in Kotor, consider a trip up into the mountains to Montenegro's historic capital, Cetinje (far more pleasant than its current, drab capital, Podgorica). Aside from the town of Cetinje itself—high on a plateau, with quaint old buildings and oodles of history—the drive there is a major attraction, twisting up, up, up above Kotor over a high-mountain pass. Inquire locally for tips if you'd like to attempt this trip.

SLEEPING

Kotor's Old Town offers some affordable beds in an atmospheric setting—though loud nightclubs can bother light sleepers, espe- cially in summer.

$$ Hotel Forza Lux, with five elegant rooms and a huge apartment, is a plush splurge buried deep in the Old Town. It's run

---

Sleep Code

(€1 = about $1.20, country code: 382, area code: 082)
S = Single, **D** = Double/Twin, **T** = Triple, **Q** = Quad, **b** = bathroom.
To help you sort easily through these listings, I've divided the rooms into two categories based on the price for a standard double room with bath in peak season:

   $$ Higher Priced—Most rooms €100 or more.
   $ Lower Priced—Most rooms less than €100.

---

by the Forza Cattaro travel agency at the main gate, where you'll check in—there's no real reception at the hotel itself (Db-€130, apartment-€180, air-con, on Trg Paštrovica, tel. 082/304-068, fax 082/304-064, www.forzakotor.com, forzacattaro@cg.yu).

$ Hotel Marija, a traditional-feeling Balkan place on an Old Town square, offers 17 rooms and wood-paneled halls. Rooms overlooking the square come with noise, so request a quieter room in the back (Sb/Db-€65, Tb-€87, on Trg od Kina, tel. 082/325-062, hotel.marija.kotor@cg.yu).

EATING

In Kotor
There's no shortage of dining options in Kotor's Old Town; even locals suggest simply wandering the streets and squares, following your nose, and choosing the ambience you like best. I ate well and scenically at **La Pasteria,** with good pizzas and pastas, and breezy outdoor tables facing St. Tryphon's Cathedral (open long hours daily, Pjaca Sv. Tripuna/Trg od Katedrale, tel. 082/322-269).

Near the Verige Strait, in Morinj
Konoba Ćatovića Mlini is a memorable restaurant worth going out of your way to reach. Hiding in a sparse forest off the main fjord-side road, this oasis is situated amidst a series of ponds, streams, waterfalls, and bubbling springs. The traditionally clad waiters are stiffly formal, and the cuisine is delicious but surprisingly afford-able. Choose between several different seating options, indoors and out. Family-run for 200 years, this place is a local institution, yet it feels like a well-kept secret (despite the crowds in summer). Reservations are essential (€7–8 pastas, €8–10 meat dishes, €8–20 fish dishes, extensive wine list—Vranac is a popular local dry red, daily 11:00–23:00, tel. 082/373-030). The most sensible plan might be to dine here on your way back to Dubrovnik from Kotor.

Getting There: Passing through the town of Morinj, watch for burgundy *Konoba Ćatovića Mlini* signs leading away from the water. You'll make several turns, but signs will take you right to the restaurant.

The Budva Riviera

Montenegrins boast, "Croatia's got islands, but we've got beaches!" Surrounding the resort town of Budva, just south of Kotor, are long swaths of coarse-sand and fine-pebble beaches. This 15-mile stretch of coast called the "Budva Riviera" is unappealingly built up, with endless strings of cheap resort hotels (and a few new five-star ones)—making it pale in comparison to the jagged saltiness of the Bay of Kotor or the romantic tidiness of Dalmatia. But the area isn't without its charm. Aside from the pleasant Old Town of the region's unofficial capital, Budva, you'll discover a near-mythical haunt of the rich and famous: the highly exclusive resort peninsula of Sveti Stefan. For me, more time in Kotor or an earlier return to Dubrovnik would be more satisfying than the trek to the Budva Riviera. But with plenty of time and a spirit of adventure, this area merits a look.

Getting to the Budva Riviera

Budva is about a 30-minute drive south of **Kotor.** The easiest approach is to continue past Kotor along the fjord (following *Budva* signs). Leaving Kotor's Old Town, you'll turn left at the traffic light, then take a right for the upper road to Budva that twists over the mountain—offering grand vistas back over the bay. (A new tunnel through this mountain—long under construction—may be open in 2007.) After winding up several switchbacks (with giddy views back over the Bay of Kotor) and cresting the hill, go right (again following *Budva* signs). You'll coast down into a valley, through the town of Lastva, then back over another mild hill that deposits you above the beaches of Budva. Descending, first you'll reach the town of **Budva** (turn right at traffic light, following brown *Stari Grad* signs to the Old Town; parking well-marked in modern complex next to Old Town). Continuing around the bay, you'll pass the busy, modern resort cluster of Bečići before reaching **Sveti Stefan.**

SIGHTS

Between the strings of resort hotels are two towns that deserve a quick visit.

Budva—The Budva Riviera's best old town has charming Old World lanes crammed with souvenir shops and holiday-making

Serbs. While far less appealing than Kotor (and Croatian towns such as Korčula, Hvar, and Trogir), Budva at least offers a taste of romance between the resort sprawl.

Budva's ancient history (dating back at least to the fifth century B.C.) is arguably more illustrious than Kotor's. It began as an "emporium" (market and trading center) for Greek seamen, and extremely valuable jewelry uncovered here indicates that some pretty important people spent time in Budva. And yet, Budva isn't about history; it's about today. As in many Mexican vacation areas, the Old Town is just one more part of the resort experience—it's basically treated as a backdrop for outdoor dining and nightclubs.

A 10-minute stroll tells you all you need to know about Budva. The layout is simple and intuitive—a peninsula (flanked by beaches) with a big Venetian-style bell tower. From the parking lot, simply go through the Old Town walls and wander up the main drag, Njegoševa; near the end of the street on the right is the **TI** (open long hours daily in summer, tel. 086/452-750, www .tob.cg.yu). Out at the tip of town, you'll find several churches and a huge citadel that's been turned into a restaurant (€2 entry, free with drink or meal purchase).

▲**Sveti Stefan**—Like a mirage hovering just offshore, the resort peninsula of Sveti Stefan beckons curious travelers. Once an actual, living town (connected to the mainland only by a narrow, natural causeway), Sveti Stefan was virtually abandoned after World War II. The Yugoslav government developed it into a giant resort hotel in the 1950s. As old homes were converted to hotel rooms, the novelty of the place—and its sterling location, surrounded by pebbly beaches and lush scenery—began to attract some seriously wealthy guests.

During this resort's heyday in the 1960s and 1970s, it ranked with Cannes or St-Tropez as *the* place to see or be seen on Europe's beaches. You could rent a room, a house, an entire block of houses, or even the entire peninsula. Anonymity was vigilantly protected, as the nicest "rooms" had their own private pools (away from public scrutiny), lockable gates, and security guards. Lured by Sveti Stefan's promise of privacy, celebrities, rock stars, royalty, and dignitaries famously engaged in

bidding wars to decide who'd be granted access to the best suites: Whoever put the most money in a sealed envelope and slipped it to the manager, won. (According to local legend, Sly Stallone's money talked.) Guests were pampered—indulged no matter how outrageous their requests. Sofia Loren, Kirk Douglas, Doris Day, and Claudia Schiffer are just a few of the big names who basked on Sveti Stefan's beaches.

In recent years, Sveti Stefan has seen a dramatic decline. Warfare in nearby places (such as Dubrovnik and Kosovo) kept away visitors, its cachet faded, and an inability to deal with wear and tear left the resort a bit rough around the edges. But the cavalry has arrived, in the form of Japanese investors. Sometime in 2007, Sveti Stefan is due to undergo an extensive renovation that promises to once again put it among the world's most exclusive, crème-de-la-crème resorts. (This means that the visiting procedure may be slightly different than described here, or the complex might even be closed to visitors.)

Visitors find that Sveti Stefan is exactly what it sounds like: a peninsular old-town-turned-hotel. Though totally lacking the charm of an actual town, and less impressive than it sounds, Sveti Stefan is undeniably cool. After parking in the lot near the causeway, cross over on foot, noticing that the beach on the left is public, while the one on the right is for hotel guests only (though the water looks the same to me). You'll pay a hefty €7 to enter the hotel (open to visitors May–Oct daily 10:00–19:00, closed Nov–April). Circle your way around the "hotel" clockwise. Stroll through the dead town, peeking through gates, hoping to spot a withered old celebrity who forgot to go home. Notice the varying degrees of privacy (each more expensive than the last): no fence, small fence, big fence. At the far end is the biggest and most famous "suite," where guests have an entire corner of the peninsula to themselves. At the top of the peninsula is a big Russian Orthodox church and a smaller Serbian Orthodox church—though both are little more than hotel decorations today. Continuing clockwise around the peninsula, find your way down to the big café terrace and look back to the mainland. You'll spot one of Tito's former vacation villas across the water, on its own little cove. If you're ready for a hike after leaving Sveti Stefan, walk over the small hill (on the left as you come across the causeway) to this villa for a look around (and more views back on Sveti Stefan).

Getting to Sveti Stefan: Sveti Stefan is just three miles (5 km) beyond Budva. Coming around the bay from Budva (following signs toward Bar), skip the first turnoff to the right that leads into Sveti Stefan. Instead, pass above the peninsula on the main road, watching for the pull-out on the right that offers great views over the resort. After snapping your photos, backtrack to the access road and head down to the town, twisting through a more recent commercial sprawl to the parking lot near the causeway (€5).

Returning to Dubrovnik from Sveti Stefan, figure two hours to the Croatian border (if you use the shortcut ferry across the Bay of Kotor—described on page 297), then another 45 minutes to Dubrovnik.

SLOVENIA

SLOVENIA

(Slovenija)

 Tiny, overlooked Slovenia is one of Europe's most unexpectedly charming destinations. At the intersection of the Slavic, German, and Italian worlds, Slovenia is an exciting mix of the best of each culture. Though it's just a quick trip away from the tourist throngs in Venice, Munich, Salzburg, and Vienna, Slovenia has stayed off the tourist track—a handy detour for in-the-know Back Door travelers.

Today, it seems strange to think that Slovenia was ever part of Yugoslavia. Both in the personality of its people and in its landscape, Slovenia feels more like Austria. Slovenes are more industrious, organized, and punctual than their fellow former Yugoslavs...yet still friendly, relaxed, and Mediterranean. Locals like the balance. Visitors expecting minefields and rusting Yugo factories are pleasantly surprised to find Slovenia's rolling countryside dotted instead with quaint alpine villages and the spires of miniature Baroque churches, with breathtaking, snowcapped peaks in the distance.

Only half as big as Switzerland, but remarkably diverse for its size, Slovenia can be easily appreciated on a brief visit. Travelers can hike on alpine trails in the morning and explore some of the world's best caves in the afternoon, before relaxing with a seafood dinner on the Adriatic.

Slovenia enjoys a powerhouse economy—the healthiest in Eastern Europe. Of the 10 new nations that joined the European Union in 2004, Slovenia was the only one rich enough to be a net donor (with a higher per-capita income than the average), and the only one already qualified to join the euro currency zone (it adopted the euro in January of 2007). Thanks to its long-standing ties to the West and can-do spirit, Slovenia already feels more Western than any other destination in this book.

The country has a funny way of making people fall in love with it. Slovenes are laid-back, easygoing, and fun. They won't win any world wars (they're too well-adjusted to even try)...but they're exactly the type of people you'd love to chat with over a cup of coffee. Many of today's American visitors are soldiers who participated in the conflict in nearby Bosnia and have good

Slovenia

memories of their vacations here in Slovenia. Now they're bringing their families back with them. They're not the only ones. One of your co-authors has decided that Slovenia is his hands-down favorite European country.

The Slovene language is as mellow as the people. While Slovenes use Serb and German curses in abundance, the worst they can say in their native tongue is, "May you be kicked by a horse." For "Darn it!" they say, "Three hundred hairy bears!"

Coming from such a small country, locals are proud of the few things that are distinctly Slovenian, such as the roofed hayrack. Foreigners think that Slovenes' fascination with these hayracks is strange... until they visit, and see them absolutely everywhere (especially in the northwest part of the country). Because of the frequent rainfall, the hayracks are covered by a

roof that allows the hay to dry thoroughly. The most traditional kind is the *toplar*, consisting of two hayracks connected by one big roof. It looks like a skinny barn with open, fenced sides. Hay hangs on the sides to dry; firewood, carts, tractors, and other farm implements sit on the ground inside; and dried hay is stored in the loft up above. But these wooden *toplarji* are firetraps, and a stray bolt of lighting can burn one down in a flash. So in recent

Slovenia Almanac

Official Name: Republika Slovenija, or simply Slovenija.

Snapshot History: After being dominated by Germans for centuries, Slovenian culture proudly emerged in the 19th century. After World War I, Slovenia merged with its neighbors to become Yugoslavia, then broke away and achieved independence for the first time ever in 1991.

Population: Slovenia's two million people (similar to Nevada) are 83 percent ethnic Slovenes who speak Slovene, plus a smattering of Serbs, Croats, and Muslim Bosniaks. The majority of the country is Catholic.

Latitude and Longitude: 46° N and 14° E (latitude similar to Lyon, France; Quebec, Canada; or Bismarck, North Dakota).

Area: At 7,800 square miles, it's about the size of New Jersey, but with a fourth the population.

Geography: Tiny Slovenia has three extremely different terrains and climates: the warm Mediterranean coastline (just 29 miles long—about one inch per inhabitant); the snow-capped, forested alpine mountains in the northwest (including 9,400-foot Mount Triglav); and the moderate-climate, central limestone plateau that includes Ljubljana and the cave-filled Karst region. If you look at a map of Slovenia and kind of squint, it really begins to look like a chicken running towards the east.

Biggest Cities: Nearly one in five Slovenes lives in the two biggest cities: Ljubljana (the capital, pop. 265,000) and Maribor (in the east, pop. 115,000). Half the country lives in rural villages.

Economy: With a Gross Domestic Product of $43 billion and a GDP per capita of nearly $21,500, Slovenia's economy is much stronger than the average Eastern European country. Slovenia's wealth comes largely from manufactured metal products (trucks and machinery) traded with a diverse group of partners.

Currency: Slovenia adopted the euro currency in January of 2007. €1 = about $1.20. For more, see "Euro Conversion" under "Practicalities" on page 316.

Government: The country is headed by Prime Minister Janez Janša, who heads up the leading vote-getting party in legislative elections. He governs along with the figurehead president, Janez Drnovšek. For health reasons, Drnovšek has adopted a vegan diet and lives in the countryside outside of Ljubljana, and has announced he will not run for re-election when his term is up in December 2007. (Drnovšek's predecessor, Milan Kučan, took a brave stand for independence as Yugoslavia was disintegrating.

Slovenia's relatively peaceful succession is credited largely to Kučan, who remains a popular figure.) The National Assembly of about 90 elected legislators (along with a second house of parliament, which has much less power) is not currently dominated by any single party. Despite the country's small size, it is divided into some 200 municipalities.

Flag: Three horizontal bands of white (top), blue, and red. A shield in the upper left shows Mount Triglav, with a wavy-line sea below and three stars above.

The Average Slovene: The average Slovene skis, in this largely alpine country, and is an avid fan of the oddly popular sport of team handball. He or she lives in a 250-square-foot apartment, earns $1,400 a month, watches 16 hours of TV a week (much of it in English with Slovene subtitles), and enjoys a drink-and-a-half of alcohol every day.

Notable Slovenes: A pair of prominent Ohio politicians—presidential candidate Dennis Kucinich and Senator George Voinovich, both from the Cleveland area—are each half-Slovene. Classical musicians might know composers Giuseppe Tartini and Hugo Wolf. Even if you haven't heard of architect Jože Plečnik yet, you'll hear his name a hundred times while you're in Slovenia—especially in Ljubljana (see page 342). Most famous of all is the illustrious Melania Knauss—a *GQ* cover girl who's also Mrs. Donald Trump.

If you follow alpine sports or team handball, you'll surely know some world-class athletes from Slovenia. NBA fans might recognize basketball players Primož Brezec and Bostjan Nachbar, as well as some lesser players. The athletic Slovenes—perhaps trying to compensate for the miniscule size of their country—have accomplished astonishing feats: Davo Karničar has skied down from the summits of some of the world's tallest mountains (including Everest, Kilimanjaro, and McKinley; www.davokarnicar.com). Benka Pulko became the first person ever to drive a motorcycle around the world (that is, all seven continents, including Antarctica; total trip: 118,000 miles in 2,000 days—also the longest solo motorcycle journey by a woman; www.benkapulko.com). Dušan Mravlje ran across all the continents (www.dusanmravlje.si). And ultra-marathon swimmer Martin Strel has swum the entire length of several major rivers, including the Danube (1,775 miles), the Mississippi (2,415 miles), and the Yangtze (3,915 miles). Next up: The Amazon (3,393 miles—follow along at www.martinstrel.com).

years, more farmers are moving to single hayracks *(enojni);* these are still roofed, but have posts made of concrete, rather than wood. You'll find postcards and miniature wooden models of both kinds of hayracks (a fun souvenir).

Another good (and uniquely Slovenian) memento is a creatively decorated front panel from a beehive *(panjske končnice).* Slovenia has a strong beekeeping tradition, and beekeepers once believed that painting the fronts of the hives made it easier for bees to find their way home. Replicas of these panels are available at gift shops all over the country. (For more on the panels and Slovenia's beekeeping heritage, see page 372.)

To really stretch your euros, try one of Slovenia's more than 200 farmhouse B&Bs, called "tourist farms" *(turistične kmetije).* Use the B&B as a home base to explore the entire country—remember, the farthest reaches of Slovenia are only a day trip away. You can get a comfortable, hotelesque double with a private bathroom— plus a traditional Slovenian dinner and a hearty breakfast—for as little as $40. Request a listing from the Slovenian Tourist Board (see page 9), or visit www.slovenia-tourism.si/touristfarms.

Slovenia is poised to become one of Eastern Europe's top destinations in the next few years. Now is the time to visit, while the locals are still friendly, the prices are still reasonable, and the lanes and trails are yours alone.

Practicalities

Euro Conversion: Slovenia has been using the euro currency only since January of 2007. This means that Slovenes are still getting used to the transition, and many still think in terms of the previous currency, the *tolar.* There were about 190 tolars in one dollar, and about 240 tolars in one euro. The prices in this book were researched before the euro was introduced, so you may find some variation from the actual prices.

Sunday Closures: In a typically mellow step to counteract Europe's race into the future, Slovenia recently passed a law mandating that virtually all retail shops in the country must be closed on Sunday. This means that buying a phone card or a sweater can become an ordeal on Sunday, even in Ljubljana—plan ahead. Fortunately, restaurants remain open, plus a select few grocery stores. In early 2007, this law was under review, and exceptions may soon be allowed in city centers.

Telephones: Insertable phone cards, sold at newsstands and kiosks everywhere, get you access to the modern public phones.

When calling locally, dial the seven-digit number. To make a long-distance call within the country, start with the area code (which begins with 0). To call a Slovenian number from abroad, dial the international access number (00 if calling from Europe,

011 from the United States or Canada) followed by 386 (Slovenia's country code), then the area code (without the initial 0) and the seven-digit number. To call out of Slovenia, dial 00, the country code of the country you're calling (see chart in appendix), the area code if applicable (may need to drop initial zero), and the local number.

Slovenian phone numbers beginning with 080 are toll-free; 090 and 089 denote expensive toll lines. Mobile phone numbers usually begin with 031, 041, 051, 040, or 070.

Slovenian History

Slovenia has a long and not very interesting history as part of various larger empires. Charlemagne's Franks conquered the tiny land in the eighth century, and, ever since, Slovenia has been a backwater of the Germanic world—first as a holding of the Holy Roman Empire, and later, the Hapsburg Empire. Slovenia often seems as much German as Slavic. But even as the capital, Ljubljana, was populated by Austrians (and called Laibach by its German-speaking residents), the Slovenian language and cultural traditions survived in the countryside.

Ljubljana rose to international prominence for half a decade (1809–1813) when Napoleon named it the capital of his "Illyrian Provinces," stretching from Austria's Tirol to Croatia's Dalmatian Coast. During this time, the long-suppressed Slovene language was used for the first time in schools and the government. Inspired by the patriotic poetry of France Prešeren, national pride surged.

The most interesting chapter in Slovenian history happened in the last century. Some of World War I's fiercest fighting occurred at the Soča (Isonzo) Front in northwest Slovenia—witnessed by young Ernest Hemingway, who drove an ambulance. After the war, from 1918 to 1991, Slovenia was Yugoslavia's smallest, northernmost, and most affluent republic. Concerned about Serbian strongman Slobodan Milošević's politics, Slovenia seceded in 1991. Because more than 90 percent of the people here were ethnic Slovenes, the break with Yugoslavia was simple and virtually uncontested. Its war for independence lasted just 10 days and claimed only a few dozen lives. (For more details, see the Understanding Yugoslavia chapter, page 436.)

After centuries of looking to the West, Slovenia became the first of the former Yugoslav republics to join the European Union in May 2004. The Slovenes are practical about this move, realizing it's essential for their survival as a tiny nation in a modern world. But there are trade-offs, and "Euroskeptics" are down on EU bureaucracy. As borders disappear, Slovenes are experiencing more crime. Local farming is threatened by EU standards. There are no more cheap bananas (because brown ones must be trashed),

Slo-what?-ia

"The only thing I know about Slovakia is what I learned firsthand from your foreign minister, who came to Texas."

—George W. Bush, to a Slovak journalist
(Bush had actually met with Dr. Janez Drnovšek, who was then Slovenia's prime minister)

Maybe it's understandable that many Americans confuse Slovenia with Slovakia. Both are small, mountainous countries that not too long ago were parts of bigger, better known, now defunct nations. But anyone who has visited Slovenia and Slovakia will set you straight—they feel worlds apart.

Slovenia, wedged between the Alps and the Adriatic, is a tidy, prosperous country with a strong economy. Until 1991, Slovenia was one of the six republics that made up Yugoslavia. Historically, Slovenia has had very strong ties with Germanic culture—so it feels German.

Slovakia—two countries away, to the northeast—is slightly bigger. Much of its territory is covered by the Carpathian Mountains, most notably the dramatic, jagged peaks of the High Tatras. In 1993, the Czechs and Slovaks peacefully chose to go their separate ways, so the nation of Czechoslovakia dissolved into the Czech Republic and the Slovak Republic (a.k.a. Slovakia). Slovakia was hit hard by the communists, and still suffers from a weak economy and high poverty levels. Slovakia was part of Hungary until the end of World War I, and feels Hungarian (especially the southern half of the country, where many Hungarians still live).

To make things even more confusing, there's also **Slavonia.** This is the thick, inland "panhandle" that makes up the northeast half of Croatia, along Slovenia's southeast border. Much of the warfare in Croatia's 1991–1995 war took place in Slavonia (including Vukovar; see Understanding Yugoslavia chapter).

I won't tell on you if you mix them up. But if you want to feel smarter than the president, do a little homework and get it right.

and "you can't sell a cucumber with more than a three-degree curve." Slovenian businesses are having difficulty competing with big German and Western firms. Before EU membership, only Slovenes could own Slovenian land. But now wealthy foreigners are buying property, driving up the cost of real estate.

As Slovenia became the first post-communist country to adopt the euro currency in January of 2007, locals worried about a

---

Pršut

In Slovenia and Croatia, *pršut* (purr-SHOOT) is one of the essential food groups. This air-cured ham (like Italian prosciutto) is soaked in salt and sometimes also smoked. Then it hangs in open-ended barns for up to a year and a half, to be dried and seasoned by the howling Bora wind. Each region produces a slightly different *pršut*. In Dalmatia, a layer of fat keeps the ham moist; in Istria, the fat is trimmed, and the *pršut* is dryer.

Since Slovenia joined the European Union, strict new standards have swept the land. Separate rooms must be used for the slaughter, preparation, and curing of the ham. While this seems fair enough for large producers, small family farms that want to produce just enough *pršut* for their own use—and maybe sell one or two ham hocks to neighbors—find they have to invest thousands of euros to be compliant.

---

potential increase in prices...even as they felt proud of their economic achievements. It seems that throughout all of the changes in the last two decades, Slovenes have maintained their sense of humor and easygoing attitude.

Slovenian Food

Slovenian cuisine has enjoyed influence from a wide variety of sources. Slovenes brag that their cuisine melds the best of Italian and German cooking—but they also embrace other international influences, especially French. Like Croatian food, Slovenian cuisine also features some pan-Balkan elements. The eggplant-and-red-bell-pepper condiment *ajvar* is popular here. For fast food, you'll find *burek*, *čevapčići*, and *ražnjići* (see "Balkan Flavors," page 39). Slovenia enjoys Italian-style fare, with a pizza or pasta restaurant on seemingly every corner. Hungarian food simmers in the northeast corner of the country (where many Magyars reside). But most of all, Slovenian food has a distinctly German vibe—including the "four S's": sausages, schnitzels, strudels, and sauerkraut.

Traditional Slovenian dishes are prepared with groats—a grainy mush made with buckwheat, barley, or corn. Buckwheat, which thrives in this climate, often appears on Slovenian menus. You'll also see plenty of *štruklji* (dumplings), which can be stuffed with cheese, meat, or vegetables. *Repa* is turnip prepared like sauerkraut. Among the hearty soups in Slovenia is *jota*—a staple for Karst peasants, made from *repa*, beans, and vegetables.

The cuisine of Slovenia's Karst region (the arid limestone plain south of Ljubljana) is notable. The small farms and wineries of this region have been inspired by Italy's "Slow Food" movement, and believe that cuisine is meant to be gradually appreciated, not rushed—making the Karst a destination for gourmet tours. Karstic cuisine is similar to France's nouvelle cuisine—several courses in small portions, with a focus on unusual combinations and preparations—but with an Italian flair. The Karst's tasty air-dried ham *(pršut),* available throughout the country, is worth seeking out (see sidebar). Istria (the peninsula just to the south of the Karst, in southern Slovenia and Croatia) produces truffles that, locals boast, are as good as those from Italy's Piedmont (see page 126).

Voda is water, and *kava* is coffee. Radenska, in the bottle with the three little hearts, is Slovenia's best-known brand of mineral water—good enough that the word *Radenska* is synonymous with bottled water all over Slovenia and throughout the former Yugoslavia.

Adventurous teetotalers should forego the Coke and sample Cockta, a Slovenian cola with an unusual flavor (which supposedly comes from berry, lemon, orange, and 11 herbs). Originally

called "Cockta-Cockta," the drink was introduced during the communist period, as an alternative to the difficult-to-get Coke. This local variation developed a loyal following...until the Iron Curtain fell, and the real Coke became readily available. Cockta sales plummeted. But in recent years—prodded by the slogan "The Taste of Your Youth"—nostalgic Slovenes are drinking Cockta once more. Aside from having happy childhood memories of sipping Cockta, Slovenes figure they can be proud that their little country produced a soft drink that rivals Coca-Cola.

To toast, say, *"Na ZDROW-yeh!"*—if you can't remember it, think of "Nice driving!" The premier Slovenian brand of *pivo* (beer) is Union (OO-nee-ohn), but you'll also see a lot of Laško, whose mascot is the Zlatorog (or "Golden Horn," a mythical chamois-like animal).

Slovenia produces some fine *vino* (wine). The Celts first made wine in Slovenia; the Romans improved the process and spread it throughout the country. Slovenia has three primary wine regions. Podravje, in the northeast, is dominated by *laški* and *renski riesling* and other top-quality wines. Posavje, in the southeast, produces both white and red wines, but is famous for the light, russet-colored *cviček* wine. Primorska, in the southwest, has a Mediterranean climate and produces mostly reds, including *teran,* made from *refošk* grapes.

Key Slovenian Phrases

English	Slovene	Pronounced
Hello. (formal)	*Dober dan.*	DOH-behr dahn
Hi. / Bye. (informal)	*Živjo.*	ZHEEV-yoh
Do you speak English?	*Ali govorite angleško?*	AH-lee goh-voh-REE-teh ahn-GLEHSH-koh
yes / no	*ja / ne*	yah / neh
Please. / You're welcome.	*Prosim.*	PROH-seem
Can I help you?	*Izvolite?*	eez-VOH-lee-teh
Thank you.	*Hvala.*	HVAH-lah
I'm sorry. / Excuse me.	*Oprostite.*	oh-proh-STEE-teh
Good.	*Dobro.*	DOH-broh
Goodbye.	*Na svidenje.*	nah SVEE-dehn-yeh
one / two	*ena / dve*	EH-nah / dveh
three / four	*tri / štiri*	tree / SHTEE-ree
five / six	*pet / šest*	peht / shehst
seven / eight	*sedem / osem*	SEH-dehm / OH-sehm
nine / ten	*devet / deset*	deh-VEHT / deh-SEHT
hundred	*sto*	stoh
thousand	*tisoč*	TEE-sohch
How much?	*Koliko?*	KOH-lee-koh
local currency	*tolar (SIT)*	TOH-lar
Where is...?	*Kje je...?*	kyeh yeh
...the toilet	*...vece*	VEHT-seh
men	*moški*	MOHSH-kee
women	*ženski*	ZHEHN-skee
water / coffee	*voda / kava*	VOH-dah / KAH-vah
beer / wine	*pivo / vino*	PEE-voh / VEE-noh
Cheers!	*Na zdravje!*	nah ZDROW-yeh
the bill	*račun*	rah-CHOON

For more Slovenian phrases, see page 459.

Slovenia's national dessert is *potica,* a rolled pastry with walnuts and sometimes also raisins. For more tasty treats, see the "Bled Desserts" sidebar on page 370. Locals claim that Ljubljana has the finest gelato outside of Italy—which, after all, is just an hour down the road.

Slovenian Language

Slovene is surprisingly different from languages spoken in the other former Yugoslav republics. While Serbian and Croatian are mutually intelligible, Slovene is gibberish to Serbs and Croats. Most Slovenes, on the other hand, know Serbo-Croatian—because, a generation ago, everybody in Yugoslavia had to learn it.

The tiny country of Slovenia borders Italy and Austria, with important historical and linguistic ties to both. For self-preservation, the Slovene population has always been forced to function in many different languages. All of these factors make Slovenes excellent linguists. Most young Slovenes speak effortless, flawless English—then admit that they've never set foot in the United States or Britain, but love watching American movies and TV shows (which are always subtitled, never dubbed).

Remember, *c* is pronounced "ts" (like "cats"). The letter *j* is pronounced as "y"—making "Ljubljana" easier to say than it looks (lyoob-lyee-AH-nah). Slovene only has one diacritical mark: the *strešica,* or "little roof." This makes *č* sound like "ch," *š* sound like "sh," and *ž* sound like "zh" (as in "measure").

The only trick: As in English, which syllable gets the emphasis is unpredictable. Slovenes use many of the same words as Croatians, but put the stress on an entirely different place.

LJUBLJANA

Slovenia's capital, Ljubljana (lyoob-lyee-AH-nah), with a lazy Old Town clustered around a castle-topped mountain, is often likened to Salzburg. It's an apt comparison—but only if you inject a healthy dose of breezy Adriatic culture, add a Slavic accent, and replace Mozart with local architect Jože Plečnik.

Ljubljana feels much smaller than its population of 265,000. While big-league museums are in short supply, the town itself is an idyllic place that sometimes feels too good to be true. Festivals fill the summer, and people enjoy a Sunday stroll any day of the week. Fashion boutiques and cafés jockey for control of the Old Town, while the leafy riverside promenade crawls with stylishly dressed students sipping *kava* and polishing their near-perfect English. Laid-back Ljubljana is the kind of place where graffiti and crumbling buildings seem elegantly atmospheric instead of shoddy.

Batted around by history, Ljubljana has seen cultural influences from all sides—most notably Prague, Vienna, and Venice. This has left the city a happy hodgepodge of cultures. Being the midpoint between the Slavic, Germanic, and Italian worlds gives Ljubljana a special spice.

People often ask me: What's the "next Prague"? And I have to answer Kraków. But Ljubljana is the *next* "next Prague."

Planning Your Time

Ljubljana deserves a full day. While there are few must-see sights, the city's biggest attraction is its ambience. You'll spend much of your time strolling the pleasant town center, exploring the many interesting squares and architectural gems, shopping the boutiques, and sipping coffee at sidewalk cafés along the river.

Here's the best plan for a low-impact sightseeing day: Begin on Prešeren Square, the heart of the city. Cross the Triple Bridge and wander through the riverside produce market before joining the town walking tour at 10:00 (daily May–Sept; less frequent off-season). After the tour, enjoy a lunch and some leisurely people-watching in the center before hiking or riding the tourist train up to the castle. After descending, wander along the Ljubljanica River to Jože Plečnik's National and University Library, French Revolution Square, and on to my favorite Ljubljana museum, the Jože Plečnik House (note this sight's limited hours, and plan accordingly: Tue–Thu 10:00–18:00, Sat 10:00–15:00, closed Sun–Mon and Fri). With more time, or if the Plečnik House is closed, stroll from Prešeren Square up Čopova street to Tivoli Park, where you can visit the Contemporary History Museum (daily until 18:00).

There are plenty of good day trips close to Ljubljana. With a second day, visit one of the two impressive caves (Škocjan or Postojna) and nearby sights in the Karst region south of the city (see The Karst chapter, page 419).

Ljubljana is dead and disappointing on Sundays (virtually all shops are closed and the produce market is quiet, but museums are generally open, a modest flea market stretches along the riverfront, and the TI's walking tour still runs). The city is also relatively quiet in August, when the students are on break and many locals head to beach resorts. They say that in August, even homeless people go to the coast.

ORIENTATION

(area code: 01)

Ljubljana—with narrow lanes, architecture that mingles the Old World and contemporary Europe, and cobbles upon cobbles of wonderful distractions—can be disorienting for a first-timer. But the charming central zone is compact, and with a little wandering, you'll quickly get the hang of it.

The Ljubljanica River—lined with cafés, restaurants, and a buzzing outdoor market—bisects the city, making a 90-degree turn around the base of a castle-topped mountain. Most sights are either on or just a short walk from the river. Visitors enjoy the distinctive bridges that span the Ljubljanica, including the landmark Triple Bridge (Tromostovje) and pillared Cobblers' Bridge (Čevljarski Most)—both designed by Jože Plečnik. Between them is a very plain wooden bridge dubbed "the Ugly Duckling." The center of Ljubljana is Prešeren Square, watched over by a big statue of Slovenia's national poet, France Prešeren.

The Story of Ljubljana

In ancient times, Ljubljana was on the trade route connecting the Mediterranean (just 60 miles away) to the Black Sea (toss a bottle off the bridge here, and it can float to the Danube and, eventually, all the way to Russia). Legend has it that Jason and his Argonauts founded Ljubljana when they stopped here for the winter on their way home with the Golden Fleece. The town was Romanized (and called Emona) before being over-run by Huns, only to be resettled later by Slavs.

In 1335, Ljubljana fell under the jurisdiction of the Hapsburg Emperors (who called it Laibach). After six centuries of Hapsburg rule, Ljubljana still feels Austrian—especially the abundant Austrian Baroque and Viennese Art Nouveau architecture—but with a Mediterranean flair.

Napoleon put Ljubljana on the map when he made it the capital of his Illyrian Provinces, a realm that stretched from the Danube to Dubrovnik, from Austria to Albania (for only four years, 1809–1813). For the first time, the Slovene language was taught in schools, awakening a newfound pride in Slovenian cultural heritage. People still look back fondly on this very brief era, which was the first (and probably only) time when Ljubljana rose to prominence on the world stage. After more than 600 years of being part of the Hapsburg Empire, Ljubljana has no "Hapsburg Square"...but they do have a "French Revolution Square."

In the mid-19th century, the railway connecting Vienna to the Adriatic (Trieste) was built through town—and Ljubljana boomed. But much of the city was destroyed by an earthquake in 1895. It was rebuilt in the Art Nouveau style so popular in Vienna, its capital at the time. A generation later, architect Jože Plečnik bathed the city in his distinctive, artsy-but-sensible, classical-meets-modern style.

In 1991, Ljubljana became the capital of one of Europe's youngest nations. Today the city is filled with university students, making it a very youthful-feeling town. Ljubljana has always felt free to be creative, and recent years—with unprecedented freedoms—have been no exception. This city is on the cutting edge when it comes to architecture, public art, and trendy pubs. But the scintillating avant-garde culture has soft edges—hip, but also non-threatening and user-friendly.

Ljubljana

1. Grand Hotel Union
2. To Union Hotel Garni
3. Hotel Emonec
4. Pri Mraku Guesthouse
5. To Hotel Park & Hostel Celica
6. Alibi Hostel
7. Sokol Restaurant
8. Gostilna As Rest. & Lounge
9. Ribca Restaurant
10. Zlata Ribica Rest.
11. Emonska Klet
12. Pizzeria Foculus
13. Ljubljanski Dvor Pizzeria
14. Paninoteka Sandwiches
15. To Nobel Burek & Olympia Burek
16. Restaurant Chez Eric & Bar Minimal
17. Čajna Hiša Teahouse
18. Zvezda Kavarna (Desserts)
19. To Krakovo Eateries
20. Kod & Kam Map Store
21. Dom Trgovina Souvenir Shops (2)
22. Funicular

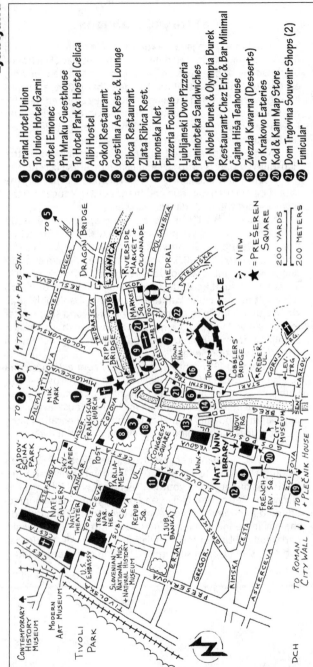

Ljubljana's Two Big Ps

Mind your Ps, and your visit to Ljubljana becomes more meaningful:

Jože Plečnik (YOH-zheh PLAYCH-neek, 1872–1957) is the architect who shaped Ljubljana, designing virtually all of the city's most important landmarks. For more information, see page 342.

France Prešeren (FRAHN-tseh preh-SHAY-rehn, 1800–1849) is Slovenia's greatest poet and the namesake of Ljubljana's main square. Some civic-minded candy shops—trying to imitate the success of Austria's "Mozart Ball" chocolates—have started marketing chocolate "Prešeren Balls."

I've organized the sights in this chapter based on which side of the river they're on: the east (castle) side of the river, where Ljubljana began, with more medieval charm; and the west (Prešeren Square) side of the river, which has a more Baroque/Art Nouveau feel and most of the urban sprawl. At the northern edge of the tourist's Ljubljana is the train station; at the southern edge is the garden district of Krakovo and the Jože Plečnik House.

Tourist Information

Ljubljana's helpful TI has an office at the **Triple Bridge** (across from Prešeren Square; daily June–Sept 8:00–21:00, Oct–May 8:00–19:00, Stritarjeva ulica, tel. 01/306-1215, www.ljubljana-tourism.si). Another TI branch is at the **train station** (daily June–Sept 8:00–22:00, Oct–May 10:00–19:00, Trg O.F. 6, tel. 01/433-9475). A third TI, at the upper, far end of the **market** at Krekov trg 10, also offers information about the rest of Slovenia and has several Internet terminals (daily June–Sept 8:00–21:00, Oct–May 8:00–19:00, tel. 01/306-4575).

At any TI, pick up a pile of free resources: the big city map, the Tourist Guide, the *Ljubljana A to Z* directory, the monthly *Where to?* events guide, *Ljubljana Life* magazine (with restaurant reviews), and a wide range of informative brochures. Skip the **Ljubljana City Card**, which includes access to public transportation and free entry or discounts at several city museums (€13/72 hrs).

Arrival in Ljubljana

By Train: Ljubljana's modern, user-friendly train station (Železniška Postaja) is on the north edge of the city center. Emerging from the passage up to track 1a, turn right to find the Tir Bar (**bike rental**—see "Getting Around Ljubljana," page 330) and the yellow arrivals hall, which has a **TI** (see above), an **ATM**, and helpful

English signs (arrivals hall open daily 5:00–22:00). Arrivals are *prihodi*, departures are *odhodi*, and track is *tir*.

The main square—and all of my recommended hotels—are within easy **walking** distance. It's a 10-minute stroll to get to the city center: Leave the arrivals hall to the right and walk a long block along the busy Trg Osvobodilne Fronte (or "Trg O.F." for short). At the post office (yellow *pošta* sign), cross Trg O.F., head straight down Miklošičeva, and you'll reach Prešeren Square.

Taxis, usually with unscrupulous cabbies, wait for you in front of the station. These mafia-type thugs are accustomed to charging you whatever they want without using the meter. The most likely scenario is that you'll pay a euro or two too much for the convenience of taking a taxi to your hotel—but *never* pay more than €5 total to any of my recommended hotels. For more on taxis—and how to avoid rip-off cabbies—see "Getting Around Ljubljana—By Taxi," page 330.

By Bus: Ljubljana's bus station (Autobusna Postaja) is a low-profile building (with ticket windows, Internet access, a bakery, and newsstands) in the middle of Trg O.F., right in front of the train station. To get into the center, see "By Train," above.

By Car: As you approach Ljubljana on the expressway, the toll road ends. Once you're on the ring road, you can take any exit, then follow bull's-eye signs for *Center*. Once you get into the city center, you'll begin to see directional signs to individual hotels. Ask your hotel about parking—most have some available, usually for a price. If you need to gas up your rental car before returning it, you'll find a huge gas station on Tivolska Cesta (just west of the train station). Otherwise, your options in the center are limited—it's better to look for a gas station on the expressway as you approach the city.

By Plane: See "Transportation Connections," page 352.

Helpful Hints

Pedestrian Safety: Ljubljana residents prefer to commute by bike. As a pedestrian, I've had many close calls with bikes that go whizzing by. Keep your eyes open and stay out of the designated bike lanes on the sidewalks (often marked in red).

Closed Days: Most Ljubljana museums (except the castle) are closed on Mondays. Remember that the highly recommended Jože Plečnik House is closed Sundays, Mondays, and Fridays—time your visit here carefully to coincide with a scheduled English tour (see page 342).

Markets: In addition to the regular **market** that sprawls along the riverfront (described under "Sights," page 335), a colorful **flea market** hops along the castle side of the Ljubljanica River (south of the TI) every Sunday 8:00–13:00.

Ljubljana Essentials

English	Slovene	Pronounced
Ljubljana Castle	Ljubljanski Grad	lyoob-lyee-AHN-skee grahd
Prešeren Square	Prešernov trg	preh-SHEHR-nohv turg
Congress Square	Kongresni Trg	kohn-GREHS-nee turg
French Revolution Square	Trg Francoske Revolucije	turg frant-SOH-skeh reh-voh-LOOT-see-yeh
Square of the Republic	Trg Republike	turg reh-POOB-lee-keh
Triple Bridge	Tromostovje	troh-moh-STOHV-yeh
Cobblers' Bridge	Čevljarski Most	chehv-LAR-skee mohst
Dragon Bridge	Zmajski Most	ZMAY-skee mohst
Jože Plečnik, the architect	Jože Plečnik	YOH-zheh PLAYCH-neek
France Prešeren, the poet	France Prešeren	FRAHN-tseh preh-SHAY-rehn

Money: Most banks are open Mon–Fri 9:00–12:00 & 14:00–17:00, Sat 9:00–12:00, closed Sun.

Internet Access: Most hotel lobbies have Internet access for guests. The TI at the upper end of the market has several terminals (see "Tourist Information," above). **Cyber Café Xplorer** is more expensive but has longer hours (Mon–Fri 10:00–22:00, Sat–Sun 14:00–22:00, across the river from the market at Petkovškovo nabrežje 23). The other TIs have free terminals allowing you to check your e-mail (but only Hotmail and Yahoo).

Post Office: The main post office *(pošta)* is in a beautiful yellow Art Nouveau building a block up Čopova from Prešeren Square, at the intersection with the busy Slovenska cesta (Mon–Fri 7:00–20:00, Sat 7:00–13:00, closed Sun).

Map Store: Kod & Kam has a huge selection of maps, English guidebooks, and other books about Slovenia (Mon–Fri 9:00–19:00, until 20:00 May–Aug, Sat 8:00–13:00, closed Sun, hiding at the bottom of French Revolution Square by the City Museum at Trg Francoske Revolucije 7, tel. 01/200-2732).

Architecture Guidebook: Ljubljana turns on architecture buffs. If you want to learn more about this city's quirky buildings, consider the excellent but expensive €30 *Architectural Guide to Ljubljana* (sold at TIs and many bookstores).

Laundry: Most hotels can do your laundry, but it's pricey. **Hostel Celica** serves as the town's self-serve launderette (€5/load, not very central at Metelkova 8, see page 348).

Car Rental: Figure about €50 per day (includes tax and insurance, no extra charge for drop-off elsewhere in Slovenia). **Europcar** (Mon–Fri 8:00–18:00, Sat 8:00–13:00 & 18:00–20:00, Sun 8:00–13:00, in City Hotel at Dalmatinova 15, tel. 01/234-9170, www.europcar.si) is slightly cheaper than **Avis** (Mon–Fri 7:00–19:00, Sat 7:00–13:00, Sun 8:00–12:00, Čufarjeva 2, tel. 01/430-8010, www.avis.si).

Best Views: Now that The Skyscraper is closed (see page 341), the best view in Ljubljana is from the castle tower. On sunny, blue-sky days, the colorful architecture on and near Prešeren Square pops, and you'll take photos like crazy along the river promenade.

Upcoming Events: Ljubljana will get lots of Europe-wide press in the coming years—in April of 2007, the city hosts the World Championship for ice hockey, and a year later, a Slovene will be elected to the European Union's rotating six-month presidency.

Getting Around Ljubljana

By Bus: Virtually all of Ljubljana's sights are easily accessible by foot, so public transportation probably isn't necessary. But just in case: A token, or *žeton*, for a bus trip costs €0.80 (buy at kiosk, bus station, or TI). If you pay on board, it's €1.25 and you need exact change. An all-day ticket costs €3.75 (sold only at bus station, TI, or LPP transit office).

By Taxi: There are several companies with different rates, but taxis usually start at about €1, and then charge €1 per kilometer. Additional "surcharges" (such as for luggage) are bogus—and are often tacked on as a surprise after you reach your destination. Crooked cabbies are a huge problem in Ljubljana (especially those hanging out at the train station and tourist attractions). A ride within the city center (such as from the station to a hotel) shouldn't cost more than €5. Your best strategy is to ask for an estimate up front. The cabbie will probably want to just take you for a flat price without using the meter. This is the easiest solution, but realize you'll probably wind up paying 10–20 percent more than you would if he used the meter. (If you're feeling stingy and feisty, try insisting on the meter.) Another common trick is to charge you the "Sunday and holidays" *(nedelja in počitnice)* rate even on weekdays. If you're suspicious, ask your cabbie to explain why he's chosen the tariff. You'll likely (but not definitely) avoid crooked cabbies if you

Ljubljana at a Glance

▲▲▲Jože Plečnik House Final digs of the famed hometown architect who shaped so much of Ljubljana, explained by an enthusiastic guide. **Hours:** English tours begin at the top of each hour Tue–Thu 10:00–18:00, Sat 10:00–15:00, last tour departs 1 hour before closing, closed Sun–Mon and Fri.

▲▲Riverside Market Lively market area in the Old Town with produce, clothing, souvenirs—even wild boar salami. **Hours:** Best in the morning, especially Sat; market hall open Mon–Sat 7:00–14:00, Thu–Fri until 16:00, closed Sun.

▲▲Ljubljana Castle Tower with good views and so-so 3-D film. **Hours:** Grounds open daily May–Sept 9:00–22:00, Oct–April 10:00–21:00; castle open daily May–Sept 9:00–21:00, Oct–April 10:00–18:00, film plays all day on the half-hour.

▲▲National and University Library Plečnik's pièce de résistance, with an intriguing facade, piles of books, and a bright reading room. **Hours:** Main stairwell open Mon–Fri 9:00–20:00, Sat 9:00–14:00, closed Sun; student reading room open to the public mid-July–mid-Aug Mon–Fri 14:00–20:00.

▲Dragon Bridge Distinctive Art Nouveau bridge adorned with the city's mascot. **Hours:** Always roaring.

▲Contemporary History Museum Baroque mansion in Tivoli Park, with exhibit highlighting Slovenia's last 100 years. **Hours:** Daily 10:00–18:00.

▲Architectural Museum of Ljubljana Castle with Plečnik exhibit on the edge of town. **Hours:** Mon–Fri 9:00–15:00, Sat 11:00–18:00, Sun 11:00–14:00.

call for a taxi. While this might sound intimidating, dispatchers generally speak a little English. Your hotel, restaurant, or maybe the TI (if they're not too busy) can call a cab for you. **Yellow Taxi** is more reputable than the norm (mobile 041-731-831); **Metro Taxi** is known for being inexpensive (mobile 041-240-200).

By Bike: Ljubljana is a cyclist's delight, with lots of well-marked bike lanes. Cheap bikes are rented all over the city, including at the market square TI, next to the big, pink Franciscan Church on Prešeren Square, and at the train station's Tir Bar (€1/2 hrs, €4.50/day, low prices subsidized by private companies that put ads on bikes).

TOURS

Most of Ljubljana's museums are disappointing; the town's ambience, architecture, and public art are its best attraction. To help you appreciate it all, taking a walking tour—either through the TI or by hiring your own local guide—is worth ▲▲.

Walking Tour—The TI organizes excellent two-hour guided town walks of Ljubljana in English, led by knowledgeable guides. From April through September, there are two tours daily: at 10:00 (a walking tour of the Old Town) and at 18:00 (a quick walking tour of the Old Town, followed by a trip by tourist train up to the castle). From October through March, the walking tour (no castle) goes only on Fridays, Saturdays, and Sundays at 11:00 (€7.50 for any of these tours, meet at Town Hall around corner from Triple Bridge TI).

Local Guide—Having an expert show you around his hometown for two hours for $45 has to be the best value in town. Ljubljana's hardworking guides lead tours on a wide variety of topics and can tailor their tour to your interests (figure €35/2 hrs, 50 percent more for same-day booking, contact TI for details, arrange at least 24 hours before). **Marijan Krišković,** who leads tours for me throughout Europe, is an outstanding guide (€35/2 hrs, mobile 040-222-739, kriskovic@yahoo.com).

Boat Cruise—Consider seeing the town from the Ljubljanica River. Various boat-cruise options (some guided, others with no guide or commentary) leave a block from the Triple Bridge TI (away from the market). Ask the TI about cruise times (€7.50 with a guide or €4 with no guide, sometimes combined with a short walking tour, weather permitting, few or no cruises Nov–March).

Bike Tour—The TI offers a bike tour of the city by request (€13, 2 hrs, 3-person minimum, arrange at least 24 hours ahead, get details at TI).

SELF-GUIDED SPIN-TOUR

Prešeren Square

The heart of Ljubljana is lively Prešeren Square (Prešernov trg). The city's meeting point is the large **statue of France Prešeren,** Slovenia's greatest poet, whose works include the lyrics to the Slovenian national anthem (and whose silhouette adorns Slovenia's €2 coin). The statue shows Prešeren, an important catalyst of 19th-century Slovenian nationalism, being inspired from overhead by the Muse. This statue provoked a scandal and outraged the bishop when it went up a hundred years ago—a naked woman sharing the square with a church! To ensure that nobody could be confused about the woman's intentions, she's conspicuously depicted with typical muse accessories: a laurel branch and a cloak.

Stand at the base of the statue to get oriented. Notice the bridge crossing the Ljubljanica River. This is one of Ljubljana's most important landmarks, Jože Plečnik's **Triple Bridge** (Tromostovje). The middle (widest) part of this bridge already existed, but Plečnik added the two side spans to more efficiently funnel the six streets of traffic on this side of the bridge to the one street on the other side. The bridge's Venetian vibe is intentional: Plečnik recognized that Ljubljana, located midway between Venice and then-capital Vienna, is itself a bridge between the Italian and Germanic worlds. Across the bridge is the TI, WCs, ATMs, market and cathedral (to the left), and the Town Hall (straight ahead).

Now turn 90 degrees to the right, and look down the first street after the riverbank. Find the pale woman in the picture frame on the second floor of the yellow house. This is **Julija**, the unrequited love of Prešeren's life. Tour guides spin romantic tales about how the couple met. But the truth is far less exciting: He was a teacher in her father's house when he was in his 30s and she was four. Later in life, she inspired him from afar—as she does now, from across the square—but they never got together. She may have been his muse, but when it came to marriage, she opted for wealth and status.

Ljubljana—especially the streets around this square—is an architecture-lover's paradise, starting with the **Hauptmann House,** to the right of Julija. This was the only building in town that survived the devastating 1895 earthquake. A few years later, the owner renovated it anyway in the then-trendy Viennese Art Nouveau style you see today. All that remains of the original is the Baroque balcony above the entrance.

Just to the right of the Hauptmann House is a car-sized **model** of the city center—helpful for orientation. The street next to it (with the McDonald's) is **Čopova,** once the route of Ljubljana's Sunday promenade. A century ago, locals would put on their Sunday best and stroll from here to Tivoli Park, listening to musicians and dropping into cafés along the way. Plečnik called it the "lifeline of the city," connecting the green lungs of the park to this urban center. Today, busy Slovenska avenue and railroad tracks cross the route, making the promenade less inviting. But in the last decade, Ljubljana has been trying to recapture its golden age, and some downtown streets are pedestrian-only on weekends once again. The new evening *paseo* thrives along the river between the Triple Bridge and Cobblers' Bridge.

Continue looking to the right, past the big, pink landmark Franciscan Church of St. Mary. To the right of the church, the street called **Miklošičeva cesta** connects Prešeren Square to the train station. When Ljubljana was rebuilding after the 1895 earthquake, town architects and designers envisioned this street as a showcase of its new, Vienna-inspired Art Nouveau image. Down the street and on the left is the prominent **Grand Hotel Union,** with a stately domed spire on the corner. When these buildings were designed, Prague was the cultural capital of the Slavic world. The new look of Ljubljana paid homage to "the golden city of a hundred spires" (and copied Prague's romantic image). There was actually a law for several years that corner buildings had to have these spires. Even the trees you'll see around town were part of the vision. When the architect Plečnik designed the Ljubljanica River embankments a generation later, he planted tall, pointy poplar trees and squat, rounded willows—imitating the spires and domes of Prague.

Across from the Grand Hotel Union (not visible from here, but worth a wander up the street) is a Secessionist building with classic red, blue, and white colors (for the Slovenian flag) next to the noisy, pink, zigzagged **Cooperative Bank.** The bank was designed by Ivan Vurnik, an ambitious Slovenian architect who wanted to invent a distinctive national style after World War I, when the Hapsburg Empire broke up and Eastern Europe's nations were proudly emerging for the first time.

On the near corner of Miklošičeva cesta, look for the characteristic glass awning of **Centromerkur**—the first big post-quake department store, today government-protected. At the top of the building is Mercury, god of commerce, watching over the square that has been Ljubljana's commercial heart since the city began. Since this was across the river from medieval Ljubljana (beyond the town's limits...and the long arm of its tax collector), this area was the best place to sell and buy goods. Today it's the heart of Ljubljana's boutique culture. Step into the Centromerkur store to admire the interior, which is exactly the same as when it was built. The old-fashioned layout isn't convenient for modern shoppers—no elevator, tight aisles—but no matter how much anyone complains, the management isn't allowed to change a thing.

Prešeren Square is the perfect springboard to explore the rest of Ljubljana. Now that you're oriented, visit some of the areas listed next.

SIGHTS

East of the River, Under the Castle

The castle side of the river is the city's most colorful and historic quarter, packed with Old World ambience.

▲▲**Riverside Market**—In Ljubljana's thriving Old Town market, big-city Slovenes enjoy buying directly from the producer. The market, worth an amble anytime, is best on Saturday mornings, when the townspeople take their time wandering the stalls. In this tiny capital of a tiny country, you may even see the president searching for the perfect melon.

Begin your walk through the market at the Triple Bridge (and TI). The riverside **colonnade** was designed by (who else?) Jože Plečnik. This first stretch—nearest the Triple Bridge—is good for souvenirs: woodcarvings, miniature painted frontboards from bee-hives, and lots of colorful candles (bubbly Marta will gladly paint a special message on your candle for no extra charge).

Farther in, the market is almost all local, and the colonnade is populated by butchers, bakers, fishermen, and lazy cafés. Peek down at the actual river and see how the architect wanted the town and river to connect. The lower arcade is a people zone, with easy access from the bridge, public WCs, inviting cafés, and a stinky fish market offering a wide variety. The restaurant just below, **Ribca,** serves fun fishy plates, beer, and coffee with great riverside seating (open Mon–Sat only until 16:00; see "Eating," page 349).

Walk along the colonnade with the river on your left. When you come to the first small market square on your right, notice the 10-foot-tall concrete **cone.** Plečnik wanted to make Ljubljana the "Athens of the North," and imagined a huge hilltop cone crowning the center of a national acropolis—a complex for government, museums, and culture. This ambitious plan never panned out, but part of Plečnik's Greek idea did: this marketplace, based on an ancient Greek *agora.* But the Slovenes haven't given up on Plečnik's vision: His never-completed giant cone adorns Slovenia's €0.10 coin (probably the only nonexistent building ever to grace a piece of currency).

At the top of this square, you'll find the 18th-century **cathedral** *(stolnica)* standing on the site of a 13th-century Romanesque church. The cathedral is dedicated to St. Nicholas, patron saint of the fishermen and boatmen who have long come to sell their catch at the market. Take a close look at the intricately decorated side door under the passageway. This remarkable door was created for Pope John Paul II's visit here in 1996. Buried deeply in the fecund soil of their ancient and pagan history, the nation's linden tree of life sprouts with the story of the Slovenes. Crusaders and Ottomans battle at the bottom. At the top is Pope John Paul II, the Pole who oversaw the fall of communism, and—below him—the man who will become Slovenia's first saint. Around back is a similar door, carved with images of the six 20th-century bishops of Ljubljana. The interior is stunning Italian Baroque.

The building at the end of this first market square is the seminary palace. In the basement is a **market hall,** with vendors selling cheeses, meats, dried fruits, and other goodies (Mon–Sat 7:00–14:00, Thu–Fri until 16:00, closed Sun). This place is worth a graze. Most merchants are happy to give you a free sample (point to what you want, and say *probat, prosim*—"a taste, please").

When you leave the market hall, continue downstream into the big **main market square,** packed with produce and clothing stands. (The colorful flower market hides behind the seminary palace/market hall.) These producers go out of their way to be old-fashioned—many of them still follow the tradition of pushing their veggies on wooden carts (called *cizas*) to the market from their garden patches in the suburbs. Once at their stalls, they handle their produce wearing special gloves—it's considered rude for customers to touch the fruits and vegetables before they're bought. Over time, shoppers develop friendships with their favorite producers. On busy days, you'll see a long line at one stand, while the other merchants stand bored. Your choice is simple: Get in line, or eat sub-par produce.

Look for the little **scales** in the wooden kiosks marked *Kontrola Tehtnica*—allowing buyers to immediately check whether the producer cheated them (not a common problem, but just in case). The Hapsburg days left locals with the old German saying, "Trust is good; control is better."

At the corner of this market square (toward Prešeren Square), you'll notice a big gap along the riverfront colonnade. This was to be the site of a huge, roofed **Butchers' Bridge** designed by Jože Plečnik, but the plans never materialized. Aware of Plečnik's newfound touristic currency, some town politicians have recently dusted off the old plans and proposed building the bridge after all these years. (If you look across the river, you'll see that the cornerstone was already put in place by an overzealous politician.) It's a controversial project, and anytime a new mayor is elected, the decision is reversed.

If you want a unique taste as you finish exploring the market, enter the colonnade near the very end and find the **Divjač'na Hubert** stand at #22, specializing in game. Ask charming Minka (it's her shop) for a *probat* (taste) of *div. prašič salama*—wild boar salami.

Just beyond the end of the market colonnade is the...

▲Dragon Bridge (Zmajski Most)—The dragon has been the symbol of Ljubljana for centuries, ever since Jason (of Argonauts

and Golden Fleece fame) supposedly slew one in a nearby swamp. While the dragon is the star of this very photogenic Art Nouveau bridge, it was officially dedicated to Hapsburg Emperor Franz Josef. (Tapping into the emp's vanity got new projects funded—vital as the city rebuilt after its devastating earthquake of 1895.) But the Franz Josef name never stuck; those dragons are just too darn memorable.

▲▲**Town Square (Mestni Trg)**—This square—just across the Triple Bridge and up the street from Prešeren Square—is home to the **Town Hall** (Rotovž), highlighted by its clock tower and pillared loggia. Step inside the Renaissance courtyard to see artifacts and a map of late-17th-century Ljubljana. Studying this map, notice how the river, hill, and wall worked together to fortify the town. Courtyards like this (but humbler) are hidden through the city. As rent in these old places is cheap, many such courtyards host funky and characteristic little businesses. Be sure to get off the main drag and poke into Ljubljana's nooks and crannies.

In the square is the **Fountain of Three Carolinian Rivers,** inspired in style and theme by Rome's many fountains. The figures with vases represent this region's three main rivers: Ljubljanica, Sava, and Krka. Over the centuries, the wild fluctuations in temperature that come with Ljubljana winters took its toll on this fountain—so recently, it's been undergoing a years-long restoration project (if it's missing, that's why).

In the early 19th century, Ljubljana consisted mainly of this single street, running along the base of Castle Hill (plus a small "New Town" across the river). Stretching south from here are two other "squares"—Stari trg (Old Square) and Gornji trg (Upper Square)—that have long since grown together into one big, atmospheric promenade lined with quaint shops and cafés (perfect for a stroll). Virtually every house along this drag has a story to tell, of a famous resident or infamous incident. As you walk, keep your eyes open for Ljubljana's mascot dragon—it's everywhere. At the end of the pedestrian zone (at Gornji trg), look uphill and notice the village charms of the oldest buildings in town (four medieval houses with rooflines slanted at the ends, different from the others on this street).

▲▲**Ljubljana Castle (Ljubljanski Grad)**—The castle above town offers enjoyable views of Ljubljana and the surrounding countryside. There has probably been a settlement on this site since prehistoric times, though the first castle here was Roman. The 12th-century

version was gradually added on to over the centuries, until it fell into disrepair in the 17th century. Today's castle was rebuilt in the 1940s, renovated in the 1970s, and is still technically unfinished (subject to ongoing additions). The castle houses a restaurant, a gift shop, temporary exhibition halls, and a Gothic chapel with Baroque paintings of the coat of arms of St. George (Ljubljana's patron saint, the dragon-slayer). Above the restaurant are two wedding halls—Ljubljana's most popular places to get married. While the castle and its attractions are ho-hum, the views are worth the climb.

It's free to enter the castle grounds (daily May–Sept 9:00–22:00, Oct–April 10:00–21:00, tel. 01/232-9994). Inside are two optional activities you have to pay for (€3.50 covers both, daily May–Sept 9:00–21:00, Oct–April 10:00–18:00): the **castle tower,** with 92 steps leading to one of the best views in town; and a 20-minute **3-D film** about the history of Ljubljana (touted as a "virtual museum," but barely worth your time; plays all day on the half-hour).

Tours of the castle in Slovene and English leave from the entry bridge daily June through mid–September at 10:00 and 16:00 (€5, tour lasts 60–90 min). The castle is also home to the Ljubljana Summer Festival, with **concerts** throughout the summer (tel. 01/426-4340, www.festival-lj.si).

Getting to the Castle: A brand-new **funicular** whisks visitors to the top in a jiff (€2, daily 10:00–21:00, catch it at Krekov trg, across the busy street from the market square TI). Another sweat-free route to the top is via the **tourist train** that leaves at the top of each hour (or more frequently, with demand) from Prešeren Square (€2.50, daily in summer 9:00–21:00, shorter hours off-season, doesn't run in snow or other bad weather). There are also two handy **trails** to the castle. The steeper-but-faster route begins near the Dragon Bridge (find Studentovska lane, just past the statue of Vodnik in the market). Slower but easier is Reber, just off Stari trg (Old Square), a few blocks south of the Town Hall (once on the trail, always bear left, then go right when you're just under the castle—follow signs).

West of the River, Beyond Prešeren Square

The Prešeren Square (west) side of the river is the heart of modern Ljubljana, and home to several prominent squares and fine museums. These sights are listed roughly in order from Prešeren Square, and can be linked to make an interesting walk.

• *Leave Prešeren Square in the direction the poet is looking, bear to your left (up Wolfova, by the picture of Julija), and walk a block to...*

Congress Square (Kongresni Trg)—This grassy, tree-lined square is ringed by some of Ljubljana's most important build-ings: the University headquarters, the Baroque Ursuline Church of the Holy Trinity, a classical mansion called the Kažina, and the Philharmonic Hall. At the top end of the square, by the entry to a pedestrian underpass, a Roman sarcophagus sits under a gilded statue of a **Roman citizen**—a replica of an artifact from 1,700 years ago, when this town was called Emona. The busy street above you has been the main trading route through town since ancient Roman times. This square hosts the big town events. Locals remember how, when President Clinton visited, tens of thousands packed the square. (When President George W. Bush came, almost nobody showed up.)

• *Take the underpass beneath busy Slovenska avenue (the town's main traffic thoroughfare) to the...*

▲Square of the Republic (Trg Republike)—This unusual square is essentially a parking lot ringed by an odd collection of buildings. While hardly quaint, the Square of the Republic gives you a good taste of a modern corner of Ljubljana. And it's historic—this is where Slovenia declared its independence in 1991.

The **twin office towers** (with the world's biggest digital watch, flashing the date, time, and temperature) were designed by Plečnik's protégé, Edvard Ravnikar. As harrowing as these seem, imagine if they had followed the original plans—twice as tall as they are now, and connected by a bridge, representing the gateway to Ljubljana. These buildings were originally designed as the Slovenian parliament—but the ambitious plans were scaled back when Tito didn't approve (since it would have made Slovenia's parliament bigger than the Yugoslav parliament in Belgrade). Instead, the **Slovenian Parliament** is across the square, in the strangely low-profile office building with the sculpted entryway. The carvings are in the Social Realist style, celebrating the noble Slovenian people conforming to communist ideals for the good of the entire society. Completing the square are a huge conference center (Cankarjev Dom, the white building behind the skyscrap-ers), a shopping mall, and some public art.

• *Just a block north (on Trg Narodni Herojev), you'll find the...*

Slovenian National Museum (Narodni Muzej Slovenije) and Slovenian Museum of Natural History (Prirodoslovni Muzej Slovenije)—These two museums share a single historic building facing a park behind the Parliament. While neither collection is particularly good, they're both worth considering if you have a special interest or if it's a rainy day (€3 for each museum, or €4.60

for both, some English descriptions, daily 10:00–18:00, Thu until 20:00, Muzejska 1, tel. 01/241-0940, www2.pms-lj.si).

The **National Museum** occupies the ground floor, featuring a lapidarium with carved-stone Roman monuments and exhibits on Egyptian mummies. (Temporary exhibits are also on this level.) Upstairs and to the right are more exhibits of the National Museum, loosely tracing Slovenian history with artifacts ranging from old armor and pottery to the museum's pride and joy, a fragment of a 45,000-year-old Neanderthal flute.

Upstairs and to the left is the **Natural History** exhibit, featuring the flora and fauna of Slovenia. You'll see partial skeletons of a mammoth and a cave bear, plenty of stuffed reptiles, fish, and birds, and an exhibit on "human fish" (*Proteus anguinus*—long, skinny, pale-pink salamanders).

Behind the museum is a pretty yellow chalet housing the **US Embassy**—my vote for quaintest embassy building in the world.

• *Just up the street are two decent but skippable art museums:*

National Gallery (Narodna Galerija)—This museum has three parts: European artists, Slovenian artists, and temporary exhibits. Find the work of Ivana Kobilca, a late-19th-century Slovenian Impressionist. Art-lovers enjoy her self-portrait in *Summer.* If you're going to Bled, you can get a sneak preview with Marko Pernhart's huge panorama of the Julian Alps (€4.25, free on Sat after 14:00, open Tue–Sun 10:00–18:00, closed Mon, enter through big glass box between two older buildings at Prešernova 24, tel. 01/241-5435, www.ng-slo.si).

Museum of Modern Art (Moderna Galerija Ljubljana)—This has a ho-hum permanent collection of modern and contemporary Slovenian artists, as well as temporary exhibits by both Slovenes and international artists (€4.25; July–Aug Tue–Sat 12:00–20:00, closed Mon; Sept–June Tue–Sat 10:00–18:00, closed Mon; Tomšičeva 14, tel. 01/241-6800, www.mg-lj.si).

• *Near the art museums, look for the...*

Serbian Orthodox Church—The church was built in 1936, soon after the Slovenes joined a political union with the Serbs. Wealthy Slovenia attracted its poorer neighbors from the south—so it built this church for that community. Since 1991, the Serb population continues to rise—people from the poorer parts of the former Yugoslavia, such as Serbia, are flocking to prosperous Slovenia. The church is decorated without a hint of the 20th century, mirroring a very conservative religion. You'll see Cyrillic script in this building, which feels closer to Moscow than to Rome. For more on the Orthodox faith, see the sidebar on page 234.

• *On the other side of the busy street is...*

Tivoli Park (Park Tivoli)—This huge park, just west of the center, is where Slovenes relax on summer weekends. The easiest access is by underpass from Cankarjeva cesta (between the National Gallery and the Museum of Modern Art). As you emerge, the Neoclassical pillars leading down the promenade clue you in that this part of the park was designed by Jože Plečnik.

• *Aside from taking a leisurely stroll, the best thing to do in the park is visit the...*

▲**Contemporary History Museum (Muzej Novejše Zgodovine)**—In a Baroque mansion (Cekinov Grad) in Tivoli Park, a well-done exhibit called "Slovenians in the 20th Century" traces the last hundred years of Slovenian history. Downstairs are temporary exhibits, and upstairs are several rooms using models, dioramas, and light-and-sound effects to creatively tell the story of one of Europe's youngest nations. It's a little difficult to fully appreciate, even with the English descriptions. But the creativity and the spunky spirit of the place are truly enjoyable. The most moving room has artifacts from the Slovenes' brave declaration of independence from a hostile Yugoslavia in 1991. The well-organized Slovenes had only to weather a 10-day skirmish to gain their autonomy. (It's chilling to think that bombers were en route to leveling this gorgeous city. The planes were called back at the last minute, because diplomatic negotiations were improving.) The free English brochure explains everything (€3.50, permanent exhibit free first Sun of the month, open daily 10:00–18:00, in Tivoli Park at Celovška cesta 23, tel. 01/300-9610, www.muzej-nz.si).

Getting There: The museum is a 20-minute walk from the center, best combined with a wander through Tivoli Park. The fastest approach: As you emerge from the Cankarjeva cesta underpass into the park, turn right and go straight ahead for five minutes, continue straight up the ramp, then turn left after the tennis courts and look for the big pink mansion.

• *On your way back to the center, consider stopping by...*

The Skyscraper (Nebotičnik)—This 1933 Art Deco building was the first skyscraper in Slovenia, for a time the tallest building in Central Europe, and one of the earliest European buildings that was clearly influenced by American architecture.

The Skyscraper has weathered an often-unlucky history. At the time it was constructed, Jože Plečnik was calling the shots when it came to Ljubljana architecture, so this building's designer had to get Plečnik's approval before he could build. Plečnik agreed, but didn't like the plan for 12 stories—so he asked to make it nine instead. After agreeing, the building's architect went ahead and built the last three stories anyway.

Ever since, say the locals, The Skyscraper has been cursed. The 12th-story observation deck—with Ljubljana's best view—had to close a few years back because it had become the most popular spot in the country for suicide attempts. Now it has been (ineffectively) retrofitted to try to prevent people from diving off. Two different restaurants on the top floor have come and gone over the last five years, and plans for a new one are constantly on-again, off-again (2 blocks from Prešeren Square at Štefanova ulica 1).

• *A few blocks south, near several Jože Plečnik sights (see below) at the river end of French Revolution Square, you'll find the...*

City Museum of Ljubljana (Mestni Muzej Ljubljana)—This highly conceptual museum, in the recently restored Auersperg Palace, offers a high-tech, in-depth look at the history of Ljubljana. The cellar features Roman ruins and medieval artifacts, while the second floor hosts a permanent exhibition about the culture, politics, and economy of Ljubljana. Rounding out the museum's collection is a wide range of special exhibitions, and a relaxing movie theater showing films about the city (free but will likely begin charging entry fee for permanent exhibit in 2007, well-described in English, Tue–Sun 10:00–18:00, closed Mon, Gosposka 15, tel. 01/241-2500, www.mm-lj.si).

Jože Plečnik's Architecture

Jože Plečnik is to Ljubljana what Antoni Gaudí is to Barcelona: a homegrown and amazingly prolific genius who shaped his town with a uniquely beautiful vision. And, as in Barcelona, Ljubljana has a way of turning people who couldn't care less about architecture into huge Plečnik fans. There's plenty to see. In addition to the top sights listed here, Plečnik designed the embankments along the Ljubljanica and Gradaščica Rivers in the Trnovo neighborhood; the rebuilt Roman wall along Mirje street, south of the center; the Church of St. Francis, with its classicist bell tower; St. Michael's Church on the Marsh; Orel Stadium; Žale Cemetery; and many more buildings throughout Slovenia.

▲▲▲Jože Plečnik House (Plečnikova Zbirka)—Ljubljana's favorite son lived here from 1921 until his death in 1957. He added on to an existing house, building a circular bedroom for himself and filling the place with bric-a-brac he designed, as well as artifacts, photos, and gifts from around the world that inspired him as he shaped Ljubljana.

Today the house is decorated exactly as it was the day Plečnik died, containing much of his equipment, models, and plans. There are very few barriers, so you are in direct contact with the world of the architect. Perhaps no other museum in Europe gives such an intimate portrait of an artist; you'll feel like Plečnik invited you over for dinner. It's still furnished with unique, Plečnik-designed furniture and ingenious, one-of-a-kind inventions. Whether or not you care about Plečnik, architecture, or design, you can't help but be tickled by this man's sheer creativity, and by the world he forged for himself to live in.

Jože Plečnik
(1872–1957)

There is probably no other single architect who has shaped one city as Jože Plečnik (YOH-zheh PLAYCH-neek) shaped Ljubljana. Everywhere you go, you

can see where he left his mark. While he may not yet register very high on the international Richter scale of important architects, the Slovenes' pride in this man's work is understandable.

Plečnik was born in Ljubljana and studied in Vienna under the Secessionist architect Otto Wagner.

His first commissions, done around the turn of the 20th century in Vienna, were pretty standard Art Nouveau stuff. Then Tomáš Masaryk, president of the new nation of Czechoslovakia, decided that the dull Hapsburg design of Prague Castle could use a new look to go with its new independence. But he didn't want an Austrian architect; it had to be a Slav. In 1921, Masaryk chose Jože Plečnik, who sprinkled the castle grounds with his distinctive touches. By now, Plečnik had perfected his simple, eye-pleasing style, which mixes modern and classical influences, with lots of columns and pyramids—simultaneously austere and playful.

By the time Plečnik finished in Prague, he had made a name for himself. His prime years were spent creating for the Kingdom of Yugoslavia (before the ideology-driven era of Tito). Plečnik returned home to Ljubljana and set to work redesigning the city, both as an architect and as an urban planner. He lived in a simple house behind the Trnovo Church (now a tourable museum—see page 342), and on his walk to work every day, he pondered ways to make the city even more livable. Wandering through town, notice how thoughtfully he incorporated people, nature, the Slovenian heritage, town vistas, and symbolism into his works—it's feng shui on a grand urban scale. Many of his ideas became reality; even more did not. (It's fun to imagine what this city would look like if Plečnik had always gotten his way.)

After his death in 1957, Plečnik was virtually forgotten by Slovenes and scholars alike. His many works in Ljubljana were taken for granted. But in 1986, an exposition about Plečnik at Paris' Pompidou Center jump-started interest in the architect. Within a few years Plečnik was back in vogue. Today, scholars hail him as a genius who was ahead of his time, while locals and tourists simply enjoy the beauty of his brilliant works. In 2007, Ljubljana celebrates the "Year of Plečnik," commemorating the 50th anniversary of the architect's death.

The house can be toured only with a guide, whose enthusiasm brings the place to life. Thirty-minute English tours begin at the top of each hour (€5, €2.50 guidebook, Tue–Thu 10:00–18:00, Sat 10:00–15:00, last tour departs 1 hour before closing, closed Fri and Sun–Mon, Karunova ulica 4, tel. 01/280-1600, www.aml.si, pz @aml.si, well-run by Ana and Natalija).

Getting There: The 15-minute stroll from the center is nearly as enjoyable as the house itself. First find your way to French Revolution Square, surrounded by other Plečnik works (described next). From the square's obelisk, walk down Emonska for about 10 minutes toward the twin-spired church. You'll pass (on the left) the delightful Krakovo district—a patch of green countryside in downtown Ljubljana. Many of the veggies you see in the riverside market come from these carefully tended gardens. (This mellow residential zone also has a pair of good restaurants—see "Eating.") When you reach the Gradaščica stream, head over the bridge (also designed by Plečnik) and go around the left side of the church to find the house.

▲▲**National and University Library (Narodna in Univerzitetna Knjižnica, or NUK)**—Just a block up from the river at Novi trg is Plečnik's masterpiece. The theme of the building is overcoming obstacles to attain knowledge. The facade has blocks of odd sizes and shapes, representing a complex numerological pattern that suggests barriers on the path to enlightenment. The sculpture on the river side is Moses—known for leading his people through 40 years of hardship to the Promised Land. On the right side  of the building, find the horse-head doorknobs—representing the winged horse Pegasus (grab hold, and he'll whisk you away to new levels of enlightenment). Step inside. The main staircase is dark and gloomy—modeled after an Egyptian tomb. But at the top, through the door marked *Velika Čitalnica*, is the bright, airy main reading room: the ultimate goal, a place of learning.

Aside from being a great work of architecture, the building also houses the most important library in Slovenia, with more than two million books (about one per Slovene). The library is supposed to receive a copy of each new book printed in the country. In a freaky bit of bad luck, this was the only building in town damaged in World War II, when a plane crashed into it. But the people didn't want to see their books go up in flames—so hundreds of locals formed a human chain, risking life and limb to get the books out of the burning building.

You can easily duck into the main stairwell (free, Mon–Fri 9:00–20:00, Sat 9:00–14:00, closed Sun). The quiet student reading room is officially open for visitors during very limited hours, when it's technically closed to students (mid-July–mid-Aug Mon–Fri 14:00–20:00). If you're not here during that one-month span, and you're really determined to see the room, you can stick close to a student going inside. To get out, follow another student—or push gently on the door (it usually opens easily).

The library is at the corner of Turjaška and Gosposka streets. To get here from Prešeren Square, simply follow the river south and turn right up Novi trg (the parking-lot square just after Cobblers' Bridge).

▲French Revolution Square (Trg Francoske Revolucije)— Many of Plečnik's finest works are on or near this square, just around the corner from the National and University Library (described earlier).

Plečnik designed the **obelisk** in the middle of the square to commemorate Napoleon's short-lived decision to make Ljubljana the capital of his Illyrian Provinces. It's rare to find anything honoring Napoleon outside of Paris, but he was good to Ljubljana. Under his rule, Slovenian culture flourished, schools were established, and roads and infrastructure were improved. The monument contains ashes of the unknown French soldiers who died in 1813, when the region went from French to Austrian control.

The Teutonic Knights of the Cross established the nearby **monastery** (Križanke, ivy-capped wall and gate, free entry) in 1230. The adaptation of these monastery buildings into the Ljubljana Summer Theatre was Plečnik's last major work (1950–1956).

▲Architectural Museum of Ljubljana (Arhitekturni Muzej Ljubljana)—If your visit to Ljubljana has infected you with Plečnik fever, you can trek out to this interesting museum, located in Fužine Castle on the outskirts of Ljubljana. The permanent exhibit features parts of the 1986 Paris exhibition that made Plečnik famous all over again. Downstairs is a display of plans and photos from Plečnik's earlier works in Vienna and Prague, and upstairs, you'll find an exhibit on his works in Slovenia, including some detailed plans and models for ambitious projects he never completed (like the huge, cone-shaped parliament building atop Castle Hill). It's worthwhile, but a bit of a hassle to reach—only true enthusiasts should pay a visit (€2.50, Mon–Fri 9:00–15:00, Sat 11:00–18:00, Sun 11:00–14:00, last entry 30 min before closing, Pot na Fužine 2, tel. 01/540-9798, www.aml.si). Take bus #20 from Congress Square (direction: Fužine) to the end of the line (about 20 min).

SHOPPING

Ljubljana, with its easygoing ambience and countless boutiques, is made to order for whiling away an afternoon shopping. It's also a fun place to stock up on souvenirs and gifts for the folks back home. Popular items include wood carvings (especially of the characteristic hayracks that dot the countryside), different flavors of schnapps (the kind with a whole pear inside—cultivated to actually grow right into the bottle—is the classiest), honey mead brandy (*medica*—sweet and smooth), and those adorable painted frontboard panels from beehives (see page 372).

The most atmospheric trinket-shopping is in the first stretch of the **market colonnade,** along the riverfront next to the Triple Bridge (see page 335). The best souvenir shop in town is **Dom Trgovina,** just a block across the Triple Bridge from Prešeren Square and facing the Town Hall (Mon–Fri 9:00–19:00, Sat 9:00–13:00, closed Sun, Mestni trg 24, tel. 01/241-8300). Another location is across from the TI on the main market square (Mon–Fri 8:00–19:00, Sat 8:00–13:00, closed Sun, Ciril-Metodov trg 5).

Another item you'll see sold all over the country are **Peko shoes.** Made in a town north of Ljubljana called Tržič, Pekos are similar to high-fashion Italian models, but much cheaper. The name is an abbreviation of its founder's name: Peter Kozina (www.peko.si).

SLEEPING

Ljubljana's accommodations scene, once abysmal, is steadily improving. Still, it's challenging. Only a handful of places are within convenient walking distance of the center, and most are overpriced. For the best value, stick with the Pri Mraku or the Emonec (though even these "good" options come with caveats). The most expensive hotels raise their prices even more during conventions (often Sept–Oct, and sometimes also June). To locate hotels and restaurants, see the map on page 326. The TI can give you a list of cheap private rooms *(sobe).*

$$$ Grand Hotel Union is as much an Art Nouveau landmark as a hotel. You'll pay dearly for its Old World elegance, hundred years of history, professional staff, big pool, and perfect location (right on Prešeren Square). The 194 plush "Executive" rooms are in the main building (Sb-€149–159, Db-€177, extra bed-€27, prices 20 percent higher during conventions, can be 20 percent cheaper during slow times—including most weekends and mid-July–mid-Aug, non-smoking floors, elevator, Internet access, parking-€12.50/day, Miklošičeva cesta 1, tel. 01/308-1270, fax 01/308-1015, www.gh-union.si, hotel.union@gh-union.si). Its 133 "Business" rooms next

---

Sleep Code

(€1 = about $1.20, country code: 386, area code: 01)
S = Single, **D** = Double/Twin, **T** = Triple, **Q** = Quad, **b** = bathroom.
Unless otherwise noted, credit cards are accepted, breakfast is
included, and the modest tourist tax (€1 per person, per night)
is not. Everyone speaks English.

    To help you easily sort through these listings, I've divided
the rooms into three categories based on the price for a standard double room with bath:

$$$ **Higher Priced**—Most rooms €110 or more.
  $$ **Moderately Priced**—Most rooms between €55–110.
   $ **Lower Priced**—Most rooms €55 or less.

---

door are a lesser value: less luxurious and almost as expensive (Sb-
€129–140, Db-€164, same price increases and deals as "Executive"
prices, non-smoking floors, elevator, parking and Internet access at
main hotel, Miklošičeva cesta 3, tel. 01/308-1170, fax 01/308-1914,
www.gh-union.si, hotel.business@gh-union.si).

    $$$ Union Hotel Garni, technically part of the Grand Hotel
Union up the street, has been threatening to change its name for
years. Whatever it's called, the hotel has 74 modern, business-class
rooms with less panache than the main Hotel Union, but it's nicely
situated between Prešeren Square and the train station (Sb-€107–
117, Db-€140, 20 percent less on weekends and mid-July–mid-Aug,
extra bed-€27, non-smoking rooms, elevator, parking garage-€11/
day, Miklošičeva cesta 9, tel. 01/308-4300, fax 01/230-1181, www
.astralhotel.net, hotel.garni@gh-union.si).

    $$ Hotel Emonec, a great value with some of the best-located
rooms in Ljubljana, hides between Prešeren and Congress squares.
Its 26 rooms—in two buildings across a courtyard from each
other—are simple and institutional, but the price is right, and you
can't be more central. If you're a light sleeper, be warned that the
hotel shares its courtyard with a disco that can be noisy into the
wee hours—request a quiet room (Sb-€57, small Db-€64, bigger
"standard" Db-€74, Tb-€89, Qb-€104, Internet access, free loaner
bikes for guests, Wolfova 12, tel. 01/200-1520, fax 01/200-1521,
www.hotel-emonec.com, hotelemonec@siol.net).

    $$ Pri Mraku Guesthouse has 36 comfortable, slightly worn
rooms in a very pleasant neighborhood near French Revolution
Square. Despite its quirks (a so-so breakfast, lots of stairs with no
elevator, occasionally frustrating staff), it's my sentimental favorite
in Ljubljana (Sb-€65–75, Db-€100, extra bed-€20, ground-floor
and top-floor rooms have air-con and cost about €10 more, prices

about 20 percent cheaper July–Aug, non-smoking floor, beautiful new breakfast room and restaurant, Rimska 4, tel. 01/421-9600, fax 01/421-9655, www.daj-dam.si, mrak@daj-dam.si).

$$ Hotel Park is housed in a soulless, 12-story communist apartment block in a dull neighborhood a 10-minute walk from Prešeren Square. Its 145 inexpensive rooms come in two types: "two-star" rooms, nicer than you'd expect from the exterior; and "one-star" rooms, with no TV, old linoleum, and worn furniture, but reasonably well-maintained. The staff is often aggravating, but the elevator, which seems possessed, always manages to top them. I'd consider this one a last resort (one-star rooms with toilet but no shower: S-€38, D-€46, 10 percent discount for hostel members for these rooms only; one-star rooms with full bathrooms: Sb-€50, Db-€64; two-star rooms: Sb-€55, Db-€71; elevator, Tabor 9, tel. 01/300-2500, fax 01/433-0546, www.hotelpark.si, hotel.park@siol.net).

$ Hostel Celica rents the cheapest beds in town in an unforgettable setting. This innovative hostel is funded by the city and run by a nonprofit student arts organization. Once an old military prison, this remarkable place has 20 cells *(celica)* converted into hostel rooms—each one unique, decorated by a different designer (tours of the hostel daily at 14:00, usually led by the architect on Tue and Wed). The top floor features more typical hostel rooms (each with its own bathroom, for 3–14 people). The building also houses an art gallery, tourist information, Internet access, self-serve laundry, restaurant, and shoes-off "Oriental café." The surrounding neighborhood—a bit run-down and remote, but safe—is gradually emerging as a happening nightlife zone; in fact, a nearby disco can make things noisy on weekends (all prices listed are per person—cell rooms: S-€45, D-€25, T-€20; bed in top-floor rooms with bathrooms: 3–5-bed room-€23, 6–7-bed dorm-€20, 14-bed dorm-€18; includes breakfast and sheets, no curfew, non-smoking, Metelkova 8, a dull 15-min walk to Prešeren Square, 10 min to the train station, tel. 01/230-9700, fax 01/230-9712, www.souhostel.si, info@souhostel.si).

$ Alibi Hostel, loosely run by Gorazd, offers 110 beds and a funkier, more laid-back scene than Celica. The rooms are colorful and scruffy, and it's ideally located right on Ljubljana's main riverfront-café drag. The imaginative graffiti murals—featuring a stripper with memorable piercings, and a certain cowboy president—are guaranteed to offend just about anyone over 30 (dorm bed-€20, D-€60, includes sheets and tax, breakfast-€2, €20 key deposit, free Internet access, Cankarjevo nabrežje 27, tel. 01/251-1244, www.alibi.si).

EATING

Though heavy, meat-and-starch Slovenian food is available, Ljubljana also offers an abundance of pizza and other Italian fare—not to mention plenty of other international options (French, Indian, Chinese, even Mexican). The main drag through the Old Town is lined with inviting eateries, their tables spilling out into the cobbled pedestrian street. Prešeren Square thrives in the evenings, often with live bands leading a celebration of life and youth. To locate these restaurants, see the map on page 326.

Mid-Range, Local-Style Cuisine

Very few places serve strictly Slovenian food; at this crossroads of cultures (and cuisines), Italian and French flavors are just as "local" as anything else. But the following eateries are as close to "real Slovenian cuisine" as you'll get.

Sokol, with brisk, traditionally clad waiters serving truly typical Slovenian food, is a reliable option (soup in a bread bowl is a favorite starter). The sprawling Slovenian-village interior is fun and woody, jaunty polka plays on the soundtrack, and the location is very central. All of this means it's deluged by tourists, so don't expect top quality or a good value (€6–18 main dishes, salads, veggie options, Mon–Sat 7:00–23:00, Sun 10:00–23:00, on castle side of Triple Bridge at Ciril-Metodov trg 18, tel. 01/439-6855).

Gostilna As Lounge, a cheaper side-restaurant of the fancy Gostilna As (described under "Upscale International" on page 351), features drinks, €5–7 salads and sandwiches, €6–8 pastas, and €8–13 main dishes. Dine in the cellar, or head outside to the lively, leafy courtyard (daily 12:00–24:00, Čopova ulica 5A, or enter courtyard with *As* sign near image of Julija, tel. 01/425-8822). The courtyard also has several other fun eateries—and, in the summer only, live music and a much-loved gelato stand.

Ribca ("Fish"), under the first stretch of market colonnade near the Triple Bridge, is your best bet for a relatively quick and cheap riverside lunch. Choose between the two menus: grilled and fried. There's a long list of straightforward fish dishes (€3–7.50 dishes, fish and chips for €6)—and, with the fragrant fish market right next door, you know it's fresh. If you just want to enjoy sitting along the river below the bustling market, this is also a fine spot for a coffee or beer (open Mon–Sat 7:00–16:00, closed Sun).

Zlata Ribica ("Golden Fish")—not to be confused with plain old Ribca, see above—is along the castle side of the embankment, with the best riverfront view in town. But the food lives up to the location: modern Slovenian cuisine (with an emphasis on fish, of course) and delicious pastas, especially gnocchi (€5–8 pastas, €10–18 main dishes, daily 8:00–24:00, between the Triple and Cobblers' Bridges at Cankarjevo nabrežje 5–7, tel. 01/241-2680).

Emonska Klet, a student favorite, is in a monastery cellar. With energetic music, Ljubljana's longest bar, and good food under a cavernous medieval vault, it's a fun dining experience. Their €5 lunch deals are a cheap way to fill the tank (€5–10 main dishes, good €5 pizzas, so-so salad bar, Mon–Sat 8:00–2:00 in the morning, Sun 12:00–24:00, go through underpass at the top of Congress Square—it's on your left as you emerge on the other side, Plečnikov trg 1, tel. 01/421-9300).

Pizzerias

Ljubljana has lots of great sit-down pizza places. Expect to pay €5–10 for an average-sized pie (wide variety of toppings).

Pizzeria Foculus, tucked in a boring alleyway a few blocks up from the river, has a loyal local following, a happening atmosphere, an innovative, leafy interior, Ljubljana's best pizza (over 50 types), and a good salad bar (Mon–Fri 10:00–24:00, Sat–Sun 12:00–24:00, just off French Revolution Square across the street from Plečnik's National and University Library at Gregorčičeva 3, tel. 01/251-5643).

Ljubljanski Dvor enjoys the most convenient location and most scenic setting...even if the pizza isn't quite as good. On a sunny summer day, the outdoor riverside terrace is unbeatable. The interior has a simple pizza parlor downstairs, with a more refined dining room upstairs (selling the same pizzas, plus €10–15 Italian main dishes; pizza parlor open daily 12:00–23:00, upstairs restaurant closed Sun, just 50 yards from Cobblers' Bridge at Dvorni trg 1, tel. 01/251-6555). For cheap take-away, go around back to the walk-up window on Congress Square (€1.50 slices to go, along with other light food, picnic in the park or down on the river—plenty of welcoming benches, Mon–Sat 9:00–24:00, closed Sun).

Fast and Cheap

Paninoteka serves €2–4 grilled sandwiches just over the Cobblers' Bridge from the castle (order at the display case or sit at a table to be waited on, Mon–Sat 8:00–1:00 in the morning, Sun 9:00–23:00, fine outdoor seating, Jurčičev trg 3, tel. 01/425-0055).

Burek, the typical Balkan snack (see "Balkan Flavors" sidebar on page 39), can be picked up at street stands around town. Most are open 24 hours and charge about €2 for a hearty portion. Try **Nobel Burek,** next to Miklošičeva cesta 30, or **Olympia Burek,** around the corner on Pražakova ulica (across the street from #1).

Upscale International

These fine restaurants—serving mostly French cuisine, with Slovenian and other influences—are good for a splurge. At either place, it's important to make a dinner reservation.

Gostilna As ("Ace"), tucked into a courtyard just off Prešeren Square, offers fish-lovers the best splurge in town. It's dressy, pricey, and pretentious (waiters recommend what's fresh, rather than what's on the menu). Everything is specially prepared each day and beautifully presented. Servings are small, so you're expected to take your time and order two or three courses (mostly fish and Italian, €8–15 starters, €15–25 main dishes, daily 12:00–24:00, enter courtyard with *As* sign near image of Julija at Čopova ulica 5A, tel. 01/425-8822). For cheaper food from the same kitchen, eat at their attached Gostilna As Lounge (see "Mid-Range, Local-Style Cuisine").

Restaurant Chez Eric is *the* place for French cuisine in town, with white-tablecloth-and-shiny-crystal formality. The dining rooms—some under medieval brick vaults, all under fancy chandeliers—are simply elegant, and the outdoor seating is on Ljubljana's most historic square (€15–20 main dishes, €25–30 fixed-price dinners, summer Mon–Sat 12:00–22:30, winter Mon–Sat 12:00–16:00 & 19:00–22:30, always closed Sun, a few doors down from Town Hall at Mestni trg 3, tel. 01/251-2839). Their three-course, fixed-price business lunch is a great deal (€9, served Mon–Fri).

In Krakovo

The Krakovo district—just south of the city center, where garden patches nearly outnumber simple homes—is a pleasant area to wander. It's also home to a pair of tasty restaurants. Consider combining a meal here with your trip to the Jože Plečnik House (which is just beyond Krakovo).

Harambaša is the closest thing to a ticket to Sarajevo. Serving Balkan grilled meats, this popular-with-students eatery has Turkish-flavored decor, old pictures, and cuisine reminiscent of the Bosnian capital. For a refresher on the meat dishes, see "Balkan Flavors" on page 39. The menu is limited, which makes ordering easy. Their handy €4.50 *pola-pola* combo-plate—with lotsa meat combined with chopped onions, *kajmak* (a buttery spread), and *lepinja* (bread)—makes for a simple but filling lunch. Vegetarians need not apply (€3–5 main dishes, Mon–Fri 10:00–22:00, Sat 12:00–22:00, Sun 12:00–18:00, Vrtna ulica 8).

Pri Škofu ("By the Bishop") is a laid-back, informal place with a focus on freshness and traditional Slovenian cuisine. There's no menu—the waiter tells you what's good today...and it is (€7 lunches, €20–25 dinners, Mon–Fri 8:00–24:00, Sat–Sun 12:00–24:00, reserve ahead, Rečna 8, tel. 01/426-4508).

Coffee, Tea, and Treats

Riverfront Cafés: Enjoying a coffee, beer, or ice-cream cone along the Ljubljanica River embankment (between the Triple and

Cobblers' bridges) is Ljubljana's single best experience. Tables spill out into the street, and some of the best-dressed, best-looking students on the planet happily fill them day and night. (A common question from first-time visitors to Ljubljana: "Doesn't anybody here have a job?") This is simply some
of the top people-watching in Europe. Rather than recommend a particular place (they're all about the same), I'll leave you to explore and find the spot with the breezy ambience you like best. When ordering, the easiest choice is a *bela kava*—"white coffee," basically a latte.

Tea House: If coffee's not your cup of tea, go a block inland to the teahouse **Čajna Hiša.** They have a shop (called "Cha") with over 100 varieties of tea, plus porcelain teapots and cups from all over (Mon–Fri 9:00–20:00, Sat 9:00–13:30, closed Sun). The café serves about 50 different types of tea, light food, and desserts (€1.50–3 sandwiches, €4–6 salads, Mon–Fri 9:00–23:00, Sat 9:00–15:00 & 18:00–23:00, closed Sun, on castle side of the river a few steps from Cobblers' Bridge at Stari trg 3, tel. 01/252-7010).

Treats: **Zvezda Kavarna,** a trendy, central place at the bottom of Congress Square, is a local favorite for cakes, pastries, and ice cream (Mon–Sat 7:00–23:00, Sun 10:00–20:00, a block up from Prešeren Square at Wolfova 14, tel. 01/421-9090).

Trendy Pub: **Bar Minimal** is my favorite of Ljubljana's many theme cafés and pubs. Stripped down to bare basics, this totally black-and-white place is as simple as it gets. While the cubical chairs aren't the most comfortable, the clever design here turns on architecture students (coffee and cocktails, €2–3 sandwiches, daily 8:00–1:00 in the morning, next to Town Hall at Mestni trg 4, tel. 01/426-0138).

Ice Cream: Ljubljana is known for its Italian gelato–style ice cream. You'll see fine options all along the Ljubljanica River embankment. Favorites include the courtyard garden at **Gostilna As** (summer only) and **Zvezda Kavarna** (both described above).

TRANSPORTATION CONNECTIONS

Note that in Slovene, Vienna is "Dunaj."

Getting to the Dalmatian Coast: If connecting directly to Croatia's Dalmatian Coast, you have three options: Train to

Zagreb (2.5 hrs), where you'll catch a cheap Croatia Air flight or a bus; take the long, once-daily train connection from Ljubljana to Split (8 hrs, requires a change in Zagreb); or, much slower, take the train to Rijeka, then cruise on a boat down the coast from there. (For specifics on flights, buses, and boats, see "Getting to the Dalmatian Coast," page 152.)

From Ljubljana by Train to: Lesce-Bled (roughly hourly, 1 hr—but bus is better), **Divača** (close to Škocjan caves and Lipica, hourly, 1.75 hrs), **Postojna** (roughly hourly, 1 hr), **Maribor** (roughly hourly, 1.75–3 hrs), **Ptuj** (3/day, 2.5 hrs—1 direct, the others transfer in Pragersko), **Zagreb** (8/day, 2.5 hrs), **Rijeka** (2–3/day direct, 2.5 hrs), **Split** (1/day, 8 hrs, transfer in Zagreb), **Vienna** (that's *Dunaj* in Slovene, 1/day direct, 6 hrs; otherwise 6/day, 7 hrs with transfer in Villach, Maribor, or Graz), **Venice** (2/day direct, 4 hrs), **Munich** (3/day direct, 7 hrs, including 1 night train; otherwise transfer in Salzburg), **Salzburg** (5/day direct, 5 hrs), **Budapest** (2/day direct, 7.75–8.5 hrs, no convenient night train). Train info: tel. 01/291-3332, www.slo-zeleznice.si.

By Bus to: Bled (Mon–Fri 11/day, Sat–Sun 8/day, 1.25 hrs, €6.25), **Divača** (close to Škocjan caves and Lipica, every 2 hrs, 1.5 hrs, €7.50), **Postojna** (at least hourly, 1 hr, €5.50), **Piran** (6/day, 2.5 hrs, €11.25), **Rovinj** (1/day in season). Bus info: tel. 090-4230 (toll number—about €0.75/min), www.ap-ljubljana.si. If you pick up the blue phone in the bus station, you'll be connected to a free information line.

Ljubljana's Airports

Slovenia's only airport, **Aerodrom Ljubljana** (airport code: LJU), is at Brnik, 14 miles north of the city—conveniently located about halfway between Ljubljana and Bled. Almost every flight is operated by Adria Airways (www.adria-airways.com), but recently, easyJet (www.easyjet.com), Wizz Air (www.wizzair.com), and Czech Airlines (www.csa.cz) have also entered the fray. Since Slovenia joined the EU, it's recommended you arrive two hours before your flight (tel. 04/206-1000, www.lju-airport.si). An airport bus connects Brnik with Ljubljana's bus station (€3.50 for 45-min ride, €4.25 for express 30-min bus, buses run hourly, some gaps in the schedule Sat–Sun—confirm in advance). There's also a private shuttle that does the same trip (€4.25, every 2 hrs, get details at TI or your hotel). Figure about €25 for a taxi to the airport.

Since Ljubljana's airport is the only one in the country and thus charges extremely high taxes and airport fees, many Slovenes prefer to fly out of Austria. The airport in **Klagenfurt** (airport code: KLU, also known as "Alpe-Adria Airport"), just over the Austrian border to the north, is subsidized by the local government to keep prices low and compete with Ljubljana's airport.

Especially if you're connecting to Bled, it's somewhat handy to reach (from Ljubljana or Bled, take the train to Villach, then to Klagenfurt's Annabichl station, which is a 5-min walk from the airport; total trip 3 hrs from Ljubljana, or 2 hrs from Bled; www .klagenfurt-airport.com). A taxi transfer to Bled runs a hefty €120 and takes about an hour (see "By Taxi" on page 360, in the "Getting Around Lake Bled (Literally)" section). Austrian Airlines (www.aua.com) flies from Klagenfurt, as do low-cost carriers such as Ryanair (www.ryanair.com) and Hapag-Lloyd Express (www. hlx.com).

All this competition is keeping Slovenia's national airline, Adria, on its toes. While it's generally pretty pricey to fly Adria, the airline often posts a few heavily discounted fares for each flight on its Web site (such as €110 one-way from Ljubljana to London or Paris; first come, first served, www.adria-airways.com).

LAKE BLED

Lake Bled—Slovenia's leading mountain resort—comes complete with a sweeping alpine panorama, a fairy-tale island, a cliff-hanging medieval castle, a lazy lakeside promenade, and the country's most sought-after desserts. While Bled has all the modern resort-town amenities, its most endearing qualities are its stunning setting, its natural romanticism, and its fun-loving wedding parties.

Since the Hapsburg days, Lake Bled (pronounced like it looks) has been *the* place where Slovenes wow visiting diplomats. Tito had one of his vacation homes here (today's Hotel Vila Bled), and more recent visitors have included Prince Charles, Madeleine Albright, and Laura Bush.

The lake's main town, also called Bled, has plenty of ways to idle away an afternoon. While the town itself is more functional than quaint, it offers postcard views of the lake and handy access to the region. Hike up to Bled Castle for intoxicating vistas. Make a wish and ring the bell at the island church. Wander the dreamy path around the lake. Then relax with some of Bled's famous desserts while you take in the view of Triglav, Slovenia's favorite mountain (see "Mount Triglav" sidebar on page 382). Bled quiets down at night—no nightlife beyond a handful of pubs—giving hikers and other holiday-makers a chance to recharge. Bled is also a great jumping-off point for a car trip through the Julian Alps (see next chapter).

Planning Your Time

Bled and its neighboring mountains deserve two days. With one day, spend it in and around Bled (or, to rush things, spend the morning in Bled and the afternoon day-tripping). With a second day and a car, drive through the Julian Alps using the self-guided tour in the next chapter. The circular route takes you up and over the stunning Vršič Pass, then down the scenic and historic Soča River Valley. Without a car, skip the second day, or spend it doing nearby day trips: Bus to Radovljica to see the bee museum, hike to Vintgar Gorge, or visit the more rustic Lake Bohinj (all described under "Near Lake Bled," at the end of this chapter).

ORIENTATION

(area code: 04)

The town of Bled is on the east end of 1.5-mile-long Lake Bled. The lakefront is lined with cafés and resort hotels. A 3.5-mile path meanders around the lake. Lake Bled is particularly peaceful, as no motorized boats are allowed.

The tourists' center of Bled is a cluster of big resort hotels, dominated by the giant, red Hotel Park (dubbed the "red can"). The busy street called **Ljubljanska cesta** leads out of Bled town towards Ljubljana and most other destinations. Just up from the lakefront, across Ljubljanska cesta from Hotel Park, is the modern **commercial center** (Trgovski Center Bled), with a travel agency, grocery store, ATM, shops, a smattering of lively cafés, and (on Thursday evenings) a traditional polka dance. Nicknamed "Gadhafi" by the people of Bled, the commercial center was designed for a Libyan city, but the deal fell through—so the frugal Slovenes built it here instead. Just up the road from the commercial center, you'll find the post office and library (with Internet access).

Bled's less-touristy Old Town is under the castle, surrounding the pointy spire of St. Martin's Church. There you'll find the bus station, several good restaurants, a few hotels, and more locals than tourists.

The mountains poking above the ridge at the far end of the lake are the Julian Alps, crowned by the three peaks of Mount Triglav. The big mountain behind the town of Bled is Stol ("Chair"), part of the Karavanke range that defines the Austrian border.

Tourist Information

Bled's helpful TI is in the long, lakefront building across from the big, red Hotel Park (as you face the lake, the TI is hiding around front at the far left end, by the casino). Pick up the map with updated prices and schedules and the free Bled guide booklet (if they have it in stock). Get advice on hikes and day trips. If you're doing any hiking, spring for a good regional map. The TI can't find you a room, but can give you a list of accommodations (open unpredictable hours, but usually July–Aug Mon–Sat 8:00–21:00,

Bled Town

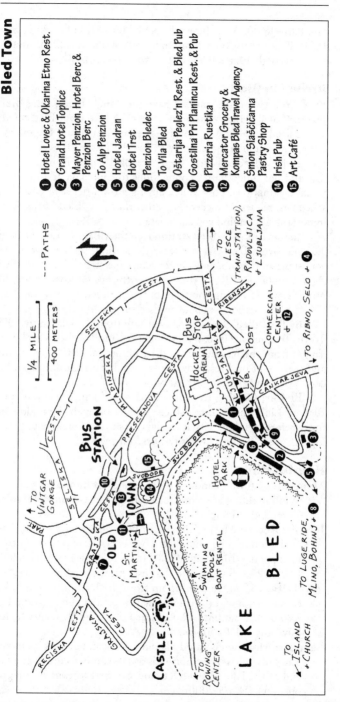

1 Hotel Lovec & Okarina Etno Rest.
2 Grand Hotel Toplice
3 Mayer Penzion, Hotel Berc & Penzion Berc
4 To Alp Penzion
5 Hotel Jadran
6 Hotel Trst
7 Penzion Bledec
8 To Vila Bled
9 Oštarija Peglez'n Rest. & Bled Pub
10 Gostilna Pri Planincu Rest. & Pub
11 Pizzeria Rustika
12 Mercator Grocery & Kompas Bled Travel Agency
13 Šmon Slaščičarna Pastry Shop
14 Irish Pub
15 Art Café

--- PATHS

¼ MILE
400 METERS

Sun 8:00–18:00; May–June and Sept Mon–Sat 8:00–19:00, Sun 11:00–17:00; Oct–April Mon–Sat 9:00–18:00, Sun 12:00–16:00; Cesta Svobode 10, tel. 04/574-1122, www.bled.si).

Arrival in Bled

By Train: Two train stations have the name "Bled." The **Bled Jezero** ("Bled Lake") station is across the lake from Bled town, and is used only by slow, tourist-oriented trains into the mountains. You're much more likely to use the **Lesce-Bled** station in the nearby village of Lesce. The Lesce-Bled station is on the main line and has much better connections to Ljubljana and international destinations. So if you're buying a train ticket or checking schedules, request "Lesce-Bled" rather than just "Bled." (This is so important, I'll remind you again later.)

The small **Lesce-Bled station** is in the village of Lesce, about 2.5 miles from Bled. As you leave the station, the nearest ATM is upstairs in the shopping center across the street. A taxi to Bled should run about €10, or you can take the bus (at least hourly, 10 min, €1.50). If taking the train out of Lesce-Bled, you can buy tickets at the station—nobody in Bled town sells tickets.

By Bus: Bled's bus station is just up from the lake in the Old Town. To reach the lake, walk straight downhill on Cesta Svobode. To get from the bus station to the commercial center, jog uphill and turn right on Prešernova cesta, which runs into Ljubljanska cesta just above the commercial center.

By Car: Coming from Ljubljana, you'll wind your way into Bled on Ljubljanska cesta, which rumbles through the middle of town before swinging left at the lake. Ask your hotel about parking. Also see "Route Tips for Drivers," on page 371.

Helpful Hints

Money: Bled town's handiest ATMs are **SKB Banka** (upstairs in round building at commercial center) and **Gorenjska Banka** (at far end of Hotel Park).

Internet Access: Most of the bigger hotels have access for guests in the lobby. The public library has fast access (free up to 1 hour per day, Mon 8:00–19:00, Tue–Fri 14:00–19:00, Sat 8:00–12:00, closed Sun, next to the post office on Ljubljanska cesta).

Post Office: If you're coming up from the lake on Ljubljanska cesta, it's just past the commercial center and library (Mon–Fri 7:00–19:00, Sat until 12:00, closed Sun, slightly longer hours July–Aug, tel. 04/575-0200).

Laundry: Most hotels can do laundry for you, but it's expensive. The only self-service option is at the campground at the far end of the lake (April–Oct only, call first to confirm they're open, tel. 04/575-2000).

Bled and the Julian Alps Essentials

English	Slovene	Pronounced
Slovenia's Biggest Mountain	Triglav	TREE-glahv
Lake Bled	Blejsko Jezero	BLAY-skoh YAY-zay-roh
The Island	Otok	OH-tohk
Bled Castle	Blejski Grad	BLAY-skee grahd
Town near Bled with Train Station	Lesce	lest-SEH
Town with Bee Museum	Radovljica	rah-DOH-vleet-suh
Gorge near Bled	Vintgar	VEENT-gar
Rustic Lake near Bled	Bohinj	BOH-heen
Scenic High-Mountain Pass	Vršič	vur-SHEECH
Historic River Valley	Soča	SOH-chah

Car Rental: The Julian Alps are ideal by car. Several big chains rent cars in Bled—figure €50–60 per day, including tax, insurance, and unlimited mileage (no extra charge for drop-off elsewhere in Slovenia). **Europcar** (in Hotel Krim, tel. 04/574-1155) usually has better rates than **Avis** (in the commercial center, tel. 04/576-8700).

Travel Agency: Kompas Bled Travel Agency, in the commercial center, exchanges money, rents bikes, sells books and maps, offers a room-booking service (including many cheap rooms in private homes—though most are away from the lake), and sells various tours around the region (Mon–Sat 8:00–19:00, Sun 8:00–12:00 & 16:00–19:00, June–Sept until 20:00, Ljubljanska cesta 4, tel. 04/572-7500, www.kompas-bled.si, kompas.bled@siol.net).

Getting Around Lake Bled (Literally)

By Bike: You can rent a mountain bike at Kompas Bled Travel Agency (above)—great for biking around the lake (€3/hr, €6.50/3 hrs, €8/half-day, €11/day). For a longer pedal, a brand-new bike path to the nearby village of Radovljica (and its bee museum) should be open in 2007 (about 4 miles each way, get details at Kompas or the TI).

By Horse and Buggy: Buggies called *fijakers* are the romantic, expensive, and easy way to get around the lake. You'll see them along the lakefront between Hotel Park and the castle (around the lake-€25, one-way up to castle-€25, round-trip to castle with 30-min wait time-€35, mobile 041-710-970).

By Tourist Train: A touristy little train makes a circuit around the lake every 40 minutes in summer (€3, daily 9:00–18:00, shorter hours off-season, weather-dependent, tel. 041-608-689).

By Tourist Bus: A handy shuttle bus passes through Bled once daily in summer. It leaves the bus station at 10:00, stops at a few hotels (including Grand Hotel Toplice), then goes up to the castle and on to the Vintgar Gorge entrance (€2.50, mid-June–Sept only, confirm schedule at TI or bus station).

By Taxi: Bled Tours, run by friendly, English-speaking Sandi Demšar, can take you to various destinations near Bled (€10 to Lesce-Bled train station, €11 to Radovljica, €45 to Ljubljana airport, €120 to Klagenfurt airport in Austria, mobile 031-205-611, info@bledtours.si). Your hotel can also call a taxi for you.

By Boat: For information on boat rental, see "Boating," page 364. For details on the characteristic *pletna* boats, see "Getting to the Island," page 362.

By Plane: If you have perfect weather and deep pockets, there's no more thrilling way to experience Slovenia's high-mountain scenery than from a small propeller plane soaring over the peaks. Flights depart from a grass airstrip near the village of Lesce, a 10-minute drive or taxi ride from Bled. Expensive...but unforgettable (€70 for 15-min hop over Lake Bled only, €120 for 30-min flight that also buzzes Lake Bohinj, €170 for deluxe 45-min version around the summit of Triglav, arrange at least a day in advance, tel. 04/532-0100, www.alc-lesce.si, info@alc-lesce.si).

TOURS

Local Guides—**Tina Hiti** and **Sašo Golub** are fine guides who enjoy sharing the town and region they love with American visitors. Hiring one of them can add immeasurably to your enjoyment and understanding of Bled (€30/2 hrs, arrange several days in advance; Tina: mobile 040-166-554, tinahiti@gmail.com; Sašo: mobile 040-524-774, sasogolub@gmail.com). Either one can drive you in their car on a long day tour into the Julian Alps—or anywhere in Slovenia—for €120. (This price is for two people; it's more expensive for three or more people, since they have to rent a van.) I've spent great days with both Tina and Sašo, and was thankful they were behind the wheel.

Excursions—To hit several far-flung day-trip destinations in one go, you could take a package tour from Bled. Destinations range from Ljubljana and the Karst region to the Austrian or Italian Alps to Venice (yes, Venice—it's doable as a long day trip from here). An all-day Julian Alps trip to the Vršič Pass and Soča Valley runs about €35 (sold by various agencies, including Kompas Bled—see page 359). This tour is handy, but two people can rent a car for the day for less and do it at their own pace using the self-guided driving tour in the next chapter. There's also a scenic "Old-Timer Train" tour connecting some of the alpine sights, but it runs infrequently (ask at Kompas Bled for details).

SIGHTS AND ACTIVITIES

Lake Bled

Bled doesn't have many "sights" (except the dull castle museum, described later). But there are plenty of rewarding and pleasant activities.

▲▲**The Island (Otok)**—Bled's little island—capped by a super-cute church—nudges the lake's quaintness level over the top. Locals call it simply "The Island" *(Otok)*. While it's pretty to look at from afar, it's also fun to visit.

The island has long been a sacred site with a romantic twist. On summer Saturdays, a steady procession of brides and grooms,

cheered on by their entourages, head for the island. Ninety-eight steps lead from the island's dock up to the Church of the Assumption on top. It's tradition for the groom to carry—or try to carry—his bride up these steps. About four out of five are successful (proving themselves "fit for marriage"). During the communist era, the church was closed, and weddings were outlawed here. But the tradition reemerged—illegally—even before the regime ended, with a clandestine ceremony in 1989.

An eighth-century Slavic pagan temple dedicated to the goddess of love and fertility once stood here; the current Baroque version (with Venetian flair—the bell tower separate from the main church) is the fifth to occupy this spot. As you enter the church (€3), look straight ahead to the painting of Mary on the wall. She doesn't quite look like other Madonnas, because she has the face of Maria Theresa—the Hapsburg empress who controlled Slovenia at the time. The Madonna at the altar in front of the church is similarly pudgy...er, imperial.

Find the rope for the church bell, hanging in the middle of the aisle just before the altar. A local superstition claims that if you ring this bell three times, your dreams will come true. Worth a try.

If you're waiting for a herd of tourists to ring out their wishes, pass the time looking around the front of the church. When the church was being renovated in the 1970s, workers dug up several medieval graves (you can see one through the glass under the bell rope). They also discovered Gothic frescoes on either side of the altar, including, above the door on the right, an unusual ecclesiastical theme: the *bris* (Jewish circumcision ritual) of Christ.

A café (with a WC) and souvenir shop (with an exhibit of nativity scenes) are near the church at the top of the steps.

To descend by a different route, walk down the trail behind the church, then follow the path around the island's perimeter back to where your *pletna* boat awaits.

Getting to the Island: The most romantic route to the island is to cruise on one of the distinctive ***pletna*** boats (€10 per person round-trip, includes 30-min wait time at the island; catch one at several spots around the lake—most convenient from in front of Grand Hotel Toplice or just below Hotel Park; generally run from dawn until around 20:00 in summer, stop earlier off-season, replaced by enclosed electric boats in winter—unless the lake freezes, mobile 031-316-575). For more on these characteristic little vessels, see the "*Pletna* Boats" sidebar. You can also **rent your own boat** to row to the island (see "Boating"). It's even possible to **swim** to the island, especially from the end of the lake nearest the island (see "Swimming")—but you're not allowed into the church in your swimsuit.

▲▲Walk Around the Lake—Strolling the 3.5 miles around the lake is enjoyable, peaceful, and scenic. At a leisurely pace, it takes about an hour and a half...not counting stops to snap photos of the ever-changing view. On the way, you'll pass some great villas, mostly from the beginning of the 19th century. The most significant one was a former residence of Marshal Tito—today the Hotel Vila Bled, a great place to stop for a coffee and pretend Tito invited you over for a visit (see "Tito's Vila Bled," next). For the more adventurous, hiking paths lead up into the hills surrounding the lake (ask TI for details and maps; or hike to Vintgar Gorge, described on page 374).

Tito's Vila Bled—Before World War II, this villa on Lake Bled was the summer residence for the Yugoslav royal family. When Tito ran Yugoslavia, he entertained international guests here (big shots from the communist and non-aligned world, from Indira Gandhi to Khrushchev to Kim Il Sung). Since 1984, it's been a classy hotel and restaurant, offering guests grand Lake Bled views and James Bond ambience. For some, this is a nostalgic opportunity to send e-mail from Tito's desk, sip tea in his lounge, and gawk at his Social Realist wall murals.

The villa is a 20-minute lakeside walk from the town of Bled at Cesta Svobode 26 (it's the big, white villa with the long staircase

Pletna Boats

The *pletna* is an important symbol of Lake Bled. These boats provide a pleasant way to reach the island and carry on an important tradition dating back for generations. In the 17th century, Hapsburg Empress Maria Theresa granted the villagers from Mlino—the little town along the lakefront just beyond Bled—special permission to ferry visitors to the  island. (Since Mlino had very limited access to farmland, they needed another source of income.) Mlino residents built their *pletnas* by hand, using a special design passed down from father to son for centuries—like the equally iconic gondolas of Venice. Eventually, this imperial decree and family tradition evolved into a modern union of *pletna* oarsmen, which continues to this day.

Today *pletna* boats are still hand-built according to that same centuries-old design. There's no keel, so the skilled oarsmen work hard to steer the flat-bottomed boat with each stroke—boats piloted by an inexperienced oarsman can slide around a bit on very windy days. There are 21 official *pletnas* on Lake Bled, all belonging to the same union. The gondoliers dump all of their earnings into one fund, give a cut to the tourist board, and divide the rest evenly among themselves. Occasionally a new family tries to break into the cartel, underselling his competitors with a "black market" boat that looks the same as the official ones. While some see this as a violation of a centuries-old tradition, others view it as good old capitalism. Either way, competition is fierce.

at the southern end of lake, near the village of Mlino). You can also ask your *pletna* gondolier to drop you off here after visiting the island. Those hiking around the lake will pass the gate leading through Tito's garden to the restaurant, where they are welcome to drop in for a meal, the salad bar, or just a cup of coffee. Tito fans might want to splurge for an overnight here (basic Db–€190, tel. 04/579-1500, www.vila-bled.com).

▲**Bled Castle (Blejski Grad)**—Bled's cliff-hanging castle, dating in one form or another from a thousand years ago, was the seat of the Austrian Bishops of Brixen, who controlled Bled in the Middle Ages. Your castle admission includes a modest castle museum (with a couple of interesting videos, creaky rooms, and good English descriptions), a small theater continuously showing a fun 20-minute movie about Bled (under the restaurant), and a rampart walk with an "herbal gallery" (gift shop of traditional-meets-modern herbal brandies, cosmetics, and perfumes). These attractions are less than thrilling, but the sweeping views over Lake Bled and the surrounding mountainscapes justify the trip (€6, daily May–Oct 8:00–20:00, Nov–April 9:00–17:00, tel. 04/578-0525).

In addition, the castle is home to a pair of interesting, old-fashioned shops: You can visit a working replica of a **printing press** from Gutenberg's time, and press your own custom-made souvenir certificate for €5 (in the castle's oldest tower—from the 11th century). Or, at the **wine cellar** *(grajska klet de Adami)*, bottle and cork your own bottle of wine (€5–17). These attractions are manned by a pair of gregarious guys, one dressed as a medieval printer and the other as a monk. Both men happen to be named Andrej (they switch costumes sometimes for a change of pace). Both shops are generally open daily 10:00–18:00 (until 16:00 Dec–Feb; if one of the shops is closed, the other should be open).

Eating at the Castle: The **restaurant** at the castle is fairly expensive, but your restaurant reservation gets you into the castle grounds for free (international cuisine and some local specialties, €8–20 main dishes, tel. 04/579-4424). Better yet, there's a scenic little **picnic spot** in the castle courtyard, with fine tables and views (buy sandwiches at the Mercator grocery store in the commercial center before you ascend—see listing under "Eating").

Getting to the Castle: Most people **hike** up the steep hill (20 min). The handiest trails are behind big St. Martin's Church: Walk past the front door of the church with the lake at your back, and look left after the first set of houses for the *Grad* signs marking the steepest route up (on this trail, bear uphill—or right—at the benches); or, for a longer but less steep route, continue past the church on the same street about five minutes, bearing uphill (left) at the fork, and find the *Grad* sign just after the Pension Bledec hostel on the left. Once you're on this second trail, don't take the sharp-left uphill turn at the fork (instead, continue straight up, around the back of the hill). Instead of hiking, you can take the 10:00 **tourist bus** (see "Getting Around Lake Bled," page 359), your **rental car,** a **taxi** (around €6), or—if you're wealthy and romantic—a **horse and buggy** (€25, €10 extra to wait 30 min and bring you back down, see "Getting Around Lake Bled").

Boating—Bled is the rowing center of Slovenia. Town officials even lengthened the lake a bit so it would perfectly fit the standard two-kilometer laps, with 100 meters more for the turn. Three world championships have been held here. The town has produced many Olympic medalists, winning gold in Sydney and silver in Athens. You'll notice that local crew team members are characters—with a tradition of wild and colorful haircuts. You'll likely see them running or rowing. This dedication to rowing adds to Bled's tranquility, since no motorized boats are allowed on the lake.

If you want to get into the action, you'll find **rental rowboats** at the swimming pool under the castle (small 3-person boat: first hour-€10.50, additional hours-€6.50 each; bigger 5-person boat: first hour-€12.50, additional hours-€7.50 each) or at the campground on the far side of the lake (4-person boat-€8.50/hr, closed in bad weather and off-season).

Swimming—Lake Bled has several suitable spots for a swim. The swimming pools under the castle are filled with lake water and routinely earn the "blue flag," meaning the water is top-quality (swim all day-€5, less for afternoon only, June–Sept daily 8:00–19:00, closed Oct–May, tel. 04/578-0528). Bled's two beaches are at the far end of the lake. Both are free; the one at the campground (southwest corner) has lots of tourists, while locals prefer the one at the rowing center (northwest corner). If you swim to the island, remember that you can't get into the church in your swimsuit.

Luge Ride (Polento Sankanje)—Bled's new "summer toboggan" luge ride allows you to scream down a steep, curvy metal rail track on a little plastic sled. A chairlift takes you to the top of the track, where you'll sit on your sled, take a deep breath, and remind yourself: Pull back on the stick to slow down, push forward on the stick to go faster. You'll drop 480 feet in altitude on the 570-yard-long track, speeding up to about 25 miles per hour as you race toward the lake. You'll see the track on the hillside just south of town, beyond the Grand Hotel Toplice (€4.50/ride, cheaper for multiple rides, chairlift only-€2, weather-dependent—if it rains, you can't go; mid-June–mid-Sept daily 9:00–12:00 & 16:00–20:00; May–mid-June Sat–Sun only 10:00–19:00, closed Mon–Fri; mid-Sept–Oct Sat–Sun only 10:00–18:00, closed Mon–Fri; closed Nov–April).

Day Trips—For details on some easy and enjoyable nearby side-trips—including a quirky bee museum, a scenic gorge hike, and a more remote lake experience—see "Near Lake Bled" at the end of this chapter.

NIGHTLIFE

Bled is quiet after hours. If you're not a drinker or a dancer, you're down to mini golf...open late in summer across from the commercial center.

Pub Crawl—Bled has several fun bars that are lively with a young crowd (all open nightly until 2:00 in the morning). Since many young people in Bled are students at the local tourism school, they're likely to speak English...and eager to practice with a native speaker. Try a "Smile," a Corona-type Slovenian lager. *Šnops* (schnapps) is a local specialty—popular flavors are plum *(slivovka)*, honey *(medica)*, blueberry (*borovničevec*), and pear (*hruškovec*).

Kick things off with the fun-loving local gang at **Gostilna Pri Planincu** near the bus station (described under "Eating"). Then head down Cesta Svobode toward the lake; just below Hotel Jelovica, you'll find the rollicking **Irish Pub** (a.k.a. "The Pub"), with Guinness and indoor or outdoor seating. For a more genteel atmosphere, duck across the street and wander a few more steps down toward the lake to find the **Art Café,** with a mellow ambience reminiscent of a van Gogh painting. Around the lake near the commercial center, **Bled Pub** (a.k.a. "The Cocktail Bar" or "Troha"—for the family that owns it) is a trendy late-night spot where bartenders sling a dizzying array of mixed drinks to an appreciative crowd (between the commercial center and the lake, above the recommended Oštarija Peglez'n restaurant). If you're still standing, several other, more low-key bars and cafés percolate the commercial center.

Polka—Slovenia is the land of polka. Slovenes claim it was invented here, and singer/accordionist Slavko Avsenik—from the nearby village of Begunje—cranks out popular oompah songs that make him bigger than the Beatles (and therefore, presumably, Jesus) in Germany. The easiest way to hear accordion music and yodeling in Bled is to attend a free polka evening with a local band at the commercial center (outside on the lower terrace; every Thu from around 20:00, mid-June–mid-Sept only). While the audience is mostly local, tourists are more than welcome. (You can spot the tourists—they're the ones who can't polka.) There's also a Slovenian folk evening once a week at a Bled hotel (ask at TI).

SLEEPING

Bled is packed with gradually decaying, communist-era convention hotels. A few have been nicely renovated, but most are stale, outmoded, and overpriced. It's a strange, incestuous little circle—the vast majority of the town's big hotels and restaurants are owned by the same company. Only a handful of Bled accommodations are modern and a good value, and I've listed them here—along with a few older places that work in a pinch. Quaint little family-run pensions are rare, and they book up fast with Germans and Brits; reserve these places as far ahead as possible. I've listed the high-season prices (May–Oct). Off-season, the big hotels lower prices 10–15 percent. For cheaper beds, consider one of the many *sobe* (rooms in private homes) scattered around the lake (about €25 per person in peak season, often with a hefty 30 percent surcharge for stays shorter than three nights). Several agencies in town can help

Sleep Code

(€1 = about $1.20, country code: 386, area code: 04)
S = Single, **D** = Double/Twin, **T** = Triple, **Q** = Quad, **b** = bathroom.
Unless otherwise noted, credit cards are accepted. Everyone
speaks English, and all of these accommodations include
breakfast. Bled levies a €1 tourist tax per person, per night (not
included in below prices unless noted).

To help you sort easily through these listings, I've divided
the rooms into three categories based on the price for a standard double room with bath:

$$$ **Higher Priced**—Most rooms €100 or more.
$$ **Moderately Priced**—Most rooms between €50–100.
$ **Lower Priced**—Most rooms €50 or less.

you find a *soba* (including Kompas Bled—see page 359). But be
sure the location is convenient before you accept.

$$$ Hotel Lovec, a Best Western, sits in a convenient
(but non-lakefront) location just above the commercial center.
Gorgeously renovated inside and out, and run by a helpful and
friendly staff, it's a welcoming, cheery, well-run alternative to
Bled's many old, dreary communist hotels. Its 60 plush rooms come
with all the comforts (Sb-€122, Db-€144, €15 more for a lake-view
balcony, €50 more for "deluxe" room with balcony and Jacuzzi, €24
less per room Nov–April, family and "executive" suites available,
delicious breakfast, elevator, Internet access, indoor pool, park-
ing garage-€8.50/day, Ljubljanska cesta 6, tel. 04/576-8615, fax
04/576-8625, www.lovechotel.com, sales@lovechotel.com).

$$$ Grand Hotel Toplice is the grande dame of Bled, with
87 rooms, an elegant view lounge, posh decor, all the amenities,
and a long list of high-profile guests—from Madeleine Albright
to Jordan's King Hussein. Rooms in the back are cheaper, but have
no lake views and overlook a noisy street—try to get one as high
up as possible (non-view: Sb-€120, Db-€150; lake view: Sb-€170,
Db-€210; suites mostly with lake views-€260; 15–20 percent less
Nov–April, elevator, Cesta Svobode 12, tel. 04/579-1000, fax
04/574-1841, www.hotel-toplice.com, info@hotel-toplice.com).
The hotel's name—*toplice*—means "spa"; guests are free to use
the hotel's natural-spring-fed indoor swimming pool (a chilly 72
degrees Fahrenheit).

$$ Mayer Penzion, perched on a bluff above Grand Hotel
Toplice, is a steep five-minute uphill walk from lake. Wonderfully
run by the Trseglav family, this place comes with 13 great-value
rooms, a friendly and professional staff, an excellent restaurant, and

an atmospheric wine-tasting cellar. They book up fast in summer with return clients, so reserve early (Sb-€45, Db-€65–75 depending on size and balcony, extra bed-€20, elevator, Želeška cesta 7, tel. 04/576-5740, fax 04/576-5741, www.mayer-sp.si, penzion @mayer-sp.si). They also rent a cute little two-story Slovenian farm cottage next door (Db-€70, Tb-€80, Qb-€90).

$$ Hotel Berc and **Penzion Berc,** run by the Berc brothers, are next door to Mayer Penzion. The new hotel building has 15 rooms with pleasantly woody decor (Sb-€40, Db-€65–70, all rooms have balconies, Pod Stražo 13, tel. 04/576-5658, fax 04/576-5659, hotel@berc-sp.si, run by Luka). The older, adjacent *penzion* offers 11 cheaper, almost-as-nice rooms (Sb-€30–35, Db-€50–60, most rooms have balconies, Želeška cesta 15, tel. & fax 04/574-1838, penzion@berc-sp.si, run by Miha). Both have cozy public spaces and are worth reserving ahead (for both: cash only, 10 percent more for 1-night stays, 10 percent less off-season, prices include tax, free Internet access, free loaner bikes, www.berc-sp.si).

$$ Alp Penzion, sitting in cornfields a 15-minute walk from the lake and just out of town, is the most tranquil and only farm-feeling option. Its 11 rooms are small and faded, but comfortable. The place is enthusiastically run by the Sršen family, who offer lots of fun activities: tennis court, summer barbecue grill, wine-tasting, and a sauna (Sb-€40, Db-€55–60, Tb-€80, 10 percent more for 1-night stays, cheaper Nov–March, family rooms, free Internet access, free loaner bikes, Cankarjeva cesta 20A, tel. 04/574-1614, fax 04/574-4590, www.alp-penzion.com, bled@alp-penzion.com).

Grand Hotel Toplice (listed earlier) runs two nearby annexes with much lower prices: **$$ Hotel Jadran,** on a hill behind the Toplice, has 45 tired, old rooms (reception tel. 04/579-1365). **$$ Hotel Trst** is less homey, but its 31 rooms are a little bigger and have been lightly renovated (reception and breakfast at the Toplice, often closed in winter). Both have the same prices and can be reserved through Grand Hotel Toplice (non-view: Sb-€56, Db-€72; lake view: Sb-€81, Db-€96; extra bed-€21, all rooms €10 less Nov–April, Cesta Svobode 12, tel. 04/579-1000, fax 04/574-1841, www.hotel-toplice.com, info@hotel-toplice.com). At either place, ask for a room on the higher floors to avoid road noise (both have elevators).

$ Penzion Bledec is just below the castle at the top of the old town. While technically an IYHF hostel, each of the 13 rooms has its own bathroom, and some can be rented as doubles (though "doubles" are actually underutilized triples and quads, with separate beds pushed together—so they're not reservable July–Aug). The friendly staff is justifiably proud of the bargain they offer (bed in 4–7-bed dorm-€19, Db-€50, Tb-€63, cheaper Nov–April, members pay 10 percent less, includes sheets and breakfast, entirely non-smoking, great family rooms, Internet access, full-service laundry for guests-€9/load, Grajska 17, tel. 04/574-5250, fax 04/574-5251, www.mlino.si, bledec@mlino.si).

EATING

Okarina Etno, run by charming, well-traveled Leo Ličof, serves a diverse array of cuisines, all of them well-executed: international fare, traditional Slovenian specialties, and Indian (Himalayan) dishes. Leo has a respect for salads and vegetables and a passion for fish. Creative cooking, fine presentation, friendly service, and an atmosphere as tastefully eclectic as the food make this place a winner (€7–12 pastas, €9–20 main dishes, handy €10 fixed-price lunch deal includes a drink; April–Oct Mon–Fri 12:00–15:00 & 18:00–24:00, Sat–Sun 12:00–24:00; Nov–March daily 12:00–15:00 & 18:00–24:00; next to Hotel Lovec at Ljubljanska cesta 8, tel. 04/574-1458). Skim the guest book to find the page with Paul McCartney's visit from May 2005.

Oštarija Peglez'n ("The Old Iron"), conveniently located on the main road between the commercial center and the lake, cooks up tasty meals with an emphasis on fish. Choose between the delightful Slovenian cottage interior or the shady streetside terrace (€5–7 salads, €6–7 pastas, €10–20 main dishes, daily 10:00–24:00, fun family-style shareable plates, Cesta Svobode 7A, tel. 04/574-4218).

Mayer Penzion, just up the hill from the lakefront, has a dressy restaurant with good traditional cooking that's worth the short hike. This is where a Babel of international tourists come to swap hiking tips and day-trip tales (main dishes €8–20, Tue–Fri 17:00–24:00, Sat–Sun 12:00–24:00, closed Mon, indoor or outdoor seating, above Hotel Jadran at Želeška cesta 7, tel. 04/576-5740).

Gostilna Pri Planincu ("By the Mountaineers") is a homey, informal bar coated with license plates and packed with fun-loving and sometimes rowdy natives. Behind the small, local-feeling pub sprawls a large dining area. The big menu features good-enough Slovenian pub grub and Balkan grilled-meat specialties (€6–10 main dishes, fish splurges up to €15, daily 9:00–23:00, huge portions, traditional daily specials, Grajska cesta 8, tel. & fax 04/574-1613).

Pizzeria Rustika, in the old town, offers good wood-fired pizzas, pastas, and salads (Tue–Sun 12:00–23:00, Mon 15:00–23:00, marked only with low-profile *pizzeria* sign at Riklijeva cesta 13, tel. 04/576-8900). Its upstairs roof terrace is relaxing on a balmy evening.

The **Mercator** grocery store, in the commercial center, has the makings for a bang-up picnic. They sell €2–3 pre-made sandwiches, or will make you one to order (point to what you want).

Bled Desserts

While you're in Bled, be sure to enjoy the town's specialty, a cream cake called **kremna rezina** (KRAYM-nah ray-ZEE-nah; often referred to by its German name, **kremšnita,** KRAYM-shnee-tah). It's a layer of cream and a thick layer of vanilla custard artfully sandwiched between sheets of delicate, crispy crust. Heavenly. Slovenes travel from all over the country to sample this famous dessert.

Slightly less renowned—but just as tasty—is **grmada** (gur-MAH-dah, "bonfire"). This dessert was developed by Hotel Jelovica as a way to get rid of their day-old leftovers. They take yesterday's cake, add rum, milk, custard, and raisins, and top it off with whipped cream and chocolate syrup.

Finally, there's prekmurska gibanica—or just **gibanica** (gee-bah-NEET-seh) for short. Originating in the Hungarian corner of the country, gibanica is an earthy pastry filled with poppy seeds, walnuts, apple, and cheese, and drizzled with rum.

These desserts are typically enjoyed with a lake-and-mountains view—the best spots are the Panorama restaurant by Grand Hotel Toplice and the terrace across from the Hotel Park (figure around €5 for cake and coffee at any of these places). For a more local (but non-lake view) setting, consider Šmon Slaščičarna (only slightly cheaper; see "Dessert," below).

This is a great option for hikers and budget travelers (Mon–Sat 7:00–19:00, Sun 8:00–12:00).

Dessert: While tourists generally gulp down their cream cakes on a hotel restaurant's lakefront terrace, local residents know the best desserts are at **Šmon Slaščičarna** (a.k.a. the "Brown Bear," for the bear on the sign). It's nicely untouristy, but lacks the atmosphere of the lakeside spots (daily 7:30–22:00, near bus station at Grajska cesta 3, tel. 04/574-1616).

TRANSPORTATION CONNECTIONS

The most convenient train connections to Bled leave from the Lesce-Bled station, about 2.5 miles away (see details under "Arrival in Bled" on page 358). Remember, when buying a train ticket to Lake Bled, make it clear that you want to go to the Lesce-Bled station (not the Bled Jezero station, which is poorly connected to the main line). No one in the town of Bled sells train tickets; buy them at the station just before your train departs. If the ticket window there is closed, buy your ticket on board from the conductor (who will likely waive the €2.50 additional fee).

Note that if you're going to **Ljubljana,** the bus (which leaves from Bled town itself) is better than the train (which leaves from the Lesce-Bled train station).

From Lesce-Bled by Train to: Ljubljana (roughly hourly, 1 hr—but bus is better), **Salzburg** (5/day, 4 hrs), **Munich** (3/day, 6 hrs), **Vienna** (that's *Dunaj* in Slovene, 5/day, 6 hrs, transfer in Villach, Austria), **Venice** (3/day with transfer in Ljubljana or Villach, 6 hrs), **Zagreb** (5/day, 3.5 hrs).

By Bus to: Ljubljana (Mon–Fri 11/day, Sat–Sun 8/day, 1.25 hrs, €6.25), **Radovljica** (Mon–Fri at least 2/hr, Sat hourly, Sun almost hourly, 15 min, €2), **Lesce-Bled train station** (at least hourly, 10 min, €1.50), **Lake Bohinj** (hourly, 30 min to Bohinj Jezero stop, 35 min to Bohinj Vogel stop, 40 min to Bohinj Zlatorog stop, €3.50-4 depending on stop), **Podhom** (20-min hike away from Vintgar Gorge, Mon–Fri 9/day, none Sat, 1/day Sun, 15 min, €1.25), **Spodnje Gorje** (also near Vintgar Gorge, take bus in direction of Krnica, hourly, 15 min, €1.25). Confirm times at the Bled bus station.

By Plane: The Ljubljana-Brnik Airport is between Lake Bled and Ljubljana, about a 45-minute drive from Bled. Connecting by taxi costs around €45 (set price up front—since it's outside of town, they don't use the meter). The bus connection from Bled to the airport is cheap (total cost: about €5), but complicated and time-consuming: First, go to Kranj (Mon–Fri 12/day, Sat–Sun 8/day, 35 min), then transfer to a Brnik-bound bus (at least hourly, 20 min). Many Bled residents prefer to fly from Klagenfurt, Austria. For details on both the Ljubljana and the Klagenfurt airports, see page 353.

Route Tips for Drivers: Bled is less than an hour north of Ljubljana. From Ljubljana, take the A-2 expressway north until it ends, diverting you onto a smaller two-lane road. (You'll notice construction on the new expressway that will connect this stretch directly to the Karavanke tunnel to Austria—due to be completed in 2008. North of Bled, the expressway is already finished.) Watch for signs to *Bled*. This road will take you directly to the lake (where it's called Ljubljanska cesta).

To reach Radovljica (bee museum) or Lesce (train station), drive out of Bled on Ljubljanska cesta toward the expressway. Watch for the turnoff to those two towns on the right (they're on the same road).

Near Lake Bled

The countryside around Bled offers several day trips that can be done easily without a car (bus connection information is described in each section). The three listed here are the best (one village/

museum experience, two hiking/back-to-nature options). They're more convenient than can't-miss, but each one is worthwhile on a longer visit, and all give a good taste of the Julian Alps. For a self-guided driving tour through farther-flung (and even more striking) parts of the Julian Alps, see the next chapter.

Radovljica

The village of Radovljica (rah-DOH-vleet-suh) is larger than Bled, perched on a plateau above the Sava River. The town itself is nothing exciting, though its old center pedestrian zone, Linhartov trg, makes for a pleasant stroll. But the town is home to a fascinating and offbeat beekeeping museum—which, with only a few rooms, still ranks as one of Europe's biggest on the topic.

Radovljica's **Apicultural Museum** (Čebelarski Muzej)—worth ▲—celebrates Slovenia's long beekeeping heritage. Since the days before Europeans had sugar, Slovenia has been a big honey producer. Slovenian farmer Anton Janša is considered the father of modern beekeeping; he was Europe's first official teacher of beekeeping (in Hapsburg Vienna).

The first two rooms of the museum trace the history of beekeeping, from the time when bees were kept in hollowed-out trees to the present day. Notice the old-fashioned **tools** in the first room. When a new queen bee is born, the old queen takes half the hive's bees to a new location. Experienced beekeepers used the long, skinny instrument (a beehive stethoscope) to figure out when the swarm would fly the coop. Then, once the bees had moved to a nearby tree, the beekeeper used the big spoons to retrieve the queen—surrounded by an angry ball of her subjects—from her new home before she could get settled in. The beekeeper transported the furious gang into a manmade hive designed for easier, more sanitary collection of the honey. You can also see the tools beekeepers used to create smoke, which makes bees less aggressive. Even today, some of Slovenia's old-fashioned beekeepers simply light up a cigarette and blow smoke on any bees that get ornery.

The third room features the museum's highlight: whimsically painted beehive **frontboards** (called *panjske končnice*). Nineteenth-century farmers, believing these paintings would help the bees find their way home, developed a tradition of decorating their hives with religious, historical, and satirical folk themes (look for the devil sharpening a woman's tongue). The depiction of a hunter's funeral shows all the animals happy...except his dog. There's everything from portraits of Hapsburg emperors, to a "true crime" sequence of a man murdering his family as they sleep, to proto-"Lockhorns" cartoons of marital strife, to 18th-century erotica (one with a woman showing some leg, and another with a flip-up, peek-a-boo panel).

Near Lake Bled

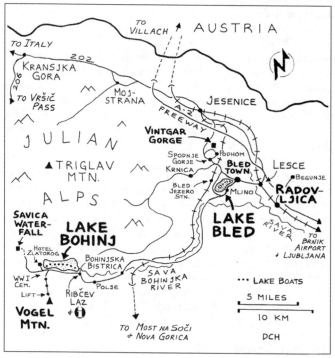

The life-size wooden statues were used to "guard" the beehives—and designed to look like fearsome Ottoman and Napoleonic soldiers.

You'll also find an interactive multimedia exhibit, a good video in English, temporary exhibitions, and—in the summer only—an actual, functioning beehive (try to find the queen). The gift shop is a good place for souvenirs, with hand-painted replicas of front-boards, honey brandy, candles, ornaments, and other bee products (museum entry-€2.50, good English descriptions, free sheet of English info, €2 English guidebook is a nice souvenir; May–Oct Tue–Sun 10:00–13:00 & 15:00–18:00, closed Mon; March–April and Nov–Dec Wed and Sat–Sun 10:00–12:00 & 15:00–17:00, closed Mon–Tue and Thu–Fri; closed Jan–Feb; Linhartov trg 1, tel. 04/532-0520, www.muzeji-radovljica.si).

Eating in Radovljica: Several Radovljica restaurants near the bee museum have view terraces overlooking the surrounding mountains and valleys. **Lectar** offers hearty Slovenian fare in a rural-feeling setting with a user-friendly, super-traditional menu. The restaurant is known for its heart-shaped cookies, decorated with messages of love (€12 plates, Wed–Mon 12:00–23:00, closed

Tue, family-friendly, Linhartov trg 2, tel. 04/537-4800). **Grajska Gostilnica** dishes up good, basic pub grub closer to the bus station (salads, pizza, pastas, open long hours daily, inside Hotel Grajski Dvor at Kranjska 2, tel. 04/531-5585).

Getting to Radovljica: When planning your day, note that the bee museum closes for two hours after lunch. **Buses** to Radovljica generally leave Bled every half-hour (fewer on weekends, check schedules at hotel or station, €2, buy ticket from driver, trip takes about 15 min). To reach the old town square and the bee museum, leave the station going straight ahead, cross the bus parking lot and the next street, then turn left down the far street (following brown sign for *Staro Mesto*). In five minutes, you'll get to the pedestrianized Linhartov trg (TI on right just before you enter pedestrian zone). At the end of this square, just before the church, you'll see the bee museum, which shares an old Baroque mansion with a music school (bee museum upstairs). Coming back to Bled, there are fewer buses; check the schedule when you arrive (usually about 2/hr, but fewer Sat–Sun). **Drivers** leave Bled on Ljubljanska cesta, then turn right at the sign for *Radovljica* and go through the village of Lesce; the road dead-ends at Radovljica's pedestrian zone, a short walk from the bee museum. A brand-new **bike** path, scenically and peacefully connecting Bled with Radovljica (about 4 miles), should open in 2007 (get details at TI).

Vintgar Gorge

Just north of Bled, the river Radovna has carved this mile-long, picturesque gorge into the mountainside. Boardwalks and bridges put you right in the middle of the action of this "poor man's Plitvice." A hike here is worth ▲. You'll cross over several waterfalls and marvel at the clarity of the water. The easy hike is on a boardwalk trail with handrails (sometimes narrow and a bit slippery). At the end of the gorge, you'll find a restaurant, WCs, and a bridge with a gorgeous view. Go back the way you came, or take a prettier return to Bled (see "Scenic Hike Back to Bled"). The gorge is easily reachable from Bled by bus or foot, and is the best option for those who are itching for a hike but don't have a car (€3, daily May–late Oct 8:00–19:00 or until dusk, June–Aug until 20:00, closed late Oct–April, tel. 04/572-5266).

Getting to Vintgar Gorge: The gorge is 2.5 miles north of Bled. You can walk (1 hour) or bus (15-min ride plus 15-min walk, or 30-min ride on summer tourist bus) to the gorge entrance. **Walkers** leave Bled on the road between the castle and St. Martin's Church and take the uphill (left) road at the fork. Soon after you pass the Pension Bledec hostel, turn right at the stop sign, then turn left at the bend in the road (following signs for *Podhom* and *Vintgar;* ignore the other *Vintgar* sign pointing back toward the way you came). At the fork just after the little bridge, go left for Podhom, then simply follow signs for *Vintgar*. In summer, the easy **tourist bus** takes you right to the gorge entrance in 30 minutes (see "Getting Around Lake Bled," page 359). Otherwise, take a **local bus** to one of two stops: Podhom (15 min, 9/day Mon-Fri, none Sat, 1/day Sun) or Spodnje Gorje (15 min, take bus in direction of Krnica, hourly). From either the Podhom or the Spodnje Gorje bus stop, it's a 15-minute walk to the gorge (follow signs for *Vintgar*). **Drivers** follow signs to *Podhom,* then *Vintgar* (see walking instructions, above).

Scenic Hike Back to Bled: If you still have energy once you reach the end of the gorge, consider this longer hike back with panoramic views. Behind the restaurant, find the trail marked *Katarina Bled.* You'll go uphill for 25 strenuous minutes (following the red-and-white circles and arrows) before cresting the hill and enjoying beautiful views over Bled town and the region. Continue straight down the road 15 minutes to the typical, narrow, old village of Zasip, then walk (about 30 min) or take the bus back to Bled.

Lake Bohinj

The pristine alpine Lake Bohinj (BOH-heen), 16 miles southwest of Bled, enjoys a quieter scene and (in clear weather) even

better vistas of Triglav and the surrounding mountains. This is a real back-to-nature experience, with just a smattering of hotels and campgrounds, rather than the well-oiled resort machine of Bled. Some people adore Bohinj; others are bored by it. If you think Bled is too touristy to allow you to really enjoy the nature, go to Bohinj.

Getting to Lake Bohinj: From Bled, hourly **buses** head for Bohinj, stopping at three different destinations: Bohinj Jezero (the village of Ribčev Laz, 30 min, €3.50), then Bohinj Vogel (a 10-minute walk from the base of the Vogel Mountain cable car, 35 min, €3.75), and finally Bohinj Zlatorog (Hotel Zlatorog and the one-hour hike to the Savica waterfall trailhead, 40 min, €4). Off-season, there are fewer buses—confirm times before you depart. **Drivers** leave Bled going south along the lakefront road, Cesta Svobode; once you reach the village of Mlino, you'll peel off from the lake and follow signs to *Boh. Bistrica* (a midsize town near Lake Bohinj). Once in the town of Bohinjska Bistrica, turn right, following *Bohinj Jezero* signs. The road takes you to the village of Ribčev Laz and along the lakefront road with all the attractions.

Sights and Activities: A visit to Bohinj has three parts: a village, a cable car (and nearby cemetery), and a waterfall hike.

Coming from Bled, your first views of Bohinj will be from the little village at the southeast corner of the lake called **Ribčev Laz** (loosely translated as "Good Fishin' Hole"). Here you'll find a TI, a handful of hotels and ice-cream stands, and the Bohinj Jezero bus stop.

The town's trademark is its church, St. John the Baptist (to your right as you face the lake, past the distinctive stone bridge). One of the area's oldest churches, St. John's features a rustic exterior and a fresco-packed interior (if it's locked, borrow key from TI). In the other direction, a five-minute stroll down the lakefront road, is a dock where you can catch an electric tourist boat to make a silent circuit around the lake (€8 round-trip, €6.50 one-way, daily 10:00-18:00, 2/hr, less off-season). The boat stops at the far end of the lake, at Camp Zlatorog—a 10-minute walk from the Vogel cable car (see next). Across from the Ribčev Laz dock is a fun concrete 3-D model of Triglav (compare to the real thing, hovering across the lake). Finally, a few more steps down the road, just beyond a boat rental dock, you'll see a statue of Zlatorog, the "Golden Horn"—a mythical chamois-like creature native to the Julian Alps.

The remaining sights are along this same road, which follows the lake to its end.

For a mountain perch without the sweat, take the cable car up to **Vogel Mountain,** offering impressive panoramic views of Mount Triglav and the Julian Alps (€10 round-trip, runs every 30 min, daily 7:00–19:00 in summer, 8:00–18:00 in winter, shorter hours and less frequent departures in spring and fall—confirm schedule before you make the trip, closed Nov, www.vogel.si). The top is a ski-in-winter, hike-in-summer area with fine views and a chairlift experience. The alpine hut Merjasec ("Wild Boar") offers tasty strudel and a wide variety of local brandies (including the notorious "Boar's Blood"—a concoction of several different flavors guaranteed to get you snorting). To reach the cable-car station, drivers follow signs to *Vogel* (to the left off the main lakefront road); by bus, get off at the Bohinj Vogel stop (request this stop from driver) and hike about 10 minutes up the steep road on the left (away from the lake).

Just beyond the cable-car station and Bohinj Vogel bus stop, look for the metal gate on the left marking a **World War I cemetery**—the final resting place for Soča Front soldiers (see sidebar on page 390). While no fighting occurred here (it was mostly on the other side of these mountains), injured soldiers were brought to a nearby hospital. Those who didn't recover ended up here. Notice that many of the names are not Slovene, but Hungarian, Polish,

Czech, and so on—a reminder that the entire multiethnic Austro-Hungarian Empire was involved in the fighting. If you're walking down from the cable-car station, the cemetery makes for a poignant detour on your way to the main road (look for it through the trees).

Up the valley beyond the end of the lake is Bohinj's final treat, a waterfall called **Slap Savica** (sah-VEET-seh). Hardy hikers enjoy following the moderate-to-strenuous uphill trail (including 553 stairs) to see the cascade, which dumps into a remarkably pure pool of aquamarine snowmelt (€2, daily in summer from 8:00 until dusk, allow about 90 min for the round-trip hike). Drivers follow the lakefront road to where it ends, right at the trailhead. Without a car, getting to the trailhead is a hassle. If you take the public bus from Bled, or the boats on the lake, they'll get you only as far as the Bohinj Zlatorog stop—the end of the line, and still a one-hour hike from the trailhead (from the bus stop, follow signs to *Slap Savica*). In summer, a sporadic shuttle bus takes you right to the trailhead. But frankly, it's not worth it if you don't have a car.

Sleeping near Lake Bohinj: Like most people who live in these parts, **$ Bojan and Ksenija Kočar** (BOH-yawn and kuh-SAYN-yah KOH-char) have spent years building their alpine home. In addition to housing the Kočars and their two teenagers, this delightful chalet also has several affordable rooms for tourists, as well as a beautifully hand-carved lounge/breakfast room. If you have a car and want to really get away from it all, consider sleeping here, in the countryside less than a mile from Lake Bohinj (about a 30-min drive from Lake Bled). Friendly, English-speaking Bojan—who's a bus driver—is often out of town, but Ksenija (who speaks less English) will take good care of you (Db-€34, or €44 for 1-night stays, includes breakfast, closed Jan–March, tel. 04/574-6660—best to call after 21:00, mobile 041-478-490, kocar .bojan@siol.net). Driving from Lake Bled, you'll go through the town of Bohinjska Bistrica, then the village of Polje; they're just beyond Polje, but before Lake Bohinj itself (the first farmhouse on the left after Polje, #49, look for *Rooms* sign).

THE JULIAN ALPS

The Vršič Pass and the Soča River Valley

The countryside around Lake Bled has its own distinctive beauty. But to get the full Slovenian mountain experience, head for the hills. The northwestern corner of Slovenia—within yodeling distance of Austria and Italy—is crowned by the Julian Alps (named for Julius Caesar). Here, mountain culture has a Slavic flavor.

The Slovenian mountainsides are laced with hiking paths, blanketed in a deep forest, and speckled with ski resorts and vacation chalets. Beyond every ridge is a peaceful alpine village nestled around a quaint Baroque steeple. And in the center of it all is Mount Triglav—ol' "Three Heads"—Slovenia's symbol and tallest mountain (see page 382).

The single best day in the Julian Alps is spent driving up and over the 50 hairpin turns of the breathtaking Vršič Pass (vur-SHEECH, open May–Oct), and back down via the Soča (SOH-chah) River Valley, lined with offbeat nooks and Hemingway-haunted crannies. As you curl on twisty roads between the cut-glass peaks, you'll enjoy stunning high-mountain scenery, whitewater rivers with superb fishing, rustic rest stops, thought-provoking World War I sights, and charming hamlets.

A pair of Soča Valley towns holds watch over the region. Bovec is all about good times (it's the whitewater adventure-sports hub), while Kobarid attends to more serious matters (WWI history). While neither is a destination in itself, both Bovec and Kobarid are pleasant, functional, and convenient home bases for exploring this gloriously beautiful region.

Getting Around the Julian Alps

The Julian Alps are best by **car**. Even if you're doing the rest of your trip by train, consider renting a car here for maximum mountain day-trip flexibility. I've included a self-guided driving tour incorporating the best of the Julian Alps (Vršič Pass and Soča Valley).

It's difficult to do the Vršič Pass and Soča Valley without your own wheels. Hiring a **local guide** with a car can be a great value, making your time not only fun, but also informative. Cheaper but less personal, you could join a day-trip **excursion** from Bled. (Both options are explained in the "Tours" section of the previous chapter, page 360.) Or stay closer to Bled, and get a taste of the Julian Alps by taking advantage of easy and frequent **bus** connections to more convenient day-trip destinations (Radovljica, the Vintgar Gorge, and Lake Bohinj—all described under "Near Lake Bled" in the previous chapter).

Julian Alps Self-Guided Driving Tour

This all-day, ▲▲▲ self-guided driving tour takes you over the highest mountain pass in Slovenia, with stunning scenery and a few quirky sights along the way. From waterfalls to hiking trails, World War I history to queasy suspension bridges, this trip has it all.

ORIENTATION

Most of the Julian Alps are encompassed by the Triglav National Park (Triglavski Narodni Park). (Some sights near Lake Bled—such as Lake Bohinj and the Vintgar Gorge—are also part of this park, but are covered in the previous chapter.) This drive is divided into two parts: the Vršič Pass and the Soča River Valley. While not for stick-shift novices, all but the most timid drivers will agree the scenery is worth the many hairpin turns. Frequent pull-outs offer plenty of opportunity to relax, stretch your legs, and enjoy the vistas.

Planning Your Time: While this drive can be done in a day, consider spending the night along the way for a more leisurely pace. You can start and end in Bled or Ljubljana. For efficient sightseeing, I prefer to begin in Bled (after appreciating the mountains from afar for a day or two) and end in the capital.

Length of This Tour: These rough estimates do not include stops: Bled to the top of Vršič Pass—1 hour; Vršič Pass to Trenta (start of Soča Valley)—30 min; Trenta to Bovec—30 min; Bovec to Kobarid—30 min; Kobarid to Ljubljana or Bled—2 hours (remember, it's an hour between Ljubljana and Bled). In other words, if you started and ended in Bled and drove the entire route without stopping, you'd make it home in less than five hours...but you'd miss so much. It takes at least a full day to really do the region justice.

Tourist Information: The best sources of information are the Bled TI (see page 356), the Triglav National Park Information Center in Trenta (page 384), and the TIs in Bovec and Kobarid (pages 386 and 389).

Maps: Pick up a good map before you begin (available at local TIs, travel agencies, and gas stations). The all-Slovenia *Autokarta Slovenija* includes all the essential roads, but several more detailed options are also available. The 1:50,000 Kod & Kam *Posoče* map covers the entire Vršič Pass and Soča Valley (but doesn't include the parts of the drive near Bled and Ljubljana).

OK...let's ride.

Part 1: Vršič Pass

From Bled or Ljubljana, take the A-2 expressway north, enjoying views of **Mount Triglav** on the left as you drive. About 10 minutes past Bled, you'll approach the industrial city of **Jesenice,** whose iron- and steelworks are now mostly closed. The nearby village of **Kurja Vas** ("Chicken Village") is famous for producing hockey players (18 of the 20 players on the 1971 Yugoslav hockey team—which went to the World Championships—were from this tiny hamlet).

As you zip past Jesenice, keep your eye out for the Hrušica exit (also marked for Jesenice, Kranjska Gora, and the Italian border; it's after the gas station, just before the tunnel to Austria). When you exit, turn left towards Kranjska Gora (yellow sign) and the Italian border.

Slovenes brag that their country—"with 56 percent of the land covered in forest"—is one of Europe's greenest. As you drive towards Kranjska Gora, take in all this greenery...and the characteristic Slovenian hayracks (recognized as part of the national heritage and now preserved; see page 313). The Vrata Valley (on the left) is a popular starting point for climbing Mount Triglav. On the right, watch for the statue of Jakob Aljaž, who actually bought Triglav back when such a thing was possible (he's pointing at his purchase). Ten minutes later, you'll cross a bridge and enjoy a great head-on view of Špik Mountain.

Entering Kranjska Gora, you'll see a turnoff to the left marked for *Vršič*. But winter sports fanatics may want to take a 15-minute

The Julian Alps and Northwest Slovenia

detour to see the biggest ski jump in the world, a few miles ahead (stay straight through Kranjska Gora, then turn left at signs for **Planica,** the last stop before the Italian border). Every year, tens of thousands of sports fans flock here to watch the ski-flying world championships. This is where a local boy was the first human to fly more than 100 meters (328 feet) on skis. Today's competitors routinely set new world records (currently 784 feet—that's 17 seconds in the air). From the ski jump, you're a few minutes' walk from Italy or Austria. This region—spanning three nations—lobbied unsuccessfully under the name Senza Confini (Italian for "without borders") to host the 2006 Winter Olympics. Despite the failed Olympic bid, this philosophy is in tune with the European Union's vision for a Europe of regions, rather than nations.

Back in Kranjska Gora, follow the signs for Vršič. Before long, you'll officially enter **Triglav National Park** and come to the first of this road's 50 hairpin turns—each one numbered and labeled with the altitude in meters. Notice that they're cobbled to provide better traction. If the drive seems daunting, remember that 50-seat tour buses routinely conquer this pass...if they can do it, so can you.

Mount Triglav

Mount Triglav ("Three Heads") stands watch over the Julian Alps and all of Slovenia. Slovenes say that its three peaks are the guardians of the water, air, and earth. This mountain defines Slovenes, even adorning the nation's flag: Look for the national seal, with three peaks. The two squiggly lines under it represent the Adriatic. Or take a look at one of Slovenia's €0.50 coins.

From the town of Bled, you'll see Triglav peeking up over the ridge on a clear day. (You'll get an even better view from nearby Lake Bohinj.)

It's said that you're not a true Slovene until you've climbed Triglav. One native took these words very seriously, and climbed the mountain 853 times...in one year. Climbing to the summit—at 9,396 feet—is an attainable goal for any hiker in decent shape. If you're here for a while and want to become an honorary Slovene, befriend a local and ask if he or she will take you to the top.

If mountain climbing isn't your style, relax at an outdoor café with a piece of cream cake and a view of Triglav. It won't make you a Slovene...but it's close enough on a quick visit.

After switchback #8, with the cute waterfall, park your car on the right and hike up the stairs to the little **Russian chapel**

(recently renovated, so it looks shiny and new). This road was built during World War I by 10,000 Russian POWs of the Austro-Hungarian Empire to supply the front lines of the Soča Front. The POWs lived and worked in terrible conditions, and several hundred died of illness and exposure. On March 8, 1916, an avalanche thundered down the mountains, killing hundreds more workers. This chapel was built where the final casualty was found. Take a minute to pay your respects to the men who built the road you're enjoying today.

After #22, at the pullout for Erjavčeva Koča restaurant, you may see tour-bus groups making a fuss about the mountain vista.

They're looking for a ghostly face in the cliff wall, supposedly belonging to the mythical figure **Ajda.** This village girl was cursed by the townspeople after correctly predicting the death of the Zlatorog (Golden Horn), a magical, beloved, chamois-like animal. Her tiny image (with a Picasso nose) is just above the tree line, a little to the right—try to get someone to point her out to you (you can see her best if you stand at the signpost near the road).

After #24, you reach the **summit** (5,285 feet). On the right, a long gravel chute gives hikers a thrilling glissade down. (From the pullout just beyond #26, it's easy to view hikers "skiing" down.) As you begin the descent, keep an eye out for old WWI debris. A lonely guard tunnel stands after #28, followed by a tunnel marked *1916* (on the left) that was part of the road's original path. Then you'll see abandoned checkpoints from when this was the border between Italy and the Austro-Hungarian Empire. At #48 is a statue of **Julius Kugy,** an Italian botanist who wrote books about alpine flora.

At #49, the road to the right (marked *Izvir Soče*) leads to the **source of the Soča River.** If you feel like stretching your legs after all that shifting, drive about five minutes down this road to a restaurant parking lot. From here, you can take a 20-minute uphill hike to the Soča source. This is also the starting point for a new, well-explained Soča Trail (Soška Pot) that leads all the way to the town of Bovec, mostly following the road we're driving today. With plenty of time and a hankering to hike rather than drive, consider taking this trail (about 12 miles one-way).

Nearing the end of the switchbacks, follow signs for Bovec. Crossing the Soča River, you begin the second half of this trip.

Part 2: Soča River Valley

During World War I, the terrain between here and the Adriatic made up the Soča (Isonzo) Front. As you follow the Soča River south, down what's nicknamed the "Valley of the Cemeteries," the scenic mountainsides around you tell the tale of this terrible warfare. Imagine a young Ernest Hemingway driving his ambulance through these same hills.

But it's not all so gruesome. There are plenty of other diversions—interesting villages and churches, waterfalls and suspension bridges, and lots more.

The last Vršič switchback (#50) sends you into the village of **Trenta.** You'll pass a church and a botanical garden of alpine plants (Alpinum Juliana), then go over a bridge. Immediately after the bridge on the right is the parking lot for the Mlinarica Gorge. While the gorge is interesting, the bridge leading to it was damaged in a severe storm and hasn't yet been rebuilt—so it's best left to hardy hikers.

As you get to the cluster of buildings in Trenta's downtown, look on the left for the **Triglav National Park Information Center,** which also serves as a regional TI (May–Oct daily 10:00–18:00, closed Nov–April, tel. 05/388-9330, www.tnp.si). The humble €4 museum here provides a look (with English explanations) at the park's flora, fauna, traditional culture, and mountaineering history. A poetic 15-minute slideshow explains the wonders and fragility of the park (included in museum entry, ask for English version as you enter).

About five miles after Trenta, in the town of Soča, visit the **Church of St. Joseph** (with red onion dome, hiding behind the big tree on the right). The church was damaged in the earthquakes of 1998 and 2004, so the interior will likely be covered with scaffolding. But if it's not covered, you'll see some fascinating art. During World War II, an artist hiding out in the mountains filled this church with patriotic symbolism. The interior is bathed in Yugoslav red, white, and blue—a brave statement made when such nationalistic sentiments were dangerous. On the ceiling is St. Michael (clad in Yugoslav colors) with Yugoslavia's three WWII enemies at his feet: the eagle (Germany), the wolf (Italy), and the serpent (Japan). The tops of the walls along the nave are lined with saints—but these are Slavic, not Catholic. Finally, look carefully at the Stations of the Cross and find the faces of hated Yugoslav enemies: Hitler (fourth from altar on left) and Mussolini (first from altar on right). Behind the church is a typical cemetery, with civilian and (on the hillside) military sections.

For a good example of how the Soča River cuts like God's bandsaw into the land, stop about two minutes past the church at **Velika Korita Soče,** where you can venture out onto a suspension bridge over a gorge. Bounce if you dare. Just beyond this bridge is the turnoff (on the left) to the Lepena Valley, home of the recommended Pristava Lepena pension—and their Lipizzaner horses (see page 387).

Roughly five miles after the town of Soča, you exit the National Park and come to a fork. The main route leads to the left, through Bovec. But first, take a two-mile detour to the right (marked *Predel*), where the WWI **Kluže Fort** keeps a close watch over the narrowest part of a valley leading to Italy (€2, daily 10:00–19:00). In the 15th century, the Italians had a fort here to defend against the Ottomans. Half a millennium later, during World War I, it was used by Austrians to keep Italians out of their territory.

Notice the ladder rungs fixed to the cliff face across the road from the fort—allowing soldiers to quickly get up to the mountaintop.

Back on the main road, continue to **Bovec.** This town, which saw some of the most vicious fighting of the Soča Front, was hit hard by a 2004 earthquake. Today, it's being rebuilt and remains the adventure-sports capital of the Soča River Valley, famous for its whitewater activities. For a good lunch stop in Bovec, see my suggestions on page 388. But if you're not eating or spending the night here, feel free to skip it (continue along the main road to bypass the town center).

Heading south along the river—with water somehow both perfectly clear and spectacularly turquoise—watch for happy kayakers. When you pass the intersection at Žaga, you're just four miles from Italy. Along the way, you'll also pass a pair of waterfalls: The well-known Boka ("Slovenia's second-longest waterfall," just before Žaga) and the hidden gem Veliki Kozjak (unmarked, on the left just before Kobarid). For either, you'll have to park your car and hike uphill to see the falls.

Signs lead to the town of **Kobarid,** home to a bustling square and some fascinating WWI sights. Even if you don't think you're interested in the Soča Front, consider dropping in the Kobarid Museum. Driving up to the Italian Mausoleum hovering over the town is a must. (These sights are described on pages 389 and 391.)

Leaving Kobarid, continue south along the Soča to **Tolmin.** Before you reach Tolmin, decide on your route back to civilization.

Finishing the Drive

To Ljubljana: From Tolmin, you have two possible driving routes to the capital. Either option brings you back to the A-1 expressway south of Ljubljana, and will get you to the city in about two hours (though the second route has fewer miles).

The option you'll encounter first (turnoff to the right before Tolmin) is the smoother, longer route southwest to **Nova Gorica** (a city divided in half by the Italian border, and packed with casinos catering to Italian gamblers). From Nova Gorica, you can hop on the expressway—but the entire route between there and Ljubljana isn't finished yet, so you'll have to transfer to a secondary road for a while. (Once this entire expressway is finished, this will be hands-down the faster route.)

I prefer the more rural second option: Continue through Tolmin, then head southeast through the hills back towards Ljubljana. Along the way, you could stop for a bite and some sightseeing at the town of **Idrija** (EE-dree-yah), known to all Slovenes for three things: its tourable mercury mine, fine delicate lace, and tasty *žlikrofi* (like ravioli). Back at the expressway (at Logatec), head north to Ljubljana or on to Bled.

To Bled: The fastest option is to load your car onto a **"Car Train"** (Autovlak) that cuts directly through the mountains. The train departs at 18:05 from Most na Soči (just south of Tolmin, along the Idrija route described above) and arrives at Bohinjska Bistrica, near Lake Bohinj, at 18:50 (about €10 for the car; confirm schedule at the Bled TI before making the trip). From Bohinjska Bistrica, it's just a half-hour drive back to Bled. No reservations are necessary, but arrive at the train station about 30 minutes before the scheduled departure to allow time to load the car.

To **drive** all the way back, the fastest route (about 2 hours) is partially on a twisty, rough, very poor-quality road (go through Tolmin, turn off at Bača pri Modreju to Podbrdo, then from Petrovo Brdo take a very curvy road through the mountains into Bohinjska Bistrica and on to Bled). For more timid drivers, it's more sane and not too much longer to start out on the Idrija route toward Ljubljana (described above), but turn off in Želin (before Idrija) towards Skofja Loka and Kranj, then on to Bled. Or take one of the two routes described above for Ljubljana, then continue on the expressway past Ljubljana and back up to Bled (allow 3 hours).

Bovec

The biggest town in the area, Bovec has a happening main square and all the tourist amenities. It's best known as a hub for whitewater adventure sports. While not exactly quaint, Bovec is charming enough to qualify as a good lunch stop or overnight home base. If nothing else, it's a nice jolt of civilization wedged between the alpine cliffs.

ORIENTATION

(area code: 05)

Tourist Information
The helpful TI on the main square offers fliers on mountain biking and water sports (summer Mon–Fri 9:00–20:00, Sat–Sun 9:30–13:00; winter Mon–Fri 9:00–17:00, closed Sat–Sun; Trg Golobarskih Žrtev 8, tel. 05/389-6444, www.bovec.si).

Arrival in Bovec
The main road skirts Bovec (BOH-vets), but you can turn off (watch for signs on the right) to take the road that goes through the heart of town, then re-joins the main road farther along. As you approach the city center, you can't miss the main square, Trg

Golobarskih Žrtev, with the TI and a pair of good restaurants (described in "Eating").

SLEEPING

In Bovec

$$$ Dobra Vila is a gorgeous new hotel with classy traditional-meets-contemporary decor that feels out of place in little, remote Bovec. Not that I'm complaining. Its 12 rooms are swanky, and the public spaces (including a sitting room/library, breakfast room/restaurant, wine cellar, small "movie theater," winter garden porch, and terrace with cozy mountain-view chairs) are welcoming. Enthusiastically run by Andrea and Sebastian Kovačič, it's a winner (Sb-€93, Db-€110, 20 percent more for 1-night stays, same prices year-round, fun old-fashioned elevator, on the left just as you enter town on the main road from the Vršič Pass at Mala Vas 112, tel. 05/389-6400, fax 05/389-6404, www.dobra-vila-bovec .com, welcome@dobra-vila-bovec.com).

$$ Martinov Hram has 12 nondescript modern rooms over a popular restaurant a few steps from Bovec's main square. While the rooms are an afterthought to the busy restaurant (reception at the bar), they're comfortable (mid-July–Aug: Sb-€36, Db-€60; a few euros less off-season, no extra charge for 1-night stays, Trg Golobarskih Žrtev 27, tel. 05/388-6214).

Near Bovec

$$$ Pristava Lepena is a relaxing oasis hiding out in the Lepena Valley just north of Bovec. Well-run by Milan and Silvia Dolenc, this place is its own little village: a series of rustic-looking cabins,

---

Sleep Code

(€1 = about $1.20, country code: 386, area code: 05)
S = Single, **D** = Double/Twin, **T** = Triple, **Q** = Quad, **b** = bathroom. Unless otherwise noted, breakfast is included and credit cards are accepted. Everyone speaks English and all of these accommodations include breakfast. These prices don't include the €1 tourist tax per person, per night.

To help you sort easily through these listings, I've divided the rooms into three categories based on the price for a standard double room with bath:

  $$$ **Higher Priced**—Most rooms €100 or more.
    $$ **Moderately Priced**—Most rooms between €50–100.
     $ **Lower Priced**—Most rooms €50 or less.

a restaurant, and a sauna/outdoor swimming pool. Hiding behind the humble split-wood shingle exteriors is surprising comfort: 13 cozy apartments (with wood-burning stoves, TV, telephone, and all the amenities) that make you feel like relaxing. This place whispers "second honeymoon" (Db rates: July–Aug-€116, May–June and Sept-€100, early Oct and late April-€84, closed in winter, multinight stays preferred, 1-night stays may be possible for 20 percent extra, dinner-€16, lunch and dinner-€27, nonrefundable 30 percent advance payment when you reserve; just before Bovec, turn left off the main road toward Lepena, and follow the white horses to Lepena 2; tel. 05/388-9900, fax 05/388-9901, www.pristava-lepena .com, pristava.lepena@siol.net). The Dolences also have four Welsh ponies and four purebred Lipizzaner horses (two mares, two geldings) that guests can ride (in riding ring-€12/hr, on trail-€15/hr, riding lesson-€18; non-guests may be able to ride for a few euros more—call ahead and ask).

$ **Tourist Farm Pri Plajerju,** on a picturesque plateau at the edge of Trenta (the first town at the bottom of the Vršič Pass road), is your budget option. Run by the Pretner family, this organic farm raises sheep and goats, and rents four apartments and one room in three buildings separate from the main house. While not quite as tidy as other tourist farms I recommend, it's the best one I found in the Soča Valley (July–Aug: Db-€30–42; March–June and Sept–Dec: Db-€26–34; price depends on size of room or apartment, closed Jan–Feb, breakfast-€4.50, dinner-€6.50, watch for signs to the left after passing through the village of Trenta, Trenta 16a, tel. & fax 05/388-9209, www.eko-plajer.com, farma_plajer@hotmail.com).

EATING

In Bovec

Letni Vrt Pizzeria, dominating the main square, is the busiest place in town—with pizzas, pastas, salads, and more (closed Tue, Trg Golobarskih Žrtev 12, tel. 05/388-6335).

Martinov Hram, run by the Berginc family, is also good. The nicely traditional decor goes well with Slovenian specialties focused on sheep (good homemade bread, closed Thu, on the main road through Bovec, just before the main square on the right at Trg Golobarskih Žrtev 27, tel. 05/388-6214).

Kobarid

Kobarid feels older, and therefore a bit more appealing, than its big brother Bovec. This humble settlement was immortalized by a literary giant, Ernest Hemingway, who drove an ambulance on the Soča Front in World War I. He described Kobarid—which he called by its Italian name, Caporetto—as "a little white town with a campanile in a valley. It was a clean little town and there was a fine fountain in the square." Sounds about right. Aside from its brush with literary greatness, Kobarid is known as a hub of Soča Front information (with an excellent WWI museum, a hilltop Italian mausoleum, and walks that connect the nearby sights), and for its surprisingly good restaurants.

ORIENTATION

(area code: 05)
The main road cuts right through the heart of little Kobarid, bisecting its main square (Trg Svobode). The Kobarid Museum is along this road, on the left before the square. To reach the museum from the main square, simply walk five minutes back toward Bovec.

Tourist Information
The TI is across the street from the Kobarid Museum (summer daily 9:00–19:00, even later in peak season; winter Mon–Fri 9:00–16:00, Sat 9:00–13:00, closed Sun; Gregorčičeva 8, tel. 05/380-0490, www.lto-sotocje.si and www.kobarid.si).

SIGHTS

▲▲▲**Kobarid Museum (Kobariški Muzej)**—This modest but world-class museum offers a haunting look at the tragedy of the Soča Front. This proud little place, with fine English descriptions, was voted Europe's best museum in 1993. The entry is lined with hastily made cement and barbed-wire gravestones, pictures of soldiers, and flags of all of the nationalities involved in the fighting. Maps show how Europe changed from 1914 to 1918. The rotating ground-floor exhibit features a different country each year.

Upon arrival, ask to watch the English version of the 19-minute film on the history of the Soča Front (plays on top floor). Upstairs are exhibits on the way these soldiers lived, the tragedies they encountered (with some horrific images of war injuries), the devastating effects of the war on civilians, the strategies involved in the various battles (including a huge model of the successful Austrian-German *Blitzkrieg* attack), and the history of this region before and after World War I. Naturally, the exhibit focuses on the crucial 12th battle of the Soča Front—the Battle of Kobarid (€4, good €3 museum guide, €10 *Soča Front* book; April–Sept Mon–Fri 9:00–18:00, Sat–Sun 9:00–19:00; Oct–March Mon–Fri 10:00–17:00, Sat–Sun 9:00–18:00; Gregorčičeva 10, tel. 05/389-0000, www.kobariski-muzej.si).

The Soča (Isonzo) Front

The northwest corner of Slovenia—called Soča in Slovene, and Isonzo in Italian—saw some of World War I's fiercest fighting. While the Western Front gets more press, this eastern border between the Central Powers and the Allies was just as significant. In a series of 13 battles involving 16 different nationalities, 300,000 soldiers died, 700,000 were wounded, and 100,000 were declared MIA. In addition, tens of thousands of civilians died. Among the injured soldiers was a young Ernest Hemingway, who drove an ambulance for the Italian army. (Later in life, he would write the novel *A Farewell to Arms* about his experiences here.)

On April 26, 1915, Italy joined the Allies. A month later, they declared war on the Austro-Hungarian Empire (which included Slovenia). Italy invaded the Soča Valley, quickly taking the tiny town of Kobarid, which they planned to use as a home base for attacks deeper into Austrian territory. For the next 29 months, Italy launched 10 more offensives, all of them unsuccessful. This was difficult warfare—Italy had to attack uphill, waging war high in the mountains, in the harshest of conditions.

In October 1917, the Central Powers of Austria-Hungary and Germany retook Kobarid, launching a downhill attack of 600,000 soldiers. For the first time ever, the Austrian-German army used a new surprise-attack technique called *Blitzkrieg*, carried out by a German general named Erwin Rommel against orders from a superior. (He was demoted for his insolence despite its success, but climbed the ranks again to become famous as Hitler's "Desert Fox" in North Africa.) The Central Powers caught the Italian forces off-guard, quickly breaking through three lines of defense. Within three days, the Italians were forced to retreat. The Austrians called it the "Miracle at Kobarid," but Italy felt differently—to this day, when an Italian finds himself in a mess, he says he had a *Caporetto* (the Italian name for Kobarid).

A year later, Italy came back—this time with the aid of British, French, and US forces. The Allies were successful, and on November 4, 1918, Austria-Hungary conceded defeat. After more than a million casualties, the fighting at Soča was finally over.

At the museum (and local TIs), you can pick up a free brochure outlining the **"Kobarid Historical Walk"** tracing WWI sites in town and the surrounding countryside (3 miles, mostly uphill, allow 3–5 hours). History buffs can also call ahead to arrange a private guide (€15/hr, tel. 05/389-0000).

In 2007, the museum—and all of Kobarid—commemorates the 90th anniversary of the end of the Soča Front warfare, culminating in a town-wide festival in October.

▲▲**Italian Mausoleum (Kostnica)**—The 55 miles between here and the Adriatic are dotted with more than a hundred cemeteries, reminders of the countless casualties of the Soča Front. One of the most dramatic is this mausoleum, overlooking Kobarid. The access road, across Kobarid's main square from the side of the church, is marked by stone gate towers (with the word *Kostnica*). One of these tow-

ers used to be topped with a star, and the other with a cross—but now the star (representing Yugoslav communism) has gone missing. Hmm.

Take the road up Gradič Hill—passing Stations of the Cross—to the mausoleum. Built in 1938 (when this was still part of Italy) around the existing Church of St. Anthony, this fascist-style octagonal pyramid holds the remains of 7,014 Italian soldiers. Names are listed alphabetically, along with mass graves for more than 1,700 unknown soldiers *(militi ignoti)*. Walk behind the church and find the WWI battlements high on the mountain's rock face (with your back to church, they're at 10 o'clock). Incredibly, the fighting was done on these treacherous ridges; civilians in the valleys only heard the distant battles. If the church is open, go inside and look above the door to see a brave soldier standing over the body of a fallen comrade, fending off enemies with nothing but rocks. When Mussolini came to dedicate the mausoleum, local revolutionaries plotted an assassination attempt that couldn't fail. But at the last minute, the triggerman had a change of heart, Mussolini had an uneventful trip, and fascism continued to thrive in Italy.

SLEEPING AND EATING

$$$ Hotel Hvala, right on the main square, is your best bet. Run by the Hvala family, its 31 simple, contemporary rooms feel a few years out of date—but they're comfortable, and the location can't be beat (late July and Aug: Sb-€65, Db-€100; April–late July and Sept–Oct: Sb-€59, Db-€88; off-season: Sb-€54, Db-€78; 20 percent more for 1-night stays, hotel closed Feb and weekdays in Nov, Trg Svobode 1, tel. 05/389-9300, fax 05/388-5322, www.hotel -hvala.si, topli.val@siol.net).

The Hotel Hvala's restaurant, **Topli Val** ("Heat Wave"), is highly regarded for its fish dishes (€8–10 pastas, €10–20 main dishes, lengthy list of Slovenian wines, daily 12:00–16:00 & 18:00–24:00, Trg Svobode 1, tel. 05/389-9300).

For other options, you won't need to look far—pizzerias, pubs, and cafés are scattered around the main square. **Kotlar Restaurant,** across the square from Hotel Hvala, is similarly priced and well-regarded, and also has rooms for rent if you're in a pinch.

LOGARSKA DOLINA
and the NORTHERN VALLEYS

The Julian Alps around Lake Bled are Slovenia's most accessible and most famous pincushion of peaks. But the high-mountain thrills don't end there. Stretching to the east, along the border with Austria, is the Kamniško Savinjske range—home to several very remote valleys. One particularly inviting nook between the cut-glass peaks is the time-passed valley called Logarska Dolina. To get way, way, way off the beaten track—with gravel roads, unpasteurized milk, and the few Slovenes who still don't speak English—Logarska Dolina and surrounding valleys are the place. Slovenes like to keep this getaway a secret; it's one of their favorite escapes from the daily grind (and, along with Lake Bled, one of the country's most popular places to get married). Travelers who find Lake Bled too touristy prefer Lake Bohinj (see page 375). But travelers who think Bohinj is too touristy...love Logarska Dolina.

Logarska Dolina—very loosely translated as "Woodsman's Valley"—is more difficult to reach than the other destinations in this book. It's best left to adventurous drivers, true back-to-nature nuts, and those intrigued by old-fashioned farming lifestyles—or, better yet, someone who's all three. Most of all, Logarska Dolina is the ideal excuse for a long drive on high-mountain roads to one of Slovenia's most traditional corners.

Planning Your Time

A trip to Logarska Dolina can be done as a long full-day circular drive from either Bled or Ljubljana. With more time, you could spend the night. If you're heading between Ljubljana/Bled and Ptuj/Maribor on the A-1 expressway, Logarska Dolina is roughly on the way (though it's a still an hour and a half off the expressway).

Getting to Logarska Dolina

I'd skip this region without a car. Public transportation to the northern valleys is extremely time-consuming. In summer only, one **bus** a day goes from the city of Celje to Solčava, then on to Logarska Dolina. But once you're there, many of the region's best attractions (such as the Panoramic Road) are unreachable by public bus.

On the other hand, Logarska Dolina is made to order by **car.** The valley is nearly due north from Ljubljana. But because of the mountains that lie between them, you'll have to boomerang substantially to the east to get there. From Ljubljana, take the A-1 expressway east (toward Celje) to the Šentrupert exit. Head north on road 225 along the Savinja River past Mozirje and Nazarje to Juvanje, where you'll continue northwest on road 428 toward Luče, then Solčava. The little valley of Robanov Kot is just before the town of Solčava, and the road up to the Panoramic Road is in Solčava. For details on getting around the valleys once you're in Solčava, see page 397. Figure about an hour from Ljubljana to the Šentrupert exit, then another hour and a half to Solčava. You'll likely return the same way (unless you want to tackle a challenging "shortcut"—described next).

A good, detailed map is essential. The *Avtokarta Slovenija* map described on page 12 will do, but consider getting one with even more detail for the region (available locally). Your map may show some seeming "shortcuts" that appear to take you more directly between Ljubljana and Logarska Dolina (for example, Ljubljana-Kamnik-Stahovica, then directly east along the Črna Dreta River through Gornji Grad to Juvanje—or the shortcut past Krivčevo north through Podvolovljek to Luče). These possibilities—on very rough and twisty roads—save you miles, but not time. The Podvolovljek shortcut is actually on a road that's largely unpaved, so it's very slow going, and often unpassable outside of summer. Another seeming shortcut via Kranj—dipping into Austria on the Jezersko-Pavličevo Sedlo road, through Vellach—is also not advisable, since the Pavličevo Sedlo border is open only to European Union citizens.

ORIENTATION

(area code: 03)

The region is tucked in the northern corner of Slovenia, just a few miles from Austria. This chapter's sights branch off from an east–west axis formed by the valley of the Savinja River. The main attraction here is the valley called **Logarska Dolina,** which cuts

Logarska Dolina

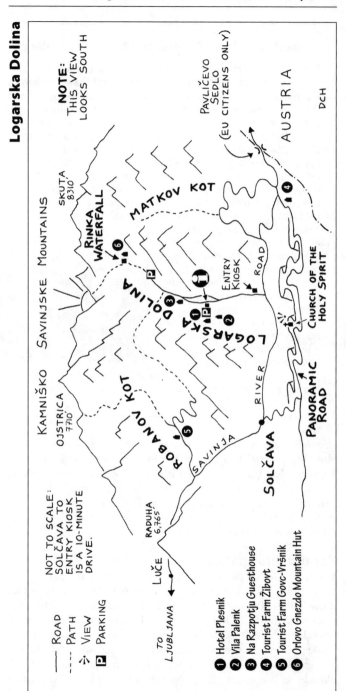

NOTE: THIS VIEW LOOKS SOUTH

AUSTRIA

PAVLIČEVO SEDLO (EU CITIZENS ONLY)

DCH

SKUTA 8310'

RINKA WATERFALL

MATKOV KOT

SAVINJSKE MOUNTAINS

KAMNIŠKO

OJSTRICA 7710'

LOGARSKA DOLINA

ENTRY KIOSK

ROAD

CHURCH OF THE HOLY SPIRIT

ROBANOV KOT

RIVER

SAVINJA

SOLČAVA

PANORAMIC ROAD

RADUHA 6,765'

LUČE

TO LJUBLJANA

NOT TO SCALE: SOLČAVA TO ENTRY KIOSK IS A 10-MINUTE DRIVE.

— ROAD
---- PATH
⋏ VIEW
P PARKING

1 Hotel Plesnik
2 Vila Palenk
3 Na Razpotju Guesthouse
4 Tourist Farm Žibovt
5 Tourist Farm Govc-Vršnik
6 Orlovo Gnezdo Mountain Hut

Farming in (and Above) the Northern Valleys

For many visitors, the most striking thing about a visit to this region is the ingenious way the intrepid locals have learned to eke out a living in such an inhospitable land. Just as throughout the Alps, the valleys and plateaus here are carefully manicured, creating cow-filled pastures wherever there's a flat patch of earth. But what's special in Logarska Dolina is the way farmers also cultivate the land at the very tops of hills. Especially from the Panoramic Road, you can see that the highest points of various ridges and foothills are shaved bare—rounded hilltops sticking up here and there like bald heads in a crowd. Cows graze even on this sharply angled land. Locals joke that these farms are so steep that cows' front legs are shorter than their rear legs to make it easier for them to climb uphill—and dogs have to hang on to the grass with their teeth and bark through their rear ends. If this type of rugged, high-mountain farming takes place elsewhere in Europe, I haven't seen it.

You'll see more traditional houses here than just about anywhere else in the country. Many have wooden roofs and siding. These shingles are generally made of larch wood—the hardest, most durable wood in these parts. The boards are not cut, but

through the mountainscape south from the Savinja River Valley. Roughly parallel to Logarska Dolina are two smaller valleys: **Robanov Kot** (to the east) and **Matkov Kot** (to the west). (Note that *dolina* means "valley," while *kot*—literally, "corner"—is a short valley.) Running along the top of the Podolševa ridge above the Savinja River is the rough, gravelly **Panoramic Road** (Panoramska Cesta)—with spectacular views over the entire region.

Tourist Information

Logarska Dolina has a modest TI kiosk, across the parking lot from Hotel Plesnik (very flexible hours but generally May–Oct daily 9:00–15:00, closed Nov–April, take left fork to hotel after you enter Logarska Dolina, Logarska Dolina 9, tel. 03/838-9004, www.logarska-dolina.si). The TI can help you find a room or plan a hike, and can arrange activities such as guided hikes, bike rental, horseback riding, rock climbing, archery, and paragliding. If it's closed—as is the case off-season—the nearby Hotel Plesnik also provides basic tourist information.

split. Each house has a tiled stove for heat, and a patch of grass to feed livestock.

It's a rough lifestyle. A farming family's primary source of income is their animals—mostly cows used for milk and meat, but also pigs and goats. Some of the farms in the Savinja River Valley raise yaks imported from Scotland, which are bred for their meat. A second source of income is forestry: The trees on a farm's property can be harvested and sold. Finally, they make a living from you and me, in the form of overnights or meals eaten at their farms.

All the tourist farms in this region are a recent phenomenon. During the Yugoslav era, people who lived here stopped farming and moved or commuted into nearby towns in the valley to work in factories. But Slovenia's industry was designed to work as a cog in the Yugoslav machine—other regions provided raw materials, and a large, ready-made market to buy the finished product. After the Slovenes declared independence from Yugoslavia, many of their factories closed, and their farmers-turned-workers returned to ancestral farming ways. To supplement their income, many families have converted their working farms into tourist farms, inviting guests to visit, stay, and dine with them, and appreciate their unique lifestyles. (I've listed a pair of tourist farms under "Sleeping," later in this chapter.) Even though many of the farms in Logarska Dolina seem as though they could be generations old, some date from only the mid-1990s.

SIGHTS AND ACTIVITIES

The road along the Savinja River, and the Panoramic Road up above, are connected at both ends—forming a handy loop that allows drivers to see everything efficiently. I suggest driving the Panoramic Road first, to get a good overview of the region, then winding down along the Savinja River to see the valleys. (If you have bad morning weather that looks like it may clear up in the afternoon, do the opposite.) The town of Solčava is the gateway to the region (see "Getting to Logarska Dolina," earlier in this chapter). In Solčava, you can head up to the Panoramic Road (follow signs to Podolševa). At the far end of this sky-high road, you'll wind your way back down into the valley. (Don't try to enter Austria at Pavličevo Sedlo, as this border crossing is only for EU citizens.) You can turn off the Panoramic Road early, for a more direct route to Logarska Dolina; or stay on longer, for a scenic detour around the smaller valley called Matkov Kot. After seeing Logarska Dolina, the Savinja River road continues back to Solčava.

If you have time, you can detour into the valley of Robanov Kot when you head south from Solčava.

▲▲▲**Panoramic Road (Panoramska Cesta)**—The Logarska Dolina valley (described below) is pretty. But the region's spec-

tacular highlight is the Panoramic Road twisting along the top of the cliff above it. At an altitude of around 4,000 feet (compared to about 2,500 feet in Logarska Dolina), this road offers one thrilling drive.

As you rattle along the rough road, all around you are vast swaths of mountain forests, broken only by hilltops covered with patches of green grass. Each of these hills is its own farm, which raises grass to feed livestock (see sidebar on page 396). Several stretches of the Panoramic Road are what Slovenes poetically call "white road"—that is, gravel (no pavement). Realize that you're just an avalanche's tumble from the Austrian border.

About halfway along the Panoramic Road, the late-19th-century **Church of the Holy Spirit** (Sveti Duh) hovers on a

hilltop above the hamlet of Podolševa. Climb up to the church for sweeping views over Logarska Dolina. If the church is open, duck inside and find a very unusual relief of three men representing the Holy Trinity. God is in the center, Jesus is on the left, and on the right, it's...the Holy Spirit, depicted not as a dove but as a balding man.

The Panoramic Road is lined with inviting tourist farms *(turistična kmetija)*, offering beds and meals to travelers—just follow the views to your favorite (Tourist Farm Žibovt, listed under "Sleeping," later in this chapter, is one good option). Some farms serve *kislo mleko,* or "soured milk"...which is exactly what it sounds like (about €3 per bowl). Fresh, unpasteurized milk is set out in the open air, usually in a darkened room. The fat rises to the top and forms a skin on top. The bottom of the milk is like yogurt, white and relatively flavorless. Meanwhile, the yellowish top layer comes

with a kick: a pungent barnyard aftertaste. I tried it—once—and enjoyed it...the experience, if not the flavor.

▲▲**Logarska Dolina**—This valley, four and a half miles long and about a quarter-mile wide, is the region's main draw. A flat,

broad meadow surrounded on all sides by sheer alpine cliffs, it's an idyllic place for a drive, hike, or bike ride. Various sights—caves, waterfalls, old log cabins, and so on—surround the valley, but it's most appealing simply as a place to commune with gorgeous Slovenian nature.

While you can enter the valley year-round, you'll have to pay a €5 entry fee per car April through October. After the valley entrance, the road forks. Take the left fork to reach the TI (see "Tourist Information," earlier in this chapter) and hotels (see "Sleeping," later in this chapter); or take the right fork to bypass them (the two forks re-join after a while).

At the far end of the valley, you'll find a parking lot with some snack stands. From here, you can follow the *Slap Rinka—10 min* signs up the moderately strenuous path to the **Rinka Waterfall.**

Relax at the little mountain hut called Orlovo Gnezdo ("Eagle's Nest") and enjoy a drink with a view of the falls, which plunge 300 feet down from the adjacent cliffs.

With more time, Logarska Dolina offers an inviting, mostly level place to go for a longer **hike,** surrounded by cow-filled meadows and towering peaks. The "Wonder Trail" is a two-hour, four-mile (one-way) hike that starts near the entrance of the valley and leads to the end of the valley. As you enter Logarska Dolina, pick up the brochure that narrates the route. This brochure and information on more adventurous hikes up into the mountains around Logarska Dolina are also available at the TI.

Robanov Kot and Matkov Kot—These smaller, sleepier valleys, dotted with traditional farm buildings, flank Logarska Dolina. They offer the same surrounded-by-mountains feeling, but are less crowded than Logarska during the peak season. With extra time, poke into one or both of these mini-valleys simply to enjoy the peaceful views. Tourist Farm Govc-Vršnik—listed under "Sleeping"—is in Robanov Kot.

SLEEPING

The accommodations listed here are in three very different settings. The hotel/villa/guesthouse are in the heart of the Logarska Dolina valley; the first tourist farm is up on the ridge above; and the second tourist farm is in a smaller, even quieter side valley called Robanov Kot.

$$ Hotel Plesnik and **Vila Palenk,** both part of the only big hotel outfit in the area, sit proudly in the middle of Logarska Dolina. The hotel, with lively public spaces and 30 modern rooms with traditional farmhouse furnishings, is a big, classy, overpriced splurge (Sb-€83, Db-€132, €5 cheaper without balcony, elevator). The nearby, smaller Vila Palenk has 11 rustic rooms with more character (Sb-€66, Db-€106, no elevator, breakfast at the main hotel). The staff at both places speaks English. Reservations for both are handled through the same office (no extra charge for 1-night stays, €10 per person for lunch or dinner at hotel restaurant, check online for weekend deals—especially off-season, outdoor swimming pool, Logarska Dolina 10, tel. 03/839-2300, fax 03/839-2312, www.plesnik.si, info@plesnik.si). After entering Logarska Dolina, you'll come to a fork; bear left to reach the hotel. They also run the 10-room **Na Razpotju Guesthouse,** a quarter-mile from the main hotel (Sb-€47, Db-€76, tel. 03/839-1650, razpotje@siol.net).

$ Tourist Farm Žibovt is dramatically situated at the far end of the Panoramic Road, a few minutes' walk from the Austrian border. It perches on a ledge with fine views of a tranquil meadow that ends at a sheer cliff plunging to the bottom of Logarska Dolina. In addition to renting six cheery rooms, the Poličnik family serves meals and turns out a wide range of dairy products—including the unforgettable *kislo mleko* ("soured milk"). Near this farm is a

---

Sleep Code

(€1 = about $1.20, country code: 386, area code: 03)
S = Single, **D** = Double/Twin, **T** = Triple, **Q** = Quad, **b** = bathroom. These accommodations include breakfast. The hotel accepts credit cards, but the tourist farms are cash only and charge 20-30 percent extra for stays of fewer than three nights. These prices don't include the €1 tourist tax per person, per night.

To help you sort easily through these listings, I've divided the rooms into two categories based on the price for a standard double room with bath:

$$ Higher Priced—Most rooms €60 or more.
$ Lower Priced—Most rooms less than €60.

modest marble quarry (Db-€46, or €55 with dinner, cash only, minimal English spoken, Logarska Dolina 24, tel. 03/584-7118, www.slovenia.info/zibovt, kmetija.zibovt@gmail.com). The farm is well-marked on the Panoramic Road. It's at the far end of the road from where it comes up at Solčava—close to the Austrian border crossing at Pavličevo Sedlo.

$ Tourist Farm Govc-Vršnik is in the smaller, relaxing valley of Robanov Kot, a 15-minute drive from Logarska Dolina. This working farm, run by the English-speaking Vršnik family, has a traditional beehive and 10 cozy rooms with bright, woody decor (Db-€46, or €58 with dinner, €6 less mid-Sept–June, cash only, Robanov Kot 34, tel. 03/839-5016, fax 03/839-5017, www.govc-vrsnik.com, govc.vrsnik@siol.net). As you enter the valley of Robanov Kot (just south of Solčava), just watch for signs.

EATING

There are no specific restaurants worth seeking out in Logarska Dolina—simply stop when you're hungry, or when you spot a place that looks good. Many of the region's tourist farms *(turistična kmetija)* serve full meals to passersby in summer, and light food and snacks at other times. Hotel Plesnik and Na Razpotju Guesthouse, listed above, also serve food to non-guests. But the best option is to bring a picnic with you, and eat whenever you find the scenic perch you like best (buy provisions before you arrive, as there's limited opportunity to buy groceries once in the valley).

PTUJ and MARIBOR

The vast majority of Slovenia's attractions are concentrated in the western third of the country: the mountains, the sea, the capital city, and the Karst. East of Ljubljana, the mountains gradually merge into plains, the towns and cities become less colorful, and "oh, wow!" turns into "so what?" But there's hope, in the form of Slovenia's oldest town (and winner of the "funniest name" award): Ptuj (puh-TOOey—the "P" is almost silent; and yes, it really does sound like someone spitting).

With a storied past, a much-vaunted castle, and easygoing locals who act like they've never met a tourist, Ptuj charms. Populated since the Early Stone Age, Ptuj has a long and colorful history that reads like a Who's Who of Central Europe: Celts and Romans, Dominican friars and Hapsburg counts, Nazis and Yugoslavs...not to mention a fuzzy monster named Kurent. The people of Ptuj are particularly proud of their Roman era, when "Poetovio" was a bustling metropolis of 40,000 people. But even as it clings to its noble past, today's Ptuj is refreshingly real, with a sleepy small-town ambience and an interesting castle museum.

While it hosts plenty of visitors (mostly Germans, who call it "Pettau"), Ptuj is hardly a tourist town. Real people, not nightclubs or T-shirt shops, populate the Old Town. If this makes Ptuj feel a bit less polished than the big-name sights in western Slovenia, so much the better—think of it as a diamond in the rough.

For a big-city complement to Ptuj, drop into Maribor—the country's second city, and the de facto capital of eastern Slovenia (see the end of this chapter).

Planning Your Time

With a week or more in Slovenia, and a desire to delve into the less-touristed areas of the country, Ptuj deserves a short visit. A few hours are enough to feel you've mastered the town; if you're a restless sightseer, it's tough to fill an entire day here. Begin by touring the castle, then enjoy a wander through the Old Town and consider Ptuj's other museums. Let your pulse slow and take a mini-vacation from your vacation. If you can't sit still that long, consider a side-trip into Maribor.

Notice that Ptuj is conveniently located on the train network, easy to reach from Ljubljana and Maribor, as well as international destinations like Zagreb and Budapest.

ORIENTATION

(area code: 02)

Ptuj is squeezed between its historic castle and the wide Drava River. With just 11,000 people (23,000 in greater Ptuj), it still ranks as Slovenia's eighth-largest town. The Old Town is shaped roughly like a triangle, formed by the castle and the two monasteries. You can walk from one end of the Old Town to the other in about 10 minutes, but since the town slopes uphill from the river to the castle, there's a lot of up and down.

Tourist Information

Ptuj's TI shares the square called Slovenski trg with its landmark City Tower. Pick up the information magazine and the free city map marked with sights, hotels, and restaurants (Mon–Fri 8:00–18:00, Sat–Sun 9:00–13:00, may be closed Sun off-season, Slovenski trg 3, tel. 02/779-6011, www.ptuj-tourism.si).

Arrival in Ptuj

The humble **train** station is about a 10-minute walk from the center (exit the station to the left, then cross the busy road and pass the bus station into the Old Town). The **bus** station is just on the edge of the Old Town. **Drivers** will find a handy parking lot on the riverfront, near the west end of town.

Helpful Hints

Local Guide: To arrange your own private guide, contact the **Ptujske Vedute agency** (€34 for a 90-min tour of the Old Town, tel. 02/778-8781, ptuj.vedute@siol.net). The TI can also help you find a guide.

Laundry: Non-guests can normally use the self-service laundry at the **Kurent Youth Hostel,** but only when its reception is

Ptuj

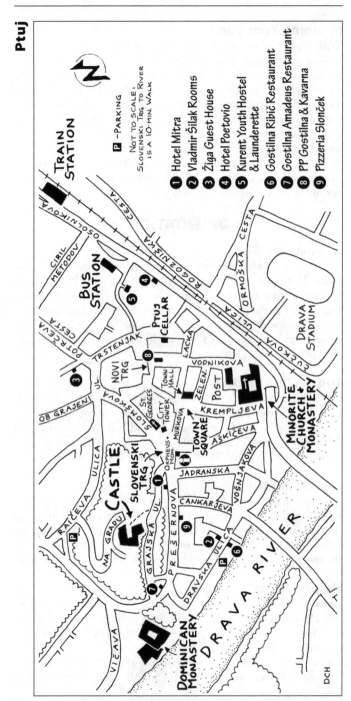

1. Hotel Mitra
2. Vladmir Šilak Rooms
3. Žiga Guest House
4. Hotel Poetovio
5. Kurent Youth Hostel & Launderette
6. Gostilna Ribič Restaurant
7. Gostilna Amadeus Restaurant
8. PP Gostilna & Kavarna
9. Pizzeria Slonček

P = Parking

Not to Scale: Slovenski Trg to River is a 10-min. walk

TRAIN STATION

BUS STATION

PTUJ CELLAR

CASTLE

SLOVENSKI TRG

TOWN SQUARE

NOVI TRG

MINORITE CHURCH + MONASTERY

DRAVA STADIUM

DRAVA RIVER

DOMINICAN MONASTERY

DCH

open (€4.50/load, daily 8:00–12:00 & 16:00–20:00, call first to confirm, tel. 02/771-0814; see "Sleeping," page 413).

SIGHTS

Ptuj Castle (Ptujski Grad)

The modest castle, rated ▲▲, is Ptuj's top sight and proudly claims to be Slovenia's most-visited museum. Overlooking the town from its perch over the Drava River, it's less than thrilling from afar. But the horseshoe-shaped castle complex hosts a series of surprisingly rich and engaging exhibits.

Cost, Hours, Information: €3, daily May–mid-Oct 9:00–18:00, mid-Oct–April 9:00–17:00, July–Aug Sat–Sun until 20:00, tel. 02/748-0360, www.pok-muzej-ptuj.si. Sparse English descriptions are posted in some rooms. English tours are rare, but you can call to ask if one is scheduled that you can join (you'll pay a measly €1 extra). Since it's unlikely you'll get on a tour, I've explained the highlights in a self-guided tour.

Getting There: You can't miss the castle, sitting over the city. Several different trails lead up from the Old Town, all well-marked with *Grad* signs.

◐ Self-Guided Tour: The core of the Ptuj Castle collection shows off the lifestyles of the castle's historic residents, while other exhibits display weapons, musical instruments, and traditional costumes used for the annual Kurentovanje festival. You're expected to follow a one-way route (described next); if you try to make your own plan, you may be herded back in line. The entrances to each exhibit are unmarked, but attendants are always around to direct you to what you want to see. Touring the whole shebang takes about two hours.

After buying your ticket, go up the stairs near the ticket office and turn right. Look over the **courtyard** for this quick history lesson: In the 11th century, the archbishops of Salzburg built a fortress here. In the 12th century, the Lords of Ptuj, who watched over the Salzburgers' land, moved in. The LoPs died out in the mid-15th century, and from then on the castle changed hands frequently.  Over the next several centuries, Ptuj Castle gradually acquired its current appearance: a Romanesque core (part of a 14th-century fortress, barely visible now) with a Renaissance arcaded courtyard (designed by Italian experts who came to fortify the castle against the Ottomans), accentuated by an austere Baroque addition (the outermost wing, with the decorated stone window frames). Most of what you'll see today came about under the Counts of Herberstein (1873–1945).

Now look over the door at the end of the arcade to see the **castle seal,** a hodgepodge of symbols representing previous owners. What's an English phrase doing on a Slovenian castle seal? It's because of a Hungarian princess, of course. In the Middle Ages, when a princess of Hungary moved to Scotland to be with her new husband, she took with her a particularly protective chamberlain. When the chamberlain buckled the princess to her horse for a treacherous river crossing, he'd fasten her on with three belts instead of just one, and shout "Grip fast!" when they came to any rough patches. That chamberlain's descendants took the name Leslie and eventually bought this castle in 1656. The family crest became those three buckles the chamberlain had used to protect his princess (in the left shield). You'll spot this insignia throughout the castle.

• *Going through the door, you enter the...*

Feudal Dwelling Culture Collection: This exhibit displays artifacts belonging to the castle's previous owners. The route takes you more or less clockwise in a roughly chronological order, from the 16th to the 19th centuries. In the first few rooms—where receptions were held and guests were (hopefully) impressed—you'll see several 17th-century tapestries from Brussels depicting the travels of Ulysses. Notice that nearly every big room has its own ceramic stove (fed from behind the wall by servants). Looking up, you'll see that while some of the rooms have exposed wooden-beam ceilings, others are adorned with cake-frosting stucco work—it's original, by highly skilled masters, and still intact after more than 280 years. At the end of the hall is a gallery of portraits of the Herbersteins, who furnished this part of the castle and were eager to establish their legitimacy as a ruling family.

Now continue clockwise into the residential part of the castle (as you enter, notice the 700-year-old Herberstein family tree on your right). The **Chinese Salon** reveals the fascination many 17th- and 18th-century Europeans had for foreign cultures. But the European artists who created these works never actually visited China, instead basing their visions on stories they heard from travelers who may or may not have had firsthand experience there. The result—European depictions of imagined Chinese culture—are highly inaccurate at best, and flights of pure fantasy at worst (look around for animals and instruments that never existed). This European interest in Chinese culture is known as *chinoiserie*. We'll see a similar fixation on Turkish culture soon.

Head through the next few rooms (ladies' salon, countess'

dressing room, old chapel). Before entering the 14th-century core—and oldest part—of the castle, keep your head up to see a very unusual chandelier: an anatomically correct (or maybe surgically enhanced?) **female dragon.**

Continue into the **bedrooms.** The first shows off what prim and proper 17th-century Europeans considered to be "erotic" art (with a mythical creature hitting on a woman), while the second is decorated in Napoleonic-era Empire-style furniture. In this room, pay special attention to the stove: Water (which could be scented) was poured into the top, then emerged at the bottom in the form of steam. Fancy. The third bedroom brings the survey of furniture up to date: 19th-century Biedermeier...simple, practical, comfortable, but still beautiful.

• *Going into the arcade, turn left to find the...*

Festival Hall: Then, as now, this hall was a preferred place for banquets and concerts. Decorating the walls is Europe's biggest collection of *turqueries*. Like the faux-Chinese stuff we saw earlier, this is a (usually highly inaccurate) European vision of Turkish culture. After the Hapsburgs militarily defeated the Ottomans and forced them out of Central Europe, the two powers began a diplomatic relationship. In the late 17th century, many Austrian officers went to Turkey and came back with souvenirs and tall tales, which were patched together to form the idiosyncratic vision of the Ottoman Empire you see here.

The left wall shows Ottoman politicians of the day—many with European features (presumably painted by artists who'd never laid eyes on an actual Turkish person). Along the back wall, we see portraits of four sultans' wives. Imagine how astonishing the notion of a harem must have been in the buttoned-down Hapsburg days. But even though these paintings are unmistakably titillating, they're still appropriately repressed. The first woman (on left) wears two different layers of semi-transparent clothing (what's the point?). And the fourth woman (on right) reaches for some fruit (symbolic of...well, you know) and teasingly pulls open her dress so we can see what's underneath, which is...more clothes.

Finally, look on the right wall, with 17th-century Eurofied visions of people from other cultures: Africans, Native Americans, and Asians, all with exaggerated features.

This quirky collection is typical of Slovenian museums: Since they can't afford great works by famous artists, they collect items that may be obscure, but have an even more interesting story to tell.

• *As you exit, go straight ahead to the end of the hall, where you'll take the tight, medieval spiral staircase up one level. At the top, turn left into the...*

France Mihelič Archive: France Mihelič was an important Slovenian painter of the mid-20th century who donated an enormous

Kurentovanje

Ptuj is famous for its distinctive Mardi Gras celebration, called Kurentovanje (koo-rent-oh-VAWN-yeh). Locals dress up in elaborate costumes and parade through the streets, celebrating the end of winter and heralding the arrival of spring. Nearby villages have similar, smaller, and more traditional processions.

It seems quaint today, but in the Middle Ages, Kurentovanje was deadly serious. The winter is particularly harsh here, so when spring began to approach, the peasants wanted to encourage it. They'd put on frightening masks and costumes and parade around making as much noise as possible to scare off the winter.

Kurentovanje's most notable character is Kurent, a fun-loving Slavic pagan god of hedonism—sort of the Slovenian Bacchus. A Kurent is covered with fur and has a long, red tongue, horns, a snout, whiskers, two red-ringed eyes, a wooden club with a spiny hedgehog skin wrapped around one end, and red or green socks. It wears a chain of five bells around its waist, and jumps around and swings its hips to get them clanging as loudly as possible. Kurents travel together in packs, so the combined noise can be deafening.

Traditionally the role of Kurent was played by young men of the village—

stash of paintings to this museum. Some are displayed here, while others are carefully archived in the big steel filing cabinets.

• *In the next room begins the...*

Sluga Collection: Donated by a local collector, this exhibit shows off more of the Biedermeier furniture that was all the rage in Central Europe during the early to mid-19th century.

• *The next two rooms are the...*

Castle Gallery: The first room displays works of art from the Baroque period, while the second (darkened) room highlights the Middle Ages. The first three sculptures on the left (#9–11) are especially precious, done by the greatest masters of the day.

• *Exit to the right. And now for something completely different...*

Carnival Masks Collection: Ptuj's Mardi Gras celebration, called Kurentovanje, is well-known for its processions of fanciful masked characters (see sidebar). This room offers an entertaining look at the complete Kurentovanje experience. The costume of the old woman carrying the old man on her back seems whimsical, but it represents a powerful theme: We carry the memory of the they were able to pull it off physically (the costume could weigh 90 pounds) and used it as an opportunity to catch the eye of a potential wife. (As the Kurents parade through the streets, young women still toss them handkerchiefs in approval.) Leading up to the procession, the young man would make his own costume in secret. That way, the monster would be all the more frightening and impressive when it was finally revealed. Ideally, they'd use the stinkiest animal hides they could find, to make the beast smell as hideous as it looked and sounded.

These processions have evolved into modern extravaganzas. These days, men and women of any age buy their Kurent costumes in a store, and Kurentovanje's daytime parades are followed by evenings of music, celebration, and general debauchery. In recent years, in a sort of "creature exchange" program, characters from Mardi Gras celebrations in other countries have come to take part in Kurentovanje.

Imagine about 350 of these hairy beasts, each one with five huge bells clanging at top volume, stomping down Prešernova street. Or come the Sunday before Ash Wednesday, and see for yourself. For details on all the festivities, check out www .kurentovanje.net.

Kurentovanje ends at midnight on Shrove Tuesday (before Ash Wednesday), when people move into the more pensive season of Lent... confident that spring will return with ease.

deceased always with us. The plow is used to symbolically "wake up the soil" and set the stage for a season of bountiful crops. The cow and horse costumes are unruly and obnoxious, testing the patience of the farmer. The Kurent costumes are especially striking—from old homemade costumes (turn an old coat inside-out to reveal the fur lining) to today's store-bought version (they run about €500).

After the Carnival Masks Collection, you'll pass through an ethnographic collection (farm implements, traditional tools, etc.), which the museum hopes to move soon to a more suitable location.
• *Head back down to the courtyard. Ask one of the attendants to direct you (across the courtyard from the ticket office) to the...*

Musical Instruments Collection: This fun and well-presented exhibit groups instruments by type of music, which you'll hear as you enter each room. You can also press the button next to the picture of the instrument you'd like to hear. The first room features a military band, and the second displays ancient Roman instruments. The tibia (in the display case), dating from the second or third century A.D., is the only one ever found; it had two pipes leading to a single mouthpiece (illustrated on the wall). Rounding out the exhibit are salon instruments (including a rare, preserved lute) and keyboard instruments.

• *Exiting, ask to be directed to the anticlimactic finale, the...*

Armory Collection: Squeezed into one corner of a huge room is an armory collection spanning several centuries, from the 1400s through World War I. They're displayed on racks, as they would have been in a real armory.

• *Your castle visit is over. Enjoy the views, then head back down into town.*

Old Town

The sights in Ptuj's Old Town are simple and not very time-consuming. Wander around, take them in at your own pace, then reward yourself with a relaxing drink on a square.

▲**Slovenski Trg**—Once Ptuj's main square, and now its most atmospheric, Slovenski trg is fronted by the TI, Hotel Mitra, and the City Tower. Around this square are several reminders of Ptuj's Roman past.

The white marble slab in the middle of the square, known as the **Orpheus Monument,** was commissioned by a Roman mayor in the second century A.D. to honor an esteemed figure...himself. Notice the musician playing the lyre (near the top, center of slab, below the naked woman). Since the lyre is commonly associated with Orpheus, the monument's nickname stuck. When Rome fell, so did many of its structures, including this one. It became buried in history, only to reappear in the 16th century as the town pillory, where criminals were punished (secured by chains that were embedded in the holes you still see in the slab). In the Middle Ages, the town mayor would come out onto the balcony over the door of his white house at the top of the square (#6) to witness justice being served.

The **City Tower** was built in the late 16th century to defend against Ottoman invaders (who were likely  to pass by here on their way to lay siege to Vienna). The tower used to be another story taller—but the top burned in a devastating fire (one of four that swept the city in the late 17th and early 18th centuries). The newly shorter tower was capped with this jaunty Baroque steeple.

Embedded in the staircase at the back of the tower are more fragments from Ptuj's Roman era. This so-called **"open-air museum"** is just a taste of the vast Roman material unearthed in Ptuj. In the middle of the staircase, make out the letters: POETOVIONA—a longer version of Ptuj's Roman name, Poetovio. (For an even more extensive Roman collection, head for the Dominican Monastery.)

Just behind the City Tower is **St. George's Parish Church** (Cerkev Svetega Jurija), which dates back before any other building in Slovenia. The current Gothic version is packed with diverse ecclesiastical art. If it's open, go inside (daily 7:00–11:00 & 18:00–18:30). As you enter, notice (on your left) the gorgeous circa-1380 statue of St. George, Ptuj's patron saint, slaying the dragon. Then go to the first big pillar on the right, where you'll see a glass-covered relief depicting throngs of admirers adoring the Baby Jes... wait—where's Jesus? (Not to mention Mary's hands?) Several years ago, Jesus was stolen from this pillar. To help prevent further vandalism, the priests reduced the opening times (notice the ridiculously long midday break).

Prešernova Street—Stretching away from the City Tower is Ptuj's main drag and oldest street. It's wider than most streets in town because it led to what was the medieval market square (now Slovenski trg), so merchants would set up market stalls all along the street. Many of the houses here have long since been renovated in Renaissance or Baroque style, making it Ptuj's most picturesque thoroughfare.

Town Square (Mestni Trg)—Today Ptuj's main square, this lively people zone (just down Murkova street from Slovenski trg) is a hub of activity. Major events and festivals—including the Kurentovanje Mardi Gras festival—take place here.

The square is watched over by the distinctive **Town Hall,** built by a visionary mayor a century ago. The three flags represent (left to right) the European Union, Slovenia, and the Municipality of Ptuj. Over the left door (on the corner) are two statues commemorating Ptuj's Roman history: on the right, Emperor Trajan, who granted Ptuj city status in the early second century A.D.; and on the left, St. Viktorin, a Ptuj bishop who wrote scholarly works on ecclesiastical themes during the late third century A.D., until he was martyred by Emperor Diocletian.

In the middle of the square is a statue of **St. Florian,** who traditionally protects towns against fire. Ptuj was devastated by four different fires in the late 17th and early 18th centuries. This statue is a 1993 replica of one that was built here after the fourth fire, in 1744. Miraculously, the town never burned again...though this might have had something to do with the fact that they started building with stone instead of wood. Largely as a result of Ptuj's

frequent fires, its rival Maribor (to the north) gradually supplanted Ptuj as the region's main center of commerce and winemaking. Ptuj's fate was sealed a century later, when the rail line from Vienna to Trieste went through Maribor. Today Maribor has 10 times as many people as Ptuj—and 10 times the industry, congestion, and urban gloominess. Hmm...maybe Ptuj got the better end of the deal, after all.

Ptuj Cellar (Ptujska Klet)—Ptuj is highly regarded for its wines. Simple wine was produced in this region as far back as the Celts. The Romans advanced the art, only to have it disappear in the Dark Ages, then be revived in the 13th century by Minorite monks. Today this enormous cellar, branching out under the Old Town, continues this proud tradition—and holds a staggering five million liters of wine (about 85 percent whites). The cellar is also home to a "wine archive" with bottles dating back to 1917. This precious archive survived World War II because it was sealed off and hidden from the Nazis behind a giant barrel.

The cellar is most proud of their award-winning Sauvignon Blanc (€4/bottle), but their best seller—at a million bottles a year—is a local wine called Haložan (a semi-dry blend of four whites, €2/bottle).

Cellar **tours** and **wine-tastings** are only available to groups, and English tours are rare—call the TI to find out if one is scheduled that you can join. If you're determined, it's easy to join a German- or Slovene-language tour. Either way, you'll pay about €4–7 for the experience, depending on how many wines you taste. The cellar tour comes with some hokey lighting effects and is followed by an even hokier audio-visual presentation during the tasting.

If you just want to pick up a bottle, stop by their **wine shop,** next door to the cellar (Mon–Fri 7:00–19:00, Sat 7:00–12:00, closed Sun, Vinarski trg 1, tel. 02/787-9810, www.ptujska-klet.si).

Minorite Church and Monastery (Minoritski Samostan)—This church, dedicated to Saints Peter and Paul, was one of the only buildings in town destroyed in World War II. (The Allies believed that the occupying Nazis were storing munitions here.) Only the foundation at the back end of the church (the part that's yellow instead of white) survived, and was left as ruins for decades. In 1989, friars celebrated their 750th anniversary in Ptuj by rebuilding the back part of the church. About a decade later, the front (white) half was also reconstructed. They followed the original plans carefully, but something's missing: Those empty niches above the door, once occupied by statues, are a sobering reminder of wartime devastation. But step into the contemporary interior (daily 7:30–18:30, Minoritski trg). There, at the altar, are the original statues that once adorned the church facade.

At the chapel at the back of the church (on the right), you'll see very contemporary Stations of the Cross. Then go through the door on the right into the peaceful cloister. A handful of friars can still be seen roaming these tranquil halls, and you're welcome to stroll here, too.

Dominican Monastery (Dominikanski Samostan)—This monastery, at the opposite end of the Old Town, no longer operates, but instead hosts a wide range of Roman artifacts—many of which are displayed on the lawn. Inside you'll find more Roman fragments scattered around a cloister with very limited explanations (€3, mid-April–Nov daily 10:00–17:00, closed in winter, Muzejski trg 1, tel. 02/787-9230).

SLEEPING

Central Ptuj has only two hotels, a hostel, and a handful of *sobe/* guest houses. While the options seem limited, the rooms are generally a very good value.

$$$ Hotel Mitra, the town's only "splurge" (and a cheap one, at that), enjoys Ptuj's best location: right on its most appealing street, a few steps from the landmark City Tower. Each of the 23 rooms has its own historical theme. A renovation planned for early 2007 might increase these prices (Sb-€61, Db-€81, €10 cheaper May–mid-Oct, lots of stairs, Prešernova 6, tel. 02/787-7455, fax

---

Sleep Code

(€1 = about $1.20, country code: 386, area code: 02)
S = Single, **D** = Double/Twin, **T** = Triple, **Q** = Quad, **b** = bathroom. No hotel in Ptuj has an elevator, but everyone speaks English. Unless otherwise noted, credit cards are accepted, breakfast is included, and the modest tourist tax (€1 per person, per night) is not.

To help you easily sort through these listings, I've divided the rooms into three categories based on the price for a standard double room with bath:

$$$ Higher Priced—Most rooms €80 or more.
  $$ Moderately Priced—Most rooms between €30–80.
    $ Lower Priced—Most rooms €30 or less.

02/787-7459, www.hotelptuj.com, info@hotelptuj.com).

$$ Vladmir Šilak rents six comfortable rooms around a charming courtyard in his gorgeously renovated, circa-1690 Old Town home. If you want to sleep in a 300-year-old house with huge medieval vaults and three-foot-thick walls, this is the place (Sb-€26–30, Db-€36–55, Tb/Qb-€51–63, extra bed-€13, price depends on size of room, no breakfast, about €7 more if you want your own kitchen, no extra charge for 1-night stays, bike rental, Dravska 13, tel. 02/787-7447, mobile 031-597-361, www.rooms -silak.com, rooms.silak@siol.net).

$$ Žiga Guest House is simpler, slightly cheaper, and less memorable. On a nondescript street between the bus station and the Old Town, its 10 outmoded rooms are a reliable budget option (Sb-€21, Db-€31, no breakfast, cash only, Panonska 1, tel. 02/748-1683, fax 02/748-1384, www.prenocisca-ziga.com, prenocisce .ziga@gmail.com, run with care by the Šoštarić family).

$$ Hotel Poetovio (named for Ptuj's Roman settlement) is your last resort. Its 24 rooms have some of the oldest, rattiest furniture I've seen, and its location—on the main road at the edge of the Old Town—leaves something to be desired (Sb-€28, Db-€38, Tb-€46, Vinarski trg 5, tel. 02/779-8201, fax 02/779-8241, www .memoria.si).

$ Kurent Youth Hostel, an IYHF hostel, is new (from 2004), institutional, comfortable, and clean. It has 53 bunks in two- to six-bed rooms, each with its own bathroom (€16 per bed, €1.50 less with hostel membership, breakfast €0.50 extra, Internet access, self-service laundry-€4.50/load, reception open daily 8:00–12:00 & 16:00–20:00, Osojnikova 9, tel. 02/771-0814, fax 02/771-0815, yhptuj@csod.si). It's hiding in the big, pinkish commercial center (with the Spar supermarket) near the bus station.

EATING

Little Ptuj isn't known for its high cuisine. You'll spot several breezy cafés and packed pizzerias, but high-quality eateries are in short supply.

Gostilna Ribič is every local's first recommendation for a splurge dinner. One of the most popular (and expensive) places in town, it has a short menu focusing on fish. Sit in the classy interior, or outside on the relaxing riverside terrace (€10–17 main dishes, open long hours daily, Dravska ulica 9, tel. 02/749-0635). If you're ready for a break from Slovenian cuisine, the Chinese restaurant across the street is also quite good.

Gostilna Amadeus serves up traditional Slovenian cuisine to tour groups, individual tourists, and a few locals. They're especially proud of their €3.50 *štruklji,* or filled dumplings. The bar, with outdoor seating, is downstairs; to eat a meal, head upstairs to their nicely appointed dining room (€5–10 main dishes, Mon–Sat 12:00–23:00, Sun 12:00–16:00, Prešernova 36, tel. 02/771-7051).

PP is frequented by locals who enjoy its inexpensive, unpretentious, stick-to-your-ribs fare—lots of meat and potatoes, plus fried...everything. It's on the town's main shopping square (Novi trg), surrounded by supermarkets and malls. There's a Kavarna (café) with light food and outdoor seating; to eat a full meal, look for the indoor Gostilna (filling €4–8 main dishes, Mon–Sat 9:00–19:00, Sun 12:00–16:00, the Kavarna has longer hours, Novi trg 2, tel. 02/749-0622). The name stands for Perutnina Ptuj, a chicken conglomerate that owns half the town (including this place, Gostilna Ribič, and the big wine cellar)—you'll see their logo everywhere.

Pizzeria Slonček has a great location right on Prešernova, with outdoor tables and good €5 pizzas (open long hours daily, Prešernova 19, tel. 02/776-1311).

TRANSPORTATION CONNECTIONS

From Ptuj by Train to: Maribor (8/day, 45–60 min), **Ljubljana** (6/day, 2–3 hrs, 1 direct, otherwise transfer in Pragersko), **Zagreb** (9/day, 3–4.5 hrs, usually requires 2 transfers), **Budapest** (1/day direct, 6.25 hrs, additional longer connections possible with transfers), **Vienna** (5/day, 4.5–6.75 hrs, most require 1–2 changes). For destinations in western Slovenia, first go to Ljubljana.

Maribor

The second-biggest city in Slovenia (with 110,000 people), Maribor lives forever in the shadow of its much glitzier big sister, Ljubljana. Maribor is too small to offer an exciting big-city experience, and too big to be charming. But this home of industry, business, and one of Slovenia's three universities is worth a quick look if you want to round out your Slovenian experience.

The lazy provincial town of Maribor woke up fast in 1846, when the Hapsburgs built the train line from Vienna to the coast through here. It quickly modernized, losing some of its quaintness but gaining an urban, industrial flavor. However, Maribor was devastated in World War II (unlike other Slovenian cities), when it served as a headquarters for occupying Nazi forces. Since the city's factories also produced plane engines and other supplies, it became a "secondary target," where Allied warplanes—mostly Americans—would drop their bombs if unable to bomb their primary targets in Germany or Austria.

Today, rebuilt Maribor feels mellow for its size. Nestled up against a gentle vineyard-covered hill, it's almost cozy. From a tourist's perspective, the town is pleasant but dull—there's little to do other than wander its pedestrians-only streets. Maribor doesn't merit a detour, but it's worth a couple of hours for a stroll if you're  passing through or have run out of diversions in Ptuj.

The countryside surrounding Maribor—called Mariborsko Pohorje—is an inviting recreational area, with vine-strewn hills beloved by hikers and bicyclists in summer and by skiers in winter. Maribor is also the center of a thriving wine-growing region—especially popular among Austrians, who flow over the border to sample wines here, then stumble home. If you have time to spare, ask the TI for details about either of these outlying activities.

ORIENTATION

Maribor lines up along the bank of the Drava River. At the center of its concrete sprawl is the mostly traffic-free Old Town, with a variety of fine squares.

Tourist Information

The main TI is at the northeast corner of the Old Town, on the far side of the Franciscan Church from Trg Svobode (Mon–Fri 9:00–19:00, Sat 9:00–17:00, Sun 9:00–12:00, Partizanska 6a, tel. 02/234-6611, www.maribor-tourism.si). A branch TI may be across the street from the train station (but could be closed in 2007). Pick up the handy city map and any other brochures that interest you. The TI can also give you a list of hotels or help you arrange for a local guide.

Arrival in Maribor

The train station (which has big €2 lockers) is a 10-minute walk east of the Old Town. Exit the station to the left and head up busy Partizanska cesta. If the branch TI across the street from the station is open, stop in to pick up a map before heading into town. Follow Partizanska as it swings right at the bus station, then continue three more blocks toward the Franciscan Church, with its twin red-brick spires. The main TI is in front of the church, and the Old Town is immediately behind the church.

SELF-GUIDED WALK

Welcome to Maribor

Maribor's Austrian-feeling Old Town lacks big-league sights, but its squares and lanes are worth a wander. This very lightly narrated walk will give you the lay of the land. You could do it in less than a half-hour, not including stops.

Entering the Old Town from the train station (on Partizanska, near the Franciscan Church with its two red-brick spires—see "Arrival in Maribor"), you find yourself on **Trg Svobode.** The oddly bulbous monument honors local Partisans who were executed by Nazis during World War II. Wine cellars honeycomb the earth under this square (most can be toured only with a group—ask at the TI).

At the end of the square is the town's **castle** (Mestni Grad), with the tall tower. The castle usually houses a good regional museum, which is likely closed for renovation in 2007.

Adjoining Trg Svobode is a second square, **Grajski trg**— Maribor's liveliest, bustling with cafés and restaurants (including the recommended Štajerc brewpub, described under "Eating," later in this section). At the top of the square is the venerable **Café Astoria,** a local landmark (open long hours daily).

Recent-history buffs may want to take a detour from here to Maribor's most interesting museum: the **Maribor National Liberation Museum** (Muzej Narodone Osvoboditve Maribor), about a five-minute walk up the street at the top of Grajski trg (between Café Astoria and the castle). This collection features a hodgepodge of items from the city's history, mostly focusing on Slovenia's turbulent 20th century. A permanent exhibit covers the early Tito years (1945–1955), and is supplemented by temporary exhibits. Enjoy the idealized propaganda posters of happy Yugoslavs, eagerly pitching in to build a new nation (€1.25, Mon–Fri 8:00–18:00, Sat 9:00–12:00, closed Sun, Ulica Heroja Tomšiča 5).

Back on Grajski trg, follow lively **Slovenska ulica,** lined with characteristic cafés, sweet shops, and happy *al fresco* diners. Take a left at Gosposka, then turn right on 10 Oktobra to find the big parking-lot square called Slomškov trg, with the city **cathedral** (skip the tower climb—the view is nothing special).

From the cathedral, walk straight down toward the river, cutting through Rotovški trg. You'll wind up on the long, narrow **Glavni trg,** surrounded by historic buildings (including the City Hall) and presided over by an impressive 18th-century plague column.

If you continue down to the riverbank, you'll find yourself in the district called **Lent,** where vintners traditionally offer tastings of their wines. While it's usually pretty quiet, this area hops each summer when Maribor hosts its Lent Festival (late June–early July, http://lent.slovenija.net). Along this embankment, look for the locally revered "old vine" stretching along a railing—it's supposedly 400 years old, and still produces wine.

EATING

Štajerc is a popular local watering hole that brews its own beer and serves up heavy, starchy, traditional food. They're particularly known for their distinctive emerald-green beer, *Štajerc Zeleno*. Sit inside, or enjoy the outdoor seating on Maribor's most happening square, Grajski trg (€5–10 meals, closed Sun, Vetrinjska 30, tel. 02/234-4234).

TRANSPORTATION CONNECTIONS

From Maribor by Train to: Ptuj (8/day, 45–60 min), **Ljubljana** (at least hourly, 1.75–3 hrs, some direct, others transfer in Zidani Most).

THE KARST

Caves, Castles, and Horses

In Slovenia's Karst region, about an hour on the A-1 expressway south of Ljubljana, you'll find some of the most impressive cave systems on the planet, a chance to see the famous Lipizzaner stallions for a fraction of what you'd pay in Vienna, and one of Europe's most dramatically situated castles—built into the face of a mountain.

The term "karst" is used worldwide to refer to an arid limestone plateau, but Slovenia's is the original. It comes from the Slovenian word "Kras"—a specific region near the Italian border. Since this limestone terrain is easily dissolved by water, karstic regions are punctuated by remarkable networks of caves and underground rivers.

Your top Karst priority is a cave visit. Choose between Slovenia's two best caves, Škocjan or Postojna—each with a handy side-trip nearby (to help you pick, see the sidebar on page 421).

In the neighborhood of Škocjan is Lipica, where the Lipizzaner stallions strut their stuff. Just up the road from Postojna is Predjama Castle, picturesquely nestled into the side of a cliff.

Sleeping: To sleep in the heart of the Karst—a short drive from all these sights—consider **Tourist Farm Hudičevec,** halfway between Škocjan and Postojna. It's as comfortable and private as a hotel. A roomy, spick-and-span double with a private bathroom—including a Slovenian dinner and farm-fresh eggs for breakfast—costs only €56 for two people (Db without dinner-€40, Razdrto 1, tel. 05/703-0300, fax 05/703-0320, www.hudicevec .com, hudicevec@siol.net, Simčič family). Idyllic and remote as this place sounds, it's actually close to the expressway—and large tour groups frequently show up for dinner.

The Karst Region

Škocjan Caves and the Lipica Stud Farm

Škocjan Caves (Škocjanske Jame)

Škocjan (SHKOHTS-yahn) offers good formations and a vast canyon with a raging underground river. You'll end up walking about two miles, going up and down more than 400 steps. While anyone in good shape can enjoy Škocjan, those who have trouble walking or tire easily are better off touring Postojna (see "Postojna Caves and Predjama Castle" later in this chapter).

Upon arrival, get a ticket for the next tour (they rarely fill up). You'll pass waiting time at a covered terrace with a tiny gift kiosk and a bar serving light meals and drinks. At tour time, your guide (toting an industrial-strength flashlight) calls everyone together, and you march silently for 10 minutes to the cave entrance. There you split into language groups and enter the cave.

The first half of the experience is the "dry caves," with wondrous formations and what seem like large caverns. Then you get to the truly colossal "finale" cavern, with a mighty river crashing

---

Postojna vs. Škocjan: Which Caves to Visit?

To Postojna or to Škocjan?—that is the question. Each cave system is massive, cut into the limestone by rivers for more than two million years. Stalagmites and stalactites—in a slow-motion love story—silently work their way towards each other until that last drip never drops. Minerals picked up by the water as it seeps through various rocks create the different colors (iron makes red, limestone makes white, and so on). Both caves were excavated and explored in the mid-19th century.

Slovenes debate long and hard about which cave system is better. The formations at Postojna are slightly more abundant, varied, and colorful, with stalagmites and stalactites as tall as 100 feet. Postojna is easier to reach by public transportation, and far less strenuous to visit than Škocjan—of the three-mile route, you'll walk only about a mile (the rest of the time, you're on a Disney World–type people-mover). But Postojna is also more expensive and much more touristy—you'll wade through tour buses and tacky souvenir stands on your way to the entrance. Most importantly, Postojna lacks Škocjan's spectacular, massive-cavern finale. Škocjan also comes with a fairly strenuous hike, leaving you feeling like you really did something adventurous. Finally, the choice of likely side-trip might help you decide: Near Postojna is the cliff-hanging Predjama Castle, while Škocjan is closer to the Lipica Stud Farm.

No matter which cave you visit, you'll find it chilly, but not really cold (a light sweater is fine). Both caves forbid photography (a laughable rule that nobody takes seriously).

---

through the bottom. You feel like a bit player in a sci-fi thriller. It's a world where a thousand evil *Wizard of Oz* monkeys could comfortably fly in formation. You hike high above the river for about a mile, crossing a breathtaking (but stable-feeling) footbridge 150 feet above the torrent. Far below, the scant remains of century-old trails from the early days of tourism are evocative. The cave finally widens, sunlight pours in, and you emerge—like lost creatures seeking daylight—into a lush canyon. A steep, somewhat strenuous hike leads to a small funicular, which lifts you back to the ticket booth/café/shop.

Cost and Hours: The guided tour is mandatory and takes about two hours (€11, June–Sept tours daily at the top of each hour 10:00–17:00, Oct–May tours daily at 10:00 and 13:00 and sometimes also at 15:00 or 15:30, call or pick up current brochure—which you'll find everywhere in Slovenia—to confirm schedule before making the trip, tel. 05/763-2840, www.park-skocjanske-jame.si).

Getting to Škocjan: By car, take the A-1 expressway south from Ljubljana about 90 minutes and get off at the Divača exit (also marked with brown signs for Lipica and Škocjanske jame) and follow signs for Škocjanske jame. (Before or after Škocjan, drivers can easily visit the Lipica Stud Farm.) The caves have free and easy parking.

By public transportation, it's trickier. Take the train or bus to Divača (see Ljubljana's "Transportation Connections," page 352), which is about three miles from the caves. Either hike in or take a taxi from the Divača station (tel. 05/734-5428). A better but less predictable option is to take one of the buses from Ljubljana to Piran that goes along the older road (not all of them do; ask for details at bus station). This bus can drop you off closer to the caves (one mile away—ask for "Škocjanske jame," SHKOHTS-yahn-skeh YAH-meh).

Lipica Stud Farm (Kobilarna Lipica)

The Lipica (LEE-peet-suh) Stud Farm, a 10-minute drive from the Škocjan Caves, was founded in 1580 to provide horses for the Hapsburg court in Vienna. Horse-loving Hapsburg Archduke Charles wanted to create the perfect animal: He imported Andalusian horses from his homeland of Spain, then mixed them with a local line to come up with an extremely intelligent and easily trainable breed. Charles' creation, the Lipizzaner stallions—known for their noble gait and Baroque shape—were made famous by Vienna's Spanish Riding School. Italian and Arabian bloodlines were later added to tweak various characteristics. These regal horses have changed shape with the tenor of the times: They were bred strong and stout during wars, frilly and slender in more cultured eras. But they're always born black, fade to gray, and turn a distinctive white in adulthood. Until World War I, Lipica bred horses for Austria's needs. Now Austria breeds its own line, and these horses prance for Slovenia—a treasured part of its cultural heritage (and featured on Slovenia's €0.20 coin).

Today you can tour the Lipizzaner stables to visit the magnificent animals, whose stalls are labeled with purebred bloodlines. Unlike in Vienna, tickets to see the horses perform here are cheap and easy to get. Visitors thrill to the Lipizzaners' clever routine—stutter-stepping sideways to the classical beat. This excursion—offering an up-close horse encounter—is less polished (and cheaper) than the Lipizzaner experience in Vienna. It's worth a visit only if you're a horse enthusiast, or if you have a car and it fits your schedule (for example, drivers visiting the Škocjan Caves are only a few minutes away).

By the way, the hills less than a mile away are in Italy. Aside from the horses, Lipica's big draw is its casino. Italians across the border are legally forbidden from gambling in their own town's casinos—for fear of addiction—so they flock here to Slovenia to try their luck. Farther north, the Slovenian border town of Nova Gorica has Europe's biggest casino, packed with gamblers from the Italian side of town.

Visiting the Stud Farm: There are three activities at Lipica: **Touring** the farm for a look at the horses; watching a **performance** of the prancing stallions; and, on days when there's no performance, watching a **training session.** If you're coming all the way to Lipica, you might as well time it so that you can do both the tour and a performance (or a training session). Call ahead to confirm performance and tour times before you make the trip (tel. 05/739-1580, www.lipica.org).

Cost: Stud farm tour only-€7, tour plus performance-€14, tour plus training session-€9.

Tours: July–Aug daily on the hour 9:00–18:00 except 12:00; April–June and Sept–Oct daily on the hour 10:00–17:00 except 12:00 (also at 9:00 and 18:00 Sat–Sun); off-season daily at 11:00, 13:00, 14:00, and 15:00 (plus 10:00 and 16:00 Sat–Sun in March). Note that on days when there's a 15:00 performance, you can tour the farm before (14:00) or after (15:40) the show; likewise, if you attend a 12:00 training session, you can do the tour before (11:00) or after (13:00).

Performances: April–Oct Tue, Wed, Fri, and Sun at 15:00, none Nov–March.

Training Sessions: April–Oct Thu at 12:00, none Nov–March.

Getting to Lipica: The Lipica Stud Farm is in Slovenia's southwest corner (a stone's throw from Trieste, Italy). By car, exit the A-1 expressway at Divača and follow brown *Lipica* signs. (As you drive into the farm, you'll go through pastures where the stallions often roam.) It's a major hassle by public transportation. You can take the train or bus from Ljubljana to Divača (see "Getting to Škocjan," earlier in this chapter)—but that's still about five miles from Lipica, with no bus connections. You could take a taxi (about €15 one-way from Divača station, tel. 05/734-5428) or try hitching a ride on a friendly tour bus. Note that there's also no bus connection between Škocjan and Lipica.

Postojna Caves and Predjama Castle

Postojna Caves (Postojnska Jama)
Postojna (poh-STOY-nah) is the most accessible—and touristy—cave experience in the region. It's the biggest cave system

in Slovenia (and, before borders shifted a few generations ago, it was the biggest in Italy...a fact that envious Italians still haven't forgotten).

Whether you arrive by car, tour bus, or on foot, you'll walk past a paved outdoor mall of shops, eateries, and handicraft vendors to the gaping hole in the mountain. Buy your ticket and board a train, which slings you deep into the mountain, whizzing past wonderful formations. (The ride alone is exhilarating.) Then you get out, assemble into language groups, and follow a guide on a well-lit, circular, paved path through more formations. You'll see 100-foot-tall stalagmites and stalactites, as well as translucent "curtains" of rock and ceilings dripping with skinny "spaghetti stalactites." You'll wind up peering at the strange "human fish" (a.k.a. olm or *Proteus anguinus*)—sort of a long, skinny, pale-pink salamander with fingers and toes. The world's biggest cave-dwelling animal, these amphibians can survive up to seven years without eating (the live specimens you see here are never fed during the four months they're on display). Then you'll load back onto the train and return to the bright daylight.

Cost and Hours: Your visit, which is by tour only, costs €18 and lasts 90 minutes. Tours leave May–Sept daily at the top of each hour 9:00–18:00 (off-season daily at 10:00, 12:00, and 14:00; April and Oct and Nov–March Sat–Sun also at 16:00; call to confirm schedule or pick up brochure at any TI). From mid-May through August, try to show up 30 minutes early for the morning tours (popular with tour buses); otherwise, aim for 15 minutes ahead. Information: tel. 05/700-0100, www.postojna-cave.com.

"Proteus Vivarium": This exhibit gives you the chance to learn more about karstic caves and about speleobiology—the study of cave-dwelling animal life. While troglodytes, science nuts, and those who just can't get enough of those human fish may get a charge out of this exhibit, it's basically just an attempt to wring a little more cash out of gullible tourists (€6; May–Sept daily 8:30–18:30; April and Oct daily 9:30–16:30; Nov–March Mon–Fri 10:30–14:30, Sat–Sun 9:30–16:00).

Getting to Postojna: The caves are just outside the town of Postojna, about an hour south of Ljubljana on the A-1 expressway (Jamska cesta 30). By car, take the expressway south from Ljubljana and get off at the Postojna exit. Turn right after the tollbooth and follow the *jama/grotte/cave* signs through town until you see the tour buses. Drivers pay €3 to park 200 yards from the cave entry. The train from Ljubljana to Postojna arrives at a station 20 minutes by foot from the caves. The bus drops you just five minutes from the caves. (For details, see Ljubljana's "Transportation Connections," page 352.)

Predjama Castle (Predjamski Grad)

Burrowed into the side of a mountain close to Postojna is dramatic Predjama Castle (prehd-YAH-mah), one of Europe's most scenic castles. Predjama is a hit with tourists for its striking setting, exciting exterior, and romantic legend.

What a wonderful site for a castle. Notice as you approach that you don't even see Predjama—crouching magnificently in its cave—until the last moment. The first castle here was actually a tiny ninth-century fortress embedded deep in the cave behind the present castle. Over the centuries, different castles were built here, and they gradually moved out to the mouth of the cave. While the original was called "the castle in the cave," the current one is *pred jama*—"in front of the cave."

While enjoying the view, ponder this legend: In the 15th century, a nobleman named Erasmus killed the emperor's cousin in a duel. He was imprisoned under Ljubljana Castle, and spent years nursing a grudge. When he was finally released, he used his castle—buried deep inside the cave above this current version—as a home base for a series of Robin Hood–style raids on the local nobility and merchants. (Actually, Erasmus stole from the rich and kept for himself—but that was good enough to make him a hero to the peasants, who hated the nobles.)

Soldiers from Trieste were brought in to put an end to Erasmus' raids, laying siege to the castle for over a year. Back then, the only way into the castle was through the cave in the valley below—then up, through an extensive labyrinth of caves, to the top. While the soldiers down below froze and starved, Erasmus' men sneaked out through the caves to bring in supplies. (They liked to drop their leftovers on the soldiers below to taunt them, letting them know that the siege wasn't working.)

Eventually, the soldiers came up with a plan. They waited for Erasmus to visit the latrine—which, by design, had to be on the thin-walled outer edge of the castle—and then, on seeing a signal by a secret agent, blew Erasmus off his throne with a cannonball. Today, Erasmus is supposedly buried under the huge linden tree in the parking lot.

As the legend of Erasmus faded, the function of the castle changed. By the 16th century, Predjama had become a castle for hunting more than for defense—explaining its current picturesque-but-impractical design.

After driving all the way here, it seems a shame not to visit the interior—but it's truly skippable. The management (which also runs the nearby Postojna Caves) is very strict about keeping the interior 16th-century in style, so there's virtually nothing inside except 20th-century fakes of 16th-century furniture, plus a few forgettable paintings and cheesy folk displays. English descriptions are sparse, and the free English history flier is not much help. But for most, the views of the place alone are worth the drive.

Cost and Hours: €7, daily May–Sept 9:00–19:00, April and Oct 10:00–18:00, Nov–March 10:00–16:00. Information: tel. 05/751-6015.

Cave Tours: If you're already visiting the caves at Postojna or Škocjan, a visit to the caves under this castle is unnecessary (€7, 45 min, May–Sept daily at 11:00, 13:00, 15:00, and 17:00, no tours Oct–April).

Getting to Predjama: Predjama Castle is on a twisty rural road 5.5 miles beyond Postojna Caves. By car, just continue on the winding road past Postojna, following signs for *Predjama* and *Predjamski Grad* (coming back, follow signs to *Postojna*). By public transportation, it's difficult. There is one bus per day from Postojna to Predjama, and another to Bukovje (about a half-mile from Predjama)—but you'll be stranded at Predjama, with no return bus. Consider hitching a ride at Postojna on a friendly Predjama-bound tour bus or tourist's car, as most visitors do both sights.

PIRAN

Croatia's 3,600-mile-long coast gets all the press, but don't overlook Slovenia's own 29 miles of Adriatic coastline. The Slovenian coast has only a handful of towns: big, industrial Koper; lived-in and crumbling Izola; and the swanky but soulless resort of Portorož. But the Back Door gem of the Slovenian Adriatic is Piran. Most Adriatic towns are all tourists and concrete, but Piran has kept itself charming and in remarkably good repair while holding the tourist sprawl at bay. In peak season, it's overrun with Italian vacationers and can feel a bit greedy at first. But as you get to know it, Piran becomes one of the most pleasant and user-friendly seaside towns this side of Dubrovnik.

Planning Your Time

You can see everything in Piran (including a pop into the Maritime Museum and a hike up the bell tower) in a quick hour-long walk. Then feel free to just bask in the town's ambience. Enjoy a gelato or a *kava* (coffee) on the sleek, marbled Tartini Square, surrounded by Neoclassical buildings and watched over by the bell tower. Wander Piran's piers and catch its glow at sunset. Piran also works as a base for visiting the caves, horses, and castles of the nearby Karst region (see previous chapter).

ORIENTATION

(area code: 05)

Piran (pee-RAHN) is small; everything is within a few minutes' walk. Crowded onto the tip of its peninsula, the town can't grow. Its population—7,500 a century ago—has dropped to

Piran

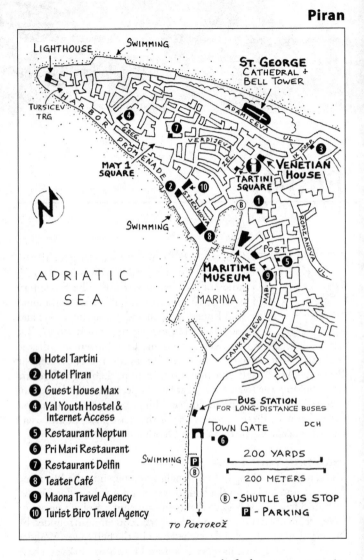

LIGHTHOUSE SWIMMING

ST. GEORGE CATHEDRAL + BELL TOWER

TURSICEV TRG

HARBOR PROMENADE

GREG.

MAY 1 SQUARE

ADAMICEVA UL.

VERDIJEVA

VENETIAN HOUSE

VLIK KORP

TARTINI SQUARE

ADRIATIC SEA

MARINA

SWIMMING

S. JENKOVA

MARITIME MUSEUM

POST

NAB.

ROMZANOVA UL.

CANKARJEVO

1 Hotel Tartini
2 Hotel Piran
3 Guest House Max
4 Val Youth Hostel & Internet Access
5 Restaurant Neptun
6 Pri Mari Restaurant
7 Restaurant Delfin
8 Teater Café
9 Maona Travel Agency
10 Turist Biro Travel Agency

BUS STATION FOR LONG-DISTANCE BUSES

TOWN GATE

DCH

200 YARDS

200 METERS

B - SHUTTLE BUS STOP
P - PARKING

SWIMMING

TO PORTOROŽ

about 4,200 today, as many young people find more opportunity in bigger cities.

Piran clusters around its boat-speckled harbor and main showpiece square, Tartini Square (Tartinijev trg). Up the hill behind Tartini Square is the landmark bell tower of the Cathedral of St. George. A few blocks towards the end of the peninsula from Tartini Square is the heart of the Old Town, May 1 Square (Trg 1 Maja).

From Tartini Square and the nearby marina, a concrete

promenade—lined with rocks to break the storm waves, and with expensive tourist restaurants to break your budget—stretches along the town's waterfront, inviting you to stroll.

Tourist Information

The TI is on Tartini Square facing the marina (daily June–Aug 9:00–13:30 & 15:00–21:00, Sept–May 10:00–17:00, at #2, tel. 05/673-4440, www.portoroz.si). For **Internet access,** get online at the Val Youth Hostel (see "Sleeping," later in this chapter).

Arrival in Piran

By Car: It's easiest to park at the big harborside lot, just outside the gate into town (€8/day, frequent shuttle buses take you right to Tartini Square, or walk there in 10 min). If you want to drive into the town, get a ticket at the gate (you'll pay as you exit, 6-hour maximum). But once you're inside town, most parking is reserved for locals. The only parking for tourists is in the congested area around Tartini Square (parking anywhere else will likely get you a ticket—ask TI for specifics). I'd only enter town to drop off things at my hotel, then take my car right back to the harborside lot.

By Bus: Piran has two bus stops. Shuttle buses from the harborside parking lot and nearby towns (such as Portorož) stop right at Tartini Square; buses to long-distance destinations (such as Ljubljana) use the low-profile bus station along the water near the entrance to town.

SIGHTS AND ACTIVITIES

In Piran

▲**Tartini Square (Tartinijev trg)**—Tartini Square, with its polished marble, was once part of a protected harbor. In 1894, the harbor smelled so bad that they decided to fill it in. Today, rather than fishing boats, it's filled with kids on skateboards.

The statue honors Giuseppe Tartini (1692–1770), a composer and violinist once known throughout Europe. While the Church of St. Peter has overlooked this spot since 1272, its current facade is Neoclassical, from the early 1800s. The Neo-Renaissance Town Hall dates from the 1870s.

The fine little red palace in the corner (at #4) evokes Venice. This **"Venetian House"** (c. 1450) is the oldest preserved house on the square. Classic Venetian Gothic, it was built by a wealthy Venetian merchant and comes

Piran History

Piran was named for the fires (*pyr* in Greek) that were lit at the tip of its peninsula to assist passing ships. Known as "Pirano" in *Italiano*, the town is home to a long-standing Italian community (about 1,500 today)—so it's legally bilingual, with signs in two languages. As with most towns on the Adriatic, it has a Venetian flavor. Piran wisely signed on with Venice as part of its trading empire in 933. Because of its valuable salt industry and strong trade, Piran managed some autonomy in later centuries. After plagues killed most of Piran's population in the 15th century, local Italians let Slavs fleeing the Ottomans repopulate the town. Piran's impressive walls were built to counter the growing Ottoman threat. Too much rain ruined the town's salt basins, but in the 19th century, the Austrian Hapsburg rulers rebuilt the salt industry. With that came a new economic boom, and Piran grew in importance once again. After World War I, this part of the Hapsburg Empire was assigned to Italy, but fascism never sat well with the locals. After World War II, the region was made neutral, then became part of Yugoslavia in 1956. And in 1991, with the creation of Slovenia, the Slovenes of Piran were finally independent.

with a legend: The merchant fell in love with a simple local girl when visiting on business, became her sugar daddy, and eventually built her this flat. When the townsfolk began to gossip about the relationship, he answered them with the relief you see today (with the Venetian lion, between the two top windows): *Lassa pur dir* ("Let them talk").

May 1 Square (Trg 1 Maja)—This square marks the center of medieval Piran, where its main streets converged. Once the administrative center of town, today it's the domain of local kids and ringed by a few humble eateries. The stone rainwater cistern dominating the center of the square was built in 1775 after a severe drought. Rainwater was captured here with the help of drains from roofs, and channeled by hardworking statues into the system. The water was filtered through sand and stored in the well, clean and ready for townspeople to draw—or, later, pump—for drinking.

Cathedral and Bell Tower of St. George (Stolna Cerkev Sv. Jurija)—Piran is proud of its many churches, numbering more than 20. While none are of any real historic or artistic importance, the Cathedral of St. George—dating from the 14th century, and decorated Baroque by Venetian artists in the 17th century—is worth a look. It dominates the Old Town with its bell tower *(campanile)*, a miniature version of the more famous one in Venice. The tower (with bells dating from the 15th century) welcomes tourists willing to pay €1 to climb 146 rickety steps for the best view in town and a chance for some bell fun (daily 10:00–17:00, until 19:00 in summer). Stand inside the biggest bell. Chant, find the resonant frequency, and ring the clapper ever so softly. Snap a portrait of you, your partner, and the rusty clapper. Brace yourself for *fortissimo* clangs on the quarter-hour.

Sergej Mašera Maritime Museum (Pomorski Muzej Sergej Mašera)—This humble museum faces the harbor and the square, filling an elegant old building with meager but faintly endearing exhibits—furniture, model ships, and paintings—about the "Slovene seamen" and the town's history (€3.50, €0.50 English booklet, otherwise borrow scant English descriptions; July–Aug Tue–Sun 9:00–12:00 & 18:00–21:00, closed Mon; Sept–June Tue–Sun 9:00–12:00 & 15:00–18:00, closed Mon; Cankarjevo nabrežje 3, tel. 05/671-0040, www.pommuz-pi.si).

Harborfront Stroll—Wandering along the harborfront is a delight: almost no pesky mopeds or cars, and virtually no American or Japanese tourists—just Slovenes and Italians. Children sell shells on cardboard boxes. Husky sunbathers lie like large limpets on the rocks. Walk around the lighthouse at the tip of the town and around the corner, checking out the cafés and fish restaurants along the way.

Swimming—While there is no sandy beach, the water is warm and clean, and swimming is a major activity in Piran. There are two pebbly beaches: one just outside of town before the big parking lot, and the other at the end of the harbor promenade past the lighthouse. Two designated swimming areas are accessible from the promenade—both with very slippery concrete embankments, ladders, and showers (one in front of Hotel Piran, the other around the corner from the lighthouse).

Near Piran

▲Sečovlje Salina Nature Park (Krajinski Park Sečoveljske Soline)—Just south of Piran, a stone's throw from the Croatian border, are enormous salt fields used since the Middle Ages for harvesting salt. As you drive by on the way to Croatia, you'll wonder what this massive complex is—so why not stop for a visit? There are two parts to this "nature park": **Lera,** to the north, harvests salt using modern techniques; while **Fontanigge,** to the south (closer to Croatia), is no longer in operation—except to demonstrate traditional salt-harvesting methods to tourists. I'd skip the Lera section (or visit it quickly), but make time for Fontanigge and its interesting museum.

At Fontanigge (within a few feet of the Croatian border, which is just over the little river), you'll see the way salt was harvested from medieval times up until the 1960s. Well-explained by posted English information and a knowledgeable docent, the exhibit demonstrates tools and methods, and explains the lifestyles of the people who eked out a hard living on these salty marshes (for example, since they all shared a communal oven, each family had their own stamp for marking their loaves of bread). If your timing's right, you may even see people gathering salt the way their ancestors did. I never thought salt could be so interesting.

The catch: The museum is about a mile and a half off the main road, reached only by a very bumpy gravel road. The management encourages people to walk (30 min one-way) instead of drive along the gravel road to the museum, but if you ask nicely, they might let you drive (especially in bad weather).

Cost, Hours, Information: Entry to both Fontanigge and Lera salt fields-€2.50, daily 8:00–18:00, summer until 20:00, winter until 17:00; museum entry-€4, daily June–Aug 9:00–20:00, April–May and Sept–Oct 9:00–18:00, closed Nov–March; tel. 05/671-0040, www.kpss.soline.si.

Getting There: Both salt fields are between Piran and the Croatian border. As you drive south (see "Route Tips for Drivers" at the end of this chapter), you'll pass the entrance to the modern Lera salt field on the right just after entering the town of Seča. For the more interesting Fontanigge, it's more complicated: You'll actually have to cross the Slovenian border. A few feet later, just before you reach the Croatian border post, you'll see a gravel road on the right, leading to the salt field. It's about a five-minute drive to the gate, where (hopefully) they'll let you continue in your car another 10 or so minutes on the very rough gravel road to the museum. Much easier: Boats from Piran can occasionally take you directly to the museum—ask at the TI.

SLEEPING

Piran's accommodations options are limited: two comparable hotels, a colorful guest house, and a youth hostel. The hotels raise their rates in peak season (mid-July–late Aug). If everyone's booked up, find a *soba* (room in a private home).

$$$ Hotel Tartini faces the main square 50 yards from the waterfront. Its 45 rooms are jaunty, colorful, and a bit faded (Sb-€66, Db-€92; peak season: Sb-€82, Db-€108; €6 more for seaside room with balcony; air-con, elevator, Internet access, Tartinijev trg 15, tel. 05/671-1000, fax 05/671-1665, www.hotel-tartini-piran.com, info@hotel-tartini-piran.com).

$$$ Hotel Piran is right on the water, with a concrete "beach" directly in front of it. Its 89 rooms are more business than resort, with a complex pricing scheme (seaview Sb-€68, non-view

---

Sleep Code

(€1 = about $1.20, country code: 386, area code: 05)
S = Single, **D** = Double/Twin, **T** = Triple, **Q** = Quad, **b** = bathroom.
Unless otherwise noted, credit cards are accepted and break-
fast is included. Everyone speaks English.

To help you sort easily through these listings, I've divided
the rooms into three categories based on the price for a standard double room with bath:

$$$ **Higher Priced**—Most rooms €85 or more.
  $$ **Moderately Priced**—Most rooms between €50–85.
   $ **Lower Priced**—Most rooms €50 or less.

Db-€83, seaview Db-€102; peak season: seaview Sb-€74, non-
view Db-€94, seaview Db-€114; "superior" rooms have air-con,
a bigger bathroom, and more soundproof windows for €10 more;
prices drop Nov–mid-April, elevator, Internet access, Kidričevo
nabrežje 4, tel. 05/676-2100, fax 05/676-2520, www.hoteli-piran.si,
marketing@hoteli-piran.si).

$$ Guest House Max is a clean-yet-funky place just under
the town's bell tower. Mellow and friendly Max welcomes travelers
with six simple, mod, and comfy rooms up a tight staircase over
a cozy breakfast room. He speaks English and enjoys sharing his
long afternoon siesta (13:00–17:00) with guests in his bar (Db-
€60, €70 in July–Aug, fans, ulica 9 Korpusa #26, tel. 05/673-3436,
mobile 041-692-928, www.maxpiran.com, info@maxpiran.com).
Since Max is a one-man show, it's essential to carefully settle on an
arrival time with him.

$ Val Youth Hostel rents the cheapest beds in this otherwise
expensive town. It's a friendly place, a half-block off the waterfront
(56 beds in 22 two-, three-, or four-bed rooms, €24 per person
mid-May–mid-Sept, €20 per person off-season, €2 more for 1-
night stays in peak season, includes breakfast and sheets, prices are
the same regardless of room size, free self-service laundry, kitchen;
free Internet access for guests, or €1/hr for non-guests; 20 yards
in from waterfront near tip of peninsula, Gregorčičeva 38A, tel.
05/673-2555, fax 05/673-2556, www.hostel-val.com, yhostel.val
@siol.net).

$ Sobe: To track down a private room, try two local travel
agencies: **Maona** (Cankarjevo nabrežje 7, tel. 05/673-4520, www
.maona.si, maonapiran@siol.net) or **Turist Biro** (Tomažičeva 3, tel.
05/673-2509, www.turistbiro-ag.si, info@turistbiro-ag.si). Piran's
sobe don't care for one- or two-nights stays (expect to pay 30–50
percent extra; may not be possible at all in peak season).

EATING

Pricey tourist bars and restaurants face the sea (figure about €20 per person), while the laid-back, funky, and colorful local joints seem to seek an escape from both the tourists and the sun in the back lanes. Get off the beaten track to find one of my recommended restaurants, and you'll enjoy a seafood-and-pasta feast for half what you'd pay in Venice (just across the sea).

Restaurant Neptun, with fresh seafood and pastas in a fish-net-strewn dining room, is far classier than the tacky tourist fish joints. The Grilj family and their three cooks work hard to please six tables of diners. Everything's made to order with fish straight out of the Adriatic—nothing's frozen. I can't resist their gnocchi with scampi (€4–8 pastas, €6–15 meat and fish dishes, daily 12:00–16:00 & 18:00–24:00, open all day in summer, Župančičeva 7, tel. 05/673-4111). Don't confuse this with Neptun Café, at the waterfront bus station.

Pri Mari Restaurant is about a 10-minute walk from Tartini Square, near the entrance to town. Gregarious Mara and Tomaž will welcome you into their cheery dining room like an old friend, then treat you to tasty Venetian-style cooking (€6–9 pastas, €7–12 meat and fish dishes, Tue–Sun 12:00–22:00, closed Mon, Dantejeva 17, tel. 05/673-4735).

Restaurant Delfin is a crank-'em-out fish restaurant with a good reputation. Run by the Pašalič family, it has a pleasant dining room as well as tables out on the Old Town's May 1 Square (€5 pastas, €6–10 meat dishes, €10–15 fish dishes, daily 11:00–24:00, Kosovelova 4, tel. 05/673-2448).

Drinks: **Teater Café** is *the* place for drinks with Adriatic views and a characteristic old interior. Catching the sunset here is a fine way to kick off your Piran evening (open long hours daily, Stjenkova 1).

TRANSPORTATION CONNECTIONS

The best way to connect Piran with **Ljubljana** is by **bus** (6/day, 2.5 hrs, €11.25). By **train,** the trip takes four hours (bus between Piran and Koper, then train between Koper and Ljubljana).

By **car,** Piran is about 90 minutes from Ljubljana. From Ljubljana, take the A-1 expressway south to Koper; once in Koper, follow *Portorož/Portorose* signs, then *Piran/Pirano.* For arrival and parking instructions, see "Arrival in Piran," earlier in this chapter.

To Istria: Public transportation between Piran and Rovinj (the best of Istria's seaside towns) is very difficult. In peak season (July–Aug), a few **buses** run daily from Piran to Istria (1/day to Rovinj departing at about 16:20, 3/day to Poreč, 2/day to Pula).

The rest of the year, there's just one bus per day from Portorož (near Piran) to Poreč, then on to Pula. So between September and June, to get from Piran to Rovinj, you'll have to take a local bus to Portorož, catch another bus to Poreč, then change to yet another bus for Rovinj. There are additional bus connections between Piran and Umag (at the northern end of Istria; 5/day in summer, 2/day in winter). From Umag, buses run to other destinations in Istria (including Rovinj and Pula).

About once weekly in summer, Venezia Lines runs **boats** between Piran and Istria (including Rovinj and Poreč; for details, visit www.venezialines.com).

To Venice: A **boat** called the *Prince of Venice*—designed for day-trippers, but also convenient for one-way transport—sails from Slovenia's coast to Venice two or three times each week in peak season. The boat generally goes from the nearby town of Izola. Occasionally the boat departs from Piran, stopping in the Croatian town of Umag en route to Venice (2.5-hr trip each way; €32–47 one-way, depending on season; departs from Izola at 8:00, or from Piran at 7:00; when boat departs from Izola, a shuttle bus picks up at Piran's Tartini Square 1 hour before departure; boat returns from Venice on the same day at 17:00, arriving Izola at 19:30; book through Kompas Travel Agency in nearby Portorož: tel. 05/617-8000, portoroz@kompas.si). Once a week from June through September, Italian-run **Venezia Lines** does a similar trip, departing directly from Piran (€43–46 one-way depending on season, usually departs Piran at 8:40 and arrives at Venice at 11:00, boat returns same day 17:00–19:20, from the US call 011-39-041-242-4000, from within Europe dial 00-39-041-242-4000, www.venezialines.com).

Route Tips for Drivers

Piran is a natural stopover between Ljubljana and Croatia's Istria. You can do the Karst sights on the way down (lined up conveniently along the A-1 expressway), sleep in Piran, then continue to Istria; or simply make a beeline to Piran and see the town before moving on to sleep in Istria.

From Piran to Istria: Leaving Piran, go through Portorož, then Lucija, then follow signs to Pula. Just after you enter Seča, signs on the right point to the salt fields. The border is just a few minutes straight ahead. (If you want to see the salt museum, remember that it's between the Slovenian and Croatian border posts—just after leaving Slovenia, keep an eye on the right for the very easy-to-miss gravel road.) Once in Croatia, follow signs to Pula to get on the *ipsilon* highway that zips you down through the middle of Istria.

UNDERSTANDING YUGOSLAVIA

Americans struggle to understand the complicated breakup of Yugoslavia (especially when visiting countries that rose from its ashes, such as Croatia and Slovenia). During the Yugoslav era, it was no less confusing. As the old joke went, Yugoslavia had eight distinct peoples in six republics, with five languages, three religions (Orthodox, Catholic, and Muslim), and two alphabets (Roman and Cyrillic), but only one Yugoslav—Tito.

Everyone you talk to in the former Yugoslavia will have a different version of events. A very wise Bosnian Muslim told me, "Listen to all three sides—Muslim, Serb, and Croat. Then decide for yourself what you think." That's the best advice I can offer. But since you likely won't have time for that on your brief visit, here's an admittedly oversimplified, as-impartial-as-possible history to get you started.

Who's Who

For starters, it helps to have a handle on the Balkans—the southeastern European peninsula between the Adriatic and the Black Sea, stretching from Hungary to Greece. The Balkan Peninsula has always been a crossroads of cultures. The Illyrians, Greeks, and Romans had settlements here before the Slavs moved into the region from the north around the seventh century. During the next millennium and a half, the western part of the peninsula—which would become Yugoslavia—was divided by a series of cultural, ethnic, and religious fault lines.

The most important influences were three religions: **Western Christianity** (i.e., Roman Catholicism, primarily brought to the western part of the region by Charlemagne, and later reinforced by the Austrian Hapsburgs), **Eastern Orthodox Christianity** (brought to the east from the Byzantine Empire), and **Islam** (in

Yugoslav Succession

the south, from the Ottomans).

Two major historical factors made the Balkans what they are today: The first was the **split of the Roman Empire** in the fourth century A.D., dividing the Balkans down the middle into Roman Catholic (west) and Byzantine Orthodox (east)—roughly along today's Bosnian-Serbian border. The second was the **invasion of the Islamic Ottomans** in the 14th century. The Ottoman victory at the Battle of Kosovo (1389) began five centuries of Islamic influence in Bosnia-Herzegovina and Serbia, further dividing the Balkans into Christian (north) and Muslim (south).

Because of these and other events, several distinct ethnic identities emerged. Confusingly, the major "ethnicities" of Yugoslavia are all South Slavs—they're descended from the same ancestors, and speak essentially the same language, but they practice

Who's Who in Yugoslavia

Yugoslavia was made up of six republics, which were inhabited by eight different ethnicities (not counting small minorities such as Jews, Germans, and Roma). This chart shows each ethnicity, and in which republic they were most concentrated. Not coincidentally, the more ethnicities in a region, the more conflict took place.

	Serbia*	Croatia	Bosnia-Herz.	Slovenia	Montenegro	Macedonia
Serbs (Orthodox)	x	x	x			
Croats (Catholic)		x	x			
Bosniaks (Muslims)			x			
Slovenes (Catholic)				x		
Macedonians (like Bulgarians)						x
Montenegrins (like Serbs)					x	
Albanians	x		x			x

*Within Serbia were two "autonomous provinces," each of which was dominated by a non-Slavic ethnic group: Hungarians in Vojvodina and Albanians in Kosovo. Tito intentionally set up these two autonomous provinces to prevent Serbia from becoming too powerful. Tito was right: Slobodan Milošević's annexation of Kosovo is precisely what tipped the balance of power in Yugoslavia, sparking the Balkan wars of the 1990s.

different religions. Catholic South Slavs are called **Croats** or **Slovenes** (mostly west of the Dinaric Mountains: Croats along the Adriatic coast, and Slovenes farther north, in the Alps); Orthodox South Slavs are called **Serbs** (mostly east of the Dinaric range); and Muslim South Slavs are called **Bosniaks** (who converted to Islam under the Ottomans, mostly living in the Dinaric Mountains). To complicate matters, the region is also home to several non-Slavic groups, including **Hungarians** (in the northern province of Vojvodina) and **Albanians,** concentrated in the southern province of Kosovo (descended from the Illyrians, who lived here long before the Greeks and Romans).

Of course, these geographic divisions are extremely general.

The groups overlapped a lot—which is exactly why the breakup of Yugoslavia was so contentious. For example, one of the biggest causes of this ethnic mixing came in the 16th century. The Ottomans were threatening to overrun Europe, and the Austrian Hapsburgs wanted a buffer zone—a "human shield." The Hapsburgs encouraged Serbs who were fleeing from Ottoman invasions to settle along today's Croatian-Bosnian border (known as *Vojna Krajina,* or "Military Frontier"). The Serbs stayed after the Ottomans had left, establishing homes in predominantly Croat communities.

After the Ottoman threat subsided in the late 17th century, some of the Balkans (basically today's Slovenia and Croatia) became part of the Austrian Hapsburg Empire. The Ottomans stayed longer in the south and east (today's Bosnia-Herzegovina and Serbia)—making the cultures in these regions even more different. Serbia finally gained its independence from the Ottomans in the mid-19th century, but it wasn't too long before World War I started...after a disgruntled Bosnian Serb nationalist killed the Austrian archduke.

South Slavs Unite

When the Austro-Hungarian Empire fell at the end of World War I, the European map was redrawn for the 20th century. After centuries of being governed by foreign powers, the South Slavs began to see their shared history as more important than their minor differences. A tiny country of a few million Croats or Slovenes couldn't have survived. Rather than be absorbed by a non-Slavic power, the South Slavs decided that there was safety in numbers, and banded together as a single state—first called the "Kingdom of the Serbs, Croats, and Slovenes" (1918), later known as Yugoslavia ("Land of the South Slavs"—*yugo* means "south"). "Yugoslav unity" was in the air, but this new union was artificial and ultimately bound to fail (not unlike the partnership between the Czechs and Slovaks, formed at the same time and for much the same reasons).

From the very beginning, the various ethnicities struggled for power within the new union. Croats in particular often felt they were treated as lesser partners under the Serbs. (For example, many Croats objected to naming the country's official language "Serbo-Croatian"—why not "Croato-Serbian?") Serbia already had a very strong king, Alexander Karađorđević, who immediately made attempts to give his nation a leading role in the federation. A nationalistic Croatian politician named Stjepan Radić, pushing for a more equitable division of powers, was shot by a Serb during a parliament session in 1928. Karađorđević abolished the parliament and became dictator. Six years later, infuriated

Croatian separatists killed him.

Many Croat nationalists sided with the Nazis in World War II in the hopes that it would be their ticket to independence from Serbia. The Nazi puppet government in Croatia (called the Ustaše) conducted an extermination campaign, murdering many Serbs (along with Jews and Roma) living in Croatia; other Serbs were forced to flee the country or convert to Catholicism. Most historians consider the Ustaše concentration camps to be the first instance of "ethnic cleansing" in the Balkans...and the Serbs' long memory of it may go far in explaining their own ethnic cleansing of the Croats in the 1990s.

At the end of World War II, the rest of Eastern Europe was "liberated" by the Soviets—but the Yugoslavs regained their independence on their own, as their communist partisan army forced out the Nazis. After the short but rocky Yugoslav union between the World Wars, it seemed that no one could hold the southern Slavs together in a single nation. But there was one man who could, and did: Tito.

Tito

Communist Party president and war hero Josip Broz—who dubbed himself with the simple nickname Tito—emerged as a political leader after World War II. With a Slovene for a mother, a Croat for a father, a Serb for a wife, and a home in Belgrade, Tito was a true Yugoslav. Tito had a compelling vision that this fractured union of the South Slavs could function. And it did. For the next three decades, Tito managed to keep Yugoslavia intact, essentially by the force of his own personality.

Tito's new incarnation of Yugoslavia aimed for a more equitable division of powers. It was made up of six republics, each with its own parliament and president: **Croatia** (mostly Catholic Croats), **Slovenia** (mostly Catholic Slovenes), **Serbia** (mostly Orthodox Serbs), **Bosnia-Herzegovina** (the most diverse—mostly Muslim Bosniaks, but with very large Croat and Serb populations), **Montenegro** (mostly Serb-like Montenegrins), and **Macedonia** (with about 25 percent Albanians and 75 percent Macedonians—who are claimed variously by Bulgarians and Serbs). There were also two autonomous provinces, each one dominated by an ethnicity that was a minority in greater Yugoslavia: Albanians in **Kosovo** (to the south) and Hungarians in **Vojvodina** (to the north). Tito hoped that by allowing these two provinces some degree of independence—including voting rights—they could balance the political clout of Serbia, preventing a single republic from dominating the union.

Each republic managed its own affairs...but always under the watchful eye of president-for-life Tito, who said that the borders between the republics should be "like white lines in a marble column."

Tito was unquestionably a political genius, carefully crafting a workable union. For example, every Yugoslav had to serve in the National Army, and Tito made sure that each unit was a microcosm of the complete Yugoslavia—with equal representation from each ethnic group. (Allowing an all-Slovene unit, stationed in Slovenia, would be begging for trouble.) There was also a dark side to Tito, who resorted to violent, strong-arming measures to assert his power, especially early in his reign. He staged brutal, Stalin-esque "show trials" to intimidate potential dissidents, and imprisoned church leaders, such as Alojzije Stepinac (see page 52). Nationalism was strongly discouraged, and this tight control—though sometimes oppressive—kept the country from unraveling. In retrospect, most former Yugoslavs forgive Tito for governing with an iron fist, believing that this was necessary for keeping the country strong and united. Today, most of them consider Tito more of a hero than a villain, and usually speak of him with reverence.

Tito's Yugoslavia was communist, but it wasn't Soviet communism; you'll find no statues of Lenin or Stalin here. Despite strong pressure from Moscow, Tito refused to ally himself with the Soviets—and therefore received good will (and $2 billion) from the United States. Tito's vision was for a "third way," where Yugoslavia could work with both East and West, without being dominated by either. Yugoslavia was the most free of the communist states: While large industry was nationalized, Tito's system allowed for small businesses. This experience with market economy benefited Yugoslavs when Eastern Europe's communist regimes eventually fell. And even during the communist era, Yugoslavia remained a popular tourist destination, keeping its standards more in line with the West than the Soviet states.

Things Fall Apart

With Tito's death in 1980, Yugoslavia's six constituent republics gained more autonomy, with a rotating presidency. But before long, the delicate union Tito had held together began to unravel. In the late 1980s, Serbian politician Slobodan Milošević took advantage of ethnic-motivated conflicts in the province of Kosovo to become president of Serbia and grab more centralized power. Other republics (especially Slovenia and Croatia) feared that he would gut their nation to create a "Greater Serbia," instead of a friendly coalition of diverse Yugoslav republics. Some of the leaders—most notably Milan Kučan of Slovenia—tried to avoid warfare by suggesting a plan for a loosely united Yugoslavia, based on the Swiss model of independent yet confederated cantons. But other parties, who wanted complete autonomy, refused. Over the next decade, Yugoslavia broke apart, with much bloodshed.

The Slovene Secession

Slovenia was the first Yugoslav republic to hold free elections, in the spring of 1990. The voters wanted the communists out—and their own independent nation. Along with being the most ethnically homogeneous of the Yugoslav nations, Slovenia was also the most Western-oriented, most prosperous, and most geographically isolated—so secession just made sense. But that didn't mean that there was no violence.

After months of stockpiling weapons, Slovenia closed its borders and declared independence from Yugoslavia on June 25, 1991. Belgrade sent in the Yugoslav National Army to take control of Slovenia's borders with Italy and Austria, figuring that who-ever controlled the borders had a legitimate claim on sovereignty. Fighting broke out around these borders. Because the Yugoslav National Army was made up of soldiers from all republics, many Slovenian soldiers found themselves fighting their own countrymen. (The army had cut off communication between these conscripts and the home front, so they didn't know what was going on—and often didn't realize they were fighting their friends and neighbors until they were close enough to see them.)

Slovenian civilians bravely entered the fray, blockading the Yugoslav barracks with their own cars and trucks. Most of the Yugoslav soldiers—now trapped—were young and inexperienced, and were terrified of the ragtag (but relentless) Slovenian militia even though their own resources were far superior.

After 10 days of fighting and fewer than a hundred deaths, Belgrade relented. The Slovenes stepped aside and allowed the Yugoslav National Army to take all of the weapons with them back into Yugoslavia, and destroy all remaining military installations. When the Yugoslav National Army had cleared out, they left the Slovenes with their freedom.

The Croatian Conflict

In April of 1990, a historian named Franjo Tuđman—and his highly nationalistic, right-wing party, the HDZ (Croatian Democratic Union)—won Croatia's first free elections (for more on Tuđman, see page 54). Like the Slovenian reformers, Tuđman and the HDZ wanted more autonomy from Yugoslavia. But Tuđman's methods were more extreme than that of the gently progressive Slovenes. Tuđman immediately invoked the spirit of the last group that led an "independent" Croatia—the Ustaše, who had ruthlessly run Croatia's puppet government under the Nazis. Tuđman reintroduced the Ustaše's red-and-white checkerboard flag and their currency (the *kuna*). The 600,000 Serbs living in Croatia, mindful of their grandparents who had been massacred by the Ustaše, saw the writing on the wall and began to rise up.

The first conflicts were in the Serb-dominated Croatian city of Knin. Among Tuđman's reforms was the decree that all of Croatia's policemen wear a new uniform, which bore a striking resemblance to Nazi-era Ustaše uniforms. Infuriated by this slap in the face, and inspired by Slobodan Milošević's rhetoric, Serb police officers in Knin refused. Over the next few months, tense negotiations ensued. Serbs from Knin and elsewhere began the so-called "tree trunk revolution"—blocking important tourist roads to the coast with logs and other barriers. Meanwhile, the Croatian government—after being denied support from the United States— illegally purchased truckloads of guns from Hungary. Tensions escalated, and the first shots of the conflict were fired on Easter Sunday of 1991 at Plitvice Lakes National Park, between Croatian policemen and Serb irregulars from Knin.

By the time Croatia declared its independence (on June 25, 1991—the same day as Slovenia), it was already embroiled in the beginnings of a bloody war. Croatia's more than half-million Serb residents immediately declared their own independence from Croatia. The Serb-dominated Yugoslav National Army swept in, supposedly to keep the peace between Serbs and Croats—but it soon became obvious that they were there to support the Serbs. The ill-prepared Croatian resistance, made up mostly of police-men and a few soldiers who defected from the Yugoslav National Army, were quickly overwhelmed. The Serbs gained control over a large swath of inland Croatia, mostly around the Bosnian bor-der (including Plitvice) and in Croatia's inland panhandle (the region of Slavonia). They called this territory—about a quarter of Croatia—the **Republic of Serbian Krajina** (*krajina* means "bor-der"). This new "country" (hardly recognized by any other nations) minted its own money and had its own army, much to the con-sternation of Croatia—which was now worried about the safety of Croats living in Krajina.

As the Serbs advanced, hundreds of thousands of Croats fled to the coast and lived as refugees in resort hotels. The Serbs began a campaign of ethnic cleansing, systematically removing Croats from their territory—often by murdering them. The bloodiest siege was at the town of **Vukovar,** which the Yugoslav army surrounded and shelled relentlessly for three months. At the end of the siege, thousands of Croat soldiers and civilians mysteriously disappeared. Many of these people were later discovered in mass graves; hun-dreds are still missing, and bodies are still being found. In a sur-prise move, Serbs also attacked the tourist resort of **Dubrovnik** (see page 224). By early 1992, both Croatia and the Republic of

Serbian Krajina had established their borders, and a tense ceasefire fell over the region.

The standoff lasted until 1995, when the now well-equipped Croatian Army retook the Serbian-occupied areas in a series of two offensives—**"Lightning"** *(Blijesak),* in the northern part of the country, and **"Storm"** *(Oluja),* farther south. Some Croats retaliated for earlier ethnic cleansing by doing much of the same to Serbs—torturing and murdering them, and dynamiting their homes. Croatia quickly established the borders that exist today, and the Erdut Agreement brought peace to the region—but most of the 600,000 Serbs who once lived in Croatia/Krajina were forced into Serbia or were killed. Today, only a few thousand Serbs remain in Croatia. While Serbs have long since been legally invited back to their ancestral Croatian homes, few have returned—afraid of the "welcome" they might receive from the Croat neighbors who killed their relatives or blew up their houses just a few years ago.

The War in Bosnia-Herzegovina

Bosnia-Herzegovina declared its independence from Yugoslavia four months after Croatia and Slovenia did. But Bosnia-Herzegovina was always at the crossroads of Balkan culture, and therefore even more diverse than Croatia—predominantly Muslim Bosniaks (mostly in the cities), but also with large Serb and Croat populations (often farmers), as well as Albanian Kosovars.

In the spring of 1992, Serbs within Bosnia-Herzegovina (with the support of Serbia) began a campaign of ethnic cleansing against the Bosniaks and Croats. Before long, the Croats did the same against the Serbs. A three-way war (between the Bosniaks, Serbs, and Croats) raged for years. Even the many mixed families were forced to choose sides. If you had a Serb mother and a Croat father, you were expected to pick one ethnicity or the other—and your brother might choose the opposite. As families and former neighbors trained their guns on each other, proud and beautiful cities such as Sarajevo and Mostar were turned to rubble, and people throughout Bosnia-Herzegovina lived in a state of constant terror.

Serb sieges of Bosnian Muslim cities—such as the notorious siege of Srebrenica in July of 1995, which ended with a massacre of about 7,000 Bosniak civilians—brought the ongoing atrocities to the world's attention. Perhaps most despicable was the establishment of so-called "rape camps"—concentration camps where Bosniak women were imprisoned and systematically raped by Serb soldiers.

The United Nations Protection Force (UNPROFOR)—dubbed "Smurfs" both for their light-blue helmets and for their ineffectiveness—exercised their limited authority to try to suppress the violence. This ugly situation was brilliantly parodied in the film *No Man's Land* (which won the Oscar for Best Foreign Film in 2002), a very dark comedy about the absurdity of the Bosnian war.

Finally, in 1995, the Dayton Peace Accords carefully divided Bosnia-Herzegovina among the different ethnicities. Today, Bosnia-Herzegovina continues to work on its tenuous peace, rebuild its devastated country, and bring its infrastructure up to its neighbors' standards.

Kosovo

The ongoing Yugoslav crisis finally reached its peak in the Serbian province of Kosovo. After years of poor treatment by the Serbs, Kosovars rebelled in 1998. Milošević sent in the army, and in March 1999, they began a campaign of ethnic cleansing. Thousands of Kosovars were murdered, and hundreds of thousands fled into Albania and Macedonia. NATO planes, under the command of US General and Supreme Allied Commander Wesley Clark, bombed Serb positions for two months, forcing the Serb army to leave Kosovo in the summer of 1999.

The Fall of Milošević

After years of bloody conflicts, Serbian public opinion had decisively swung against their president. The transition began gradually in early 2000, spearheaded by Otpor and other nonviolent, grassroots, student-based opposition movements. These organizations used clever PR strategies to gain support and convince Serbians that real change was possible. As anti-Milošević sentiments gained momentum, opposing political parties banded together and got behind one candidate, Vojislav Koštunica. Public support for Koštunica mounted, and when the arrogant Milošević called an early election in September 2000, he was soundly defeated. Though Milošević tried to claim that the election results were invalid, determined Serbs streamed into their capital, marched on their parliament, and—like the Czechs and Slovaks a decade before—peacefully took back their nation.

In 2001, Milošević was arrested and sent to The Hague, in the Netherlands, to stand trial before the International Criminal Tribunal for the Former Yugoslavia (ICTY). Milošević served as his own attorney as his trial wore on for five years, frequently delayed due to his health problems. Then, on March 11, 2006—as his trial was coming to a close—Milošević was found dead in his cell. Ruled a heart attack, Milošević's death, like his life, was controversial. Supporters claimed that Milošević was denied suitable medical care while on trial, some speculated that he was poisoned, and others suspected that he'd intentionally worsened his heart condition to avoid the completion of his trial. Whatever the cause, it seems that in the end Milošević avoided coming to justice—he was never found guilty of a thing.

Finding Their Way:
The Former Yugoslav Republics

Today, Slovenia and Croatia are as stable as Western Europe, Bosnia-Herzegovina is slowly putting itself back together, Macedonia feels closer to Bulgaria than to Belgrade, and the last two united parts of "Yugoslavia"—Serbia and Montenegro—have peacefully parted ways, leaving six independent countries where once there was one.

It's important to remember that there were no "good guys" and no "bad guys" in these wars—just a lot of ugliness on all sides. If there were any victims, they were the Bosniaks and the Kosovars—but even they were not blameless. When considering specifically the war between the Croats and the Serbs, it's tempting for Americans to take Croatia's "side"—because we saw them in the role of victims first; because they're Catholic, so they seem more "like us" than the Orthodox Serbs; and because we admire their striving for an independent nation. But in the streets and the trenches, it was never that clear-cut. When Croatians retook the Serb-occupied areas in 1995, they were every bit as brutal as the Serbs had been a few years before. Both sides resorted to ethnic cleansing, both sides had victims, and both sides had victimizers.

Perhaps the only "easy" villains in this conflict were Serbian President Slobodan Milošević and Croatian President Franjo Tuđman. Even after the deaths of both men, information continually emerges that makes these two leaders out to be even more ruthless than once thought. It's increasingly clear that Tuđman and Milošević secretly orchestrated the whole brutal war in close association with each other, using their citizens as pawns in a giant war game. (Their ultimate plan was to partition Bosnia-Herzegovina between their newly independent countries, much as Hitler and Stalin secretly plotted to divide Poland.)

It's easy to blame these conflicts on some deep-seated, inevitable cultural hatred among the Yugoslav ethnic groups. But this is an oversimplification, and ignores the fact that Serbs, Croats, Bosniaks, and Kosovars coexisted more or less peacefully and happily during the Tito era. While some long-standing tensions and misunderstandings did exist, it wasn't until Milošević and Tuđman expertly colluded to manipulate them that the country fell into war. By vigorously fanning the embers of ethnic grudges, and carefully controlling media coverage of the escalating violence, these two leaders turned a healthy political debate into a holocaust.

Tension still exists throughout the former Yugoslavia—especially areas that were most war-torn. When Serbs or Croats encounter other Yugoslavs in their travels, they immediately evaluate each other's accent to determine: Are they one of us, or one of them?

But, with time, these hard feelings are fading. The younger generations don't look back—teenaged Slovenes no longer learn Serbo-Croatian, can't imagine not living in an independent little country, and get bored (and a little irritated) when their old-fashioned parents wax nostalgic about the days of a united Yugoslavia. A middle-aged Slovene friend of mine thinks fondly of his months of compulsory service in the Yugoslav National Army, when his unit was made up of Slovenes, Croats, Serbs, Bosniaks, Kosovars, Macedonians, and Montenegrins—all of them countrymen, and all good friends. To these young Yugoslavs, minor ethnic differences didn't matter. He still often visits with his army buddy from Dubrovnik—600 miles away, not long ago part of the same nation—and wishes there had been a way to keep it all together. But he says, optimistically, "I look forward to the day when the other former Yugoslav republics also join the European Union. Then, in a way, we will all be united once again."

APPENDIX

Let's Talk Telephones

To make international calls, you need to break the codes: the international access codes and country codes. For specifics on making local, long-distance, and international calls, please see the "European Calling Chart" on the next page. You'll find more information on telephones in the Introduction on page 30.

Country Codes

After you've dialed the international access code (011 if you're calling from the US or Canada; 00 if you're calling from virtually anywhere in Europe), dial the code of the country you're calling.

Austria—43
Belgium—32
Bosnia-Herzegovina—387
Britain—44
Canada—1
Croatia—385
Czech Rep.—420
Denmark—45
Estonia—372
Finland—358
France—33
Germany—49
Gibraltar—350
Greece—30
Hungary—36

Ireland—353
Italy—39
Montenegro—382
Morocco—212
Netherlands—31
Norway—47
Poland—48
Portugal—351
Slovakia—421
Slovenia—386
Spain—34
Sweden—46
Switzerland—41
Turkey—90
US—1

European Calling Chart

Just smile and dial, using this key:
AC = Area Code, LN = Local Number.

European Country	Calling long distance within ...	Calling from the US or Canada to ...	Calling from a European country to ...
Austria	AC + LN	011 + 43 + AC (without the initial zero) + LN	00 + 43 + AC (without the initial zero) + LN
Belgium	LN	011 + 32 + LN (without initial zero)	00 + 32 + LN (without initial zero)
Bosnia-Herzegovina	AC + LN	011 + 387 + AC (without initial zero) + LN	00 + 387 + AC (without initial zero) + LN
Britain	AC + LN	011 + 44 + AC (without initial zero) + LN	00 + 44 + AC (without initial zero) + LN
Croatia	AC + LN	011 + 385 + AC (without initial zero) + LN	00 + 385 + AC (without initial zero) + LN
Czech Republic	LN	011 + 420 + LN	00 + 420 + LN
Denmark	LN	011 + 45 + LN	00 + 45 + LN
Finland	AC + LN	011 + 358 + AC (without initial zero) + LN	999 + 358 + AC (without initial zero) + LN
France	LN	011 + 33 + LN (without initial zero)	00 + 33 + LN (without initial zero)
Germany	AC + LN	011 + 49 + AC (without initial zero) + LN	00 + 49 + AC (without initial zero) + LN
Greece	LN	011 + 30 + LN	00 + 30 + LN
Hungary	06 + AC + LN	011 + 36 + AC + LN	00 + 36 + AC + LN
Ireland	AC + LN	011 + 353 + AC (without initial zero) + LN	00 + 353 + AC (without initial zero) + LN

European Country	Calling long distance within ...	Calling from the US or Canada to ...	Calling from a European country to ...
Italy	LN	011 + 39 + LN	00 + 39 + LN
Montenegro	AC + LN	011 + 382 + AC (without initial zero) + LN	00 + 382 + AC (without initial zero) + LN
Netherlands	AC + LN	011 + 31 + AC (without initial zero) + LN	00 + 31 + AC (without initial zero) + LN
Norway	LN	011 + 47 + LN	00 + 47 + LN
Poland	LN	011 + 48 + LN (without initial zero)	00 + 48 + LN (without initial zero)
Portugal	LN	011 + 351 + LN	00 + 351 + LN
Slovakia	AC + LN	011 + 421 + AC (without initial zero) + LN	00 + 421 + AC (without initial zero) + LN
Slovenia	AC + LN	011 + 386 + AC (without initial zero) + LN	00 + 386 + AC (without initial zero) + LN
Spain	LN	011 + 34 + LN	00 + 34 + LN
Sweden	AC + LN	011 + 46 + AC (without initial zero) + LN	00 + 46 + AC (without initial zero) + LN
Switzerland	LN	011 + 41 + LN (without initial zero)	00 + 41 + LN (without initial zero)
Turkey	AC (if no initial zero is included, add one) + LN	011 + 90 + AC (without initial zero) + LN	00 + 90 + AC (without initial zero) + LN

- The instructions above apply whether you're calling a land line or mobile phone.
- The international access codes (the first numbers you dial when making an international call) are 011 if you're calling from the US or Canada, or 00 if you're calling from virtually anywhere in Europe (except Finland, where it's 999).
- To call the US or Canada from Europe, dial 00, then 1 (the country code for the US and Canada), then the area code and number. In short, 00 + 1 + AC + LN = Hi, Mom!

US Embassies

Croatia: Ulica Thomasa Jeffersona 2, Zagreb, tel. 01/661-2200, consular services tel. 01/661-2300, www.usembassy.hr.

Slovenia: Prešernova 31, Ljubljana, tel. 01/200-5500, www.usembassy.si.

Montenegro: Ljubljanska b.b., Podgorica, tel. 081/225-417, fax 081/241-358.

Bosnia-Herzegovina: Alipašina 43, Sarajevo, tel. 033/445-700, on weekends and after hours call the same number and press 0 after the recording, fax 033/221-837, www.usembassy.ba. There's also a branch office in Mostar (Mostarskog Bataljona b.b., tel. 036/580-580).

Croatian and Slovenian Festivals and Holidays in 2007

Note that this isn't a complete list; holidays strike without warning. As both Croatia and Slovenia are Catholic, religious holidays are a big deal. For more details on holidays, check with each country's tourist office (see page 9).

Jan 1	New Year's Day, Croatia and Slovenia
Jan 6	Epiphany, Croatia and Slovenia
Feb 8	National Day of Culture, Slovenia (celebrates Slovenian culture and national poet France Prešeren)
March 22–25	Ski Flying World Championships, Planica, Slovenia (www.planica.info)
April 8–9	Easter Sunday and Monday, Croatia and Slovenia
April 27	National Resistance Day, Slovenia
May 1	Labor Day, Croatia and Slovenia
May 17	Ascension Day, Croatia and Slovenia
May 27	Pentecost, Croatia and Slovenia
Early June	Dance Week Festival, Zagreb, Croatia (www.danceweekfestival.com)
June 7	Corpus Christi, Croatia and Slovenia
June 22	Antifascist Struggle Day, Croatia
June 25	National Day, Slovenia; Statehood Day, Croatia
July 10–Aug 25	Dubrovnik Summer Festival, Croatia (www.dubrovnik-festival.hr)
Early July–late Aug	Ljubljana Summer Festival, Slovenia (www.festival-lj.si)
July 20–22	Marco Polo Festival, Korčula, Croatia (www.marcopolofest.hr)
Late July	International Folklore Festival, Zagreb, Croatia (costumes, songs, dances from all over Croatia; www.msf.hr)

2007

JANUARY
S	M	T	W	T	F	S
	1	2	3	4	5	6
7	8	9	10	11	12	13
14	15	16	17	18	19	20
21	22	23	24	25	26	27
28	29	30	31			

FEBRUARY
S	M	T	W	T	F	S
				1	2	3
4	5	6	7	8	9	10
11	12	13	14	15	16	17
18	19	20	21	22	23	24
25	26	27	28			

MARCH
S	M	T	W	T	F	S
				1	2	3
4	5	6	7	8	9	10
11	12	13	14	15	16	17
18	19	20	21	22	23	24
25	26	27	28	29	30	31

APRIL
S	M	T	W	T	F	S
1	2	3	4	5	6	7
8	9	10	11	12	13	14
15	16	17	18	19	20	21
22	23	24	25	26	27	28
29	30					

MAY
S	M	T	W	T	F	S
		1	2	3	4	5
6	7	8	9	10	11	12
13	14	15	16	17	18	19
20	21	22	23	24	25	26
27	28	29	30	31		

JUNE
S	M	T	W	T	F	S
					1	2
3	4	5	6	7	8	9
10	11	12	13	14	15	16
17	18	19	20	21	22	23
24	25	26	27	28	29	30

JULY
S	M	T	W	T	F	S
1	2	3	4	5	6	7
8	9	10	11	12	13	14
15	16	17	18	19	20	21
22	23	24	25	26	27	28
29	30	31				

AUGUST
S	M	T	W	T	F	S
			1	2	3	4
5	6	7	8	9	10	11
12	13	14	15	16	17	18
19	20	21	22	23	24	25
26	27	28	29	30	31	

SEPTEMBER
S	M	T	W	T	F	S
						1
2	3	4	5	6	7	8
9	10	11	12	13	14	15
16	17	18	19	20	21	22
23/30	24	25	26	27	28	29

OCTOBER
S	M	T	W	T	F	S
	1	2	3	4	5	6
7	8	9	10	11	12	13
14	15	16	17	18	19	20
21	22	23	24	25	26	27
28	29	30	31			

NOVEMBER
S	M	T	W	T	F	S
				1	2	3
4	5	6	7	8	9	10
11	12	13	14	15	16	17
18	19	20	21	22	23	24
25	26	27	28	29	30	

DECEMBER
S	M	T	W	T	F	S
						1
2	3	4	5	6	7	8
9	10	11	12	13	14	15
16	17	18	19	20	21	22
23/30	24/31	25	26	27	28	29

Aug 5	National Thanksgiving Day, Croatia
Aug 15	Assumption of Mary, Croatia and Slovenia
Early Sept	Marco Polo Naval Battle Reenactment, Korčula, Croatia
Oct 8	Independence Day, Croatia
Oct 31	Reformation Day, Slovenia
Nov 1	All Saints' Day/Remembrance Day, Croatia and Slovenia (religious festival, some closures)
Nov 11	St. Martin's Day (official first day of wine season), Croatia and Slovenia
Dec 24–25	Christmas Eve and Christmas Day, Croatia and Slovenia
Dec 26	Boxing Day/St. Stephen's Day, Croatia and Slovenia; Independence and Unity Day, Slovenia

Numbers and Stumblers

- Europeans write a few of their numbers differently than we do: 1 = $\mathit{1}$, 4 = $\mathit{4}$, 7 = $\mathit{7}$. Learn the difference or miss your train.
- Europeans write dates as day/month/year (Christmas is 25/12/07).
- Commas are decimal points, and decimals are commas. A dollar and a half is 1,50. There are 5.280 feet in a mile.
- When counting with fingers, start with your thumb. If you hold up your first finger to request one item, you'll probably get two.
- What we Americans call the second floor of a building is the first floor in Europe.
- Europeans keep the left "lane" open for passing on escalators and moving sidewalks. Keep to the right.

Climate

Here is a list of average temperatures (first line—average daily low; second line—average daily high; third line—days of rain). This can be helpful in planning your itinerary, but I have never found European weather to be particularly predictable, and these charts ignore humidity.

J	F	M	A	M	J	J	A	S	O	N	D

CROATIA • Dubrovnik

J	F	M	A	M	J	J	A	S	O	N	D
42°	43°	57°	52°	58°	65°	69°	69°	64°	57°	51°	46°
53°	55°	58°	63°	70°	78°	83°	82°	77°	69°	62°	56°
13	13	11	10	10	6	4	3	7	11	16	15

SLOVENIA • Ljubljana

J	F	M	A	M	J	J	A	S	O	N	D
25°	25°	32°	40°	48°	54°	57°	57°	51°	43°	36°	30°
36°	41°	50°	60°	68°	75°	80°	78°	71°	59°	47°	39°
13	11	11	13	16	16	12	12	10	14	15	15

Temperature Conversion: Fahrenheit and Celsius

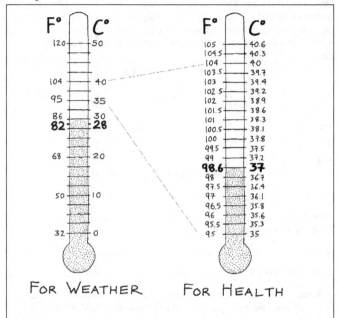

Europe takes its temperature using the Celsius scale, while we opt for Fahrenheit. For weather, remember that 28°C is 82°F—perfect. For health, 37°C is just right.

Metric Conversion (approximate)

1 inch = 25 millimeters	32°F = 0°C
1 foot = 0.3 meter	82°F = about 28°C
1 yard = 0.9 meter	1 ounce = 28 grams
1 mile = 1.6 kilometers	1 kilogram = 2.2 pounds
1 centimeter = 0.4 inch	1 quart = 0.95 liter
1 meter = 39.4 inches	1 square yard = 0.8 square meter
1 kilometer = 0.62 mile	1 acre = 0.4 hectare

Making Your Hotel Reservation

Most hotel managers know basic "hotel English." Faxing or e-mailing are the preferred methods for reserving a room. They're more accurate than telephoning and much faster than writing a letter. Use this handy form for your fax or find it online at www.ricksteves.com/reservation. Photocopy and fax away.

One-Page Fax

To: _____ @ _____
           hotel   *fax*

From: _____@ _____
            name   *fax*

Today's date: _____ / _____ / _____
                 day   *month*   *year*

Dear Hotel _____ ,
Please make this reservation for me:

Name: _____

Total # of people:_____ # of rooms: _____ # of nights: _____

Arriving: _____ /_____ /_____   My time of arrival (24-hr clock): _____
          day   *month*   *year*   (I will telephone if I will be late)

Departing:____ /____/____
         day   *month*   *year*

Room(s): Single _____ Double ____ Twin _____ Triple ____ Quad____

With: Toilet _____ Shower_____ Bath _____ Sink only _____

Special needs: View____ Quiet ____ Cheapest ____ Ground Floor ____

Please fax, mail, or e-mail confirmation of my reservation, along with the type of room reserved and the price. Please also inform me of your cancellation policy. After I hear from you, I will quickly send my credit-card information as a deposit to hold the room. Thank you.

_____
Signature

_____
Name

_____
Address

_____
City   *State*   *Zip Code*   *Country*

_____
E-mail Address

Croatian Survival Phrases

When using the phonetics, pronounce ī / Ī as the long I sound in "light."

English	Croatian	Phonetics
Hello. (formal)	Dobar dan.	DOH-bahr dahn
Hi. / Bye. (informal)	Bog.	bohg
Do you speak English?	Govorite li engleski?	GOH-voh-ree-teh lee EHN-glehs-kee
Yes. / No.	Da. / Ne.	dah / neh
I (don't) understand.	(Ne) razumijem.	(neh) rah-ZOO-mee-yehm
Please. / You're welcome.	Molim.	MOH-leem
Thank you (very much).	Hvala (ljepa).	HVAH-lah (LYEH-pah)
Excuse me. / I'm sorry.	Oprostite.	oh-PROH-stee-teh
problem	problem	proh-BLEHM
No problem.	Nema problema.	NEH-mah proh-BLEH-mah
Good.	Dobro.	DOH-broh
Goodbye.	Do viđenija.	doh veed-JAY-neeah
one / two	jedan / dva	YEH-dahn / dvah
three / four	tri / četiri	tree / CHEH-teh-ree
five / six	pet / šest	peht / shehst
seven / eight	sedam / osam	SEH-dahm / OH-sahm
nine / ten	devet / deset	DEH-veht / DEH-seht
hundred / thousand	sto / tisuća	stoh / TEE-soo-chah
How much?	Koliko?	KOH-lee-koh
local currency	kuna	KOO-nah
Write it?	Napišite?	nah-PEESH-ee-teh
Is it free?	Da li je besplatno?	dah lee yeh BEH-splaht-noh
Is it included?	Da li je uključeno?	dah lee yeh OOK-lyoo-cheh-noh
Where can I find / buy...?	Gdje mogu pronaći / kupiti...?	guh-DYEH MOH-goo PROH-nah-chee / KOO-pee-tee
I'd like / We'd like...	Želio bih / Željeli bismo...	ZHEH-lee-oh beeh / ZHEH-lyeh-lee BEES-moh
...a room.	...sobu.	SOH-boo
...a ticket to ___.	...kartu do ___.	KAR-too doh
Is it possible?	Da li je moguće?	dah lee yeh MOH-goo-cheh
Where is...?	Gdje je...?	guh-DYEH yeh
...the train station	...željeznička stanica	ZHEH-lyehz-neech-kah STAH-neet-sah
...the bus station	...autobusna stanica	OW-toh-boos-nah STAH-neet-sah
...the tourist information office	...turističko informativni centar	TOO-ree-steech-koh EEN-for-mah-teev-nee TSEHN-tahr
...the toilet	...vece (WC)	VEHT-SEH
men	muški	MOOSH-kee
women	ženski	ZHEHN-skee
left / right	lijevo / desno	LEE-yeh-voh / DEHS-noh
straight	ravno	RAHV-noh
At what time...	U koliko sati...	oo KOH-lee-koh SAH-tee
...does this open / close?	...otvara / zatvara?	OHT-vah-rah / ZAHT-vah-rah
(Just) a moment.	(Samo) trenutak.	(SAH-moh) treh-NOO-tahk
now / soon / later	sada / uskoro / kasnije	SAH-dah / OOS-koh-roh / KAHS-nee-yeh
today / tomorrow	danas / sutra	DAH-nahs / SOO-trah

In the Restaurant

I'd like to reserve...	**Rezervirao bih...**	reh-zehr-VEER-ow beeh
We'd like to reserve...	**Rezervirali bismo...**	reh-zehr-VEE-rah-lee BEES-moh
...a table for one / two.	**...stol za jednog / dva.**	stohl zah YEHD-nog / dvah
Non-smoking.	**Za nepušače.**	zah NEH-poo-shah-cheh
Is this table free?	**Da li je ovaj stol slobodan?**	dah lee yeh OH-vī stohl SLOH-boh-dahn
Can I help you?	**Izvolite?**	EEZ-voh-lee-teh
The menu (in English), please.	**Jelovnik (na engleskom), molim.**	yeh-LOHV-neek (nah EHN-glehs-kohm) MOH-leem
service (not) included	**posluga (nije) uključena**	POH-sloo-gah (NEE-yeh) OOK-lyoo-cheh-nah
cover charge	**couvert**	KOO-vehr
"to go"	**za ponjeti**	zah POHN-yeh-tee
with / without	**sa / bez**	sah / behz
and / or	**i / ili**	ee / EE-lee
fixed-price meal (of the day)	**(dnevni) meni**	(duh-NEHV-nee) MEH-nee
specialty of the house	**specijalitet kuće**	speht-see-yah-LEE-teht KOO-cheh
half portion	**pola porcije**	POH-lah PORT-see-yeh
daily special	**jelo dana**	YEH-loh DAH-nah
fixed-price meal for tourists	**turistički meni**	TOO-ree-steech-kee MEH-nee
appetizers	**predjela**	PREHD-yeh-lah
bread	**kruh**	krooh
cheese	**sir**	seer
sandwich	**sendvič**	SEND-veech
soup	**juha**	YOO-hah
salad	**salata**	sah-LAH-tah
meat	**meso**	MAY-soh
poultry	**perad**	PEH-rahd
fish	**riba**	REE-bah
seafood	**morska hrana**	MOHR-skah HRAH-nah
fruit	**voće**	VOH-cheh
vegetables	**povrće**	POH-vur-cheh
dessert	**desert**	deh-SAYRT
(tap) water	**voda (od slavine)**	VOH-dah (ohd SLAH-vee-neh)
mineral water	**mineralna voda**	MEE-neh-rahl-nah VOH-dah
milk	**mlijeko**	mlee-YEH-koh
(orange) juice	**sok (od naranče)**	sohk (ohd NAH-rahn-cheh)
coffee	**kava**	KAH-vah
tea	**čaj**	chī
wine	**vino**	VEE-noh
red / white	**crno / bijelo**	TSEHR-noh / bee-YEH-loh
sweet / dry / semi-dry	**slatko / suho / polusuho**	SLAHT-koh / SOO-hoh / POH-loo-soo-hoh
glass / bottle	**čaša / boca**	CHAH-shah / BOHT-sah
beer	**pivo**	PEE-voh
Cheers!	**Živjeli!**	ZHEE-vyeh-lee
More. / Another.	**Još. / Još jedno.**	yohsh / yohsh YEHD-noh
The same.	**Isto.**	EES-toh
Bill, please.	**Račun, molim.**	RAH-choon MOH-leem
tip	**napojnica**	NAH-poy-neet-sah
Delicious!	**Izvrsno!**	EEZ-vur-snoh

Slovenian Survival Phrases

When using the phonetics, pronounce ī / Ī as the long I sound in "light."
The vowel "eh" sometimes sounds closer to "ay" (depending on the speaker).

Hello. (formal)	**Dober dan.**	DOH-behr dahn
Hi. / Bye. (informal)	**Živjo.**	ZHEEV-yoh
Do you speak English?	**Ali govorite angleško?**	AH-lee goh-voh-REE-teh ahn-GLEHSH-koh
Yes. / No.	**Ja. / Ne.**	yah / neh
I (don't) understand.	**(Ne) razumem.**	(neh) rah-ZOO-mehm
Please. / You're welcome.	**Prosim.**	PROH-seem
Thank you (very much).	**Hvala (lepa).**	HVAH-lah (LEH-pah)
Excuse me. / I'm sorry.	**Oprostite.**	oh-proh-STEE-teh
problem	**problem**	proh-BLEHM
No problem.	**Ni problema.**	nee proh-BLEH-mah
Good.	**Dobro.**	DOH-broh
Goodbye.	**Na svidenje.**	nah SVEE-dehn-yeh
one / two	**ena / dve**	EH-nah / dveh
three / four	**tri / štiri**	tree / SHTEE-ree
five / six	**pet / šest**	peht / shehst
seven / eight	**sedem / osem**	SEH-dehm / OH-sehm
nine / ten	**devet / deset**	deh-VEHT / deh-SEHT
hundred / thousand	**sto / tisoč**	stoh / TEE-sohch
How much?	**Koliko?**	KOH-lee-koh
local currency	**euro**	EE-oo-roh
Write it?	**Napišite?**	nah-PEESH-ee-teh
Is it free?	**Ali je brezplačno?**	AH-lee yeh brehz-PLAHCH-noh
Is it included?	**Ali je vključeno?**	AH-lee yeh vuk-LYOO-cheh-noh
Where can I find / buy...?	**Kje lahko najdem / kupim...?**	kyeh LAH-koh NĪ-dehm / KOO-peem
I'd / We'd like...	**Želel / Želeli bi...**	zheh-LEEoo / zheh-LEH-lee bee
...a room.	**...sobo.**	SOH-boh
...a ticket to ___.	**...vozovnico do ___.**	voh-ZOHV-neet-soh doh
Is it possible?	**Ali je možno?**	AH-lee yeh MOHZH-noh
Where is...?	**Kje je...?**	kyeh yeh
...the train station	**...železniška postaja**	zheh-LEHZ-neesh-kah pohs-TĪ-yah
...the bus station	**...avtobusna postaja**	OW-toh-boos-nah pohs-TĪ-yah
...the tourist information office	**...turistično informacijski center**	too-REES-teech-noh een-for-maht-SEE-skee TSEHN-tehr
...the toilet	**...vece (WC)**	VEHT-SEH
men	**moški**	MOHSH-kee
women	**ženski**	ZHEHN-skee
left / right	**levo / desno**	LEH-voh / DEHS-noh
straight	**naravnost**	nah-RAHV-nohst
At what time...	**Ob kateri uri...**	ohb kah-TEH-ree OO-ree
...does this open / close?	**...se odpre / zapre?**	seh ohd-PREH / zah-PREH
(Just) a moment.	**(Samo) trenutek.**	(sah-MOH) treh-NOO-tehk
now / soon / later	**zdaj / kmalu / pozneje**	zuh-DĪ / kuh-MAH-loo / pohz-NEH-yeh
today / tomorrow	**danes / jutri**	DAH-nehs / YOO-tree

In the Restaurant

I'd like to reserve...	Rezerviral bi...	reh-zehr-VEE-rahl bee
We'd like to reserve...	Rezervirali bi...	reh-zehr-VEE-rah-lee bee
...a table for one / two.	...mizo za enega / dva.	MEE-zoh zah EH-neh-gah / dvah
Non-smoking.	Za nekadilce.	zah NEH-kah-deelt-seh
Is this table free?	Ali je ta miza prosta?	AH-lee yeh tah MEE-zah PROH-stah
Can I help you?	Izvolite?	eez-VOH-lee-teh
The menu (in English), please.	Jedilni list (v angleščini), prosim.	yeh-DEEL-nee leest (vuh ahn-GLEHSH-chee-nee) PROH-seem
service (not) included	postrežba (ni) vključena	post-REHZH-bah (nee) vuk-LYOO-cheh-nah
cover charge	pogrinjek	poh-GREEN-yehk
"to go"	za s sabo	zah SAH-boh
with / without	z / brez	zuh / brehz
and / or	in / ali	een / AH-lee
fixed-price meal (of the day)	(dnevni) meni	(duh-NEW-nee) meh-NEE
specialty of the house	specialiteta hiše	speht-see-ah-lee-TEH-tah HEE-sheh
half portion	polovična porcija	poh-loh-VEECH-nah PORT-see-yah
daily special	dnevna ponudba	duh-NEW-nah poh-NOOD-bah
fixed-price meal for tourists	turistični meni	too-REES-teech-nee meh-NEE
appetizers	predjedi	prehd-yeh-DEE
bread	kruh	krooh
cheese	sir	seer
sandwich	sendvič	SEND-veech
soup	juha	YOO-hah
salad	solata	soh-LAH-tah
meat	meso	meh-SOH
poultry	perutnina	peh-root-NEE-nah
fish	riba	REE-bah
seafood	morska hrana	MOHR-skah HRAH-nah
fruit	sadje	SAHD-yeh
vegetables	zelenjava	zeh-lehn-YAH-vah
dessert	sladica	slah-DEET-sah
(tap) water	voda (iz pipe)	VOH-dah (eez PEE-peh)
mineral water	mineralna voda	mee-neh-RAHL-nah VOH-dah
milk	mleko	MLEH-koh
(orange) juice	(pomarančni) sok	(poh-mah-RAHNCH-nee) sohk
coffee	kava	KAH-vah
tea	čaj	chī
wine	vino	VEE-noh
red / white	rdeče / belo	ahr-DEH-cheh / BEH-loh
sweet / dry / semi-dry	sladko / suho / polsuho	SLAHD-koh / SOO-hoh / POHL-soo-hoh
glass / bottle	kozarec / steklenica	koh-ZAH-rehts / stehk-leh-NEET-sah
beer	pivo	PEE-voh
Cheers!	Na zdravje!	nah ZDROW-yeh
More. / Another.	Še. / Še eno.	sheh / sheh EH-noh
The same.	Isto.	EES-toh
Bill, please.	Račun, prosim.	rah-CHOON PROH-seem
tip	napitnina	nah-peet-NEE-nah
Delicious!	Odlično!	ohd-LEECH-noh

INDEX

Travel smart...carry on!

The latest generation of Rick Steves' carry-on travel bags is easily the best—benefiting from two decades of on-the-road attention to what really matters: maximum quality and strength; practical, flexible features; and no unnecessary frills. You won't find a better value anywhere!

Rick Steves' Convertible Carry-On

This is the classic "back door bag" that Rick Steves lives out of for three months every summer. It's made of rugged, water-resistant 1000-denier nylon. Best of all, it converts easily from a smart-looking suitcase to a handy backpack with comfortably-curved shoulder straps and a padded waistbelt.

This roomy, versatile 9" x 21" x 14" bag has a large 2500 cubic-inch main compartment, plus three outside pockets (small, medium and huge) that are perfect for often-used items. And the cinch-tight compression straps will keep your load compact and close to your back—not sagging like a sack of potatoes.

Wishing you had even more room to bring home souvenirs? Pull open the full-perimeter expando-zipper and its capacity jumps from 2500 to 3000 cubic inches. When you want to use it as a suitcase or check it as luggage (required when "expanded"), the straps and belt hide away in a zippered compartment in the back. Choose from five great traveling colors: black, navy, blue spruce, evergreen or merlot.

Rick Steves' 21" Roll-Aboard

At 9" x 21" x 14" our sturdy 21" Roll-Aboard is rucksack-soft in front, but the rest is lined with a hard ABS-lexan shell to give maximum protection to your belongings. We've spared no expense on moving parts, splurging on an extra-long button-release handle and big, tough inline skate wheels for easy rolling on rough surfaces.

Wishing you had even more room to bring home souvenirs? Pull open the full-perimeter expando-zipper and its capacity jumps from 2500 to 3000 cubic inches.

Rick Steves' 21" Roll-Aboard features exactly the same three-outside-pocket configuration and rugged 1000-denier nylon fabric as our Convertible Carry-On, plus a full lining and a handy "add-a-bag" strap.

Choose from five great traveling colors: black, navy, blue spruce, evergreen or merlot.

For great deals on a wide selection of travel goodies, begin your next trip at the Rick Steves Travel Store!

Visit the Rick Steves Travel Store at
www.ricksteves.com

Start your trip at
www.ricksteves.com

Rick Steves' Web site is packed with over 3,000 pages of timely travel information. It's also your gateway to getting FREE monthly travel news from Rick— and more!

Free Monthly European Travel News

Fresh articles on Europe's most interesting destinations and happenings. Rick will even send you an e-mail every month (often direct from Europe) with his latest discoveries!

Timely Travel Tips

Rick Steves' best money-and-stress-saving tips on trip planning, packing, transportation, hotels, health, safety, finances, hurdling the language barrier…and more.

Travelers' Graffiti Wall

Candid advice and opinions from thousands of travelers on everything listed above, plus whatever topics are hot at the moment (discount flights, packing tips, scams…you name it).

Rick's Annual Guide to European Railpasses

The clearest, most comprehensive guide to the confusing array of rail-pass options out there, and how to choo-choose the railpass that best fits your itinerary and budget. Then you can order your railpass (and get a bunch of great freebies) online from us!

Great Gear at the Rick Steves Travel Store

Enjoy bargains on Rick's guidebooks, planning maps and TV series DVDs, and on his custom-designed carry-on bags, roll-aboard bags, day packs and light-packing accessories.

Rick Steves Tours

This year more than 10,000 lucky travelers will explore Europe on a Rick Steves tour. Learn more about our 25 different one-to-three-week itineraries, read uncensored feedback from our tour alums, and sign up for your dream trip online!

Rick on Radio and TV

Download free podcasts of our weekly *Travel with Rick Steves* public radio show; read the scripts and see video clips from public television's *Rick Steves' Europe*.

Respect for Your Privacy

Ordering online from us is secure. When you buy something from us, join a tour, or subscribe to Rick's free monthly travel news e-mails, we promise to never share your name, information, or e-mail address with anyone else. You won't be spammed!

Have fun raising your Travel I.Q. at
www.ricksteves.com

![Rick Steves]

More *Savvy*. More *Surprising*. More *Fun.*

COUNTRY GUIDES 2007

Croatia & Slovenia
England
France
Germany & Austria
Great Britain
Ireland
Italy
Portugal
Scandinavia
Spain
Switzerland

CITY GUIDES 2007

Amsterdam, Bruges & Brussels
Florence & Tuscany
Istanbul
London
Paris
Prague & The Czech Republic
Provence & The French Riviera
Rome
Venice

BEST OF GUIDES

Best of Eastern Europe
Best of Europe

As the #1 authority on European travel, Rick gives you inside information on what to visit, where to stay, and how to get there—economically and hassle-free.

www.ricksteves.com

PHRASE BOOKS & DICTIONARIES

French
French, Italian & German
German
Italian
Portuguese
Spanish

MORE EUROPE FROM RICK STEVES

Easy Access Europe
Europe 101
Europe Through the Back Door
Postcards from Europe

RICK STEVES' EUROPE DVDs

All 43 Shows 2000-2005
Britain
Eastern Europe
France & Benelux
Germany, The Swiss Alps & Travel Skills
Ireland
Italy
Spain & Portugal

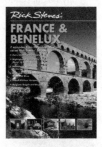

PLANNING MAPS

Britain & Ireland
Europe
France
Germany, Austria & Switzerland
Italy
Spain & Portugal

CREDITS

Contributor

Gene Openshaw
Gene is the co-author of eight Rick Steves books. For this book, he wrote material on Europe's art, history, and contemporary culture. When not traveling, Gene enjoys composing music, recovering from his 1973 trip to Europe with Rick, and living everyday life with his wife and daughter.

IMAGES

Location	
Title Page: Bled Island, Slovenia	Cameron Hewitt
Croatia (full-page image): Old Town, Dubrovnik	Cameron Hewitt
Zagreb: Jelačić Square	Cameron Hewitt
Plitvice Lakes National Park: Plitvice	Rick Steves
Istria: Motovun	Cameron Hewitt
Kvarner Gulf: Jablanac	Cameron Hewitt
Split: Riva Promenade and Old Town	Cameron Hewitt
Hvar: Hvar Harbor	Cameron Hewitt
Korčula: View of Old Town	Cameron Hewitt
Dubrovnik: View of Old Town	Cameron Hewitt
Near Dubrovnik: Neptune Fountain, Trsteno Arboretum	Cameron Hewitt
Bosnia-Herzegovina (full-page image): Coppersmiths' Street, Mostar	Cameron Hewitt
Bosnia-Herzegovina: Old Bridge, Mostar	Cameron Hewitt
Montenegro (full-page image): Perast	Cameron Hewitt
Montenegro: Perast and the Bay of Kotor	Cameron Hewitt
Slovenia (full-page image): Soča River Valley	Cameron Hewitt
Ljubljana: Ljubljana Castle overlooking Prešeren Square	Cameron Hewitt
Lake Bled: *Pletna* Boat on Lake Bled	Cameron Hewitt
The Julian Alps: Mountain Hut	Cameron Hewitt
Logarska Dolina and the Northern Valleys: Logarska Dolina	Cameron Hewitt
The Karst: Predjama Castle	Rick Steves
Piran: Breakwater	Rick Steves
Ptuj: View of Old Town	Cameron Hewitt

Rick Steves' Guidebook Series

Country Guides
Rick Steves' Best of Europe
Rick Steves' Best of Eastern Europe
Rick Steves' Croatia & Slovenia (new in 2007)
Rick Steves' England
Rick Steves' France
Rick Steves' Germany & Austria
Rick Steves' Great Britain
Rick Steves' Ireland
Rick Steves' Italy
Rick Steves' Portugal
Rick Steves' Scandinavia
Rick Steves' Spain
Rick Steves' Switzerland

City and Regional Guides
Rick Steves' Amsterdam, Bruges & Brussels
Rick Steves' Florence & Tuscany
Rick Steves' Istanbul (new in 2007)
Rick Steves' London
Rick Steves' Paris
Rick Steves' Prague & the Czech Republic
Rick Steves' Provence & the French Riviera
Rick Steves' Rome
Rick Steves' Venice

Rick Steves' Phrase Books
French
German
Italian
Spanish
Portuguese
French/Italian/German

Other Books
Rick Steves' Europe Through the Back Door
Rick Steves' Europe 101: History and Art for the Traveler
Rick Steves' Easy Access Europe
Rick Steves' Postcards from Europe
Rick Steves' European Christmas

(Avalon Travel Publishing)

For a complete list of Rick Steves' guidebooks, see the previous page.

Avalon Travel Publishing
1400 65th Street, Suite 250
Emeryville, CA 94608

AVALON
publishing group incorporated

Avalon Travel Publishing
An Imprint of Avalon Publishing Group
Text © 2007 by Rick Steves
Cover © 2007 by Avalon Travel Publishing, Inc. All rights reserved.
Maps © 2007 by Europe Through the Back Door
Printed in the USA by Worzalla. First printing March 2007.

Portions of this book were originally published in *Rick Steves' Best of Eastern Europe*
© 2007, 2006, 2005, 2004 by Rick Steves and Cameron Hewitt.

For the latest on Rick Steves' lectures, guidebooks, tours, public radio show, and public
television series, contact Europe Through the Back Door, tel. 425/771-8303, fax 425/771-
0833, www.ricksteves.com, rick@ricksteves.com.

ISBN (10) 1-59880-055-8
ISBN (13) 978-1-59880-055-5
ISSN 1935-7419

Europe Through the Back Door Senior Editor: Cameron Hewitt
ETBD Editors: Jennifer Madison Davis, Cathy McDonald
ETBD Managing Editor: Risa Laib
Avalon Travel Publishing Editor and Series Manager: Madhu Prasher
Avalon Travel Publishing Project Editor: Patrick Collins
Copy Editor: Ellie Behrstock
Proofreader: Janet Walden
Indexer: Stephen Callahan
Production & Typesetting: McGuire Barber Design
Cover Design: Kari Gim, Laura Mazer
Interior Design: Laura Mazer, Jane Musser, Amber Pirker
Maps & Graphics: David C. Hoerlein, Laura VanDeventer, Lauren Mills, Barb Geisler,
    Mike Morgenfeld
Photography: Cameron Hewitt, Rick Steves, David C. Hoerlein
Front Matter Color Photos: Page i: Bled Island, Slovenia © Cameron Hewitt
Cover Photos: Front: Dragon Bridge, Ljubljana, Slovenia © Cameron Hewitt; back:
    Korčula, Croatia © Michael Potter

Distributed to the book trade by Publishers Group West, Berkeley, California